MICROSOFT® WORD 2013

QuickSteps®

About the Authors

Marty and **Carole Matthews** have used computers for over 40 years, from some of the early mainframe computers to recent personal computers. They have done this as programmers, systems analysts, managers, and company executives. As a result, they have firsthand knowledge of not only how to program and use a computer, but also how to make the best use of all that can be done with one.

Over 25 years ago, Marty and Carole wrote their first computer book on how to buy mini-computers. Not long after, they began writing books as a major part of their occupation. In the intervening years, they have written over 70 books, including ones on desktop publishing, web publishing, Microsoft Office, and Microsoft operating systems, beginning with MS-DOS. Recent books published by McGraw-Hill include *Windows 8 QuickSteps, Facebook for Seniors QuickSteps, Genealogy for Seniors QuickSteps, iPad QuickSteps, Microsoft Office Excel 2013 QuickSteps,* and *Microsoft Office 2013 QuickSteps.*

Marty and Carole live on an island in Puget Sound.

MICROSOFT® WORD 2013

QuickSteps®

Marty Matthews

Carole B. Matthews

New York Chicago San Francisco
Lisbon London Madrid Mexico City
Milan New Delhi San Juan
Seoul Singapore Sydney Toronto

Cataloging-in-Publication Data is on file with the Library of Congress

McGraw-Hill Education books are available at special quantity discounts to use as premiums and sales promotions, or for use in corporate training programs. To contact a representative, please e-mail us at bulksales@mcgraw-hill.com.

Microsoft® Word 2013 QuickSteps®

1 2 3 4 5 6 7 8 9 0 QVR QVR 1 0 9 8 7 6 5 4 3

ISBN 978-0-07-180597-1
MHID 0-07-180597-4

SPONSORING EDITOR / Roger Stewart
EDITORIAL SUPERVISOR / Patty Mon
PROJECT MANAGER / Sheena Uprety, Cenveo® Publisher Services
ACQUISITIONS COORDINATOR / Amanda Russell
COPY EDITOR / Lisa McCoy
PROOFREADER / Vicki Wong
INDEXER / Valerie Perry
PRODUCTION SUPERVISOR / James Kussow
COMPOSITION / Cenveo Publisher Services
ILLUSTRATION / Erin Johnson
ART DIRECTOR, COVER / Jeff Weeks
COVER DESIGNER / Pattie Lee
SERIES CREATORS / Marty and Carole Matthews
SERIES DESIGN / Mary McKeon

To Daniel and Pherron Mulhaney…

Dear friends who are much in our thoughts these days.

—Marty and Carole

Contents at a Glance

Chapter 1 **Stepping into Word** 1
Start and exit Word; explore the Word window; use the ribbon, mouse, touch screen, Word screen, and Help; customize Word

Chapter 2 **Working with Documents** 27
Create a new document; use templates; locate and import a document; enter, select, copy, move, and delete text; save a document

Chapter 3 **Formatting a Document** 57
Apply character, paragraph, and page formatting; create special effects, drop caps, and numbered lists; add borders and shading

Chapter 4 **Customizing a Document** 89
Create and use themes, styles, templates, or columns; add tabs, headers/footers, or footnotes; create an index and table of contents

Chapter 5 **Printing and Using Mail Merge** 129
Set up a printer; preview and print documents, envelopes, and labels; send faxes; send email; create a merge document and a list

Chapter 6 **Using Tables** 155
Create or draw a table; change a table's size, row height, and column width; repeat headings; merge and split cells; format tables

Chapter 7 **Working with Illustrations** 179
Add pictures; use clip art; position pictures in two ways; work with AutoShapes, curves, and color; resize and rotate graphics

Chapter 8 **Using Special Features** 207
Create, modify, and use forms; translate to and from another language; create, format, and work with charts

Chapter 9 **Creating Webpages** 229
Create and save a Word document as a webpage, configure web options, understand HTML, insert hyperlinks, create HTML elements

Chapter 10 **Using Word with Other People** 243
Track and review changes, create reviewing shortcuts, add comments, highlight objects, use multiple copies, compare documents

Index 257

Contents

Acknowledgments.. xv

Introduction xvii

Chapter 1 **Stepping into Word** 1

Open and Exit Word 2
- Use Windows 7 to Open Word 2
- Using Touch 3
- Start Word in Windows 8 4

Explore Word 4
- Open a Document 4
- Close a Document 4
- Exit Word 4
- Explore the Word Window 4
- Become Familiar with the Ribbon 7
- Use the Mouse 8
- Use the Mini Toolbar in Word 8
- Use Tabs and Menus 9
- Use Views in Word 9

Personalize and Customize Word 11
- Work with File View 11
- Customize the Ribbon 11
- Customize the Quick Access Toolbar 15
- Show or Hide ScreenTips 18
- Add Identifying Information to Documents 18
- Set Preferences 20
- Understanding Versions of Office 2013 21

Get Help 22
- Open Help 22
- Use the Thesaurus 22
- Define a Word 23
- Translate a Document 24

Chapter 2 **Working with Documents** 27

- Understanding Word Files 28

Create a New Document 28
- Using Templates 28
- Select a Template on Your Computer 30
- Open a Blank Document 32

Open an Existing Document 32
- Locate an Existing Document 32
- Using SkyDrive 34
- Import a Document 36

Write a Document 36
- Enter Text 36

Determine Where Text Will Appear 37
Insert Text or Type Over It 37
Insert Symbols or Special Characters 38
Insert Line or Page Breaks 39
Select Text 40
Delete Text 41
Copy and Move Text 42
Use the Office Clipboard 43
Edit a Document 45
Move Around in a Document 45
Find and Replace Text 47
Use Wildcards 50
Complete and Save a Document 51
Check Spelling and Grammar 51
Get SkyDrive for Your Files 53
Save a Document for the First Time 53
Save a Document Automatically 56
Save a Document 56

3 Chapter 3 **Formatting a Document** 57
Format Text 57
Apply Character Formatting 58
Reset Font Defaults 63
Change Character Spacing and OpenType Features 63
Change Capitalization 68
Create a Drop Cap 68
Format a Paragraph 69
Set Paragraph Alignment 69
Indenting a Paragraph 71
Use the Ruler for Indents 73
Understand Line and Paragraph Spacing 73
Set Line Spacing 73
Use Numbered and Bulleted Lists 76
Define New Multilevel Lists 81
Add Horizontal Lines, Borders, and Shading 81
Format a Page 84
Turn On Formatting Marks 84
Set Margins 85
Copy Formatting 85
Use a Dialog Box to Format a Page 86
Use Mirror Margins 87
Determine Page Orientation 87
Specify Paper Size 87
Track Inconsistent Formatting 87
Set Vertical Alignment 88

4 Chapter 4 **Customizing a Document** 89
Use Styles 89
Understanding Themes, Styles, and Templates 90
Identify Text with a Style 90
Apply Predefined Style Sets to a Document 90
Create a New Style 91

Modify a Style 93
Clear a Style from Text or a Document 94
Delete Styles from the Gallery 94
Examine Current Styles 95
Use Themes 96
Assign a Theme to Your Document 96
Change a Theme 96
Create a Custom Theme 99
Use Templates 100
Apply a Template to a New Document 100
Create a Template 100
Work with Documents 103
Create Section Breaks 103
Create and Use Columns 104
Use Tabs 105
Add Headers and Footers 107
Add Footnotes and Endnotes 110
Create an Index 112
Create a Table of Contents 114
Create and Use Outlines 116
Use View Buttons 118
Use Word Writing Aids 118
Implement AutoCorrect 118
Use AutoFormat 120
Use Building Blocks 121
Count Characters and Words 122
Use Highlighting 123
Add Hyphenation 124
Explore the Thesaurus 125
Enter an Equation 125

Chapter 5 **Printing and Using Mail Merge** 129
Print Documents 129
Set Up Your Printer 129
Define How a Document Is Printed 130
Preview What You'll Print 132
Print a Document 135
Print an Envelope 137
Print Labels 140
Fax a Document 141
Send an Email 142
Merge Lists with Letters and Envelopes 143
Perform a Mail Merge Using the Wizard 144
Use Rules 150
Merge to Envelopes 151
Merge to Labels 152

Chapter 6 **Using Tables** 155
Create Tables 155
Create a Table 155
Dissecting a Table 156

5

6

Use Table Tools 158
Select Tables, Rows, Columns, or Cells 159
Change the Table Size 160
Change Column Width and Row Height 162
Work with Tables 164
Enter Information into Tables 164
Sort Data 164
Move and Copy Tables, Columns, and Rows 166
Calculate Values Using Formulas 167
Working with Formulas 167
Convert Tables to Text and Text to Tables 168
Repeat Header Rows 169
Remove a Table 170
Format Content 170
Change a Table's Appearance 172
Merge and Split Cells 172
Change a Table's Alignment 172
Wrap Text Around a Table 173
Change Cell Margins 174
Apply Shading and Border Effects 174
Apply Styles to a Table Automatically 175

7 Chapter 7 **Working with Illustrations** 179
Work with Pictures 179
Add Pictures from a Computer 179
Linking Picture Files 185
Use the Picture Tools Format Tab 185
Crop Unwanted Areas of a Photo 185
Position "In-Line" Pictures 187
Reduce a Picture's File Size 188
Wrap Text Around a Picture 188
Create Drawings 189
Add Shapes 190
Use Color Effects 190
Work with Curves 192
Add Special Effects to Text 193
Create a Diagram 195
Add Objects from Other Programs 198
Take Screenshots 198
Modify Illustrations 201
Resize and Rotate Illustrations Precisely 201
Position Illustrations 202
Understanding Illustration Positioning 203
Use Handles and Borders to Position Objects 205
Position Illustrations Other Ways 205
Combine Illustrations by Grouping 206

8 Chapter 8 **Using Special Features** 207
Work with Forms 207
Use Microsoft Form Templates 207
Modify a Template 209

Create a Form 211
Use a Form 213
Translate Text 214
Translate a Word or Phrase 214
Translate Selected Text 215
Translate an Entire Document 215
Understanding Data Series and Axes 217
Work with Charts 217
Create a Chart 217
Determine the Chart Type 220
Select Chart Items 221
Work with Chart Items 223
Format Chart Items 226
Format Text 226
Work with the Data Table 227

Chapter 9 **Creating Webpages** 229
Create and Save a Webpage in Word 229
Understanding HTML and How Word Uses It 230
Create a Webpage 230
Save Word Documents as Webpages 231
Choosing Suitable Web File Formats 232
Use Word to Create HTML Elements 232
Work with Webpages in Word 233
Configure Web Options in Word 233
Understanding Hyperlinks 237
Insert a Hyperlink 237
Verify How a Page Will Look 240
Remove Personal Information from the File Properties 241
Remove Word-Specific Tags from a Document 242

Chapter 10 **Using Word with Other People** 243
Mark Changes 243
Track Changes 245
Review Changes 249
Add Comments 252
Highlight Text 254
Work with Multiple Documents 255
Save Several Copies of a Document 255
Compare Documents 255

Index 257

9

10

Acknowledgments

This book is a team effort of truly talented people. Among them are:

Roger Stewart, sponsoring editor, believed in us enough to sell the series, and continues to stand behind us as we go through the fourth edition. Thanks, Roger!

Patty Mon and **Sheena Uprety**, project editors, greased the wheels and straightened the track to make a very smooth production process. Thanks, Patty and Sheena!

Lisa McCoy, copy editor, added greatly to the readability and understandability of the book while always being a joy to work with. Thanks, Lisa!

Valerie Perry, indexer, who adds so much to the usability of the book, and does so quickly and without notice. Thanks, Valerie!

Introduction

QuickSteps® books are recipe books for computer users. They answer the question "How do I…?" by providing quick sets of steps to accomplish the most common tasks in a particular program. The sets of steps ("QuickSteps") are the central focus of the book and show you how to quickly perform many functions and tasks. Notes, Tips, and Cautions augment the steps, and are presented next to the text they relate to. The brief introductions are minimal rather than narrative, and numerous illustrations and figures, many with callouts, support the steps.

QuickSteps® books are organized by function and the tasks needed to perform that function. Each function is a chapter. Each task contains the steps needed for accomplishing the function along with relevant Notes, Tips, Cautions, and screenshots. Tasks will be easy to find through:

- The table of contents, which lists the functional areas (chapters) and tasks in the order they are presented
- A QuickSteps list of tasks on the opening page of each chapter
- The index, with its alphabetical list of terms used in describing the functions and tasks
- Color-coded tabs for each chapter or functional area, with an index to the tabs just before the table of contents

Conventions Used in This Book

Microsoft® Word 2013 QuickSteps® uses several conventions designed to make the book easier for you to follow:

- A ✓ in the table of contents references a QuickFacts sidebar in a chapter.
- **Bold** type is used for words on the screen that you are to do something with, such as click **Save As** or **Open**.
- *Italic* type is used for a word or phrase that is being defined or otherwise deserves special emphasis.
- <u>Underlined</u> type is used for text that you are to type from the keyboard. SMALL CAPITAL LETTERS are used for keys on the keyboard, such as **ENTER** and **SHIFT**.
- When you are expected to enter a command, you are told to press the key(s). If you are to enter text or numbers, you are told to type them. Specific letters or numbers to be entered will be underlined.
- A pipe (|) indicates that you are to enter items in sequence. For instance, "Click **Insert | Page Number | Current Position**" would tell you to first click the Insert tab, then the Page Number command, then find and click Current Position on the submenu.

QuickSteps to...

- Use Windows 7 to Open Word
- Start Word in Windows 8
- Open a Document
- Close a Document
- Exit Word
- Explore the Word Window
- Become Familiar with the Ribbon
- Use the Mouse
- Use the Mini Toolbar in Word
- Use Tabs and Menus
- Use Views in Word
- Work with File View
- Customize the Ribbon
- Customize the Quick Access Toolbar
- Show or Hide ScreenTips
- Add Identifying Information to Documents
- Set Preferences
- Open Help
- Use the Thesaurus
- Define a Word
- Translate a Document

Chapter 1

Stepping into Word

Microsoft Word is the most widely used of all word-processing programs, and Word 2013 is the latest version in that line. While maintaining the core features and functionality of Word from years past, this version continues the evolution of Office products from a menu-driven user interface (the collection of screen elements that allows you to use and navigate the program) to that of a touchable, customizable *ribbon,* an organizational scheme to better connect tools to tasks.

New features include touch mode, a flatter look of the ribbon, a new way to access programs (in place of the Start menu), new alignment lines when moving objects, online picture support, resume reading mode, and better PDF support. Along with these and other infrastructure enhancements, Word 2013 adds several new ease-of-use features such as a *live layout and alignment* so you can better place images in a document, and this version improves collaboration with a new simple markup view and the ability to edit PDF documents in Word. While preserving the simple elegance of producing a professional-looking document, Microsoft continues to find ways to make working with documents easier and more intuitive as it adds features to use and distribute information in more meaningful ways.

In this chapter you will become familiar with Word; see how to start and exit it; use Word's windows, panes, ribbon, toolbars, and menus; learn how to get help; and find out how to customize Word and the ribbon.

OPEN AND EXIT WORD

Word can be opened using several methods, depending on which operating system you have, what method you consider to be convenient, your personal style, and the appearance of your desktop. In this section you'll see several ways to start Word using either Windows 7 or 8. You'll also see how to exit Word.

 Use Windows 7 to Open Word

With Windows 7, you can open Word using the Start menu, the keyboard, the taskbar, or from a shortcut on your desktop.

Open Word from the Start Menu

1. Start your computer, if it is not already running, and log on to Windows if necessary.
2. Click **Start**. The Start menu opens.
3. Click **All Programs**, scroll down the menu if needed by clicking the bar on the right, click **Microsoft Office 2013**, and click **Word 2013**.

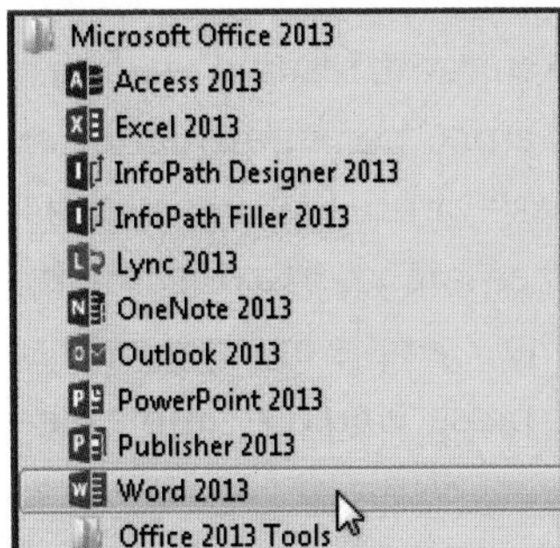

Pin a Word Shortcut to the Start Menu or Taskbar

When you *pin* something, you place a shortcut icon to it in a menu or taskbar. You can pin a shortcut to Word to the Start menu itself or to the taskbar at the bottom of your screen, and then use either of the shortcut icons to open Word. Here is how to pin Word to the Start menu or taskbar using Windows 7.

1. Click **Start** to open the Start menu, click **All Programs**, scroll down (if needed), and click **Microsoft Office 2013**.
2. Right-click (click the right mouse button) **Word 2013:**
   - Click **Pin To Start Menu** to place a shortcut on the Start menu itself.
   - Click **Pin To Taskbar** to place a shortcut to Word on the taskbar.

Word can then be started using the next set of steps.

TIP The Start menu's contents and sequence of items change depending on how often you use the various programs. The icons of the programs you use most often are automatically displayed on the left side of the Start menu. You can also add items to the list. This is a great way to place favorite programs in a handy place. If you want a program to be more accessible, you can "pin" it to the Start menu using the steps in this chapter.

Start Word Using a Shortcut

If you have pinned a shortcut to the Start menu (or use the program frequently enough that it is placed there automatically) or to the taskbar, you'll find Word's icon displayed there. To use the shortcuts to start Word:

1. To open Word using the Start menu shortcut, click **Start**. The Start menu opens.

2. Hover over the **Word** icon and, if you have used a previous version of Word, a list of files most recently accessed will be displayed. Otherwise, you'll not see the recent files.
   - If you have a list of recent files, click **Word** to open it without also opening a file; then click a filename to open Word with the selected file.
   - If you have no recent files, click **Word** and you'll see the list of templates. Click the template you want.

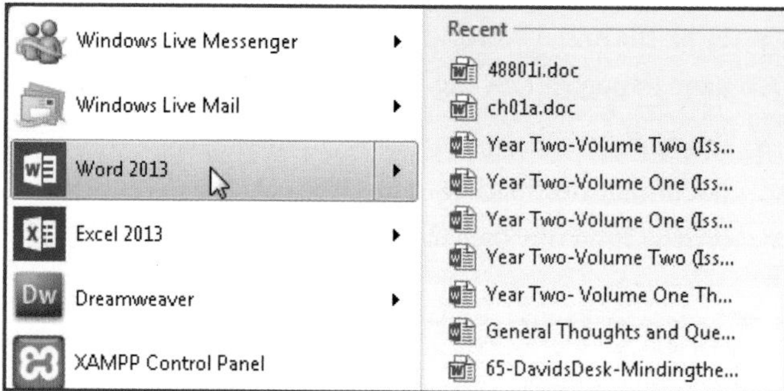

–Or–

To open Word using the taskbar shortcut, click the **Word** icon on the taskbar.

   - If you have already used Word during this computer session, Word will open with a blank document pane. Just begin typing to start a new file, or click **File | Open** to open an existing file.
   - If you are starting Word for the first time this computer session, Word will open and you'll see a list of templates, perhaps with a list of recent files. Click a template for a new document, or click a listed recent file to open an existing file.

Create a Desktop Shortcut

An easy way to start Word is to create a shortcut icon on the desktop and use it to start the program.

1. Click **Start**, click **All Programs**, and click **Microsoft Office 2013**.
2. Right-click **Word 2013**, click **Send To**, and click **Desktop (Create Shortcut)**.

In this case, Word is started by double-clicking (pressing the mouse button twice in rapid succession) it.

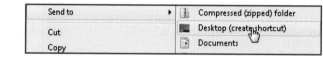

QuickFacts

Using Touch

Many newer computers running Windows 8 have a touch-sensitive screen that can be used in place of the mouse and occasionally the keyboard. In the earlier part of this chapter, we've included both mouse and touch commands to perform the steps. To keep this from getting laborious, from here on we'll just refer to the mouse commands, but you can use Table 1-1 for the relevant touch command for each mouse command. For further information on using touch and/or the keyboard in place of or in addition to the mouse, see *Windows 8 QuickSteps*. That book has tear-out tables inside the back cover that compare the mouse, touch, and keyboard commands. These tables are also available at quickstepsbooks.com/windows8cheats. Click **Download Tables**.

Table 1-1: Touch vs. Mouse Commands for Various Actions

Action	With a Mouse	With Touch
Select an object or start an app in the Start screen	**Click** the object	**Tap** the object
Open an object or start an app on the desktop	**Double-click** the object	**Double-tap** the object
Open an object's context menu or the app bar for an app	**Right-click** the object	**Touch** and hold for a moment; then swipe down
Move an object on the screen	**Drag** the object with the mouse	**Drag** the object with your finger

1 2 3 4 5 6 7 8 9 10

Start Word in Windows 8

Windows 8 will give you a very different way to open Word. With a normal installation of Office 2013 on Windows 8, you should see a tile for Word 2013 on the Start screen.

Click or tap that tile to start Word.

If you don't see the Word tile on the Start screen:

1. Right-click or swipe up from the bottom of the screen, and click or tap **All Apps**. You should see the Word tile under Microsoft Office 2013.

2. Before selecting it, right-click or touch and hold for a moment and then swipe down the tile to open the command bar. Note the two options on the left:

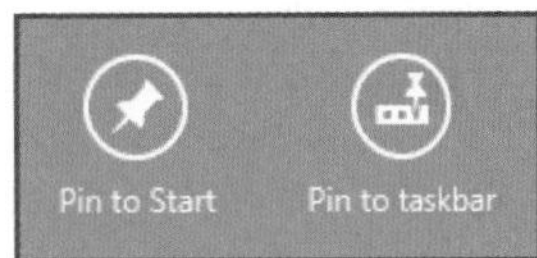

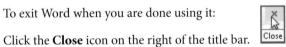

3. If you will be using Word a great deal, click or tap **Pin To Start** and/or **Pin To Taskbar** to pin the Word tile either to the Start screen or on the desktop's taskbar so you can start it in the future with fewer steps.
4. In any case, click or tap the **Word** tile to start it.

EXPLORE WORD

Word uses a wide assortment of windows, ribbon tabs, toolbars, menus, and special features to accomplish its functions. Much of this book explores how to find and use all of those items. In this section you'll learn to use the most common features of the default Word window, including the parts of the window, the tabs on the ribbon, and the task pane.

Open a Document

You may open an existing document or a new one. If you are starting Word for the first time during a computer session, you'll see the initial Word screen, which displays the files and templates for you to open. If you have already used Word in this computer session, you will see a blank document. See Chapter 2 for a more detailed description of how to open a template or document. Here is briefly how to open a document:

1. Open Word using one of the techniques described earlier.
2. Do one of the following to open a new or existing document:
   - From the initial Word screen, under Recent, click a filename to open a recently used document.
   - From the initial Word screen, click the template listed in the right pane to open a new file.
   - From a document pane screen, click **File | Open**, click the document destination, and click either a recent document or browse for a file. (See Chapter 2.)

Close a Document

To close a document when you are done using it:

Click **File | Close**.

Exit Word

To exit Word when you are done using it:

Click the **Close** icon on the right of the title bar.

Explore the Word Window

The Word window has many features to aid you in creating and editing documents. The view presented to you when you first start Word is shown in Figure 1-1. It allows you to quickly either click a document you've recently used or create a new one. In Figure 1-2, you can see the primary parts of the Word working document, including the structure of the ribbon. The principal features of the Word window, including the various ribbon tabs, are described further in this and other chapters of this book.

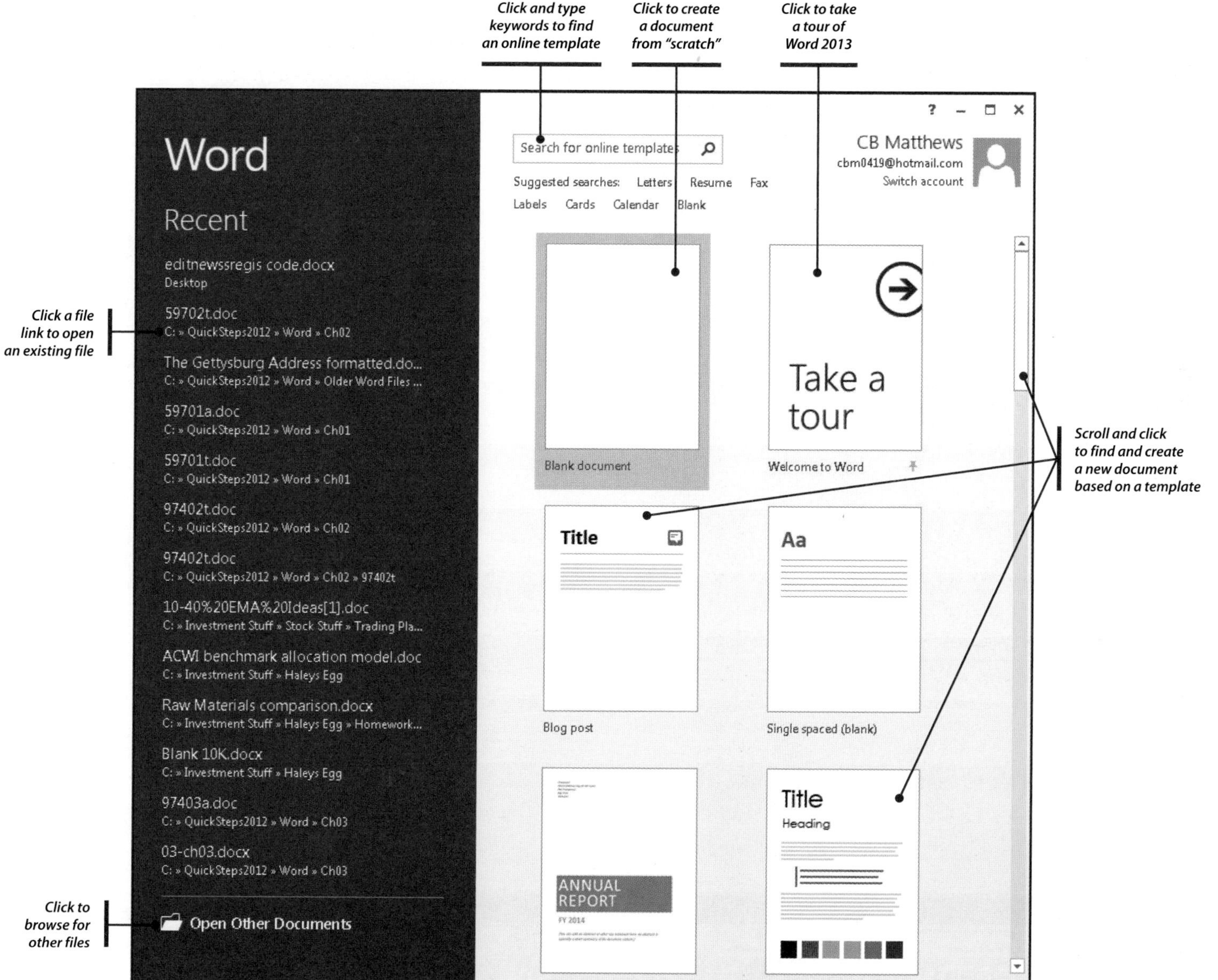

***Figure 1-1:** When you first load Word 2013, you'll see a selection of files you recently used, a selection of templates you may want to use, and a Welcome Tour.*

1

2

3

4

5

6

7

8

9

10

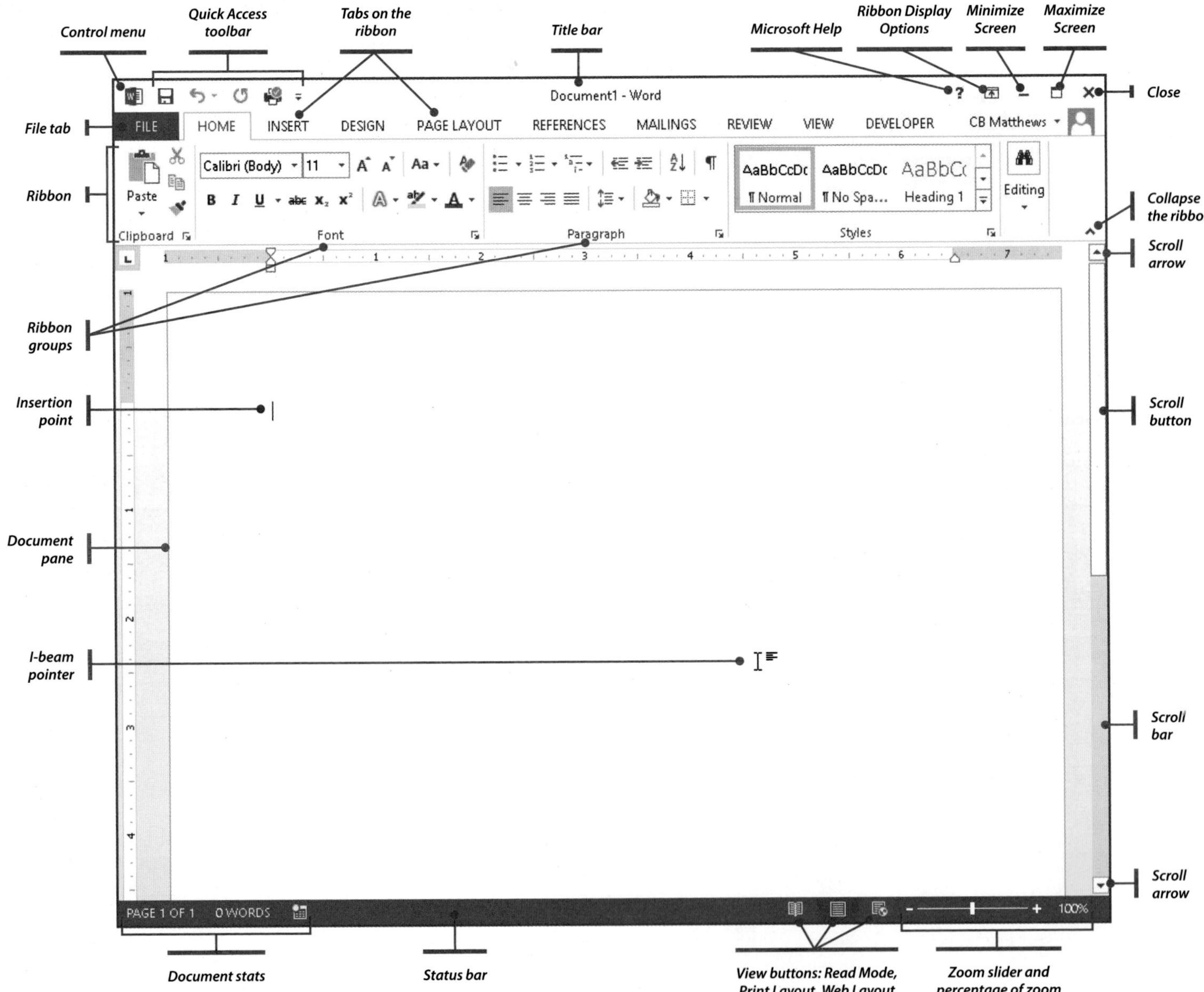

Figure 1-2: **The default Word window used for creating and editing documents**

 Become Familiar with the Ribbon

Microsoft uses the *ribbon* to contain tools and features you'll use when working with Word (see Figure 1-2). The ribbon collects tools for a given function into *groups*—for example, the Font group provides the tools to work with text. Groups are then organized into tabs for working on likely tasks. For instance, the Insert tab contains groups for adding components, such as tables, links, and charts, to your document (or spreadsheet or slide presentation). Each Office program has a default set of tabs, with additional *contextual* tabs that appear as the context of your work changes. For example, when you select a picture, a Format tab containing shapes and drawing tools that you can use with the particular object appears beneath the defining tools tab (such as the Picture Tools Format tab shown in Figure 1-3); when the object is unselected, the Format tab disappears.

The ribbon contains labeled buttons you can click to use a given command or tool. Depending on the tool, you are then presented with additional options in the form of a list of commands, a dialog box or task pane, or galleries of choices that reflect what you'll see in your work. Groups that contain several more tools than can be displayed in the ribbon include a *Dialog Box Launcher* icon that takes you directly to these other choices.

The ribbon also takes advantage of Office features, including a live preview of many potential changes (for example, you can select text and see it change color as you point to various colors in the Font Color gallery).

TIP The ribbon adapts to the size of your Word window and your screen resolution, changing the size and shape of buttons and labels. You can see the difference yourself by increasing or decreasing the size of the window. For instance, if your Word window is initially not maximized, click **Maximize** and notice how the ribbon appears, and then click the **Restore Down** button on the title bar and again notice the ribbon. Drag the right border of the Word window toward the left, and see how the ribbon changes to reflect its decreasing real estate.

At the left end of the ribbon is the File tab, and above the left end of the ribbon is the Quick Access toolbar. The File tab provides access to the File view, which lets you work *with* your document (such as saving it), as opposed to the ribbon, which centers on working *in* your document (such as editing and formatting). The Quick Access toolbar provides an always-available location for your favorite tools. It starts out with a small default set of tools, but you can add to it. See the accompanying sections and figures for more information on the ribbon and the other elements of the Word window.

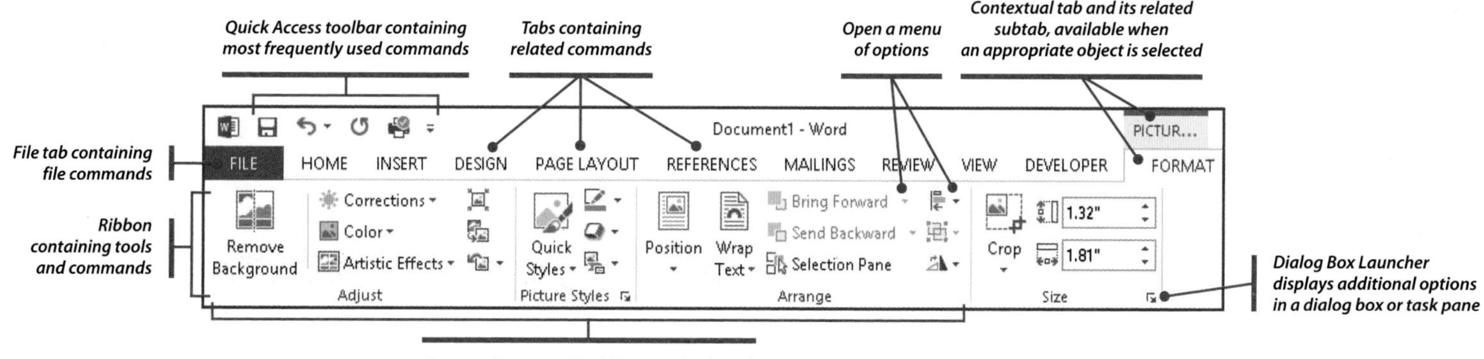

***Figure 1-3:* Organized into tabs and groups, the commands and tools on the ribbon are how you create, edit, and otherwise work with documents.**

> **TIP** To gain working space in the document pane, you can minimize the size of the ribbon. To do this, click the **Collapse The Ribbon** icon [^] in the upper-right of the ribbon's tab bar, or press **CTRL+F1** to toggle the size of the ribbon. You can also double-click the active tab name to minimize the ribbon and then restore it.

Use the Mouse

Most readers by now are familiar with using a mouse and understand how to use it and the terminology surrounding it. If you are a beginning computer user, you might find this section useful. Otherwise, you're good to go.

A *mouse* is any pointing device—including trackballs, pointing sticks, and graphic tablets—with two or more buttons. This book assumes you are using a two-button mouse. Moving the mouse moves the pointer on the screen. You *select* an object on the screen by moving the pointer so that it is on top of the object and then pressing the left button on the mouse.

You may control the mouse with either your left or right hand; therefore, the buttons may be switched. (See *Windows 7 QuickSteps* or *Windows 8 QuickSteps,* published by McGraw-Hill, for how to switch the buttons.) This book assumes the right hand controls the mouse and the left mouse button is "*the* mouse button." The right button is always called the "right mouse button." If you switch the buttons, you must change your interpretation of these phrases.

Five actions can be accomplished with the mouse:

- **Point** at an *object* on the screen (a button, an icon, a menu or one of its options, or a border) to highlight it. To *point* means to move the mouse so that the tip of the pointer is on top of the object.
- **Click** an object on the screen to *select* it, making that object the item that your next actions will affect. Clicking will also open a menu, select a menu option, or activate a button or "tool" on a toolbar or the ribbon. *Click* means to point at an object you want to select and quickly press and release the left mouse button.
- **Double-click** an object to open or activate it. *Double-click* means to point at an object you want to select and then press and release the left mouse button twice in rapid succession.
- **Right-click** an object to open a context menu containing commands used to manipulate that object. *Right-click* means to point at an object that you want to select and then quickly press and release the right mouse button. For example, right-clicking text opens this context menu:

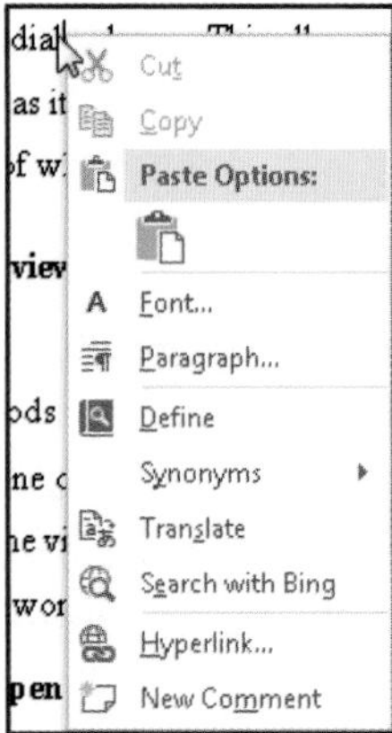

- **Drag** an object to move it on the screen to where you want it located within the document. *Drag* means to point at an object you want to move and then hold down the left mouse button while moving the mouse. The object is dragged as you move the mouse. When the object is where you want it, release the mouse button.

Use the Mini Toolbar in Word

When you select (highlight) text, a mini toolbar is displayed that allows you to perform an action directly on that text, such as making it bold or centering a paragraph. This toolbar contains a subset of the tools contained in the Fonts and Paragraph groups of the Home tab.

Display the Text Mini Toolbar

Select text by dragging over it. The mini toolbar will appear. If it fades as you move the mouse, move it directly over the toolbar to make it clearer.

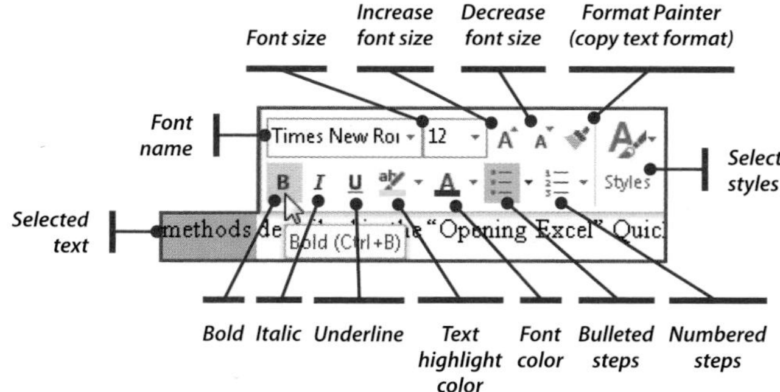

Use a Text Tool

Click the button or icon on the mini toolbar that represents the tool you want to use, as described earlier.

Hide the Mini Toolbar

You can hide the mini toolbar by moving the mouse pointer away from it or by pressing ESC. You can also hide the mini toolbar so it doesn't appear at all by changing the default setting, which is to show it.

1. Click **File | Options | General**.
2. Click **Show Mini Toolbar On Selection** to remove the check mark.

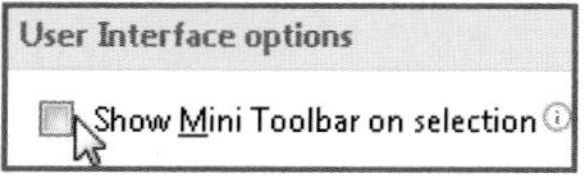

3. Click **OK** to finalize the choice.

Use Tabs and Menus

Command tabs are displayed at the top of the ribbon or in a dialog box. Examples are Home and Insert. Menus are displayed when you click a down arrow on a button on the ribbon, a dialog box, or a toolbar. You can use tabs and menus in the following ways:

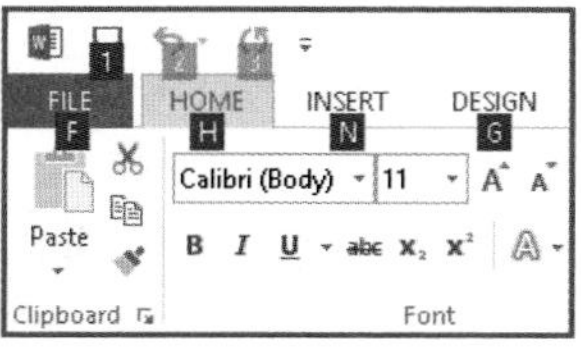

- To open a tab or menu with the mouse, click the tab or menu.
- To open a tab or menu with the keyboard, press ALT and the letter or number that appears in a small box for the object, tab, or menu name. For example, press ALT+F to open the **File** tab.
- To select an option on a tab or menu, click the tab or menu to open it, and then click the option.

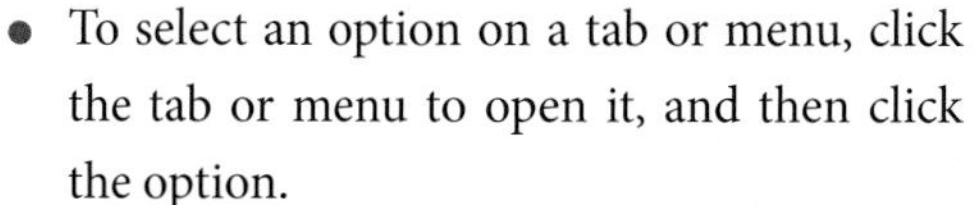

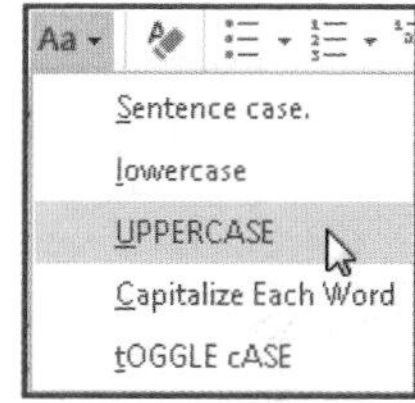

NOTE A number of menu options have a right-pointing arrow on their right to indicate that a submenu is associated with that option. To open this type of menu, hover the mouse pointer over the path to the submenu. After the submenu appears, move the pointer to the the submenu, and click the desired option. As an example, click **Insert | Table | Quick Tables** to see the submenu.

Use Views in Word

Word presents text in several views, allowing you to choose which one facilitates the task you are doing. To access a view, click the **View** tab, and then click a Views group button:

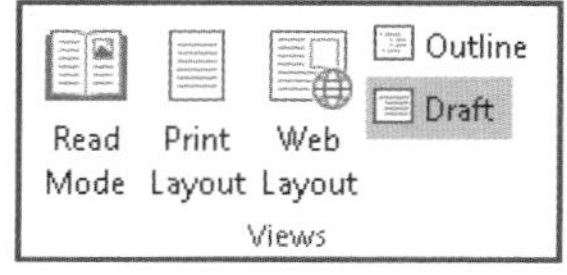

- **Read Mode** displays the text without the ribbon, giving you a larger reading space.
- **Print Layout** displays the text as it looks on a printed page.
- **Web Layout** shows how the text will look as a webpage. Creating web layout pages is discussed in Chapter 9.

- **Outline** displays the text in outline form, with a contextual Outlining tab on the ribbon, shown in Figure 1-4. You can use this view to promote and demote levels of text and rearrange levels, available in the Outline Tools group. With the Show Document button, you can toggle commands to extend your ability to create, insert, unlink, merge, split, and lock the document. Click **Close Outline View** to return to Normal view. Outlining is discussed further in Chapter 4.
- **Draft** displays the text of the document in draft status for quick and easy editing. Headers and footers may not be visible.

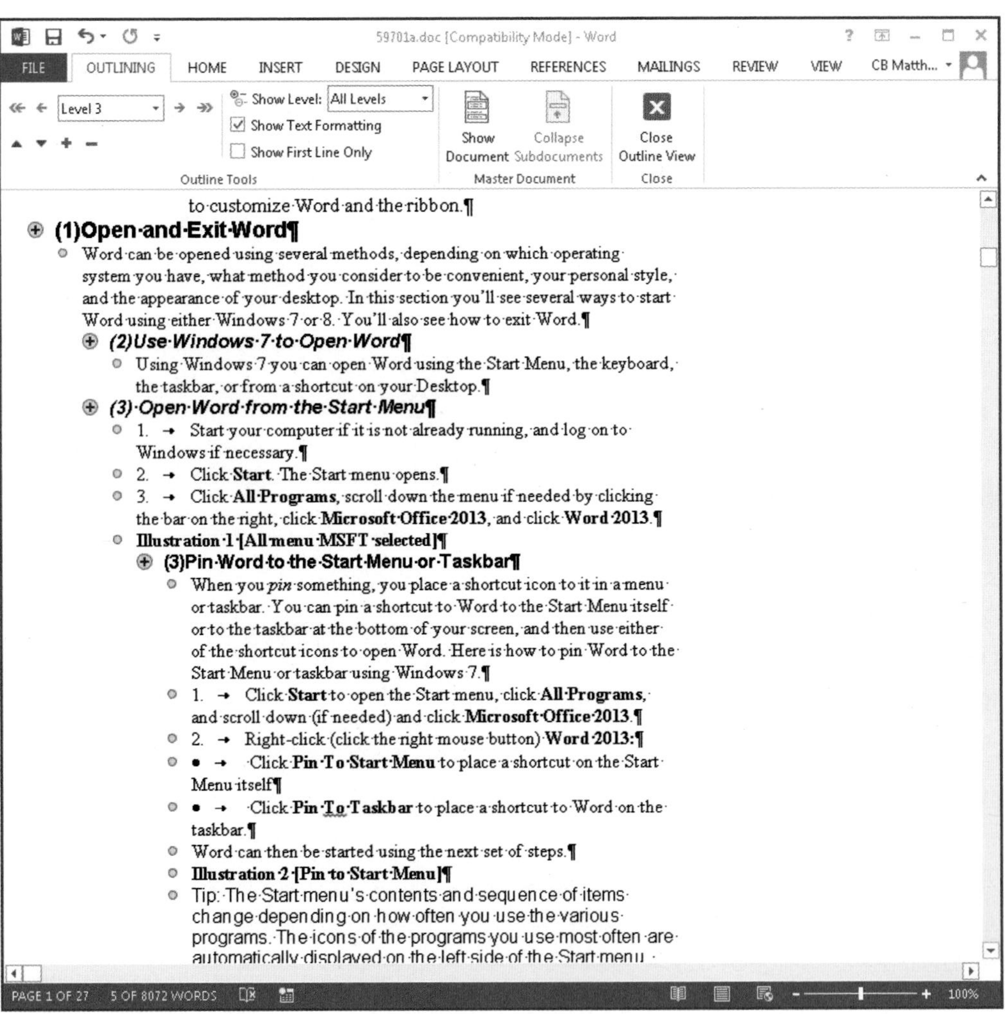

Figure 1-4: ***The Outline view displays a special outlining ribbon that provides commands to manipulate and create outlines in your text.***

NOTE A file created with an earlier version of Word will be identified as such with "Compatibility Mode" in the title bar, as shown in Figure 1-4. Such a file can be saved as a Word 2013 file, bringing it up to current standards.

PERSONALIZE AND CUSTOMIZE WORD

You can personalize Word, or make it your own, by changing the settings Word has for options such as the layout and contents of the ribbon, the tools available on the Quick Access toolbar, or your user name and initials. You can customize Word by changing the general default settings with regard to editing, proofing, display, and other options. Many of these options are discussed in the other chapters. Here we will look at customizing the ribbon, the Quick Access toolbar, the display, and other options. We'll begin by looking at Office 2013's new File view.

Work with File View

Word 2013 shares with the other Office 2013 programs an improved way to customize tasks as well as to manipulate settings that affect the total document, such as opening, closing, printing, and saving from one screen, avoiding the need to open several dialog boxes. These settings are accessed via the File view, which, as you might guess, handles file-related tasks like saving or opening a file. Figure 1-5 shows the File view.

To display the File view:

1. Open Word and a document using one of the methods described earlier in this chapter.
2. Click the **File** tab, and then click one of the areas of interest on the left of the window. For example, clicking Print provides a document preview and options for printing your work.

3. When finished, to return to working with a document, click the LEFT ARROW at the top of the File view.

Customize the Ribbon

The default ribbon consists of nine tabs, including File (see Figure 1-2), each tab containing several groups and subgroups that combine related tasks. While Word strives to provide a logical hierarchy to all the tasks available to you, you may not find its way of organizing functions to be the most convenient. Consequently, Word offers you the ability to change how things are organized. You can remove groups from the existing main tabs, create new tabs and groups, and populate your new groups from a plethora of available commands/tasks.

NOTE You'll see two types of tabs on the ribbon. The *main* tabs appear when you open a document and contain a generalized set of tools. *Tool* tabs are contextual, and appear when you are working with specific Word features, such as pictures, and contain tools for working with these features (see Figure 1-3).

To customize the ribbon:

Click the **File** tab, and in the left pane, click **Options**. In the Word Options dialog box, also in the left pane, click **Customize Ribbon**.

–Or–

Right-click any tool on the ribbon and click **Customize The Ribbon**.

In either case, the Customize The Ribbon And Keyboard Shortcuts view, shown in Figure 1-6, displays the list of available commands/tasks/tools on the left and a hierarchy of tabs and groups on the right.

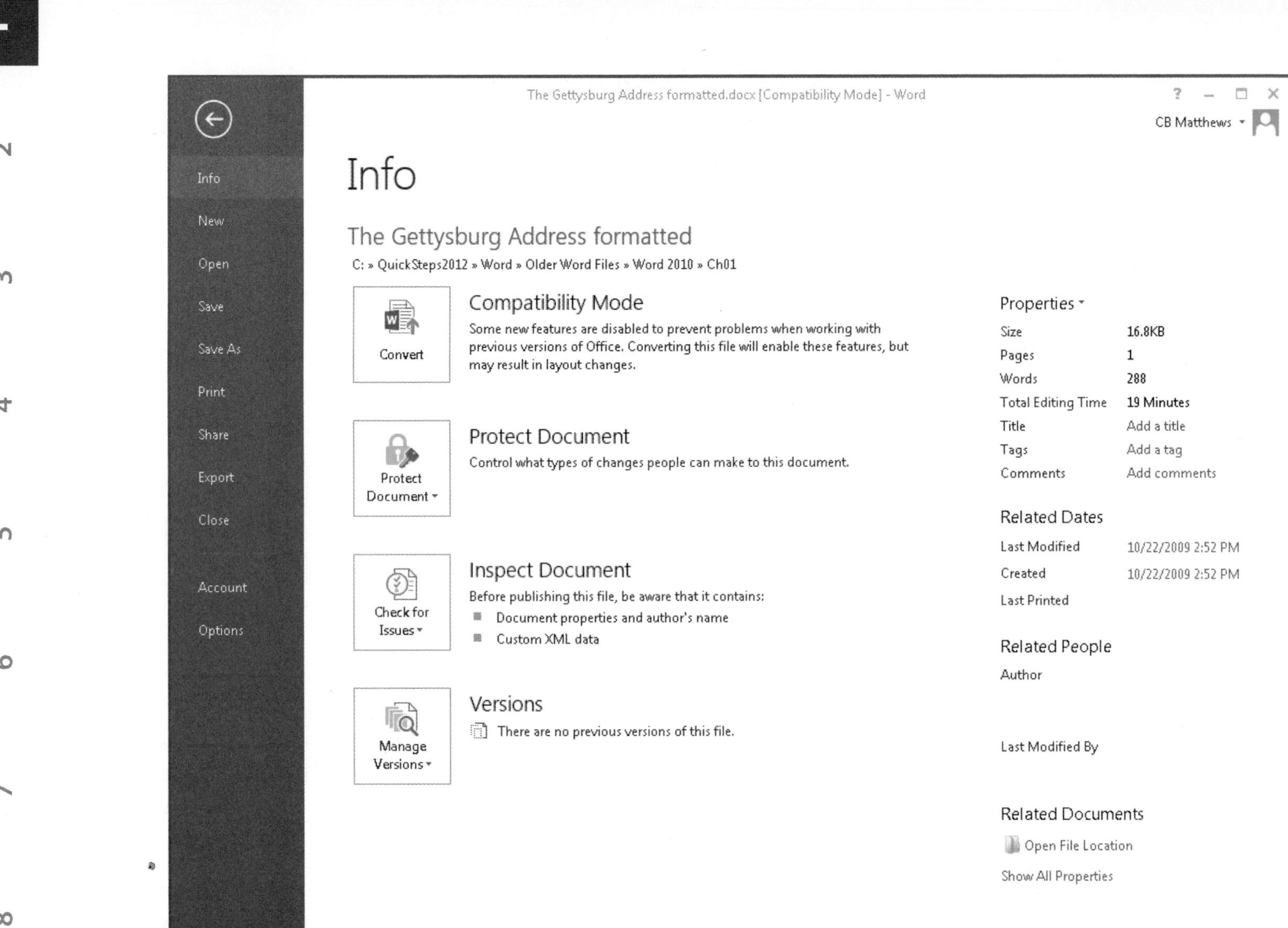
The Gettysburg Address formatted.docx [Compatibility Mode] - Word
CB Matthews
Info
New
Open
Save
Save As
Print
Share
Export
Close
Account
Options
Info
The Gettysburg Address formatted
C: » QuickSteps2012 » Word » Older Word Files » Word 2010 » Ch01
Convert
Compatibility Mode
Some new features are disabled to prevent problems when working with previous versions of Office. Converting this file will enable these features, but may result in layout changes.
Protect Document
Protect Document
Control what types of changes people can make to this document.
Check for Issues
Inspect Document
Before publishing this file, be aware that it contains:
Document properties and author's name
Custom XML data
Manage Versions
Versions
There are no previous versions of this file.
Properties
Size 16.8KB
Pages 1
Words 288
Total Editing Time 19 Minutes
Title Add a title
Tags Add a tag
Comments Add comments
Related Dates
Last Modified 10/22/2009 2:52 PM
Created 10/22/2009 2:52 PM
Last Printed
Related People
Author
Last Modified By
Related Documents
Open File Location
Show All Properties

Figure 1-5: File (or Info) view provides information about the document and handles many file-related tasks.

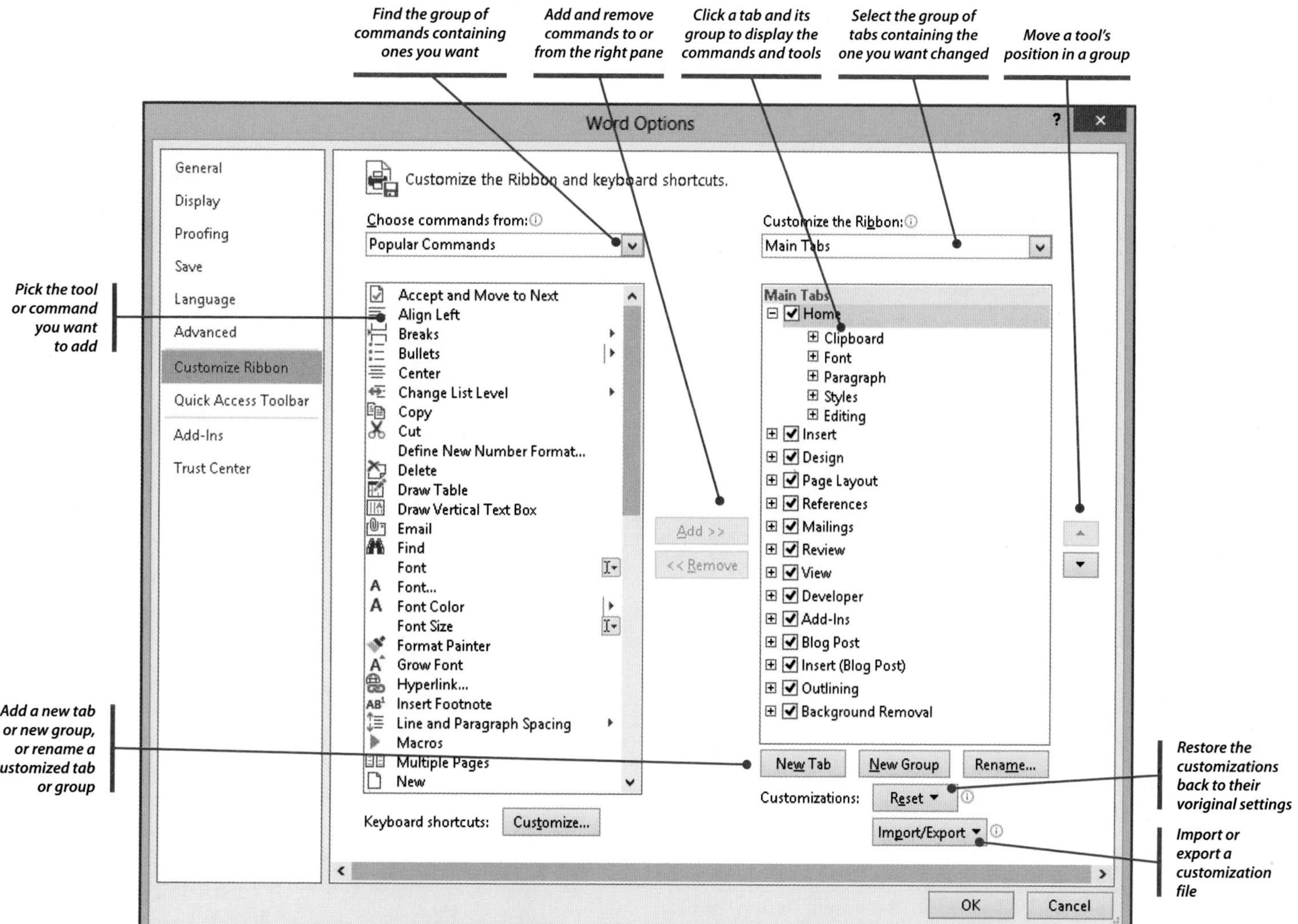

Figure 1-6: **You can easily modify or rearrange tabs and groups on the ribbon and assign tools where you want them.**

Rearrange Tabs and Groups

You can easily change the order in which your tabs and groups appear on the ribbon.

1. On the Customize The Ribbon And Keyboard Shortcuts view, click the **Customize The Ribbon** down arrow on the right, and select the type of tabs that contain the groups you want to work with.
2. To rearrange tabs, select the tab whose position on the ribbon you want to change, and click the **Move Up** and **Move Down** arrow on the right side of the tabs list to reposition the tab. (The topmost items in the list appear as the leftmost on the ribbon.)

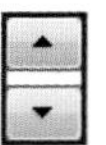

3. To rearrange groups, click the plus sign next the tab name to display its groups, and then click the **Move Up** and **Move Down** arrow to the side of the tabs list to reposition the group.
4. When finished, click **OK** to close the Word Options dialog box.

Create New Tabs and Groups

You can create new tabs and groups to collect your most often used tools. In a top-down structure, you first add a new tab and then the groups that you want beneath it. Finally, you add the commands and tools that will populate each group.

To add a new tab from within the Word Options dialog box, Customize Ribbon option:

1. Click **New Tab** at the bottom of the tabs list. You'll see both a new custom tab and group added to the list. You'll want to first handle the new tab.
2. Click the new tab to select it and move it where you want it (click the up and down arrows on the right as described in the previous section "Rearrange Tabs and Groups").
3. Rename the new tab by selecting it and clicking **Rename** at the bottom of the tabs list.

   –Or–

   Right-click the tab and click **Rename**.

   In either case, type a new name and click **OK**.

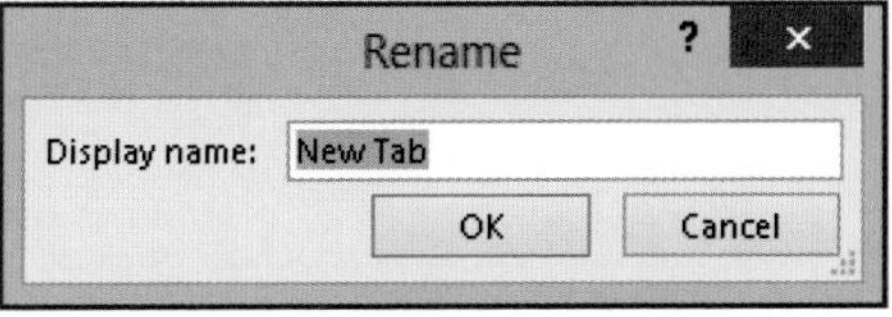

TIP If you have added a new tab, a new group is automatically added at the same time. You can rename it along with the new tab.

To add a new group:

1. Select the tab where you want to add a new group, and then click **New Group** found at the bottom of the tabs list. An empty New Group (Custom) item is added to the list for that tab.
2. Rename and rearrange the group within the tab as previously described.
3. If finished, click **OK** to close the Word Options dialog box.

TIP Don't be afraid to experiment with your ribbon by adding tabs and groups. You can always revert back to the default Word ribbon layout by clicking **Reset** under the tabs list and then choosing to either restore a selected tab or all tabs.

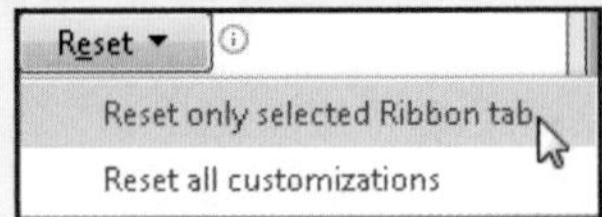

Add or Remove Commands/Tools

Once you have the tabs and groups created, named, and organized, you can add the tools you want to your custom groups. You can't add tools to an existing group. You will select commands or tools from the left column and add them to a custom group on the right.

1. On the Customize The Ribbon And Keyboard Shortcuts view, click the **Choose Commands From** down arrow. You will see a menu of categories of commands and tabs, such as Commands Not In The Ribbon or Tool Tabs. Choose a category of commands or tabs, or choose **All Commands** to see the full list. Expand the tab list by clicking the plus sign until you find and click (to select it) the tool you want to add to a custom group.
2. In the tabs list on the right, select the custom group to which you want to add the tool.
3. Click **Add** between the lists of commands and tabs. The command/tool is added under your group.
4. Repeat steps 1 through 3 to populate your custom groups with all the tools you want.
5. If you make a mistake, remove a tool from a custom group by selecting it and clicking **Remove**. To restore it as it was originally, click **Reset**.
6. Use the **Move Up** and **Move Down** arrows to the right of the tabs list to organize the added tools within your groups, and click **OK** when finished.

Customize the Quick Access Toolbar

The Quick Access toolbar can become a "best friend" if you modify it so that it fits your personal way of working.

Add to the Quick Access Toolbar

The Quick Access toolbar should contain the commands you most commonly use. The default tools are Save, Undo, and Redo. You can add commands to it if you want.

1. Click the down arrow to the right of the Quick Access toolbar and select one of the commands on the drop-drop menu to add it to the toolbar.

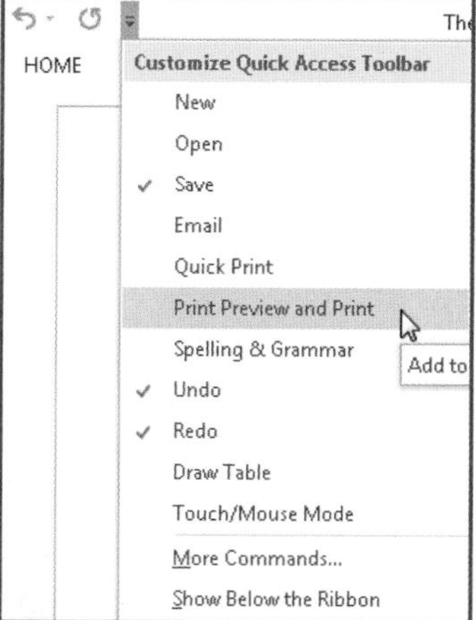

-Or-

Click the Quick Access toolbar down arrow, and click **More Commands** to view a more expansive list of Word tools.

-Or-

Click the **File** tab, click **Options**, and click **Quick Access Toolbar**.

In either of the last two cases, the Word Options dialog box appears with the Quick Access toolbar customization options, as displayed in Figure 1-7.

2. Open the **Choose Commands From** drop-down list, and select the source of the commands you want from the available options.

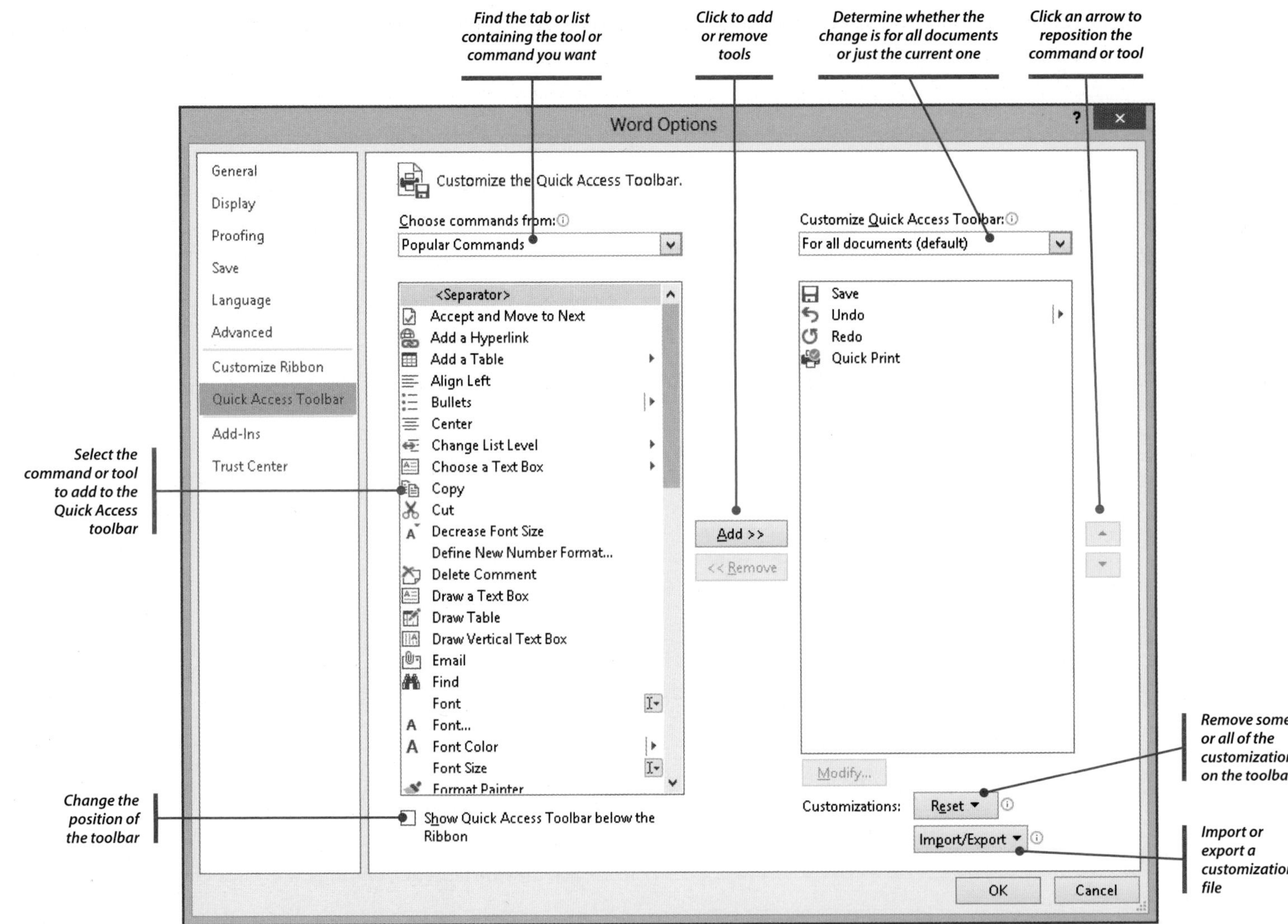

Figure 1-7: ***You can customize the Quick Access toolbar by adding to and removing from it commands for easy and quick access.***

3. In the leftmost list box, find and click the command you want to add to the toolbar, and then click **Add** to move its name to the list box on the right. Repeat this for all the commands you want in the toolbar.
4. Click **OK** when you are finished.

NOTE You can add a command to the Quick Access toolbar from the ribbon by right-clicking the button and choosing **Add To Quick Access Toolbar**.

Move the Quick Access Toolbar

You can display the Quick Access toolbar at its default position (above the ribbon) or directly below the ribbon using one of the following methods:

Right-click the tool on the Quick Access toolbar or on the ribbon, and click **Show Quick Access Toolbar Below The Ribbon** (once located below the ribbon, you can move it above the ribbon in the same manner).

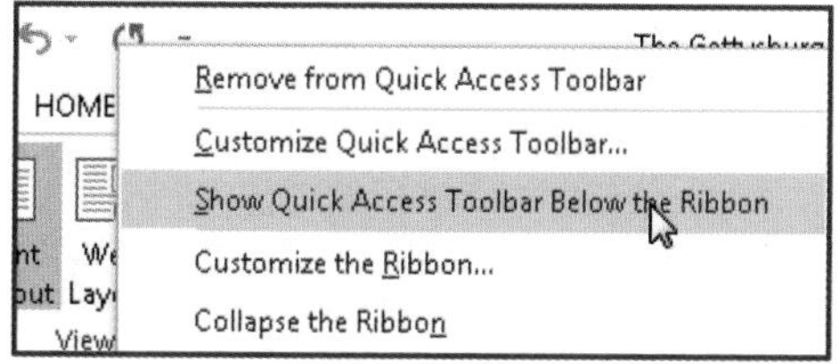

–Or–

Right-click a tool in the Quick Access toolbar, and click **Customize Quick Access Toolbar** to open the Word Options dialog box, and the Customize The Ribbon pane. Click the **Show Quick Access Toolbar Below The Ribbon** check box in the lower left, and click **OK** (to return the toolbar above the ribbon, open the pane and clear the check box).

Customize the Quick Access Toolbar for a Document

By default, changes made to the Quick Access toolbar are applicable to all documents. You can create a toolbar that only applies to the document you currently have open.

1. In the Customize The Quick Access Toolbar dialog box, click the **Customize Quick Access Toolbar** down arrow.
2. Click the option that identifies the document the toolbar will apply to.

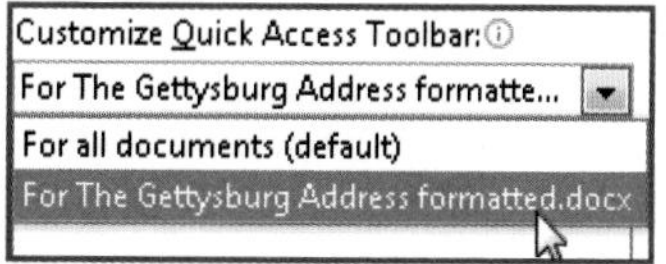

3. Click **OK** when finished.

Rearrange Tools on the Quick Access Toolbar

You can change the order in which tools appear on the Quick Access toolbar.

1. In the Customize The Quick Access Toolbar pane, select the tool in the list on the right whose position you want to change.
2. Click the **Move Up** or **Move Down** arrow to the right of the list to move the tool. Moving the tool up moves it to the left in the on-screen toolbar; moving it down the list moves it to the right in the on-screen toolbar.
3. Click **OK** when finished.

Show or Hide ScreenTips

When you hold the mouse pointer over a command or tool, a ScreenTip is displayed. The tip may be just the name of the tool or command, or it may be enhanced with a small description. You can hide the tips or change whether they are enhanced or not.

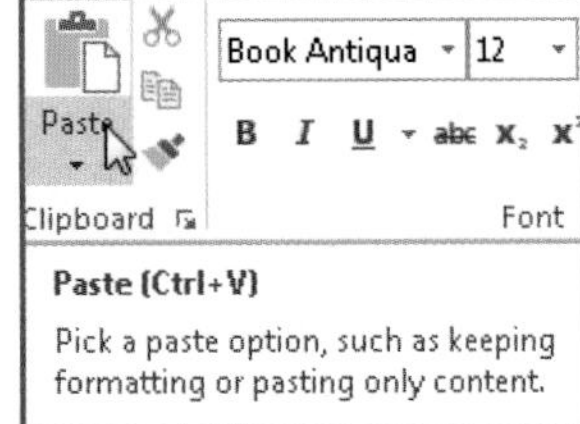

1. Click **File | Options | General**.
2. Open the **ScreenTip Style** drop-down list, and choose the option you want.

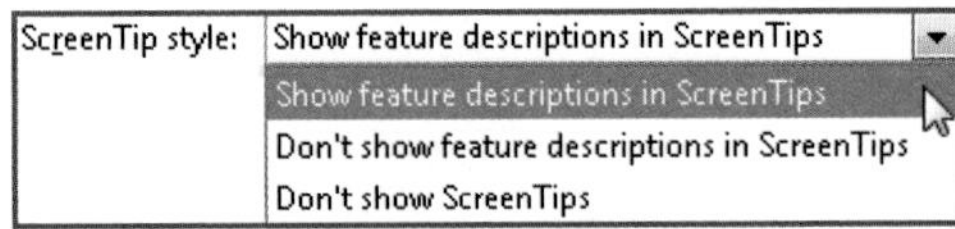

3. Click **OK** to finalize the choice.

Change the Window Background Color or Design

You can change the background color of the Word window, which is set to white by default, to light or dark gray instead.

1. Click **File | Options | General**.
   - To change the background color, click the **Office Theme** down arrow, and click the color you want.
   - To change the background design on the top edge of the screen, click the **Office Background** down arrow, and click the design you want.
2. Click **OK** to save the change.

Add Identifying Information to Documents

You can add identifying information to a document to make it easier to organize your documents and to find them quickly during searches,

TIP To open the Word Options dialog box and change keyboard shortcuts for a specific command, click **File | Options | Customize Ribbon**. On the bottom left, click **Customize**. Under Categories, click a tab. The commands on that tab will be displayed under Commands. Click the command for which you want to change or specify a shortcut key. Under Current Keys, you'll see the shortcut key currently in use, if any. To add a new shortcut key, click in the **Press New Shortcut Key** box and then press the key combination you want and click **Assign**. To remove a shortcut key combination, click it under Current Keys and click **Remove**. Click **Reset All** to restore the original shortcuts. Click **Close**.

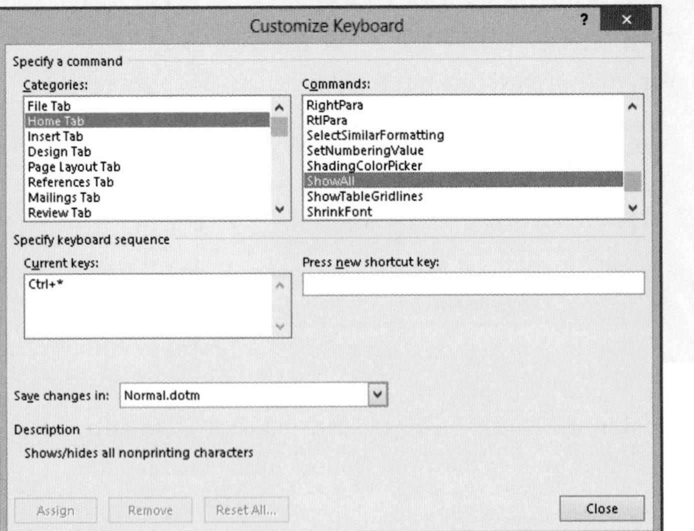

especially in a shared environment (see Chapter 9 for more on removing this document information).

1. Click **File** | **Info** (the default view), click **Properties** in the far-right pane, and click **Show Document Panel**. A Document Information panel containing standard identifiers displays under the ribbon, as shown in Figure 1-8.
2. Type identifying information, such as title, subject, and keywords (words or phrases that are associated with the document).

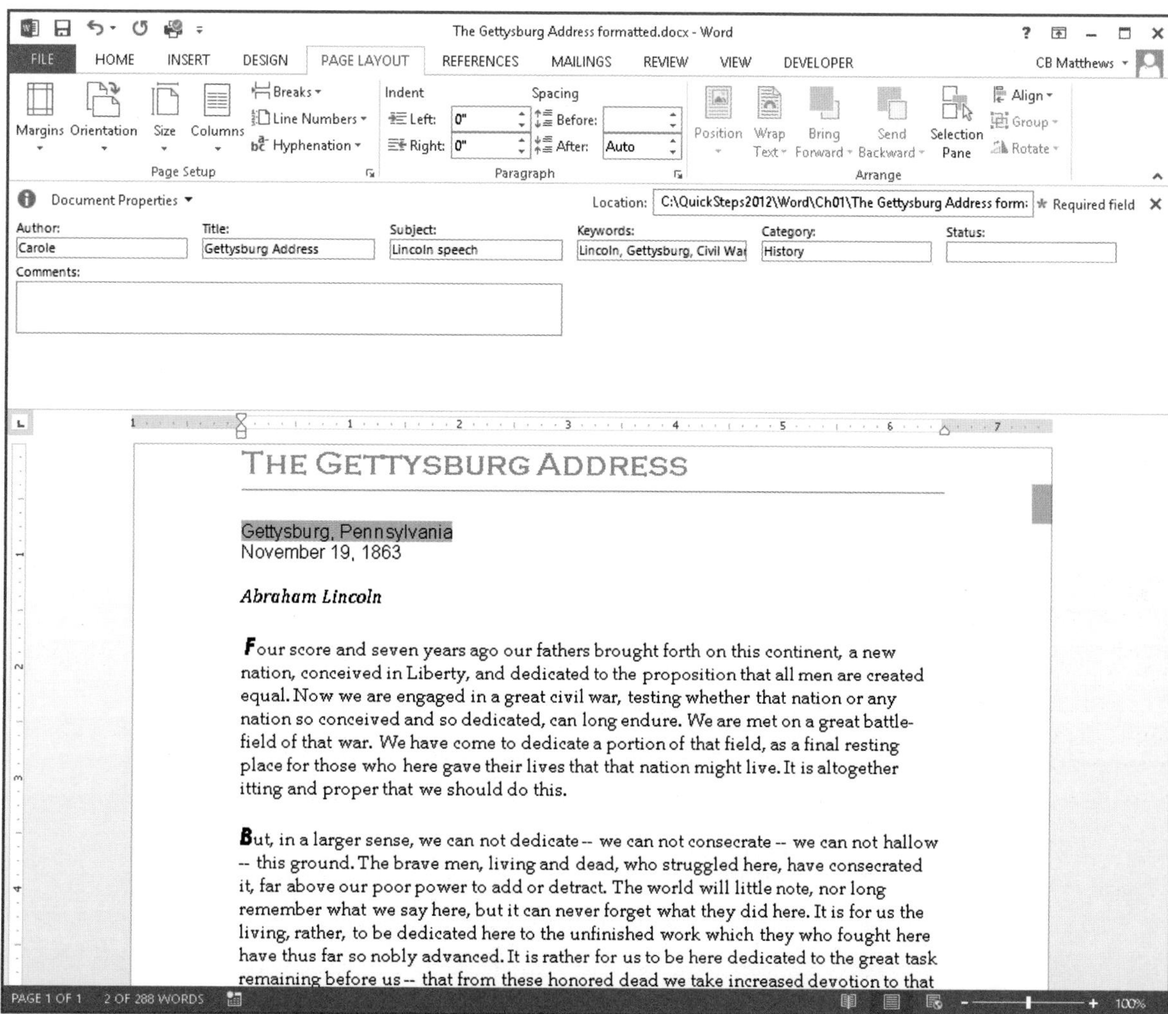

***Figure 1-8:* A Document Information panel beneath the ribbon allows you to more easily locate a document using search tools through the identifying data.**

3. To view more information about the document, click the **Document Properties** down arrow in the panel's title bar, and click **Advanced Properties**. Review each tab in the Properties dialog box to see the information available and make any changes or additions.

4. Click **Close** to remove the Properties dialog box when you are finished.

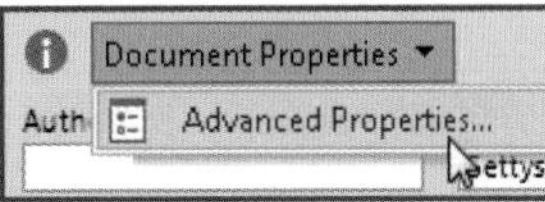

5. When you are finished with the Document Information panel, click the **X** at the rightmost end of the panel's title bar to close it.

Set Preferences

Setting preferences allows you to adapt Word to your needs and inclinations. The Word Options dialog box provides access to these settings. To access the dialog box:

Click **File** | **Options**.

Select the Display Elements That You Want to Appear

Click the **Display** option, as shown in Figure 1-9:

- Click the options in the Page Display Options area that you want.

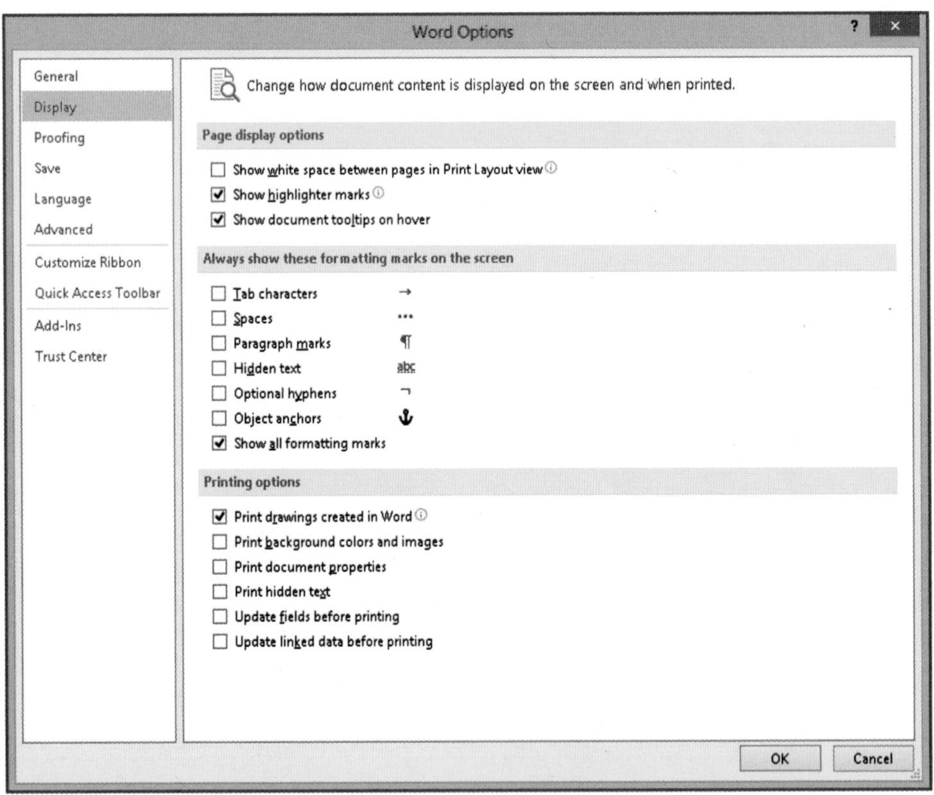

***Figure 1-9:* The Display options in the Word Options dialog box provide page display, formatting, and printing preferences.**

- Click the formatting marks you want to see—Show All Formatting Marks is a good choice.
- Click the options that you want in the Printing Options area.

Set General Options

- Click the **General** option:
    - Review and click the check boxes that are relevant for your situation. Earlier in this chapter, you saw how to disable the mini toolbar, show and hide ScreenTips, and change the color scheme of the Word window. If you are unsure about other options, keep the default and see how well those settings work for you.
    - Type the user name you want displayed in documents revised using the Track Changes feature.
    - Type the initials associated with the user name that will be displayed in comments you insert into a document.
- When you have set the General and Display Options as you want, click each of the other options, review the settings, and make any applicable changes. These are discussed further in the relevant chapters.
- When you have finished selecting your preferences, click **OK** to close the Word Options dialog box.

Understanding Versions of Office 2013

Office 2013 has an expanded set of versions and platforms upon which Office will run. Office is now available on five separate platforms (pricing is as of late fall 2012, is meant only for comparison purposes, and is subject to change):

- Office 365 is a subscription-based product, which, for a modest annual fee, you can install and run full versions of the Office 2013 apps on multiple computers running Windows 7 or 8 with multiple users and get extended storage on SkyDrive beyond the 7GB available to everybody for free. Office 365 is a set of "click-to-run" apps that are streamed to whatever computer you choose to use. You also get all upgrades of the apps for free that come out during the year. There are four versions of Office 365:
    - Office 365 Home Premium provides Office 2013 Access, Excel, OneNote, Outlook, PowerPoint, Publisher, and Word, or Office:Mac on up to five computers or tablets, with 20GB of SkyDrive storage and 60 minutes per month of free international calls using Skype, all currently for $99 per year.
    - Office 365 Small Business Premium provides all of the Office 2013 apps in Home Premium plus InfoPath, Lync, and access to Exchange and SharePoint servers on up to five computers or tablets each for up to ten users, with up to 25GB of Exchange and 10GB of SharePoint shared storage, plus an additional 500MB per user, all currently for $149.99 per user, per year.
    - Office 365 ProPlus and Office 365 Enterprise provide all of the Office 2013 apps in Small Business Premium for a larger number of users, more storage, and more servers under volume licensing plans.
- Office 2013 is a resident set of apps running on the user's computer or tablet that are similar to the Office apps that have been available for many years, and are generally referred to as the "desktop platform." They can only be installed on a single computer.
    - Office 2013 Starter is only available preinstalled on a new computer without additional cost, includes versions of Excel and Word with reduced functionality, and is supported by advertising. It can be directly upgraded to one of the following three full versions of Office 2013 through a product key card purchased online or through a retail outlet.
    - Office 2013 Home & Student is available to be installed from a DVD or via Click-To-Run over the Internet, and contains the full version of Excel, Word, OneNote, and PowerPoint. It currently costs $139.99.
    - Office 2013 Home & Business is available to be installed from a DVD or via Click-To-Run over the Internet, contains all the features of Office Home & Student, and adds Outlook. It currently costs $219.99.
    - Office 2013 Professional is available to be installed from a DVD or via Click-To-Run over the Internet, contains all the features of Office Home & Business, and adds Access and Publisher. It currently costs $399.99.

(continued)

- Office 2013 RT comes preinstalled and without additional cost on the Microsoft Surface RT tablet. It includes touch-enhanced versions of Word, Excel, PowerPoint, and OneNote.
- Office 2013 Web Apps is a web browser–based product that you can access through Internet Explorer or other browsers with a free account on SkyDrive.com or Outlook.com and includes access to somewhat limited versions of Excel, OneNote, PowerPoint, and Word.
- Office Mobile, accessed through a mobile device such as a smartphone, is another available platform.

There are also additional enterprise editions available only through a volume license. Office Standard adds Publisher to Office Home & Business, and Office Professional Plus adds SharePoint Workspace and InfoPath to Office Professional.

This book, which covers the full version of Word 2013, is applicable to all the editions with a full version of Word and, to a limited extent, those features that are included in Office Starter and Office Web Apps.

GET HELP

Help can be accessed both locally and online from Microsoft servers. A different kind of help, which provides the Thesaurus and Research features, is also available.

Open Help

The online Word Help system is maintained online at Microsoft. It is easily accessed.

Click the **Help** icon, and the Word Help window will open, shown in Figure 1-10. On the toolbar at the top of the Word Help window are several options for navigating through the topics and printing one out.

- Find the topic you want, and click it.

  –Or–

- Type keywords in the Search text box, and click **Search**.

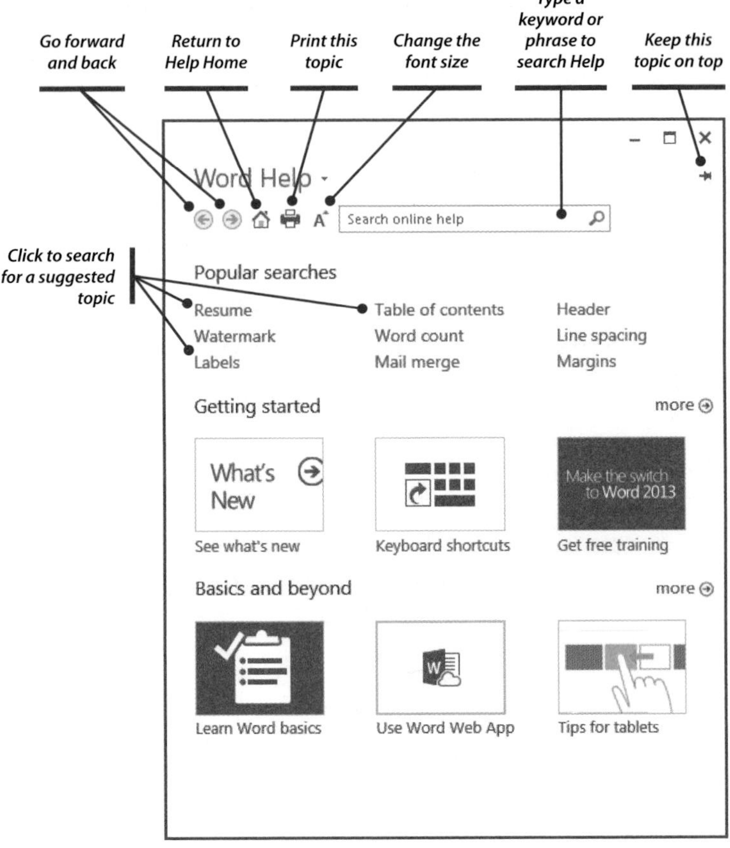

Figure 1-10:* *When you click the Help icon, the Word Help dialog box appears, where you can click the topic you want or search for specific keywords.

Use the Thesaurus

You can find synonyms for words using the Thesaurus feature.

1. To use the Thesaurus, first select the word that you want a synonym for.

2. Click **Review | Thesaurus** in the Proofing group. The Thesaurus task pane will appear on the right with the most likely synonyms listed:

   - Click a listed word to search for its synonyms.
   - Click the word down arrow to insert, copy, or look up the word.

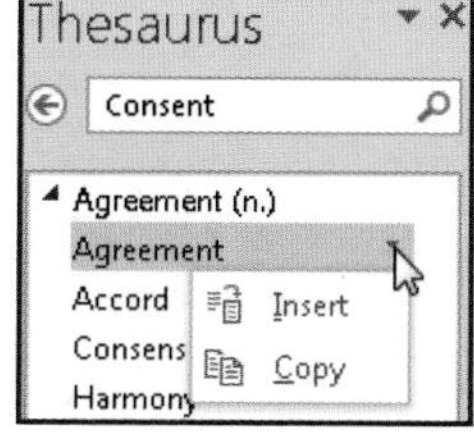

3. Click **Close** to close the task pane.

TIP You can also access the Thesaurus by pressing **SHIFT+F7**.

NOTE Remember that if your screen is minimized, the icon will be different, such as seen here:

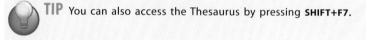

Define a Word

Define allows you to access an online dictionary to find the meaning of a word. To use this, you first need to download the dictionary you want to use. You have three choices—all for free: the *Merriam-Webster Dictionary*, the *English Dictionary*, and the *Bing Dictionary (English)*. Once you have downloaded the dictionary, you'll be able to look up words endlessly.

1. Click **Review | Define** in the Proofing group. The Dictionaries task pane is opened on the right of your window.
2. Click **Terms & Conditions** and **Privacy Policy** to find out how the various vendors will use your data and how it will be protected.
3. Click **Download** for the online dictionary you want to use. When you download a dictionary, you are agreeing to the terms and conditions and to the privacy provisions. The dictionary is loaded and its task pane is displayed so that you can look up a word.

Look Up a Word Definition

When you define a word, you can either enter it in the Search text box or select it in your document text, as shown in Figure 1-11.

1. To find the definition of a word, first select a word by highlighting it in your document.
2. Click **Review | Define** in the Proofing group. A selection of definitions is displayed in the task pane, as shown in Figure 1-11.
3. Verify that the definition you want is shown. For instance, the definitions shown in Figure 1-11 do not show the appropriate definition for the text we are viewing.
   - To find a more complete list of definitions, download additional entries by clicking the link at the bottom of the definitions.

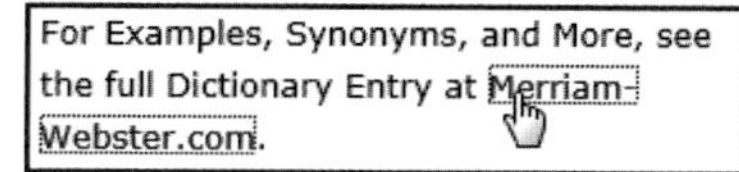
For Examples, Synonyms, and More, see the full Dictionary Entry at Merriam-Webster.com.

   - Scroll through the list of definitions and examples to find what you need. When you are finished, click **Close** on the top right of the window to return to the document and task pane.
4. Click the **X** on the upper right of the task pane to close it.

NOTE If you are a poet, you can find rhyming words in the extended online dictionary. You can also find examples of how to use the word, word origins, synonyms, how your selected word is related to other words, and more.

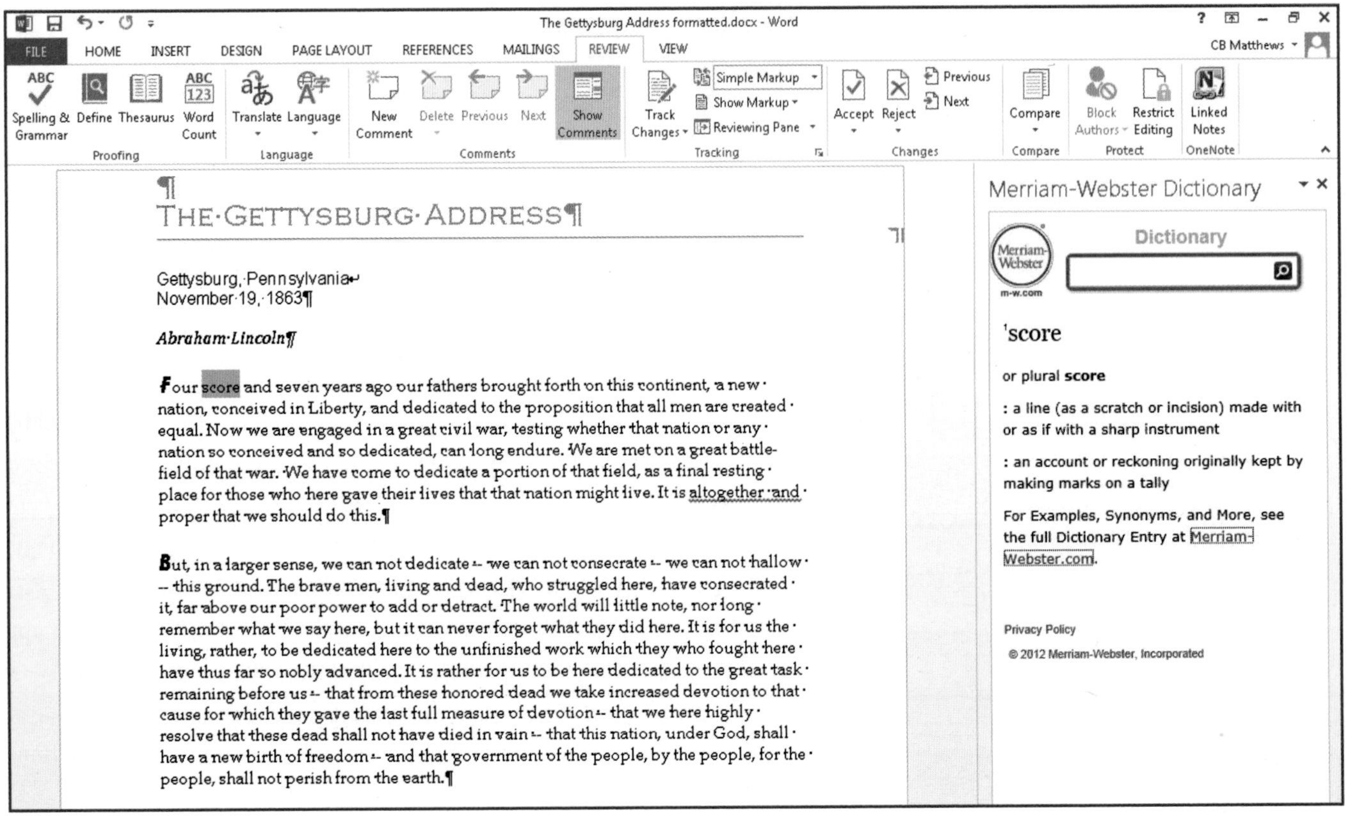

Figure 1-11: ***An online dictionary can be used to define a word in your document or find synonyms.***

 Translate a Document

Sometimes you might want to translate text into another language. For example, perhaps you have just a phrase or word in another language that you'd like to understand better. In this case, you might use the Mini Translator where you highlight the text and click the Translator for a quick translation. Or, you might want to translate a whole document from one language to another. If this is the case, you'd send the document online to another program, which would translate it and return it.

Set Up the Translator

On your first use of the Translator, you'll need to upload the appropriate translators:

1. Click **Review | Translate** in the Language group, and click **Translate Selected Text**. The Research dialog box will appear.
2. In the Research task pane, click **Translation Options**. The Translation Options dialog box will open. Listed are the options for translations. All are selected by default.
3. Simply click **OK** to accept all of them.

Translate a Word or Phrase

To translate a word or phrase in a document:

1. Select the word or phrase by dragging the pointer over it, highlighting it.
2. Press ALT and click the selected word or phrase. The word or phrase will appear in the Research task pane and a translation will appear, as shown in Figure 1-12.

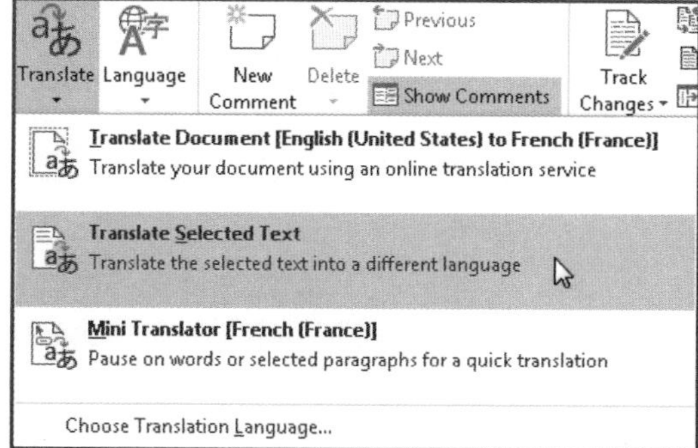

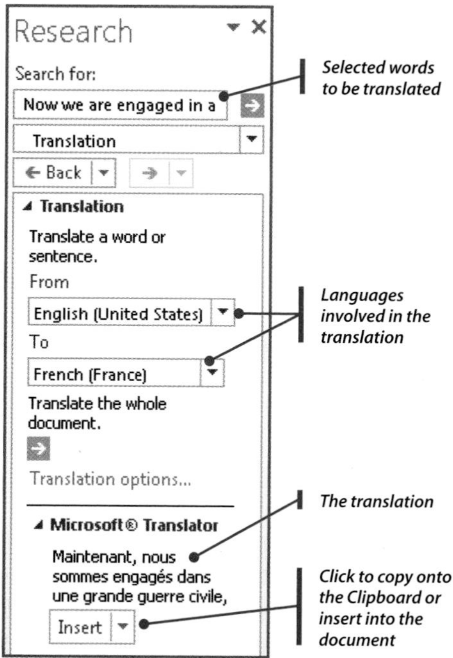

Figure 1-12: You can translate a word or phrase, or a whole document.

Translate a Whole Document

1. Click **Review | Translate** in the Language group, and click **Translate Document**. You will see a message that your document will be sent over the Internet, unsecured, to be translated by the Microsoft Translator Service.
2. Click **OK** to begin the translation.

   –Or–

   If your Research task pane is open, click the arrow opposite **Translate The Whole Document**. You'll see the same message.
3. Click **Send** to start the translation. Your translated document will appear in a browser window, as shown in Figure 1-13.

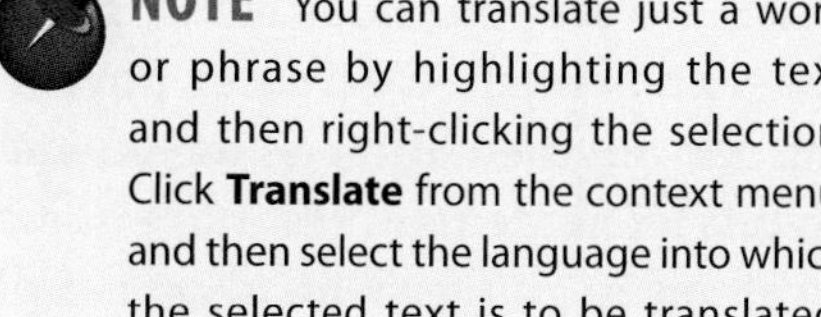

NOTE You can translate just a word or phrase by highlighting the text and then right-clicking the selection. Click **Translate** from the context menu, and then select the language into which the selected text is to be translated. The translation will appear in the Research task pane.

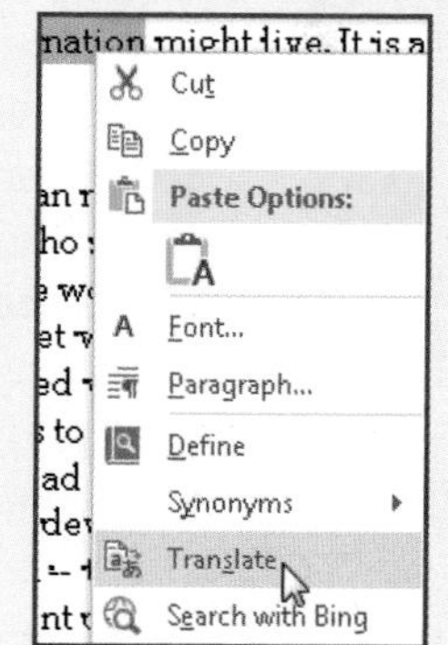

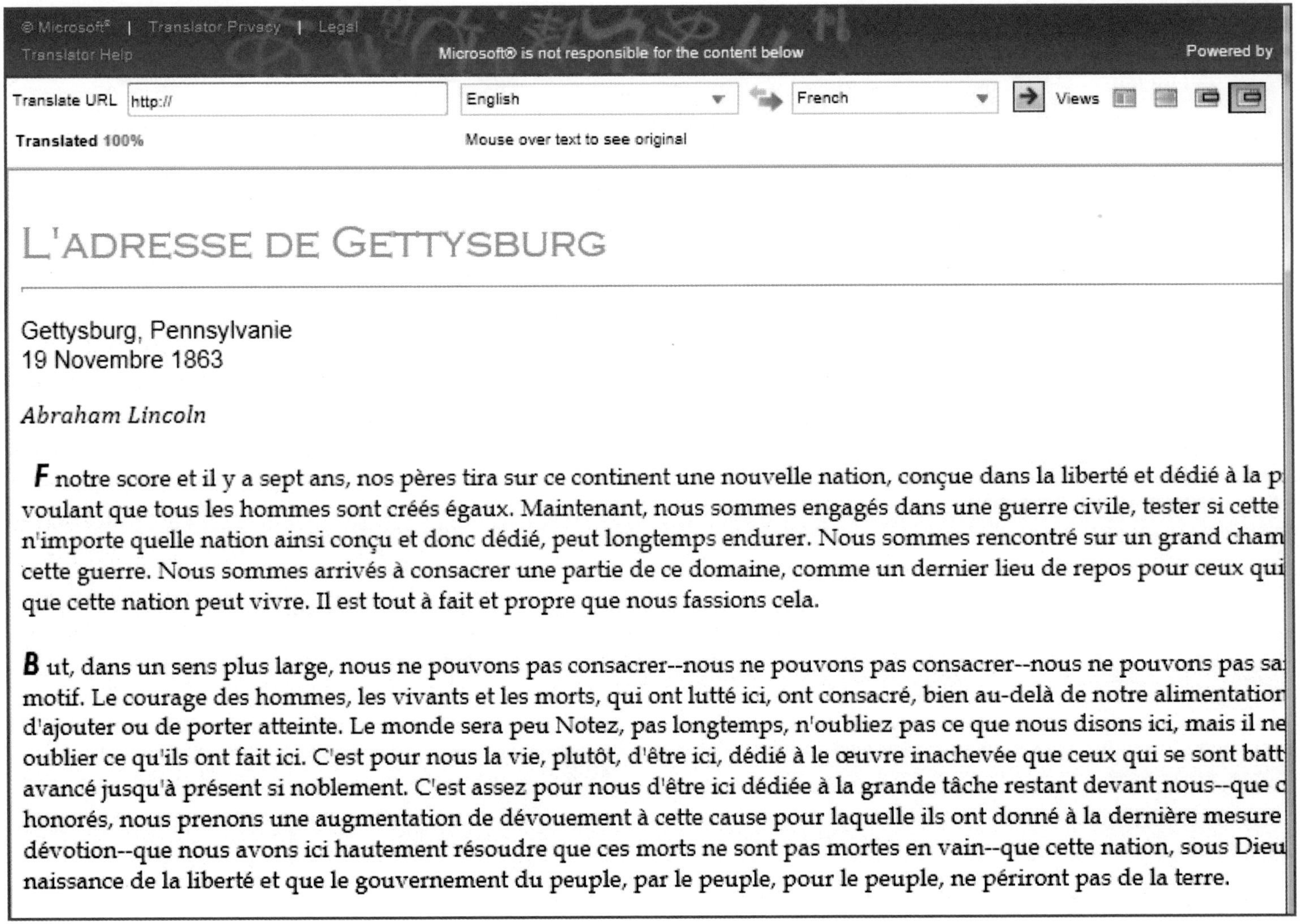

© Microsoft® | Translator Privacy | Legal
Translator Help   Microsoft® is not responsible for the content below   Powered by

Translate URL http://   English → French   Views

Translated 100%   Mouse over text to see original

L'ADRESSE DE GETTYSBURG

Gettysburg, Pennsylvanie
19 Novembre 1863

Abraham Lincoln

F notre score et il y a sept ans, nos pères tira sur ce continent une nouvelle nation, conçue dans la liberté et dédié à la p
voulant que tous les hommes sont créés égaux. Maintenant, nous sommes engagés dans une guerre civile, tester si cette
n'importe quelle nation ainsi conçu et donc dédié, peut longtemps endurer. Nous sommes rencontré sur un grand cham
cette guerre. Nous sommes arrivés à consacrer une partie de ce domaine, comme un dernier lieu de repos pour ceux qui
que cette nation peut vivre. Il est tout à fait et propre que nous fassions cela.

B ut, dans un sens plus large, nous ne pouvons pas consacrer--nous ne pouvons pas consacrer--nous ne pouvons pas sa
motif. Le courage des hommes, les vivants et les morts, qui ont lutté ici, ont consacré, bien au-delà de notre alimentation
d'ajouter ou de porter atteinte. Le monde sera peu Notez, pas longtemps, n'oubliez pas ce que nous disons ici, mais il ne
oublier ce qu'ils ont fait ici. C'est pour nous la vie, plutôt, d'être ici, dédié à le œuvre inachevée que ceux qui se sont batt
avancé jusqu'à présent si noblement. C'est assez pour nous d'être ici dédiée à la grande tâche restant devant nous--que c
honorés, nous prenons une augmentation de dévouement à cette cause pour laquelle ils ont donné à la dernière mesure
dévotion--que nous avons ici hautement résoudre que ces morts ne sont pas mortes en vain--que cette nation, sous Dieu
naissance de la liberté et que le gouvernement du peuple, par le peuple, pour le peuple, ne périront pas de la terre.

Figure 1-13: ***An example of an English-to-French translation of the whole Gettysburg Address.***

QuickSteps to...

- Select a Template on Your Computer
- Open a Blank Document
- Locate an Existing Document
- Import a Document
- Enter Text
- Determine Where Text Will Appear
- Insert Text or Type Over It
- Insert Symbols or Special Characters
- Insert Line or Page Breaks
- Select Text
- Delete Text
- Copy and Move Text
- Use the Office Clipboard
- Move Around in a Document
- Find and Replace Text
- Use Wildcards
- Check Spelling and Grammar
- Get SkyDrive for Your Files
- Save a Document for the First Time
- Save a Document Automatically
- Save a Document

Chapter 2

Working with Documents

Microsoft Office Word 2013 allows you to create and edit documents, such as letters, reports, invoices, plays, and books. In this chapter you'll see how to create new documents and edit existing ones. This includes ways to enter, change, and delete text, as well as ways to find and select text. A new feature in Word 2013 is the enhanced ability to use SkyDrive to store your files on the *cloud,* an online storage location. Also, you'll learn how to use the Clipboard to transfer text from one part of Word to another, or to another application, such as Excel. If you have worked with Word previously, you'll still find this chapter a good review and one that explains some differences in how you perform these basic tasks compared to earlier Word versions.

Understanding Word Files

The book you are reading now was written in Word. Documents from Word can be printed on one or more pages and bound by anything from a paper clip to stitch binding. In the computer, a document is called a file and is stored on a disk drive. The filename identifies it as a Word document. For example, the name given to the file for this chapter is Chap02.docx. "Chap02" is the filename, and ".docx" is the file extension. You may or may not see the file extension, depending on how Windows is configured. Most files produced by editions of Word prior to 2007 used the .doc extension. Documents saved with Word 2007 and on are, by default, saved with the .docx extension. You can read, edit, and retain documents created in earlier versions of Word. These older files are marked with the words "*Compatibility Mode*" in the title. When you see these words, you'll know you're working with an older document. The 2013 Word tools and commands may not all work correctly with older files, although most do. You can save older documents in the 2013 newer .docx format. Word converts the document to the newer format, trying to maintain your intent as best it can. I've not found a situation where it fails.

CREATE A NEW DOCUMENT

As you saw in Chapter 1, when you start Word, you can immediately choose what kind of a document you are opening—a new one or an existing one—as seen in Figure 2-1. Existing documents are listed under Recent on the left pane (see "Open an Existing Document"), while new document possibilities are listed on the right pane. For instance, if you click Blank Document, you'll open a document with a "normally" formatted template. If you open any other new name displayed (other than Take A Tour), you'll open a document with a template that has a specific design or format. See "Using Templates" QuickFacts. Regardless of the template applied, opening a new document displays a blank document pane into which you can start typing the new content immediately. If you don't see a template you like, you can search online for more suggestions, as described in "Use an Office Online Template" later in this chapter.

You can create a new document when you open Word.

From the initial Word screen, select a template from the right pane that you want.

NOTE The remainder of this chapter assumes that Word has been started and is open on your screen.

TIP You can also open a new file from an existing one. If you have opened a file and find it is the wrong one, or if you want to transfer some information from an older file to a new one, you can get to the new page by clicking **File | New** from the document screen.

Using Templates

A template is a special kind of document that is used as a pattern or the basis for other documents you create. For instance, you might want to create a calendar or business letter with the appropriate design and format already applied. The template is said to be "attached" to the document, and every Word document must have a template attached to it. The template acts as the framework around which you create your document. The document that is opened automatically when you start Word 2013 uses a default template called Normal.dotm (versions prior to 2007 used Normal .dot). This is referred to as "the Normal template" and contains standard formatting settings. Other templates can contain boilerplate text, design or formatting options for the types of documents they create, and even automating procedures. Word is installed on your computer with a number of templates that you can use, and you can access other templates, both on your computer and through Office Online. You can create your own templates for your business or organization that make all of your documents similar in appearance.

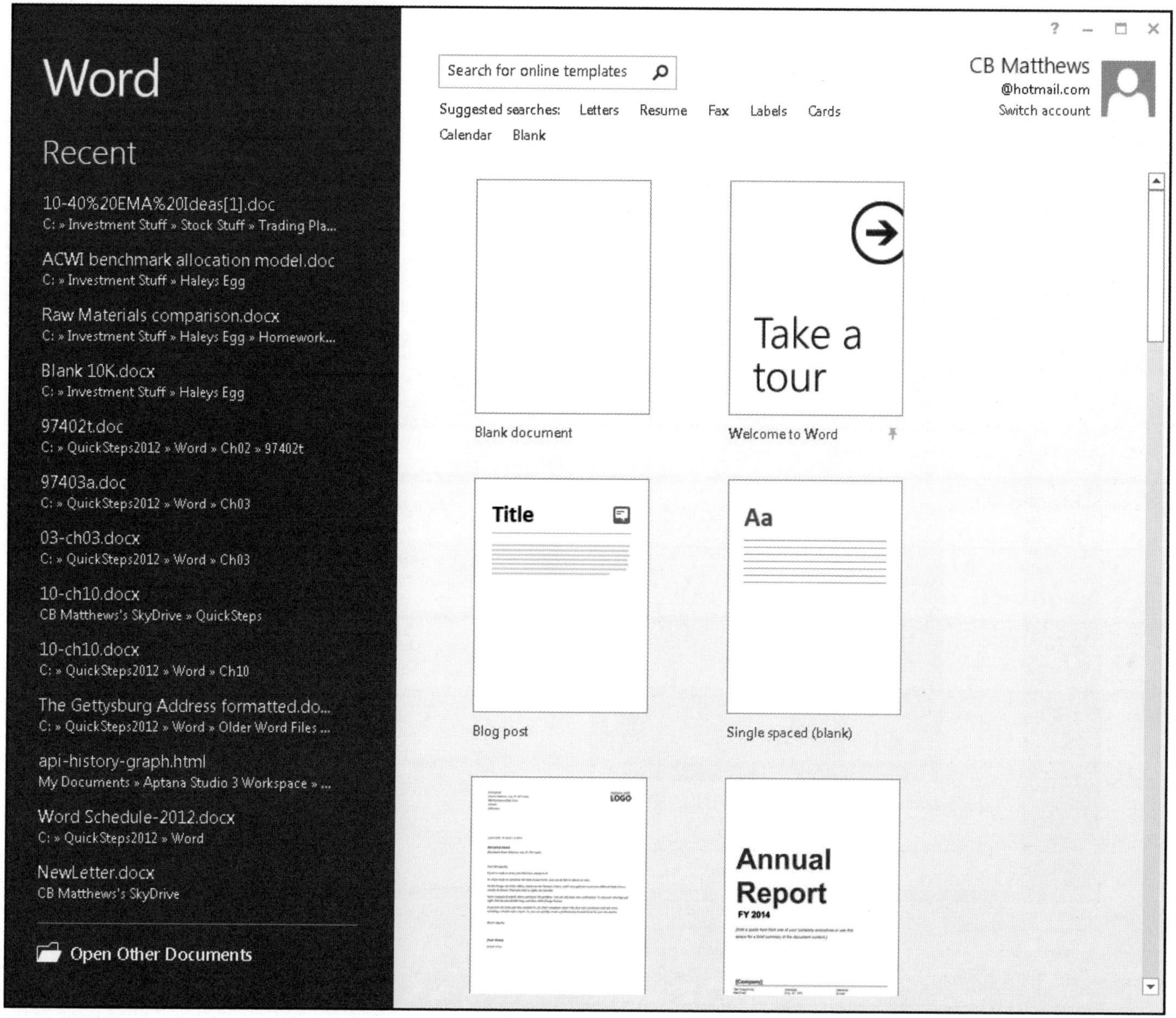

Figure 2-1: The initial Word screen allows you to open a recently used document or create a new one, perhaps with a specially designed template rather than the "normal" one.

Select a Template on Your Computer

After having opened Word 2013, you'll have a list of templates available on the right of your screen, shown earlier in Figure 2-1. From this list of templates you can select one that meets your intention for your document most closely. Here are the steps to finding the template you want for your new document:

1. Scroll through the list of available templates, viewing some of the following options:
   - **Blank Document** To use a new blank template "from scratch" where you can apply your own formatting and design
   - **Blog Post** To create a simple blog post
   - **Single Space (Blank)** Template for a single-spaced modern document
   - **Ion Design (Blank)** Template for a document featuring the Ion design, a clean look with a touch of personality
2. When you find a design you'd like to see more of, click it. You'll see the design expanded with a short description of what the template offers, such as what is shown in Figure 2-2.
3. When you find a template you want, click **Create**. A document based on the selected template will open.

Create

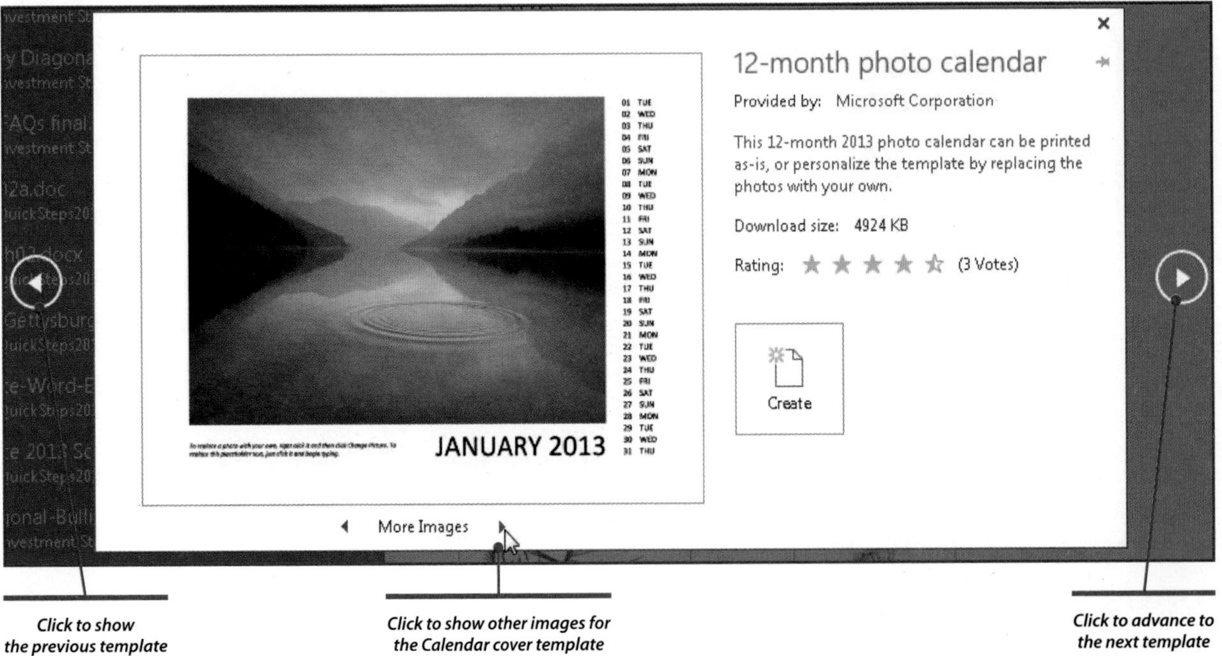
12-month photo calendar
Provided by: Microsoft Corporation
This 12-month 2013 photo calendar can be printed as-is, or personalize the template by replacing the photos with your own.
Download size: 4924 KB
Rating: (3 Votes)
Create
JANUARY 2013
More Images
Click to show the previous template
Click to show other images for the Calendar cover template
Click to advance to the next template

***Figure 2-2:* Clicking a template opens a view of it allowing you to scroll through other templates as well as to explore additional images of the current one.**

Use an Office Online Template

If you don't see a template that you want, you can search the Microsoft online templates directory.

1. Locate Microsoft's online templates above the listed templates, on either the initial Word screen or click **File | New**. You'll find a number of ways to search for online templates.

2. Select the type of template for which you want to search:

   - **Search For Online Templates** In this case, in the search text box, type the category or keyword describing the type of template for which you are searching. For instance, typing "billing" or "birthdays" will display a list of those categories of templates, such as what you see in Figure 2-3.

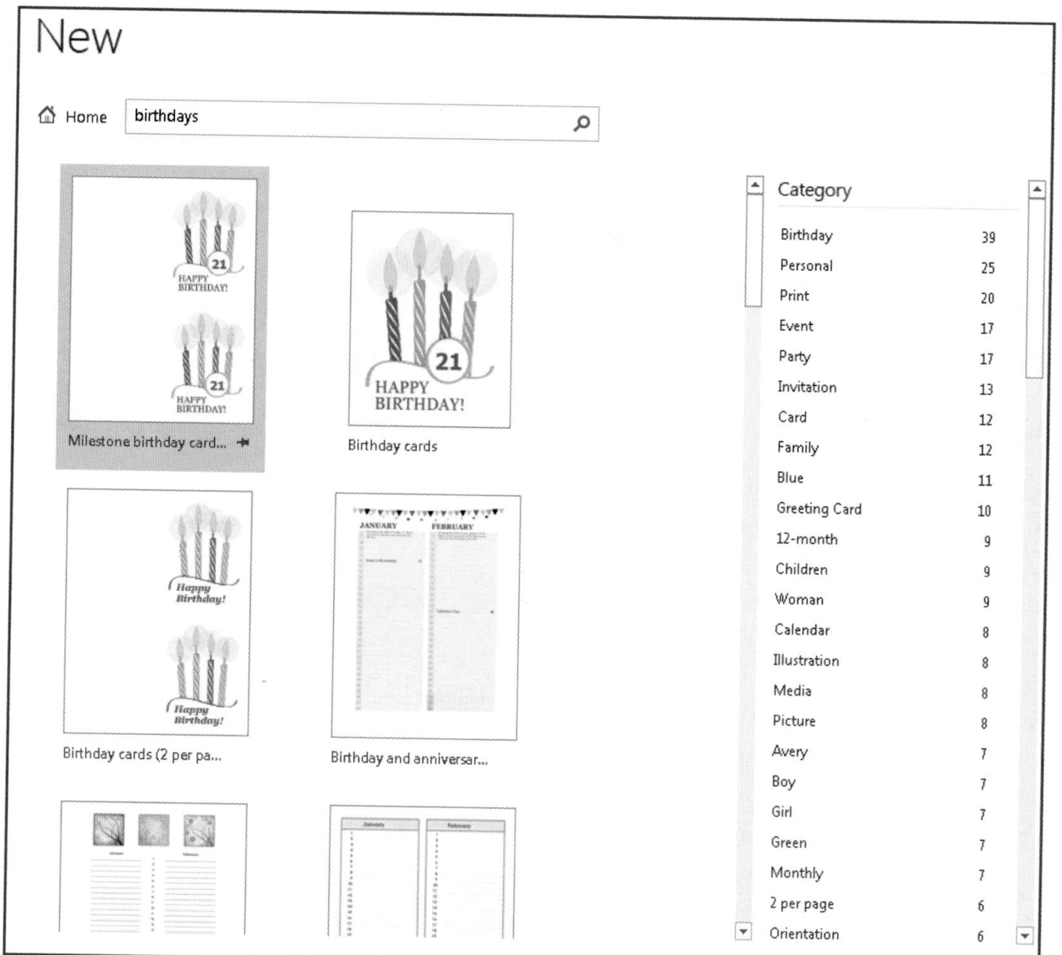

*Figure 2-3: **Microsoft offers many templates online, both for Word and for its other Office products.***

1 2 3 4 5 6 7 8 9 10

- **Suggested Searches** Suggested links to online templates are listed beneath the search text box. Click one of them, such as **Letters** or **Resume**, and a list of those templates is displayed.
- **Category List** On the right of the template list window is the Category pane listing all the categories of templates you can find online. Scroll through the list to find a category you want and click it.

3. Scroll through the list of templates: Either use the scroll bar on the right of the screen, or expand a template by clicking it and scroll using the backward and forward arrows (previously seen in Figure 2-2.)
4. When you find the one you want, expand the template view if you have not done so already (click it) and click **Create**. A new document is opened with the selected template active.

NOTE You can also create and use your own templates, as described in Chapter 4.

Open a Blank Document

When you create a new file "from scratch," you are starting with a blank page and developing your document as you go. As you have seen, you can create a new document in two ways: using the default (or "normal") document template, shown in Figure 2-4, or using a unique template. (See the "Using Templates" QuickFacts.) Opening a new document displays a blank document pane (perhaps with a template containing a design or formatting already applied) into which you can start typing the content of a new document. The blinking vertical bar in the upper-left corner of the document pane, called the *insertion point*, indicates where the text you type will appear, as you see in Figure 2-4. The mouse pointer tells you where your cursor actually is. You'll want to be aware of where they both are, or you'll be inserting characters where they don't belong.

1. To start a new document, click in the document pane where you want the next character to be inserted and start typing.
2. When you want to format a character, word, or paragraph, drag over it to select it and apply formatting. You'll see how to do this later in this chapter.
3. When you want to save and close the document, click **File | Save As | Computer** (or other storage device), click the destination folder in which you want to store the file, type the filename, and then click **Save**. Close your document. How you do these actions are described in detail later in this chapter.

OPEN AN EXISTING DOCUMENT

After creating and saving a document, you may want to come back and work on it later. You may also want to open and work on a Word document created by someone else or created in a different program. To do this, you must first locate the document, and then open it in Word. You can either locate the document directly from Word, or search for it in Word or Windows.

NOTE Not all documents created in other programs can be opened by Word, although many can. See "Import a Document."

Locate an Existing Document

When you first open Word, you'll see the screen shown earlier in Figure 2-1. If the file is one you've used recently, it will be listed on the left beneath "Recent." If the file has not been opened recently with Word, you'll have to search for it.

1. To open a file from the initial Word screen, as seen in Figure 2-1, look through the files listed under Recent and click the one you want to open. The Word document pane opens with the selected document present.

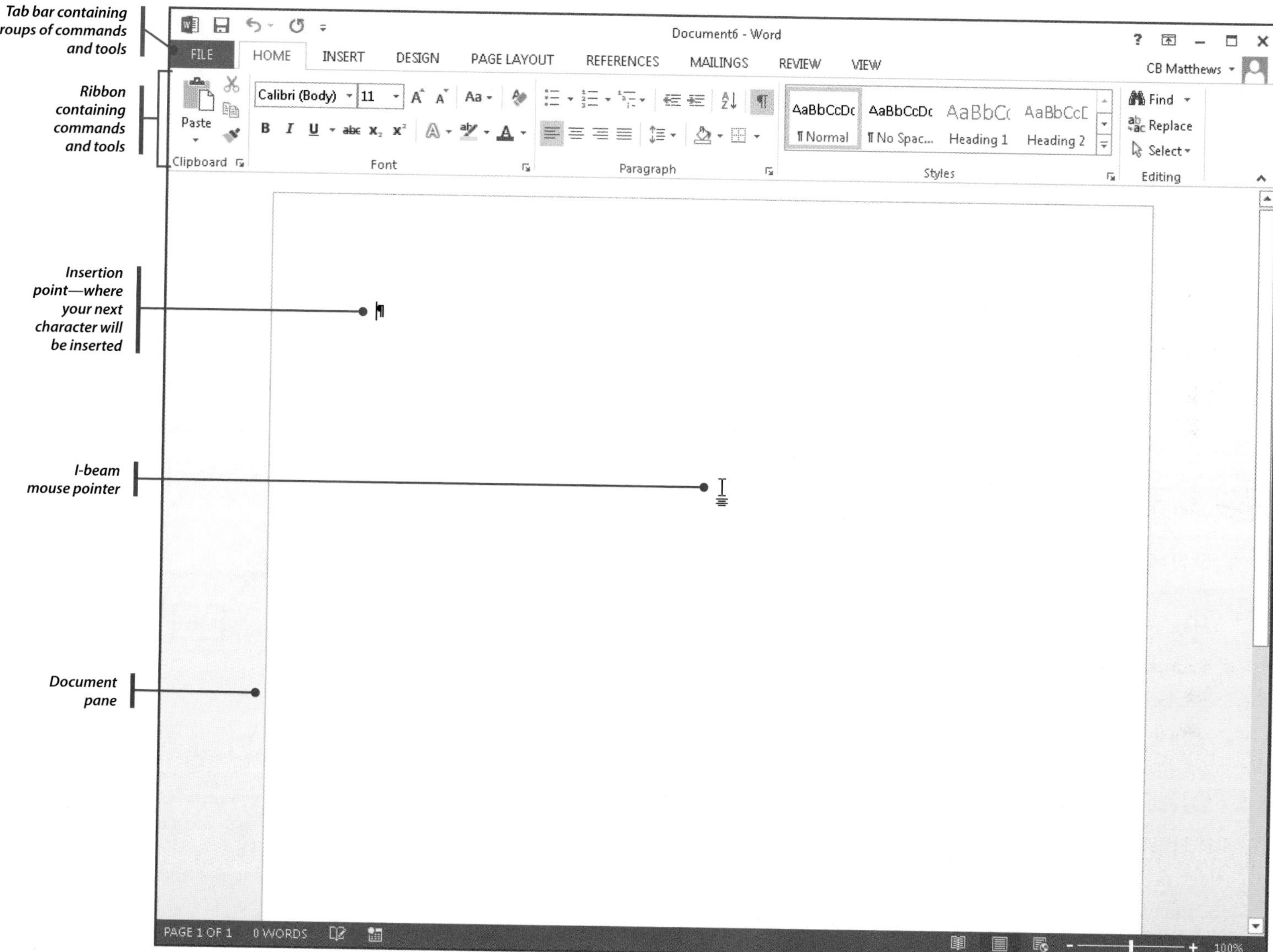

Figure 2-4: When you first start Word, you can choose to open a blank document pane, ready for you to create a new document immediately. It may or may not have formatting applied to its template.

2. If the list of recent documents doesn't contain the one you want, click **Open Other Documents** at the bottom of the list and go to step 4.

   –Or–

   To open a file from the document pane when another Word document is already open, click **File | Open**.

3. You have a choice of four sources of where the document might be found:

   - **Recent Documents** Lists the documents that have been opened recently. If you see the one you want, just click it and it will open in the document pane.

   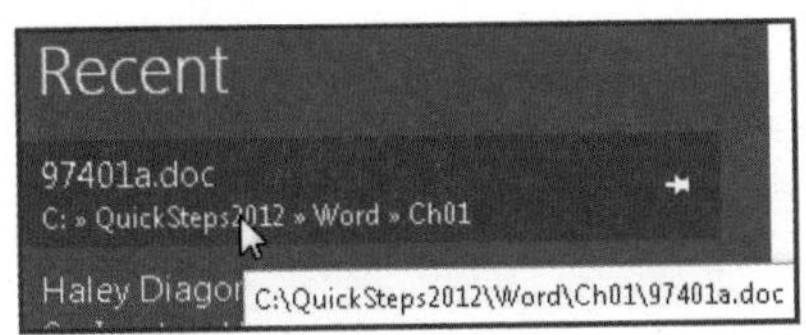

   - **SkyDrive** Click this if your document is stored on the SkyDrive rather than on your computer. (See the "Using SkyDrive" QuickFacts for more information.)
   - **Computer** Allows you to search your computer using Windows Explorer if the document is stored on your hard disk.
   - **Add A Place** Allows you to specify a new location where your document may be found. This might be on a different computer on your network, for instance, or on a removable disk.

4. Select the location of where the file is stored. Double-click the drive, folder, or sequence of folders you need to open in order to find the document.

5. When you have found the document you want to open, double-click it. It will appear in Word, ready for you to begin your work.

If you have a hard time finding a document using the direct approach just described, you can search for it either in Word or in Windows.

Using SkyDrive

We've all heard of *"the cloud,"* where you can store your documents, videos, and photos online rather than on a hard disk. SkyDrive is the cloud for Microsoft Office. You can easily store and retrieve documents from SkyDrive in Word 2013 using Windows Explorer. On your hard disk, you establish a SkyDrive folder. Everything you want on SkyDrive is put there. Everything in the folder is automatically uploaded to SkyDrive, and Microsoft synchronizes the content between your computer and SkyDrive. That is, every time you change something in the computer folder, it is also changed in the SkyDrive copy, and vice-versa. Your documents are always updated. SkyDrive is structured similarly to what you would find on your hard disk, with files and folders. See "Get SkyDrive for Your Files" to create an online folder.

Using SkyDrive has several advantages. If you are traveling, for instance, you can access your files from anywhere, even from an unfamiliar computer, such as a laptop or Internet café. If you have a document you want to share with someone else, you can make it available just to them. This is particularly handy for larger files, where you can bypass email delivery, downloading documents more rapidly without requiring storage space on a computer. If anyone changes the SkyDrive document, everyone sees the updates.

Search for a Document in Word

You can search for a document in Word based on a piece of text that is contained within the document or within some property of the document, such as the name of the author, the creation date, or the name of the file. Your computer or SkyDrive can be searched. The basic search looks for text within the document.

1. From the initial Word screen, click **Open Other Documents** beneath the Recent list. The Open view is displayed.

   –Or–

   From the document pane, click **File | Open**. The Open view is displayed.

2. Click your storage device, such as **SkyDrive** or **Computer**, to identify where to find the document. Click **Browse** and the Open dialog box will open, as shown in Figure 2-5.

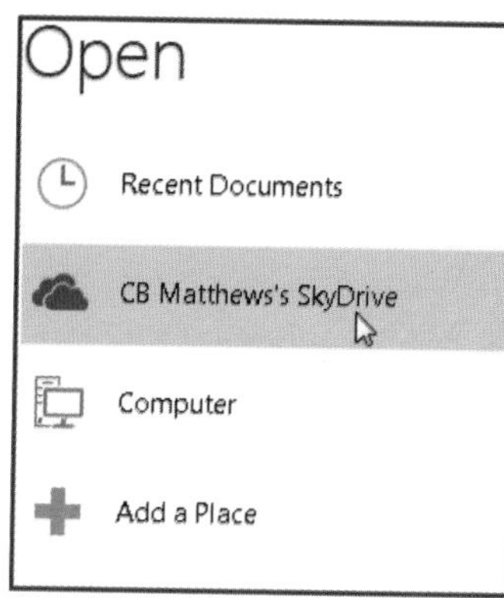

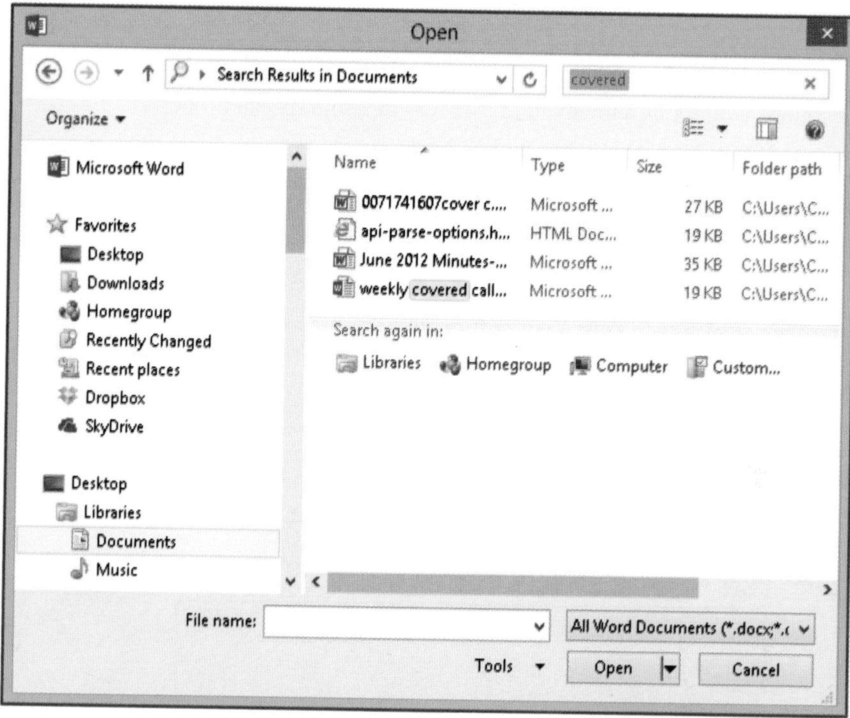

Figure 2-5: As you type the text into the search text box, the search automatically begins and the results are listed beneath the search text.

3. In the search text box on the upper-right area of the dialog box, begin to enter the text for which you are searching (see Figure 2-5). As you type, the search will begin. The results are listed in the right pane of the dialog box, beneath the search text.

4. Double-click the file you want, or select it and click **Open** to open it in Word.

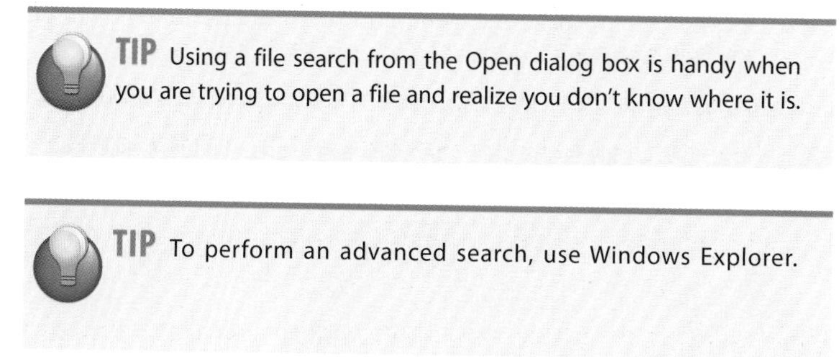

TIP Using a file search from the Open dialog box is handy when you are trying to open a file and realize you don't know where it is.

TIP To perform an advanced search, use Windows Explorer.

Use the Search and Sort Features

You can sort the files within the search results list using the column headings. Doing this allows you to sort files by some special property, such as name, date, folder type, author, or tag.

1. Display the Open dialog box (see the preceding set of steps), locate the drive or folder containing the file you want, and type your search text. The search results will be listed below as you type.
2. Click the **Change Your View** button on the right in the toolbar, and click **Details** if it is not already selected.

3. Point to a column heading on which you want to sort the results, and click. The files and folders will be sorted on that column.

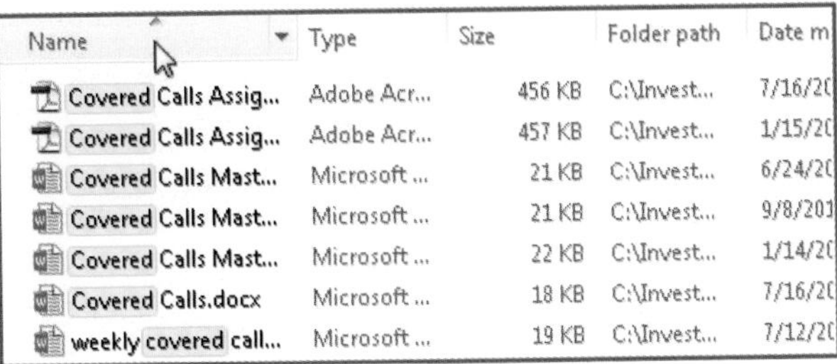

Name	Type	Size	Folder path	Date m
Covered Calls Assig...	Adobe Acr...	456 KB	C:\Invest...	7/16/2(
Covered Calls Assig...	Adobe Acr...	457 KB	C:\Invest...	1/15/2(
Covered Calls Mast...	Microsoft ...	21 KB	C:\Invest...	6/24/2(
Covered Calls Mast...	Microsoft ...	21 KB	C:\Invest...	9/8/201
Covered Calls Mast...	Microsoft ...	22 KB	C:\Invest...	1/14/2(
Covered Calls.docx	Microsoft ...	18 KB	C:\Invest...	7/16/2(
weekly covered call...	Microsoft ...	19 KB	C:\Invest...	7/12/2(

4. Click the column heading again, and the files and folders will be re-sorted into their original order.

TIP To quickly find a folder that you have used previously, click the **Recent Pages** down arrow to the left of the folder name.

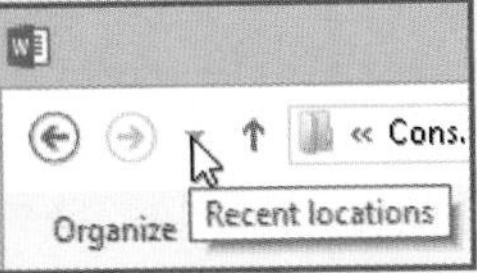

 Import a Document

If you have a word-processing document created in a program other than Word, you can most likely open it and edit it in Word.

1. From the initial Word screen, click **Open Other Documents** beneath the Recent list. The Open view is displayed.

   –Or–

   From the document pane, click **File | Open Computer (or another storage device)**. The list of folders is displayed.
2. Click a listed folder, or click **Browse** to open the drive, folder, or sequence of folders you need to open in order to find the document.
3. Click the down arrow on the right of the file type drop-down list box to display the list of files that you can open directly in Word (see Table 2-1 for a complete list).

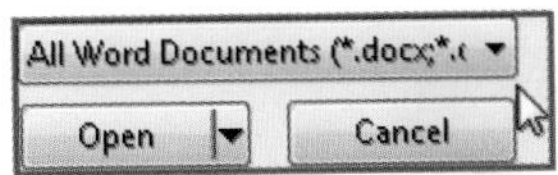

4. Click the file type that you want to open. The Open dialog box will list only files of that type.
5. Double-click the file that you want to open.

WRITE A DOCUMENT

Whether you create a new document or open an existing one, you will likely want to enter and edit text. Editing, in this case, includes adding and deleting text, as well as selecting, moving, and copying it.

 Enter Text

To enter text in a document that you have newly created or opened, simply start typing. The characters you type will appear in the document pane at the insertion point and in the order that you type them.

Table 2-1: File Types That Word Can Open Directly

File Type	Extension
Open Document text files	.odt
PDF files	.pdf
Plain-text files	.txt
Rich-text format files	.rtf
Text in any file	.*
Web page files	.htm, .html, .mht, .mhtml
Word 97 to 2003 files	.doc
Word 97 to 2003 template files	.dot
Word 2007 to 2013 document files (macro-enabled)	.docx (.docm)
Word 2007 to 2013 template files (macro-enabled)	.dotx (.dotm)
WordPerfect 5.*x* and 6.*x* files	.doc, .wpd
Works 6.0 to 9.0 files	.wps
XML files	.xml

Determine Where Text Will Appear

The *insertion point*, the blinking vertical bar shown earlier in Figure 2-4, determines where text that you type will appear. In a new document, the insertion point is obviously in the upper-leftmost corner of the document pane. It is also placed there by default when you open an existing document. You can move the insertion point within or to the end of existing text using either the keyboard or the mouse.

Move the Insertion Point with the Keyboard

When Word is open and a document is active, the insertion point moves every time you press a character or directional key on the keyboard (unless a menu or dialog box is open or the task pane is active). The directional keys include **TAB**, **BACKSPACE**, and **ENTER**, as well as the four arrow keys and **HOME**, **END**, **PAGE UP**, and **PAGE DOWN**.

Insertion|Point

Move the Insertion Point with the Mouse

When the mouse pointer is in the document pane, it appears as an I-beam, as you saw in Figure 2-4. The reason for the I-beam is that it fits between characters on the screen. You can move the insertion point by moving the I-beam mouse pointer to where you want the insertion point and then clicking.

I-beam·Mouse·Pointer·

Insert Text or Type Over It

When you press a letter or a number key with Word in its default mode (as it is when you first start it), the insertion point and any existing text to the right of the insertion point is pushed to the right and down on a page. This is also true when you press the **TAB** or **ENTER** key. This is called *insert mode.*

In versions of Word prior to 2007, if you press the **INSERT** (or **INS**) key, Word is switched to *overtype* mode, and the OVR indicator was enabled in the status bar. In Word 2007–2013, this capability is turned off by default, and the **INSERT** (or **INS**) key does nothing. The reason is that more often than not, the **INSERT** (or **INS**) key gets pressed by mistake, and you don't find out about this until after you have typed over a lot of existing text you didn't want to replace. You can turn on this capability, however.

1. Click **File | Options | Advanced.**
2. Under Editing Options, click **Use The Insert Key To Control Overtype Mode.**
3. Click **OK.**

Use the Insert key to control overtype mode
Use overtype mode

1 2 3 4 5 6 7 8 9 10

In overtype mode, any character key you press types over (replaces) the existing character to the right of the insertion point. Overtype mode does not affect the **ENTER** key, which continues to push existing characters to the right of the insertion point and down. The **TAB** key in overtype mode does replace characters to the right, *unless* it is pressed at the beginning of the line—in which case, it is treated as an indent and pushes the rest of the line to the right.

CAUTION! In Word 2013, there is no "OVR" in the status bar to indicate that you are in overtype mode.

NOTE In both insert and overtype modes, the directional keys move the insertion point without regard to which mode is enabled.

Insert Symbols or Special Characters

Keyboard characters take only a keystroke to type into a document, but many other characters and symbols exist beyond those that appear on the keyboard, for example: ©, £, Ã, ´Ω, and ☺ that you may also want to enter into a document. Some of the more common symbols are collected into a Special Characters list so they can be found easily, such as an em dash, copyright symbol, trademark, etc. You can enter these characters using either the Symbol dialog box or a sequence of keys (also called a keyboard shortcut).

TIP You can insert multiple symbols or special characters, one after the other, by repeating the steps.

1. Move the insertion point where you want to insert the symbol or special character.
2. Click **Insert | Symbols** in the Symbols group. A Symbol menu will open containing the most commonly used symbols.
3. Click the symbol in the menu if you see the one you want.
4. Click **More Symbols** if you don't see the symbol you want. The Symbol dialog box opens, seen in Figure 2-6:
   - Click the **Symbols** tab for characters found within font styles
   - Click the **Special Characters** tab to select common standard characters.
5. If you've chosen the Symbols tab, click the **Font** down arrow to select a font. The fonts vary on which characters they contain. You may need to scroll through a few before finding the exact symbol you want.

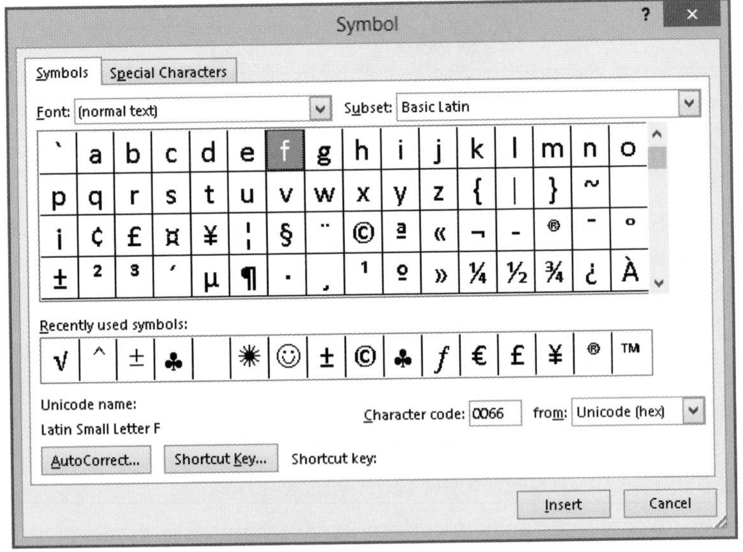

Figure 2-6: The Symbol dialog box allows you to insert special characters and symbols in various fonts and languages.

6. Scroll through the symbols or special characters. When you find the one you want, select it and click **Insert** to insert it into your document where your insertion point is located.

TIP If you use a particular symbol frequently, you can use the shortcut key to insert it. The key will be shown in the Symbol dialog box. If your symbol does not have a shortcut key, you can create one by clicking **Shortcut Key**.

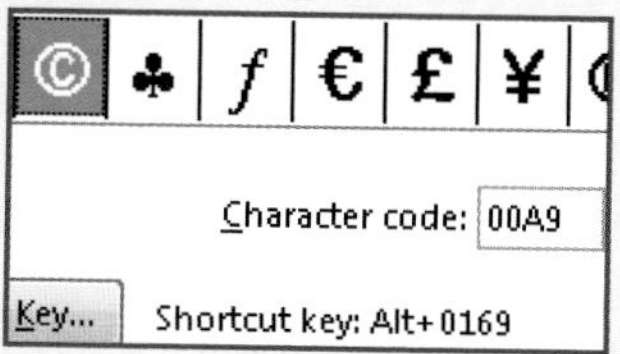

NOTE The AutoCorrect As You Type feature, which is discussed in Chapter 4, also provides a quick way of entering commonly used special characters, such as copyright, trademark, and registered symbols and en and em dashes.

Enter Special Characters from the Keyboard

You can use keyboard shortcuts to enter symbols and special characters. The numeric part of the shortcut must be entered on the numeric keypad.

1. Move the insertion point to where you want to insert the special characters.
2. Press NUM LOCK to put the numeric keypad into numeric mode.
3. Hold down ALT while pressing all four digits (including the leading zero) on the numeric keypad.
4. Release ALT. The special character will appear where the insertion point was.

The shortcut keys for some of the more common special characters are shown in Table 2-2.

Table 2-2: Shortcut Keys for Common Characters (see accompanying Note)

Character	Name	Shortcut Keys
•	Bullet	ALT+0149
©	Copyright	ALT+CTRL+C
TM	Trademark	ALT+CTRL+T
®	Registered	ALT+CTRL+R
¢	Cent	CTRL+/ , C
£	Pound	ALT+0163
€	Euro	ALT+CTRL+E
–	En dash	CTRL+NUM-
—	Em dash	ALT+CTRL+NUM-

NOTE In Table 2-2, the comma (,) means to release the previous keys and then press the following key(s). For example, for a ¢, press and hold **CTRL** while pressing /, then release **CTRL** and press **C**. In addition, "NUM" means to press the following key on the numeric keypad. So, "NUM-" means to press "-" in the upper-right corner of the numeric keypad.

Insert Line or Page Breaks

In Word, as in all word-processing programs, you simply keep typing and the text will automatically wrap around to the next line. Only when you want to break a line before it would otherwise end must you manually intervene. There are four instances where manual line breaks are required:

- At the **end of a paragraph**—to start a new paragraph, press ENTER.
- At the **end of a short line** within a paragraph—to start a new line, press SHIFT+ENTER.

- At the **end of a page**—to force the start of a new page, press **CTRL+ENTER**.
- At the **end of a section**—to start a new section, press **CTRL+SHIFT+ENTER**.

You can also enter a page break using the mouse.

With the insertion point placed where you want the break, click **Insert | Page Break** in the Pages group. A page break will be inserted in the text. (If your screen is reduced in size, you may need to click **Insert | Pages | Page Break**.)

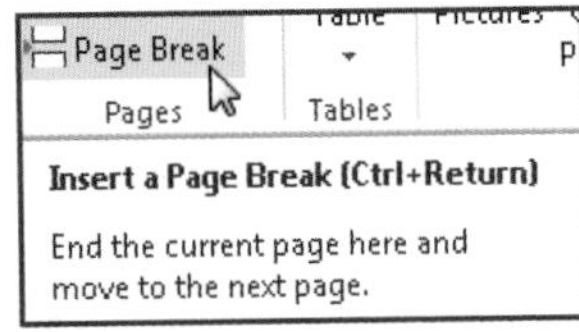

NOTE Section breaks are used to define columns within a page and to define different types of pages, as you might have with differently formatted left and right pages. The use of section breaks, columns, and different types of pages is described in Chapter 4.

Select Text

In order to copy, move, or delete text, you first need to select it. *Selecting text* means to identify it as a separate block from the remaining text in a document. You can select any amount of text, from a single character up to an entire document. As text is selected, it is highlighted with a colored background, as the example paragraph shown in Figure 2-7. You can select text with either the mouse or the keyboard.

Select Text with the Mouse

You can select varying amounts of text with the mouse.

- **Select a single word** by double-clicking it.
- **Select a single line** by clicking on the far left of the line when the I-beam mouse pointer becomes an arrow (this area on the left where the mouse pointer becomes an arrow is called the *selection bar*).

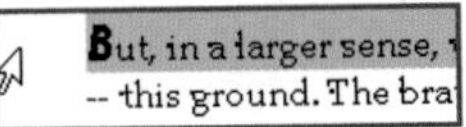

- **Select a single sentence** by holding down **CTRL** while clicking in the sentence.
- **Select a single paragraph** by double-clicking in the selection bar opposite the paragraph (or by clicking three times in the paragraph).
- **Select an entire document** by holding **CTRL+SHIFT** while clicking in the selection bar anywhere in the document (or by clicking **CTRL+A**).
- **Select one or more characters** in a word, or select two or more words, by doing the following:
  1. Click to place the insertion point to the left of the first character.
  2. Hold **SHIFT** while clicking to the right of the last character. The selected text will be highlighted.
- **Select one or more characters** in a word, or to select two or more words by dragging:
  1. Move the mouse pointer to the left of the first character.
  2. Hold down the mouse button while dragging the mouse pointer to the right of the last character. The selected text will be highlighted.

TIP After selecting one area using the keyboard, the mouse, or the two together, you can select further independent areas by holding down **CTRL** while using any of the mouse selection techniques described here.

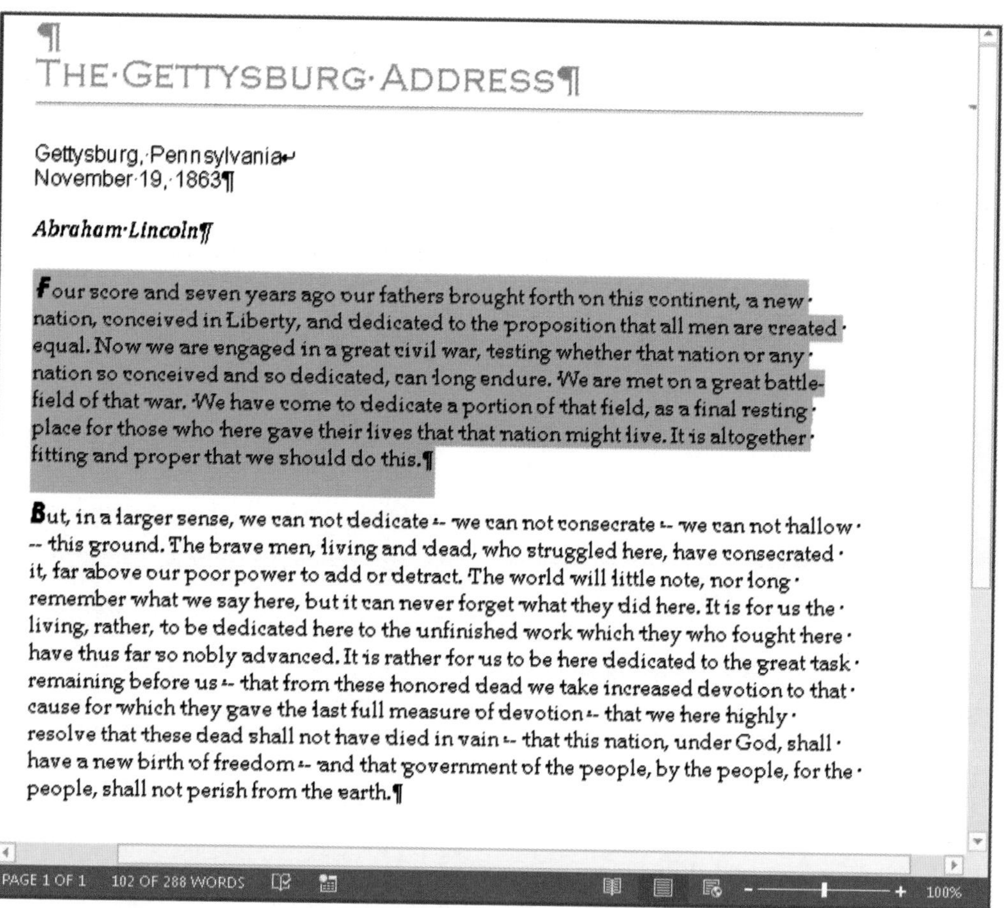

THE GETTYSBURG ADDRESS

Gettysburg, Pennsylvania
November 19, 1863

Abraham Lincoln

Four score and seven years ago our fathers brought forth on this continent, a new nation, conceived in Liberty, and dedicated to the proposition that all men are created equal. Now we are engaged in a great civil war, testing whether that nation or any nation so conceived and so dedicated, can long endure. We are met on a great battle-field of that war. We have come to dedicate a portion of that field, as a final resting place for those who here gave their lives that that nation might live. It is altogether fitting and proper that we should do this.

But, in a larger sense, we can not dedicate -- we can not consecrate -- we can not hallow -- this ground. The brave men, living and dead, who struggled here, have consecrated it, far above our poor power to add or detract. The world will little note, nor long remember what we say here, but it can never forget what they did here. It is for us the living, rather, to be dedicated here to the unfinished work which they who fought here have thus far so nobly advanced. It is rather for us to be here dedicated to the great task remaining before us -- that from these honored dead we take increased devotion to that cause for which they gave the last full measure of devotion -- that we here highly resolve that these dead shall not have died in vain -- that this nation, under God, shall have a new birth of freedom -- and that government of the people, by the people, for the people, shall not perish from the earth.

Figure 2-7: ***You will always know what you are moving, copying, or deleting because it is highlighted on the screen.***

Select Text with the Keyboard

Use the arrow keys to move the insertion point to the left or right of the first character you want to select. For example:

- Hold down **SHIFT** while using the arrow keys to move the insertion point to the right or left of the last character you want to select.
- To select a line, place the pointer at the beginning of a line. Hold **SHIFT** and press **END**.
- To select the entire document using the keyboard, press **CTRL+A**.

 Delete Text

Deleting text removes it from its current location *without* putting it in the Clipboard. To delete a selected piece of text:

Press **DELETE** or **DEL**.

 Copy and Move Text

Copying and moving text are similar actions. Think of copying text as moving it and leaving a copy behind. Both copying and moving are done in two steps.

1. Selected text is copied or cut from its current location to the Clipboard.
2. The contents of the Clipboard are pasted to a new location, as identified by the insertion point.

Use the Clipboard

The *Clipboard* is a location in the computer's memory that is used to store information temporarily. Two Clipboards can actually be used:

- The **Windows Clipboard** can store one object, either text or a picture, and pass that object within or among other Windows programs. Once an object is cut or copied to the Windows Clipboard, it stays there until another object is cut or copied to the Clipboard or until the computer is turned off. The Windows Clipboard is used by default.
- The **Office Clipboard** can store up to 24 objects, both text and pictures, and pass those objects within or among other Office programs. Once the Office Clipboard is enabled, all objects that are cut or copied to it are kept on the Office Clipboard until the 25th object is cut or copied, which will replace the first object. All objects on the Office Clipboard are lost when the computer is turned off.

Cut Text

When you *cut* text, you place it on the Clipboard and delete it from its current location. When the Clipboard contents are pasted to the new location, the text has been *moved* and no longer exists in its original location. To cut and place text on the Clipboard, first select it and then:

- Press CTRL+X.

  –Or–

- Click **Home | Cut** in the Clipboard group.

Copy Text

When you *copy* text to the Clipboard, you leave it in its original location. Once the Clipboard contents are pasted to the new location, you have the same text in two places in the document. To copy text to the Clipboard, first select it and then:

- Press CTRL+C.

  –Or–

- Click **Home | Copy** in the Clipboard group.

Paste Text

To complete a copy or a move, you must *paste* the text from the Clipboard to either the same or another document where the insertion point is located. A copy of the text stays on the Clipboard and can be pasted again. To paste the contents of the Clipboard:

- Press CTRL+V.

  –Or–

- Click **Home | Paste** in the Clipboard group.

Use the Paste Options Smart Tag

The Paste Options smart tag appears when you paste text. It asks you if you want to keep source formatting (the original formatting of the text—the leftmost icon), merge with destination formatting (change the formatting to that of the surrounding text—the middle icon), or keep text only (remove all formatting from the text—the rightmost icon). The Set Default Paste option displays the Word Options dialog box so that you can set defaults for pasting text during a cut or copy action. The Paste Options smart tag is most valuable when you can see that the paste operation has resulted in formatting that you don't want.

The Paste Options smart tag allows you to preview the result of a paste with its selected formatting before you complete it. Simply point at one of the three formatting options in the smart tag menu, and the formatting of the pasted text will temporarily change to reflect that option. If you move the pointer to another option, the formatting will immediately change to the other option. Even after you make a decision and click an option, so long as the smart tag is still visible, you can reopen it, preview another choice, and make the change if you want.

Use the Office Clipboard

As mentioned, the Office Clipboard is shared by all Office products. You can copy objects and text from any Office application and paste them in another application. The Office Clipboard contains up to 24 items. The 25th item will overwrite the first one.

Open the Clipboard

To display the Office Clipboard, click the **Home** tab, and then click the **Clipboard Dialog Box Launcher** in the Clipboard group. The Clipboard task pane will open.

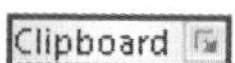

Add Items to the Clipboard

When you cut or copy text with the Clipboard task pane open, it is automatically added to the Office Clipboard. If the Office Clipboard is not open, you can open and copy to it by pressing **CTRL+C** or **CTRL+X** twice rapidly on the same item.

Paste Items from the Clipboard

To paste one item:

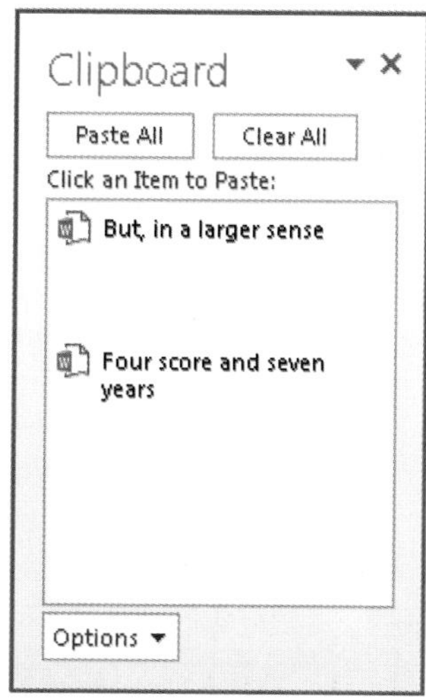

1. Click to place the insertion point in the document or text box where you want the item from the Office Clipboard inserted.
2. Click the item on the Clipboard to be inserted.

–Or–

1. With the Clipboard item selected but no insertion point placed, right-click where you want the item.
2. The context menu will appear. Like the smart tag, there are four formatting options to choose from: Use Destination Theme, Keep Source Formatting, Merge Formatting, and Keep Text Only.
3. Pointing at any of these options will temporarily show you the item pasted at the insertion point with the formatting from what is pointed at. Moving the pointer off one of the options will undo the paste.

4. Click one of the paste options to complete the paste.

To paste all items:

1. Click to place the insertion point where you want the items from the Office Clipboard inserted.
2. Click **Paste All** on the Clipboard.

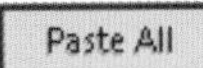

Delete Items on the Clipboard

To delete all items, click **Clear All** on the Clipboard task pane.

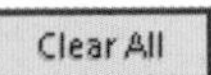

To delete a single item, move the pointer to the item, click the down arrow to the right of the item, and click **Delete**.

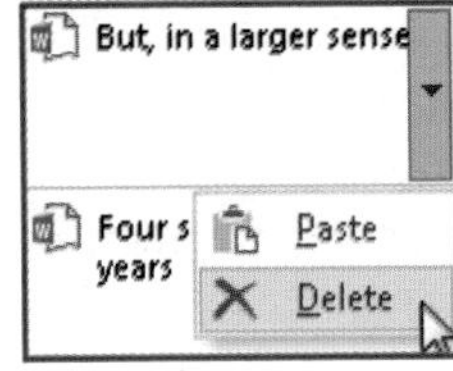

Set Clipboard Options

1. On the Clipboard task pane, click **Options** on the bottom. A context menu is displayed.

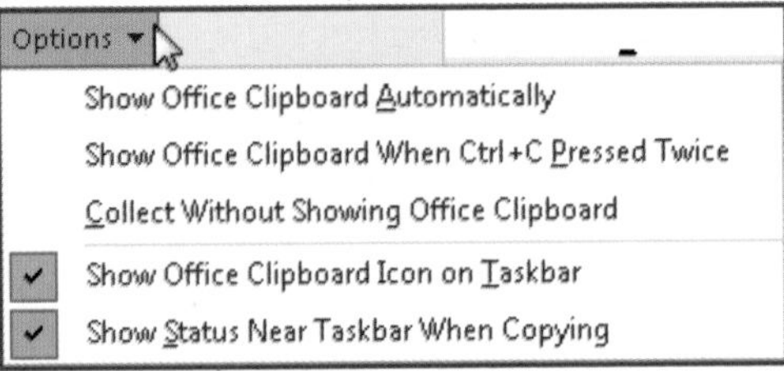

2. Click one of the following options to select or clear it:
   - **Show Office Clipboard Automatically** always shows the Office Clipboard when copying.
   - **Show Office Clipboard When CTRL+C Pressed Twice** shows the Office Clipboard when you press CTRL+C twice rapidly on the same item.
   - **Collect Without Showing Office Clipboard** copies items to the Clipboard without displaying it.
   - **Show Office Clipboard Icon On Taskbar** displays the icon on the right of the Windows taskbar when the Clipboard is being used (this may be hidden, in which case you can click the up arrow to see it).

   - **Show Status Near Taskbar When Copying** displays a momentary message about the items being added to the Clipboard as copies are made.

Undo or Redo a Move or Paste Action

You can undo or redo a move or paste action.

- To undo an action, press **CTRL+Z** or click **Undo** on the Quick Access toolbar.
- To redo an action, press **CTRL+Y** or click **Redo** on the Quick Access toolbar.

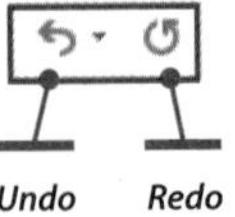

- You can generally undo the last several operations by repeating an Undo command.
- Under certain circumstances, especially while formatting, the Redo option becomes the Repeat option.

NOTE To close the Office Clipboard and revert to the Windows Clipboard, click **Close** at the top of the task pane. The items you placed on the Office Clipboard while it was open will stay there until you shut down Word, but only the last item you cut or copied to the Office Clipboard can be pasted without reopening the Office Clipboard.

TIP Place your pointer over the Office Clipboard icon in the taskbar to see how many items are currently on it.

EDIT A DOCUMENT

After entering all the text into a document, you'll want to edit it and, possibly, revise it at a later date. You'll want to be able to move around the document, quickly moving from location to location, to do this.

Move Around in a Document

You can easily move the insertion point by clicking in your text anywhere on the screen, but how do you move to some place you cannot see? You have to change what you are looking at. Word provides a number of ways to move around in a document using the mouse and the keyboard.

Use the Mouse

Word provides scroll bars to use with the mouse to move to another place, as shown in Figure 2-8.

NOTE You can recover deleted text using the Undo command in the same way that you can reverse a cut or paste action.

Use the Scroll Bars

There are two scroll bars: one for moving vertically within the document and one for moving horizontally. These are only displayed when your document is too wide or too long to be completely displayed within its window. Each scroll bar contains four controls for getting you where you want to go. Using the vertical scroll bar, you can:

- **Move upward one line** by clicking the upward-pointing *scroll arrow*.
- **Move upward or downward** by dragging the *scroll button* in the corresponding direction.
- **Move up or down the screen's height** by clicking in the *scroll bar* above the scroll button to move toward the beginning of the document or by clicking below the scroll button to move toward the end of the document.
- **Move downward by one line** by clicking the downward-pointing *scroll arrow*.

The horizontal scroll bar has similar controls, only these are used for moving in a horizontal fashion.

NOTE You select a picture by clicking it. Once selected, a picture can be copied, moved, and deleted from a document in the same ways as text, using either the Windows or Office Clipboard. See Chapter 7 for a further discussion about working with pictures.

NOTE The view buttons in the lower-right corner of the Word window change the way the document is displayed, not your location in the document. They are the same as the Document Views group in the View tab, which is described in Chapter 1.

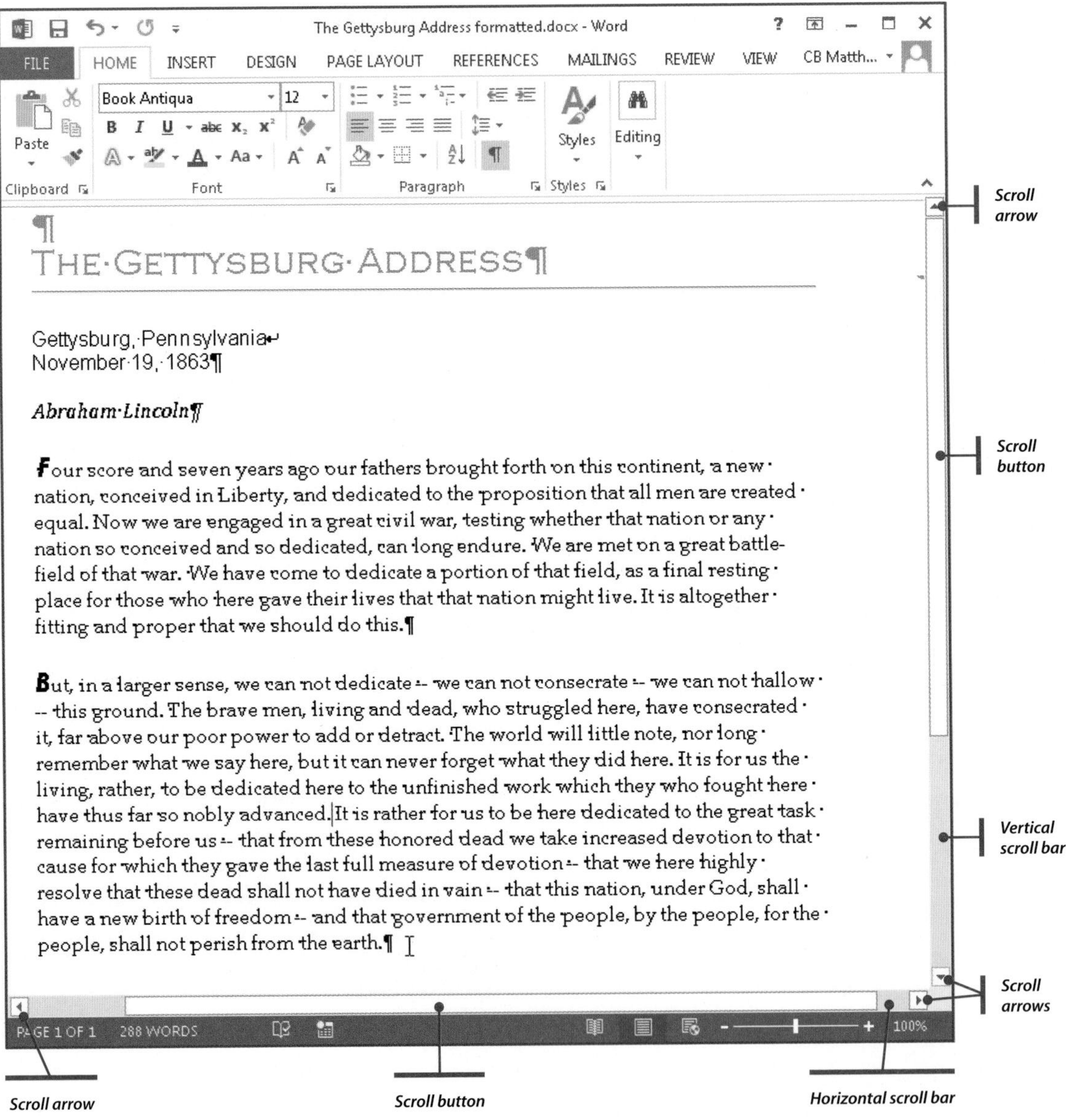

***Figure 2-8:* The scroll bars allow you to move easily to different locations within your document.**

Use the Keyboard

The following keyboard commands, used for moving around in your document, also move the insertion point:

- Press the **LEFT** or **RIGHT ARROW** key to move one character to the left or right.
- Press the **UP** or **DOWN ARROW** key to move one line up or down.
- Press **CTRL+LEFT ARROW** or **CTRL+RIGHT ARROW** to move one word to the left or right.
- Press **CTRL+UP ARROW** or **CTRL+DOWN ARROW** to move one paragraph up or down.
- Press **HOME** or **END** to move to the beginning or end of a line.
- Press **CTRL+HOME** or **CTRL+END** to move to the beginning or end of a document.
- Press **PAGE UP** or **PAGE DOWN** to move one screen up or down.
- Press **CTRL+PAGE UP** or **CTRL+PAGE DOWN** to move to the previous or next instance of the current browse object.
- Press **CTRL+ALT+PAGE UP** or **CTRL+ALT+PAGE DOWN** to move to the top or bottom of the window.

Go to a Particular Location

The Go To command opens the Go To tab in the Find And Replace dialog box, shown in Figure 2-9. This allows you to go immediately to the location of some object, such as a page, a footnote, or a table. To open the dialog box:

- Press **CTRL+G**.
- Click **Home | Find | Go To**.
- Click the left end of the status bar on the Page X Of Y area. The Navigation task pane opens. Click the **Search** text box down arrow, and select **Go To**.

After opening the dialog box, select the object you want to go to from the list on the left, and then enter the number or name of the object in the text box on the right. For example, click **Page** on the left and type 5 on the right to go to page 5 in your document.

NOTE You can also move a certain number of items relative to your current position by typing a plus sign (+) or a minus sign (–) and a number. For example, if Page is selected and you type -3, you will be moved backwards three pages.

Find and Replace Text

Often, you may want to find something that you know is in a document, but you are not sure where, or even how many times, that item occurs. This is especially true when you want to locate names or words that are sprinkled throughout a document. For example, if you had repeatedly referred to a table on page 4 and the table was subsequently moved to page 5, you would need to search for all occurrences of "page 4" and change them to "page 5." In this example, you not only want to *find* "page 4," but you also want to *replace* it with "page 5."

Word allows you to do a simple search for a word or phrase, as well as to conduct an advanced search for parts of words, particular capitalization, and words that sound alike.

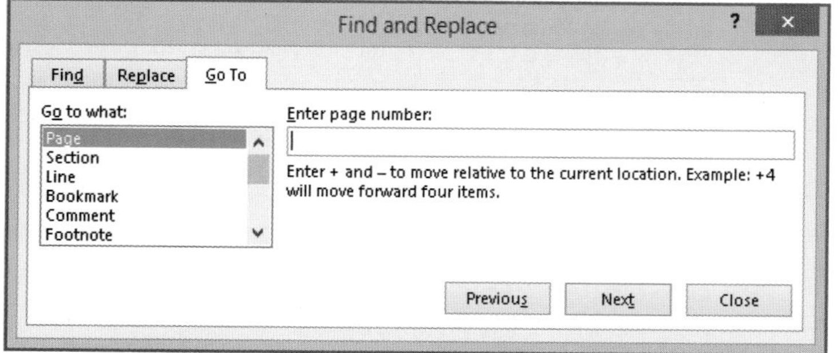

***Figure 2-9:* The Go To command allows you to go to a particular page, as well as to locate other items within a document.**

1 2 3 4 5 6 7 8 9 10

1

2

3

4

5

6

7

8

9

10

Find Text with the Navigation Pane

If you just want to search for a word or phrase:

1. Click **Home | Find** in the Editing group on the right. The navigation pane appears on the left of the Word window with the insertion point in a text box at the top of the pane.
2. Type the word or phrase for which you want to search in the text box. The results are displayed as you type. All occurrences of the word or phrase will be highlighted in the document and listed in the navigation pane, as you can see in Figure 2-10.
3. To select a result, click it in the navigation pane and the border will be highlighted. The word in the text will be highlighted with a different color, letting you know which result you have selected. To advance through the selections in the navigation pane, you can select the next occurrence by clicking the down arrow at the top of the navigation

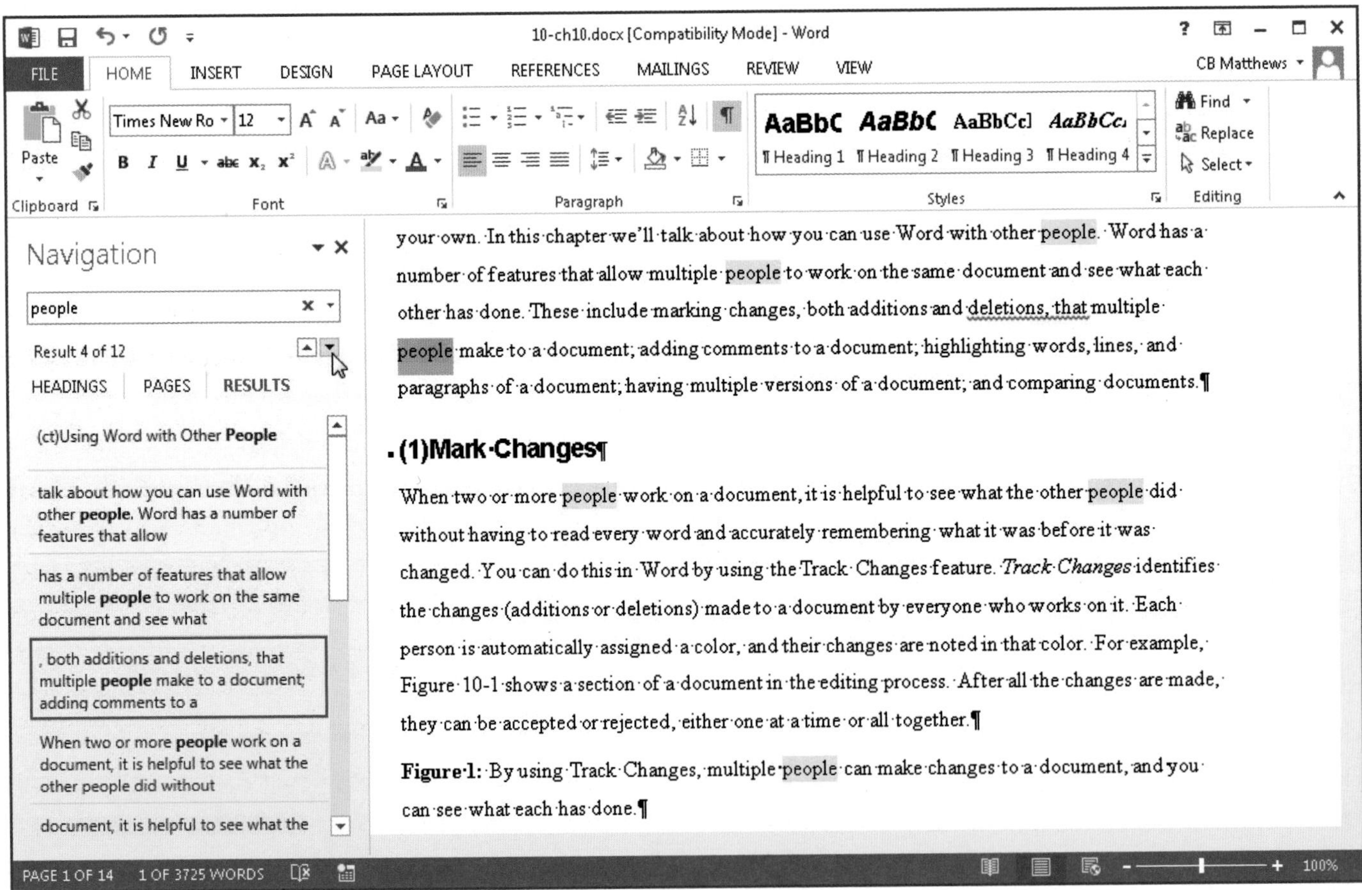

***Figure 2-10:* When you search for a word or phrase with the Find command, all occurrences of the word or phrase will be highlighted in the document.**

pane or clicking the occurrence in the navigation pane. When you are done, click **Close** in the navigation pane.

Replace Text

Sometimes, when searching for a word or phrase, you might want to replace it with something else. Word lets you use all the features of Find and then replace what is found.

1. Click **Home | Replace** in the Editing group. The Find And Replace dialog box appears with the Replace tab displayed.
2. Enter the word or phrase for which you want to search in the Find What text box.
3. Enter the word or phrase you want to replace the found item(s) with in the Replace With text box, as shown in Figure 2-11.
4. Click **Find Next**. The first occurrence in the document below the current insertion point will be highlighted.
5. Choose one of the following options:
   - Click **Replace** if you want to replace the current instance that was found with the text you entered. Word replaces this instance and automatically finds the next one.
   - Click **Find Next** if you don't want to replace the text that was found and want to find the next occurrence.
   - Click **Replace All** if you want to replace all occurrences of the word that are found in the document.
6. When you are done, click **Close**.

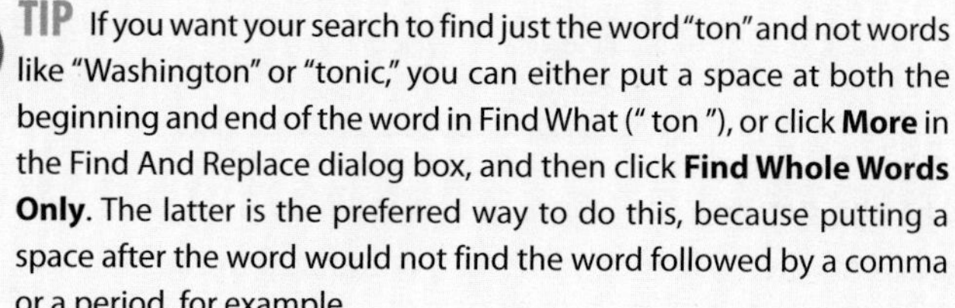

TIP If you want your search to find just the word "ton" and not words like "Washington" or "tonic," you can either put a space at both the beginning and end of the word in Find What (" ton "), or click **More** in the Find And Replace dialog box, and then click **Find Whole Words Only**. The latter is the preferred way to do this, because putting a space after the word would not find the word followed by a comma or a period, for example.

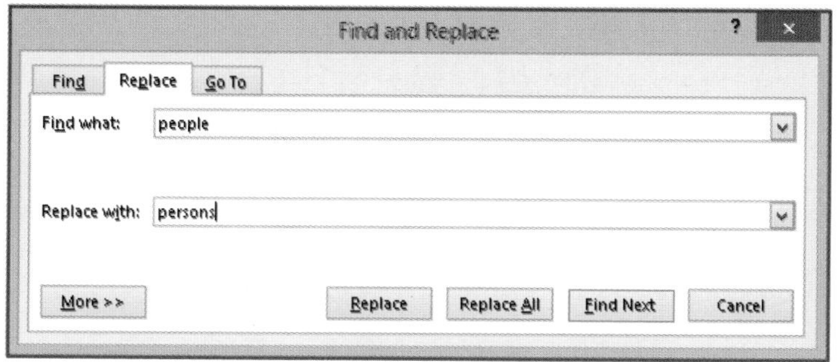

***Figure 2-11:** You can replace words and phrases either individually or all at once.*

Use an Advanced Find and Replace

There is an advanced Find And Replace dialog box, which allows for advanced searches, such as finding and replacing parts of words, particular capitalization, and words that sound alike. To open the advanced Find And Replace dialog box:

Click the **Find** down arrow | **Advanced Find** in the Home tab's Editing group. In the Find And Replace dialog box, click **More** to expand the dialog box.

–Or–

Click **Find** in the Home tab's Editing group to open the navigation pane. Then click the down arrow in the Search Document text box and click **Advanced Find**. The dialog box opens.

By clicking **More** in the Find And Replace dialog box, you will find that Word provides a number of features to make your search more sophisticated (see Figure 2-12). These include specifying the direction of the search, as well as the following additional search options:

- **Match Case** Find a specific capitalization of a word or phrase.
- **Find Whole Words Only** Find whole words only, so when searching for "equip," for example, you don't get "equipment."

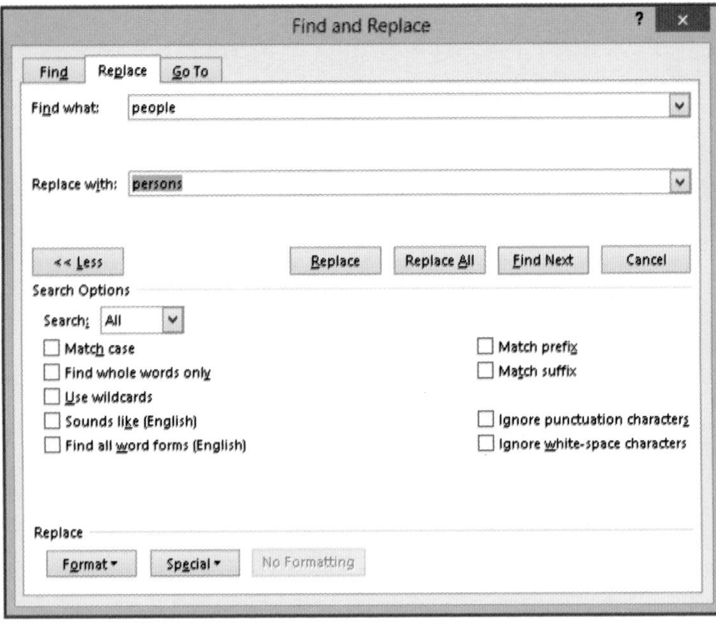

Figure 2-12: ***Word offers a number of advanced ways to search a document.***

- **Use Wildcards** Find words or phrases that contain a set of characters by using wildcards to represent the unknown part of the word or phrase (see "Use Wildcards" next).
- **Sounds Like** Find words that sound alike but are spelled differently (homonyms).
- **Find All Word Forms** Find a word in all its forms—noun, adjective, verb, or adverb (for example, ski, skier, and skiing).
- **Match Prefix Or Match Suffix** Find words containing a common prefix or suffix.
- **Ignore Punctuation Characters** Find words, regardless of punctuation. This is especially useful when a word might be followed by a comma or period.
- **Ignore White-Space Characters** Find characters, regardless of spaces, tabs, and indents.
- **Format** Find specific types of formatting, such as for fonts, paragraphs, etc.

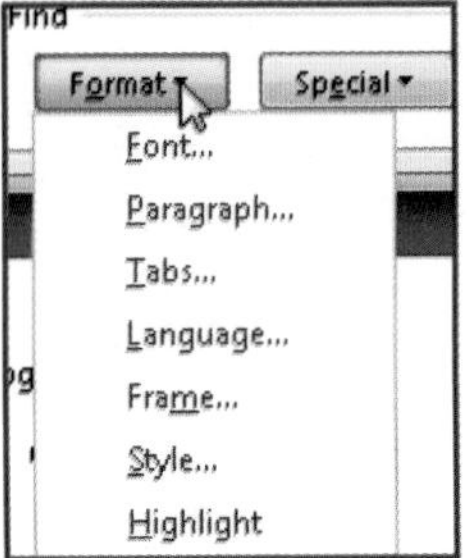

- **Special** Find special characters, such as paragraph marks, em dashes (—), or nonbreaking spaces (can't be the first or last character in a line).

Use Wildcards

Wildcards are characters that are used to represent one or more characters in a word or phrase when searching for items with similar or unknown parts. You must select the **Use Wildcards** check box in the Find And Replace dialog box, and then type the wildcard characters, along with the known characters, in the Find What text box. For example, typing page ? will find both "page 4" and "page 5." The "?" stands for any single character.

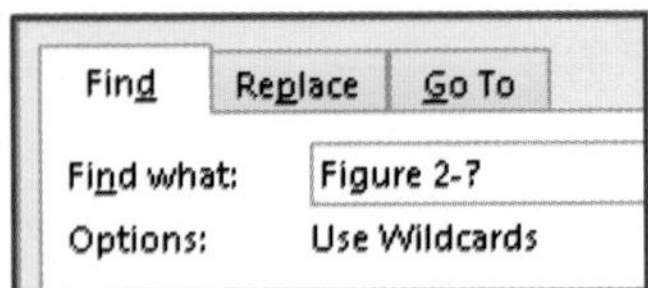

Word has defined the characters shown in Table 2-3 as wildcard characters when used with the Find command to replace one or more characters.

Table 2-3: Wildcard Characters Used with the Find Command

Character	Used to Replace	Example	Will Find	Won't Find
?	A single character	Page ?	Page 4 or Page 5	Page1
*	Any number of characters	Page *	Page 4 and Page 5	Pages1-5
<	The beginning of a word	<(corp)	Corporate	Incorporate
>	The end of a word	(ton)>	Washington	Toner
\	A wildcard character	What\?	What?	What is
[*cc*]	One of a list of characters	B[io]b	Bib or Bob	Babe
[*c-c*]	One in a range of characters	[l-t]ook	look or took	Book
[!*c-c*]	Any character except one in the range	[!k-n]ook	book or took	Look
{*n*}	*n* copies of the previous character	Lo{2}	Loo or Look	Lot
{*n*,}	*n* or more copies of the previous character	Lo{1,}	Lot or Look	Late
{*n*,*m*}	*n* to *m* copies of the previous character	150{1,3}	150 to 15000	15
@	Any number of copies of the previous character	150@	15, 150, or 1500	1400

COMPLETE AND SAVE A DOCUMENT

When you have completed working in a document, or if you feel that you have done enough to warrant saving it and putting it aside for a while, you should go through a completion procedure that includes checking the spelling and grammar, determining where to save the document, and then actually saving it.

 Check Spelling and Grammar

By default, Word checks spelling and grammar as you type, so it might be that these functions have already been performed. You can tell if Word is checking the spelling and grammar by noticing if Word automatically places a wavy red line under words it thinks are misspelled, a wavy blue line under two or more words that are contextually wrong, and a wavy green line beneath words and phrases whose grammar is questioned. You can turn off the automatic spelling and grammar checker. You can also have these features run using an array of options. You can ask Word to perform a spelling and/or grammar check whenever you want—most importantly, when you are completing a document.

> **But, in a latger sense, we can not dedidate -- we can not consecrate -- we can not hallow -- this ground. The brave men, living and dead, who struggled here, have**

Control the Spelling and Grammar Checker

Word provides a number of settings that allow you to control how the spelling and grammar check is performed.

1. Click **File | Options**, and click the **Proofing** option on the left. The dialog box shown in Figure 2-13 will appear.
2. If you wish to turn off the automatic spelling checker, beneath When Correcting Spelling And Grammar In Word, clear **Check Spelling As You Type**.
3. If you wish to turn off the automatic grammar checker, clear **Mark Grammar Errors As You Type**.

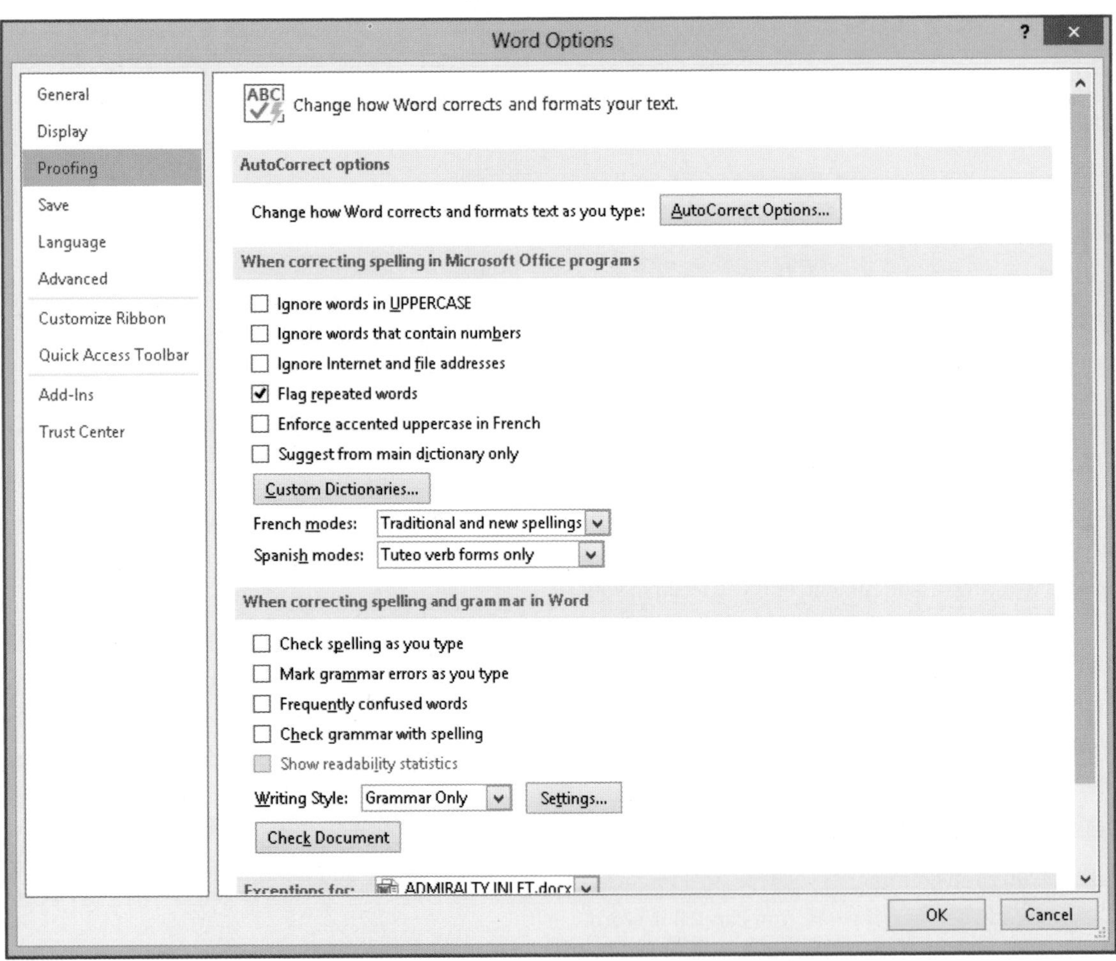

Figure 2-13: ***By default, Word checks spelling and grammar as you type, but you can disable those utilities in the Word Options dialog box.***

4. Click **Settings** to the right of Writing Style: Grammar Only to set the rules by which the grammar check is done.
5. Click **OK** twice to close both the Grammar Settings and Options dialog boxes.

Initiate Spelling and Grammar Check

To manually initiate the spelling and grammar check:

1. Click **Review | Spelling & Grammar** in the Proofing group. A Spelling or Grammar task pane will appear on the right and begin checking your document. When a word is found that Word believes might not be correct, the dialog box will display both the perceived error and one or more suggestions for its correction (see Figure 2-14).

2. You have these options for handling flagged spellings:
   - If you wish not to correct the perceived error, click **Ignore** for this instance, or click **Ignore All** for all instances of the selected word.
   - Click **Change** for this one instance, or click **Change All** for all instances if you want to replace the perceived error with the highlighted suggestion. If one of the other suggestions is a better choice, click it before clicking **Change** or **Change All**.
   - Click **Add** if you want Word to add your spelling of the word to the dictionary to be used for future documents.
   - Click **See More** to display the additional suggestions for the highlighted word.
   - Click **Undo** to reverse the last action.
3. When Word has completed checking the spelling and grammar, you'll see a message to that effect. Click **OK**.

Get SkyDrive for Your Files

If you want to store your files online in the "cloud," you can establish an account with SkyDrive and create a SkyDrive folder on your computer. Then you can easily store and retrieve your files online, with all the benefits (see the "Using SkyDrive" QuickFacts).

1. Click **File | Open** and click **SkyDrive**.
2. Click **Learn More** and then **Download**. When you click this, you are agreeing to the privacy statement and service agreement. It's a good thing to read these before you download SkyDrive.
3. Click **Run** to run SkyDrive, and then **Yes** to allow Microsoft to access your computer. SkyDrive will be installed on your computer. It is available for you to store and retrieve documents, photos, videos, and other content.

Save a Document for the First Time

The first time you save a document, you have to specify where you want to save it—that is, the disk drive and the folder or subfolder in which you want it saved. If this is your first time saving the file, the Save As page will appear so that you can specify the location and enter a filename.

1. Click **File | Save As**.
2. On the Save As page, click the destination device:
   - Click **SkyDrive** to save the file online in the cloud.
   - Click **Computer** to save it on your hard disk.
   - Click **Add A Place** to add a new disk or network destination to your Save As places.

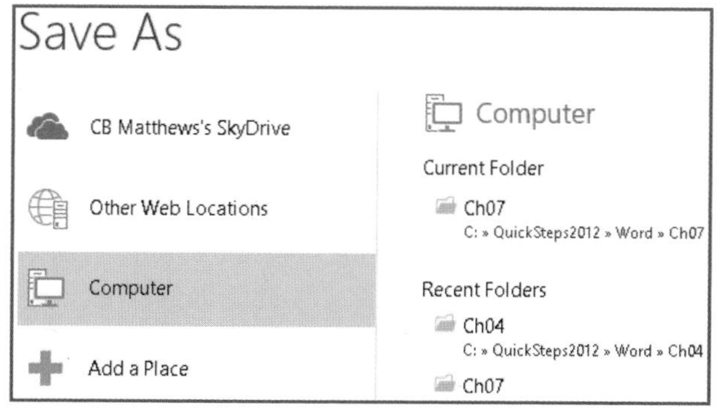

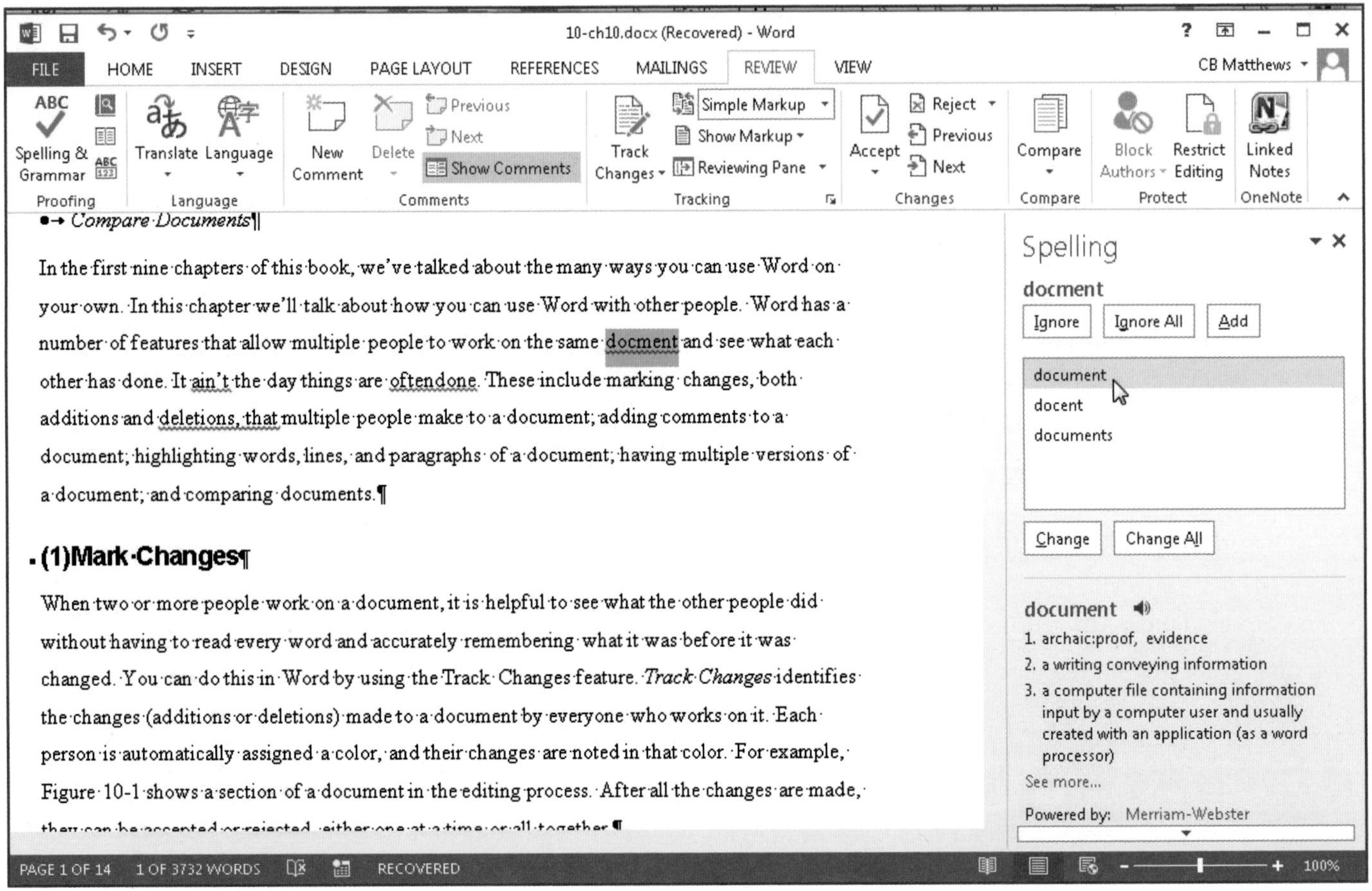

Figure 2-14: The spelling checker is a gift to those of us who are "spelling challenged"!

Save to SkyDrive

1. On the Save As page, click **SkyDrive | Browse** and then **Open**. The dialog box is displayed.
2. If you have an appropriate folder you want to use for this document within the SkyDrive folder already set up, double-click that and click **Save**. Your document is added to the online folder.
3. If you do not have a folder, click **New Folder**, name it, and click **Open** or double-click it to select it.

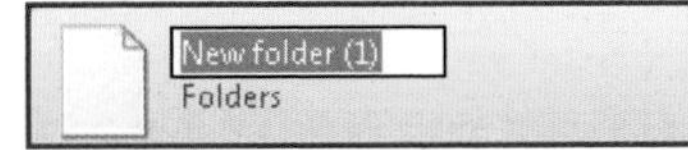

4. Click **Save** to save it.

Save to Your Computer

1. On the Save As page, click **Computer**.
2. Under Recent Folders, find the one you want, if it is listed, and double-click it. In the Save As dialog box (an example is shown in Figure 2-15), click **Save**.

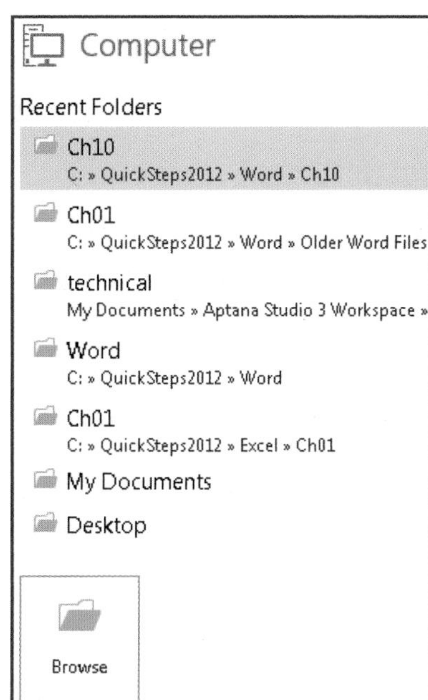

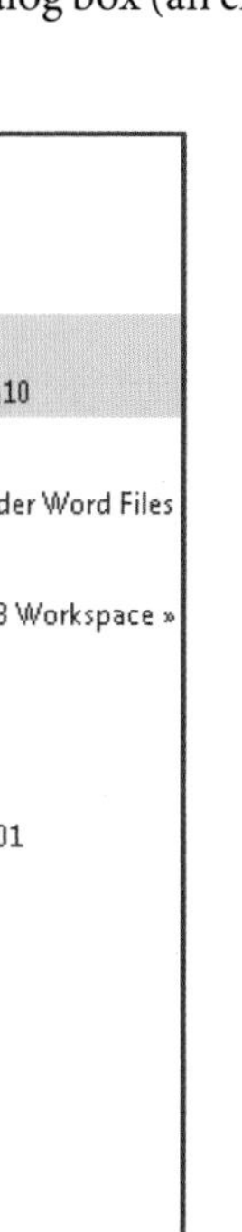

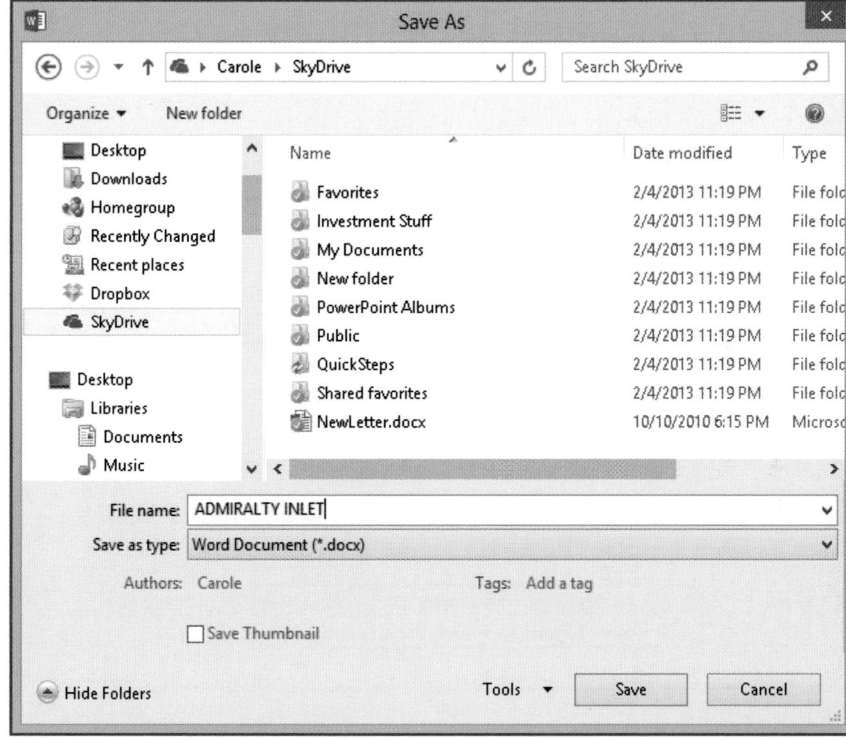

***Figure 2-15:** When saving a file, you don't have to enter a file extension. The ".docx" extension will be supplied by Word automatically.*

3. If the folder you want is not listed under Recent Folders, click **Browse**, find the folder, and double-click it. Then click **Save**.
4. If you want to store your new document in a new folder, click **New Folder** in the toolbar, type the name of the new folder, and press ENTER. Click **Open** and then **Save**.
5. When you have the folder(s) open in which you want to store the document, enter the name of the document, as shown in Figure 2-15, and then click **Save**.

Add Another New Place

You can add another place to save and retrieve your files with the Add A Place option. You are given two initial possibilities: a SharePoint designation and SkyDrive. In both cases, you'll have to sign in with your Windows Live ID before you can access the files.

1. Click **Office 365 Share Point** or **SkyDrive**. A Sign-in To Office dialog box is displayed.
2. Click **Sign In** and follow the prompts to enter your ID and password.

 Save a Document Automatically

It is important to save a document periodically as you work. Having Word save it automatically will reduce the chance of losing data in case of a power failure or other interruption. Although the option to save automatically and the time interval are set by default, you can change these.

1. Click **File | Options**, and click the **Save** option on the left.
2. Beneath Save Documents, make sure the **Save AutoRecover Information Every** check box is selected.
3. The save interval is initially set at 10 minutes. If you wish to change that, use the arrows in the Minutes box to select a time for how often Word is to save your document.
4. Click **OK** to close the dialog box.

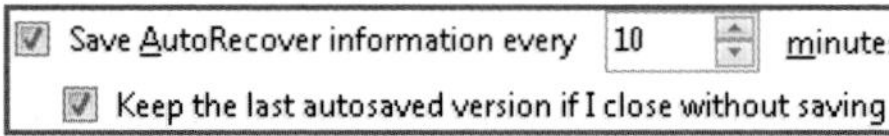

TIP As good as Word's automatic saving is, I manually save my document frequently (like a couple of times an hour) on two different disk drives. I am truly paranoid about this after experiencing the frustration of working several hours on a document only to lose it.

TIP AutoRecover is a reserve parachute that you don't want to test unless you must. AutoRecover might give you the impression that you have lost your work. In fact, if you follow the instructions and choose to recover the AutoRecover document, you may not lose anything—at most, you might lose only the very last thing that you did.

Save a Document

After you have initially saved a document and specified its location, you can quickly save it whenever you wish.

Save a Document

To save a file:

- Click **File | Save**.

  –Or–

- Click the **Save** icon on the Quick Access toolbar.

  –Or–

- Press CTRL+S.

Save a Copy of Your Document

When you save a document under a different name, you create a copy of it.

1. Click **File | Save As**. Click the destination drive: **Computer** or **SkyDrive**. Click the folder name or click **Browse**.
2. In the Save As dialog box, enter the new name in the File Name text box.
3. Click **Save**.

Save a Document as a Template

To save a newly created document as a template from which to create new documents:

1. Click **File | Save As**. Click the destination drive: **Computer** or **SkyDrive**.
2. Click the folder name from the Recent Folders, or click **Browse**. Select the folder(s) in which to store the template and enter a name (without an extension) for it in the File Name text box.
3. In the Save As dialog box, open the **Save As Type** drop-down list box, and click **Word Template (*.dotx)**.

4. Click **Save**.

QuickSteps to...

- Apply Character Formatting
- Reset Font Defaults
- Change Character Spacing and OpenType Features
- Change Capitalization
- Create a Drop Cap
- Set Paragraph Alignment
- Use the Ruler for Indents
- Set Line Spacing
- Use Numbered and Bulleted Lists
- Define New Multilevel Lists
- Add Horizontal Lines, Borders, and Shading
- Turn On Formatting Marks
- Set Margins
- Copy Formatting
- Use a Dialog Box to Format a Page
- Use Mirror Margins
- Determine Page Orientation
- Specify Paper Size
- Track Inconsistent Formatting
- Set Vertical Alignment

Chapter 3

Formatting a Document

Plain, unformatted text conveys information, but not nearly as effectively as well-formatted text, as you can see by the two examples in Figure 3-1. Word provides numerous ways to format your text. Most fall under the categories of text formatting, paragraph formatting, and page formatting, which are discussed in the following sections of this chapter. Additional formatting that can be applied at the document level is discussed in Chapter 4.

This chapter discusses the direct, or manual, application of formatting. Much of the character and paragraph formatting discussed in this chapter is commonly applied using styles that combine a number of different individual formatting steps, saving significant time over direct formatting. (Styles are discussed in Chapter 4.) Direct formatting is usually applied only to a small amount of text that needs formatting that is different from its style.

FORMAT TEXT

Text formatting is the formatting that you can apply to individual characters, and includes the selection of fonts, font size, color, character spacing, and capitalization.

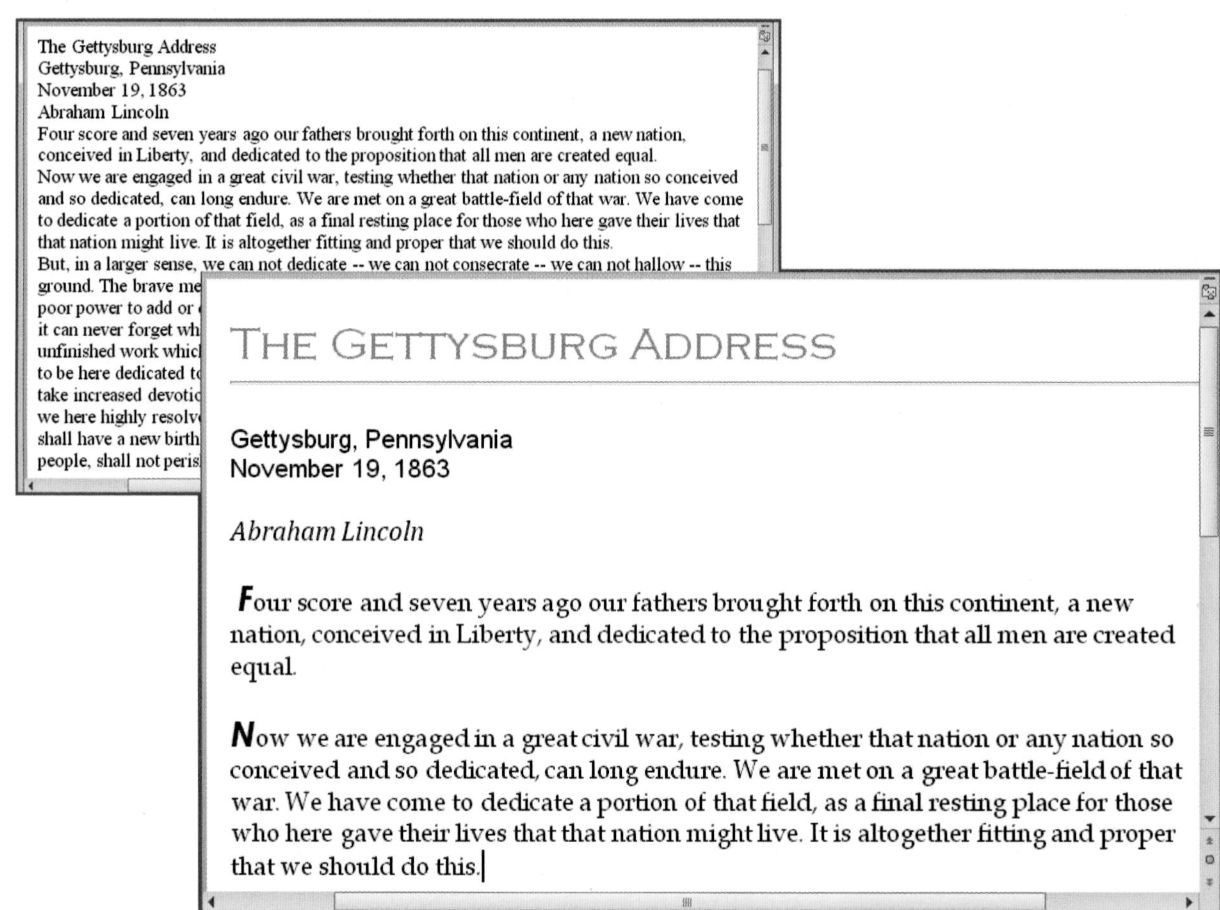
The Gettysburg Address
Gettysburg, Pennsylvania
November 19, 1863
Abraham Lincoln
Four score and seven years ago our fathers brought forth on this continent, a new nation, conceived in Liberty, and dedicated to the proposition that all men are created equal.
Now we are engaged in a great civil war, testing whether that nation or any nation so conceived and so dedicated, can long endure. We are met on a great battle-field of that war. We have come to dedicate a portion of that field, as a final resting place for those who here gave their lives that that nation might live. It is altogether fitting and proper that we should do this.
But, in a larger sense, we can not dedicate -- we can not consecrate -- we can not hallow -- this
THE GETTYSBURG ADDRESS
Gettysburg, Pennsylvania
November 19, 1863
Abraham Lincoln
Four score and seven years ago our fathers brought forth on this continent, a new nation, conceived in Liberty, and dedicated to the proposition that all men are created equal.
Now we are engaged in a great civil war, testing whether that nation or any nation so conceived and so dedicated, can long endure. We are met on a great battle-field of that war. We have come to dedicate a portion of that field, as a final resting place for those who here gave their lives that that nation might live. It is altogether fitting and proper that we should do this.

Figure 3-1: Formatting makes text both more readable and more pleasing to the eye.

Apply Character Formatting

Character formatting can be applied using keyboard shortcuts, the Home tab on the ribbon, and a Formatting dialog box. Of these, clicking the **Home** tab and clicking the **Font Dialog Box Launcher** to open the Font dialog box (see Figure 3-2) provides the most comprehensive selection of character formatting and spacing alternatives. In the sections that follow, the Font dialog box is used to accomplish the task being discussed. Font and Paragraph groups on the Home tab (see Figure 3-3) often provide a quicker way to accomplish the same task, as

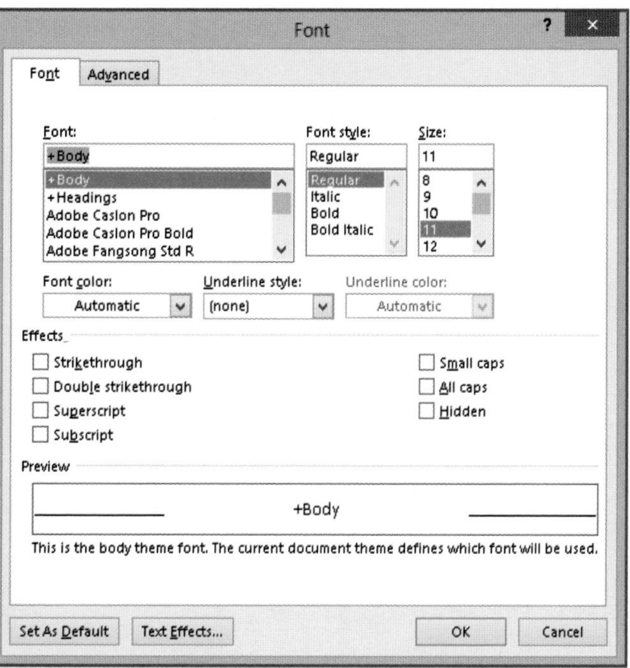

***Figure 3-2:* The Font dialog box provides the most complete set of character-formatting controls.**

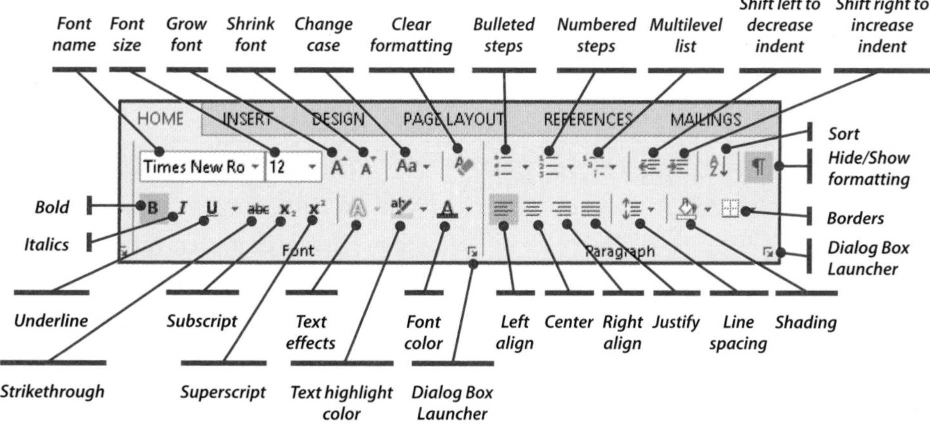

***Figure 3-3:* The Font and Paragraph groups on the Home tab provide fast formatting with the mouse.**

does using keyboard shortcuts (summarized in Table 3-1), which allows you to keep your hands on the keyboard.

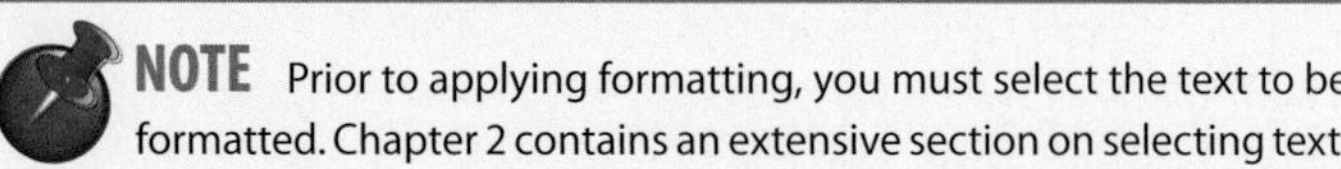

NOTE Prior to applying formatting, you must select the text to be formatted. Chapter 2 contains an extensive section on selecting text.

Table 3-1: Formatting Shortcut Keys

Apply Formatting	Shortcut Keys	Apply Formatting	Shortcut Keys
Align left	CTRL+L	Indent paragraph	CTRL+M
Align right	CTRL+R	Italic	CTRL+I
All caps	CTRL+SHIFT+A	Justify paragraph	CTRL+J
Bold	CTRL+B	Line space—single	CTRL+1
Bulleted list	CTRL+SHIFT+L	Line space—1.5 lines	CTRL+5
Center	CTRL+E	Line space—double	CTRL+2
Change case	SHIFT+F3	Normal style	CTRL+SHIFT+N
Copy format	CTRL+SHIFT+C	Paste format	CTRL+SHIFT+V
Decrease font size	CTRL+SHIFT+<	Reset character formatting	CTRL+SPACEBAR
Increase font size	CTRL+SHIFT+>	Reset paragraph formatting	CTRL+Q
Decrease font size one point	CTRL+[	Small caps	CTRL+SHIFT+K
Increase font size one point	CTRL+]	Subscript	CTRL+=
Open Font dialog box	CTRL+D	Superscript	CTRL+SHIFT+=
Font name	CTRL+SHIFT+F	Symbol font	CTRL+SHIFT+Q
Hang paragraph	CTRL+T	Unhang paragraph	CTRL+SHIFT+T
Heading level 1	ALT+CTRL+1	Unindent paragraph	CTRL+SHIFT+M
Heading level 2	ALT+CTRL+2	Underline (continuous)	CTRL+U
Heading level 3	ALT+CTRL+3	Underline (double)	CTRL+SHIFT+D
Hidden character	CTRL+SHIFT+H	Underline (word)	CTRL+SHIFT+W

Use the Mini Toolbar

You will see the mini toolbar when you select text. You can also see it when you right-click text, when you will also see a context menu (see the accompanying Tip). The toolbar has several of the buttons also available in the Home tab's Font and Paragraph groups. Consequently, you can most likely access the same functions with the mini toolbar as you can with the Font or Paragraph groups. However, to reduce repetition, using the mini toolbar to carry out these tasks will not be discussed. The following steps describe how you access and use the mini toolbar.

1. To display the mini toolbar, select the text to be formatted. It will appear above and to the right of the selection. If the mini toolbar becomes dim, just move your pointer over it to make it clearer.
2. Click the formatting command you want.

TIP The mini toolbar and a context menu with font and paragraph formatting, as well as other options, can be displayed by selecting and right-clicking the text you want formatted. You can then click the necessary options.

Select a Font

A *font* is a set of characters that share a particular design, which is called a *typeface*. When you install Windows, and again when you install Office, a number of fonts are automatically installed on your computer. You can see the fonts available by clicking the down arrow next to the font name in the Home tab Font group and then scrolling through the list (your most recently used fonts are at the top, followed by all fonts listed alphabetically). You can also see the list of fonts in the Font dialog box, where you can select a font in the Font list and see what it looks like in the Preview area at the bottom of the dialog box.

By default, the Calibri font is used for body text in all new documents using the default Normal template. To change this font:

1. Select the text to be formatted (see Chapter 2).
2. Click **Home | Font** down arrow in the Font group. Scroll through the list until you see the font that you want, and then click it.

NOTE Several types of fonts are included in the default set that is installed with Windows and Office. Alphabetic fonts come in two varieties: serif fonts, such as Times New Roman or Century Schoolbook, where each letter is designed with distinctive ends, or *serifs*, on each of the character's lines, and *sans-serif* ("without serifs") fonts, such as Arial and Century Gothic, without the ends. Sans-serif fonts are generally used for headings and lists, while serif fonts are generally used for body text in printed documents, but often the reverse in webpages. Finally, there are symbol fonts, such as Wingdings and Webdings, with many special characters, such as smiling faces ("smilies"), arrows, and pointing fingers.

Apply Bold or Italic Style

Fonts come in four styles: regular (or "roman"), bold, italic, and bold-italic. The default is, of course, regular, yet fonts such as Arial Black and Eras Bold appear bold. To make fonts bold, italic, or bold-italic:

1. Select the text to be formatted (see Chapter 2).
2. Press CTRL+B to make it bold, and/or press CTRL+I to make it italic.

   –Or–

   Click the **Bold** icon in the Font group, and/or click the **Italic** icon. 

TIP You can also open the Font dialog box by right-clicking the selected text you want to format, and then clicking **Font**; or by clicking **Home | Font Dialog Box Launcher** in the Font group.

Change Font Size

Font size is measured in *points*, which is the height of a character, not its width. For most fonts, the width varies with the character, the letter "i" taking up less room than "w." (The Courier New font is an exception, with all characters having the same width.) There are 72 points in an inch.

The default font size is 11 points for body text, with standard headings varying from 11 to 14 points. The 8-point type is common for smaller print; anything below 6 point is typically unreadable. To change the font size of your text:

1. Select the text to be formatted (see Chapter 2).
2. Click **Home | Font Size** down arrow in the Font group, scroll through the list until you see the font size you want, and then click it.

   –Or–

   Press CTRL+SHIFT+< to decrease the font size, or press CTRL+SHIFT+> to increase the font size.

TIP At the top of the Font Size list box, you can type in half-point sizes, such as 10.5, as well as sizes that are not on the list, such as 15.

Underline Text

Several forms of underlining can be applied.

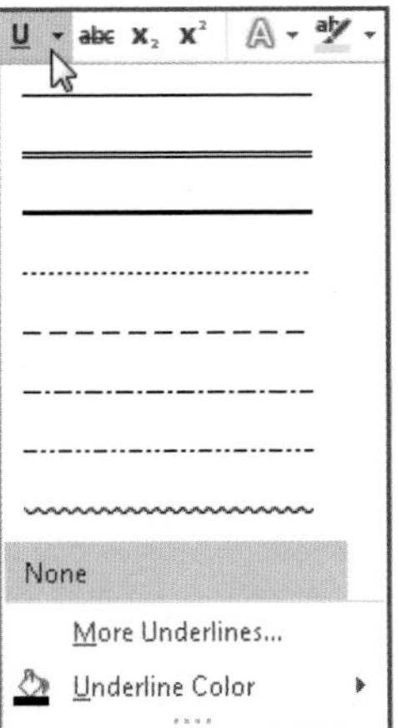

Select the text to be formatted (see Chapter 2). You have these options:

- Click **Home | Underline** down arrow in the Font group, and click the type of underline you want.
- Press CTRL+U to apply a continuous underline to the entire selection (including spaces).
- Press CTRL+SHIFT+W to apply an underline to just each word in the selection.
- Press CTRL+SHIFT+D to apply a double underline to the entire selection.

TIP The Underline Style drop-down list in the Font dialog box, as with the Underline button in the ribbon, contains underline choices beyond those the other methods provide—dotted, wavy, and so on.

Use Font Color

To change the color of text:

1. Select the text to be formatted (see Chapter 2).
2. Click **Home | Font Color** in the Font group to apply the currently selected color.

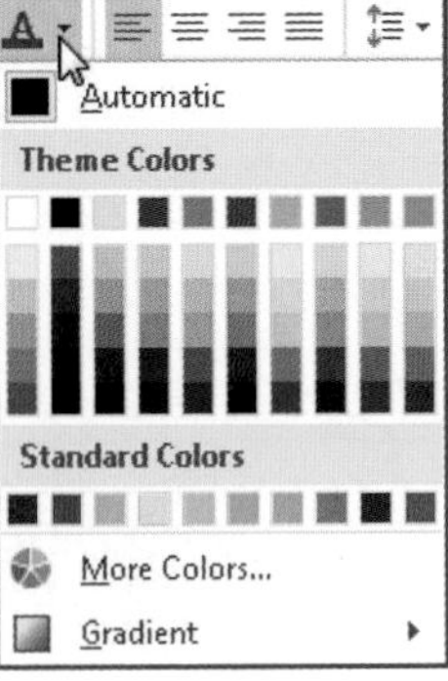

–Or–

Click the **Font Dialog Box Launcher** for the Font dialog box. Click the **Font Color** down arrow, click the color you want, and click **OK**.

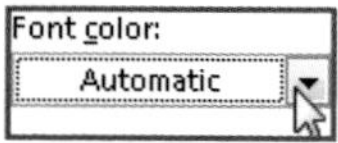

3. If, in selecting a color from either the Home tab Font group or the Font dialog box, you do not find the color you want within the 40-color palette, click **More Colors** to open the Colors dialog box. In the Standard tab, you can pick a color from a 145-color palette, or you can use the Custom tab to choose from an almost infinite range of colors by clicking in the color spectrum or by entering the RGB (red, green, and blue) values, as you can see in Figure 3-4, or the HSL (hue, saturation, and luminescent) values.

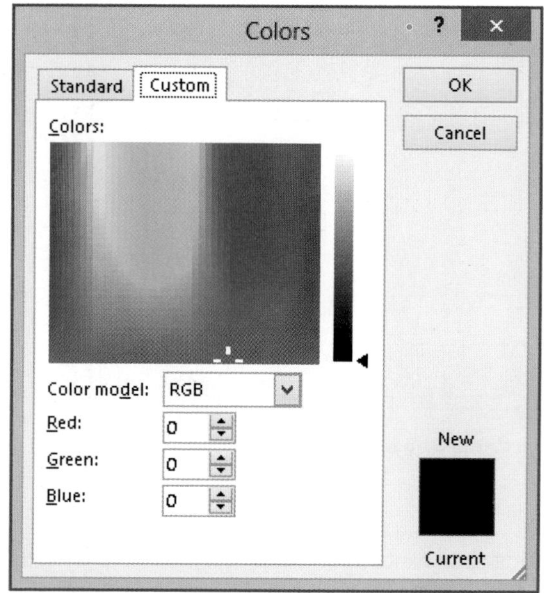

***Figure 3-4:* You can create any color you want in the Custom tab of the Colors dialog box.**

Reset Text

Figure 3-5 shows some of the formatting that has been or will be discussed. All of those can be reset to the plain text or the default formatting. To reset text to default settings:

1. Select the text to be formatted (see Chapter 2).
2. Click **Home | Clear Formatting** in the Font group.

   –Or–

   Press **CTRL+SPACEBAR.**

Reset Font Defaults

Word comes with a default set of formatting parameters for body text composed of Calibri, 11-point regular type, and black color. You can change this in the Font dialog box.

1. Click the **Font Dialog Box Launcher** in the Home tab.
2. In the Font dialog box, Font tab, select the font, style, size, and color you want.
3. Click **Set As Default**, and select either **This Document Only** or **All Documents Based On The Normal.dotm Template**.
4. Then click **OK** to make those settings the new default set.

Change Character Spacing and penType Features

Word provides the ability to change two groups of advanced font features that deal with character spacing and OpenText features. Both of these are set in the Advanced tab of the Font dialog box, which is shown in Figure 3-6.

NOTE Character spacing, especially kerning, is predominantly used when you are creating something like a brochure, flyer, or newspaper ad in which you want to achieve a professional look.

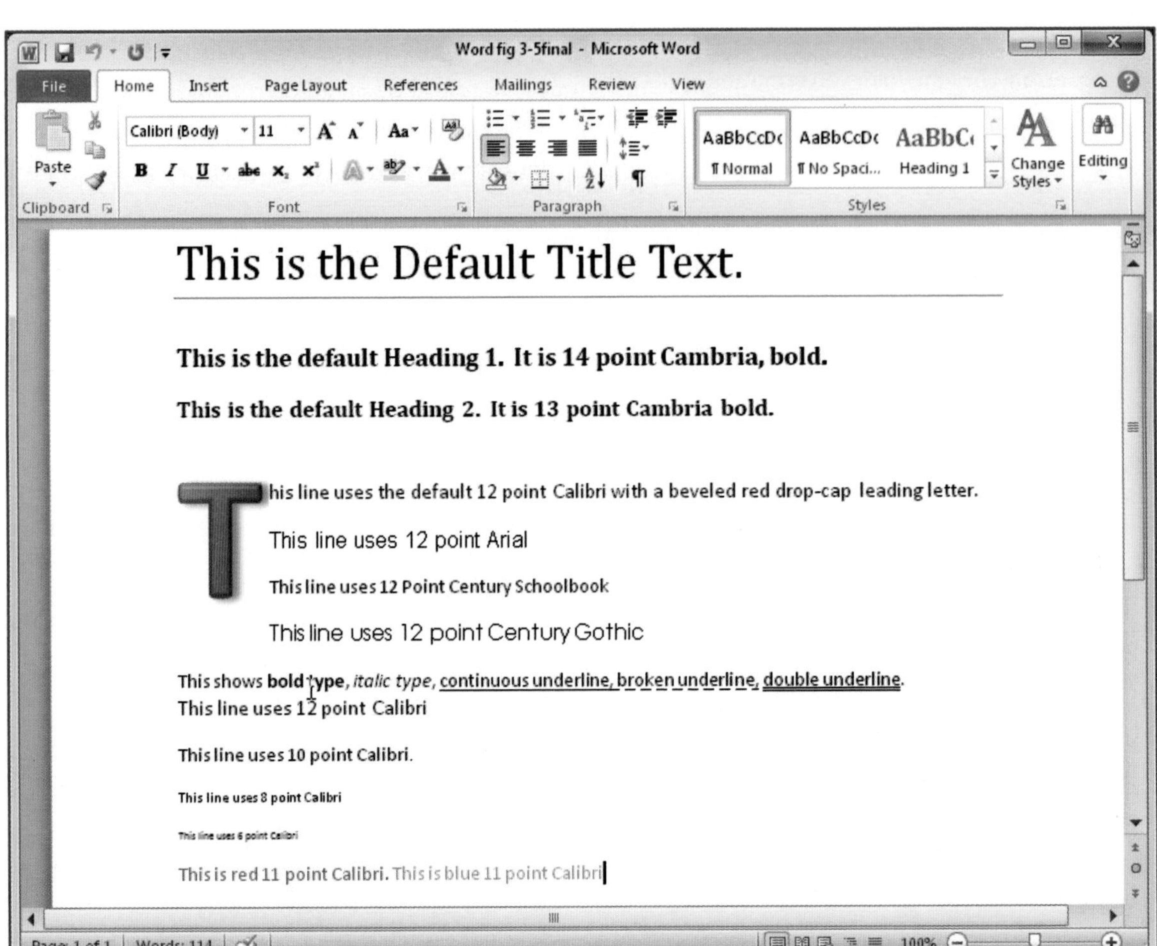

Figure 3-5: Character formatting must be applied judiciously, or it will detract from the appearance of a document.

Set Character Spacing

Character spacing, in this case, is the amount of space between characters on a single line. Word gives you the chance to increase and decrease character spacing, as well as to scale the size of selected text, raise and lower vertically the position of text on the line, and determine when to apply kerning (how much space separates certain character pairs, such as "A" and "V," which can overlap). To apply character spacing:

1. Select the text to be formatted, click **Home | Font Dialog Box Launcher** to open the Font dialog box, and click the **Advanced** tab. You have these character spacing options:

- **Scale** Select the percentage scale factor that you want to apply. (This is not recommended. It is better to change the font size so as not to distort the font).
- **Spacing** Select the change in spacing (expanded or condensed) that you want and the amount of that change in points (pt).
- **Position** Select the change in position (raised or lowered) that you want and the amount of that change in points.
- **Kerning For Fonts** Determine if you want to apply kerning rules and the point size at which you want to do that (it becomes more important in larger point sizes).

2. Check the results in the preview area, an example of which is shown in Figure 3-6. When you are satisfied, click **OK**.

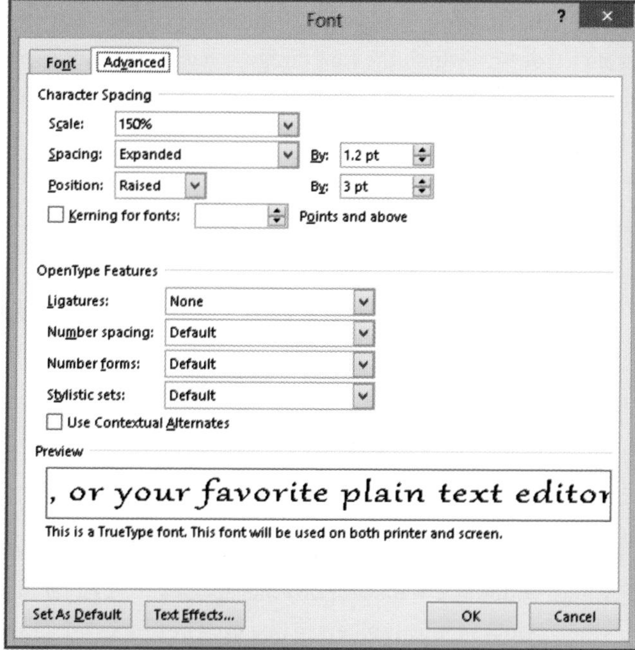

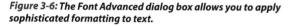

Figure 3-6: The Font Advanced dialog box allows you to apply sophisticated formatting to text.

Use Text Effects

Word provides a number of text effects that can be applied directly from the Fonts group in the Home tab, such as superscript, subscript, and strikethrough, or from the Font dialog box's effects area (see Figure 3-2), such as double strikethrough, small caps, and hidden. In addition, Word 2013 has a Text Effects button and menu in the Home tab Fonts group that allows you to apply a number of visual effects to selected characters, such as shadow, glow, and bevel.

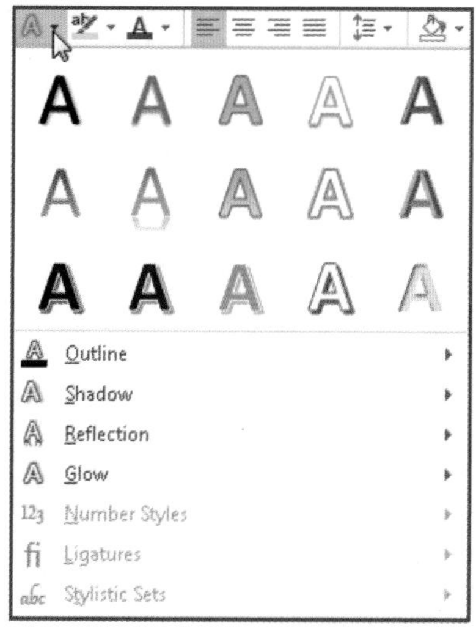

1. Select the text to which you want to apply the effect.
2. Click **Home | Text Effects** in the Font group to open the text effects drop-down menu.
3. Slowly hover the mouse pointer over the various effects to see the results on the selected text.
4. After looking at each of the 15 letter-style options, hover over each of the submenus at the bottom that are available with your selected text (not all submenus are available, depending on the font selected). Each contains a submenu with further choices.

1 2 3 4 5 6 7 8 9 10

5. Try various combinations of Outline, Shadow, Reflection, Glow, Number Styles, Ligatures, and Stylistic Sets. You have many possibilities. Depending on the active font selected, a submenu may not be available.
6. On most of the submenu items, the last item will be a "*named* Option," such as "Shadow Options." If you click that, you'll see a Format Text Effect task pane on the right with even more possibilities, shown in Figure 3-7.

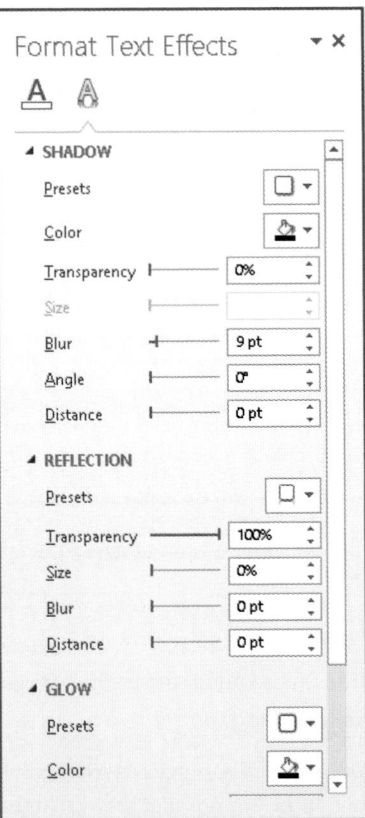

***Figure 3-7:** Using either the Text Effects drop-down menu or the Format effect task panes, such as the one shown here, you can make characters look any way you want.*

7. Select the effects you want to use, previewing them on your page. When you are satisfied, if you are using the Format Text Effects task pane, click **Close** in the upper right corner of the task pane to close it.

Set OpenType Features

OpenType is an open specification for defining computer fonts that is quite flexible, both in its ability to represent a great many of the world's alphabets and in its ability to be easily scaled or sized. OpenType was started by Microsoft and added to by Adobe Systems and others to create a substantial enhancement to its predecessor, TrueType. OpenType is the predominant method used to create fonts on most computers today.

The Advanced tab of Word's Font dialog box contains a group of settings that provide stylistic alternatives for certain OpenType fonts, in addition to the control of the use of ligatures (stylistic pairs of letters like Æ) and the spacing and forms of numbers. These settings are applicable to fonts in which the font designer has added these options. One such font that is available with Windows 7, Windows 8, and Office 2013 is Gabriola. Figure 3-8 shows the Gabriola font at 20 points with various OpenType features selected.

1. Select the text to be formatted, click **Home | Font Dialog Box Launcher** to open the Font dialog box, and click the **Advanced** tab, shown in Figure 3-6. The OpenType features available are (see the following Note):
   - **Ligatures** Select from among None, Standard, Standard And Contextual, Historical And Discretionary, or All on various levels of styling pairs of letters like Æ.
   - **Number Spacing** Select Default, Tabular, or Proportional, depending on whether you are using the number in a sentence, where you might want proportional spacing, or in a tabular list where you want the numbers to line up. The proportional setting tends to take less horizontal space, but tabular is the default. Try this with the Calibri font.

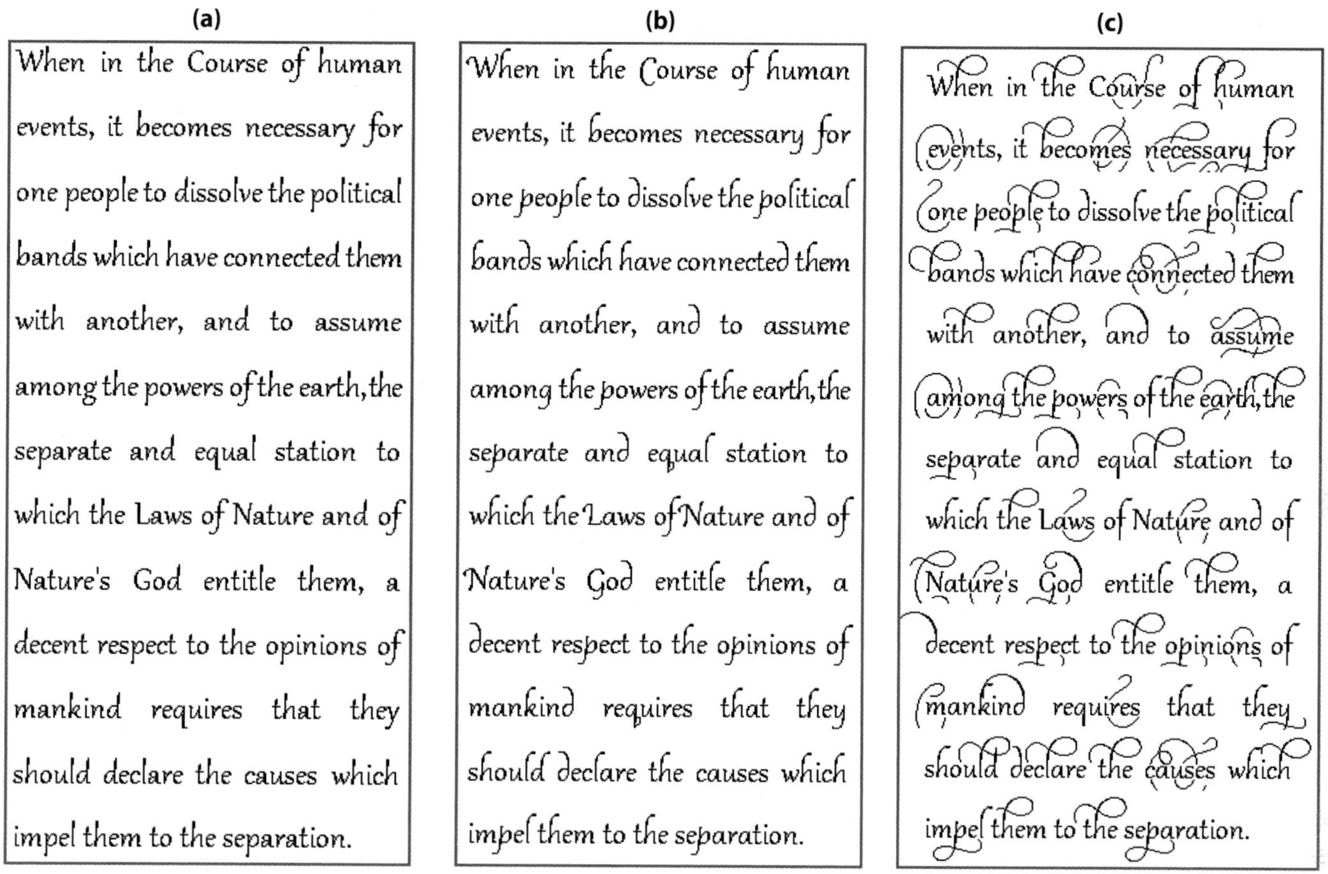

(a)

When in the Course of human events, it becomes necessary for one people to dissolve the political bands which have connected them with another, and to assume among the powers of the earth, the separate and equal station to which the Laws of Nature and of Nature's God entitle them, a decent respect to the opinions of mankind requires that they should declare the causes which impel them to the separation.

(b)

When in the Course of human events, it becomes necessary for one people to dissolve the political bands which have connected them with another, and to assume among the powers of the earth, the separate and equal station to which the Laws of Nature and of Nature's God entitle them, a decent respect to the opinions of mankind requires that they should declare the causes which impel them to the separation.

(c)

When in the Course of human events, it becomes necessary for one people to dissolve the political bands which have connected them with another, and to assume among the powers of the earth, the separate and equal station to which the Laws of Nature and of Nature's God entitle them, a decent respect to the opinions of mankind requires that they should declare the causes which impel them to the separation.

***Figure 3-8:** OpenType fonts give the font designer many added features that can be used in a given font. Here the Gabriola font is shown: (a) in its default configuration, (b) with stylistic set 5, and (c) with stylistic set 7 with Use Contextual Alternates checked.*

- **Number Forms** Select Default, Lining, where the tops and bottoms of the numbers line up, or Oldstyle, where the tops and bottoms of the numbers don't line up. Lining is the default, shown on the top in this example of Calibri numbers.

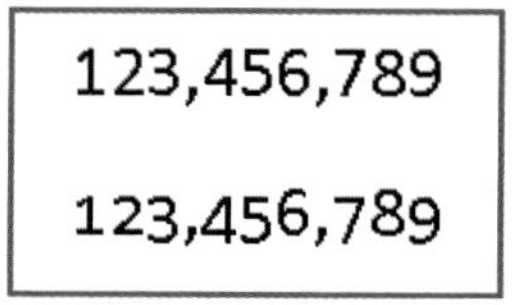

123,456,789

123,456,789

- **Stylistic Sets** Select from up to 20 alternative embellishments to a font that have been added by the font designer
- **Use Contextual Alternatives** When selected, this applies added flourishes that the designer wants used in only certain contextual circumstances, such as the first character in a line, as you can see in example (c) in Figure 3-8.

2. After making a selection, click **OK** and look at the effect on your page. The preview area does not do justice to these changes.

NOTE The meaning of "standard," "default," "contextual," and the various stylistic sets in OpenType features are at the discretion of the font designer. Generally, the stylistic sets go from "1" being the least embellished to "20" being the most embellished, although some fonts only use some of these sets, such as Gabriola, which uses seven. The only way for you to know which fonts use these features and how the various feature selections look is for you to try them out. Do so at larger point sizes.

NOTE You can use **SHIFT+F3** to toggle between uppercase, lowercase, and sentence case or capitalize each word on selected text. For instance, if you select a complete sentence with a period at the end and press **SHIFT+F3** three times, you will get all caps, all lowercase, and sentence caps (only the first letter of the sentence capitalized), respectively. If the selection does not include a sentence-ending period, then each word will have leading caps with the final press of **SHIFT+F3**.

Change Capitalization

You can, of course, capitalize a character you are typing by holding down **SHIFT** while you type. You can also press **CAPS LOCK** to have every letter that you type be capitalized and then press **CAPS LOCK** again to turn off capitalization. You can also change the capitalization of existing text.

1. Select the text whose capitalization you want to change.
2. In the Home tab Font group, click **Change Case**. Select one of these options:

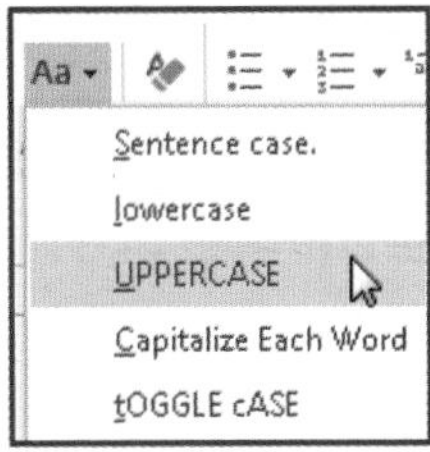

- **Sentence case** capitalizes the first letter of the first word of every selected sentence.
- **lowercase** displays all selected words in lowercase.
- **UPPERCASE** displays all selected words in all caps. All the characters of every selected word will be capitalized.
- **Capitalize Each Word** puts a leading cap on each selected word.
- **tOGGLE cASE** changes all lowercase characters to uppercase and all uppercase characters to lowercase.

 Create a Drop Cap

A *drop cap* is an enlarged capital letter at the beginning of a paragraph that extends down over two or more lines of text (see the red "t" in Figure 3-5 earlier in this chapter). To create a drop cap:

1. Select the character or word that you want to be formatted as a drop cap.
2. Click **Insert | Drop Cap** in the Text group. A context menu will open. You have these choices:

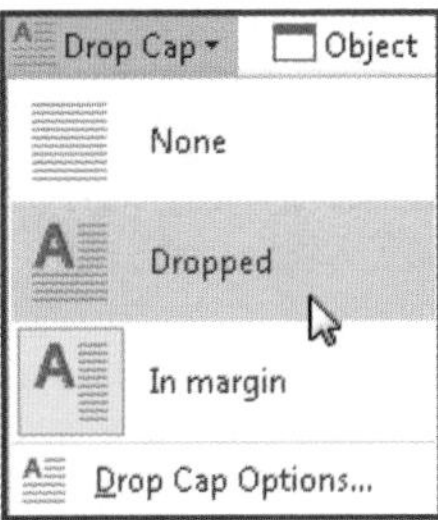

- **None**, the default, keeps a standard letter.
- Click **Dropped** to have the first letter dropped within the paragraph text.
- Click **In Margin** to set the capital letter off in the margin.
- Click **Drop Cap Options** to see further options. You can change the font, specify how many lines will be dropped (3 is the default), and specify how far from the text the dropped cap will be placed.

Click **OK** to close the Drop Cap dialog box.

3. Make the choice you want to use.

The paragraph will be reformatted around the enlarged capital letter. On the left are the two examples of putting the dropped cap in the paragraph or in the margin.

NOTE To remove a drop cap, select the character or word, click **Insert | Drop Cap** in the Insert tab Text group, and click **None** on the context menu.

FORMAT A PARAGRAPH

Paragraph formatting, which you can apply to any paragraph, is used to manage alignment, indentation, line spacing, bulleted or numbered lists, and borders. In Word, a paragraph consists of a paragraph mark (created by pressing **ENTER**) and any text or objects that appear between that paragraph mark and the previous paragraph mark. A paragraph can be empty, or it can contain anything from a single character to as many characters as you care to enter.

 Set Paragraph Alignment

Four types of paragraph alignment are available in Word (see Figure 3-9): left aligned, centered, right aligned, and justified. Left aligned, right aligned, and centered are self-explanatory. Justified means that the text in a paragraph is spread out between the left and right margins. Word does this by adding space between words, except for the last line of a paragraph. To apply paragraph alignment:

Click in the paragraph you want to align. (You don't need to select the entire paragraph.)

- For left alignment, press **CTRL+L**.
- For right alignment, press **CTRL+R**.
- For centered, press **CTRL+E**.
- For justified, press **CTRL+J**.

–Or–

In the Home tab Paragraph group, click the **Align Left**, **Center**, **Align Right**, or **Justify** button, depending on what you want to do.

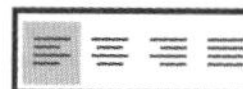

–Or–

In the Home tab Paragraph group, click the **Paragraph Dialog Box Launcher** to open the Paragraph dialog box. On the Indents And Spacing tab, click the **Alignment** down arrow, click the type of alignment you want, and click **OK**.

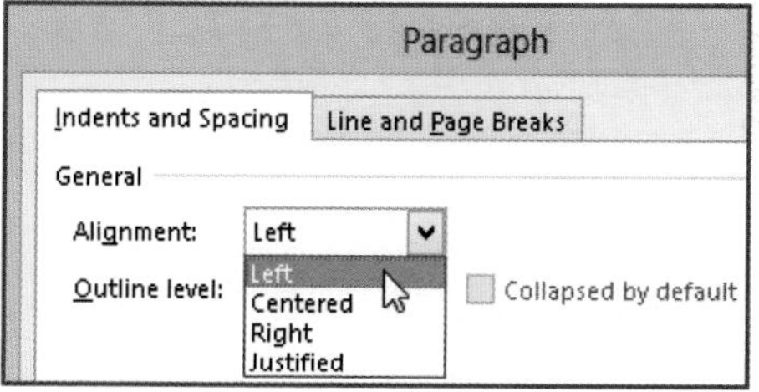

TIP You can also open the Paragraph dialog box by right-clicking the paragraph you want to format and clicking **Paragraph**.

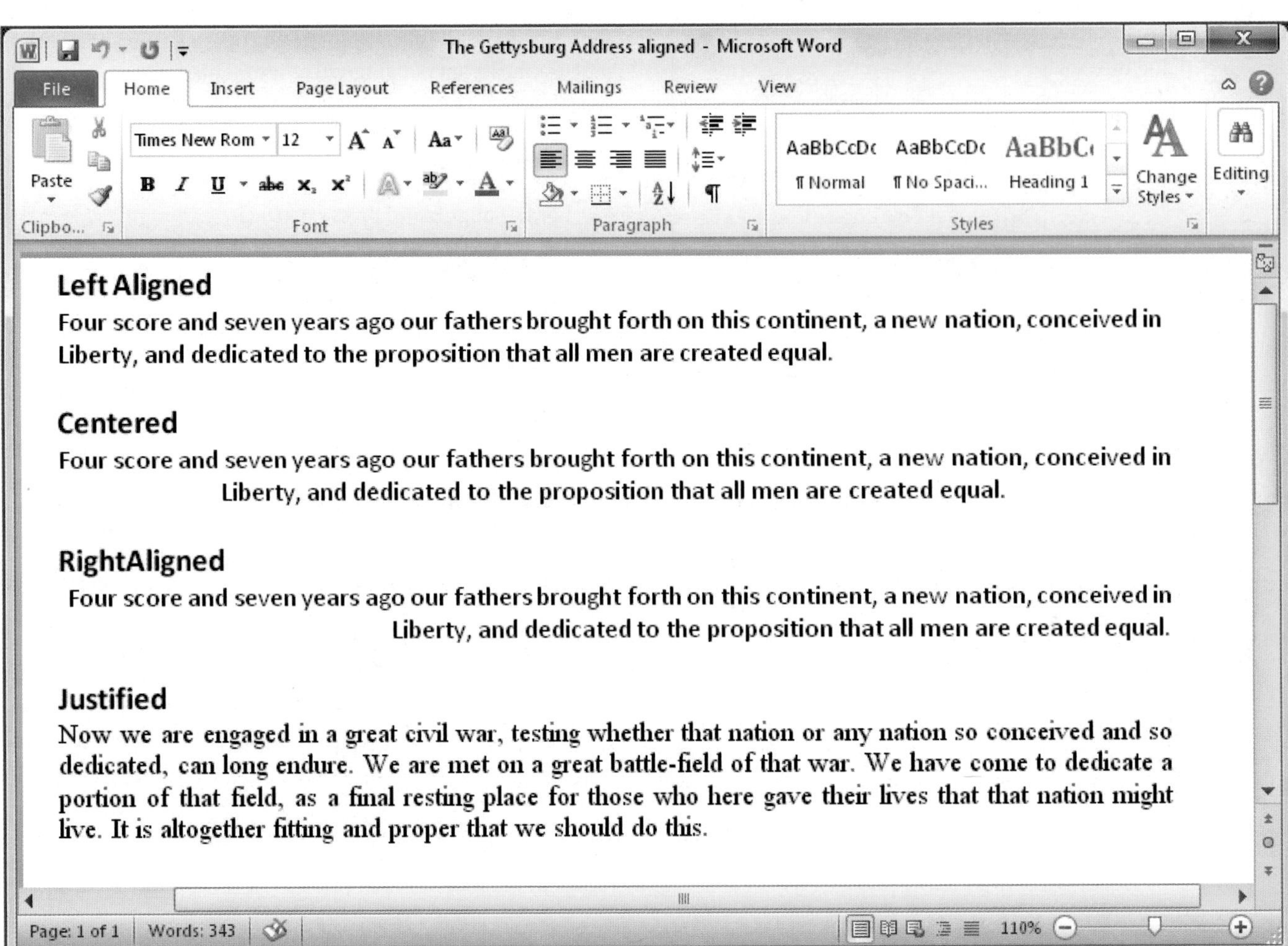
The Gettysburg Address aligned - Microsoft Word
File
Home
Insert
Page Layout
References
Mailings
Review
View
Paste
Times New Rom
12
Aa
¶ Normal
¶ No Spaci...
Heading 1
Change Styles
Editing
Clipbo...
Font
Paragraph
Styles
Left Aligned
Four score and seven years ago our fathers brought forth on this continent, a new nation, conceived in Liberty, and dedicated to the proposition that all men are created equal.
Centered
Four score and seven years ago our fathers brought forth on this continent, a new nation, conceived in Liberty, and dedicated to the proposition that all men are created equal.
RightAligned
Four score and seven years ago our fathers brought forth on this continent, a new nation, conceived in Liberty, and dedicated to the proposition that all men are created equal.
Justified
Now we are engaged in a great civil war, testing whether that nation or any nation so conceived and so dedicated, can long endure. We are met on a great battle-field of that war. We have come to dedicate a portion of that field, as a final resting place for those who here gave their lives that that nation might live. It is altogether fitting and proper that we should do this.
Page: 1 of 1
Words: 343
110%

Figure 3-9: Paragraph alignment provides both visual appeal and separation of text.

Indenting a Paragraph

As illustrated in Figure 3-10, indenting a paragraph in Word means to move the left or right edge (or both) of the paragraph inward toward the center. You can also move the left side of the first line away from the center, for a *hanging indent*.

Specific types of indenting can be seen in the following examples:

- **Bulleted and numbered lists** are used to organize and group pieces of text so they can be viewed as elements within a given topic.
- **An indented paragraph**, either just on the left or on both the left and right, is used to separate and call attention to a piece of text.
- **An outline** is used to provide a hierarchical structure.
- **Indenting the first line** of a paragraph is used to indicate the start of a new paragraph.
- **Hanging indents** indent all of the lines in a paragraph except the first line, which hangs out to the left.

Indentation is a powerful formatting tool when used correctly. Like other formatting, it can also be overused and make text hard to read or to understand. Ask yourself two questions about indentation: Do I have a good reason for it? Does it improve the readability and/or understanding of what is being said?

Normal Paragraph

Now we are engaged in a great civil war, testing whether that nation or any nation so conceived and so dedicated, can long endure. We are met on a great battle-field of that war. We have come to dedicate a portion of that field, as a final resting place

Indented Paragraph

Now we are engaged in a great civil war, testing whether that nation or any nation so conceived and so dedicated, can long endure. We are met on a great battle-field of that war. We have come to dedicate a portion of that field, as a final resting place

First Line Indent

Now we are engaged in a great civil war, testing whether that nation or any nation so conceived and so dedicated, can long endure. We are met on a great battle-field of that war. We have come to dedicate a portion of that field, as a final resting place

Hanging Indent

Now we are engaged in a great civil war, testing whether that nation or any nation so conceived and so dedicated, can long endure. We are met on a great battle-field of that war. We have come to dedicate a portion of that field, as a final resting place

Figure 3-10: Indenting allows you to separate a block of text visually.

Change the Left Indent

To move the left edge of an entire paragraph to the right, you have the following choices:

Click in the paragraph to select a paragraph:

- Click **Home | Increase Indent**, Paragraph group one or more times to indent the left edge a half-inch each time (the first click will move the left paragraph edge to the nearest half-inch or inch mark).

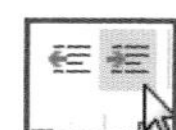

- Press **CTRL+M** one or more times to indent the left edge a half-inch each time.
- Click **Page Layout | Left Indent** spinner, Paragraph group, and click to increase it.
- Click **Home | Paragraph Dialog Box Launcher**, Paragraph group. On the Indents And Spacing tab, under Indentation, click the **Left** spinner's up arrow until you get the amount of indentation you want, and then click **OK**.

Remove a Left Indent

To move the left edge of an entire paragraph back to the left, you have these choices:

Click in the paragraph to select it.

- Click **Home | Decrease Indent**, Paragraph group one or more times to unindent the left edge a half-inch each time.

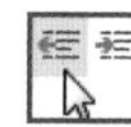

- Press **CTRL+SHIFT+M** one or more times to unindent the left edge a half-inch each time.

- Click **Home | Paragraph Dialog Box Launcher**, Paragraph group to open the Paragraph dialog box. In the Indents And Spacing tab, under Indentation, click the **Left** spinner's down arrow until you get the amount of indentation you want, and then click **OK**.

Change the Right Indent

To move the right edge of an entire paragraph to the left, you have these choices:

Click in the paragraph to select it.

- Click **Page Layout | Right Indent** spinner, Paragraph group.

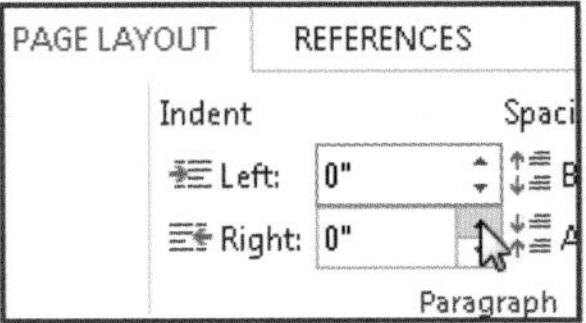

- Click **Home | Paragraph Dialog Box Launcher**, Paragraph group. In the Indents And Spacing tab, under Indentation, click the **Right** spinner's up arrow until you get the amount of indentation you want, and then click **OK**.

Indent the First Line

When indenting the first line, you can either move the first line only or move the entire paragraph except for the first line (see "Make and Remove a Hanging Indent"). To move only the first line of a paragraph to the right or left, you have these choices:

- Click on the left edge of the first line of the paragraph and press TAB.
- Click **Home | Paragraph Dialog Box Launcher**, Paragraph group. In the Indents And Spacing tab, under Indentation, click the **Special** down arrow, and click **First Line**. If you want an indent different than the .5" default, click the **By** spinner to set the amount of indentation you want, and click **OK**.

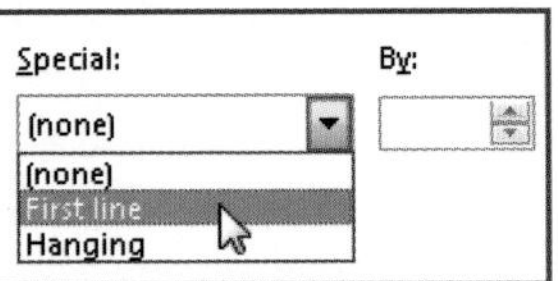

Make and Remove a Hanging Indent

To indent all of a paragraph except for the first line, you have these choices:

Click in the paragraph to select it.

- Press CTRL+T one or more times to indent the left edge of all but the first line a half-inch each time.
- Click **Home | Paragraph Dialog Box Launcher**, Paragraph group. In the Indents And Spacing tab, under Indentation, click the **Special** down arrow, and select **Hanging**. Enter the amount of the indent, and click **OK**.

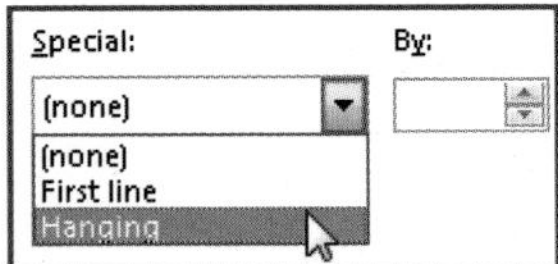

To unindent all but the first line of a paragraph:

Click in the paragraph to select it.

- Press CTRL+SHIFT+T one or more times to unindent the left edge of all but the first line a half-inch each time.
- Click **Home | Paragraph Dialog Box Launcher**, Paragraph group. In the Indents And Spacing tab, under Indentation, click the **Special** down arrow, and click **None**. Click **OK**.

TIP You can reset *all* paragraph formatting, including indents, hanging indents, alignment, and paragraph spacing, to their default settings by pressing **CTRL+Q**.

 Use the Ruler for Indents

You can use the horizontal ruler to set tabs and indents.

Display the Rulers

To display the rulers, if they are not already visible, you have these choices:

Click **View | Ruler** in the Show group. Vertical and horizontal rulers will be displayed on the top and left sides of the document window.

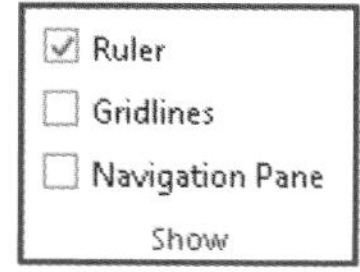

Set a Paragraph Indent on the Left

To move the paragraph to the left:

1. Click to select the paragraph to be indented.
2. Drag the left indent tab to where you want the paragraph indented.

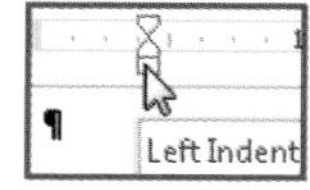

Set a Paragraph Indent on the Right

To move the right side of the paragraph to the left:

1. Click to select the paragraph to be indented.
2. Drag the right indent tab on the right of the ruler to where you want the paragraph indented.

Set a First-Line Indent

To indent the first line to the right of the rest of the paragraph:

1. Click to select the paragraph to be indented.
2. Drag the first-line indent tab on the left of the ruler to where you want the paragraph indented.

Set a Hanging Indent

To indent all but the first line of a paragraph to the right of the first line:

1. Click to select the paragraph to be indented.
2. Drag the hanging indent tab on the left of the ruler to where you want the paragraph indented.

UNDERSTAND LINE AND PARAGRAPH SPACING

The vertical spacing of text is determined by the amount of space between lines, the amount of space added before and after a paragraph, and where you break lines and pages.

 Set Line Spacing

The amount of space between lines is most often set in terms of the line height, with *single-spacing* being one times the current line height, *double-spacing* being twice the current line height, and so on. You can also specify line spacing in points, as you do the size of type. Single-spacing is approximately 14 points for 12-point type. To set line spacing for an entire paragraph:

Click in the paragraph for which you want to set the line spacing. You have these options:

- Click **Home | Line Spacing** in the Paragraph group. Then click the line spacing, in terms of lines, that you want to use.

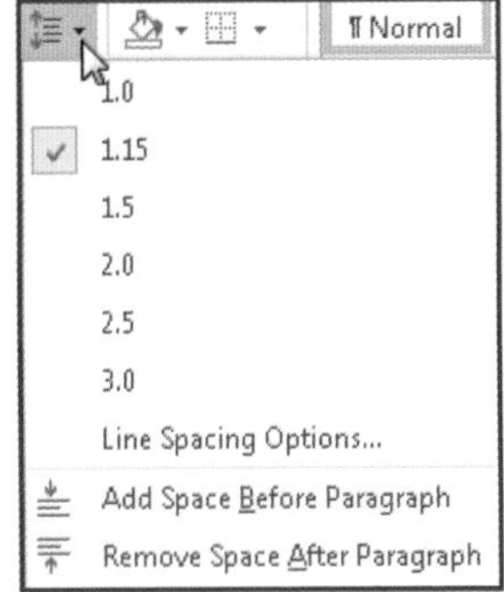

- Press **CTRL+1** for single-line spacing, press **CTRL+5** for one-and-a-half-line spacing, and press **CTRL+2** for double-line spacing.
- Click **Home | Paragraph Dialog Box Launcher** to open the Paragraph dialog box. In the Indents And Spacing tab, under Spacing, click the **Line Spacing** down arrow. From the menu that appears, select the line spacing you want to use, as shown in Figure 3-11. Click **OK**.

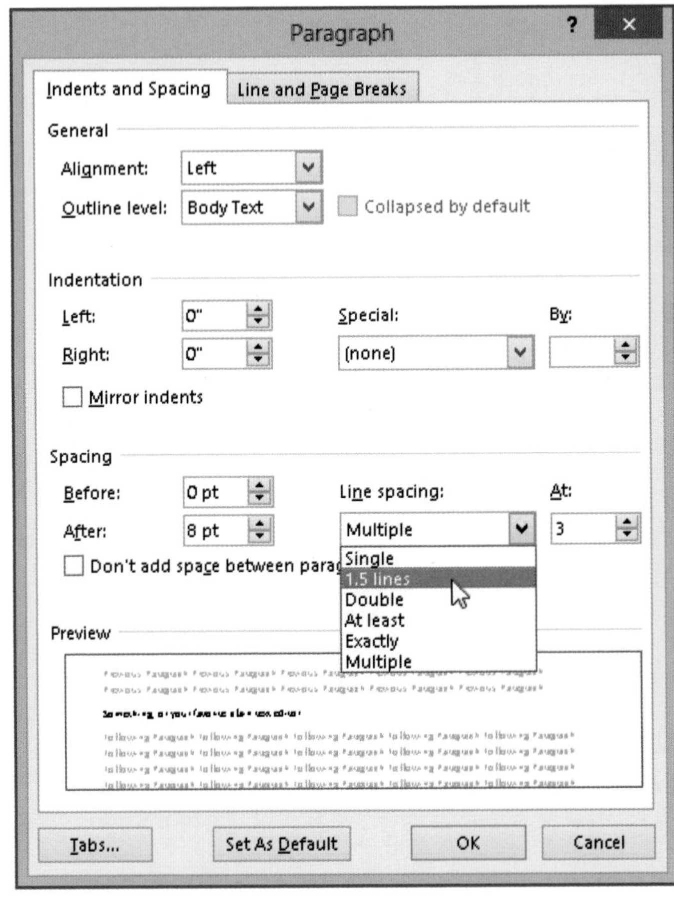

***Figure 3-11:** If a document is going to be edited on paper, it is a good idea to use double spacing to allow room for writing between the lines.*

Add Space Between Paragraphs

In addition to specifying space between lines, you can add extra space before and after paragraphs. With typewriters, many people would add an extra blank line between paragraphs. That has carried over to computers, but it does not always look good. If you are using single spacing, leaving a blank line will leave an extra 14 points (with 12-point type) between paragraphs. Common paragraph spacing is to leave 3 points before the paragraph and 6 points afterward, so if you have two of these paragraphs, one after the other, you would have a total of 9 points, in comparison to the 14 points from an extra blank line. To add extra space between paragraphs:

Click in the paragraph to which you want to add space. You have these options:

- Click **Page Layout | Spacing** in the Paragraph group spinners to set the spacing before and after the paragraph.

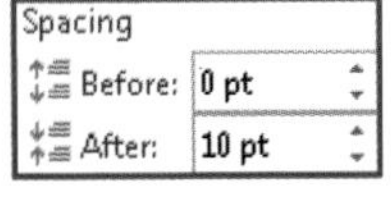

- Click **Home | Paragraph Dialog Box Launcher** in the Paragraph group to open the Paragraph dialog box. In the Indents And Spacing tab, under Spacing, click the **Before** spinner or enter a number in points ("pt") for the space you want to add before the paragraph. If desired, do the same thing for the space after the paragraph. When you are ready, click **OK**.

NOTE In the Paragraph dialog box, you can specify the amount of space between lines in a format other than the number of lines. From the Line Spacing drop-down list, click **Exactly**, and then enter or select the number of points to use between lines. With 12-point type, single-line spacing is about 14 points, one-and-a-half-line spacing (1.5) is about 21 points, and so on. With 11-point type, single spacing is about 12 points.

CAUTION! If you reduce the line spacing below the size of the type (below 12 points for 12-point type, for example), the lines will begin to overlap and become hard to read.

Set Line and Page Breaks

The vertical spacing of a document is also affected by how lines and pages are broken and how much of a paragraph you force to stay together or be with text either before or after it.

You can break a line and start a new one, thereby creating a new line, a new paragraph, or a new page.

- **Create a new paragraph** by moving the insertion point to where you want to break the line and pressing **ENTER**.
- **Advance to a new line while staying in the same paragraph** by moving the insertion point to where you want to break the line and pressing **SHIFT+ENTER**.
- **Break a page and start a new one** by pressing **CTRL+ENTER**.

  –Or–

  Click **Insert | Page Break** in the Pages group.

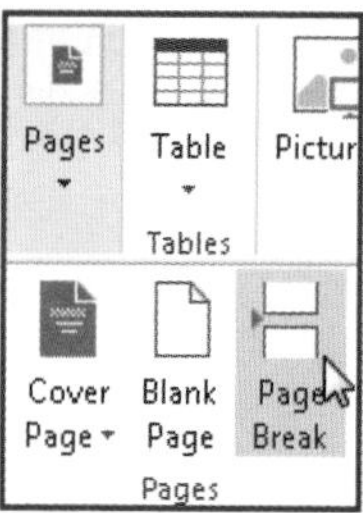

  –Or–

  Click **Page Layout | Breaks** in the Page Setup group. Click **Page** from the menu.

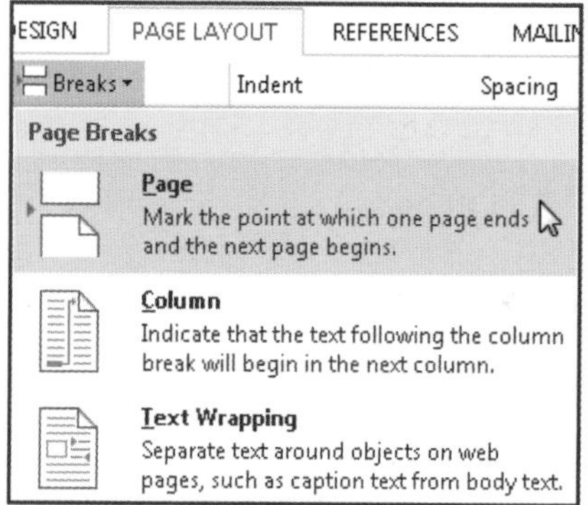

TIP If you format a single paragraph the way you want a group of paragraphs to look, you can often just press **ENTER** to begin a new paragraph with the same formatting. See the discussion of styles in Chapter 4.

Handle Split Pages

When a paragraph is split over two pages, you have several ways to control how much of the paragraph is placed on which page.

1. Click in the paragraph you want to change.
2. Click **Home | Paragraph Dialog Box Launcher** in the Paragraph group, and click the **Line And Page Breaks** tab.
3. Click the following options that are correct for your situation, and then click **OK**:
   - **Widow/Orphan Control** adjusts the pagination to keep at least two lines on one or both pages. For example, if you have three lines, without selecting Widow/Orphan Control, one line is on the first page and two are on the second. When you select this option, all three lines will be placed on the second page. Widow/Orphan Control is selected by default.

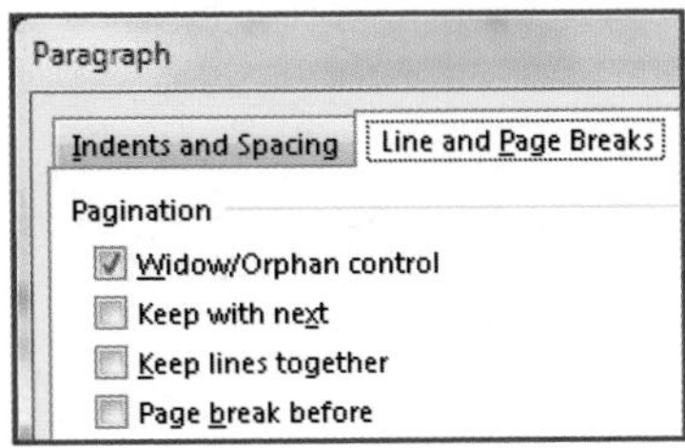

   - **Keep With Next** forces the entire paragraph to stay on the same page with the next paragraph. This option is used with paragraph headings that you want to keep with the first paragraph.
   - **Keep Lines Together** forces all lines of a paragraph to be on the same page. This option can be used for a paragraph title where you want all of it on one page.
   - **Page Break Before** forces a page break before the start of the paragraph. This option is used with major section headings or titles that you want to start on a new page.

Use Numbered and Bulleted Lists

Word provides the means to automatically number or add bullets to paragraphs and then format the paragraphs as hanging indents so that the numbers or bullets stick out to the left (see Figure 3-12).

Create a Numbered List Using AutoCorrect

You can create a numbered list as you type, and Word will automatically format it according to your text. Word's numbered lists are particularly handy, because you can add or delete paragraphs in the middle of the list and have the list automatically renumber itself. To start a numbered list:

1. Press ENTER to start a new paragraph.
2. Type 1., press either the SPACEBAR *two* times or press TAB once, and then type the rest of what you want in the first item of the numbered list.

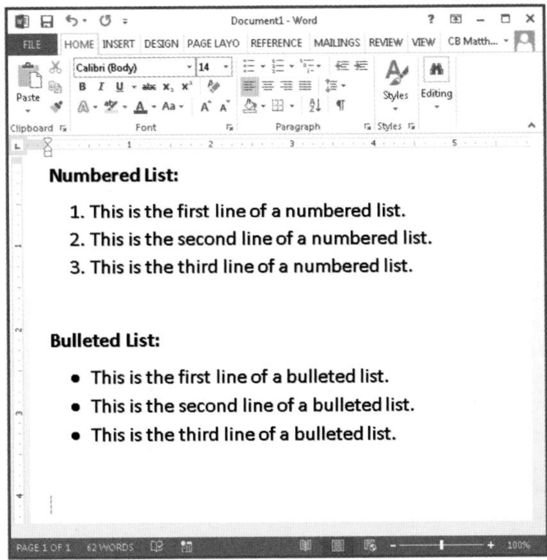

Figure 3-12: Bullets and numbering help organize thoughts into lists.

3. Press **ENTER**. The number "2." automatically appears, and both the first and the new lines are formatted as hanging indents. Also, the AutoCorrect lightning icon appears when you press **ENTER** on the first line.

1. This is the first line in a new numbered list.
2. |

4. After typing the second item in your list, press **ENTER** once again. The number "3." automatically appears. Type the item and press **ENTER** to keep numbering the list.
5. When you are done, press **ENTER** twice. The numbering will stop and the hanging indent will be removed.

If you click the **AutoCorrect** icon, you may choose to undo the automatic numbering that has already been applied, stop the automatic creation of numbered lists, and control the use of AutoCorrect (see Chapter 4 for more information on AutoCorrect).

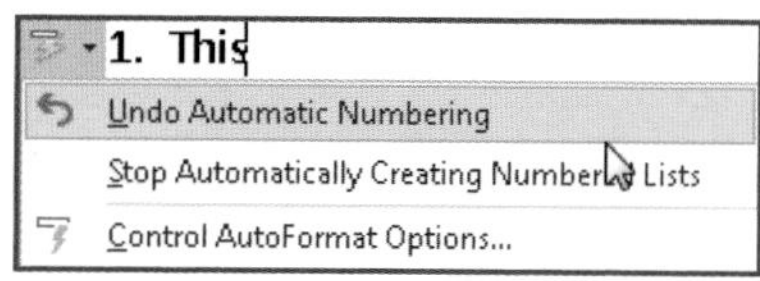

TIP You can type 1 with or without a period, and 2 will be formatted in the same way. If you type the period and press **TAB** or two spaces, the AutoCorrect icon appears immediately. It disappears when you press **ENTER**.

Create a Numbered, Bulleted, or Multilevel List Before You Type Text

You can also set up the formatting for a numbered, bulleted, or multilevel list before you start typing the text it will contain.

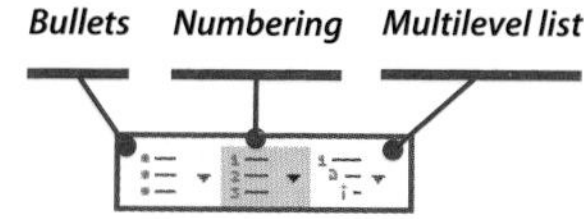

1. Press **ENTER** to start a new paragraph.
2. Click **Home | Numbering** in the Paragraph group to begin a numbered list; click **Bullets** to start a bulleted list, or click **Multilevel List** to start a multilevel tiered list. If you click Multilevel List, you'll need to also select a type of list from the menu.
3. Type the first item, and press **ENTER** to start the second numbered or bulleted item with the same style as the first. When you are done creating the list, press **ENTER** twice to stop the automatic list.

   –Or–

   Click **Home | Numbering** (or Bullets or Multilevel List) in the Paragraph group to end the list.

TIP To select a number or bullet other than the default, click the **Numbering** or **Bullets** down arrow and click your choice from the context menu, as shown in Figure 3-13. See "Customize Bullets and Numbers" later in this chapter for additional ideas on how to vary bullets and numbering formats.

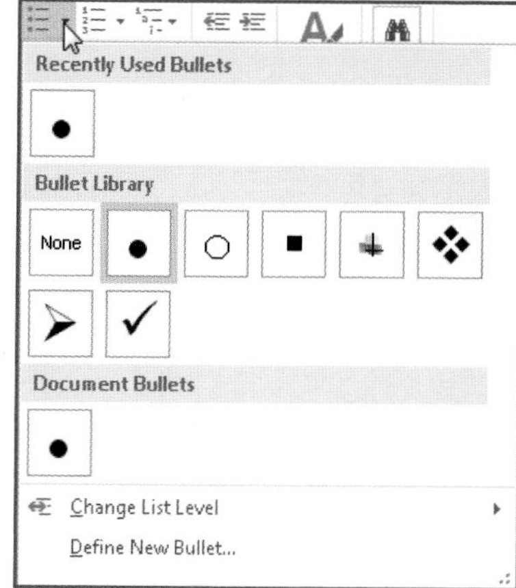

Figure 3-13: Clicking the Bullets down arrow displays a list of choices for formatting bullets. A similar menu is displayed when you click the Numbering down arrow.

1 2 3 4 5 6 7 8 9 10

Customize Bullets and Numbers

You saw in Figure 3-13 that Word offers seven different types of bullets. Word also offers eight different styles for numbering paragraphs, as you can see in Figure 3-14, and nine for multilevel lists in Figure 3-15. For those who feel eight or nine choices is not enough, there is a Define New option for bullets, numbering, and multilevel lists that includes the ability to select from hundreds of pictures and to import others to use as bullets. To use custom bullets or numbering (multilevel lists are handled separately later):

1. Click **Home | Bullets** or **Numbering** down arrow to open the Bullets or Numbering context menu.
2. Depending on whether you are using bullets or numbering, you have these choices:
   - For bullets, click **Define New Bullet**. The Define New Bullet dialog box appears (see Figure 3-16). Use one of the following:
   - Click **Font** and then select the font and other attributes in the dialog box for the character that you want to use. Click **OK** to close the Font dialog box when you are ready.

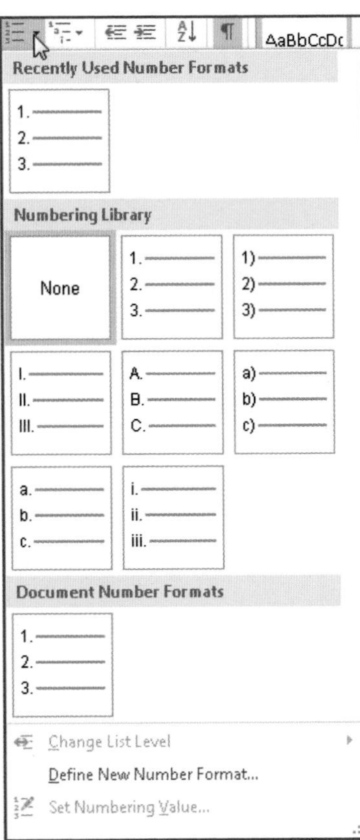

Figure 3-14: Numbered paragraphs can use numbers, letters, or even uppercase or lowercase roman numerals.

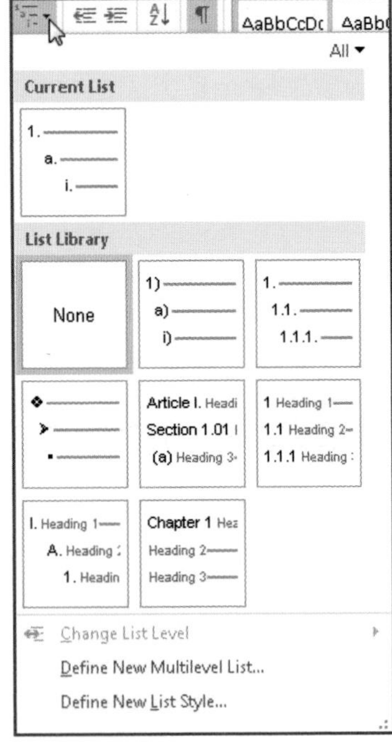

Figure 3-15: Multilevel paragraphs use a variety of characters to identify and format a multilevel list, including numbers, bullets, and text.

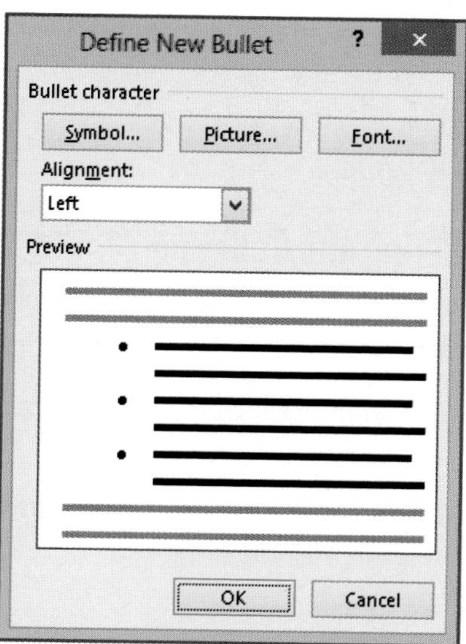

Figure 3-16: You can select any character in any font to use as a bullet.

- Click **Symbol** to select a symbol, and then click **OK**.
- Click **Picture** to choose from your own computer or SkyDrive, or online on Office's clip art catalog (see Figure 3-17), or the Internet via a Bing Image Search. To use your own picture, click **Browse** for either your computer or SkyDrive, select the picture from the files stored there, and click **Insert**. On the Define New Bullet dialog box, arrange the alignment, and then click **OK** to close the dialog box. The new bullet will appear on your page.
- To access Office's clip art, in the Search Office.com text box, type in a keyword, such as flowers, and click the **Search** icon. You'll see a collection of pictures you might use for the bullet image. Similarly, to search the Internet with Bing Image Search, type a keyword in the Search text box and click the **Search** icon. Select

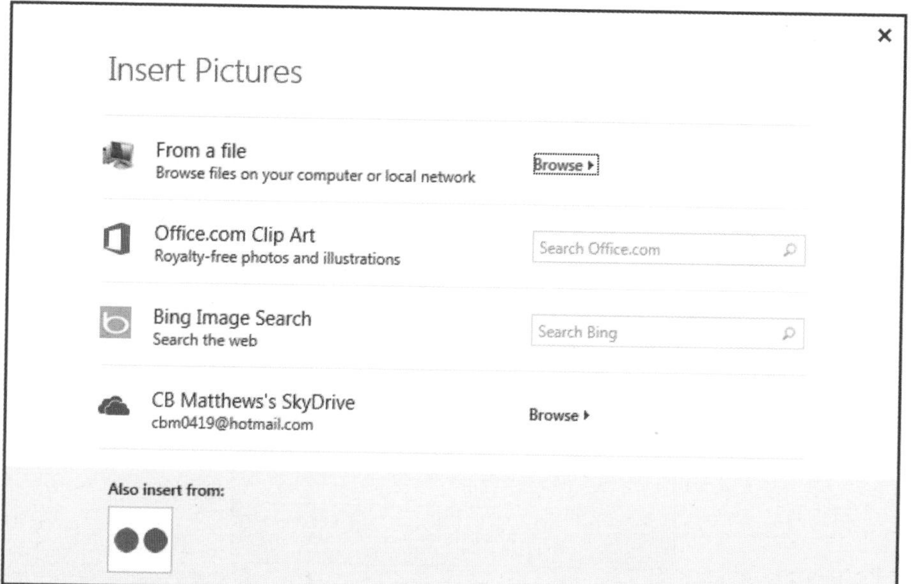

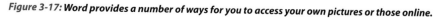

Figure 3-17: Word provides a number of ways for you to access your own pictures or those online.

an image and click **Insert**. Set the alignment in the Define New Bullet dialog box, and click **OK.**

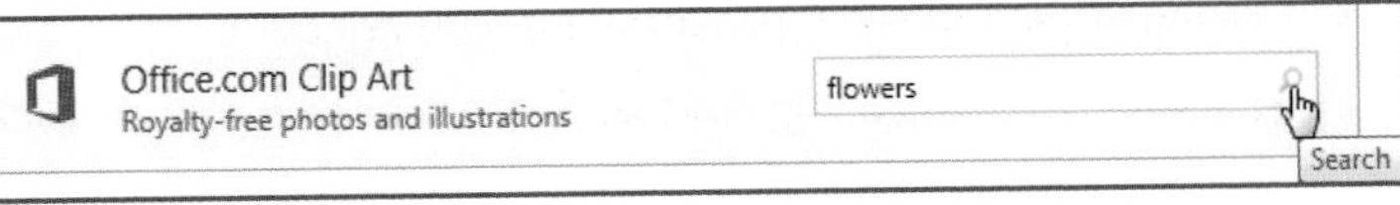

For numbering, click **Define New Number Format**. The Define New Number Format dialog box appears. Click the **Number Style** down arrow to choose the style (numbers, capital letters, lowercase letters, roman numerals, and so on). Click **Font** to choose the numbers formatted with a particular font, and click **OK** to close the Font dialog box. Press **TAB** to make any additions to the number in the Number Format text box. For example, delete the period for a number without the period or add a prefix such as "A-" to produce numbers A-1, A-2, and so on, as shown in Figure 3-18. Click the **Alignment** down arrow to choose between right alignment, left alignment, or centered. Click **OK** to apply the customized numbering.

Remove Numbering and Bulleting

To remove the numbering or bulleting (both the numbers or bullets and the hanging indent):

1. Select the paragraphs from which you want to remove the numbering or bulleting.
2. Click **Home | Numbering** in the Paragraph group, or **Bullets** or **Multilevel** List, as appropriate.

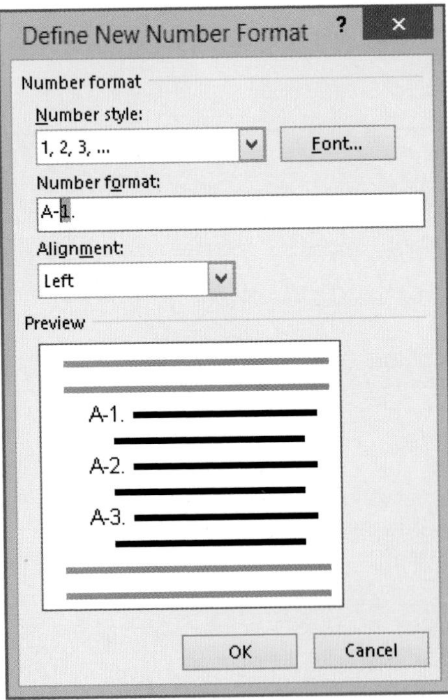

Figure 3-18: ***You can add a recurring prefix or suffix to automatically generated numbers.***

Define New Multilevel Lists

Defining new multilevel lists is handled much like bullets and numbering, but is slightly more complicated.

1. Click **Home | Multilevel List** down arrow to open the context menu.
2. Click **Define New Multilevel List**. The Define New Multilevel List dialog box will open. You have these choices:
   - Click the specific level to be modified.

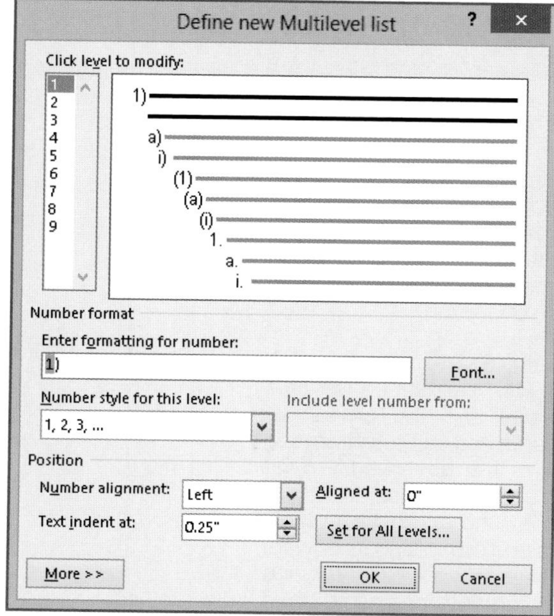

   - Click in the **Enter Formatting For Number** text box and modify the level if needed. An example would be to add a preface, such as "a-1," for instance.
   - Click **Font** to select a specific font or make changes to the formatting, such as Bold or Small Caps. It will be reflected to the left.
   - Click the **Number Style For This Level** down arrow and select a different numbering style if desired.
   - Click **Include Level Number From** down arrow and select another level to be attached to the selected numbering scheme. It will be placed before the current level number.
   - Select a **Position** setting to align the level or indent it.
   - Click **More** to open an additional group of modifications to refine the changes you can make to the multilevel list.

Add Horizontal Lines, Borders, and Shading

Borders and shading allow you to separate and call attention to text. You can place a border on any or all of the four sides of selected text, paragraphs, and pages; and you can add many varieties of shading to the space occupied by selected text, paragraphs, and pages—with or without a border around them (see Figure 3-19). You can create horizontal lines as you type, and you can add other borders from both the Formatting toolbar and the Borders And Shading dialog box.

TIP You can switch a numbered list to a bulleted one or vice versa by selecting the list and clicking the other icon in the Home tab Paragraph group.

Create Horizontal Lines as You Type

Horizontal lines can be added on their own paragraph as you type.

Hyphens------

Equal Signs ====

Underscores ______

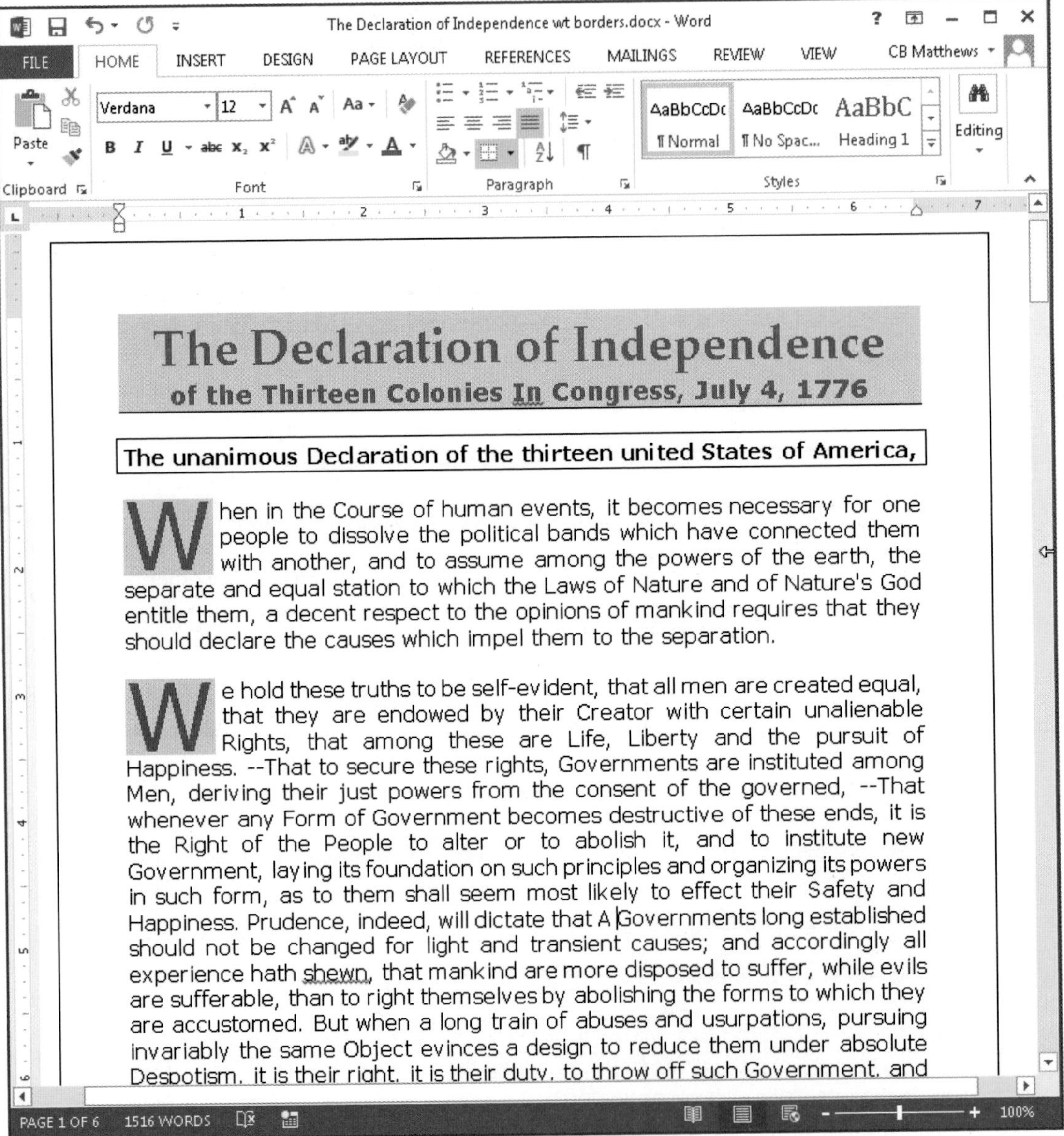
The Declaration of Independence wt borders.docx - Word
FILE
HOME
INSERT
DESIGN
PAGE LAYOUT
REFERENCES
MAILINGS
REVIEW
VIEW
CB Matthews
Paste
Verdana
12
Clipboard
Font
Paragraph
Styles
AaBbCcDc
¶ Normal
AaBbCcDc
¶ No Spac...
AaBbC
Heading 1
Editing
The Declaration of Independence
of the Thirteen Colonies In Congress, July 4, 1776
The unanimous Declaration of the thirteen united States of America,
When in the Course of human events, it becomes necessary for one people to dissolve the political bands which have connected them with another, and to assume among the powers of the earth, the separate and equal station to which the Laws of Nature and of Nature's God entitle them, a decent respect to the opinions of mankind requires that they should declare the causes which impel them to the separation.
We hold these truths to be self-evident, that all men are created equal, that they are endowed by their Creator with certain unalienable Rights, that among these are Life, Liberty and the pursuit of Happiness. --That to secure these rights, Governments are instituted among Men, deriving their just powers from the consent of the governed, --That whenever any Form of Government becomes destructive of these ends, it is the Right of the People to alter or to abolish it, and to institute new Government, laying its foundation on such principles and organizing its powers in such form, as to them shall seem most likely to effect their Safety and Happiness. Prudence, indeed, will dictate that A Governments long established should not be changed for light and transient causes; and accordingly all experience hath shewn, that mankind are more disposed to suffer, while evils are sufferable, than to right themselves by abolishing the forms to which they are accustomed. But when a long train of abuses and usurpations, pursuing invariably the same Object evinces a design to reduce them under absolute Despotism, it is their right, it is their duty, to throw off such Government, and
PAGE 1 OF 6
1516 WORDS
100%

Figure 3-19: ***Borders and shading can be applied to text, blank paragraphs, phrases, characters, and words.***

Press **ENTER** to create a new paragraph. You have these choices:

- Type --- (three hyphens) and press **ENTER**. A single, light horizontal line will be created between the left and right margins.
- Type === (three equal signs) and press **ENTER**. A double horizontal line will be created between the left and right margins.
- Type ___ (three underscores) and press **ENTER**. A single, heavy horizontal line will be created between the left and right margins.

Add Borders and Shading to Text

Borders and shading can be added to any amount of text, from a single character to several pages.

1. Select the text for which you want to have a border or shading.
2. Click **Home | Borders** down arrow in the Paragraph group, and then select the type of border you want to apply. If you have selected less than a full paragraph, you can only select a four-sided box (you actually can select less, but you will get a full box).

   –Or–

   Click **Home | Borders** down arrow in the Paragraph group, and click **Borders And Shading** on the context menu. The Borders And Shading dialog box will appear, as shown in Figure 3-20.

   - To add text or paragraph borders, click the **Borders** tab, click the type of box (click **Custom** for fewer than four sides), the line style, color, and width you want. If you want fewer than four

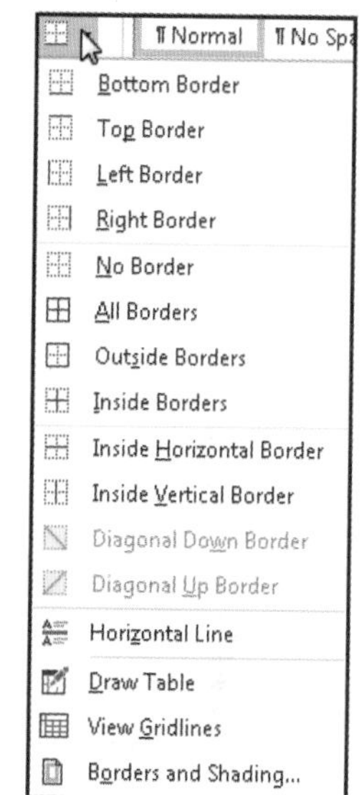

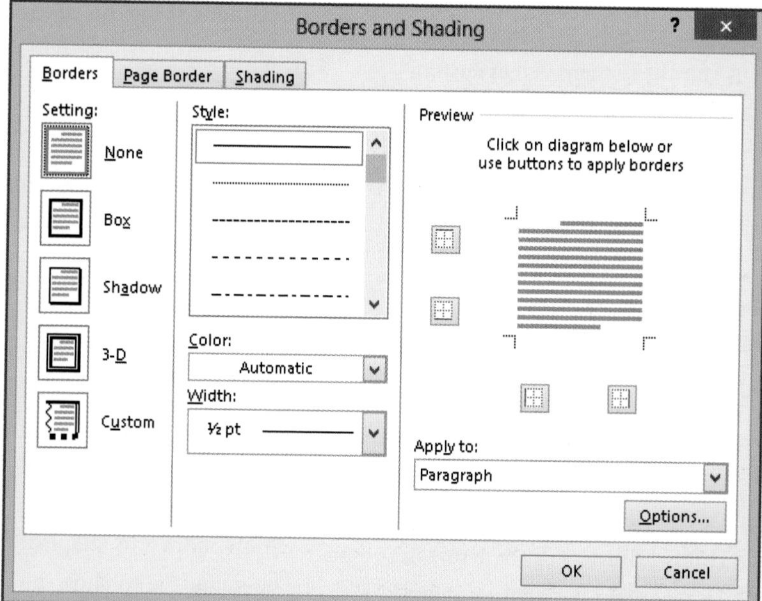

Figure 3-20: Borders can be created with many different types and widths of lines.

sides and are working with paragraphs, click the sides you want in the preview area. Click **Options** to set the distance the border is away from the text.

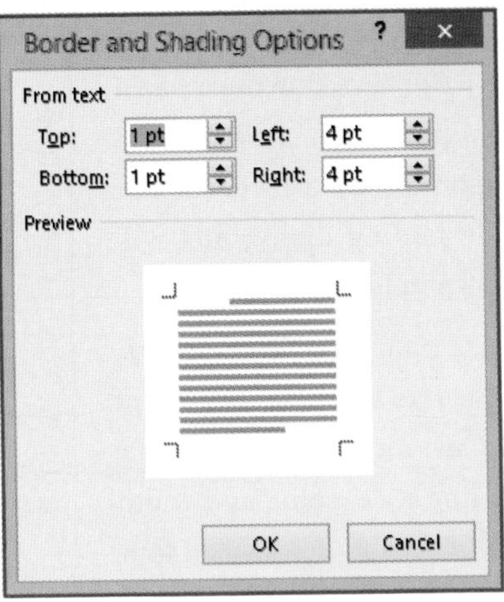

- To add page borders, click the **Page Border** tab, click the type of box (click **Custom** for fewer than four sides), the line style, color, width you want, and art you want to use for the border, such as custom drawn lines or a row of miniature company logos. If you want fewer than four sides, click the sides you want in the Preview area. Click **Options** to set the distance the border is away from either the edge of the page or the text. To add shading, click the **Shading** tab, and click the color of shading, or *fill*, you want. If desired, select a pattern (this is independent of the fill), and choose whether to apply it to the entire page, paragraph, or just to the selected text.

When you are done with the Borders And Shading dialog box, click **OK** to close it.

–Or–

- To add a graphic horizontal line, click the spot in the document where you want the line. Click **Home | Borders** down arrow in the Paragraph group, and click **Horizontal Line** on the context menu. A line will be placed in your document. If you have not identified the spot where it should be accurately, just click **Undo** and repeat.

NOTE Borders will be discussed further as they relate to tables in Chapter 6.

FORMAT A PAGE

Page formatting has to do with the overall formatting of items, such as margins, orientation, size, and vertical alignment of a page. You can set options for page formatting either from the Page Layout tab or in a dialog box.

Turn On Formatting Marks

Turning on formatting marks helps you see what is making your document look the way it does. To make it easier to see any formatting and what is causing the spacing in a document, you can display some or all of the formatting marks.

- Click **Home | Show/Hide Formatting Marks**, Paragraph group ¶ to show all of the formatting marks—tabs, spaces, and paragraph marks, among other characters.

→ This·has·a·tab,·spaces···,·and·a·paragraph·mark¶

- To fine-tune exactly which formatting marks to display, click **File | Options | Display**. Under Always Show These Formatting Marks On The Screen, you can choose which marks to display. The default is to show no formatting marks.

Always show these formatting marks on the screen	
☐ Tab characters	→
☐ Spaces	···
☐ Paragraph marks	¶
☐ Hidden text	abc
☐ Optional hyphens	¬
☐ Object anchors	⚓
☑ Show all formatting marks	

Set Margins

Margins are the space between the edge of the paper and the text. To set margins:

1. Open the document whose margins you want to set (see Chapter 2). If you want the margins to apply only to a selected part of a document, select that part now.
2. Click **Page Layout | Margins** in the Page Setup group. A menu will open, as shown in Figure 3-21.

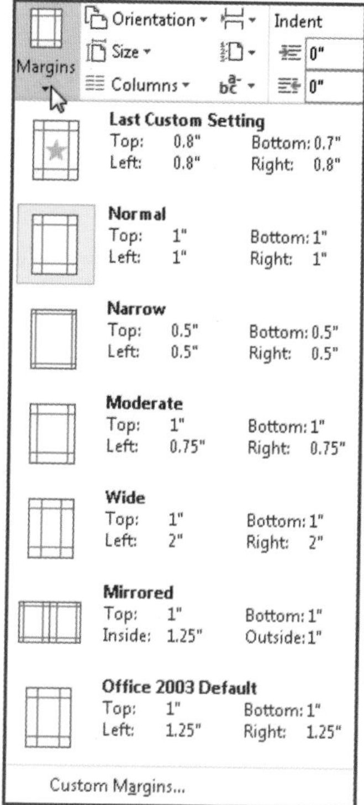

***Figure 3-21:** You can select from a group of predefined margins, according to the needs of your document, or you can create a custom set of margins.*

3. Click the option you want.

CAUTION! Remember that page formatting changes the margins and other formatting for whole pages. If you select a part of the document to have special formatting, it will separate that section by pages. To change formatting for smaller sections of text, use indenting.

Copy Formatting

Often, you'll want a word, phrase, or paragraph formatted like an existing word, phrase, or paragraph. Word allows you to copy just the formatting. You can copy a single occurrence or several scattered throughout the document. You can use the keyboard as well to do this.

Use the Format Painter for a Single Copy

1. Select the word, phrase, or paragraph from which you want to copy the formatting. In the case of a paragraph, make sure you have included the paragraph mark (see "Turn On Formatting Marks").
2. Click **Home | Format Painter** in the Clipboard group.

3. With the special pointer (brush and I-beam), select the word, phrase, or paragraph (including the paragraph mark) you want formatted.

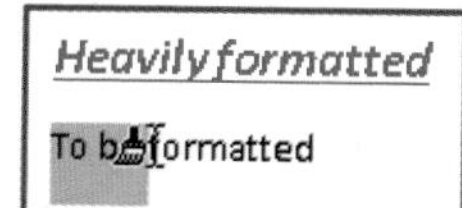

Copy Formatting to Several Places

To copy formatting to several separate pieces of text or paragraphs:

1. Drag across the source text with the formatting you want to copy.
2. Double-click **Home | Format Painter** in the Clipboard group.

3. Simply select each piece of text or paragraph that you want to format. It will automatically be formatted.
4. When you are done, to remove the Format Painter action, click **Home | Format Painter** again or press ESC.

Copy Formats with the Keyboard

1. Select the word, phrase, or paragraph whose formatting you want to copy.
2. Press CTRL+SHIFT+C to copy the format.
3. Select the word, phrase, or paragraph (including the paragraph mark) you want formatted.
4. Press CTRL+SHIFT+V to paste the format.

Use a Dialog Box to Format a Page

You can do a lot of page formatting using the Page Layout dialog box.

1. Click **Page Layout | Page Setup Dialog Box Launcher**. The Page Setup dialog box appears, as shown in Figure 3-22.
2. Click the **Margins** tab, if it isn't already visible. You have these options:
   - Under Margins, click the spinners or manually enter the desired distance in inches between the particular edge of the paper and the start or end of text.
   - Under Orientation, click either **Portrait** or **Landscape**, depending on which you want.
   - Under Pages, click the **Multiple Page** down arrow, and select an option: Click **Mirror Margins** when the inside gutter (the combined inside margin of two bound pages) is larger (if you will be printing and binding the document, for example). Click **2 Pages Per Sheet** when a normal sheet of paper is divided into two pages, and click **Book Fold** when you are putting together a section of a book ("a signature") with four, eight, or more pages in the signature.
   - If you want these changes to apply only to the selected part of a document, click **This Point Forward** under Preview Apply To.
3. When you are done setting margins, click **OK**.

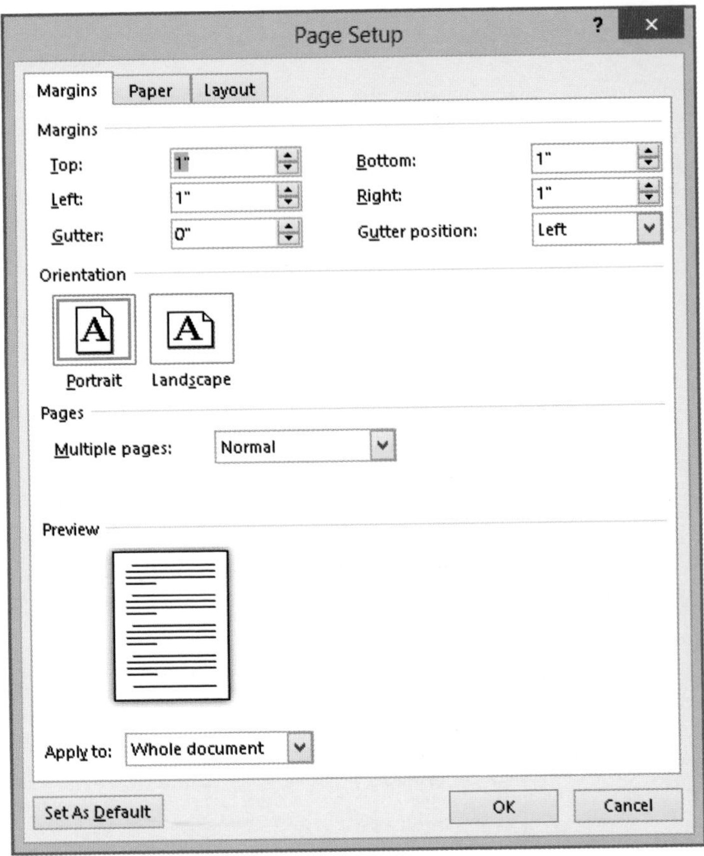

Figure 3-22: Many page-formatting tasks can be done in the Page Setup dialog box.

TIP If you are going to bind the document and want to add an extra amount of space on one edge for the binding, click the **Gutter** spinner to set the extra width you want, and click the **Gutter Position** down arrow to select the side that the gutter is on.

TIP If you want to further differentiate between the left and right pages, you need to use sections (described in Chapter 4).

Use Mirror Margins

Mirror margins allow you to have a larger "inside" margin, which would be the right margin on the left page and the left margin on the right page, or any other combination of margins that are mirrored between the left and right pages. To create mirror margins:

1. Open the document whose margins you want mirrored (see Chapter 2).
2. Click **Page Layout | Margins** in the Page Setup group.
3. Click **Mirrored**. When you do that, the left and right margins change to inside and outside margins.

Determine Page Orientation

Page orientation specifies whether a page is taller than it is wide ("portrait") or wider than it is tall ("landscape"). For 8½-inch by 11-inch letter size paper, if the 11-inch side is vertical (the left and right edges), which is the standard way of reading a letter, then it is a portrait orientation. If the 11-inch side is horizontal (the top and bottom edges), then it is a landscape orientation. Portrait is the default orientation in Word and most documents. To change it:

1. Open the document whose orientation you want to set (see Chapter 2). If you want the orientation to apply only to a selected part of a document, select that part now; but you can only select whole pages to have a particular orientation.
2. Click **Page Layout | Orientation** in the Page Setup group.

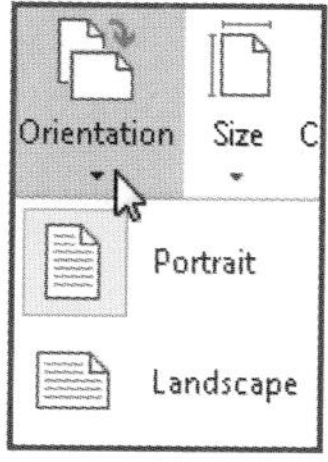

3. On the menu, click the option you want.

Specify Paper Size

Specifying the paper size gives you the starting perimeter of the area within which you can set margins and enter text or pictures.

1. Click **Page Layout | Size** down arrow in the Page Setup group. A menu will open, shown in Figure 3-23.
2. Click the size of paper you want.

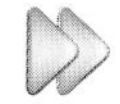

Track Inconsistent Formatting

When you turned on the formatting marks (see "Turn On Formatting Marks" earlier in the chapter), you might have felt a bit disappointed that

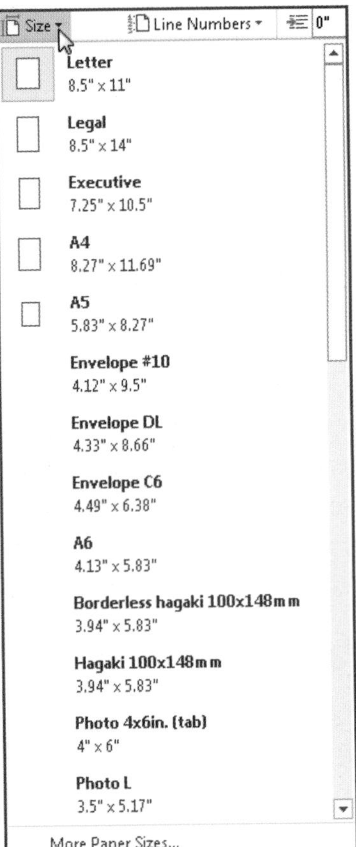

Figure 3-23: Choose the paper size from a selection of popular sizes in the Page Layout tab.

they didn't tell you more. You can direct Word to track inconsistencies in your formatting as you type.

1. Click **File | Options | Advanced** on the left pane.
2. Under Editing Options, click both **Keep Track Of Formatting** and **Mark Formatting Inconsistencies**.

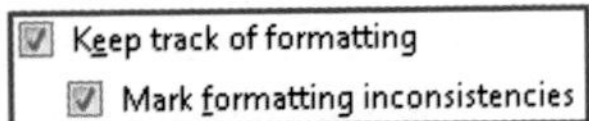

Set Vertical Alignment

Just as you can right align, center, left align, and justify text between margins (see "Set Paragraph Alignment"), you can also specify vertical alignment so that text is aligned with the top, bottom, or center of the page or justified between the top and bottom.

1. Click **Page Layout | Page Setup Dialog Box Launcher**. The Page Setup dialog box appears.

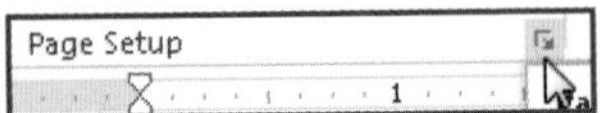

2. In the Layout tab, under Page, click the **Vertical Alignment** down arrow, and click the vertical alignment that you want to use.

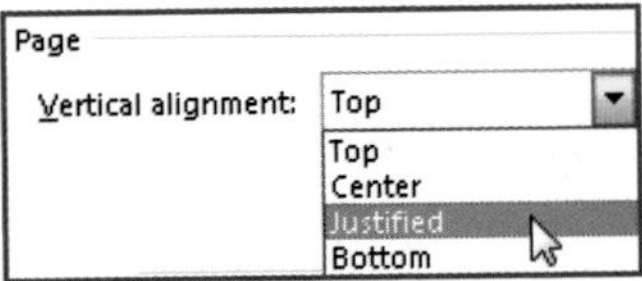

3. Click **OK** when you are done.

QuickSteps to...

- Identify Text with a Style
- Apply Predefined Style Sets to a Document
- Create a New Style
- Modify a Style
- Clear a Style from Text or a Document
- Delete Styles from the Gallery
- Examine Current Styles
- Assign a Theme to Your Document
- Change a Theme
- Create a Custom Theme
- Apply a Template to a New Document
- Create a Template
- Create Section Breaks
- Create and Use Columns
- Use Tabs
- Add Headers and Footers
- Add Footnotes and Endnotes
- Create an Index
- Create a Table of Contents
- Create and Use Outlines
- Use View Buttons
- Implement AutoCorrect
- Use AutoFormat
- Use Building Blocks
- Count Characters and Words
- Use Highlighting
- Add Hyphenation
- Explore the Thesaurus
- Enter an Equation

Chapter 4

Customizing a Document

Microsoft Word 2013 provides a number of tools that combine text creation, layout, and formatting features that you can use to customize your documents. Two of the most common tools used at a broad level are styles and templates. Word also provides several other features, such as AutoFormat and AutoText, that help make document creation and formatting easier.

This chapter discusses creating documents through the use of styles and templates; formatting your documents using tabs, headers and footers, and outlines; and inserting front and end matter, such as tables of contents and indexes. The chapter also discusses Word's writing aids, such as AutoText, hyphenation, an equation builder, and the thesaurus.

USE STYLES

Word 2013 provides a gallery of styles that provides you with sets of canned formatting choices, such as font, bold, and color, that you can apply to headings, titles, text, and lists. You use styles by identifying what kind of formatting a selected segment of text needs, such as for a header or title. Then, using style sets, you select the style of formatting you want to apply to the document. Formatting will be applied to the whole document smoothly and easily. You can easily change style sets and create new ones.

1

2

3

4

5

6

7

8

9

10

QuickFacts

Understanding Themes, Styles, and Templates

Word allows you to quickly and easily apply formatting to your documents to make them look professional and consistent by using ready-made themes, styles, and templates. A *theme* changes the background, layout, color, fonts, and effects used in a document. Themes can be similar throughout most of the Office suite, so if you choose a theme in Word, you likely will be able to apply that theme to Excel or PowerPoint documents as well. Every document has a theme.

A *style* applies a specific set of formatting characteristics to individual characters or to entire paragraphs within the theme. For example, you can apply styles to headings, titles, lists, and other text components. Consequently, styles determine how the overall design comes together in its look and feel. Styles are beneficial to document creation, because they provide an integrated and consistent platform to all text selected for formatting. Every theme has a certain set of styles assigned to it. You can change styles within a theme and change themes within a document.

A *template* contains a theme, with its unique style of formatting, and is used to set up a document for the first time. You open a template file, save it as a document file, and then enter your own contents into it. In this way, you can standardize the look of all documents that are based on a given template. You can create your own templates.

Identify Text with a Style

Within your document you have components, such as headings, titles, lists, regular paragraphs, and so on. For Word to know how to format these according to a given style, each component must be identified. You can do this by selecting text and clicking the matching style.

1. Select the text to be formatted, for example, a title or heading.
2. Click **Home | Styles More** down arrow in the Styles group. The Style gallery is displayed, as shown in Figure 4-1.

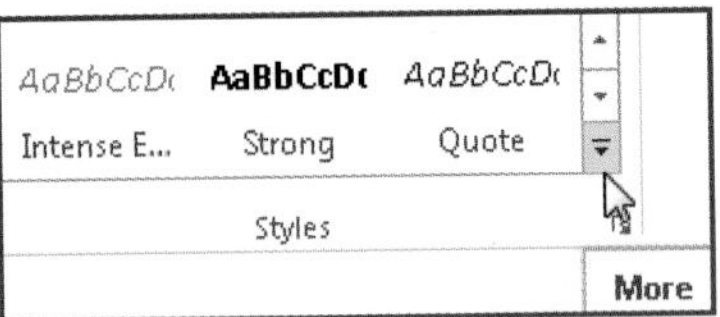

3. Point at the thumbnail of the component that matches the type of style you want to assign to the selected text. For example, select your main heading text, and then click **Heading 1** in the Style menu.

TIP If you do not find the style you want in the Style gallery for a segment of text, press **CTRL+SHIFT+S** to display the Apply Styles dialog box. Click the **Style Name** down arrow and scroll down to find the style you want. Click **Close (x)** to remove the dialog box.

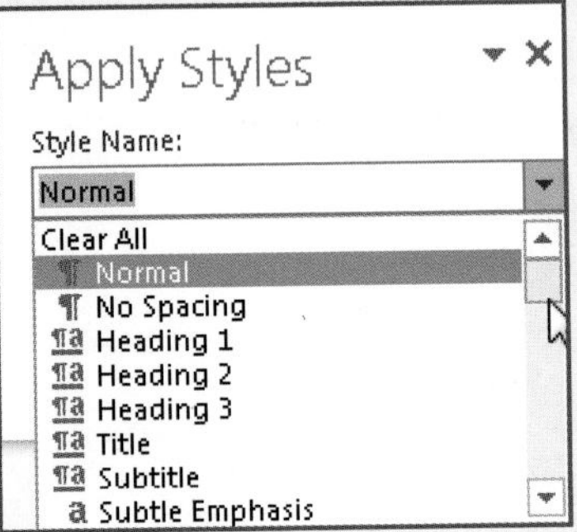

Apply Predefined Style Sets to a Document

A predefined *style set* is a group of styles that have been defined and made available to you in the Design tab. You can change or apply style sets before you begin entering text, or to an existing document. You will not see all the effects of a style set until you have identified the components

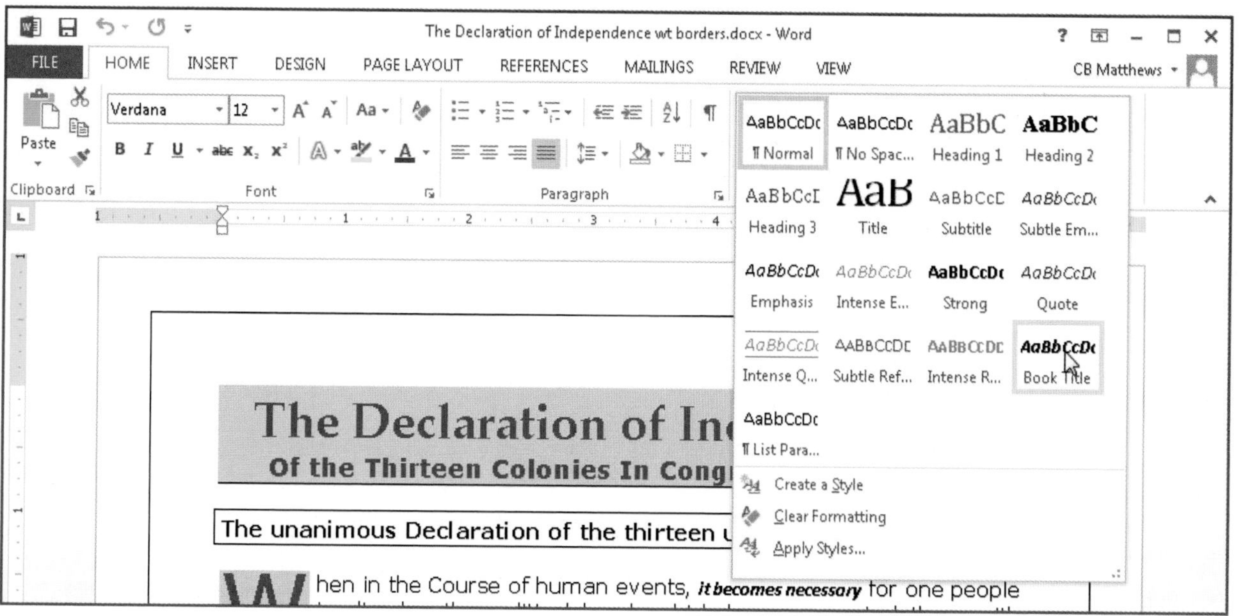

***Figure 4-1:** The Style gallery shows you ready-made options for formatting headings, text, and paragraphs.*

in your document, such as headings or titles. You can see how a style set will affect a document by selecting it and seeing what happens to the color, styles, and fonts of the document.

1. Open the document that you want to contain a style set. It can be either a blank document or one that has already had the components identified, such as title, headings, and lists. (You can define the components later, but you won't be able to see the effects of the style sets until they are defined.)
2. Click **Design** and in the Document Formatting group, click a style set you want to consider. You'll see it reflected in the document. Figure 4-2 shows an example. Remember that if you have components that are not identified with the styles, such as headings, they will not receive the formatting properly.

Create a New Style

You may want to create a new style that is immediately available to you for your documents. To create a new style option that will appear in the Style gallery:

1. Format the text using the mini formatting toolbar or the commands in the **Home | Font** and **Paragraph** groups. (See Figure 3-3 for a visual guide.)
2. Select the newly formatted text that represents the new style.
3. Click **Home | Styles Dialog Box Launcher** for the Styles task pane.
4. Click the **New Style** icon on the bottom of the task pane. The Create New Style From Formatting dialog box is displayed.
5. Type the name you want for the style, verify the settings, and click **OK**. It will appear in the Style gallery in the Home | Styles group.

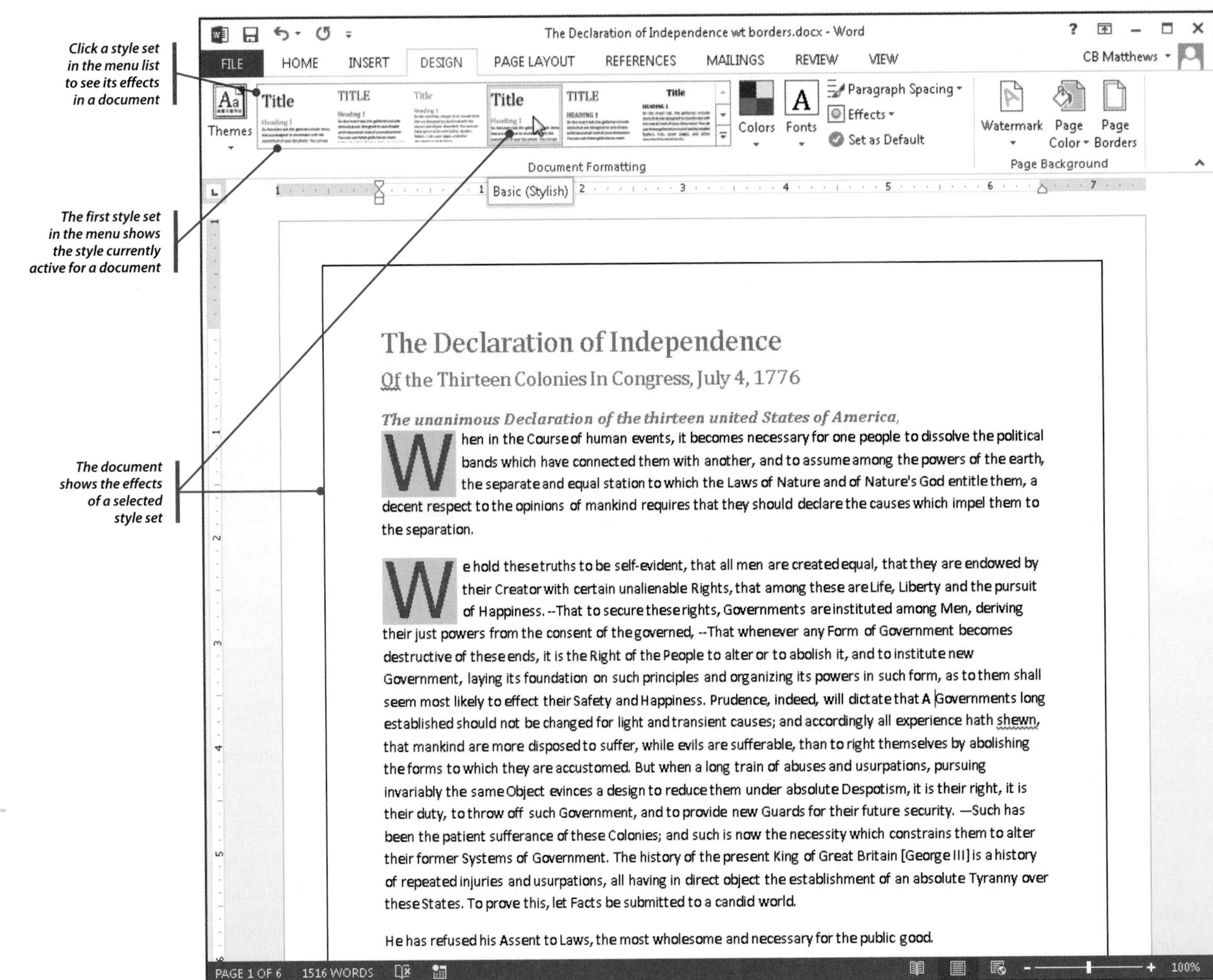
Click a style set in the menu list to see its effects in a document
The first style set in the menu shows the style currently active for a document
The document shows the effects of a selected style set
The Declaration of Independence wt borders.docx - Word
FILE
HOME
INSERT
DESIGN
PAGE LAYOUT
REFERENCES
MAILINGS
REVIEW
VIEW
CB Matthews
Themes
Title
TITLE
Colors
Fonts
Paragraph Spacing
Effects
Set as Default
Watermark
Page Color
Page Borders
Document Formatting
Page Background
Basic (Stylish)
The Declaration of Independence
Of the Thirteen Colonies In Congress, July 4, 1776
The unanimous Declaration of the thirteen united States of America,
When in the Course of human events, it becomes necessary for one people to dissolve the political bands which have connected them with another, and to assume among the powers of the earth, the separate and equal station to which the Laws of Nature and of Nature's God entitle them, a decent respect to the opinions of mankind requires that they should declare the causes which impel them to the separation.
We hold these truths to be self-evident, that all men are created equal, that they are endowed by their Creator with certain unalienable Rights, that among these are Life, Liberty and the pursuit of Happiness. --That to secure these rights, Governments are instituted among Men, deriving their just powers from the consent of the governed, --That whenever any Form of Government becomes destructive of these ends, it is the Right of the People to alter or to abolish it, and to institute new Government, laying its foundation on such principles and organizing its powers in such form, as to them shall seem most likely to effect their Safety and Happiness. Prudence, indeed, will dictate that A Governments long established should not be changed for light and transient causes; and accordingly all experience hath shewn, that mankind are more disposed to suffer, while evils are sufferable, than to right themselves by abolishing the forms to which they are accustomed. But when a long train of abuses and usurpations, pursuing invariably the same Object evinces a design to reduce them under absolute Despotism, it is their right, it is their duty, to throw off such Government, and to provide new Guards for their future security. —Such has been the patient sufferance of these Colonies; and such is now the necessity which constrains them to alter their former Systems of Government. The history of the present King of Great Britain [George III] is a history of repeated injuries and usurpations, all having in direct object the establishment of an absolute Tyranny over these States. To prove this, let Facts be submitted to a candid world.
He has refused his Assent to Laws, the most wholesome and necessary for the public good.
PAGE 1 OF 6
1516 WORDS
100%

Figure 4-2: Style sets are used to provide consistent styles throughout a document.

NOTE You can also create a new style by highlighting the formatted text containing the new style, clicking the **Styles More** down arrow to expand the Styles menu, and clicking **Create A Style**. You can name and modify the style as you wish.

Modify a Style

You can modify an existing style. To do this:

1. Click **Home | Styles** group, and click the **Styles More** down arrow to expand the Styles menu. The Style gallery is displayed.
2. Right-click the style to be changed, and click **Modify** (note that some styles cannot be changed). The Modify Style dialog box appears, as shown in Figure 4-3.

   –Or–

   From the bottom of the expanded Quick Style gallery, click **Apply Styles.** The Apply Styles dialog box appears. Click the **Style Name** down arrow, and select the name of the style you wish to change (note that some styles cannot be changed). Click **Modify**, and the Modify Style dialog box appears.

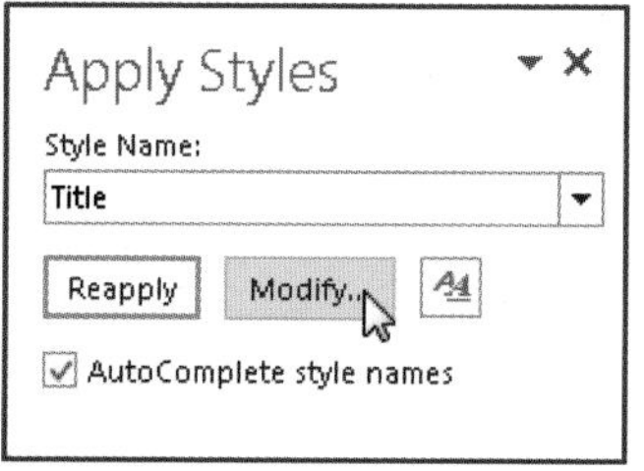

3. Change any formatting options you want. Here are some choices you have:
   - To display more options, click **Format** in the bottom-left corner, and then click the attribute—for example, **Font** or **Numbering**—that you want to modify. Make that change and click **OK.** Repeat this step for any additional attributes you want to change, clicking **OK** each time you are finished.

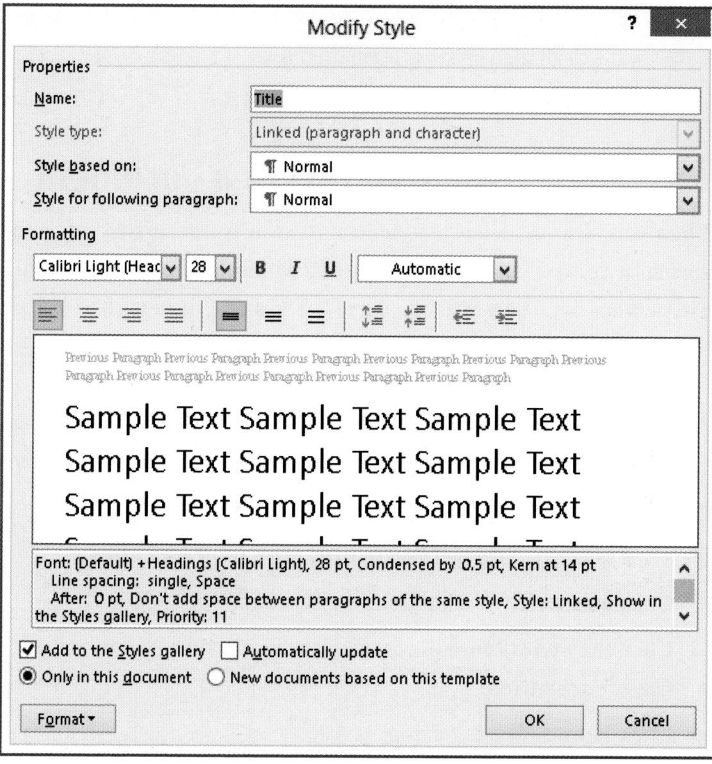

***Figure 4-3:** You can change a style by altering it in the Modify Style dialog box.*

- To add a modified style to the Styles gallery, click the **Add To Styles Gallery** check box.

- To automatically apply updates to the document, click the **Automatically Update** check box. Word will automatically update the document with the modifications for the defined styles.
- To determine whether this style will be redefined for this document only, or for all new documents with this style, click the appropriate check box.

- To create a new style, type a new name for the style, unless you want to change existing formatted text.

4. Click **OK** to close the Modify Styles dialog box.

Clear a Style from Text or a Document

When you clear or delete a style from text, it is reformatted with the Normal style. To clear the formatting of a whole document or of certain text, perhaps because you have applied the wrong style or wish to change it, follow these options.

Delete Style from Selected Text

Highlight specific text that you wish to clear of formatting. You then have these choices:

- Click **Home | Clear All Formatting** in the font group.
- Click an alternative style from the Styles gallery.
- Click the **Styles More** down arrow to expand the menu, and click **Clear Formatting**.
- Click **Home | Styles Dialog Box Launcher** for the Styles task pane. Select the style to be removed, click the down arrow to the right of the style, and click **Clear Formatting of *n* Instance(s)**. (Clear the **Show Preview** check box to see the Clear Formatting option.)

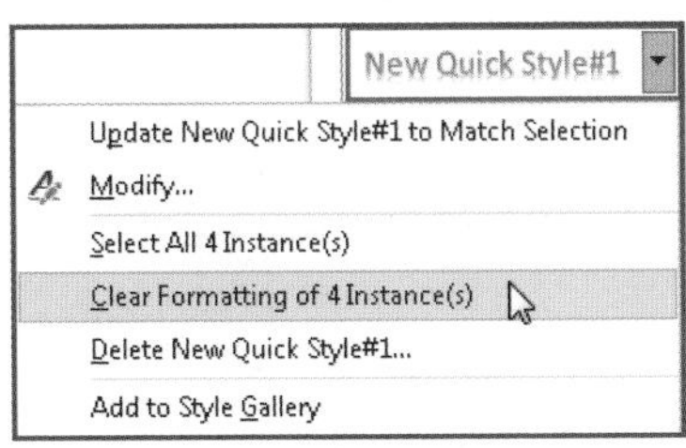

Delete Style from the Whole Document

1. To delete a style from a whole document, click **Home | Styles Dialog Box Launcher** for the Styles task pane.
2. Select the style to be removed, click the down arrow to the right of the style, and click **Delete *name of style***.
3. Click **Yes** to confirm that you want to remove the formatting from the whole document.

Delete Styles from the Gallery

Styles are kept in the Styles list and displayed in the Style gallery. You can add and delete styles from the gallery, but they will remain in the Styles list unless specifically deleted. If you delete any style from a document, the text formatted with that style will be reformatted with the Normal style. However, some styles cannot be deleted; the command to delete them will be unavailable, or grayed out, or ineffective, such as with the Normal style.

Delete/Restore a Style from the Gallery

To delete a style from the gallery, perhaps that you created for a one-time-use document and don't ever plan to use again, or to restore it in case of a mistake or change of mind:

1. Click **Home | Styles More** down arrow to display the Style gallery.
2. Right-click the style you want to delete, and click **Remove From Style Gallery**. The style will be removed from the Style gallery. However, this does not mean that the style is gone; it is still in the list of styles.

To restore the style to the gallery:

1. Click **Home | Styles Dialog Box Launcher**. The Styles task pane is displayed.
2. Right-click the style that you want to restore, and click **Add To Style Gallery**.

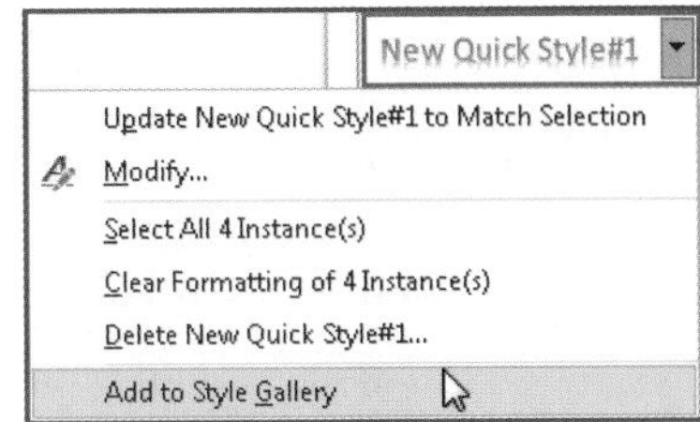

 Examine Current Styles

The Styles task pane contains a couple of ways you can look at the content of styles. For instance, you may wish to see what a style looks like before applying it, or see what styles have been applied to selected text.

Show a Preview of Styles

In addition to the Styles gallery, which shows an example of what the style looks like, you can see it in the Styles task pane.

1. Click **Home | Styles Dialog Box Launcher**, and the Styles task pane will appear.
2. Click **Show Preview** to see how the styles will appear.
3. Click the style to apply it to selected text.
4. Click **Close (x)** to close the task pane.

Inspect a Style

Perhaps you want to see what formatting has been applied to selected text.

1. Select the text whose style you want to inspect.
2. Click **Home | Styles Dialog Box Launcher**, and the Styles task pane will appear.
3. Click the **Style Inspector** icon to open the Style Inspector dialog box. You can see the essential formatting of the selected text. You have these choices:
   - To the right of a formatting style, click a **Reset** or **Clear** icon to reset or clear one component's formatting.
   - Click **Clear All** to reset or clear all the formatting for this style.
   - Click **New Style** to create a new style from the one currently selected. The Create New Style From Formatting dialog box is displayed.

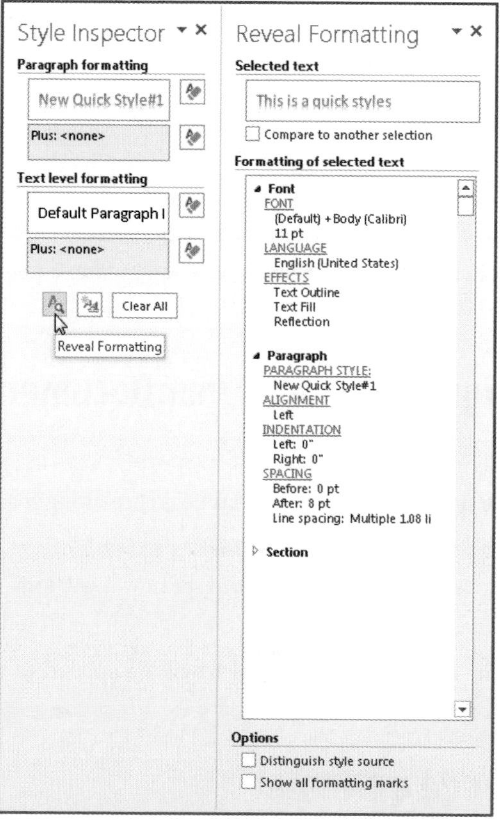

***Figure 4-4:** The Style Inspector displays the formatting for the style of selected text, and allows you to reveal formatting in more detail.*

- Click **Reveal Formatting** to see further detail of the selected formatting, as seen in Figure 4-4. By clicking **Distinguish Style Source** you can see where a style originates.

1 2 3 4 5 6 7 8 9 10

USE THEMES

One way that you can make a document look professional is by using themes. Themes contain styles with coordinated colors, fonts (for body text and headings), and design effects (such as special-effect uses for lines and fill effects) to produce a unique look. You can use the same themes with PowerPoint and Excel as well, thereby standardizing a look. All documents have themes; one is assigned to a new document by default.

Assign a Theme to Your Document

To apply a theme to a document:

1. Click **Design | Themes** in the Document Formatting group to display a gallery of themes, as seen in Figure 4-5.
2. Mouse over the menu of themes to see how it will look in your current document.
3. Click the theme you want, and it will be applied to the current document.

Change a Theme

In addition to changing the overall theme of a document, you can customize a theme by altering the fonts, color, and design effects.

Change the Color of a Theme

Each theme consists of a set of four colors for text and background, six colors for accents, and two colors for hyperlinks. You can change any single color element or all of them. When you change the colors, the font styles and design elements remain the same.

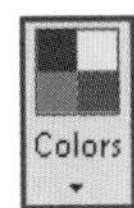

1. With your document open, click **Design | Colors**. The Theme Colors menu of color combinations will be displayed, as seen in Figure 4-6.
2. As you point at the rows of color combinations, you can see how the colors will change the document beneath. Mouse over the colors to see which ones appeal to you.
3. When you find the one you want, click it.

NOTE For a new theme's styles to be applied, the text must already be formatted with common style types, such as titles, headings, normal text, and lists.

Change Theme Fonts

Each theme includes two fonts: The *body* font is used for general text entry, and a *heading* font is used for headings. The default fonts used in Word for a new document are Calibri for body text and Cambria for headings. After you have assigned a theme to a document, the fonts may be different, and they can be changed.

1. Click **Design | Fonts** in the Document Formatting group. The Theme Fonts drop-down list displays various theme fonts. Custom Font Themes will be displayed above other Office Font Themes. The current theme font combination is highlighted in its place in the list.

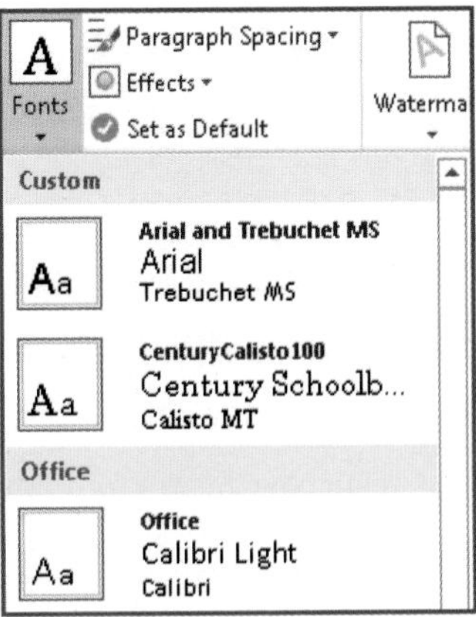

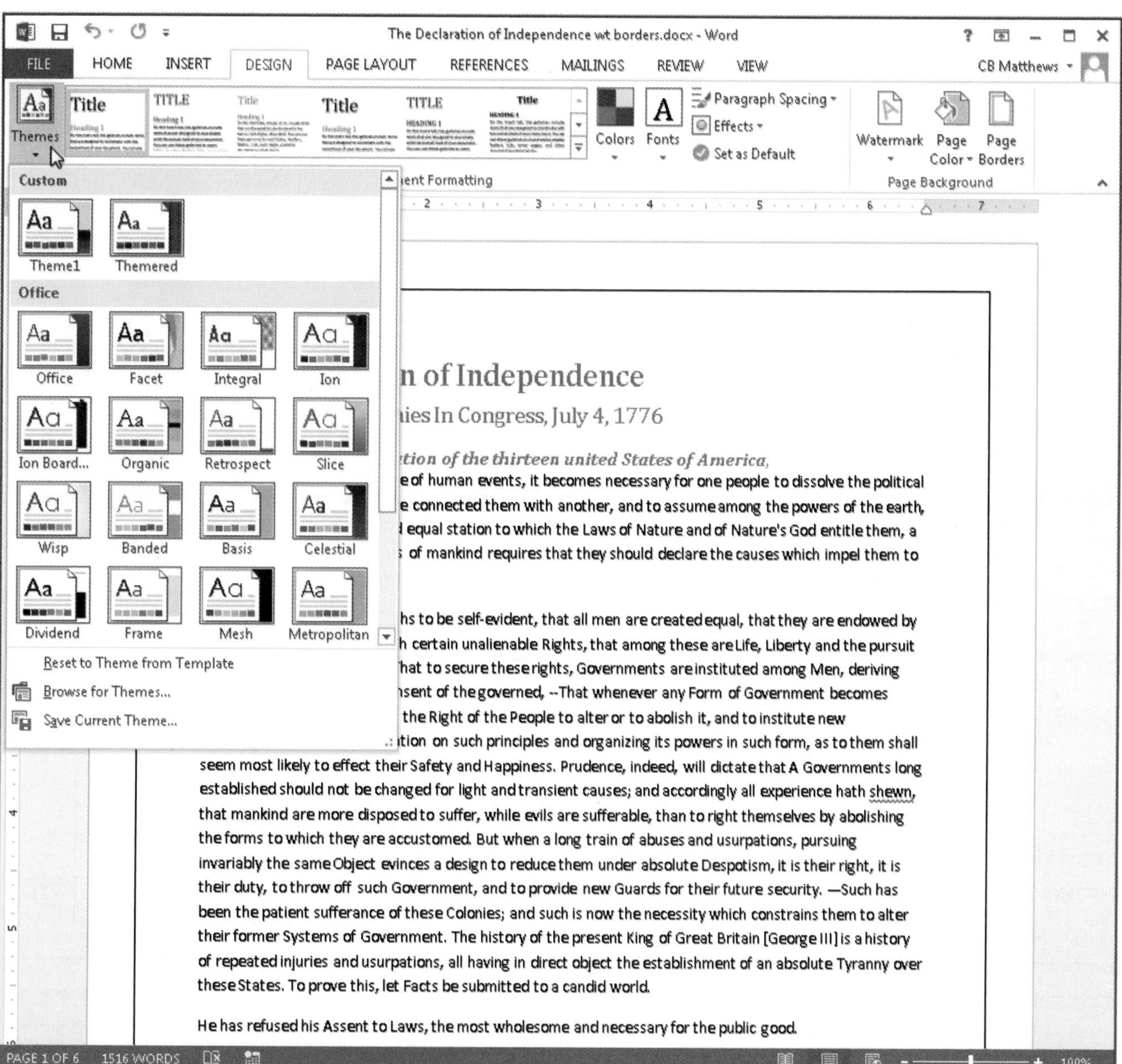

***Figure 4-5:* Use themes to standardize your documents with other Office products, such as PowerPoint and Excel.**

1 2 3 4 5 6 7 8 9 10

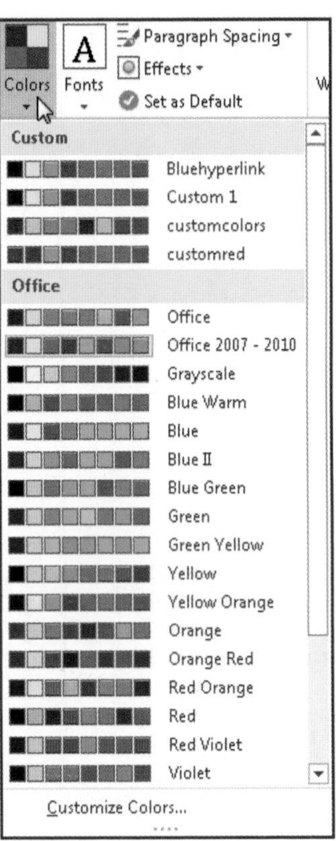

Figure 4-6: The menu of color combinations offers alternatives for your theme colors.

2. Point to each font combination to see how the fonts will appear in your document.
3. Click the font name combination you decide upon. When you click a font name combination, the fonts will replace both the body and heading fonts in your document on one or selected pages.

Create a Custom Font Theme Set

You may also decide that you want a unique set of fonts for your document. You can create a custom font set that is available in the list of fonts for your current and future documents.

1. Click **Design | Fonts | Customize Fonts**. The Create New Theme Fonts dialog box is displayed.

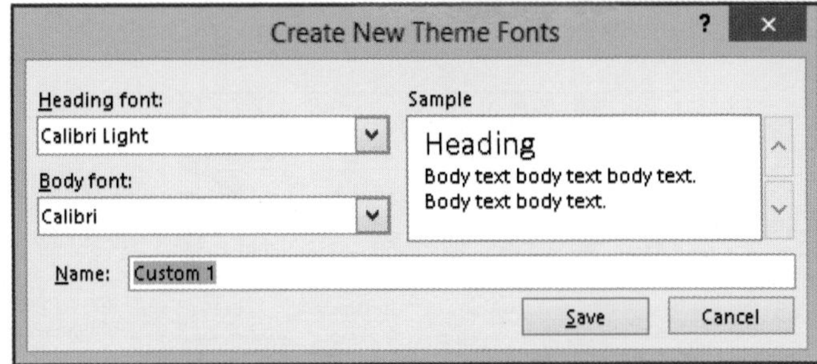

   Click either or both the Heading Font and Body Font down arrows to select a new font combination. Click your choice(s) to view the new combination in the Sample area on the right.

2. Type a new name for the font combination you've selected, and click **Save**. Custom fonts are displayed at the top of the Theme Fonts drop-down list.

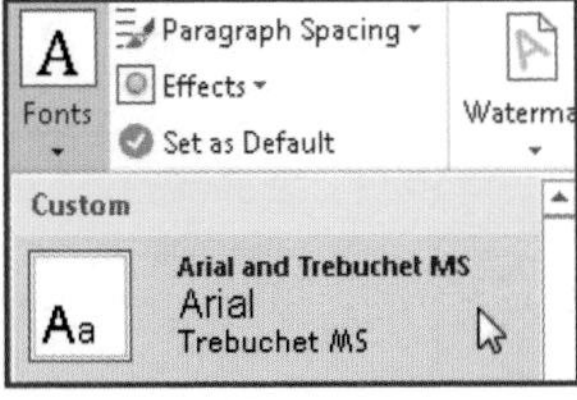

TIP Remember that you can preview what a theme, color, or font looks like by simply selecting your text, opening one of the menus described here, and hovering your mouse over an option to see how it looks with your text.

Change Themed Graphic Effects

Shapes, illustrations, pictures, and charts include graphic effects that are controlled by themes. Themed graphics are modulated in terms of their lines (borders), fills, and effects (such as shadowed, raised, and shaded). For example, some themes simply change an inserted rectangle's fill color, while other themes affect the color, the weight of the border, and whether it has a 3-D appearance. Theme effects do not affect text.

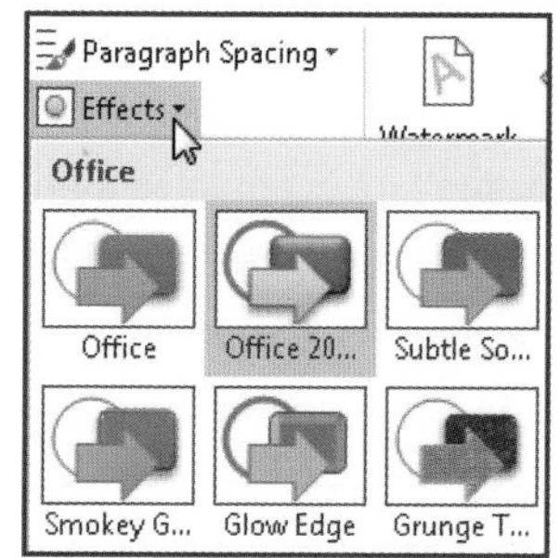

1. Click **Design | Effects** to open the Theme Effects drop-down list, which displays a gallery of effects combinations. The current effects combination is highlighted.
2. Point to each combination to see how the effects will appear in your document, assuming you have a graphic or chart inserted on the document page (see Chapters 6, 7, and 8 for information on inserting tables, charts, graphics, and drawings).
3. Click the effects combination you want.

Create a Custom Theme

You can create a new theme, save it, and use it for documents that you want to be unique and distinctively yours. This is done by selecting a group of text, background, accent, and hyperlink colors, and then giving them a collective name.

1. Click **Design | Colors | Customize Colors**. The Create New Theme Colors dialog box appears, as shown in Figure 4-7.
2. To select a color for one of the color groups, click the text/background, accent, or hyperlink down arrow, and click the color you want to test. It will be displayed in the Sample area.
3. Go through each set of colors that you want to change.

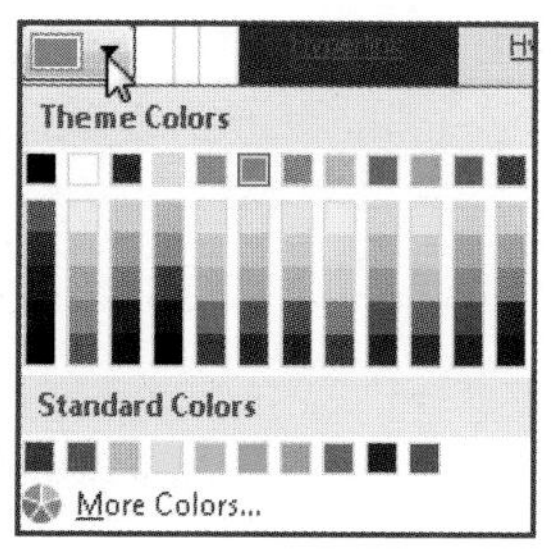

Selected colors are reflected in the Sample area

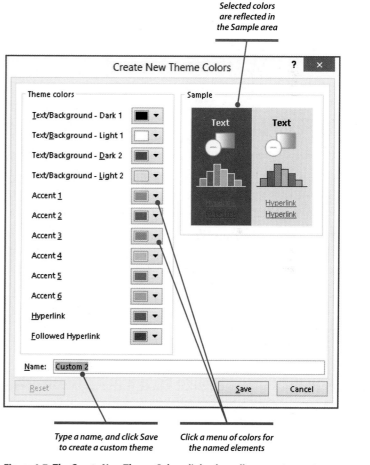

Type a name, and click Save to create a custom theme

Click a menu of colors for the named elements

Figure 4-7: The Create New Theme Colors dialog box allows you to create a new theme to use with multiple documents.

4. When you have selected a group of colors that you like, type a name in the Name text box, and click **Save**.

TIP To restore the original colors in the Sample area in the Create New Theme Colors dialog box and start over, click **Reset**.

NOTE You may find that you want to change something in a custom theme after you've been using it for a while. To edit a custom theme, click the **Colors** button in the Design Document Formatting group, right-click the custom theme you want to edit, and click **Edit**. The Edit Theme Colors dialog box, similar to that shown in Figure 4-7, will appear.

USE TEMPLATES

A *template* contains a particular theme with its collection of styles, associated formatting and design features, and colors used to determine the overall appearance of a document. Examples are letters, resumes, calendars, invitations, business reports, Christmas cards, and Valentines. What you don't find supplied with Word itself, you'll find online. A Word 2013 template file has a different extension of .dotx, which identifies it as a template rather than a normal Word file. All documents have a template attached to it, as you saw in Chapter 2.

Apply a Template to a New Document

Word comes with predefined templates, and you can access additional templates online.

1. Click **File | New** to display a list of templates, as seen in Figure 4-8.
2. Search for one that most closely matches what you're looking for:
   - Choose **Blank Document** for a document with no content, basic formatting, using the Normal.dotx template.
   - Choose another template to get themes and styles more colorfully defined, and a template of where to place heading, content, and so forth.
3. Click the template you want to use and click **Create**. A new document opens formatted with the selected template.
4. Save the file as a normal Word document (.docx). Click **File | Save As**, click the destination (your computer, for instance), click **Browse**, find the folder, name the file, select the Save As Type to be **Word Document (*.docx)**, and click **Save**.
5. Add content and additional formatting to the document as desired and save.

NOTE To find additional templates, search online. Click **File | New**, and in the Search text box type a keyword for the type of template you want. Suggestions are given for popular choices, such as Letters, Resume, Fax, etc. Click **Search** and then scroll through the choices until you find a template you like. On the right will be a category to help filter the available choices. Click the one you like and click **Create**.

Create a Template

To create a new template, start with an existing one and modify it to suit your ongoing needs. Be sure to change the name of the template when you save it so that the original is not modified. This is particularly important for the Normal.dotx template.

1. Find and create a new document with a template as described in "Apply a Template to a New Document."

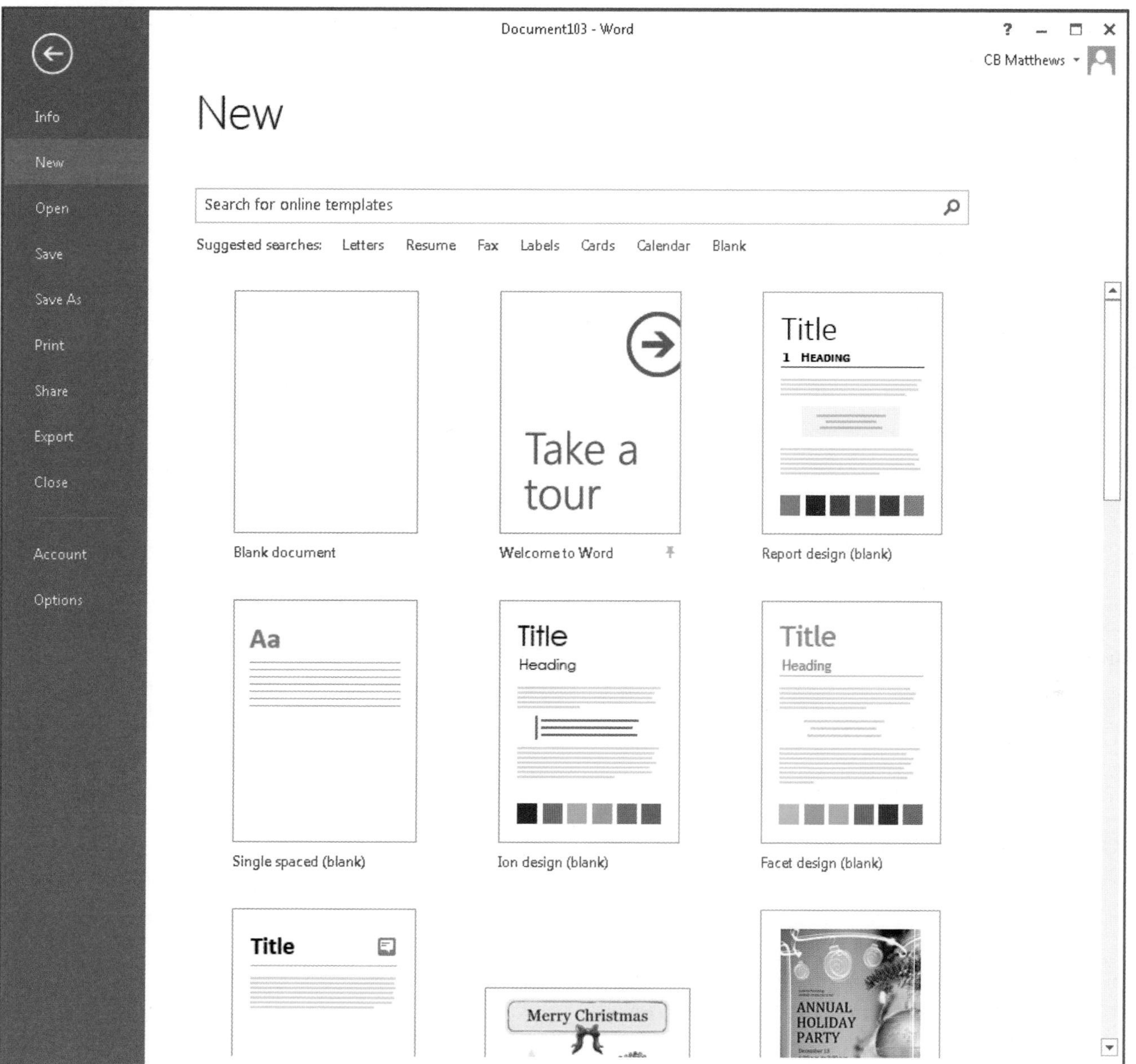

Figure 4-8: ***Word supplies a variety of templates for almost any occasion.***

2. Add the recurring text, images, and formatting that you want to be in the new template and, therefore, in each document that is created based upon the template you're creating.
3. Click **File | Save As**, click the destination (Computer, for instance), click **Browse**, find the folder, name the template file, select the Save As Type to be **Word Template (*.dotx)**, and click **Save**. The template should be saved in the default template folder.

CAUTION! Keep in mind that any changes you make to the Normal template will be applied to any future documents you create, unless you specifically save it under a different name.

NOTE If the Normal.dotx template is renamed, damaged, or moved, Word automatically creates a new version (with the original default settings) the next time you start it. The new version will not include any changes or modifications you made to the version that you renamed or moved.

Find Existing Templates

When you first upgrade to Word 2013, you may already have templates created with previous versions of Word. Existing templates are often stored under %appdata%\Microsoft\Templates\. To find them:

NOTE "%appdata%" is shorthand that tells Windows Explorer to look in the user's appdata folder for \Microsoft\Templates\ folders.

1. Copy and paste **%appdata%\Microsoft\Templates** into your Windows Explorer window address box and click the **Search** icon.

The address will transform into the real one, and you'll see a list of templates.

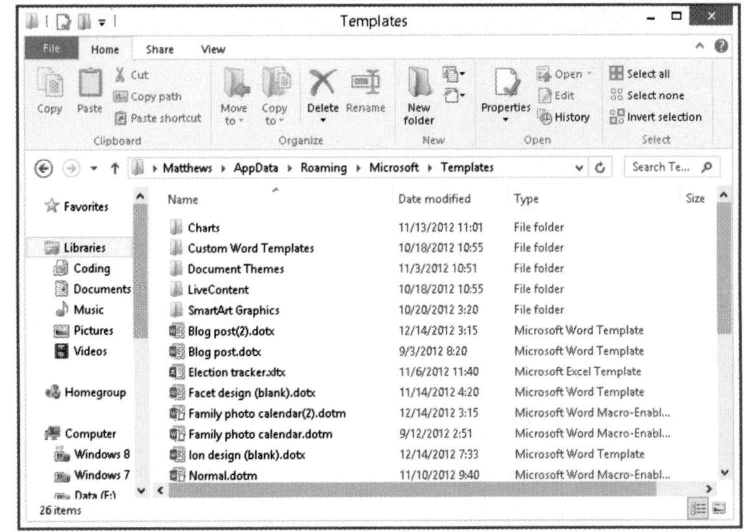

2. Click the template you want.

Change the Default Storage Folder

You can establish your own folder destination for new templates.

1. Click **File | Options | Save**.
2. Under Save Documents, to the right of Default Local File Location, click **Browse**. Find the folder you want to use to store the templates.
3. Copy the address of the new template folder from the Windows Explorer address box or the Address box in Word's Save As dialog box, and paste it into the **Default Personal Templates Location** text box.
4. Click **OK** to save the setting and close the dialog box.

New templates will be saved to the default location.

WORK WITH DOCUMENTS

In addition to using styles and templates to format your documents, you can use section breaks, columns, tabs, headers and footers, tables of contents, and indexes to further refine your documents.

 Create Section Breaks

A *section break* indicates the end of a section in a document. You can use section breaks to vary the layout of a document within a page or between pages. For example, you might choose to format the introduction of a magazine article in a single column and format the body of the article in two columns. You must separately format each section, but the section break allows them to be different. Section breaks allow you to change the number of columns, page headers and footers, page numbering, page borders, page margins, and other characteristics and formatting within a section. The section break retains the formatting above it, not after it.

Insert a Section Break

1. Open the document and click where you want to insert a section break.
2. Click **Page Layout | Breaks** in the Page Setup group. The Breaks menu appears as shown in Figure 4-9.
3. To create a new section, in the Section Break Types area, select what comes after the break. You have the following options:
   - Click **Next Page** to begin a new section on the next page.
   - Click **Continuous** to begin a new section on the same page.
   - Click **Even Page** to start the new section on the next even-numbered page.
   - Click **Odd Page** to start the new section on the next odd-numbered page.

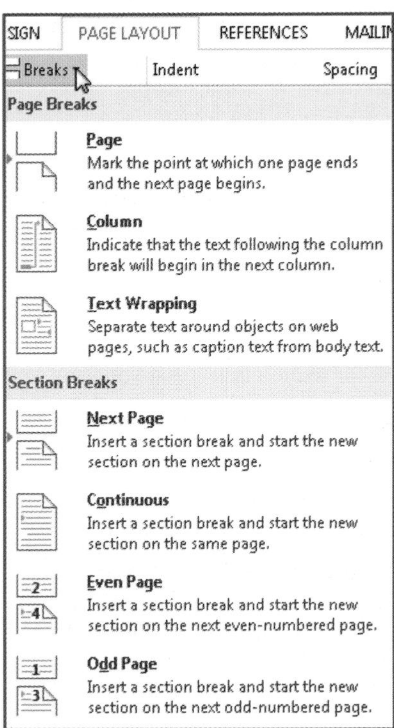

***Figure 4-9:* Insert breaks in a document to separately format sections of text.**

4. When you click the option you want, the section break is inserted. If the Show/Hide Formatting feature is turned on (in the Home tab Paragraph group), you'll be able to see the section breaks in the text.

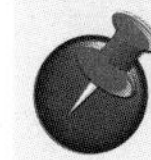

NOTE When you delete a section break, you also delete the specific formatting for the text in the paragraphs immediately above that break. That text becomes part of the following section and assumes the relevant formatting of that section.

TIP If you don't see section breaks displayed in your document, click **Home | Show/Hide** ¶ in the Paragraph group.

Delete a Section Break

When a section break is inserted on a page, you will see a note to that effect if the Show/Hide Formatting feature is turned on. You can delete the break by selecting that note.

1. Click the note for section break that you want to delete.
2. Press DELETE.

NOTE You can change the type of section break by clicking the section break line in the document and then clicking **Page Layout | Breaks** in the Page Setup group. Click the change you would like from the drop-down menu.

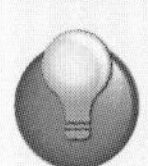

TIP You can also set or change a section break from the Page Setup dialog box. Click **Page Layout | Page Setup Dialog Box Launcher | Layout** in the Page Setup group. The section settings are at the top of the dialog box.

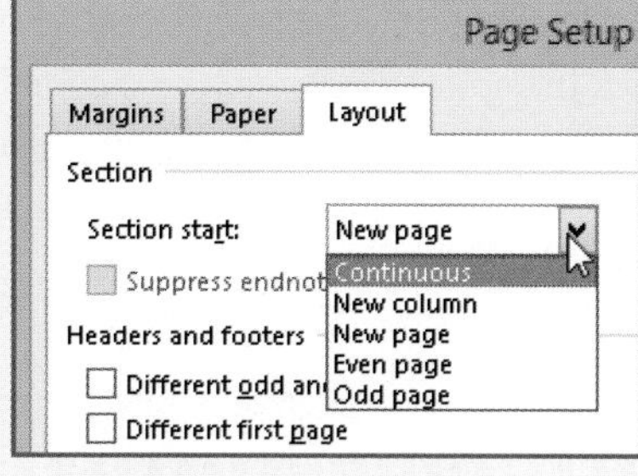

Create and Use Columns

You can format your documents in a single column or in two or more columns, like text found in newspapers or magazines. You must first create either a continuous break or a page break, not a column break, before you create the columns in order to prevent them from forming in the previous section. To create columns in a document:

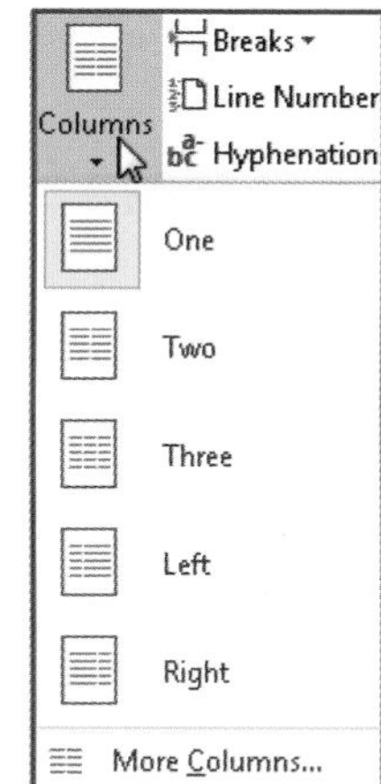

1. Place the insertion point at the place where you want the columns to begin. Click **Page Layout | Breaks | Continuous** in the Page Setup group. (You can also select Page in place of Continuous if the columns are to start on the next page.)
2. Then to define the columns, click **Page Layout | Columns** in the Page Setup group to display a menu.
3. Click the thumbnail option that corresponds to the number or type of columns you want.

   –Or–

   If you do not see what you want, click **More Columns** at the end of the menu to display the Columns dialog box (see Figure 4-10). Then:

   - Click an icon in the Presets area, or type a number in the Number Of Columns box to set the number of columns you want.
   - Use the options in the Width And Spacing area to manually determine the dimensions of your columns and the amount of space between columns. If One Preset is selected, the Equal Column Width check box is not meaningful and is therefore dim. (Clicking any other preset will make the check box available; clicking Left or Right will clear it.)
   - Click the **Line Between** check box if you want Word to insert a vertical line between columns.
   - Use the **Apply To** list box to select the part of the document to which you want your selections to apply: Whole Document, This Section, or This Point Forward. Click **This Point Forward**, and

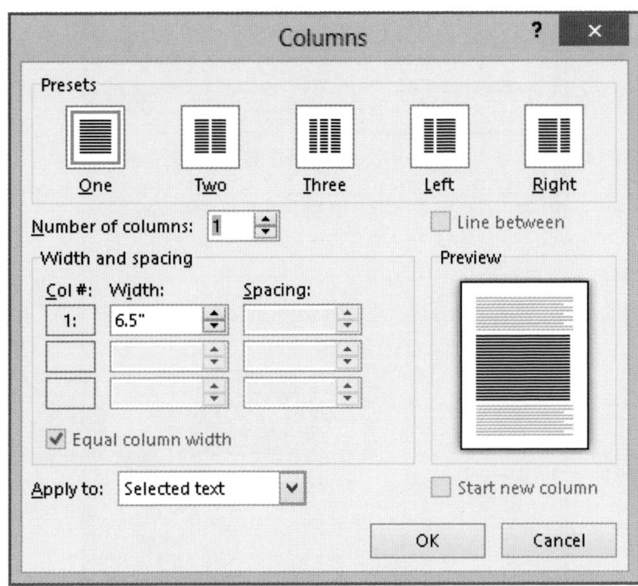

***Figure 4-10:* Use the Columns dialog box to create and format columns in your documents.**

then click the **Start New Column** check box if you want to insert a column break at an insertion point. If the text is selected, you'll see an option for Selected Text that is the default.

4. Click **OK** when finished.

TIP The preview area in the Columns dialog box displays the effects as you change the various column settings.

Use Tabs

A *tab* is a type of formatting usually used to align text and create simple tables. By default, Word has *tab stops* (the horizontal positioning of the insertion point when you press TAB) every half-inch. Tabs are better than space characters in such instances, because tabs are set to specific measurements, while spaces may not always align the way you intend due to the size and spacing of individual characters in a given font.

To align text with a tab, press the TAB key before the text you want aligned.

TIP To see tabs, the ruler needs to appear on the screen. If you do not see the ruler, click **View | Ruler** in the Show group.

Set Tabs and Indents Using the Ruler

To set tabs and indents using the ruler at the top of a page, you can use two techniques. The first, described here, is performed by clicking the tab area to the left of the ruler. The second technique manipulates the indent stops to set first line indents, hanging indents, and left and right indents, and is described in Chapter 3.

Word supports five kinds of tabs:

- **Left tab** left-aligns text at the tab stop.
- **Center tab** centers text at the tab stop.
- **Right tab** right-aligns text at the tab stop.
- **Decimal tab** aligns the decimal point of tabbed numbers at the tab stop.
- **Bar tab** left-aligns text with a vertical line that is displayed at the tab stop.

There are also four forms of indentation:

- **First Line Indent** indents the first line to the right according to the indentation setting.
- **Hanging Indent** indents the first line to the left of the rest of the paragraph according to the indentation setting.
- **Left Paragraph Indent** indents all lines of a paragraph to the right of a normal paragraph according to the indentation setting.

- Right Paragraph Indent indents all lines of a paragraph to the left of a normal paragraph according to the indentation setting.

1. Select the text, from one line to an entire document, in which you want to set one or more tab stops or indents.
2. To the left of the horizontal ruler, click the **Left Tab** icon until it changes to the type of tab you want: Left Tab, Center Tab, Right Tab, Decimal Tab, Bar Tab. The last two icons, First Line Indent and Hanging Indent, as well as Left and Right Paragraph Indent, which are described in Chapter 3, operate only by dragging the existing icons on the ruler.
3. Click the horizontal ruler where you want to set a tab stop.
4. Once you have the tabs set, you can:
   - Drag a tab off the ruler to get rid of it.
   - Drag a tab to another spot on the ruler to change its position.

Set Tabs Using Measurements

To set tabs according to specific measurements:

1. Click **Home | Paragraph Dialog Box Launcher**, and click **Tabs** at the bottom-left corner of the Paragraph dialog box that appears.

   –Or–

   Double-click a tab or an indent in the ruler.

   In either case, the Tabs dialog box will appear, as shown in Figure 4-11.
2. Enter the measurements you want in the Tab Stop Position text box and the tab alignment option you want for the Tab Stop Position.
3. Click **Set**.
4. Repeat steps 2 and 3 for as many tabs as you want to set. Click **OK** to close the dialog box.

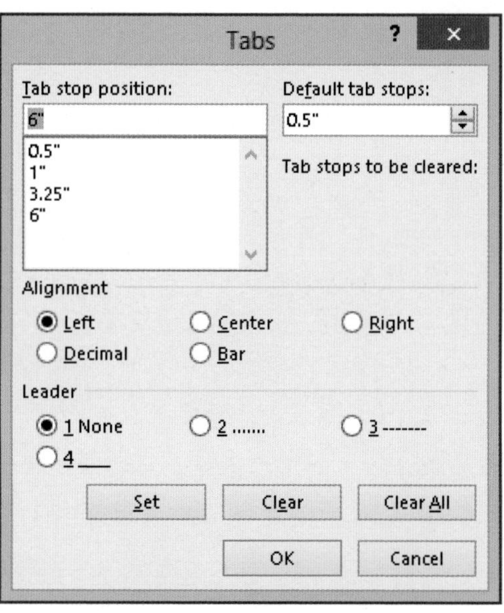

Figure 4-11: From the Tabs dialog box, you can format specific tab measurements and set tab leaders.

Set Tabs with Leaders

You can also set tabs with *tab leaders*—characters that fill the space otherwise left by a tab—a dotted line, a dashed line, or a solid underscore.

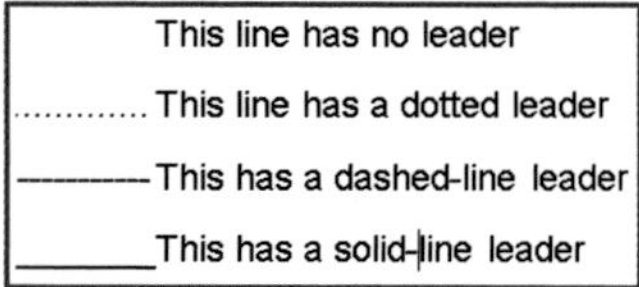

1. Open the Tabs dialog box shown in Figure 4-11 using either method described in the previous section.
2. In the Tab Stop Position text box, type the position for a new tab, or select an existing tab stop to which you want to add a tab leader.
3. In the Alignment area, select the alignment for text typed at the tab stop.

4. In the Leader area, select the leader option you want, and then click **Set**.
5. Repeat steps 2–4 for additional tabs. When you are done, click **OK** to close the dialog box.

TIP When working with tabs, it's a good idea to display text formatting so that you can distinguish tabs from spaces. To display formatting, click **Home | Show/Hide** in the Paragraph group.

Add Headers and Footers

Headers and footers are parts of a document that contain information such as page numbers, revision dates, the document title, and so on. The header appears at the top of every page, and the footer appears at the bottom of every page. Figure 4-12 shows the buttons available on the Header & Footer Tools Design tab.

You can enter a header or footer from scratch or using a predefined header format.

Create a Header or Footer from Scratch

When you first click Header or Footer, choose **Blank**, **Edit Header**, or **Edit Footer**; or double-click the blank area at the top or bottom of the page to provide a blank header or footer, as follows:

1. Open the document to which you want to add a header or footer.

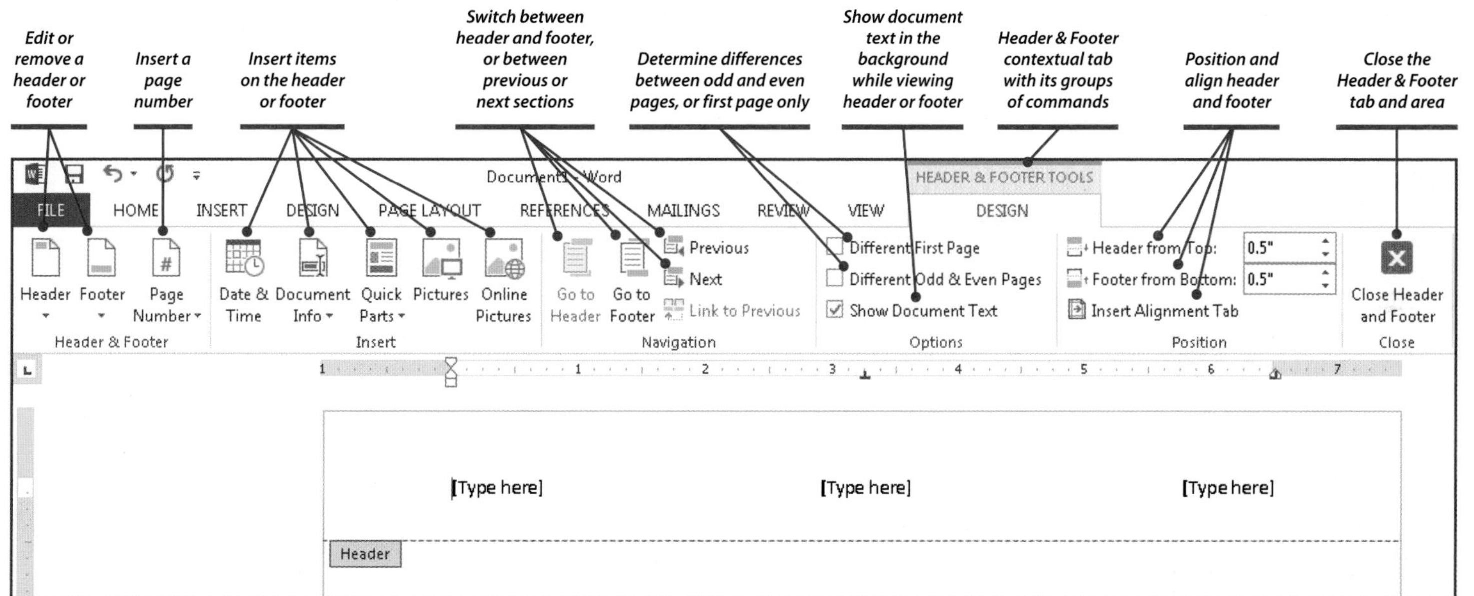

Figure 4-12: Headers and footers provide consistent information across the tops and bottoms of your document pages. These areas can also have unique tabs and other formatting.

1 2 3 4 5 6 7 8 9 10

2. You have several ways to open the header or footer area:
   - Click **Insert | Header** or **Footer** in the Header & Footer group and click **Blank**, which gives you a clean header or footer; or click **Edit Header** or **Edit Footer**, which also gives you a clean header or footer. The header or footer area will be displayed along with the special contextual Header & Footer Tools Design tab, shown in Figure 4-12.
   - Alternatively, if you have some white space above your top line of text, double-click in the top area of the document where a header would be. If you do not have white space but you have content on at least two pages, double-click the split between pages, and then double-click the header or footer area. (If the page break and header area are hidden, you can't use the double-click method.)

Here are some of your options with a blank header:

- To enter a left-aligned date, a centered title, and a right-aligned page number, either type the date or insert a date and/or time by clicking **Date & Time** in the Insert group and then clicking one of the available formats to insert a date or time. Press **TAB.**
- Type the text you want displayed for the centered title in the header or footer, and align and format it. Press **TAB.**
- Insert a right-aligned page number by clicking **Page Number** in the Header & Footer group, clicking a location in the drop-down menu (given you are already in the header or footer, choose **Current Position**), scrolling down, and clicking a format. If desired, type Page in front of the number and leave a space.

3. When you are finished, click **Close Header And Footer** or double-click outside the header area to return to the normal document pane.

TIP Switch between typing text in the header and typing it in the footer by clicking the **Go To Header** or **Go To Footer** button in the Navigation group, and typing the text you want.

TIP To go to the next or last section to enter a different header or footer, click **Previous** or **Next** in the Navigation group.

Create a Header or Footer from Menus

1. Open the document to which you want to add a header or footer.
2. Click **Insert | Header** or **Footer** in the Header & Footer group. A list of predefined headers and footers will be shown. Click one in the list. A preformatted header or footer area will be displayed (without content) with the special contextual Header & Footer Tools Design tab, shown in Figure 4-12.

3. Click in the predefined areas and type your text. If you want something different than the predefined content, click in the area and use the elements contained within the Design tab, such as the page number on the Header & Footer group, or the Date & Time on the Insert group, to select content. (See "Create a Header or Footer from Scratch" for suggestions.)
   - To enter a left-aligned date, a centered title, and a right-aligned page number, select the **Blank (Three Columns)** item from the Header menu.
   - Click in the **Type Here** area to select it, and either type the date or click **Date & Time** in the Insert group.
   - Click in the next **Type Here** area and type the title.
   - Click in the right-most **Type Here** area and, if desired, type <u>Page</u>, and leave a space. With the insertion point immediately after "Page" and the space in the tab, click **Page Number**, click **Current Position**, and click **Plain Number**. If desired, adjust the tab marks in the ruler.

2/5/2013 This is My Heading Page 2

Header

   - Format the text as desired using the Home tab.
4. When finished, double-click in the document area or click **Close Header And Footer**.

Edit a Header or Footer

1. Open the document in which you want to edit a header or footer.
2. Open the header or footer area by double-clicking the header area. You can also click **Insert | Header** or **Footer** in the Header & Footer group, and select **Edit Header** or **Edit Footer**. The header or footer area will be displayed along with the special contextual Header & Footer Tools Design tab, as shown in Figure 4-12.
3. If necessary, click **Previous** or **Next** in the Navigation group to display the header or footer section you want to edit.

Previous
Next

4. Edit the header or footer. For example, you might revise text, change the font, apply bold formatting, or add a date or time.
5. When finished, double-click in the document area or click **Close Header And Footer** in the Close group.

NOTE When you edit a header or footer, Word automatically changes the same header or footer throughout the document, unless the document contains different headers or footers in different sections.

NOTE When you delete a header or footer, Word automatically deletes the same header or footer throughout the entire document. To delete a header or footer for part of a document, you must first divide the document into sections, and then create a different header or footer for part of a document. (See "Create Section Breaks" earlier in this chapter for more information.)

Delete a Header or Footer

1. Double-click the header or footer area of the document. Or, if you can't see the header or footer, first double-click the split between pages, and then double-click the header or footer area. The header or footer area will be displayed along with the Header & Footer Tools Design tab, shown in Figure 4-12.
2. If necessary, click **Previous** or **Next** in the Navigation group to move to the header or footer section you want to delete.
3. Select the text or graphics you want to delete, and press DELETE.

   –Or–

   Click **Header** or **Footer | Remove Header** or **Remove Footer** in the Header & Footer group.

In either case, the *content* of the header or footer will be removed, but the blank header or footer area will remain. These are removed by redefining the layout of the page by clicking **Page Layout | Page Setup Dialog Box Launcher | Layout**.

Use Different Left and Right Headers

Different left and right pages use section breaks to allow different margins and tabs. Sometimes, you might want to create a document that has different left and right headers and/or footers. For example, you might have a brochure, pamphlet, or manuscript in which all odd-numbered pages have a title in the header and all even-numbered pages have the section name or other information.

To create different left and right headers and/or footers:

1. Display the header and/or footer and its Design tab by either double-clicking in the header area or clicking the appropriate option in the Insert tab, as explained in previous sections.
2. In the Options group, click **Different First Page** to enter a separate title or no title for the first page. Create a different first page in the First Page Header area, create the normal header in the Header area of the second page, and so on.

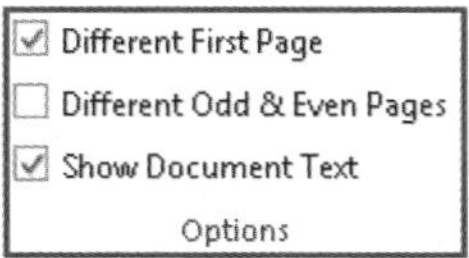

–Or–

Click **Different Odd And Even Pages** to have a different heading on the odd- and even-numbered pages. For instance, perhaps your page number is on the left for even-numbered pages and on the right for odd-numbered pages. Create the header or footer for odd-numbered pages in the Odd Page Header or Odd Page Footer area, and create the header or footer for even-numbered pages in the Even Page Header or Even Page Footer area.

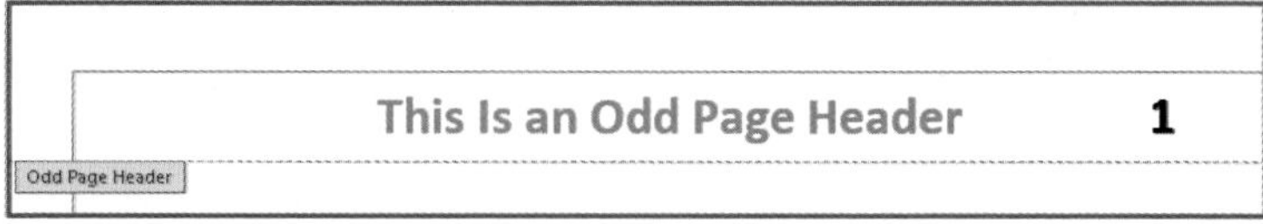

3. When finished, double-click in the document area or click Close Header & Footer in the Close group.

Add Footnotes and Endnotes

Footnotes and *endnotes* are types of annotations in a document usually used to provide citation information or to provide additional information for readers. The difference between the two is where they appear in a document. Footnotes appear either after the last line of text on the page or at the bottom of the page on which the annotated text appears. Endnotes appear either at the end of the section in which the annotated text appears or at the end of the document.

Insert a Footnote or Endnote

You'll need to view the document in Print Layout mode.

1. To display the Print Layout view, click **View | Print Layout** in the Views group.
2. In the Print Layout view, position the insertion point immediately after the text you want to annotate.
3. Click **References | Insert Footnote** or **Insert Endnote** in the Footnotes group. For a footnote, the insertion point will be positioned at the bottom of the page; for an endnote, it will be positioned at the end of the document.

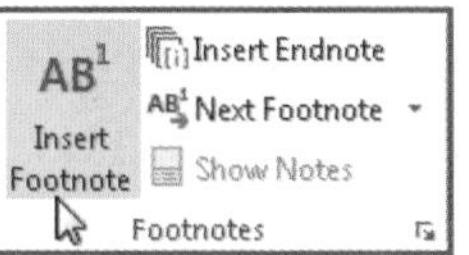

4. Type the text of the endnote or footnote.
5. To return to the text where the footnote reference was placed, right-click the footnote and click **Go To Footnote** or **Go To Endnote**. Before continuing to type, move the cursor to the right of the footnote/endnote reference symbol or number.

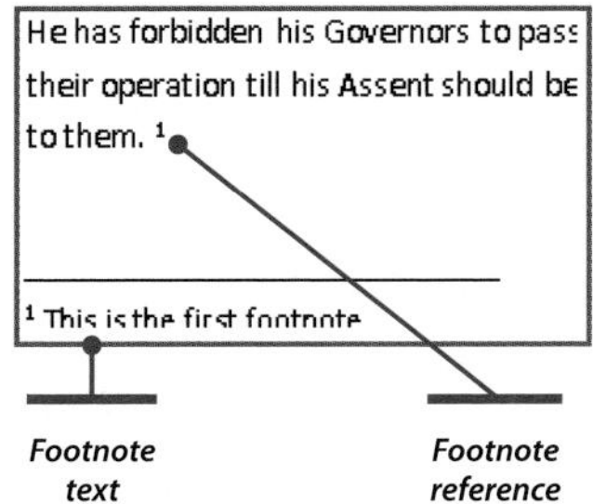

TIP If you find that your footnotes skip pages, make sure you have enough room on the bottom of the page for the notes.

Change Footnotes or Endnotes

If you want to change the numbers or formatting of footnotes or endnotes, or if you want to add a symbol to the reference, use the Footnotes dialog box.

1. Click **References | Footnotes Dialog Box Launcher** in the Footnotes group. The Footnote And Endnote dialog box appears (see Figure 4-13).
2. You have these options:
   - In the Location box, click the **Footnotes** or **Endnotes** option, and click the down arrow to the right to choose where the footnote or endnote will be placed.
   - Beneath Footnote Layout, click the **Columns** down arrow and select an option if it applies.
   - Beneath Format, click the **Number Format** down arrow, and select the type of numbering you want from the drop-down list.
   - To select a custom mark (a character that uniquely identifies a footnote or endnote), click the **Symbol** button. A dialog box appears. Scroll through the symbols, and double-click the one you want to select. It will be displayed in the Custom Mark text box. Click **Insert** to insert it in your text. You can also just type a character into the text box and then click **Insert** to place it in your text.
   - Click the **Numbering** down arrow, and choose how the numbering is to start.
   - Click the **Apply Changes To** down arrow to select the part of the document that will contain the changes.

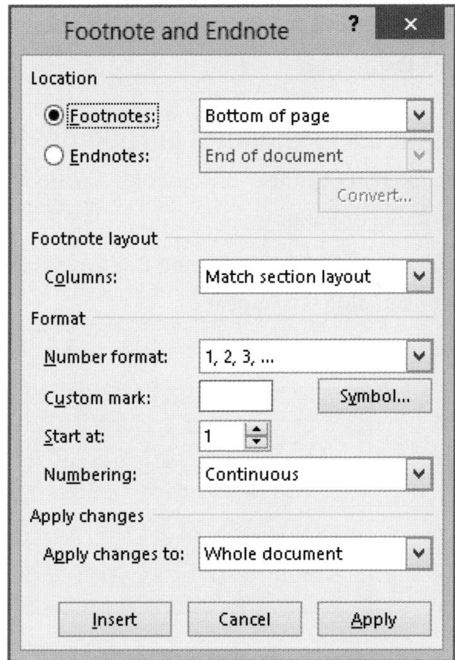

Figure 4-13: ***Footnotes and endnotes provide supplemental information to the body of your document. Use the dialog box to control location and formatting.***

3. Click **Insert**. Word makes the changes you made.
4. Type the note text.
5. When finished, return the insertion point to the body of your document, and continue typing.

TIP Sometimes it is easier to see a footnote or endnote than the text to which it refers. To quickly find the text in the document that a footnote or endnote refers to, right-click the footnote or endnote, and click **Go To Footnote** or **Go To Endnote**. The pointer will be positioned at that location in the text.

Delete a Footnote or Endnote

In the document, select the number of the note you want to delete, and then press DELETE. Word automatically deletes the footnote or endnote and renumbers the notes.

Convert Footnotes to Endnotes or Endnotes to Footnotes

1. Select the reference number or symbol in the body of a document for the footnote or endnote.
2. Click **References | Footnotes Dialog Box Launcher**. The Footnote And Endnote dialog box appears.
3. Click **Convert**. The Convert Notes dialog box appears.

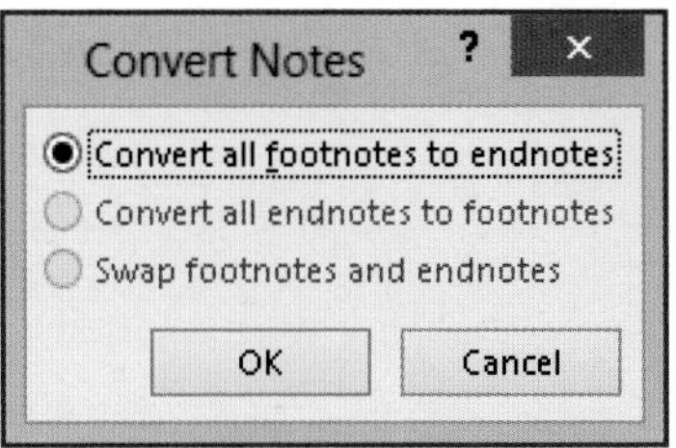

4. Select the option you want, and then click **OK**.
5. Click **Close**.

NOTE When deleting an endnote or footnote, make sure to delete the number corresponding to the annotation and not just the actual text in the note. If you delete the text but not the number, the placeholder for the annotation will remain.

Create an Index

An *index* is an alphabetical list of words or phrases in a document and the corresponding page references. Indexes created using Word can include main entries and subentries as well as cross-references. When creating an index in Word, you first need to tag the index entries and then generate the index.

Tag Index Entries

1. In the document in which you want to build an index, select the word or phrase that you want to use as an index entry. If you want an index entry to use text that you separately enter instead of using existing text in the document, place the insertion point in the document where you want your new index entry to reference.
2. Click **References | Mark Entry** in the Index group (you can also press ALT+SHIFT+X). The Mark Index Entry dialog box appears (see Figure 4-14).

3. Type or edit the text in the Main Entry box. Customize the entry by creating a subentry or by creating a cross-reference to another entry, if desired.
4. Click the **Bold** or **Italic** check box in the Page Number Format area to determine how the page numbers will appear in the index.
5. Click **Mark**. To mark all occurrences of this text in the document, click **Mark All**.
6. Repeat steps 3–5 to mark additional index entries on the same page.
7. Click **Close** to close the dialog box when finished.
8. Repeat steps 1–7 for the remaining entries in the document.

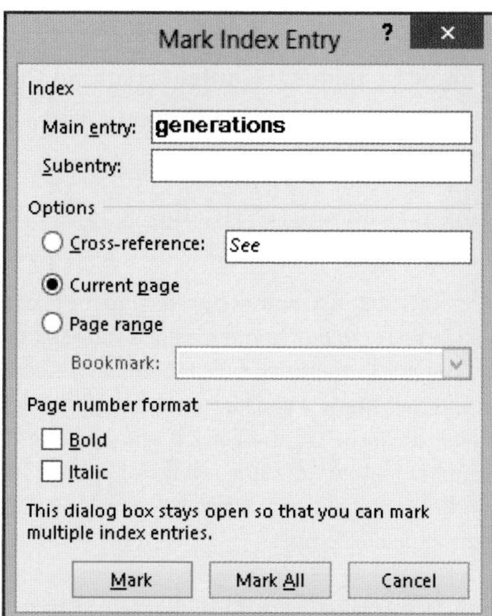

Figure 4-14: You need to tag index entries before you can generate an index.

Generate an Index

1. Position the insertion point where you want to insert the finished index (this will normally be at the end of the document).
2. Click **References | Insert Index** in the Index group. The Index dialog box appears (see Figure 4-15).

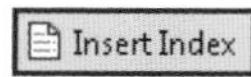

3. In the Index tab of the Index dialog box, set the formatting for the index. You have these options:
   - Click the **Type** option to indent subentries beneath and indented, or click **Run-In** to print subentries beside the upper-level category.
   - Click the **Columns** spinner to set the number of columns in the index page.

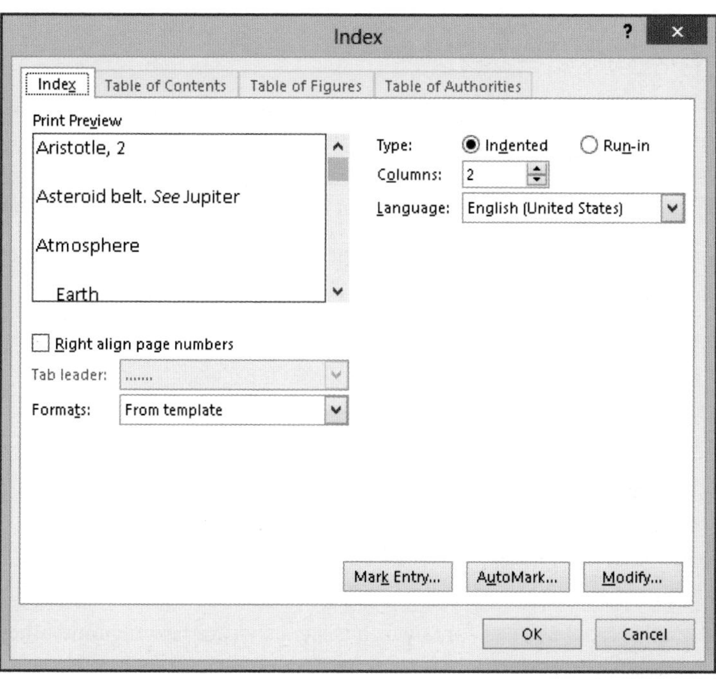

Figure 4-15: Use the options and settings in the Index dialog box to determine how your index will look.

   - Click the **Language** down arrow to set the language for the index.
   - Click **Right Align Page Numbers** to right-align the numbers.
   - Click **Tab Leader** to print a leader between the entry and the page number.
   - Click the **Formats** down arrow to use an available design template, such as Classic or Fancy.

4. Click **OK** when finished. Word generates the index.

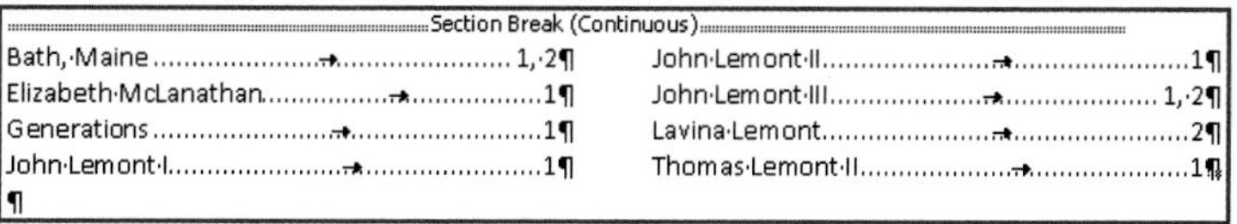

Section Break (Continuous)

Bath, Maine → 1, 2¶
Elizabeth McLanathan → 1¶
Generations → 1¶
John Lemont I → 1¶
John Lemont II → 1¶
John Lemont III → 1, 2¶
Lavina Lemont → 2¶
Thomas Lemont II → 1¶
¶

 Create a Table of Contents

A *table of contents* is a list of the headings in the order in which they appear in the document. If you have formatted paragraphs with heading styles, you can automatically generate a table of contents based on those headings. If you have not used the heading styles, then, as with indexes, you must first tag table of contents (or TOC) entries and then generate the table of contents. (See "Use Styles" earlier in this chapter.)

TIP To make sure that your document is paginated correctly (and, therefore, that the index has the correct page numbers), you need to hide field codes and hidden text. If the XE (Index Entry) fields are visible, click the **Show/Hide** button in the Home tab Paragraph group.

Tag Entries for the Table of Contents

Use the Quick Style gallery to identify a segment of text within your document so that it can contain a consistent style for headings and other text that you want contained in a table of contents.

1. Select the text to be formatted, for example, a title or heading.
2. Click **Home | Styles More** down arrow in the Styles group.
3. Point at each thumbnail to determine which style it represents, and then click the thumbnail of the style you want to apply.

Place Other Text in a Table of Contents

To add text other than identified headings in a table of contents:

1. Highlight the text or phrase to be shown in the table of contents.
2. Click **References | Add Text** in the Table Of Contents group. A menu is displayed.

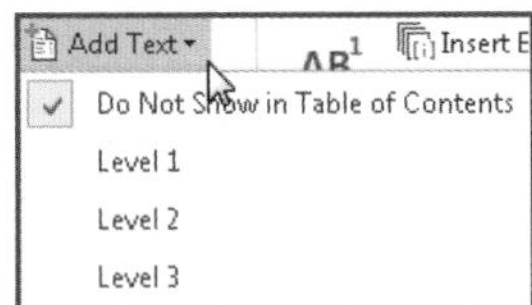

3. Click the option you want. You have these choices:
   - **Do Not Show In Table Of Contents** removes the identification that something should be included in the TOC.
   - **Level 1**, **Level 2**, or **Level 3** assigns selected text to a level similar to Heading 1, Heading 2, or Heading 3.

TIP You can also tag TOC entries by selecting the text that you want to include in your table of contents. Press **ALT+SHIFT+O**. The Mark Table Of Contents Entry dialog box appears. In the Level box, select the level and click **Mark**. If you have multiple tables of contents, you can identify to which TOC the current entry belongs by using the Table Identifier feature. To mark additional entries, select the text, click in the **Entry** box, and click **Mark**. When you have finished adding entries, close the dialog box.

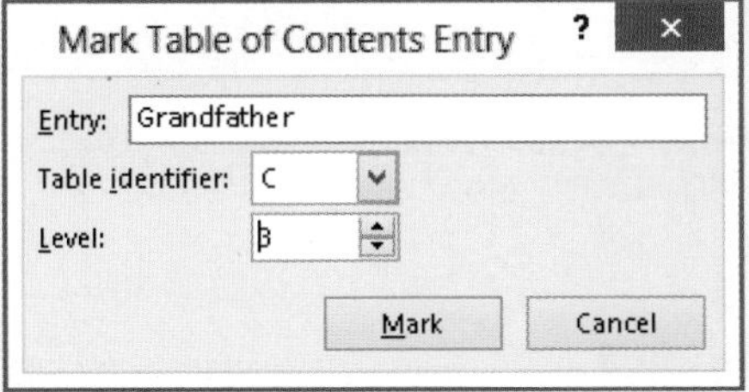

Use the Outlining Tab for the Table of Contents

The outlining tab contains an easy way to tag or identify entries for the table of contents (see "Create and Use Outlines" later in this chapter). For a table of contents, use the Promote and Demote controls to create a hierarchy of headings in your document that can be used for a table of contents.

1. Click **View | Outline** in the Views group. An Outlining tab will become available (see Figure 4-16). Within the Outlining tab, Figure 4-17 shows the Master Document group from which you can insert and manipulate subdocuments.
2. Click the right or left arrows to promote or demote the levels, respectively.

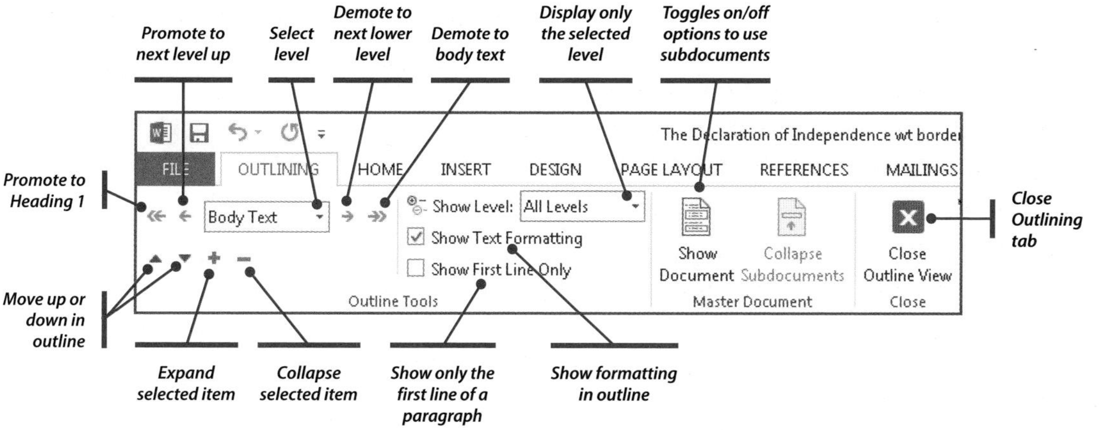

***Figure 4-16:* Use the Outlining tab to mark entries for a table of contents. The Outlining toolbar provides a number of ways to work with outlines.**

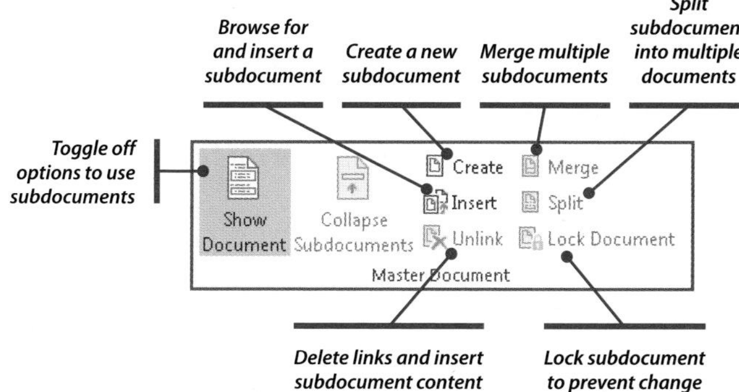

***Figure 4-17:* The subdocument commands appear when Show Documents on the Outlining tab is clicked. These commands allow subdocuments to be inserted and manipulated.**

3. Click **Close Outline View** when you are finished and ready to generate the table of contents.

Generate a Table of Contents

1. Place the insertion point where you want to insert the table of contents (normally, at the beginning of the document).
2. Click **References | Table Of Contents** in the Table Of Contents group. A menu is displayed, as shown in Figure 4-18. You have these options:
   - Click one of the two built-in **Automatic Table 1** or **2** styles that will automatically insert the assigned titles and indented levels. Just pick the format you prefer.
   - Click the **Manual Table of Contents** for a formatted structure, and then fill in the headings yourself.
   - Click **Custom Table Of Contents** to automatically generate a table of contents with formatting that you specify. In the latter case, the Table of Contents dialog box, shown in Figure 4-19, is displayed.
3. If you selected the Custom Table of Contents, Print Preview and Web Preview show how the TOC will appear based on the options selected. You have these options:
   - Clear the **Show Page Numbers** check box to suppress the display of page numbers.

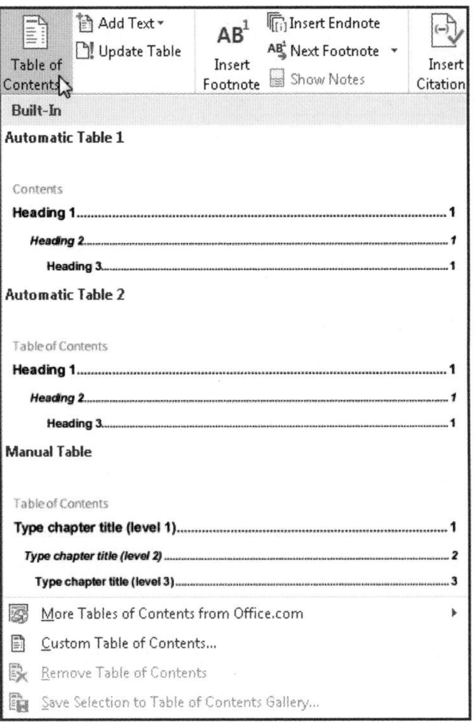

Figure 4-18: A table of contents can have several formats.

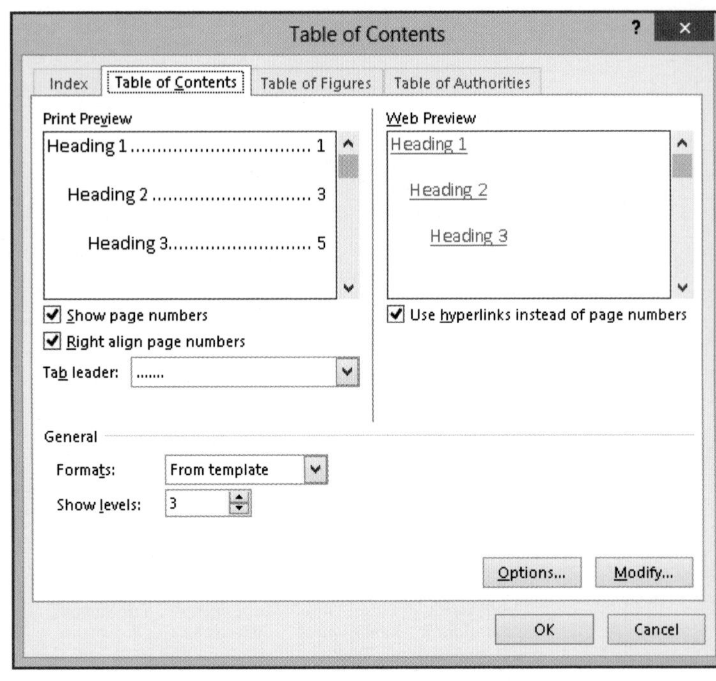

Figure 4-19: Use the options and settings in the Table Of Contents dialog box to determine how your table of contents will look.

- Clear the **Right Align Page Numbers** check box to allow page numbers to follow the text immediately.
- Clear the **Use Hyperlinks Instead Of Page Numbers** check box to use page numbers in place of hyperlinks.
- Click the **Tab Leader** down arrow, and click **(None)** or another option for a leader between the text in the TOC and the page number.
- Under General, click the **Formats** down arrow to use one of the available designs.
- Click the **Show Levels** down arrow, and click the highest level of heading you want to display in the TOC.

4. Click **OK** when finished.

 Create and Use Outlines

An *outline* is a framework upon which a document is based. It is a hierarchical list of the headings in a document. You might use an outline to help you organize your ideas and thoughts when writing a speech,

⊕ **Working with Illustrations**

- Table of Contents
- *Illustration* is a term used to describe several forms of visual enhancements that can be added to a document. Illustrations include pictures, clip art, drawings, shapes, SmartArt, charts, and Screenshots. In this chapter you will learn how to insert, format, and manage illustration files, such as digital photos and clip art images.

⊕ **(1)Work with Pictures**

- *Pictures*, which include both digital photos and *clip art* (small drawings or commercial photos), are separate files that can be manipulated in a number of ways once you have them within Word. You can organize your picture collections, resize images, and move them into the exact positions that you want.

  ⊕ ***(2)Linking Picture Files***

  - 1. To link a picture file when you are inserting a picture into a document, click the **Insert** tab, and click **Picture** in the Illustrations group to open the Insert Picture dialog box.
  - 2. Click the **Insert** down arrow in the lower-right corner, and click **Link To File**.
  - **Illustration 1 [Insert button context menu]**

  ⊕ ***(2)Add Pictures***

  - You can browse for picture files, use the Clip Art task pane to assist you, drag them from other locations, or import them directly from a scanner or digital camera.

    ⊕ **(3)Browse for Pictures**

    - 1. Place your insertion point in the Word paragraph or table where you want to insert the picture.
    - 2. In the Insert tab, click **Picture** in the Illustrations group. The Insert Picture dialog box appears, as shown in Figure 7-1.

    ⊕ **(3)Add Clip Art**

    - 1. Place your insertion point in the paragraph or table where you want to insert the picture.
    - 2. In the Insert tab Illustrations group, click **Clip Art Pane**. The Clip Art task pane opens.

    ⊕ **(3)Add Pictures Directly**

    - In addition to adding pictures to Word from files on your computer or from clip art, you can directly bring pictures into Word from a camera plugged into your computer.

Figure 4-20: Outlines are an excellent way to begin writing a document. Start with the overall ideas and drill down to your core thoughts.

a term paper, a book, or a research project. The Outline tab in Word makes it easy to build and refine your outlines, as shown in Figure 4-20.

1. Open a new blank document (see Chapter 1). Click **View | Outline** in the Document Views group. Word switches to the Outlining tab, displayed earlier in Figures 4-16 and 4-17.
2. Type your first-level heading text, and press **ENTER**. Word formats the headings using the built-in heading style Heading 1. Demote your heading level and type your second-level heading text, and continue throughout the document. You have these ways of setting the levels:

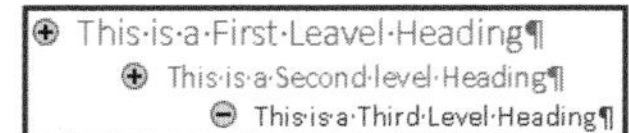

This·is·a·First·Leavel·Heading¶
This·is·a·Second·level·Heading¶
This·is·a·Third·Level·Heading¶

   - Assign a heading to a different level by clicking the **Level *no*** drop-down list box.

   –Or–

   Place the insertion point in the text, and then click the **Promote** or **Demote** button on the Outlining toolbar until the text is at the level you want.

   - To move a heading to a different location, place the insertion point in the heading, and then click the **Move Up** or **Move Down** button on the Outlining tab Outline Tools group until the heading is where you want it. (If a heading is collapsed, the subordinate text under the heading moves with it.)

3. You can display as much or as little of the outline as you want by collapsing or expanding it. To collapse the sublevels under a heading in the outline, double-click the plus sign opposite the heading. To expand the same heading, double-click the plus sign again.

   –Or–

   Select the heading and click the **Expand** or **Collapse** button on the Outlining tab Outline Tools group.

4. When you're satisfied with the organization, click **Close Outline View**, which automatically switches to Print Layout view (see "Use View Buttons" for more information).

1 2 3 4 5 6 7 8 9 10

Use View Buttons

Word 2013 contains five views that you can use to display your document in different ways. To see the views, click **View**, and in the Views group, click the one you want.

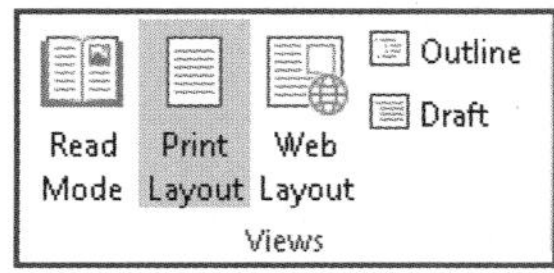

- **Read Mode** displays the document as a "book" with facing pages. You can "flip" through the pages rather than scroll through them. This view uses the full screen in order to display as much of the document as possible. On the top is a restricted toolbar with limited options for using the document. To return from the Read Mode to Print Layout, click **View | Edit Document**.
- **Print Layout** is the default view in Word and shows text as you will see it when the document is printed.
- **Web Layout view** displays a document as it would look as a webpage.
- **Outline view** displays the document's framework as it has been laid out, with the various levels of headers identified.
- **Draft** suppresses headings and footers and other design elements in order to display the text in draft form so that you can have an unobstructed view of the contents.

TIP You can also immediately display one of three document views by clicking an icon in the status bar.

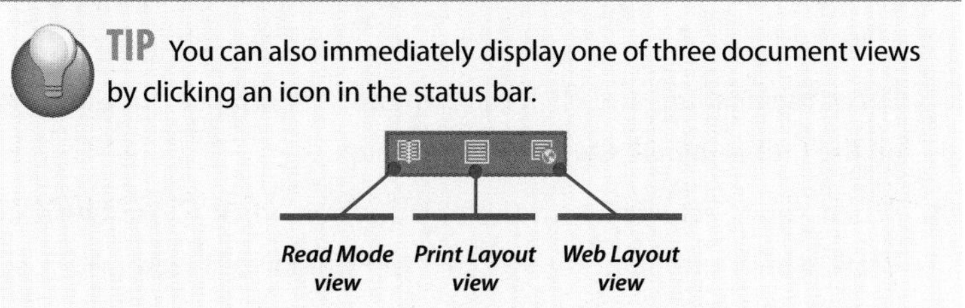

USE WORD WRITING AIDS

Word 2013 provides several aids that can assist you in not only creating your document, but also in making sure that it is as professional-looking as possible. These include AutoCorrect, AutoFormat, AutoText, AutoSummarize, an extensive equation-writing capability, character and word counts, highlighting, hyphenation, and a thesaurus.

Implement AutoCorrect

The AutoCorrect feature automatically corrects common typographical errors when you make them. While Word 2013 comes preconfigured with hundreds of AutoCorrect entries, you can also manually add entries.

Configure AutoCorrect

1. Click **File | Options | Proofing** in the left column, and click **AutoCorrect Options**. The AutoCorrect: *Language* dialog box appears.
2. Click the **AutoCorrect** tab (if it is not already displayed), and select from the following options, according to your preferences (see Figure 4-21):
   - **Show AutoCorrect Options Buttons** displays a small blue button or bar beneath text that was automatically corrected. Click this button to see a menu, where you can undo the correction or set AutoCorrect options.

     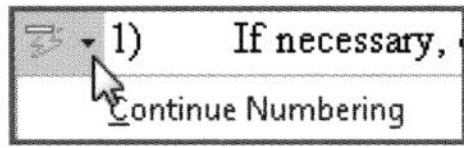

   - **Correct TWo INitial CApitals** changes the second letter in a pair of capital letters to lowercase.
   - **Capitalize The First Letter Of Sentences** capitalizes the first letter following the end of a sentence.

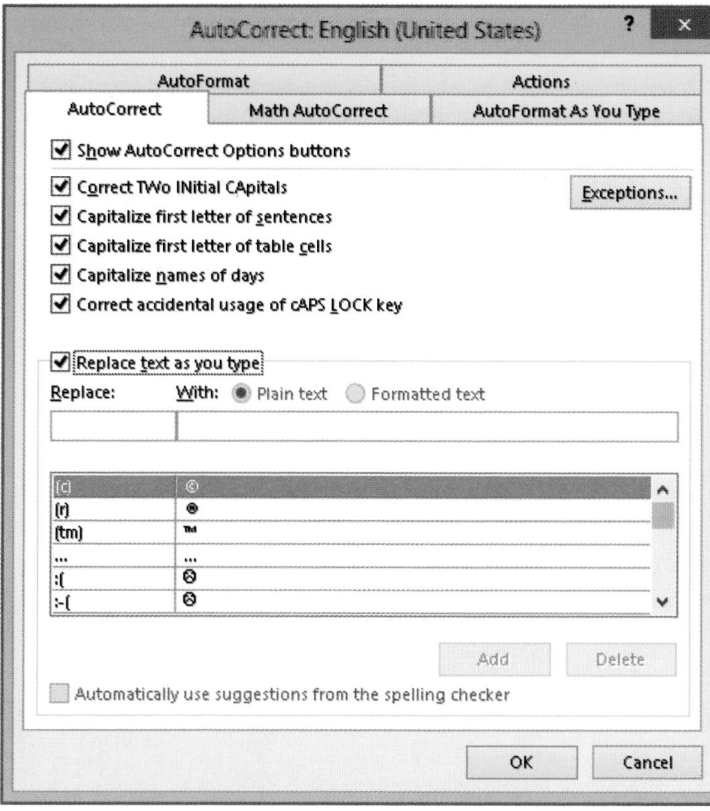

Figure 4-21:* *Use the AutoCorrect tab to determine what items Word will automatically correct for you as you type.

- **Capitalize The First Letter Of Table Cells** capitalizes the first letter of a word in a table cell.
- **Capitalize Names Of Days** capitalizes the names of the days of the week.
- **Correct Accidental Usage Of cAPS LOCK Key** corrects capitalization errors that occur when you type with the CAPS LOCK key depressed and turns off this key.
- **Replace Text As You Type** replaces typographical errors with the correct words as shown in the list beneath it.
- **Automatically Use Suggestions From The Spelling Checker** tells Word to replace spelling errors with words from the dictionary as you type.

3. Click **OK** when finished.

Add an AutoCorrect Entry

1. Click **File | Options | Proofing** in the left column, and click **AutoCorrect Options**. The AutoCorrect: *Language* dialog box appears.
2. Click the **AutoCorrect** tab (if it is not already displayed).
3. Type the text that you want Word to automatically replace in the Replace box. Type the text that you want to replace it with in the With box.
4. Click **Add** and click **OK**.

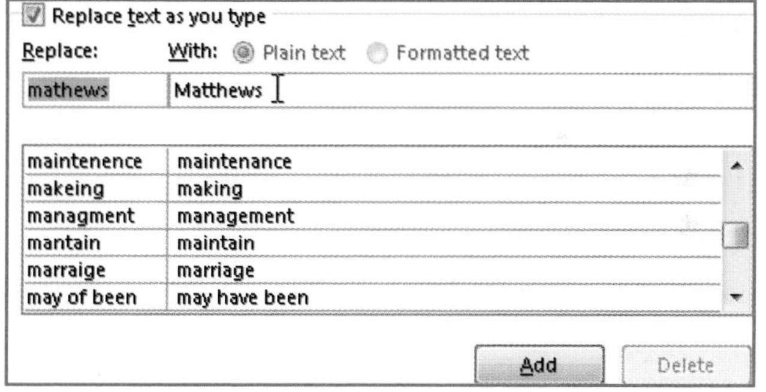

Delete an AutoCorrect Entry

1. Click **File | Options | Proofing** in the left column, and click **AutoCorrect Options**. The AutoCorrect: *Language* dialog box appears.
2. Click the **AutoCorrect** tab (if it is not already displayed).

3. Scroll through the list of AutoCorrect entries, and click the entry you want to delete.
4. Click **Delete** and click **OK**.

Use AutoFormat

AutoFormat automatically formats a document as you type it by applying the associated styles to text, depending on how it is used in the document. For example, Word will automatically format two dashes (--) into an em dash (—) or will automatically format Internet and email addresses as hyperlinks.

To choose the formatting you want Word to apply as you type:

1. Click **File | Options | Proofing** in the left column, and click **AutoCorrect Options**. The AutoCorrect: *Language* dialog box appears. Click the **AutoFormat As You Type** tab.
2. Select from among the following options, depending on your preferences (see Figure 4-22):
   - **"Straight Quotes" With "Smart Quotes"** replaces plain quotation characters with curly quotation characters.
   - **Ordinals (1st) With Superscript** formats ordinal numbers (numbers designating items in an ordered sequence) with a superscript. For example, 1st becomes 1st.
   - **Fractions (1/2) With Fraction Character (½)** replaces fractions typed with numbers and slashes with fraction characters. This only works for ½, ¼, and ¾.
   - **Hyphens (--) With Dash (—)** replaces a single hyphen with an en dash (–) and two hyphens with an em dash (—).
   - ***Bold* And _Italic_ With Real Formatting** formats text enclosed within asterisks (*) as bold and text enclosed within underscores (_) as italic.

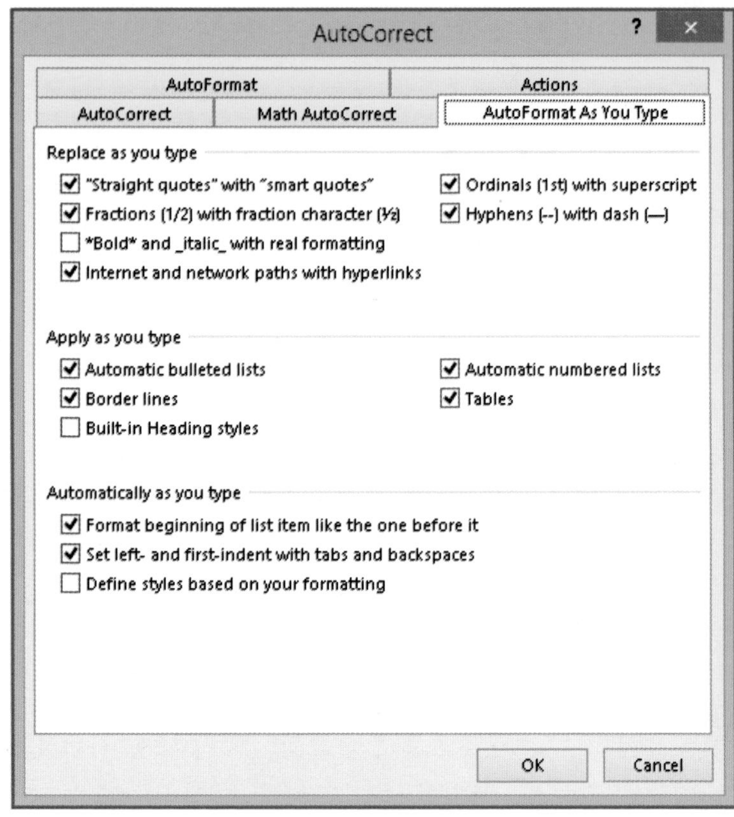

Figure 4-22: Use the AutoFormat As You Type tab to determine what items Word will automatically format for you as you type.

   - **Internet And Network Paths With Hyperlinks** formats email addresses and URLs (Uniform Resource Locator—the address of a webpage on the Internet or an intranet) as clickable hyperlink fields.
   - **Automatic Bulleted Lists** applies bulleted list formatting to paragraphs beginning with *, >, or – followed by a space or tab character.
   - **Border Lines** automatically draws a line consisting of the following characters, when you apply three or more of them and

press **ENTER**: tildes (~), hyphens, underscores, or equal signs (=), #, or *.

- **Built-In Heading Styles** applies heading styles to heading text of fewer than five words not ending with a period or ending punctuation. To format Heading 1, type the text, and press **ENTER** two times; precede Heading 2 text with a single tab and click **ENTER** twice; precede Heading 3 with two tabs and press **ENTER** twice.
- **Automatic Numbered Lists** applies numbered list formatting to paragraphs beginning with number 1 followed by a period or a tab character. Press **ENTER** twice to end the list.
- **Tables** creates a table row when you type a series of plus signs or pipes (|) to define the row edges, followed by hyphens to indicate column widths. For instance, typing +----+-----------------+ or |------------|------------| creates a two-column table row, the width equal to the number of hyphens. To create a second row, press **ENTER** at the end of the row where you want the new one.
- **Format Beginning Of List Item Like The One Before It** repeats character formatting that you apply to the beginning of a list item. For example, if you format the first word of a list item in bold, the first word of all subsequent list items are formatted in bold.
- **Set Left- And First-Indent With Tabs And Backspaces** allows you to indent the first line of a paragraph by placing the cursor before the first line and pressing **TAB**, or indenting the paragraph by placing the cursor before any other line except the first and pressing **TAB**. To remove the indents, place your cursor before the indenting tab and press **BACKSPACE**.
- **Define Styles Based On Your Formatting** automatically creates or modifies styles based on manual formatting that you apply to your document.

3. Click **OK** when finished.

Use Building Blocks

Building blocks are blocks of text and formatting that you can use repeatedly, such as cover pages, a greeting, phrases, headings, or a closing. Word provides a number of these for you, but you can identify and save your own building blocks, and then use them in different documents.

Create a Building Block

1. Select the text or graphic, along with its formatting, that you want to store as a building block. (Include the paragraph mark in the selection if you want to store paragraph formatting.)
2. Click **Insert | Quick Parts** [Quick Parts ▾] in the Text group, and then click **Save Selection To Quick Parts Gallery**.
3. The Create New Building Block dialog box appears. Accept the suggested name for the building block, or type a short abbreviation for a new one. For example, I changed this one to "mt" for Matthews Technology.

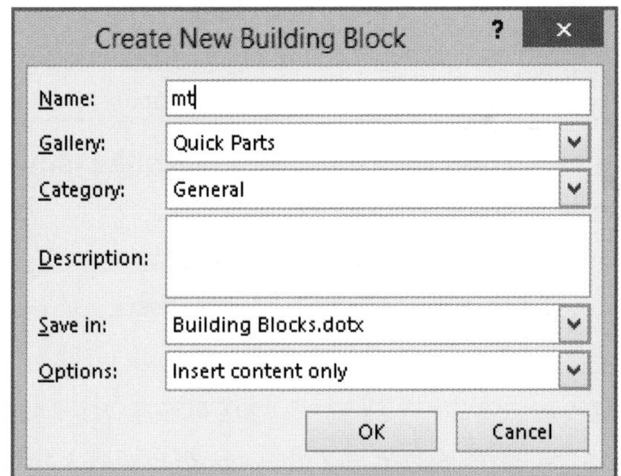

4. In most cases, you will accept the Quick Parts gallery, the General category, and the Building Blocks.dotx filename, since those provide for the easiest retrieval.

5. Click the **Options** down arrow, and, depending on what you are saving in your building block, click the option that is correct for you. If you want paragraph formatting, you must include the paragraph mark.
6. Click **OK**.

Insert One of Your Building Blocks

1. Place the insertion point in the document where you want to insert the building block.
2. Click **Insert | Quick Parts** in the Text group, and then double-click the entry you want, as shown in Figure 4-23.

   –Or–

   At the point in the document where you want to insert the building block, type its name or the short abbreviation you entered in place of the name, and press **F3**. For example, if I type <u>mt</u> and press **F3**, I get "Matthews Technology."

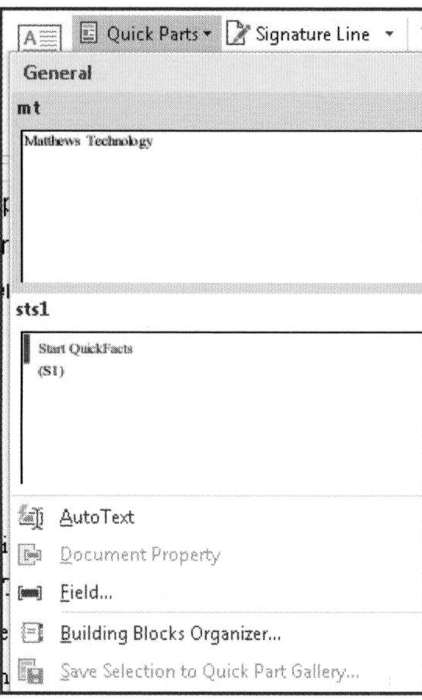

Figure 4-23: Quick Parts provides direct access to your building block entries so that you can insert them in documents.

Insert One of Word's Building Blocks

There are many predefined building blocks in Word. It will be worth your time to scroll through them just to see what is available.

1. Place the insertion point in the document where you want to insert the building block.
2. Click **Insert | Quick Parts | Building Blocks Organizer**. The Building Blocks Organizer dialog box appears.
3. Scroll through the list of building blocks until you find the one that you want. Click the entry to see it previewed on the right.
4. When you have selected one you want to use, click **Insert**.

Delete a Building Block

1. Click **Insert | Quick Parts | Building Blocks Organizer**. The Building Blocks Organizer dialog box appears.
2. Scroll through the list of building blocks until you find the one that you want. Click the entry to see it previewed on the right.
3. When you have selected the entry you want to delete, click **Delete**, click **Yes** to confirm the deletion, and click **Close**.

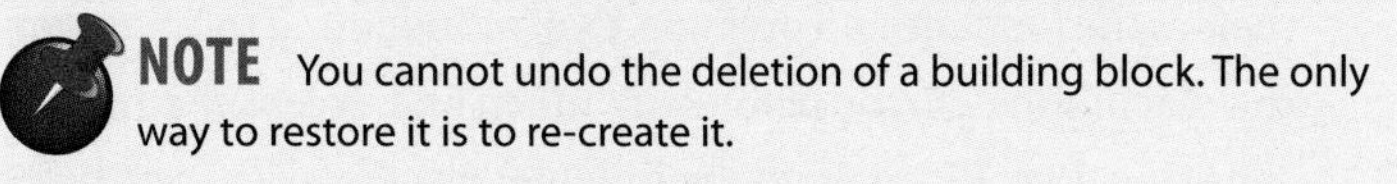

NOTE You cannot undo the deletion of a building block. The only way to restore it is to re-create it.

Count Characters and Words

Word can tell you the number of characters and words in a document or in just a portion of the document you select.

Click **Review | Word Count** in the Proofing group. The Word Count dialog box appears, displaying information about your document.

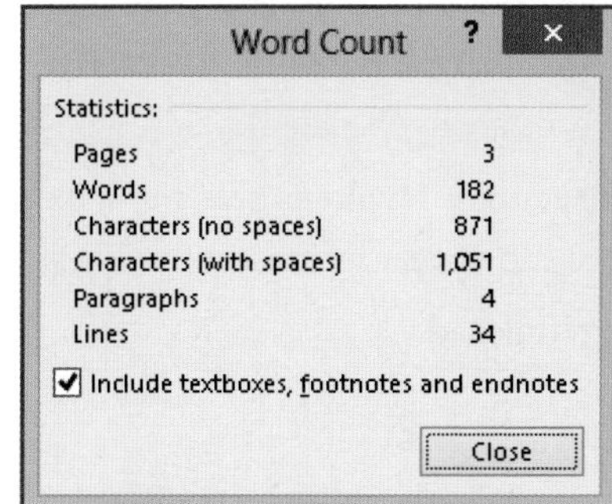

Use Highlighting

The Highlight feature is useful for marking important text in a document or text that you want to call a reader's attention to. Keep in mind, however, that highlighting parts of a document works best when the document is viewed online. When printed, the highlighting marks often appear gray and may even obscure the text you're trying to call attention to.

Select the Highlighting down arrow to see a menu of colors; click the Highlighting icon itself to apply the previously selected color.

Apply Highlighting

1. Click **Home | Highlight** down arrow in the Font group. Select the color you want.
2. Select the text or graphic that you want to highlight. The highlighting is applied to your selection.
3. To turn off highlighting, click **Highlight** again or press ESC.

TIP You can also apply highlighting by selecting the text first and then clicking **Home | Highlight** in the Font group. If you press the down arrow, you see the menu of colors. If you press the icon only, you'll highlight your text with the currently selected color.

Remove Highlighting

1. Select the text that you want to remove highlighting from, or press CTRL+A to select all of the text in the document.
2. Click **Home | Highlight**.

   —Or—

   Click **Home | Highlight** down arrow in the Font group, and then click **No Color**.

Change Highlighting Color

In the Home tab Font group, click the **Highlight** drop-down arrow, and then click the color that you want to use.

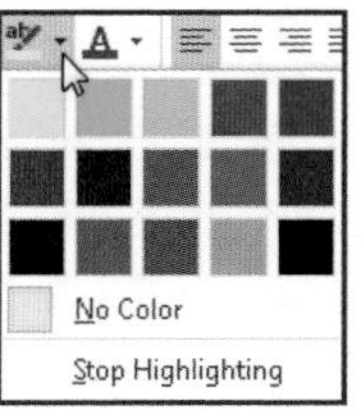

Find Highlighted Text in a Document

1. Click **Home | Find** in the Editing group.
2. In the navigation pane that opens, click the magnifying glass, and click **Advanced Find** to open the Find dialog box.
3. If you don't see the Format button, click the **More** button.
4. Click the **Format** button, and then click **Highlight**.
5. Click **Find Next** and repeat this until you reach the highlight you are searching for or the end of the document.
6. Click **OK** when the message box is displayed indicating that Word has finished searching the document, and click **Close** in the Find And Replace dialog box.

1 2 3 4 5 6 7 8 9 10

Add Hyphenation

The Hyphenation feature automatically hyphenates words at the ends of lines based on standard hyphenation rules. You might use this feature if you want words to fit better on a line, or if you want to avoid uneven margins in right-aligned text or large gaps between words in justified text. (See Chapter 3 for information on text alignment.)

Set Hyphenation Rules

You can set some overall rules about how a document can be hyphenated. To automatically hyphenate a document, hyphenate capitalized words, establish a hyphenation zone, or set the maximum number of hyphens in a line of text:

1. Click **Page Layout | Hyphenation** in the Page Setup group. A drop-down menu appears.
2. Click **Hyphenation Options** to open the Hyphenation dialog box. Select the option you want (see Figure 4-24):
   - **Automatically Hyphenate Document** either enables automatic hyphenation as you type or after the fact for selected text (this option is turned off in Word by default).

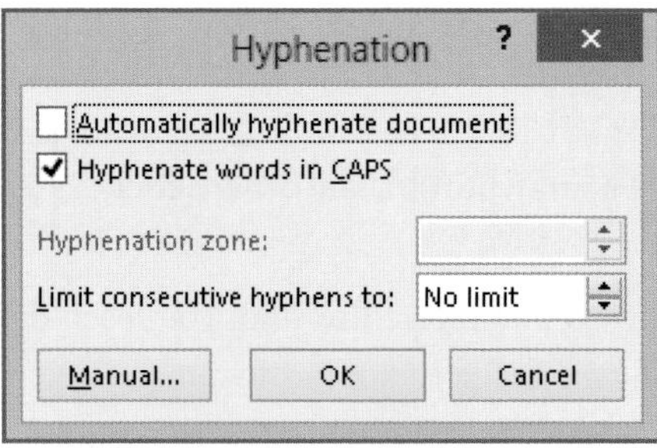

Figure 4-24: ***You can determine how Word will automatically hyphenate words.***

   - **Hyphenate Words in CAPS** hyphenates words typed in all uppercase letters.
   - **Hyphenation Zone** sets the distance from the right margin within which you want to hyphenate the document (the lower the value, the more words are hyphenated).
   - **Limit Consecutive Hyphens** sets the maximum number of hyphens that can appear in consecutive lines.
3. Click **OK** when finished.

Manually Hyphenate Text

1. Click **Page Layout | Hyphenation** in the Page Setup group. A drop-down menu appears.
2. Click **Manual**.
3. Word searches for possible words to hyphenate. When it finds one, the Manual Hyphenation dialog box appears.

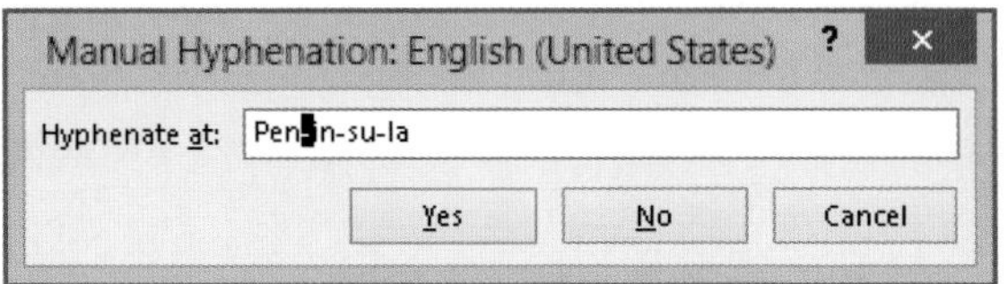

4. Do one of the following:
   - Click **Yes** to hyphenate the word at the suggested blinking hyphen.
   - Click one of the other hyphen choices, if there are more than one, and then click **Yes**.
   - Click **No** to continue without hyphenating the word.
5. Word will continue searching for words to hyphenate and display the Manual Hyphenation dialog box until the entire document has been searched. A message box is displayed to that effect. Click **OK**.

Explore the Thesaurus

A *thesaurus* is a book or list of synonyms (words that have similar meanings), and Word contains a Thesaurus feature that will help you find just the right word to get your message across.

1. Select the word in your current document for which you want a synonym. You can also type a word later.
2. Press **SHIFT+F7**.

   –Or–

   Click **Review | Thesaurus** in the Proofing group.
3. In either case, the Thesaurus task pane is displayed (see Figure 4-25).
4. If you did not select a word in step 1, type the word you want to find synonyms for in the Search field and press **ENTER**.
5. A list of possible words is displayed. Point to the word you want to use. Click the arrow that appears, and click **Insert**.

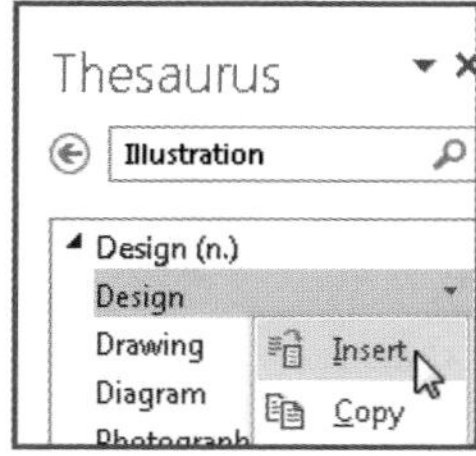

6. Close the Thesaurus pane when finished by clicking **Close**.

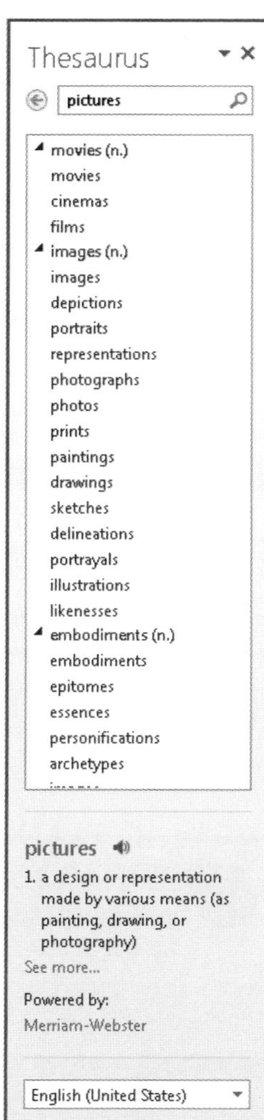

Figure 4-25: The Thesaurus feature enables you to find exactly the right word.

Enter an Equation

If you include mathematical equations in the documents you create, Word has several helpful tools for producing them. These include ready-made equations, commonly used mathematical structures, a large standard symbol set, and many special mathematical symbols that can be generated with Math AutoCorrect. These tools allow you to create equations by modifying a ready-made equation, using an equation text box with common mathematical structures and symbols, and simply typing an equation as you would ordinary text.

TIP If your Word window is smaller in size, you'll find the Equations command contained within a submenu when you click the Symbols command in the Symbols group, rather than positioned on with the Symbols command as it is in a maximized window.

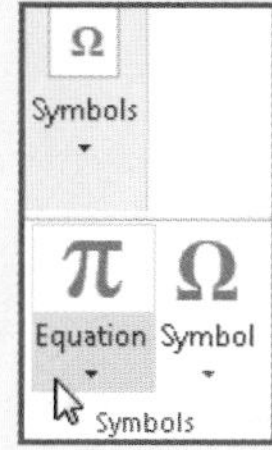

Modify a Ready-Made Equation

1. Click at the location in the document where you want the equation.
2. Click **Insert | Equation** down arrow in the Symbols group. The list of built-in equations appears, as shown in Figure 4-26.
3. Click the equation you want to insert. An equation text box will appear, containing the equation, and the Equation Tools Design tab will display, as shown in Figure 4-27.
4. Click in the equation, and make any needed changes. Use the **RIGHT ARROW** and **LEFT ARROW** keys to move through the text.

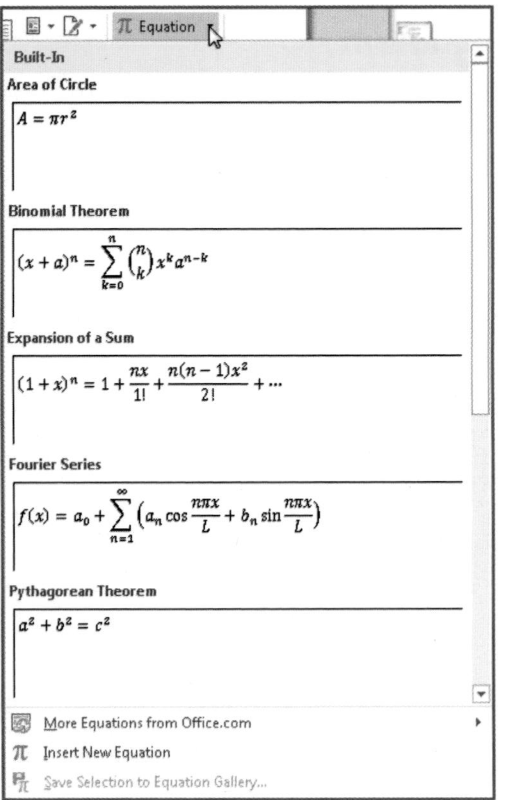

Figure 4-26: ***Word provides a number of ready-made equations for your use.***

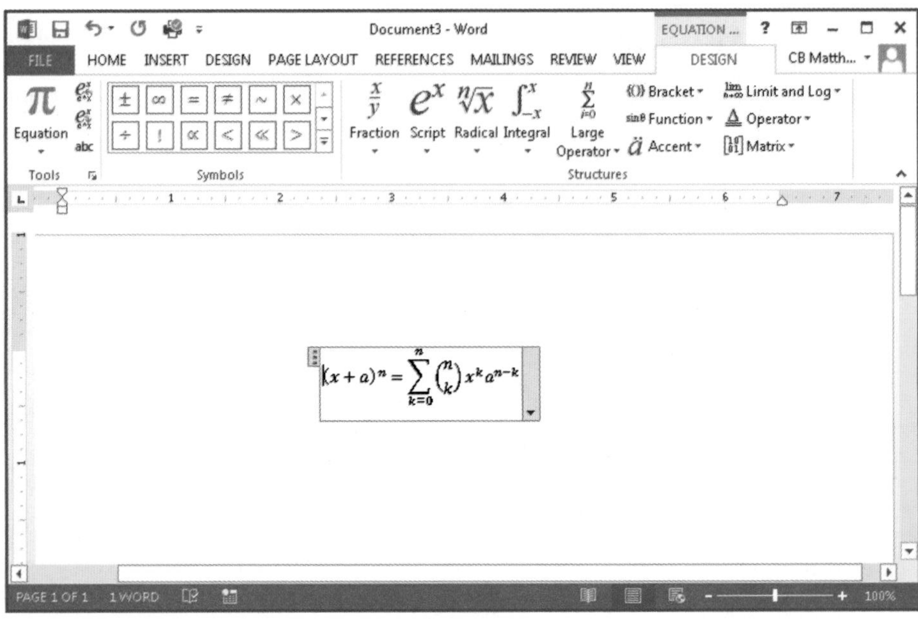

Figure 4-27: ***The equation text box automatically formats equations, which can be built with the structures and symbols in the Equation Tools Design tab.***

NOTE Treat an equation in its text box as you would ordinary text and the text box itself as an object in a line of text.

NOTE If you save a document with an equation in any format prior to Word 2007, the equation will be converted to a .tif image and you will not be able to edit it after you reopen it.

5. When you have completed the equation, click outside the text box to close it and leave the equation looking like it is part of ordinary text. Type your normal text outside the equation text box.

> An example of a complex theorem is the Binomial Theorem: $(x + a)^n = \sum_{k=0}^{n} \binom{n}{k} x^k a^{n-k}$ which in an early form was discussed by Euclid in the 4th century BC and a number of other mathematicians. Its current form was described by Blaise Pascal in the 17th century.

Create an Equation in a Text Box

You can open an equation text box and use the Equation Tools Design tab to create a professional-looking equation.

1. Click at the location in the document where you want to insert the equation.
2. Click **Insert | Equation** (not the down arrow) in the Symbols group. An empty equation text box appears.

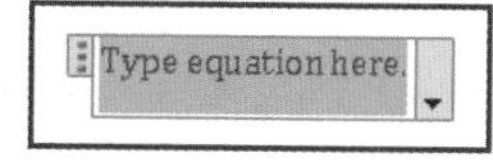

3. Either begin typing the equation or click one of the structures in the Structures group on the Equation Tools Design tab. If a drop-down menu appears, click the specific format you want. You have these choices:

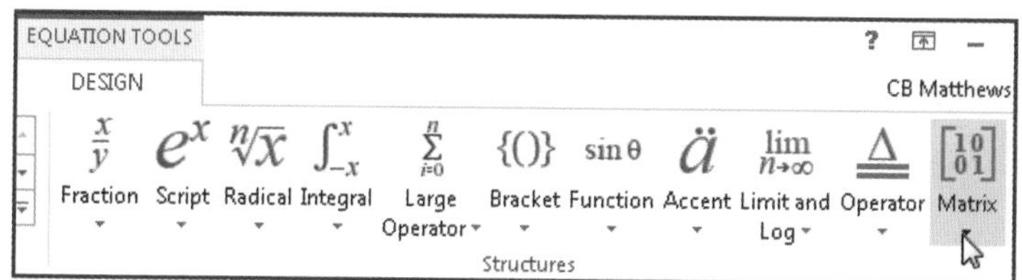

- If you use one of the structures containing text boxes, click in them and type the characters.

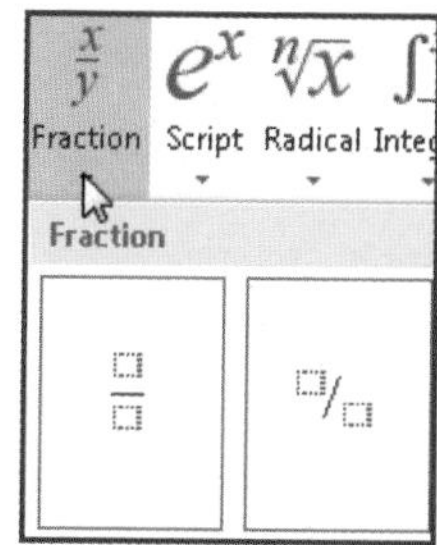

- From the Equation Tools Design tab, select the appropriate symbols from the Symbols group.
- Finish the equation using additional structures, symbols, and normal characters, if needed.

4. When you have completed the equation, click outside the text box to close it and leave the equation looking like it is part of ordinary text.

NOTE You can see the Math AutoCorrect text sequences by clicking **File | Options | Proofing | AutoCorrect Options**, and clicking the **Math AutoCorrect** tab. Scroll through the list to see the text sequences (see Figure 4-28). Click the option at the top of the dialog box to have Math AutoCorrect work outside of an equation text box. Click **OK** twice to close both dialog boxes.

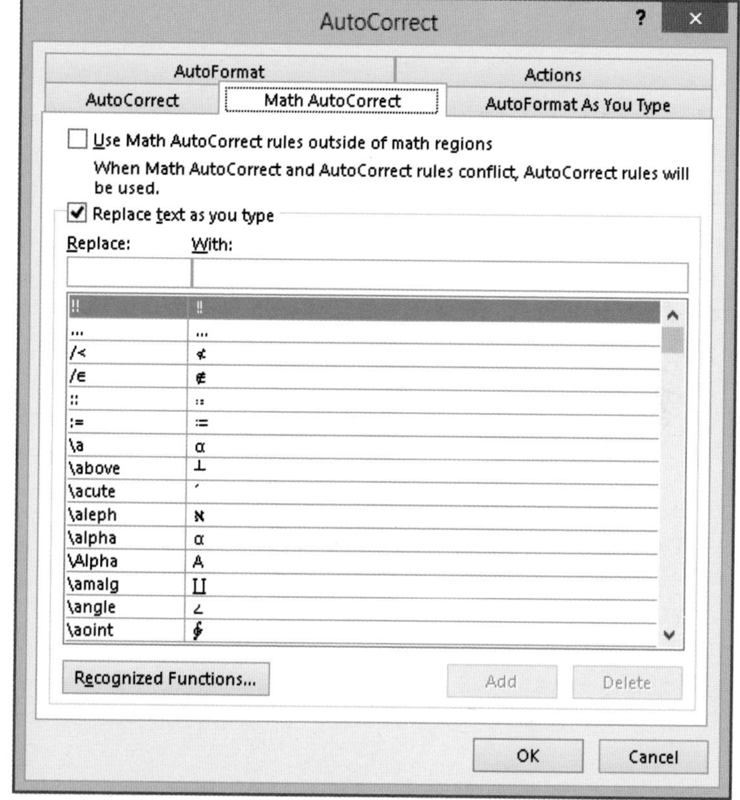

Figure 4-28: Math AutoCorrect allows you to insert math symbols by typing text sequences.

Create an Equation from Scratch

You can also type an equation in a line of text using standard keyboard keys plus special symbols and then convert it to a professional-looking equation.

1. Click at the location in the document where you want to insert the equation.
2. Begin typing using the keys on your keyboard, and, when needed, enter special characters by either:
   - Typing one of the Math AutoCorrect text sequences, like \sqrt to get a square root symbol.

     –Or–
   - Clicking **Insert | Symbol** in the Symbols group, and clicking the symbol you want if you see it; or clicking **More Symbols**, scrolling through the symbols list until you see the one you want, double-clicking it, and clicking **Close**.
3. Finish the equation using the techniques in step 2. When you have completed it (Figure 4-29 shows a quadratic equation created in this manner), select the entire equation, and click **Insert | Equation** in the Symbol group. An equation text box forms around the new equation.

X=(-b±√(b^2-4ac))/2a

(a)

$$X = \frac{-b \pm \sqrt{b^2 - 4ac}}{2a}$$

(b)

Figure 4-29: You can type an equation with normal text (a), and then convert it to a professional-looking equation (b).

4. In the Equation Tools Design tab, click Professional [Professional] in the upper-right area of the Tools group. Click outside the text box to close it. The professionally formatted quadratic equation looks like Figure 4-29b.

TIP To see how to format typed equations, select several of the ready-made equations, and click **Normal Text** [abc Normal Text] in the Equation Tools Design tab Tools group.

QuickSteps to...

- Set Up Your Printer
- Define How a Document Is Printed
- Preview What You'll Print
- Print a Document
- Print an Envelope
- Print Labels
- Fax a Document
- Send an Email
- Perform a Mail Merge Using the Wizard
- Use Rules
- Merge to Envelopes
- Merge to Labels

Chapter 5

Printing and Using Mail Merge

The printing capabilities provided by Word 2013 go beyond just printing a document. You can preview your document before printing it and set specific parameters with regard to what is printed. Word also includes a convenient feature called Mail Merge that you can use to merge mailing lists into documents, including letters or envelopes.

This chapter covers these topics and more, including how to print envelopes and labels and how to set up a name and address list.

PRINT DOCUMENTS

While printing documents may seem like a fairly basic function, there are several tasks associated with it that deserve attention, including setting up your printer, using Print Preview, and printing envelopes and labels.

Set Up Your Printer

Your printer will come with documentation that specifically tells you how to set it up, but there are two basic areas that you need to consider when setting up a printer: installing it on your computer and setting it as the default printer.

1 2 3 4 5 6 7 8 9 10

NOTE Due to the wide variety of printers available, this chapter cannot cover them all. The examples and figures in this chapter use an HP Photosmart 2600 printer. Depending on your printer model and how it's configured, you may see differences between your screen and what is shown in the figures and illustrations here.

NOTE If there is a green check mark next to the Printer icon, that printer is already set as the default printer.

Install a Printer

Follow the manufacturer's instructions to unpack, set up, and connect the printer to your computer or identify the network printer you want to use. If you install a Plug and Play printer, and almost all recent ones are, it will automatically install itself and you can ignore the following instructions. Otherwise, to install a printer:

1. From Windows 7, click **Start** and then click **Devices And Printers**. The Devices And Printers window opens, as shown in Figure 5-1.

   –Or–

   From Windows 8, right-click the lower-left corner, click **Control Panel**, and in Category view, click **Hardware And Sound | Devices and Printers**.
2. Click **Add A Printer** in the toolbar. The Add Printer Wizard starts.
3. Follow the instructions in the Add Printer Wizard, clicking **Next** as needed.
4. If you are using a local printer and you want to print a test page, make sure the printer is turned on and ready to print. When you are done, click **Finished**.

Set a Default Printer

1. From Windows 7, click **Start** and then click **Devices And Printers**, if it isn't already displayed.

   –Or–

   From Windows 8, right-click the lower-left corner, click **Control Panel**, and in Category view, click **Hardware And Sound | Devices and Printers**, if it isn't already displayed.
2. Right-click the icon for the printer you want to use as the default printer, and then click **Set As Default Printer** from the context menu that appears. A green check mark is displayed next to the icon you have selected.

   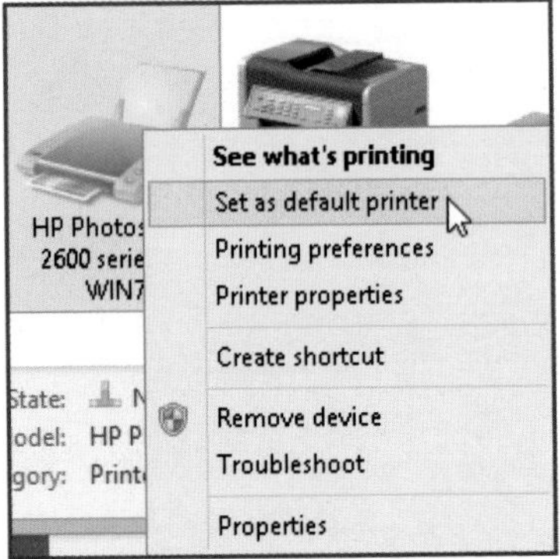

3. Click **Close** in the Devices And Printers window.

Define How a Document Is Printed

The Properties dialog box for your printer is where you define how your document will be printed. From here, you can set such things as orientation, number of copies to print, effects, and so on. An example of a Properties dialog box for an HP Photosmart 2600 printer is shown in Figure 5-2. Keep in mind that the Properties dialog box for your printer will probably have some different options, and can even be different for the same printer, depending on whether the printer is connected

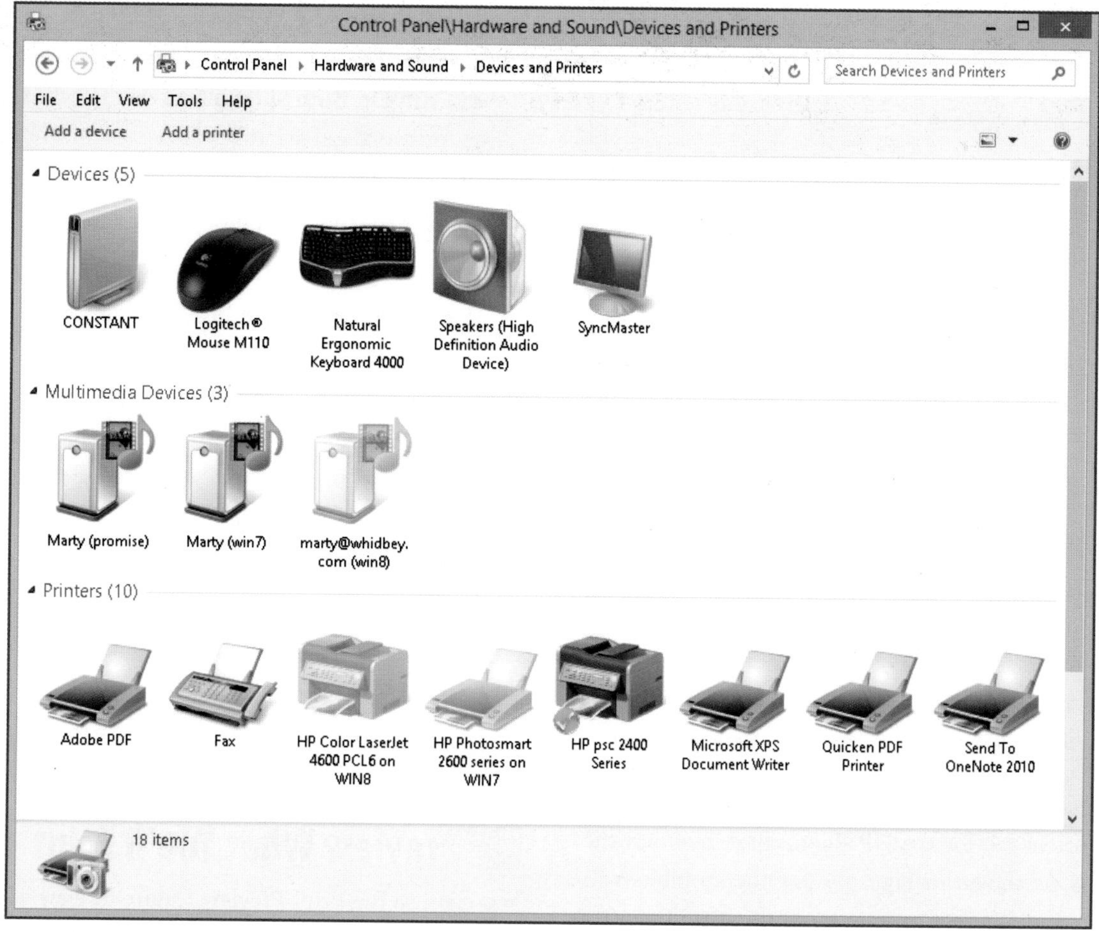

Figure 5-1: ***In addition to your printers the Devices And Printers window may display one or more virtual printers that produce files, not paper output, such as an Adobe PDF "printer."***

directly to the computer or is accessed over the network. Consult the documentation that came with your printer for specific instructions.

To open the Properties dialog box for your printer:

1. In Word, click **File | Print**.
2. In the Print window, beneath the Printer selection drop-down list, click **Printer Properties**. The Document Properties dialog box for your printer appears (see Figure 5-2). This particular printer model has five tabs in its dialog box.

1 2 3 4 5 6 7 8 9 10

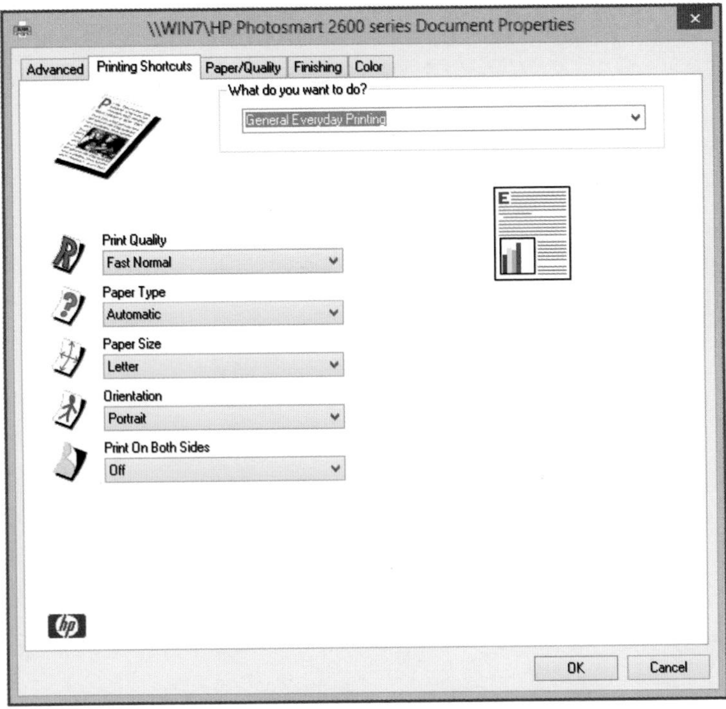

Figure 5-2:** **Use the Properties dialog box for your printer to define how your documents will be printed.

3. The Printing Shortcut tab for the HP Photosmart 2600 has the following options, as shown in Figure 5-2. Other printers will have different tabs and different options, but within the Properties dialog box, they will generally cover the same functions. Make your selections accordingly.
   - **Print Quality** determines the quality of your print job. You can choose speed over quality or quality over speed.
   - **Paper Type** determines the type of paper you are printing on, for example, plain or photo glossy.
   - **Paper Size** determines the size of the paper you are printing on, for example, letter, legal, or postcard.
   - **Orientation** determines how the document is aligned on the page: vertically (Portrait) or horizontally (Landscape).
   - **Print On Both Sides** allows you to select from several options for two-sided printing.
4. Other tabs will have a variety of options, depending on your printer. Some of the more common options are:
   - **Copies** determines the number of copies to be printed.
   - **Collate Copies** determines whether multiple copies of a document are printed one at a time. In other words, all the pages of one copy are printed, then the next copy is printed, and so on.
   - **Source** determines which of several paper trays, if you have more than one, is used as the source of the paper.
   - **Rotate** allows you to rotate the printing on the page by either a fixed or selectable number of degrees.
   - **Pages Per Sheet** allows you to print two or more pages on a single sheet of paper, either directly (if the pages are sized accordingly) or by scaling.
5. When you have the settings the way you want them, click **OK** to close the dialog boxes.

Preview What You'll Print

You can use the Print Preview feature to view your document on the screen before you print it. Print Preview displays the page(s) of your document as they will appear when printed. You can also see page breaks and margins using this feature.

To use Print Preview:

Click **File | Print**. You'll see a preview of what will print in the right pane, as shown in Figure 5-3.

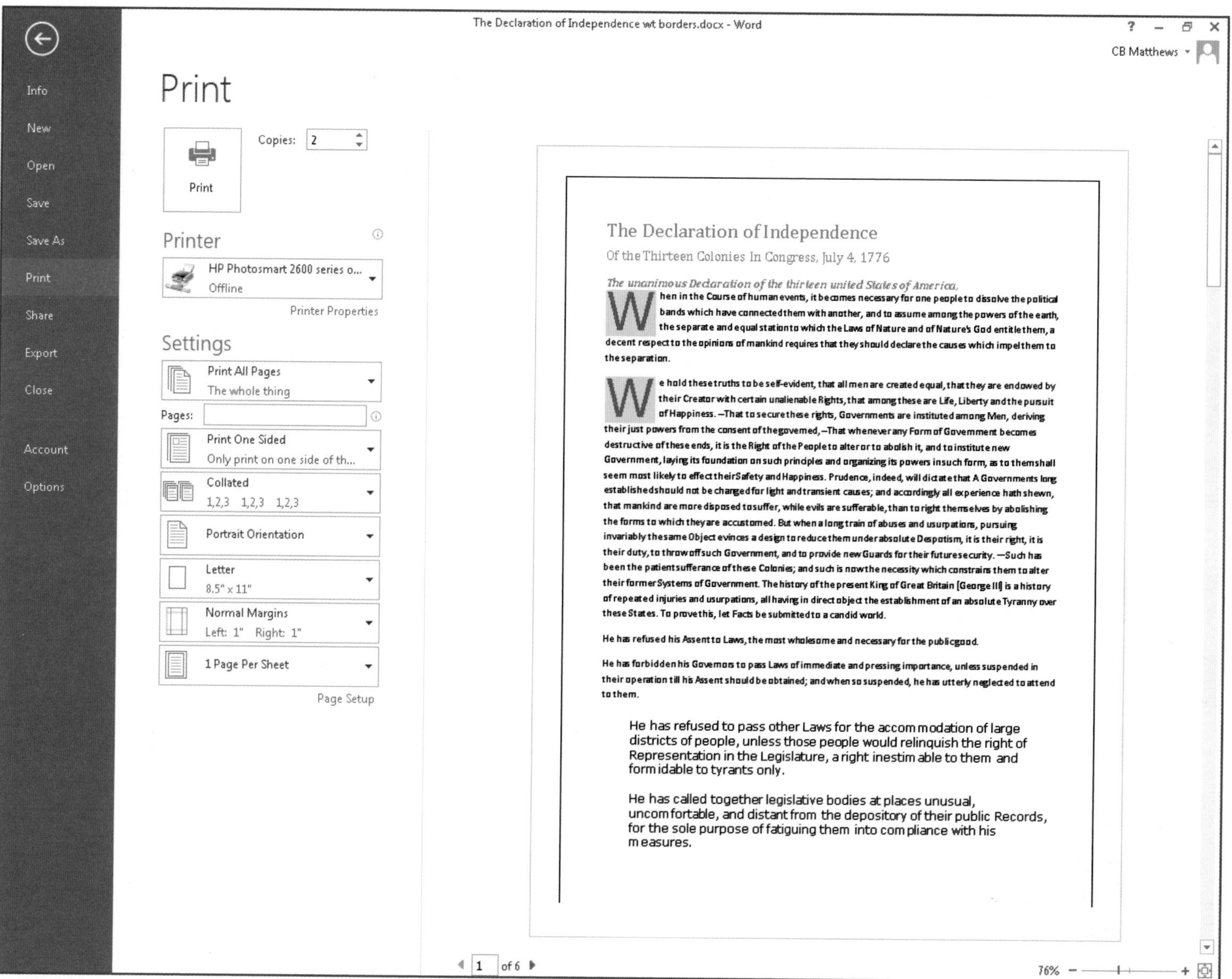
The Declaration of Independence wt borders.docx - Word
CB Matthews
Info
New
Open
Save
Save As
Print
Share
Export
Close
Account
Options
Print
Copies: 2
Print
Printer
HP Photosmart 2600 series o...
Offline
Printer Properties
Settings
Print All Pages
The whole thing
Pages:
Print One Sided
Only print on one side of th...
Collated
1,2,3 1,2,3 1,2,3
Portrait Orientation
Letter
8.5" x 11"
Normal Margins
Left: 1" Right: 1"
1 Page Per Sheet
Page Setup
The Declaration of Independence
Of the Thirteen Colonies In Congress, July 4, 1776
The unanimous Declaration of the thirteen united States of America,
He has refused to pass other Laws for the accommodation of large districts of people, unless those people would relinquish the right of Representation in the Legislature, a right inestimable to them and formidable to tyrants only.
He has called together legislative bodies at places unusual, uncomfortable, and distant from the depository of their public Records, for the sole purpose of fatiguing them into compliance with his measures.
1 of 6
76%

***Figure 5-3:* By displaying your document in Print Preview, you can see how it will look when printed.**

NOTE Print Layout view, set in the View tab Documents Views group, provides almost the exact same view as Print Preview view, and the View tab provides many of the same options.

Zoom In and Out

Word 2013 Print Preview has a set of controls that allow you to increase or decrease the magnification of the print image, as shown in Figure 5-3. These are:

- **The zoom tools** in the lower-right corner of the Print Preview area provide five separate tools:

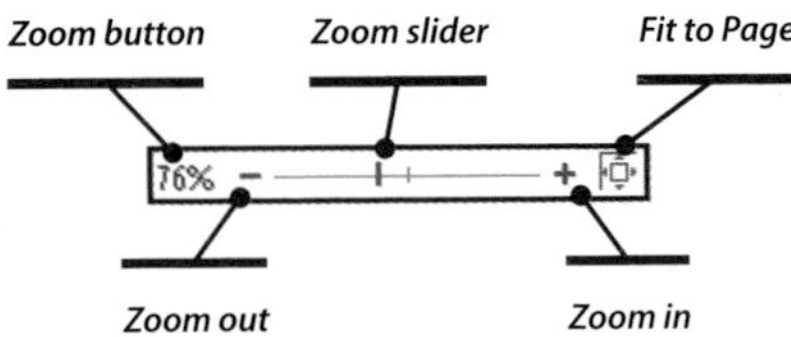

  - **The Zoom button** on the left, which shows you the current percentage of magnification. Clicking this button opens the Zoom dialog box.
  - **Zoom Out**, which is clicked to reduce the magnification and see more of the page.
  - **Zoom slider**, which you can drag in either direction to increase or decrease the magnification. The smaller center mark is for the 100% magnification effect.
  - **Zoom In**, which is clicked to increase the magnification and see less of the page.
  - **Fit To Page**, which, when clicked, reduces the magnification so the entire page can be seen in the Print Preview area.
- **The Zoom dialog box**, which is opened by clicking the **Zoom** button (the percentage number on the left of the slider) allows you to use one of the preset percentages, directly enter a percentage, or use the spinner to set the level of magnification you want. You can also click **Many Pages** to view a number of page thumbnails on one page. Click each thumbnail to see the magnification of that page below in the smaller preview and to the left in the Percent box.

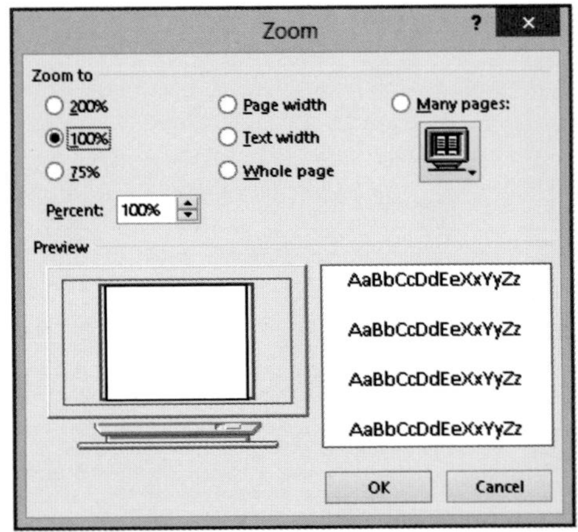

NOTE The zoom tools in the lower-right corner of most Word windows are the same as the zoom tools in the Print Preview pane. In addition, on the View tab Zoom group, you'll find similar tools, one of which, Zoom, displays the Zoom dialog box.

Change Margins

The Print option of Word's File window, shown in Figure 5-3, provides the same margin menu and access to the Page Setup dialog box as available in the Page Layout tab Page Setup group (see Chapter 3 for more information on setting margins).

1. Click **File | Print | Margins** (depending on what was previously selected, it will have a different title—the default is "Normal Margins"). A pop-up menu of margin options will open.

1 2 3 4 5 6 7 8 9 10

2. Select the option that is correct for your document, or click **Custom Margins** at the bottom of the menu to open the Page Setup dialog box. There you can directly enter or select the individual margins you want to use (see Figure 5-4).

   –Or–

   Click **Page Setup** at the bottom of the Print option window to open the Page Setup dialog box.

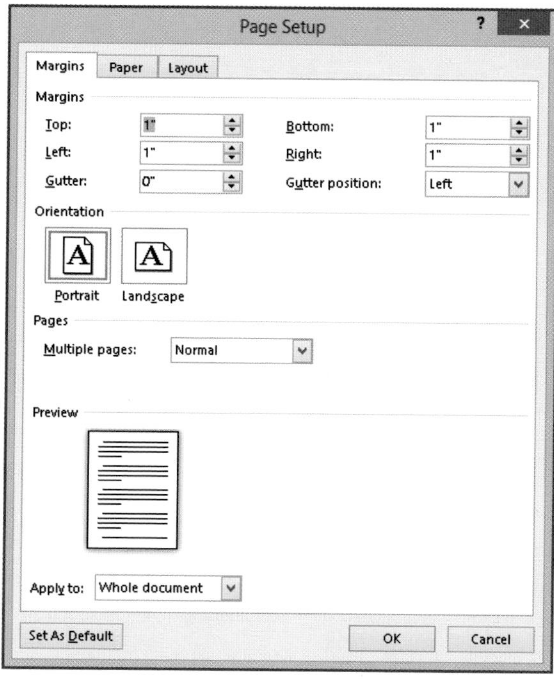

Figure 5-4: ***You can either select preset margins from the Margin drop-down menu or enter the custom margins you want in the Page Setup dialog box.***

Move from Page to Page

In the lower-left area of the Print Preview pane, click **Previous Page** or **Next Page** to move forward or backward one page at a time, or enter a page number in the text box.

Exit Print Preview

In the Print window, click the left arrow at the top left of the window to return to a normal Word window.

Print a Document

If you're in a hurry, or if you don't care about changing margins, then printing a document can be as easy as clicking a Print icon on the Quick Access toolbar. By default, that icon isn't on that toolbar, but you can add it. To set specific options before printing your document, you need to use the Print option of the File window.

Add the Quick Print Icon

Clicking the Quick Print icon in the Quick Access toolbar immediately prints the open document without further interruptions.

To add a single-click Print icon to the Quick Access toolbar:

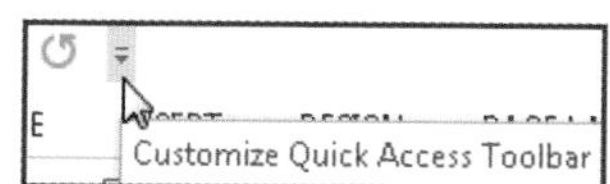

1. Click **Customize** on the right of the Quick Access toolbar.
2. Click **Quick Print**. The Quick Print icon is added.

Customize a Print Job

Customizing the print settings is done in the Print option of Word's File tab window.

1. Click **File | Print**. The Print options appear with the Print Settings area in the left part of the window, as shown in Figure 5-5.
2. Type or use the **Copies** spinner to set the number of copies you want to print.
3. Under Printer, the default printer is displayed automatically in the list box. If more than one printer is available to you and you want to consider alternatives, click the down arrow and select the printer you want to use from the Printer drop-down list.
4. By default, all the pages in the document are printed. If you want to further customize that, the options beneath Settings allow you to either:

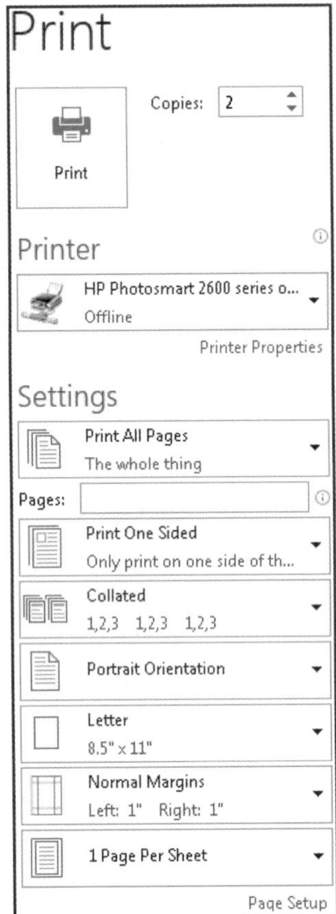

*Figure 5-5: **The Print Settings area provides many options for printing your document.***

- Retain the default, print all pages, or, beneath Print All Pages, click in the **Pages** text box and enter the specific pages to be printed in a list of pages separated by commas (1, 4, 7), or a range of pages separated by a hyphen (3-5), or a combination of the two (1-3, 6, 8-10, 12).

  Settings
  Custom Print
  Type specific pages, section...
  Pages: 1-3, 6, 8-10, 12

  –Or–

- Click the down arrow beside Print All Pages and select one of the following options, shown in Figure 5-6:
  - **Print All Pages** prints your entire document (the default).
  - **Print Selection** prints only the content you have selected. Select text to print by dragging over it to highlight it.
  - **Print Current Page** prints the currently selected page or the page in which the insertion point is active.
  - **Custom Print** allows you to select specific pages to be printed in the Page text box, as described earlier.

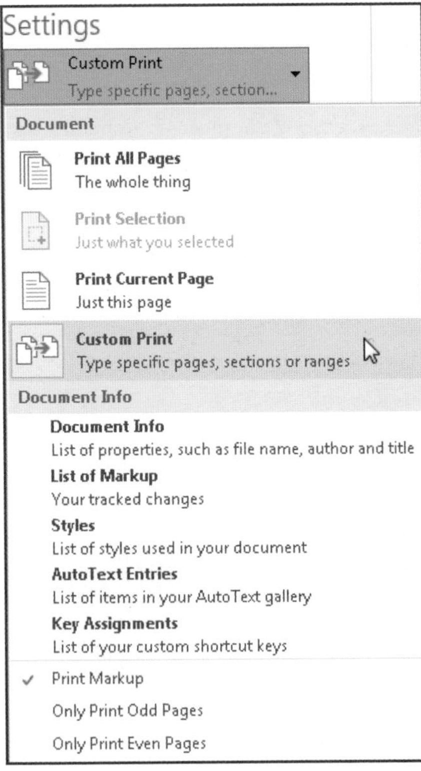

*Figure 5-6: **You can select what pages you want printed in a document.***

5. In addition, from the Print drop-down list you can choose to print several special areas:
   - **Document Info** prints the information about the document, such as the filename, the date the document was created, and when it was last saved.
   - **List Of Markup** prints the revision marks that are present. These are the changes made to the document while Track Changes is enabled. (See Chapter 10 for more information on revision marks.)
   - **Styles** prints a list of the styles used in the document. (See Chapter 4 for more information on styles.)
   - **AutoText Entries** prints a list of AutoText entries. (See Chapter 4 for more information on AutoText.)
   - **Key Assignments** prints a list of shortcut keys defined by the user and available in Word. (See Chapter 6 for more information on shortcut keys.)
   - **Print Markup** prints the selected pages, showing the changes that have been made while using Track Changes.
   - **Only Print Odd Pages** prints all the odd-numbered pages in the document or in the range you specify (an alternative to step 4).
   - **Only Print Even Pages** prints all the even-numbered pages in the document or in the range you specify (an alternative to step 4).

NOTE Word 2013 gives you the option of Quick Print, where you don't have worry about any other settings and a very detailed set of options to produce professional-looking documents.

6. Under Settings, you have six additional settings that you can control by clicking the down arrow on each option:
   - **Print One Sided** allows you to choose options for two-sided printing if your printer supports it.
   - **Collated** allows you to choose between collated, where all the pages of a document are printed before a second document is printed, and uncollated.
   - **Print Orientation** allows you to choose between portrait orientation (taller than it is wide) and landscape orientation (wider than it is tall).
   - **Letter** allows you to choose the size of paper you will use in your printer.
   - **Normal Margins** allows you to reset the document margins. (See "Change Margins" earlier in this chapter, as well as in Chapter 3.)
   - **1 Page Per Sheet** allows you to choose the number of pages to print on a sheet of paper. You may wish to print more than one page per sheet for handouts, proofing, or speech notes, for instance.
   - **Scale To Paper Size**, which is at the bottom of the pages per sheet pop-up menu, allows you to select a paper size and have your document scaled to that size. For example, you might select Executive (7.25 × 10.5 in) and have your document shrunk to that size paper.
7. When you have selected all the options you want and are ready to print your document, click **Print** at the top of the Print Settings area. Your document is printed.

Print an Envelope

You can print a mailing address on an envelope to give your correspondence a more professional look. If you have a business letter with an address in the normal location, Word will pick up that address and suggest it for the envelope. If you don't have a letter, you can still create and print an envelope.

1. Click **Mailings | Envelopes** in the Create group. The Envelopes And Labels dialog box appears with the Envelope tab selected, as shown in Figure 5-7.

Figure 5-7: ***Printed envelopes give your correspondence a professional look.***

2. In the Delivery Address box, if an address wasn't picked up from a letter, enter the mailing address.
3. In the Return Address box, accept the default return address, or enter or edit the return address. (If you are using preprinted envelopes, you can omit a return address by clicking the **Omit** check box.)
4. Click the **Add Electronic Postage** check box if you have separately installed electronic postage software and want to add it to your envelope. (If you do and want it, click this check box and you'll see a message where you can download electronic postage software.)
5. To set options for the electronic postage programs that are installed on your computer, click **E-postage Properties**.
6. To select an envelope size, address fonts, and other specifications, click **Options**, select the options you want, and then click **OK**.

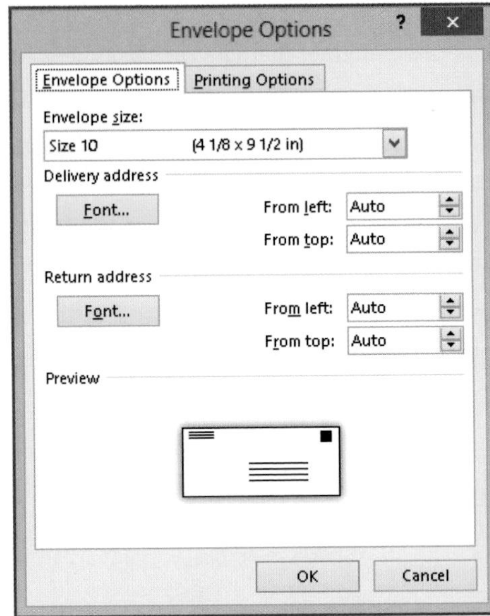

7. To print the envelope now, insert an envelope in the printer, as shown in the Feed area in the lower-right area (see the accompanying Note), and then click **Print**.
8. To attach the envelope to a document you are currently working on and print it later, click **Add To Document**. The envelope is added to the document in a separate section, as shown in Figure 5-8.

NOTE The Feed area in the lower-right area of the Envelopes And Labels dialog box (see Figure 5-7) shows a default view that may be totally wrong for your printer. You need to use trial and error (which you can do on plain paper to save envelopes) to find the correct way to feed envelopes. When you find the correct pattern, click the feed image, select the correct image, and click **OK**.

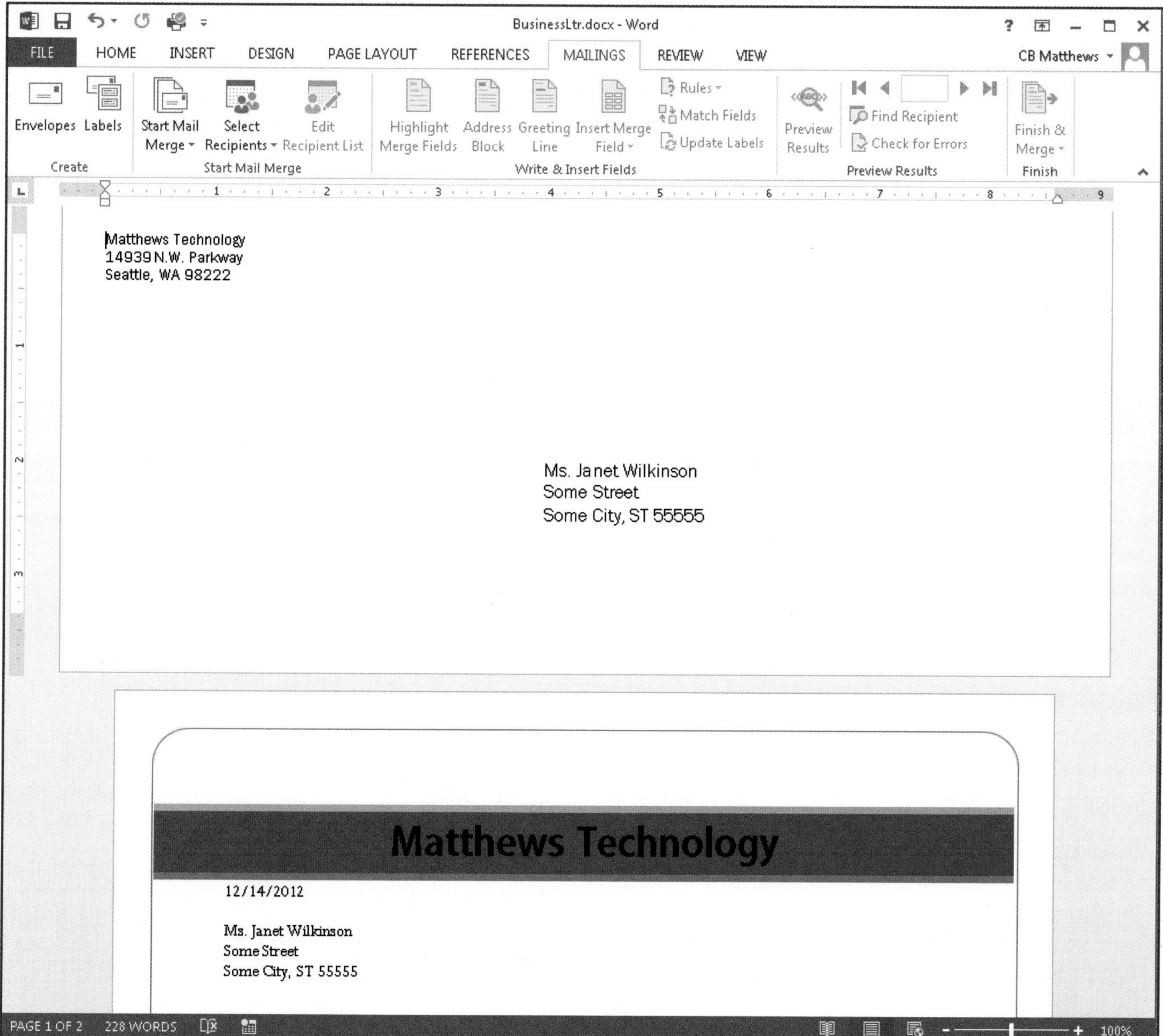

Figure 5-8: ***Word can create a printed envelope for you from a business letter.***

TIP For many HP inkjet printers, the envelopes are fed with the flap up on the left of the envelope and positioned on the far right of the feed tray, like this:

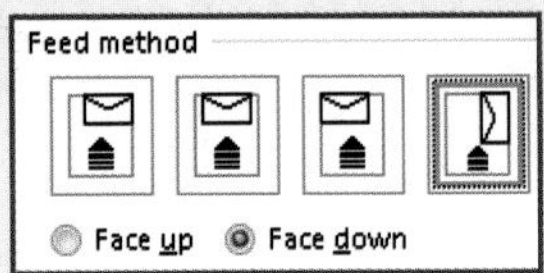

Print Labels

You can print labels for a single letter or for a mass mailing, such as holiday cards, invitations, or for marketing purposes. See the section "Merge to Labels" later in this chapter for instructions on how to create labels for a mass mailing.

To print a single label:

1. Click **Mailings | Labels** in the Create group. The Envelopes And Labels dialog box appears with the Labels tab displayed, as shown in Figure 5-9.
2. In the Address box, do one of the following:
   - If you have a business letter open in Word with an address in the normal location, that address will appear in the Address box and can be edited.
   - If you are creating a mailing label, enter or edit the address.
   - If you want to use a return address, click the **Use Return Address** check box, and then edit the address if necessary.
   - If you are creating another type of label, such as labels for file folders, type the text you want.
3. In the Print area, do one of the following:
   - Click the **Single Label** option to print a single label. Then type or select the row and column number on the label sheet for the label you want to print.
   - Click **Full Page Of The Same** Label to print the same information on a sheet of labels.
4. To select the label type, the type of paper feed, and other options, click **Options.** In the Label Options dialog box, select the options you want, and then click **OK**. Pay attention to the Label Vendors choice since that determines the product numbers you'll see. If the type of label you want to use is not listed in the Product Number box, you might be able to use one of the listed labels, or you can click **New Label** to create your own custom label.

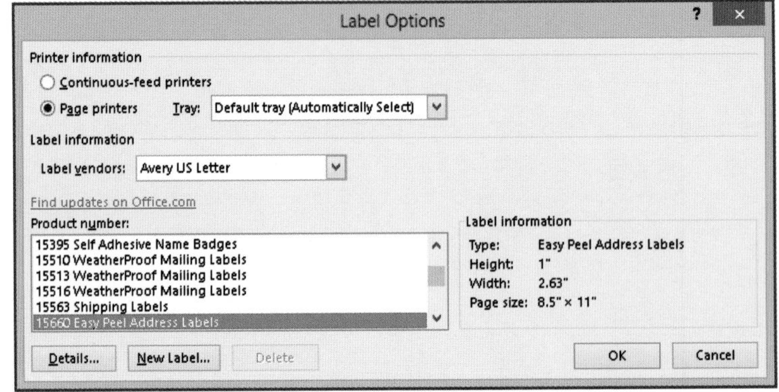

5. To print one or more labels, insert a sheet of labels into the printer, and then click **Print**.
6. To save a sheet of labels for later editing or printing, click **New Document**, and the labels will be displayed in the regular Word window. Save the labels document by clicking **File | Save As** and following the standard steps to save a file.

NOTE In the Label Options dialog box, you can use the Find Updates On Office Online link to locate newly introduced labels as well as changes to existing labels.

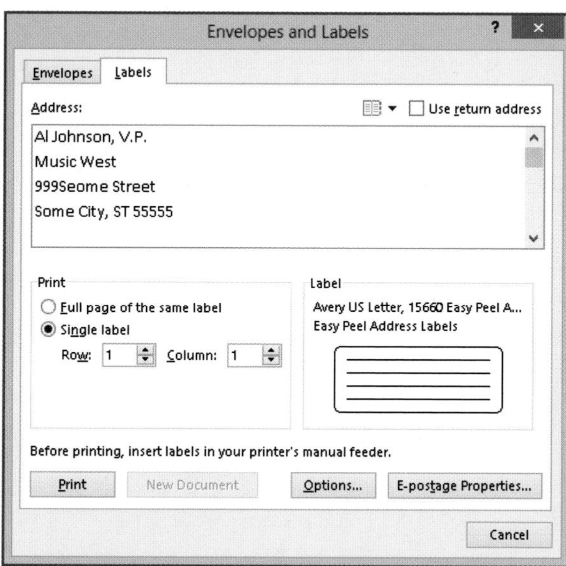

Figure 5-9: ***You can print a sheet of labels one at a time by specifying the row and column to be printed.***

NOTE Later in this chapter, in the "Merge to Labels" section, we'll discuss printing many different labels on one or more sheets.

 Fax a Document

You can send faxes directly from your computer using Word. There are two ways to send faxes: via a faxing service and via a fax modem. When you send a fax, you will create a cover letter with the current document attached.

Use a Fax Service

To send a fax using an online fax service (also called "eFax"):

1. Click **File | Share | Email | Send As Internet Fax**.
2. The first time you use fax services, you will be directed to a webpage listing fax services. Read the descriptions and click **Sign Up With *[the fax service]***. The webpage of the fax service will open. Read the information here, as there is usually a fee for this service. If you wish to go ahead, follow the sign-up instructions on the website.
3. When finished, close your web browser, and then repeat step 1. An email message will open with your document attached as an image file.
4. Click and type in the name of the **Fax Recipient** text box, the subject into the **Subject** text box, and the **Fax Number**.
5. Click **Send**.
6. If the email message does not open, or you get an error message, click **Send As Attachment** instead of Send As Internet Fax in step 1.
7. In the **TO** field, enter the recipient's fax number followed by your fax service's email address—for example: 1-888-555-1234@fax.com, where @fax.com is your service's email address.
8. Add a subject, type any fax cover information in the body of the message, and click **Send.**

Use a Fax Modem

This procedure requires that your fax modem be set up as a printer on your system. To send a fax using a fax modem:

1. Click **File | Print**. The Print view appears displaying the print settings.
2. Click the **Printer** drop-down list to open it, click **Fax**, select what to print and other settings, and click **Print**. The first time you do this, the Fax Setup dialog box will open. After that, you'll go directly to the New Fax message form and you can jump to step 4.
3. Click **Connect To A Fax Modem**, enter a name for the fax, and click **Next**. Select how you want to receive faxes, and click **Next** when Windows asks for confirmation.

1 2 3 4 5 6 7 8 9 10

4. A New Fax message form will open, as shown in Figure 5-10. Your Word document will be attached as an image file. Type the fax recipient name in the To text box, the subject, and any message.
5. Click **Send**. You should hear your modem dialing the number and sending the fax.

> **NOTE** If you want to send just a single copy of a mail-merge letter, you can simply send the Word document in the body of an email message using your basic copy and paste tools. While in Word, select as much of the document as you want to send, and use the **Copy** command or press **CTRL+C** to copy it. In your email program, open a new message form; fill in the **To**, **Cc**, and **Subject** fields; click in the message body field; and use the **Paste** command or press **CTRL+V** to paste the document in the message field. When ready, click **Send**.

Send an Email

You can email documents that you create in Word as attachments to email messages. To attach and send a document in an email:

1. Click **File | Share | Email.** You'll have a choice about how you want to send the open Word document to your email message:
   - As an attached Word (.docx) file that can be edited by the recipient
   - As a link to a file that has been stored on an Internet or intranet shared server
   - As an attached Adobe PDF file that is difficult to edit
   - As an attached Microsoft XPS file that is difficult to edit
   - As an Internet fax, as explained in "Fax a Document"
2. Click your choice. A new email message is opened with your document title automatically displayed in the Subject line and the document automatically attached to the email.
3. Fill in the To and possibly Cc or Bcc fields (if you are sending the document to multiple recipients), add anything you want to the body of the message, and click **Send**. Your email message is sent with the document attached.

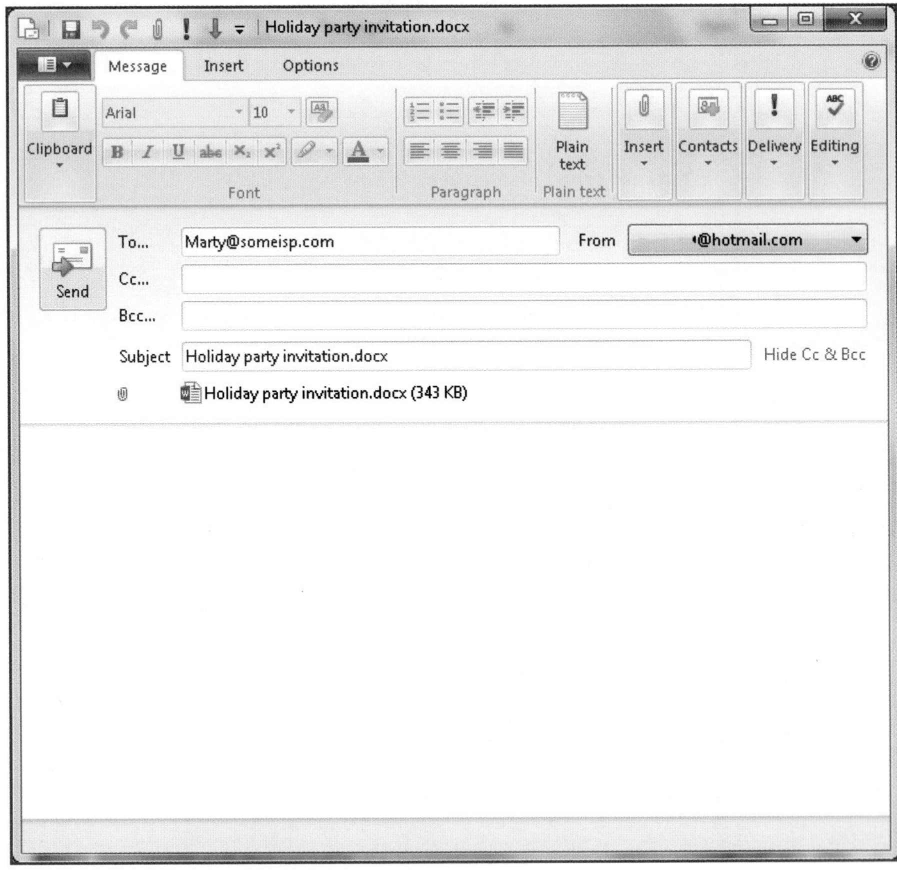

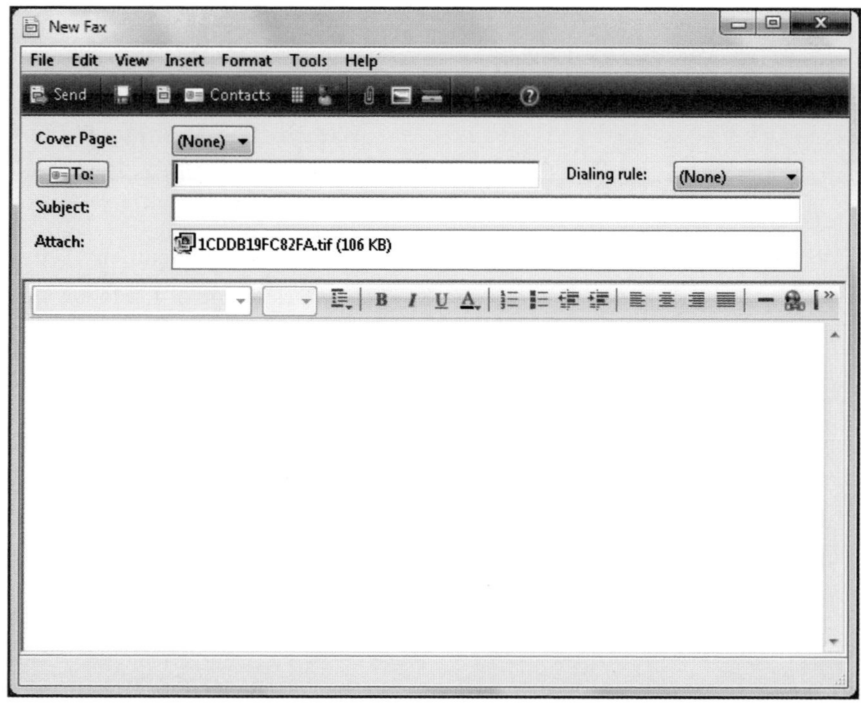

Figure 5-10: **Now that we have email, faxing has become less popular, but it is still useful.**

MERGE LISTS WITH LETTERS AND ENVELOPES

The *Mail Merge* feature allows you to combine a mailing name list with a document to send the same Word document to a number of people. You can merge a mailing list with letters, envelopes, labels, and email messages. A mail merge combines two kinds of documents: the *main document,* which is the text of the document—for example, the body of a letter—and the *data source,* which is the information that changes with each copy of the document—for example, the individual names and addresses of the people who will be receiving the letter.

The main document has two parts: static text and merge fields. *Static text* is text that does not change—for example, the body of a letter. *Merge fields* are placeholders that indicate where information from the list or data source goes. For example, in a form letter, "Dear" would be static text, while <<First Name>> <<Last Name>> are merge fields. When the main document and the data source are combined, the result is "Dear John Doe," "Dear Jane Smith," and so on.

The following sections will show you how to create a data source, create a main document, and then merge them together using the six-step Mail Merge Wizard. You can also start out with an existing main document, an existing data source, or both and just use the parts of the wizard that you want to use.

1 2 3 4 5 6 7 8 9 10

TIP You cannot use the Mail Merge feature unless a document is open, although it can be a blank document.

NOTE Word also allows you to take a list other than a mailing list—a parts list, for example, and merge it with a document to create a catalog or directory.

Perform a Mail Merge Using the Wizard

You can compose the static text in a document first and then insert the merge fields, or you can compose the static text and insert the merge fields as you go. You cannot insert merge fields into a main document until you have created the data source and associated it with your main document.

The mail-merge process consists of the following six steps, which are described in the following sections:

1. Select a document type (letter, envelope, or labels, for instance).
2. Identify the starting document, which may be blank to start with.
3. Select recipients (the data source), which can be an existing or new name list you will create now.
4. Finalize the main document, adding merge fields.
5. Preview the merge.
6. Complete the merge.

Select the Type and Identify the Document

To begin the mail-merge process:

1. In Word, open the document you want to use as your primary document, or open a new document.
2. Click **Mailings | Start Mail Merge** in the Start Mail Merge group, and click **Step By Step Mail Merge Wizard**. The Mail Merge task pane is displayed, as shown in Figure 5-11.

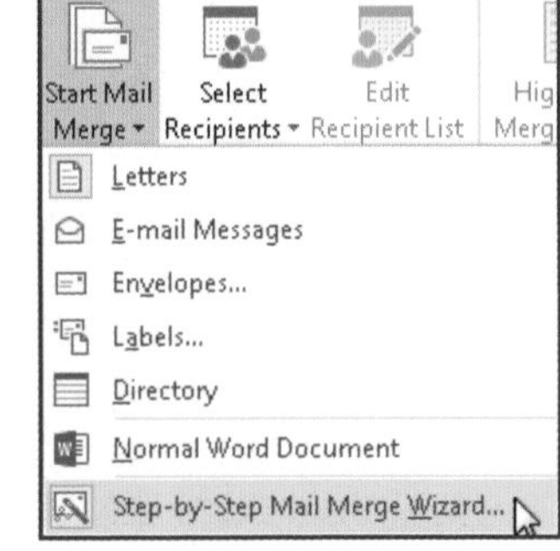

3. In the Select Document Type area, select one of the following options:
   - **Letters** are form letters designed to be sent to multiple people.
   - **E-mail Messages** are form letters designed to be sent to multiple people via email.
   - **Envelopes** are envelopes addressed to multiple people.
   - **Labels** are labels addressed to multiple people.
   - **Directory** is a collection of information regarding multiple items, such as a parts catalog or phone directory.
4. Click **Next: Starting Document** at the bottom of the task pane.
5. In the Select Starting Document area, select one of the following options:

   - **Use The Current Document** uses the currently open document as the main document for the mail merge (it can initially be blank).
   - **Start From A Template** uses a template you designate as the basis for the main document of the mail merge.

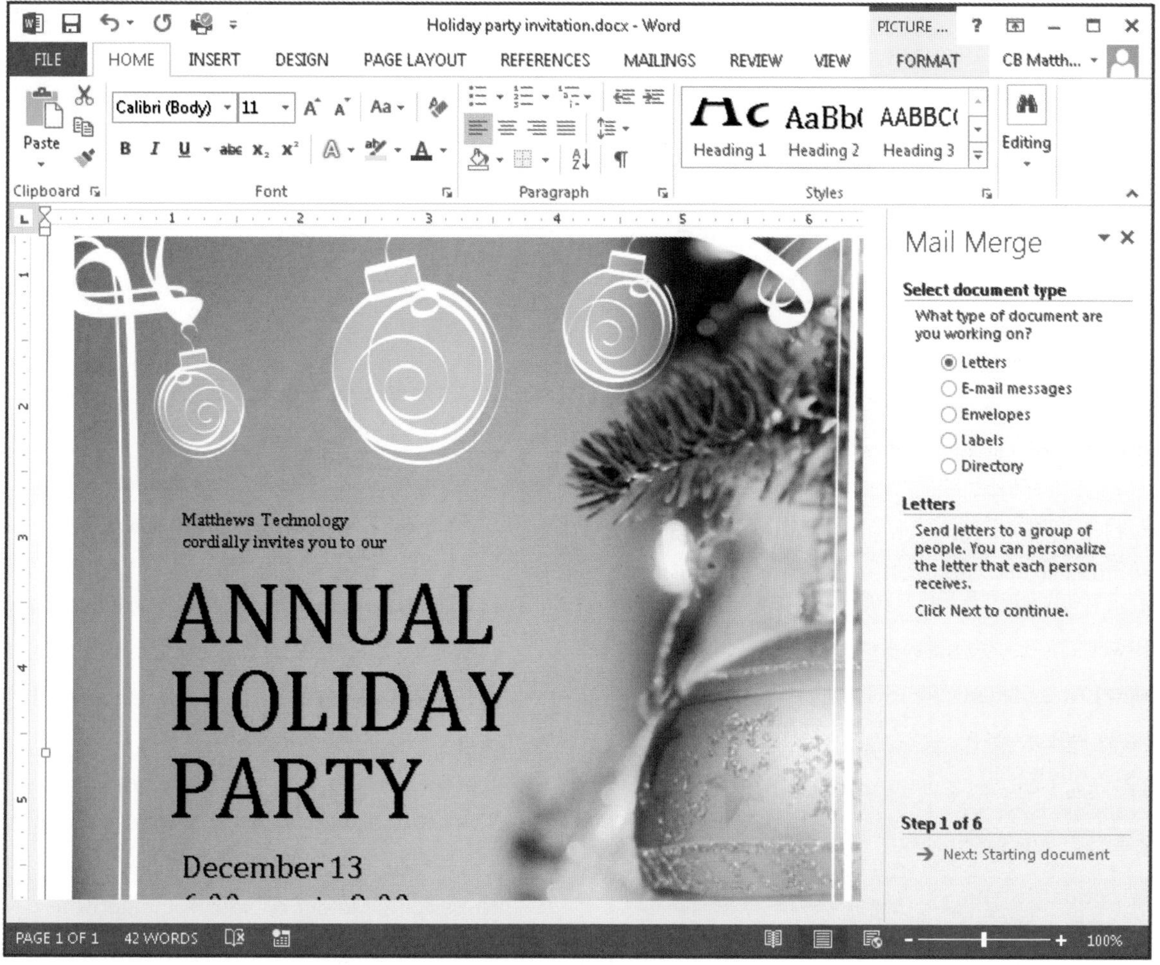

Figure 5-11: ***The Mail Merge task pane is where you begin the merge process.***

- **Start From Existing Document** uses an existing document you can retrieve from your computer or network and designate as the main document for the mail merge.

6. Click **Next: Select Recipients**.

Select Recipients

Your recipients are a name and address list, which is a data source. A data source has two parts: fields and records. A *field* is a category of information. For example, in a mailing list, First Name, Last Name, and Street Address are examples of fields. A *record* is a set of information across the fields for an individual. For example, in a mailing list, the record for John Doe would include information for all the relevant fields for this individual—his first and last name, street address, city, state, and ZIP code.

To set up a name and address list continuing from the previous section:

1. Having clicked **Next: Select Recipients** at the bottom of the task pane, now, in the Select Recipients area, you have these options:
   - **Use An Existing List** Allows you to browse for an existing name list that you have already created.
   - **Select From Outlook Contacts** Provides an opportunity for you to choose a Contacts folder from your Outlook contacts to use as a starting point in establishing your data source.
   - **Type A New List** Allows you to create a new list. These are the steps we'll continue to describe, since many of the steps in using existing lists or contacts are used here as well.

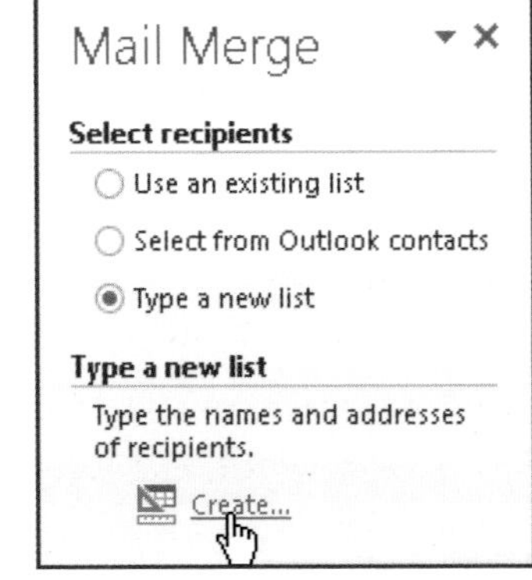

2. Click **Type A New List**, and then click **Create** in the Type A New List area. The New Address List dialog box appears, as shown in Figure 5-12.
3. You have these options as you enter the information for the first record in the fields you want to use:
   - Press **TAB** to move from field to field, or press **SHIFT+TAB** to move back to the previous field.
   - Click **New Entry** to add a new record for the next entry.
   - Click **Customize Column** to delete some of the columns or reorder them to facilitate entering data.

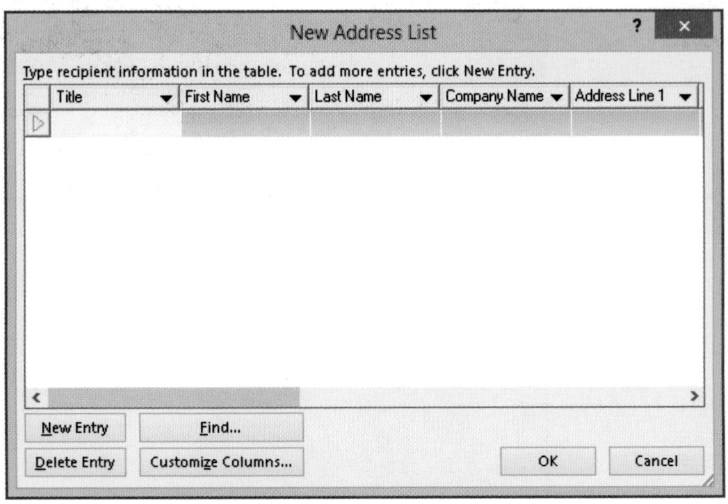

Figure 5-12: ***Use the New Address List dialog box to create your mailing list.***

   - Click **Delete Entry** to delete an existing entry.
   - To correct an incorrect entry, just click in the field and change it.
   - Click **Find** to find a particular entry, perhaps to see if you've already entered that name.
4. Repeat entering names and addresses until you have added all the records you want to your list. When you are done, click **OK**.
5. A Save Address List dialog box appears. Type a filename for the list, select the folder on your computer where you want to save it, and click **Save**.
6. The Mail Merge Recipients dialog box appears, as shown in Figure 5-13. You have these choices:
   - To delete names you do not want to include in the list, clear the check boxes next to those recipients.
   - To make further changes to the name list, select the filename in the Data Source list box, and click **Edit**. When you're finished, click **OK** to close it, and click **Yes** to update your recipient list.

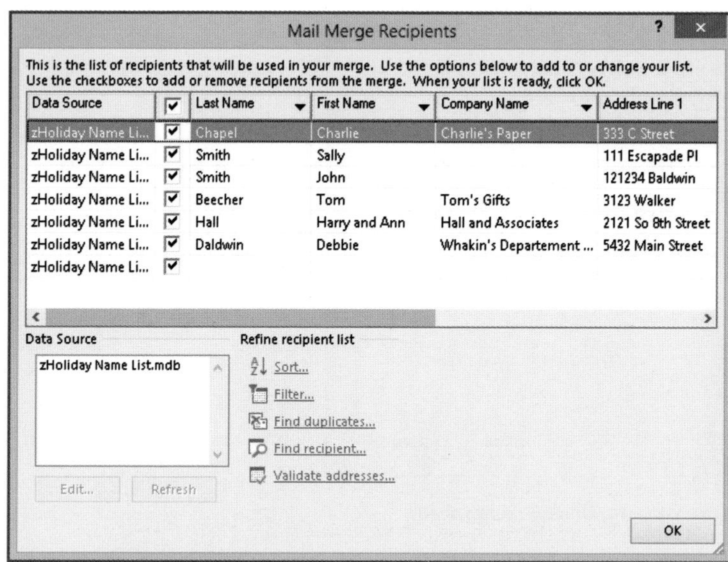

Figure 5-13: ***Use the Mail Merge Recipients dialog box to manage your mailing list prior to completing the merge.***

- To sort the recipient list using multiple fields, click **Sort** and then click the down arrows next to the sort levels to specify the order of the sort. Click **Ascending** or **Descending** for each sort level. (See the accompanying Tip for sorting single fields.)
- Click **Filter** to select certain records to include in the list—perhaps you only want to include people within a particular business or ZIP code.
- Click **Find Duplicates** to see if you have included more than one record for a recipient.
- Click **Find Recipient** to find the record for one entry.
- Click **Validate Addresses** to verify your address. To do this you'll need special software installed. Click this option to find out more.

7. Click **OK** to close the Mail Merge Recipients dialog box.
8. Click **Next: Write Your Letter** at the bottom of the Mail Merge task pane.

TIP Sort the merge recipients by clicking the field name at the top of the list that will provide the sort order. For example, if you want the list ordered alphabetically by last name, click **Last Name**.

Finalize the Main Document

After creating the data source, you need to finalize the main document and insert the merge fields. This section will tell you how, after creating the main document, to insert merge fields in general. The example uses a letter; additional sections will show you how to use merge fields when creating envelopes and labels.

1. Continuing from the previous two sections, having clicked **Next: Write Your Letter** at the bottom of the Mail Merge task pane, you're ready to continue. In the document pane, if it has not already been done, write the body of the letter—don't necessarily worry about the addressee and the greeting until you're satisfied with the text. (Although you can enter the fields and text together if you find it makes more sense to you.)
2. Place the cursor in the document where you want to insert a merge field, such as the addressee. Do one of the following:
   - Select one of the three items in the top of the Mail Merge task pane if you want to insert a predefined block of merge fields, such as a complete address or a greeting. If you select anything other than More Items, a dialog box will appear and ask you to select options and formatting for that item (see Figure 5-14). You can preview the block

Figure 5-14: **You can customize the predefined field blocks to meet your mail-merge needs.**

by clicking the Preview arrows. When the block is the way you want it, click **OK**.

- Click **More Items** (the fourth item in the list) to insert an individual merge field. The Insert Merge Field dialog box appears. Verify that **Database Fields** is selected, and then select the field that you want to insert (for example, First Name or Last Name). Click **Insert** to insert the merge field into your document. Click **Close** when you are done inserting all the fields you need.

3. Add commas, spaces, and other punctuation marks to the address as needed. If you have some conditional fields that are printed only if some condition is met, like printing the country if it isn't the "United States," see "Use Rules." Figure 5-15 shows an example of a holiday invitation with merge fields inserted.

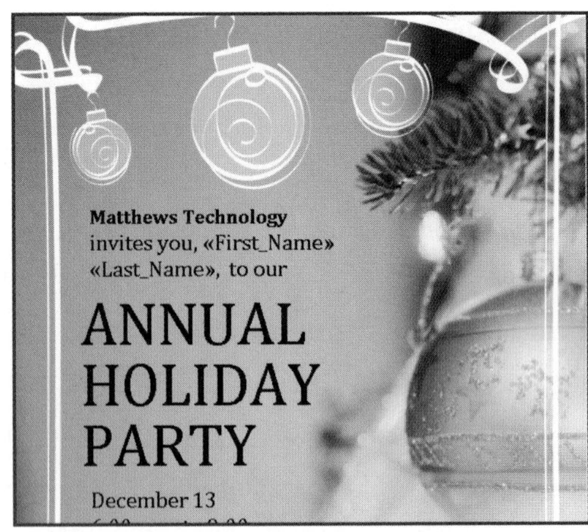

Matthews Technology
invites you, «First_Name»
«Last_Name», to our
ANNUAL
HOLIDAY
PARTY
December 13

Figure 5-15: **Merge fields are a convenient way to create a form letter for multiple recipients.**

4. Click **Next: Preview Your Letters** at the bottom of the Mail Merge task pane.

Preview the Merge

Prior to actually completing the merge, the Mail Merge task pane presents you with an opportunity to review what the merged document will look like. This way, you can go back and make any last-minute changes to fine-tune your merge.

To preview a merge:

1. Continuing from the previous sections, click **Next: Preview Your Letters** at the bottom of the Mail Merge task pane.

2. Use the right and left arrow buttons under Preview Your Letters in the Mail Merge task pane to scroll through the recipient list.
3. Click **Find A Recipient** to enter a recipient name and search for it in all fields or a particular field.

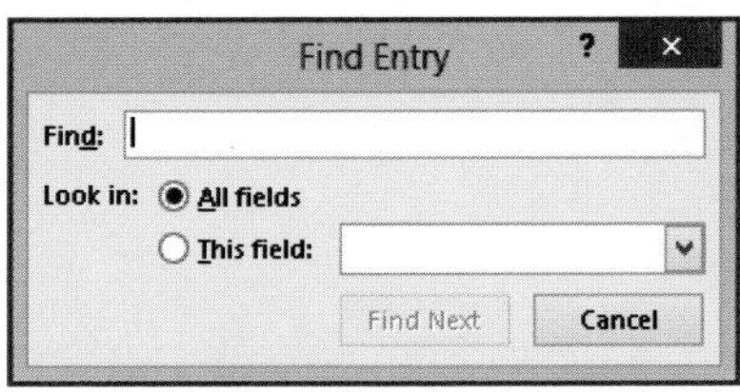

4. If you want to exclude a particular recipient from the merge, while that recipient is displayed, click **Exclude This Recipient**. (You can add the excluded recipient back by placing a check mark next to the name in the Mail Merge Recipient dialog box, which is displayed when you click **Edit Recipient List**.)

   –Or–

   Click **Edit Recipient List** to edit a particular recipient's information. If you click this link, the Mail Merge Recipients dialog box appears again (see Figure 5-13). Click the filename under the lower data source, click **Edit**, modify the information, click **OK**, and click **Yes** to update the recipient list. Click **OK** again to close the Mail Merge Recipients dialog box.
5. Click **Next: Complete The Merge** at the bottom of the Mail Merge task pane.

Complete the Merge

The last step in performing a mail merge is to complete the merge; that is, to accept the preview of how the merge will look and direct Word to perform the merge. The result of this step is that you will create and save, if you want, a document assigned to a particular recipient list, which can be printed and also modified and used again in the future.

To complete a merge:

1. Continuing from the previous sections, click **Next: Complete The Merge** at the bottom of the Mail Merge task pane.
2. If you wish, click **Edit Individual Letters** and select the letters to edit. You can use this to make unique changes to specific documents. The merged letters will appear as their own document in a new Word window, where you can make any changes you want and then print and save them as you normally would.

3. Click **Print** in the Merge area. The Merge To Printer dialog box appears.

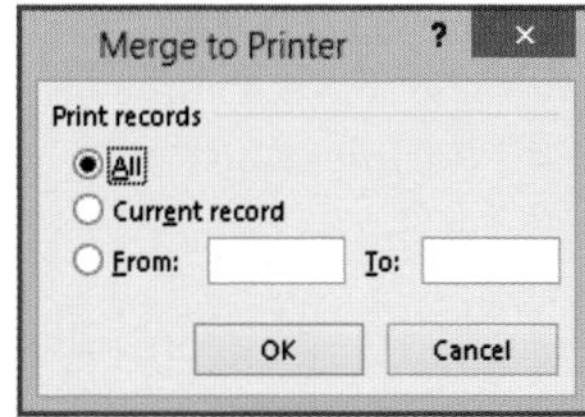

4. Select one of the following options:
   - **All** prints all records in the data source that have been included in the merge.
   - **Current Record** prints only the record that is displayed in the document window.
   - **From/To** prints a range of records you specify. Enter the starting and ending numbers in the text boxes.
5. Click **OK** when ready. The Print dialog box appears.
6. Select the print options you want, and click **OK**. Your merged document is printed.
7. When you are ready, click **File | Save** to save your merge document.

Use Rules

Rules (also called *Word Fields*) apply to merge fields or static text if certain conditions are met. One of the most common variable fields is the IF/THEN/ELSE rule. The IF rule performs one of two alternative actions, depending on a condition you specify. For example, the statement, "If the weather is sunny, we'll go to the beach; if not, we'll go to the museum," specifies a condition that *must* be met (sunny weather) for a certain action to take place (going to the beach). If the condition is not met, an alternative action occurs (going to the museum).

This is an example of how using an IF rule in Word looks with the field codes turned on:

{IF { MERGEFIELD City } = "Seattle" "Please call our office." "Please call our distributor."}

This works as follows: If the current data record contains "Seattle" in the City field, then the first text ("Please call our office.") is printed in the merged document that results from that data record. If "Seattle" is not in the City field, then the second set of text ("Please call our distributor.") is printed. Using a rule is easy and doesn't require writing such a complex statement at all.

To insert a variable field into a merge document:

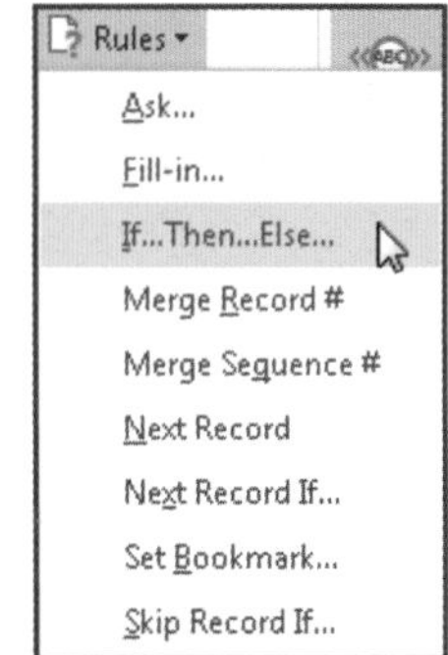

1. Position the insertion point where you want the rule.
2. Click **Mailings | Rules** [Rules] in the Write & Insert Fields group. A drop-down list appears.
3. Select the rule you want, for example, If…Then…Else.
4. The Insert Word Field dialog box appears. Fill in the text boxes with your criteria, and click **OK** when finished.

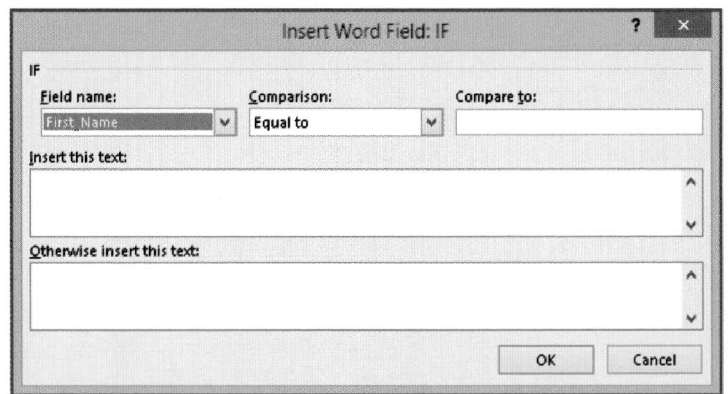

Merge to Envelopes

The process for merging to envelopes is similar to that for merging to letters: you must first define your envelope, type your return address if you don't have one defined, find your source of recipient addresses, insert the merge fields, preview your envelope results, finish the merge, and print the envelopes. This can be done with the Mail Merge Wizard, as described earlier with letters, or by using the options on the Mailings tab.

The following steps use the options on the Mailing tab.

1. In Word, open a new document. Click **Mailings | Start Mail Merge | Envelopes** in the Start Mail Merge group. The Envelope Options dialog box appears, as shown in Figure 5-16.
2. Select the options you want from the Envelope Options and Printing Options tabs. (See "Print an Envelope" earlier in this chapter to see an explanation for the Print options.) Click **OK** when finished.
3. An envelope will appear with your default return address in the upper-left corner (if you have entered one, see "Print an Envelope" earlier in this chapter) and, if you have Show Paragraph Marks turned on, an indented paragraph mark where you will put the addressee. Type a return address, if needed, or make any changes you want to the return address and any other static text that you want. This will be printed on all envelopes.
4. Click **Mailings | Select Recipients** in the Start Mail Merge group, choose the type of list you are using, and follow the steps needed to identify or create the list. (See the earlier section "Select Recipients.")

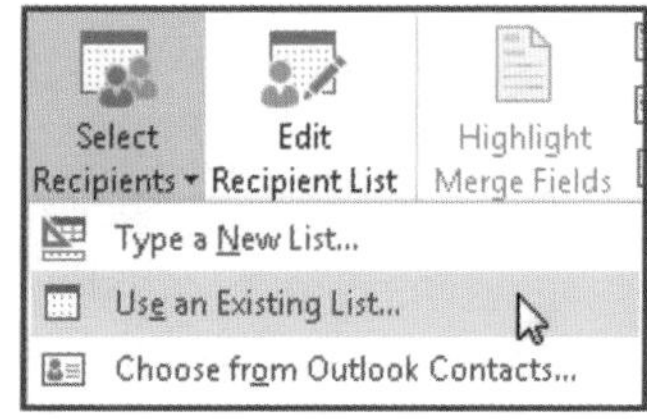

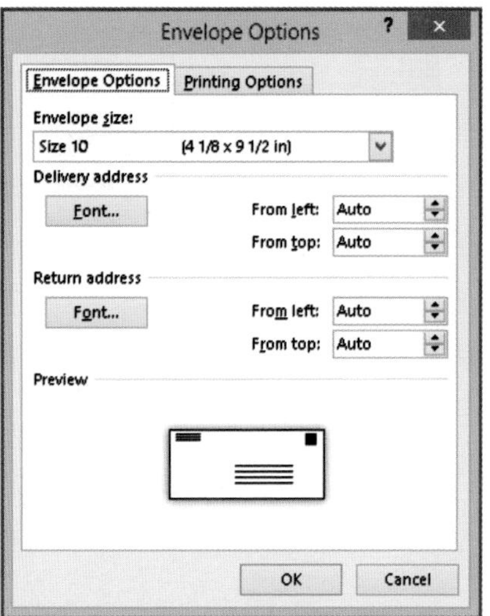

***Figure 5-16:** Word provides almost as many envelope sizes as it does paper sizes that you can use in printing.*

5. When you have your recipient list ready, click in the addressee area of the envelope. You'll see the address text box defined. Then click **Mailing | Address Block** or **Insert Merge Field** in the Write & Insert Fields group, depending on whether you want to work with the address as a single predefined block or a set of discrete elements, and complete the steps needed to place the merge fields on the envelope. You may need to insert spaces and punctuation after you've inserted all the merge fields. If you need help, see "Finalize the Main Document" earlier in this chapter.
6. Click **Mailings | Preview Results** in the Preview Results group. Your envelope should look similar to that shown in Figure 5-17. Use the **Previous Record** and **Next Record** arrows, or the record number text box to look through your merged envelopes.
7. When you are ready, click **Mailings | Finish & Merge** in the Finish group. If you want to make changes to some of the envelopes before they are printed, click **Edit Individual Documents**. The data will be

1 2 3 4 5 6 7 8 9 10

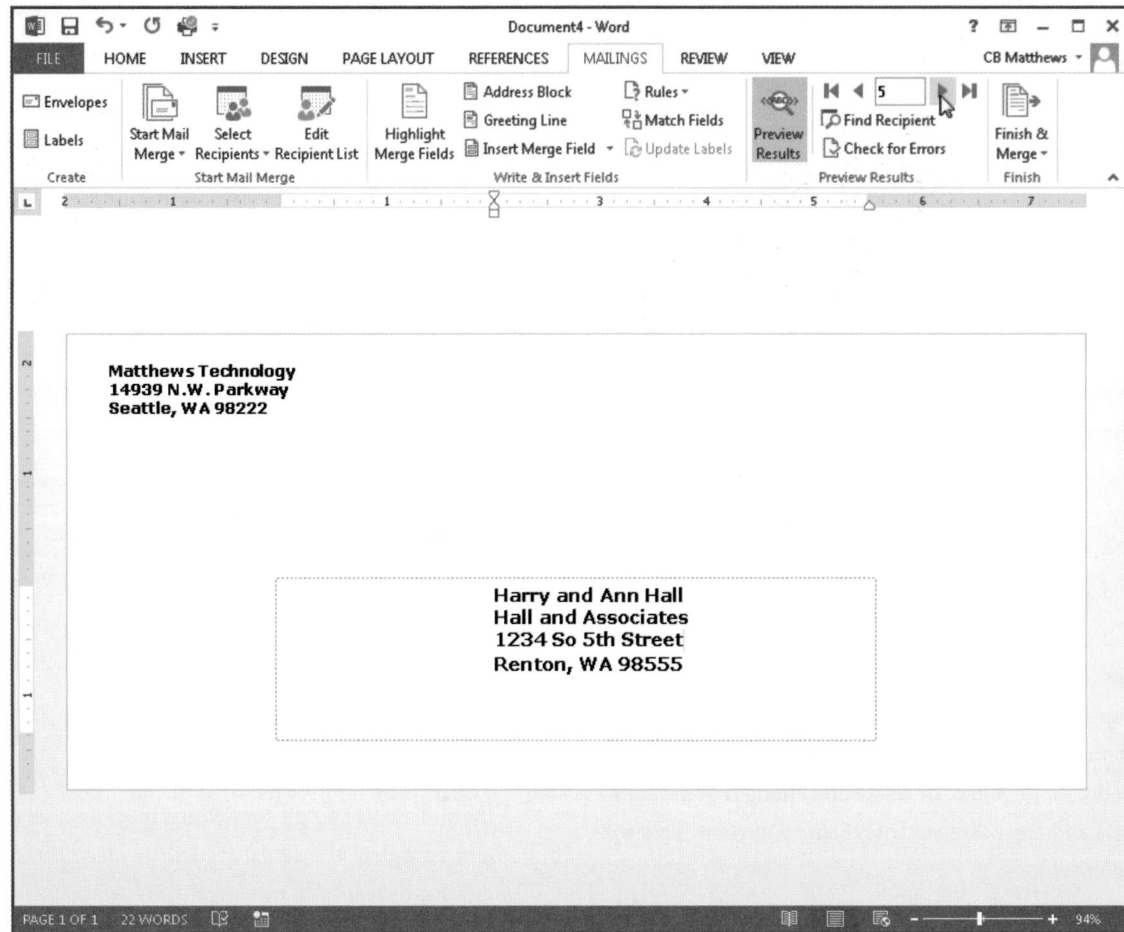

Figure 5-17: ***You can see how your merged envelope will look when completed prior to printing.***

merged to a new document that can then be modified. Otherwise, click **Print Documents**. Choose the records to be printed, and click **OK** to open the Print dialog box, where you can choose your printer options.

Merge to Labels

The process for merging to labels is similar to that for merging to letters and envelopes, and can be done with the Mail Merge Wizard, as described earlier with letters, or by using the options on the Mailings tab, as described with envelopes. The following steps use the options on the Mailing tab.

1. In Word, open a new document. Click **Mailings | Start Mail Merge | Labels** in the Start Mail Merge group. The Label Options dialog box appears.

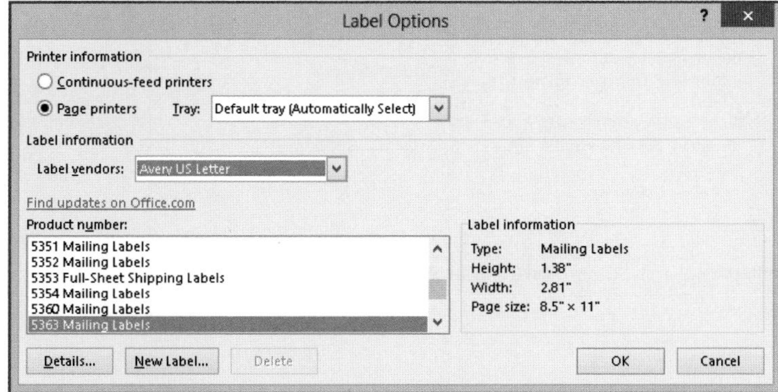

2. Select the options you want. Be sure to identify the label vendor you want for the specific label, or click **New Label** for a custom one. Click **OK** when finished. A page formatted for labels will appear in Word—you may not see the formatting just yet.
3. Click **Mailings | Select Recipients** in the Start Mail Merge group, choose the type of list you are using, and follow the steps needed to identify or create the list. (See the earlier section "Select Recipients.") The page should show <<Next Record>>merge fields.

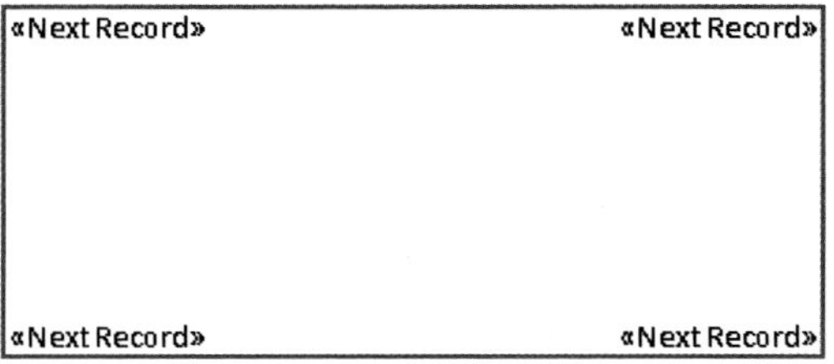

4. When you have your recipient list ready, click in the empty space for the first label. Then, click **Mailings |** and **Address Block** or **Insert Merge Field** in the Write & Insert Fields group, depending on whether you want to work with the address as a single predefined block or a set of discrete elements, and complete the steps needed to place the merge fields on the envelope. See "Finalize the Main Document" earlier in this chapter.
5. Click **Mailings | Update Labels** in the Write & Insert Fields group to copy the fields in the first label to all the labels, as shown in Figure 5-18. In that case, the individual address fields are treated as one block.
6. Click **Mailings | Preview Results** in the Preview Results group. Your labels should look something like this:

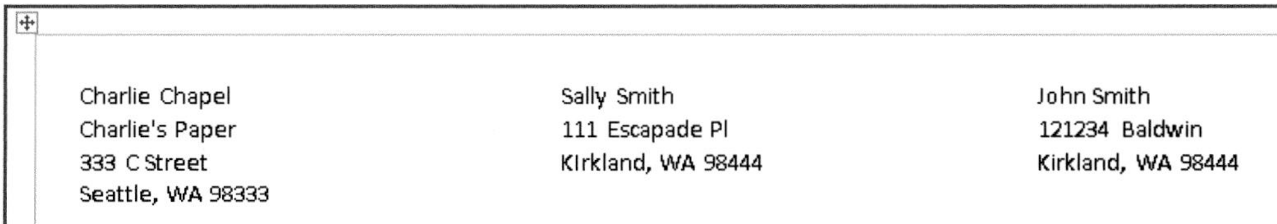

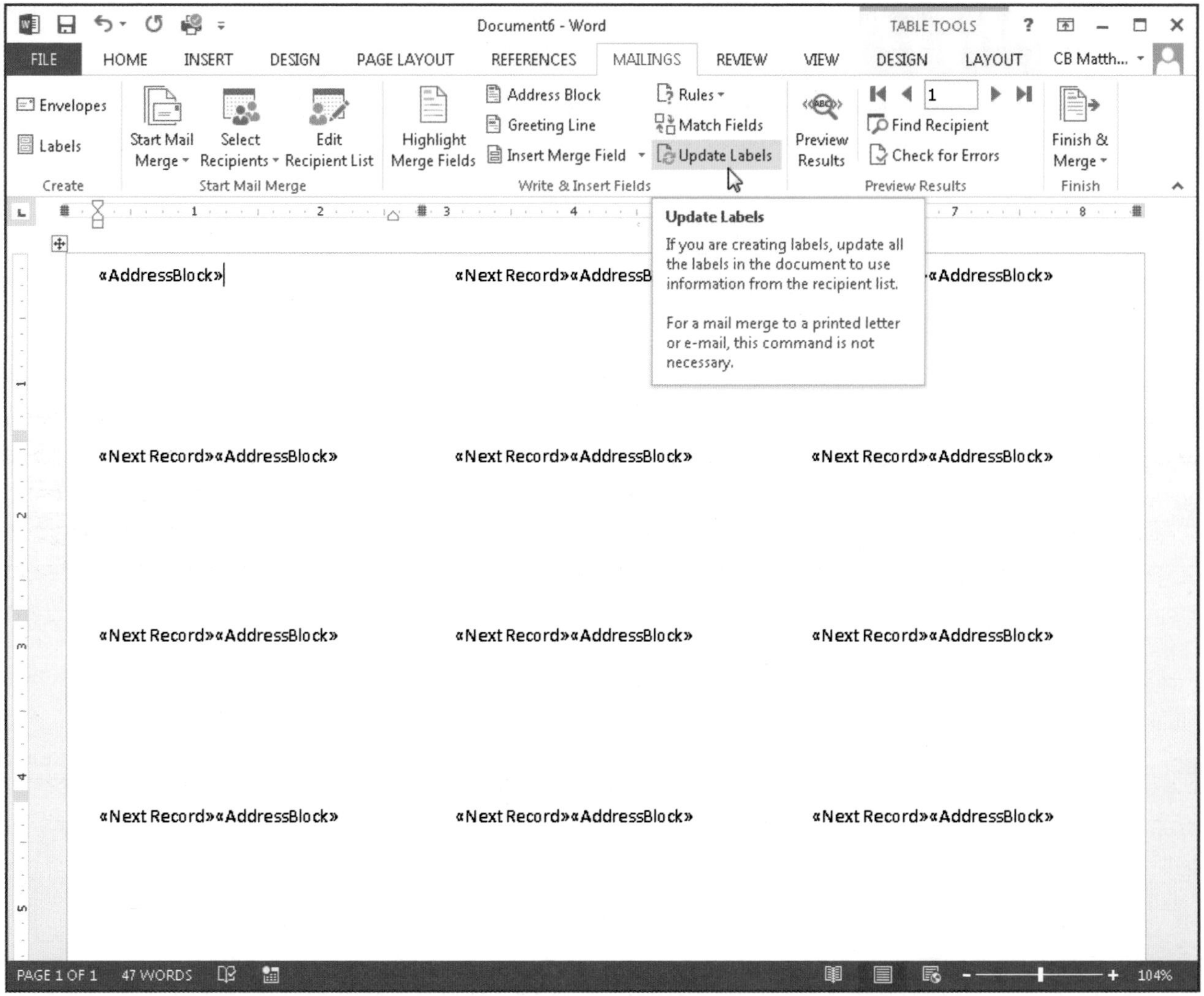

Figure 5-18: ***You can replicate the fields (or Address Block field as in this case) in the first label to all the other labels.***

7. When you are ready, click **Mailings | Finish & Merge** in the Finish group. If you want to make changes to some of the envelopes before they are printed, click **Edit Individual Documents**. The data will be merged to a new document that can then be modified. Otherwise, click **Print Documents**. Choose the records to be printed, and click **OK** to open the Print dialog box, where you can choose how the envelopes will be printed.

QuickSteps to...

- Create a Table
- Use Table Tools
- Select Tables, Rows, Columns, or Cells
- Change the Table Size
- Change Column Width and Row Height
- Enter Information into Tables
- Sort Data
- Move and Copy Tables, Columns, and Rows
- Calculate Values Using Formulas
- Convert Tables to Text and Text to Tables
- Repeat Header Rows
- Remove a Table
- Format Content
- Merge and Split Cells
- Change a Table's Alignment
- Wrap Text Around a Table
- Change Cell Margins
- Apply Shading and Border Effects
- Apply Styles to a Table Automatically

Chapter 6

Using Tables

Documents can be composed of text only, but using visual elements to support information helps emphasize, organize, and clarify your written words. *Tables* provide a familiar column-and-row matrix that lets you easily define terms, list items, and lay out data in a convenient and organized manner. Word provides extensive features that support creating, using, and formatting tables to accomplish a variety of purposes. (See Chapters 7 and 8 for more information on the use of tables—Chapter 7 covers graphics, and Chapter 8 describes using charts.)

CREATE TABLES

Tables allow you to divide a portion of a page into rows and columns that create *cells* at their intersections. Tables can be used to systematically arrange information in rows and columns, or they can be used to lay out text and graphics in a document.

Create a Table

When you create a table, you can specify the number of rows and columns in it. In addition, depending on how you created the table, you can select how the columns' width is determined and choose a table style. In all cases, you can easily modify the table attributes after the original table displays in your document. With the document open in Word, place the insertion point at the appropriate location in the document where you want a table.

1 2 3 4 5 6 7 8 9 10

QuickFacts

Dissecting a Table

A table comes with an extensive vocabulary of terms that describe many of its elements, features, and how it's used, as shown in Figure 6-1.

Some of the ways that you can use tables are:

- Tabular data display, with or without cell borders
- Side-by-side columns of text
- Aligning labels and boxes for forms
- Separating and positioning text and graphics
- Placing borders around text or graphics
- Placing text on both sides of graphics or vice versa
- Adding color to backgrounds, text, and graphics

Insert a Table Quickly

The Insert tab Tables group offers a variety of methods for creating a table using the default settings. The quickest method is to use the Insert tab.

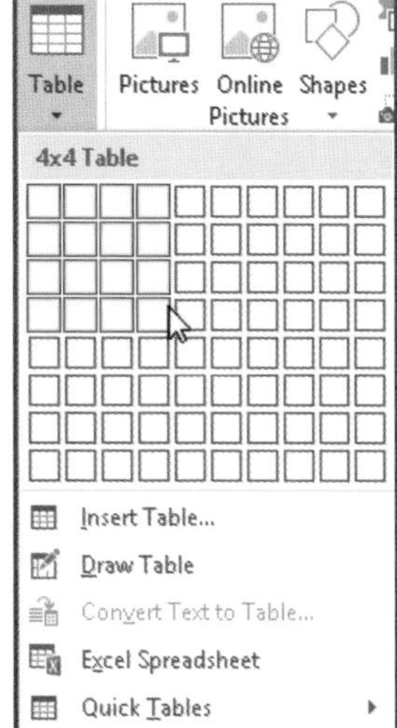

1. Click **Insert | Table** down arrow in the Tables group. In the drop-down menu that opens, click the lower-right cell needed to give you the number of rows and columns you want.
2. Type the information you want in the table, pressing TAB as needed to move from cell to cell (see "Enter Information into Tables" later in this chapter).

TIP If you want to insert a table that is larger than the 8 rows by 10 columns shown in the Table drop-down menu, you can easily add rows or columns to an initial table that you create from the menu. See "Change the Table Size" later in this chapter.

Insert a Table from a Dialog Box

The Insert Table dialog box provides several options when initially setting up a table.

1. Click **Insert | Table** down arrow in the Tables group. In the drop-down menu that opens, click **Insert Table**. The Insert Table dialog box appears, as shown in Figure 6-2.

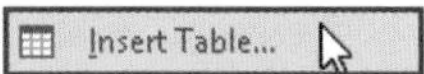

   a. Under Table Size, click the respective spinners or enter a value to determine the number of rows and columns in the table.

   b. Under AutoFit Behavior, choose a fixed column width by clicking the spinner or entering a value (*Auto*, the default, sizes the columns equally so that they fill the available width of the table), have Word set each column's width to fit the contents in each column, or have Word size the columns to fit the window the table is in. (See "Change Column Width and Row Height" later in the chapter for more ways to adjust column width after a table is created.)

2. If you want the size settings you choose to apply to future tables you create, select the **Remember Dimensions For New Tables** check box.
3. Click **OK** to display the table in your document.

Draw a Table

The most hands-on way to create a table is to draw it.

1. With the document open in Word, scroll to the location where you want to draw a table.

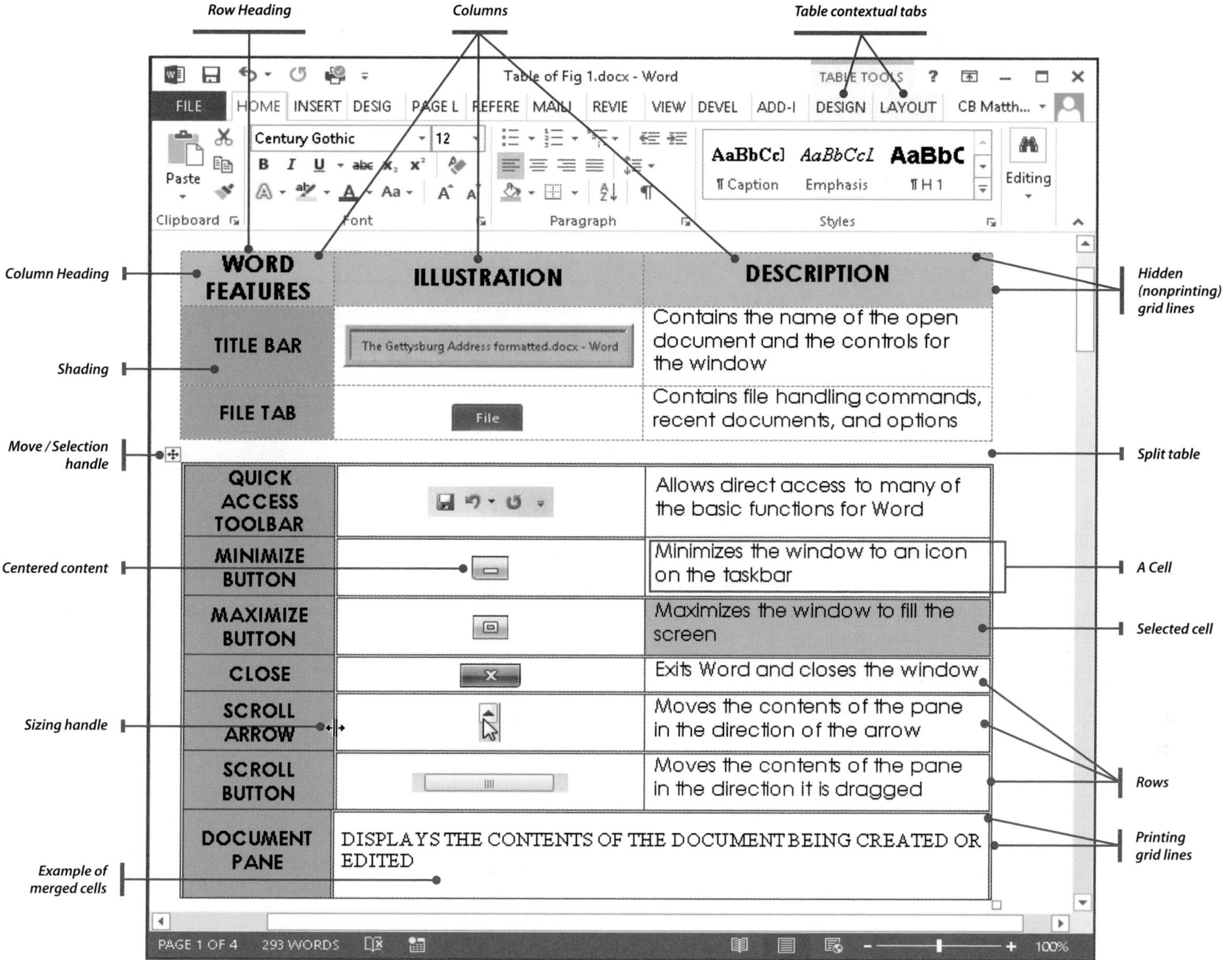

Figure 6-1: ***Tables have a vocabulary all their own.***

Figure 6-2: ***You can determine several table attributes when creating a table using the Insert Table dialog box.***

2. Click **Insert | Table** down arrow in the Tables group. In the drop-down menu that opens, click **Draw Table**. The mouse pointer turns into a pencil.
3. Place the pencil-shaped pointer where you want the upper-left corner of the table, and drag it diagonally across and down the page, creating a table outline that is the height and width of the outer border of the table you want.
4. Create the columns and rows by dragging the pencil-shaped pointer, placing the row or column where you want it in the table. You can make the columns and rows the size you want, and place them however the content demands.

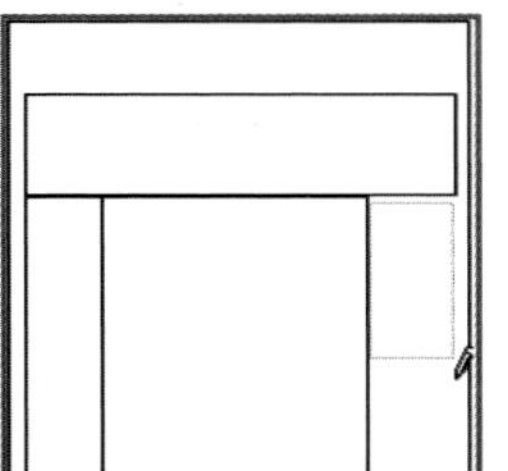

5. Repeat for as many rows and columns that you want.
6. When you are done drawing, press **ESC** to return the pencil-shaped pointer to the I-beam pointer.
7. If you want to adjust the location of any of the outer borders or the row or column borders, point at the border you want to adjust. The mouse pointer will turn into a double-headed resize arrow. Drag the selected line to the location you want it.
8. Enter the information you want in the table, pressing **TAB** as needed to move from cell to cell.

NOTE It is not important to get the initial size and grid perfectly aligned. You can adjust them after the table has been drawn.

NOTE If you make a mistake or change your mind, you can erase individual table segments with the Table Eraser. See the Note near "Remove Cells, Rows, and Columns," later in this chapter.

Use Table Tools

Once you have created a table, you have two sets of tools with which to work with it: the table contextual tabs in the ribbon and the context menus that open when you right-click in a table.

Use the Table's Contextual Tabs

When you create a table in Word 2013, the ribbon automatically displays two table-related tabs: Table Tools Design and Table Tools Layout. The Table Tools Design tab, shown in Figure 6-3, allows you to apply various styles to tables, as well as apply shading, customize the border, and draw and erase tables or their segments.

The Table Tools Layout tab, shown in Figure 6-4, allows you to modify tables in many different ways, including selecting, deleting, and inserting various table elements, as well as working with cells and their contents.

Both contextual tabs are discussed throughout this chapter.

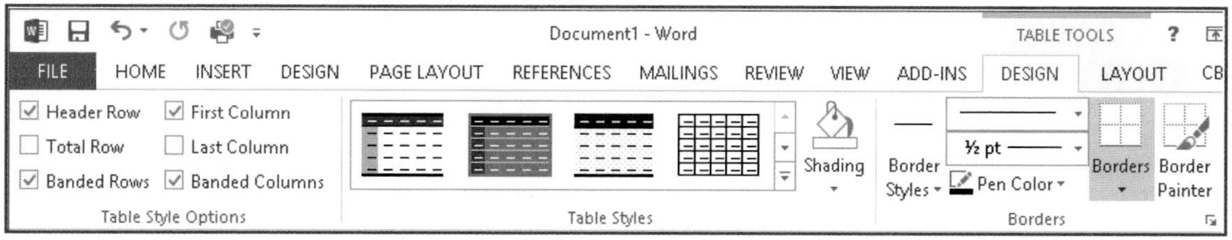

Figure 6-3: ***The Table Tools Design tab is used to change the style of a table.***

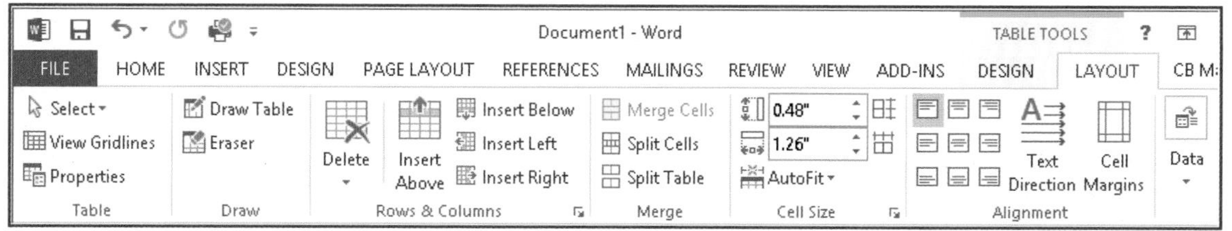

Figure 6-4: ***The Table Tools Layout tab is used to modify tables.***

Use the Table's Context Menu

When you right-click a table or its contents, you see a context menu that, depending on what you clicked, may look similar to Figure 6-5. This context menu allows you to do many of the formatting tasks in the Home tab, as well as many of the table modification tasks in the Layout tab.

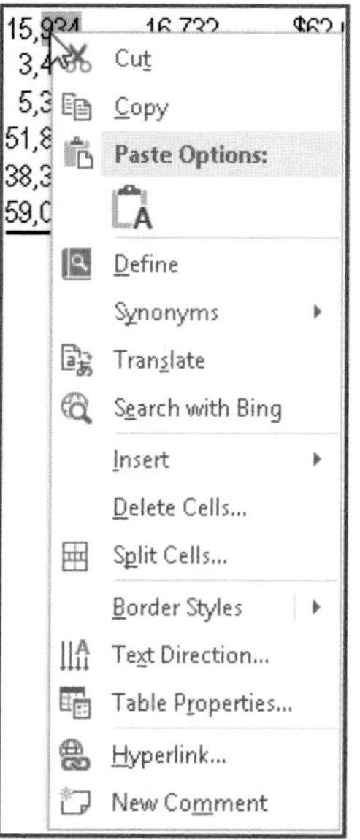

Figure 6-5: ***The context menu allows you to format and modify tables.***

Select Tables, Rows, Columns, or Cells

Before you can perform many actions in a table, you must first select the element you are working with. With the table open in Word, perform any of the actions discussed in the following sections.

Select a Table

Click inside the table and then click the **Move Handle** icon located in the upper-left area of the table.

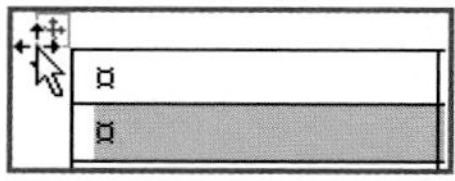

–Or–

Click anywhere in the table, and then click **Table Tools Layout | Select** in the Table group, and click **Select Table**.

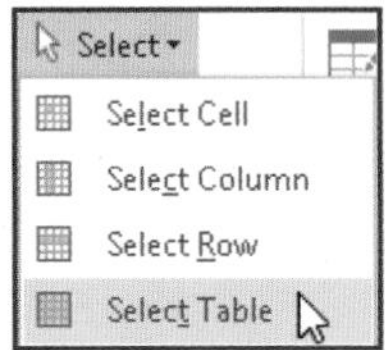

Select Rows or Columns by Clicking

- Move the mouse pointer to the left border, if selecting rows, so that the pointer becomes an angled rightward-pointing arrow, and then click.

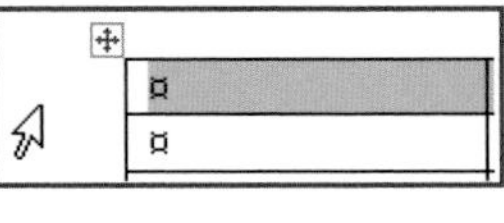

- Move the mouse pointer to the top border, if selecting columns, so that the pointer becomes a vertical black arrow, and then click.

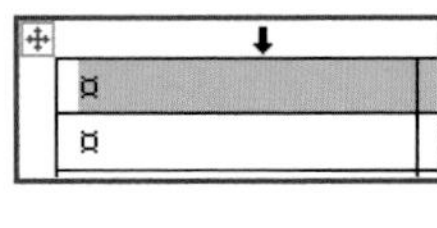

- Click anywhere in the table, and then click **Table Tools Layout | Select** in the Table group, and click **Select Column** or **Select Row**.

Select Rows or Columns by Dragging

Move the mouse to the first cell of the row or column to be selected, and drag to the last cell. You can easily select multiple rows and/or columns this way.

Select a Cell by Clicking

1. Inside the cell, move the mouse pointer to the left border so that the pointer becomes an angled rightward-pointing black arrow.
2. Click the mouse to select the cell.

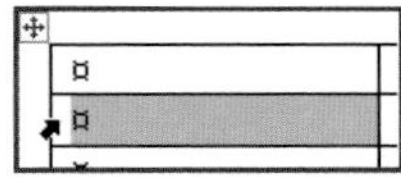

Superior Office Supply	1st Qtr	2nd Qtr	3rd Qtr	4thQtr	Total
Paper Supplies	$23,567	$35,938	$38,210	$39,876	$137,591
Writing Instruments	5,482	5,836	5,923	6,082	$23,323
Cards and Books	14,986	15,021	15,934	16,732	$62,673
Forms	2,342	2,756	3,456	3,678	$12,232
Labels	3,522	4,621	5,361	5,476	$18,980
Equipment	45,328	47,934	51,830	55,638	$200,730
Furniture	37,278	38,429	38,328	39,103	$153,138
Total	$132,505	$150,535	$159,042	$166,585	$608,667

Click here…
…and drag…
…to here to select a range of cells

Figure 6-6: ***The fastest way to select contiguous cells is to drag across them.***

Select a Cell from the Menu

1. Click your mouse in the cell you want selected.
2. Click **Table Tools Layout | Select**, and click **Select Cell**.

Select Cells by Dragging

Place your mouse pointer in the upper-leftmost cell you want to select, and drag down and to the right across the remaining cells in the range you want selected, as shown in Figure 6-6. (If you are left-handed, you might find it easier to click in the upper-rightmost cell and then drag down and to the left.)

Change the Table Size

Rows, columns, and cells can be added to a table using the Layout tab Rows & Columns group or the context menus. You can also change a table's size by removing elements, splitting a table, or resizing the overall dimensions.

Add Cells

Cells can be added to a table above and to the left of existing cells.

1. Select the cells adjacent to where you want to add the new cells. (To add a single cell, select only the cell below or to the right of where you want the new cell. If adding more than one cell, you can select

1 2 3 4 5 6 7 8 9 10

the number of cells you want added, and an equal number will be added above or to the left of your selection.) See "Select Tables, Rows, Columns, or Cells."

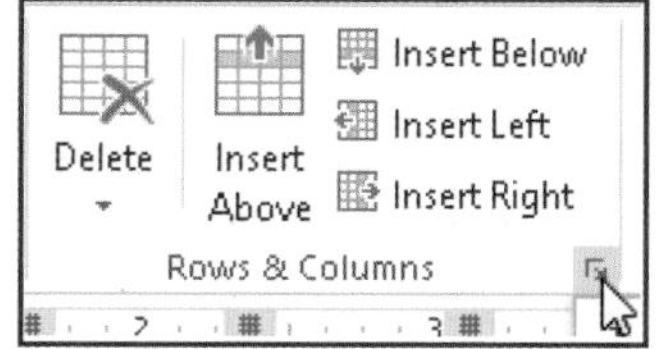

2. In the Layout tab Rows & Columns group, click the **Dialog Box Launcher**.

   –Or–

   Right-click the existing cell, and click **Insert | Insert Cells**.

   In either case, the Insert Cells dialog box appears.

3. In the Insert Cells dialog box, click **Shift Cells Right** (existing cells are "pushed" to the right, inserting the new cell or cells to the left of the existing cells).

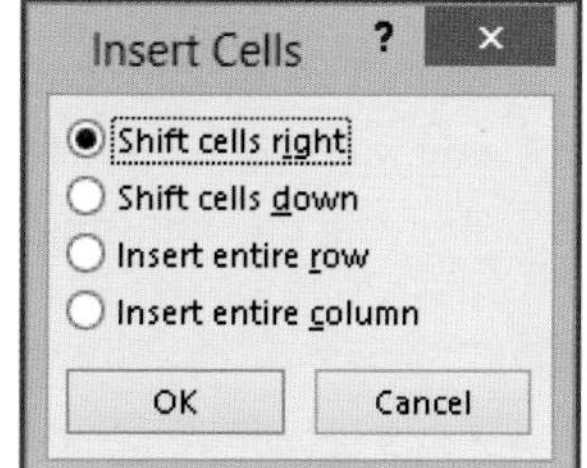

   –Or–

   Click **Shift Cells Down** (existing cells are "pushed" down, inserting the new cells above the existing cells).

4. Click **OK**.

CAUTION! It's usually better to add entire rows or columns instead of individual cells, especially when adding cells to a row. You can wind up with cells hanging to the right of your table that appear to be in a column of their own. Also, if your table contains data in a spreadsheet or list format, adding cells can easily jumble the data organization.

Insert Rows or Columns

You can quickly add rows or columns from either the Layout tab Rows & Columns group or the context menu.

1. Select the rows or columns in the table next to where you want to add rows or columns (the number of rows or columns added will equal the number of rows or columns selected).

2. Click **Table Tools Layout | Insert Above** in the Rows & Columns group, or **Insert Below** (for new rows) or **Insert Left** or **Insert Right** (for new columns).

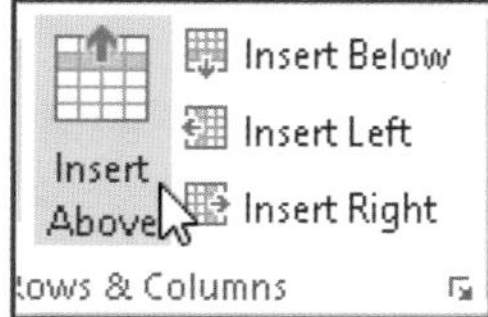

   –Or–

   Right-click an existing row or column and from the context menu, click **Insert | Insert Columns To The Left**, **Insert Columns To The Right**, **Insert Rows Above**, or **Insert Rows Below**.

Resize by Dragging

1. Click **View | Print Layout** in the Views group (the sizing handle doesn't display in other views).

2. Place your mouse over the table whose size you want to change, and drag the sizing handle (the double-headed arrow drags the handle) that appears in the lower-right corner of the table to increase or decrease the table size. The rows and columns increase or decrease proportionately within the constraints of the cell contents.

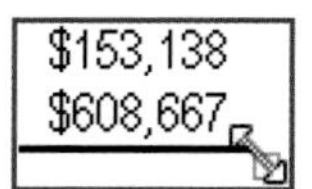

Add Rows at the Bottom of a Table

As you are entering information into a table and you reach the bottom-rightmost cell, simply pressing **TAB** will add another row to the table.

Remove Cells, Rows, and Columns

1. Select the cells, rows, or columns you want to remove (see "Select Tables, Rows, Columns, or Cells").

2. Right-click the selection. Depending on your selection, you can now:

   - Click **Delete Columns** to remove selected columns.

     –Or–

   - Click **Delete Rows** to remove selected rows.

–Or–

- Click **Delete Cells** to open the Delete Cells dialog box. Choose whether to fill the vacant area of the table by shifting cells to the left or up.

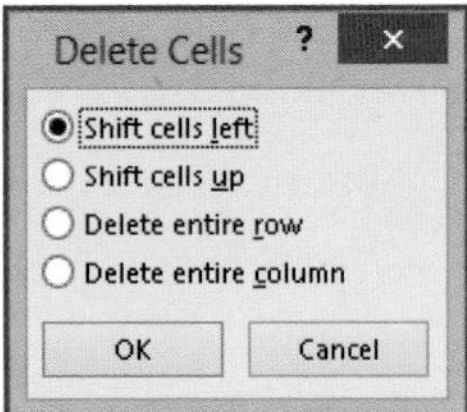

3. Click **OK**.

NOTE You can also remove parts of a table by erasing the elements you don't want. You might do this to merge cells, for instance. Click **Table Tools Layout | Eraser** in the Draw group. Drag the eraser pointer over the elements you want removed. Or click one segment of a border. The borders of the elements to be removed within the red rectangular selection are bolded. Release the mouse button to remove the selected elements (when cells are removed within the interior of the table, the "hole" that remains is one large merged cell). Press **ESC** to return to the standard pointer, or click the **Eraser** button again.

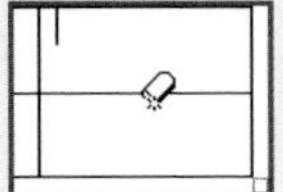

CAUTION! Removing cells also deletes any text or graphics contained within them.

Split a Table

You can divide a table along any of its rows to split it into segments. Word will divide longer tables when it creates automatic page breaks, although you might find it handy to be able to control exactly where the break occurs in the table.

1. Click a cell in the row below where you want the split to occur.
2. Click **Table Tools Layout | Split Table** in the Merge Group. A blank paragraph is inserted between the two tables (see Figure 6-1).

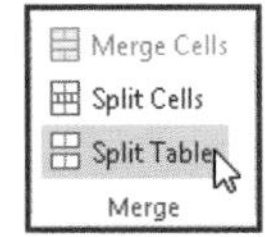

Change Column Width and Row Height

By default, tables are created with equal column widths spanning the width of the table (margin to margin across the document) unless you manually draw them. You can change each column to a specific width you set or use AutoFit to adjust the width to fit the longest entry in the column. Row heights change vertically as needed to accommodate multiple lines of text or larger font sizes (all cells in a row increase to match the highest cell in the row).

Change Column Width and Row Height by Dragging

1. Place the mouse pointer on the right border of the column whose width you want to change or on the bottom border of the row height you want to change. The mouse pointer changes to a resize pointer, showing the opposing directions in which you can drag.

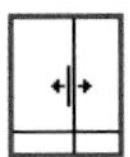

2. Drag the border to increase or decrease the size.

TIP To see the dimensions of each column's width or each row's height, hold down **ALT** as you drag a column or row border. The horizontal ruler displays the column widths, and the vertical ruler displays the row heights.

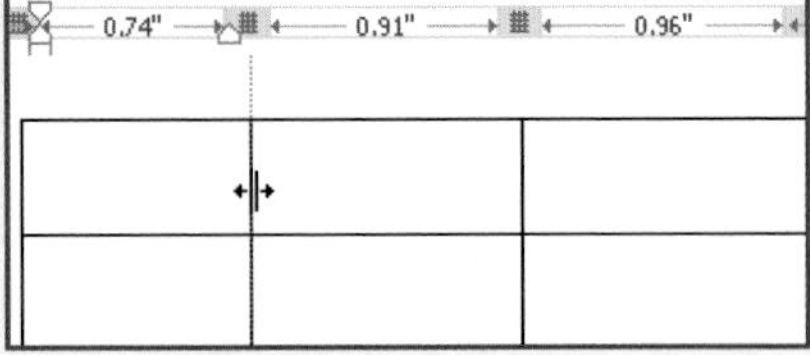

Change Column Width Precisely

1. Right-click the table to select it and click **Table Properties** on the context menu.

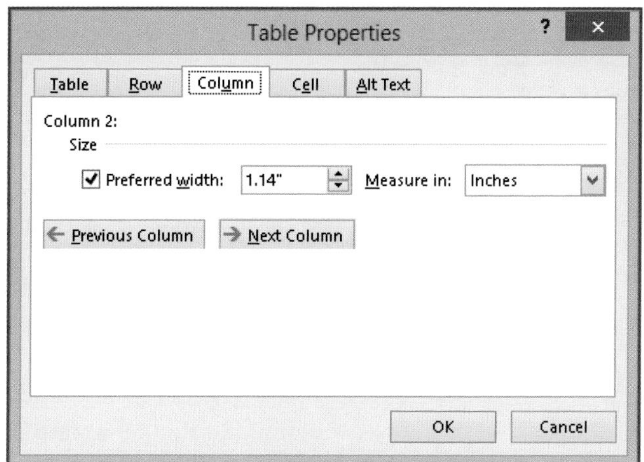

Figure 6-7: ***You can set exact dimensions for each column's width or as a percentage of the table width.***

2. In the Table Properties dialog box, click the **Column** tab, shown in Figure 6-7.
3. Click **Previous Column** or **Next Column** to select the initial column you want to set. (You may need to drag the dialog box to one side to see the table beneath it.)
4. Click the **Preferred Width** check box, and set a width in inches or as a percentage of the table width.
5. Repeat steps 3 and 4 to change the width of other columns.
6. Click **OK**.

Change Column Width to Fit or Fixed

You can use AutoFit to dynamically adjust the column widths in a table to fit the longest single-line entry in that column, to fit the size of the window, or to be of a defined fixed width.

1. Click in a table that needs its columns adjusted.
2. Click **Table Tools Layout | AutoFit** in the Cell Size group. A menu is displayed. You have these options:

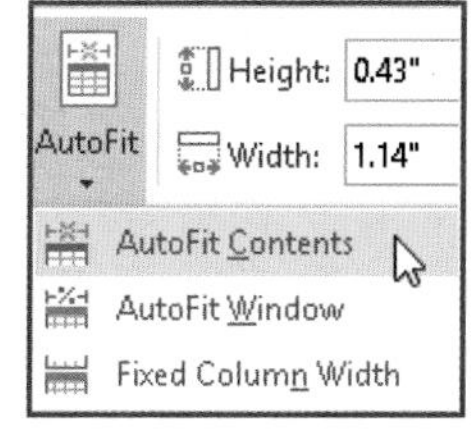

- **AutoFit Contents** automatically adjusts the columns to accommodate the size of its content.
- **AutoFit Window** automatically adjusts the table to fit the size of the page, including the margins.
- **Fixed Column Width** resizes the columns depending on the Height and Width settings in the Cell Size group.

Right-click the table whose columns you want to adjust to fit their content, click **AutoFit**, and click **AutoFit To Contents**.

TIP You can manually adjust column width and row heights to fit contents by selecting the columns or rows you want to adjust, pointing at the columns' rightmost border or the rows' lowermost border, and double-clicking when the pointer changes to a resizing icon.

TIP Distributing columns or rows evenly is particularly useful when you draw a table manually.

Space Column Widths or Row Heights Equally

Select the columns or rows that you want to make the same size, and right-click that selection to open the context menu. You have these options:

- Click **Distribute Columns Evenly** to space selected column widths equally.
- Click **Distribute Rows Evenly** to space selected row heights equally.

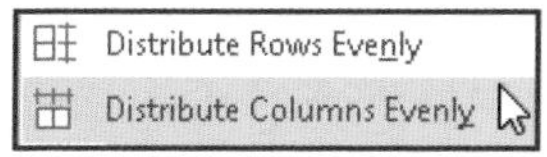

WORK WITH TABLES

Tables can be set up for many purposes, and Word provides features to support many of them. You can use special shortcut key combinations to move through the cells in a table, you can sort lists, and you can work with formulas. You can also move, copy, and delete tables.

Enter Information into Tables

Typing text in table cells is similar to typing text elsewhere in the document. You can use familiar tools, such as bullets, tabs, and other options found on the Home, Insert, and Page Layout tabs. See Chapters 2 through 4 for basic techniques used when working with text.

Type Text Above a Table

Place the insertion point in the upper-leftmost cell in the table (to the left of any text in the cell), and press **SHIFT+CTRL+ENTER**. A new paragraph is created above the table where you can enter text for a title or other annotation that will be a part of, but outside of, the table.

Move Around in a Table

The most straightforward way to move between cells in a table as you are entering data is to press **TAB**. You can also simply click the cell where you want to add text or graphics. However, if you're adding a lot of data to a table, it's more efficient to keep your hands on the keyboard. See Table 6-1 for several keyboard shortcuts you can use.

Move Content Around

You can cut and copy text and other content using the same techniques for basic text. Just select the content in the cells you want and, for example, press **CTRL+C** to copy the content. When pasting the content into other cells in the table, place the insertion point in the cell where you want the content to appear. Press **CTRL+V**. Any content in existing cells overlaid by the range of pasted cells will be overwritten with the new content.

Table 6-1: Keyboard Shortcuts to Move Around in a Table

To move to...	Press...
Cells to the right and down at row end (with cell contents selected)	TAB
Cells to the left and up at row end (with cell contents selected)	SHIFT+TAB
First cell in a column	ALT+PAGE UP
Last cell in a column	ALT+PAGE DOWN
First cell in a row	ALT+HOME
Last cell in a row	ALT+END

Sort Data

You can sort information in ascending or descending order according to the values in one or more columns. You can sort an entire table or selected cells (all data in the table or range is realigned so that the data in each row remains the same, even though the row might be placed in a different order than it was originally) or just a column (data in columns outside the sorted column does not change order).

Sort a Table or Selected Cells

1. Place your insertion point in the table you want to sort, or select a range of cells to sort.
2. Click **Table Tools Layout | Sort** in the Data group. The Sort dialog box appears, as shown in Figure 6-8.
3. Click the **Sort By** down arrow, and click the column of primary importance in determining the sort order in the drop-down list (if the columns have headings, select one of the titles; if there are no headings, select a column based on numbers that start with the leftmost column).

Figure 6-8: ***You can reorganize information in a table by sorting by one or more columns in ascending or descending order.***

4. Click the **Type** down arrow, and click whether the column contains numbers, dates, or anything else (the Text option sorts anything). Click **Ascending** or **Descending**.

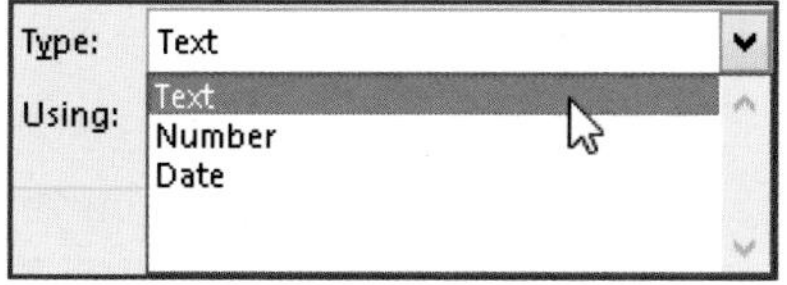

5. Click the first **Then By** down arrow, and click the column in the drop-down list that you want to base the sort on that is secondary in importance. Select the type of information in the column, and click **Ascending** or **Descending**.
6. Repeat, if necessary, for the second Then By section to sort by a third column of information.
7. Under My List Has, click whether the table or selection has a heading row.
8. Click **OK** when finished. An example of a table sorted by two columns is shown in Figure 6-9.

Primary sort arranges list by publisher

Secondary sort arranges list by date within publisher

ISBN-13	Category	Title	Author	Pub Date	Price
9780072229387	Computers	HT DO EVERYTHING W/ACCESS 2003	ANDERSEN VIRGINIA	8/1/2003	26.99
9780072232288	Computers	MS OFFICE EXCEL 2003 QUICKSTEP	CRONAN JOHN	1/1/2004	19.99
9780072232295	Computers	MS OFFICE ACCESS 2003 QUICKSTE	CRONAN JOHN	2/1/2004	16.99
9780072263725	Computers	MICROSOFT OFFICE EXCEL 2007 QU	CRONAN JOHN	11/1/2006	19.99
9780072263718	Computers	MICROSOFT OFFICE ACCESS 2007 Q	CRONAN JOHN	1/1/2007	16.99
9780071601450	Computers	BUILD AN EBAY BUSINESS QUICKST	CRONAN JOHN	12/1/2008	19.99
9780071487672	Computers	QUICKBOOKS 2007 QUICKSTEPS	FOX CINDY	1/1/2007	19.99
9780071497879	Computers	CISSP ALLINONE EXAM GDE E04	HARRIS SHON	11/1/2007	79.99
9780072263879	Computers	HOW TO DO EVERYTHING W/IPOD	HART-DAVIS GUY	1/1/2008	24.99
9780071487641	Computers	A+ CERTIFICATION STUDY GDE	HOLCOMBE JANE	6/1/2007	49.99

Figure 6-9: ***Sort by multiple columns to arrange entries that have the same secondary sort value.***

NOTE Sorting in Word is determined by a specified *sort order*. Each of the three types of information (text, numbers, and dates) recognized by Word contains its own sort order. For example, with text entries, which can contain all characters, punctuation characters are sorted first, followed by text with numbers, and finally text starting with letters. When sorting is based on the Numbers type (determined by having a number first in the cell), all characters other than numbers are ignored. Dates are recognized by the separators used to define days, months, and years. Periods, hyphens (-), forward slashes (/), and commas are valid date separators.

Sort a Single Column

You can sort a single column, independent of the rest of the table, but make sure that is what you want, because there is no way to return the table to the way it was originally.

1. Select the column you want to sort (see "Select Tables, Rows, Columns, or Cells").
2. Click **Table Tools Layout | Sort** in the Data group. The Sort dialog box appears, as shown earlier in Figure 6-8.
3. In the Sort dialog box, click **Options**.

4. In the Sort Options dialog box, click the **Sort Column Only** check box. (This won't be available to you if you have not previously selected the column.)

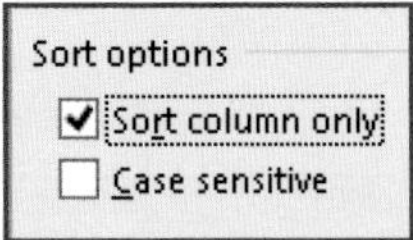

5. Click **OK** once to close the Sort Options dialog box, and again to sort the table.

TIP You can sort by four columns, but you have to "trick" Word a bit by doing the sort in two steps. First, sort by the least specific column in the Sort dialog box, and click **OK**. Next, complete a second sort in the Sort dialog box as you normally would, from the most to the least specific column, using the three sorting sections. Click **OK** to close the Sort dialog box a second time.

NOTE If the sort is on a column other than the first, you have to set the **Sort Columns Only** option for the selected column, exit both dialog boxes, click **Sort** again with the column still selected, and click **OK**. The single column is all that will be sorted. Be careful with this feature that you do not scramble your data.

Sort by More Than One Field in a Column

If you combine two or more fields of information in a single column, such as city, county, and state (for example, Everett, Snohomish, WA), instead of splitting them out into separate columns, you can sort your list by choosing which fields to sort by.

1. Place your insertion point in the table.
2. Click **Table Tools Layout | Sort** in the Data group. The Sort dialog box appears, as shown earlier in Figure 6-8.
3. In the Sort dialog box, click **Options**. In the Sort Options dialog box, under Separate Fields At, click the character used to separate the fields in a single column, or click **Other** and type the separator character. Click **OK** to close the Sort Options dialog box.

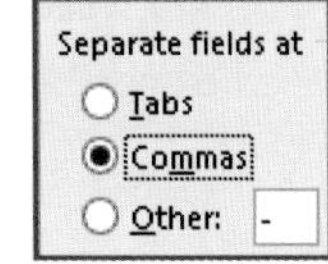

4. In the Sort dialog box, click the **Sort By** down arrow, and click the primary column that contains multiple fields. Click the **Type** down arrow, click an information type, and click **Ascending** or **Descending**. Click the **Using** down arrow, and click the record group, such as paragraphs, or Field 1, Field 2, etc.
5. Use the **Then By** sections if you want to sort by additional columns or fields.
6. Click **OK** when finished.

Move and Copy Tables, Columns, and Rows

A table is easily moved or copied by dragging its move handle (the move handle is only displayed when viewing the document in Print Layout view). Columns and rows also can be dragged into new positions.

Move a Table

1. Click anywhere in the table you want to move to display its move handle.
2. Drag the table to the position you want.

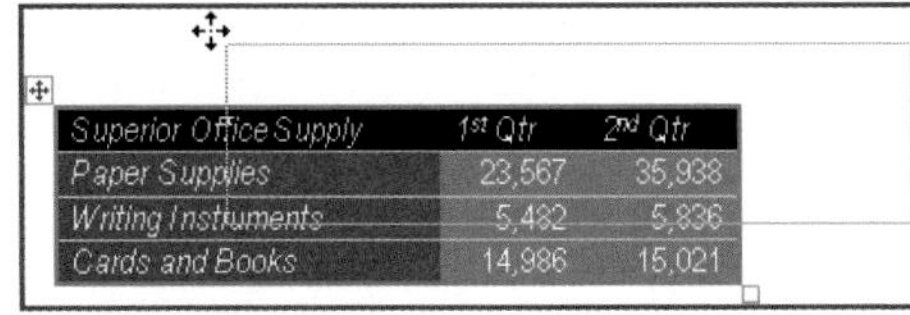

Superior Office Supply	1st Qtr	2nd Qtr
Paper Supplies	23,567	35,938
Writing Instruments	5,482	5,836
Cards and Books	14,986	15,021

Copy a Table

Hold CTRL and drag the table's move handle to position where you want the copy of the table.

–Or–

Click **Table Tools Layout | Select** in the Table group, and then click **Select Table** to select the table. (You can also simply click the table's move handle.) Press CTRL+C to copy the table to the Clipboard. Place your insertion point where you want the new table, and press CTRL+V.

Move or Copy Columns and Rows

1. Select the columns or rows you want to move (see "Select Tables, Rows, Columns, or Cells" earlier in the chapter).
2. Press **CTRL+X** to cut the selected row to be moved, or press **CTRL+C** to copy it.
3. Select the columns or rows that will be to the right (if a column) or below (if a row) of where you want the elements moved. Press **CTRL+V** to paste the selected row in its new position.

Calculate Values Using Formulas

You can use formulas in tables to perform arithmetic calculations and provide a result, either by putting together your own formulas or using an AutoSum feature.

TIP To see the underlying formula in a document's table, select the field and click **Table Tools Layout | Formula** in the Data group. It will appear in the Formula field of the Formula dialog box.

TIP You must manually update formulas after changing an underlying cell value. To recalculate a formula, select the current value in the field, and press **F9**.

Assemble Your Own Formulas

1. Place your mouse pointer in the cell where you want the result displayed.
2. Click **Table Tools Layout | Formula** [fx Formula] in the Data group. The Formula dialog box appears, as shown in Figure 6-10.
3. In the Formula text box, keep the Word-suggested formula, apply a number format, and click **OK** to display the result.

–Or–

Working with Formulas

Word provides a basic spreadsheet capability with tables to perform calculations on numeric entries. Knowing a number of terms and concepts used when working with formulas will make using them in tables much easier. (Any number-crunching other than basic calculations using simple formulas should be relegated to Microsoft Excel, the Office product devoted to performing serious work with numbers. See *Microsoft Office Excel 2013 QuickSteps,* published by McGraw-Hill, for more information on working with formulas, functions, and worksheets.) Common terms and concepts are as follows:

- **Syntax** is the set of rules Word uses for you to communicate how to perform calculations with formulas. For instance, to identify to Word that a calculation is to be performed, you must precede the calculation with an equal sign.
- **Cell reference** is the scheme formulas use to provide a unique address for each cell, consisting of its column-and-row intersection. Columns are designated alphabetically, starting with the leftmost column as "A"; rows are sequentially numbered from top to bottom, with the topmost row as "1." For example, the third cell from the left in the second row would be identified as cell C2. You must manually determine what the cell reference is; Word does not help. You can, however, use attributes like ABOVE, BELOW, LEFT, and RIGHT if you want all cells from the one you've selected in a row or column to be included.
- **Cell reference operators** are the syntax used to identify multiple cells in a formula. For example, to add the values in cells A1, A2, B1, and B2, you use commas to list the cells the function is to sum: =SUM(A1,A2,B1,B2) or use a colon (:) operator to identify a range of contiguous cells: =SUM(A1:B2).
- **Functions** are prewritten formulas that you can use to perform specific tasks. For example, some functions perform arithmetic calculations, such as SUM and AVERAGE; some apply Boolean logic, such as AND, TRUE, and NOT; others are used for unique purposes, such as to COUNT the number of values in a list.
- **Attributes** communicate instructions to a function to perform an action. For example, if you click the bottom cell in a column and open the Formula dialog box, Word suggests a formula: =SUM(ABOVE). The ABOVE attribute eliminates the need for you to reference each cell in the column above the selected cell. Another frequently used attribute is LEFT, as in =COUNT(LEFT) to count the numeric entries in the cells to the left of the selected cell. BELOW and RIGHT also are available.

Figure 6-10: **The Formula dialog box provides tools to set up formulas for basic calculations.**

1. Delete everything except the equal (=) sign.
2. Click the **Paste Function** down arrow, and click the function you want to use.

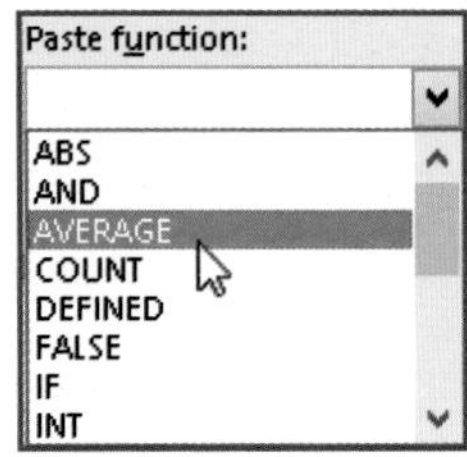

3. In the Formula text box, type the cell references or attribute the function applies to between the parentheses following the function name.
4. Click the **Number Format** down arrow, and click the style you want applied to the result.

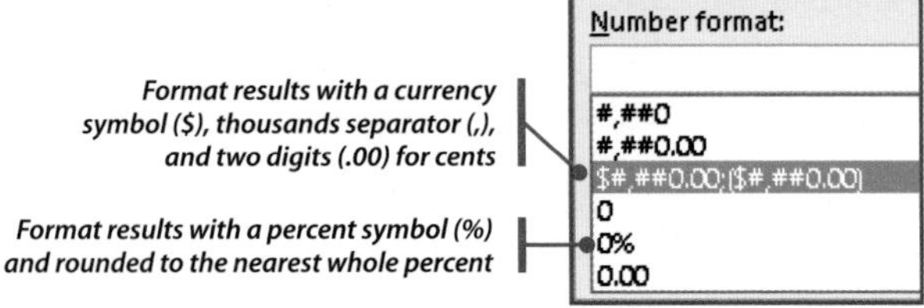

5. Click OK to display the result.

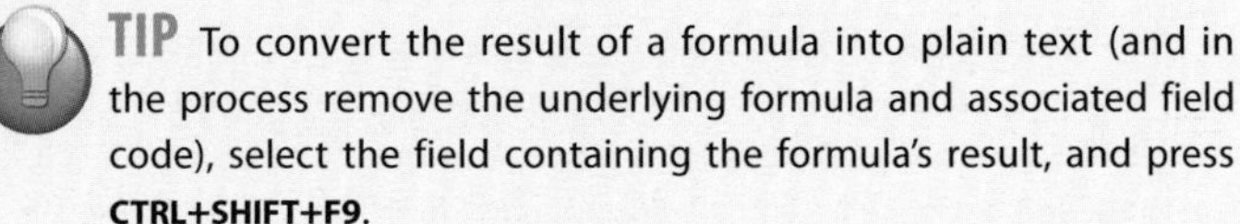

TIP To convert the result of a formula into plain text (and in the process remove the underlying formula and associated field code), select the field containing the formula's result, and press **CTRL+SHIFT+F9**.

TIP Formulas may be copied using **CTRL+C** or other copying techniques, and if you use the attributes ABOVE and LEFT, they will be automatically adjusted for the contents of the cells above or to the left of where the formulas is copied after you select the calculated field contents and press **F9**.

Convert Tables to Text and Text to Tables

If you have information in text format, Word can convert it to a table and similarly convert information in a table to ordinary text.

Convert Text to a Table

Converting text to a table requires that the text be appropriately formatted with tabs, commas, or another character between columns and a separate character, like a paragraph mark, between rows.

1. Drag to select the text you want to convert to a table.
2. Click **Insert | Table** in the Tables group, and click **Convert Text To Table**. The Convert Text To Table dialog box appears. Do not be concerned if the number of rows and columns do not yet match your expectations.

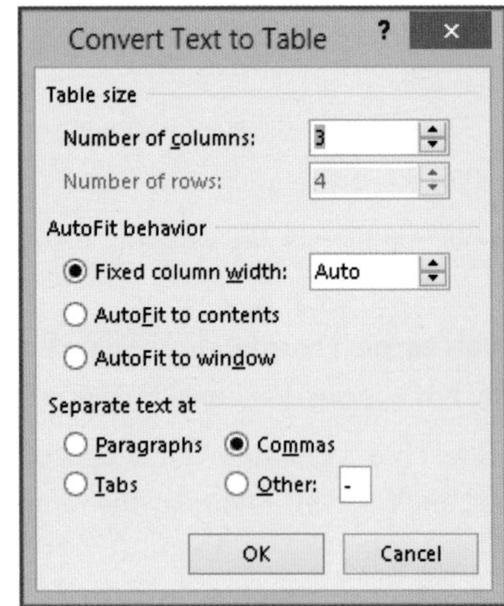

3. Under Separate Text At, click the character used to separate columns of text, or click **Other** and type the character. The number of columns and rows should now reflect how you formatted the text to be displayed in a table.
4. Under AutoFit Behavior, choose a fixed column width by clicking the spinner or entering a value (Auto, the default, sizes columns equally so that they fill the available width of the table), having Word set each column's width so that the contents fit in each column, or having Word size the columns to fit the window the table is in. (AutoFit To Window is primarily used when sizing tables in webpages. See Chapter 9 for more information on saving Word documents as webpages.)
5. Click **OK** when finished. Figure 6-11 shows the original text data, as well as the resulting table that was created from it. (Under normal circumstances, the table replaces the text. Here, a copy was converted to show both states.)

Superior Office Supply, 1st Qtr, 2nd Qtr,

Paper Supplies, 23567, 35938

Writing Instruments, 5482, 5836

Cards and Books, 14986, 15021

Superior Office Supply	1st Qtr	2nd Qtr
Paper Supplies	23567	35938
Writing Instruments	5482	5836
Cards and Books	14986	15021

Figure 6-11: ***Text properly formatted with separators is easily converted to a table in Word.***

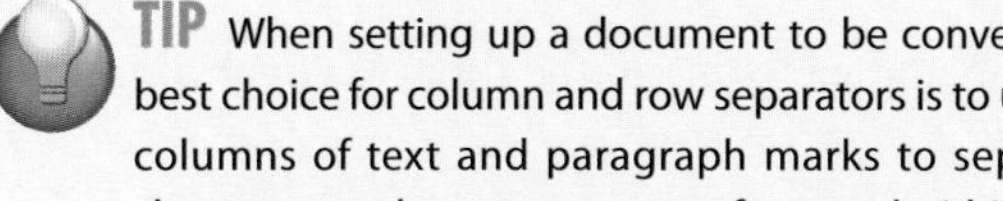

TIP When setting up a document to be converted to a table, the best choice for column and row separators is to use tabs to separate columns of text and paragraph marks to separate rows. Other characters, such as commas, are often used within text and can cause unpredictable results during the conversion.

Convert a Table to Text

Converting a table to text converts the contents of each cell to normal text separated by a character you choose, with each row becoming a separate paragraph.

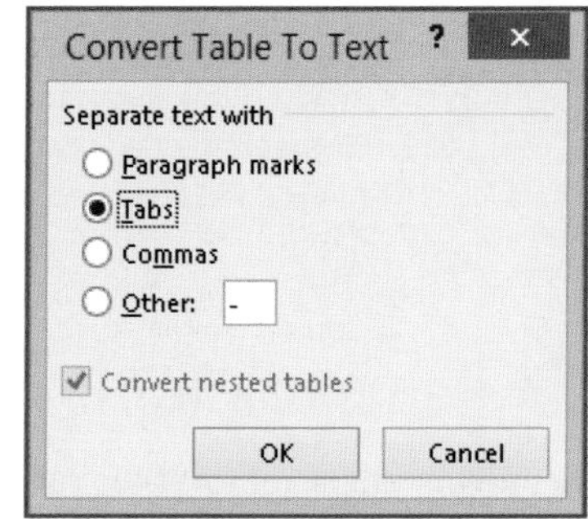

1. Select the table that you want to convert to text (see "Select Tables, Rows, Columns, or Cells").
2. Click **Table Tools Layout | Convert To Text** in the Data group. The Convert Table To Text dialog box appears.
3. Under Separate Text With, click the formatting character you want to use to separate text in columns, or click **Other** and type the character you want.
4. If you have a table within a table, click the **Convert Nested Tables** check box to convert the nested table(s) as well.
5. Click **OK** when finished.

Repeat Header Rows

Headers are the column identifiers placed in the first row of a table (see Figure 6-1) to distinguish different categories of information. In tables, you can repeat the heading rows at the top of each page so that they span multiple document pages. The reader then does not have to remember the column category or keep returning to the beginning of the table. (Repeated headers only apply to Word-generated page breaks, not those you create manually.)

1. Click **View | Print Layout** in the Views group, if it isn't already selected, so that you can see the headers displayed.
2. Select the header rows (see "Select Tables, Rows, Columns, or Cells").

1 2 3 4 5 6 7 8 9 10

3. Click **Table Tools Layout | Repeat Header Rows** in the Data group.

NOTE You can apply most of the formatting features to text within a table as you can to narrative text outside a table—for example, you can add numbered and bulleted lists and change the color of text. Use the Home, Page Layout, and Table Tools Design tabs or the formatting context menu (opened by right-clicking selected text) to add spice to your table contents!

Remove a Table

Removing a table removes the rows and columns of the table along with any text or data.

1. Place the insertion point in the table you want to remove.
2. Click **Table Tools Layout | Delete** in the Rows & Columns group, and click **Delete Table**.

–Or–

Click **Table Tools Layout | Eraser** in the Draw Borders group. Drag a rectangle using the eraser pointer over the table border, and then release the mouse button. Press **ESC** to return to the standard pointer.

–Or–

Click the move handle in the upper-left corner, just outside the table, to select the table, and press **CTRL+X**; or click **Home | Cut** in the Clipboard group [ ]. The table is removed but is available to be pasted elsewhere. (See Chapter 2 for information on using the Office Clipboard to paste material in Word documents.)

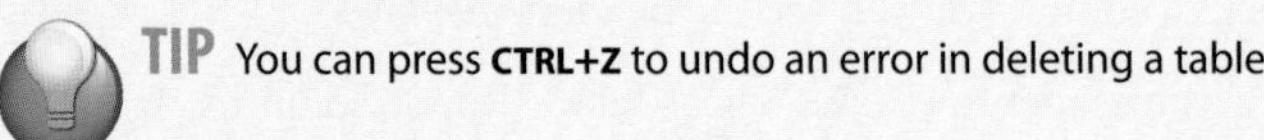

TIP You can press **CTRL+Z** to undo an error in deleting a table.

 Format Content

Tables provide several formatting features specifically focused on working with content in cells.

Align Content Within a Cell

By default, content is aligned with the upper-left corner of a cell. You can change this to several other configurations.

1. Select the cells whose content alignment you want to change.
2. Click **Table Tools Layout** and then select one of the nine alignment options in the Alignment group.

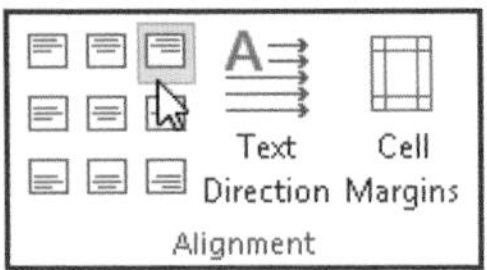

–Or–

Right-click the selected cells, click **Table Properties** on the context menu, and on the Table tab click one of the three alignment options, or click the **Indent From Left** spinner for the correct indentation.

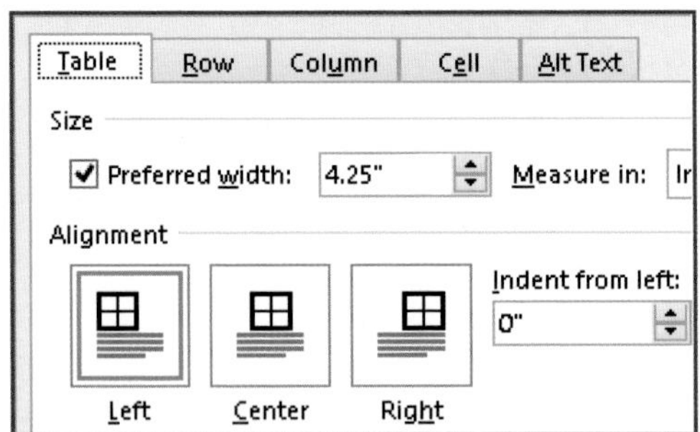

3. Click the **Cell** tab and click one of the three **Vertical Alignment** choices.

Change Text Wrapping in a Cell

By default, text is wrapped in a cell to the next line when it extends to the right border of the cell. (You can override this behavior by using AutoFit to adjust column widths to the content. See "Change Column Width to Fit or Fixed" earlier in this chapter.) To remove text wrapping in cells:

1. Select the cells for which you do not want text to wrap.
2. Right-click the selected cells, click **Table Properties** on the context menu, and click the **Cell** tab, if it isn't already selected.
3. Click **Options** to open the Cell Options dialog box. Under Options, clear the **Wrap Text** check box. (Fit Text changes the font size to fit the cell size.)

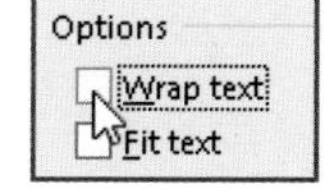

4. Click **OK** twice to close the Cell Options and Table Properties dialog boxes.

NOTE Turning off the word-wrap option does not cause text to not wrap unless the AutoFit option is selected. In other words, text continues to wrap onto the next line, regardless of the option selected, if the AutoFit option is not selected.

Orient Text Direction in a Cell

For a special effect, you can change the typical horizontal text orientation to one of two vertical arrangements, as shown in Figure 6-12.

1. Select the cells whose text orientation you want to change.
2. Right-click the selected cells, and click **Text Direction** on the context menu. In the Text Direction – Table Cell dialog box, click an orientation and click **OK**.

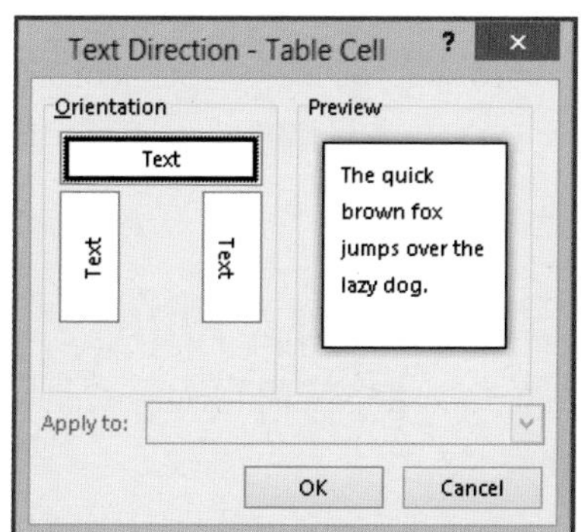

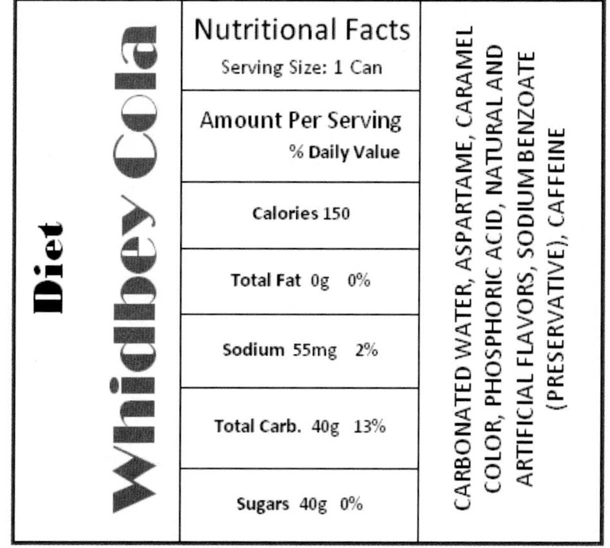

Figure 6-12: ***Vertical text provides interesting opportunities for laying out logos and other information.***

–Or–

Click **Table Tools Layout | Text Direction** in the Alignment group to cycle through the one horizontal and two vertical orientation options.

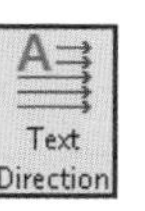

TIP Check out the alignment, lists, and indent options on the Home (and formatting mini toolbar), Page Layout, and Table Tools Layout tabs after you click a cell whose text direction has changed. The option faces become oriented vertically as well!

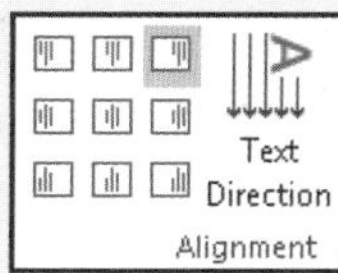

CHANGE A TABLE'S APPEARANCE

A table chock full of data is informative, but not necessarily appealing. Word offers special features to help with this, including text wrapping and orientation options. You can also change the look of the table's structure by merging and splitting cells; adjusting margins surrounding cells; aligning the table on the document page; and applying color, shading, and emphasis to backgrounds and borders.

Merge and Split Cells

Cells can be *merged* by combining two or more cells into one cell. Merged cells can be used to create a banner that spans the width of a table, as a placeholder for larger inserted graphics, and for other special effects. You can also accomplish the opposite effect by subdividing a cell into multiple columns and/or rows by splitting the cell.

Merge Cells

1. Select the cells you want to combine into one cell. (See "Select Tables, Rows, Columns, or Cells.") You have these options of how to merge cells:

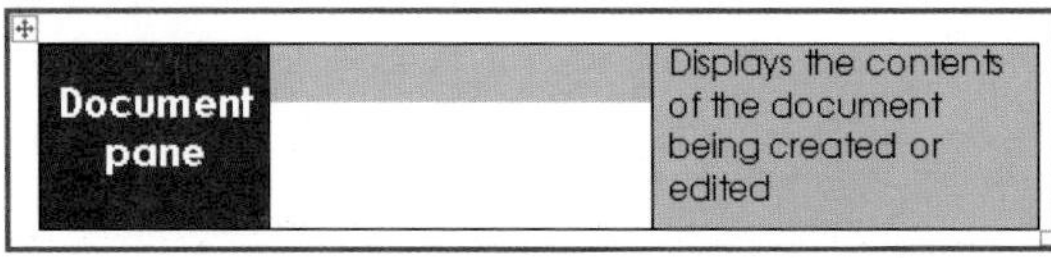

   - Right-click the selection and click **Merge Cells** from the context menu.
   - Click **Layout | Merge Cells** in the Merge group.

2. Any content in either cell now spans the merged cell.

Split Cells

1. Select the cell or cells you want to split into more columns or rows. You can open a dialog box to split cells in a couple of ways:
   - For a single cell, right-click it and click **Split Cells**.
   - With one or more selected cells, click **Layout | Split Cells** in the Merge group.
2. In both cases, the Split Cells dialog box will appear.

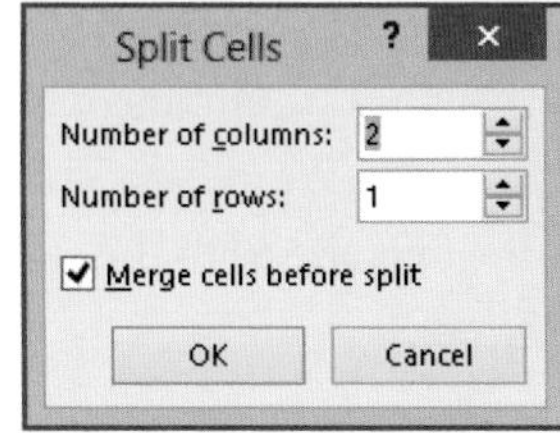

3. Click the **Number Of Columns** spinner or enter a value to divide the selected cell vertically.

   –And/or–

4. Click the **Number Of Rows** spinner or enter a value to divide the selected cells horizontally. (Other cells in the rows of the cells being split increase their height to accommodate the increase.)
5. To split each selected cell into the number of rows or columns entered, clear the **Merge Cells Before Split** check box.

   –Or–

   To split the merged block of selected cells into the number of rows or columns entered, select the **Merge Cells Before Split** check box.
6. Click **OK**.

Change a Table's Alignment

You can change a table's alignment from left aligned, centered, or right aligned.

Align a Table Quickly

1. Point just above the leftmost column, and click the table sizing handle.
2. Click **Home | Align Left**, **Center**, or **Align Right** in the Paragraph group. (See Chapter 3 for an explanation of the alignment buttons. Justify alignment doesn't work in tables.)

Align and Indent a Table

1. Right-click the table you want to align, click **Table Properties** on the context menu, and click the **Table** tab, as shown in Figure 6-13.
2. Click the **Left Alignment** icon.

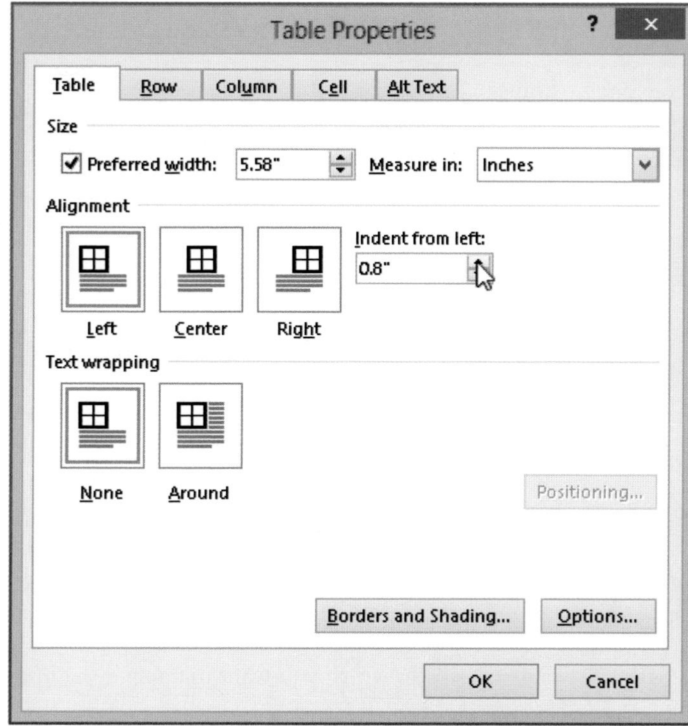

Figure 6-13: ***Use the Table tab of a table's properties dialog box to align and indent a table, as well as to size and determine text-wrapping options.***

3. Click the **Indent From Left** spinner or enter a value to shift the left edge of the table relative to the page margin (use negative values to shift the left edge to the left of the margin).
4. Click **OK**.

Wrap Text Around a Table

By default, tables are inserted *inline* with other text and objects in the document so that the other content is either above or below the table's position. You can choose to have adjacent text wrap on either side of the table, as well as adjust how the table is positioned relative to the text.

1. Right-click the table you want to align, click **Table Properties** on the context menu, and click the **Table** tab (see Figure 6-13).
2. Under Text Wrapping, click the **Around** icon to wrap text around the sides of the table (the table's width must be less than the margin width for text to appear on the sides).
3. Click **Positioning** to open the Table Positioning dialog box, shown in Figure 6-14.
   - Under Horizontal and Vertical, set values to position the table relative to margin, page, column, or paragraph.
   - Under Distance From Surrounding Text, determine how much of a gap you want to exist between the table and surrounding text.
   - Select the **Move With Text** check box if you want the table to move with text flow; clear it to keep the table in a fixed position, regardless of whether content is added or removed on the page.
   - Select **Allow Overlap** to let text flow over on top of the table.
4. Click **OK** twice.

TIP You may have to play with the Horizontal/Vertical and Distance From Surrounding Text controls to get a handle on how they work.

1 2 3 4 5 6 7 8 9 10

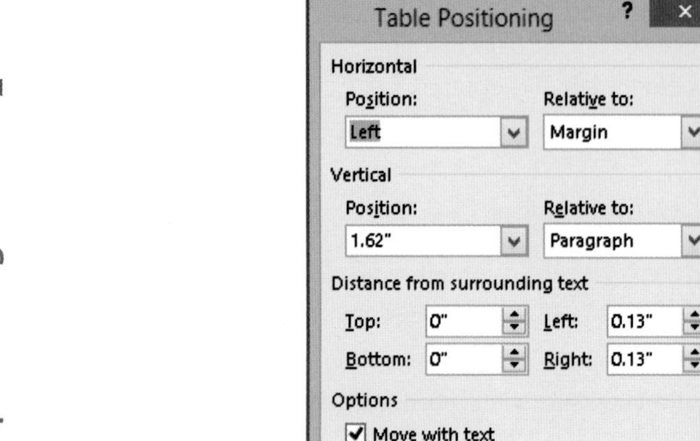

Figure 6-14: ***You can lock a table's position relative to a document's elements and set options for how text displays near the table.***

Change Cell Margins

You can change the distance between content and the cell borders, both for an entire table and for selected cells.

Set Margins for All Cells in a Table

1. Right-click the table whose default cell margins you want to change, and click **Table Properties** on the context menu.
2. On the Table tab, click **Options**.
3. In the Table Options dialog box, under Default Cell Margins, change the **Top**, **Bottom**, **Left**, and **Right** values as needed by clicking their respective spinners or entering numbers.
4. Click **OK** twice.

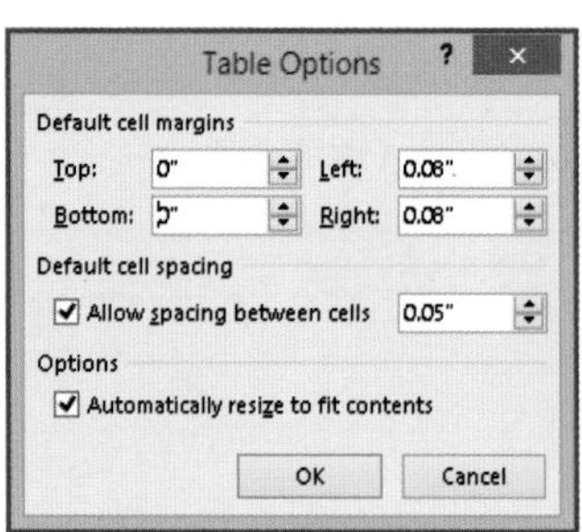

Set Margins for Selected Cells

1. Select the cells whose default cell margins you want to change, right-click them, and click **Table Properties** on the context menu.
2. Click the **Cell** tab, and click **Options**.
3. In the Cell Margins dialog box, clear the **Same As The Whole Table** check box, and change the **Top**, **Bottom**, **Left**, and **Right** values as needed by clicking their respective spinners or entering numbers.
4. Click **OK** twice.

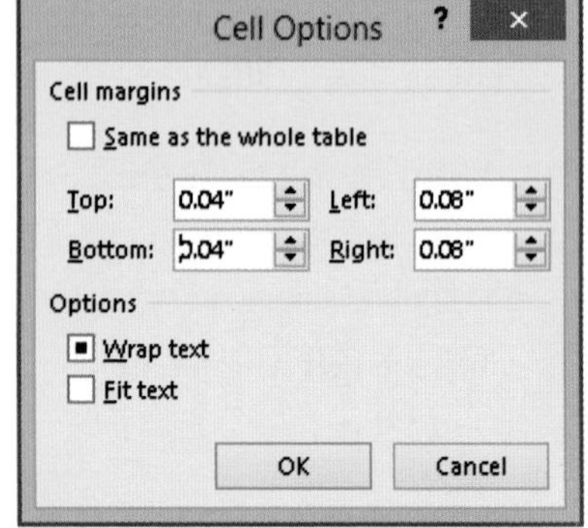

TIP Besides setting the margins for content within a cell, you can also create spacing between cells. In the Table Options dialog box (see "Set Margins for All Cells in a Table"), select the **Allow Spacing Between Cells** check box, and use the spinner or enter a value. (The accompanying illustration has borders that help demonstrate the cell spacing.)

Superior·Office·Supply¤	1st·Qtr¤	2nd·Qtr¤
Paper·Supplies¤	23,567¤	35,938¤
Writing·Instruments¤	5,482¤	5,836¤
Cards·and·Books¤	14,986¤	15,021¤

Apply Shading and Border Effects

Tables and individual cells can be emphasized using Word's broad set of tools to apply shading and border outlines.

1. Select the table or cells to which you want to apply a shading or border effect.

2. Open the Borders And Shading dialog box, shown in Figure 6-15, by one of the following means:
   - Click **Table Tools Design | Dialog Box Launcher** in lower right of the Borders group.

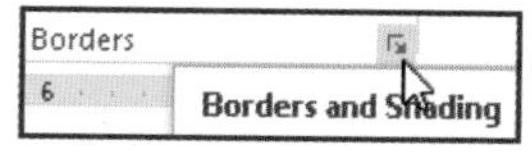

   - Click **Table Tools Layout | Properties** in the Table group, and on the Table tab of the Table Properties dialog box, click **Borders And Shading**.
3. Click the **Borders** tab to establish the border's position, width, and color.
4. Click the **Shading** tab to determine what color to use to fill the selected cells and how dense or which patterns you want for the color fill. (See Chapter 3 for information on how to apply borders and shading to text.)

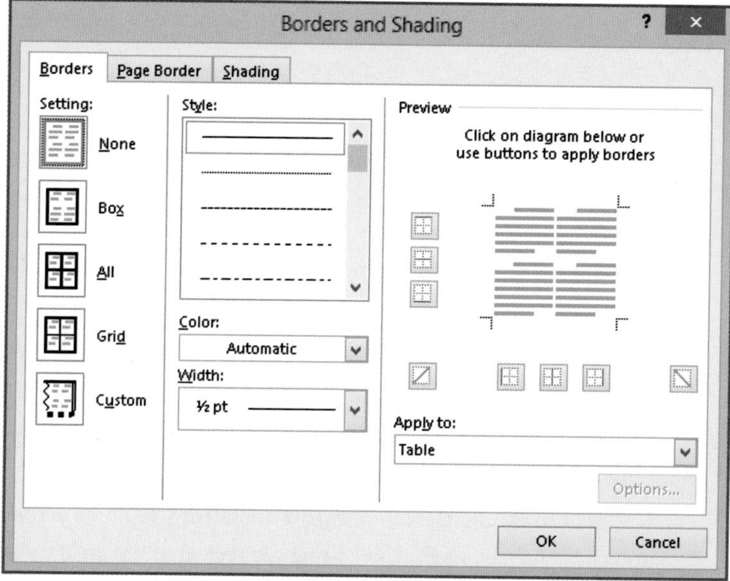

Figure 6-15: ***You can choose borders for each side of cells and the table, as well as provide background fills and patterns.***

Apply Styles to a Table Automatically

Tables are easily changed after they are created, but when in a hurry, it is often helpful to give Word the first crack at applying a consistent look to a table. You can always modify the styles or start over with a different appearance. In addition, you can create a format style from scratch and save it, or modify an existing format style and save it.

1. Select the table that you want to have Word format with an existing style automatically. (You can also automatically format a table as you create it using the Insert Table dialog box. See "Insert a Table from a Dialog Box" earlier in the chapter.)
2. In the Table Tools Design tab Table Styles group, a gallery of table styles is displayed, as shown in Figure 6-16.

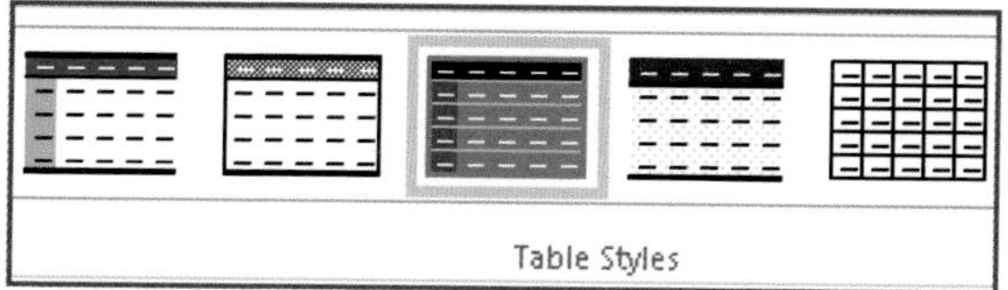

Figure 6-16: ***You can apply a preformatted table style, modify an existing style, or create your own and save any changes for future use.***

Apply a Table Style

1. Select the table you want to style.
2. In the Table Tools Design tab Table Styles group, scroll through the gallery of table styles, and point the mouse at each one to see a preview of your table with that style. Figure 6-17 shows three examples of the options available. As you point, you'll see how that style will look on your table.
3. When you find the one that you want, click that style to select it.

Superior Office Supply	1st Qtr	2nd Qtr
Paper Supplies	23,567	35,938
Writing Instruments	5,482	5,836
Cards and Books	14,986	15,021

Superior Office Supply	1st Qtr	2nd Qtr
Paper Supplies	23,567	35,938
Writing Instruments	5,482	5,836
Cards and Books	14,986	15,021

Superior Office Supply	1st Qtr	2nd Qtr
Paper Supplies	23,567	35,938
Writing Instruments	5,482	5,836
Cards and Books	14,986	15,021

Figure 6-17: ***Word provides a number of attractive table styles you can apply.***

Change or Create a Table Style

The Modify Style and Create New Style dialog boxes provide a number of options and tools that you can use to change or create a table style. (The Modify Style dialog box is shown in Figure 6-18.)

1. In the Table Tools Design tab Table Styles group, click **More** beneath the scroll arrows on the right of the style gallery.

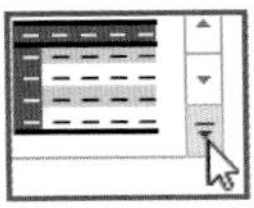

   - To change an existing style, click **Modify Table Style** at the bottom of the styles list, as seen in Figure 6-18.
   - To create a new one, click **New Table Style**.

2. In either dialog box, you use the Style Based On and the Apply Formatting To options to apply an effect to the entire table or to just part of it. In this back-and-forth manner (set the effect, select the table part), you create the overall table effect for which you're looking:
   - Under Properties, enter a name for the style, click the **Style Based On** down arrow, and click a style to start with (the style appears in the Preview area—unfortunately, you cannot mouse over an option to see the preview results).
   - Under Formatting, click the **Apply Formatting To** down arrow, and click the part of the table to which you want the style to be applied. Use the formatting tools in the center of the dialog box. Or, you can click **Format** at the bottom of the dialog box to open

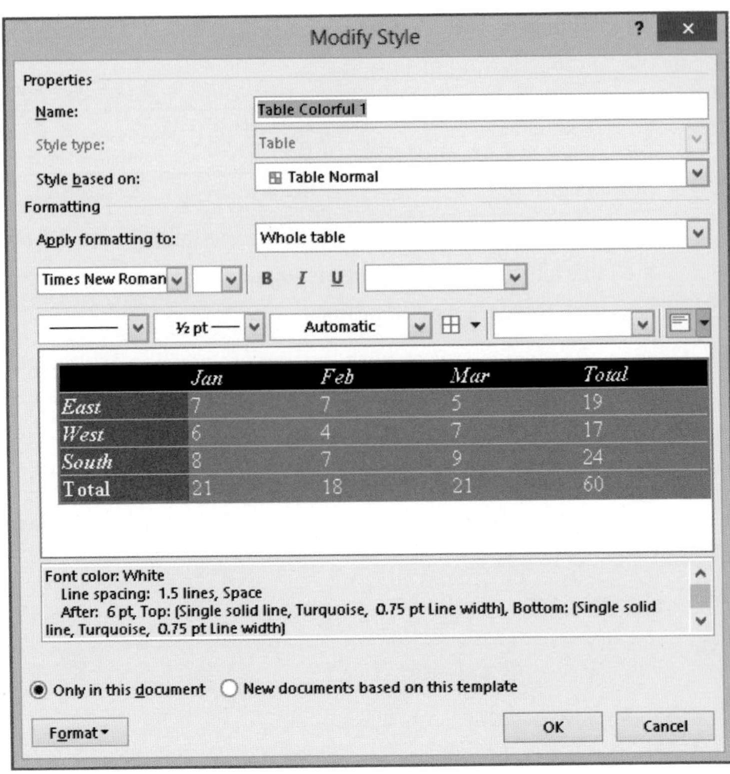

Figure 6-18: ***There is no shortage of formatting options available to you when changing or creating a table style.***

a drop-down list of options that open additional dialog boxes with even more formatting choices.

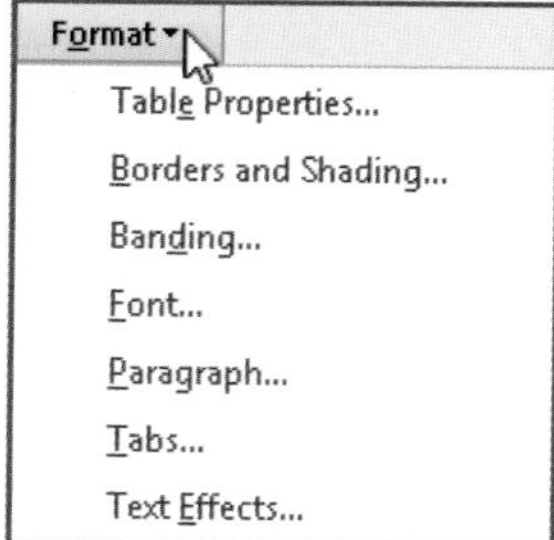

- Click **Only In This Document** if you want the formatting to apply only to your current document. Click **New Documents Based On This Template** if you want the style available to other documents.

3. Click **OK** to close all open dialog boxes when done.

CAUTION! When modifying an existing table style, provide a new name for the style in the Name text box; otherwise, the original style will be overwritten with any changes you make and you won't be able to return to "square one" if need be.

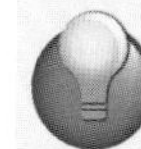

TIP You can choose a table style to be the default style for tables in the current document or for all of those that use the Normal template. Right-click the style you want from the table style gallery in the Design tab. Click **Set As Default**, click the applicable option in the Microsoft Word default table style dialog box, and click **OK**.

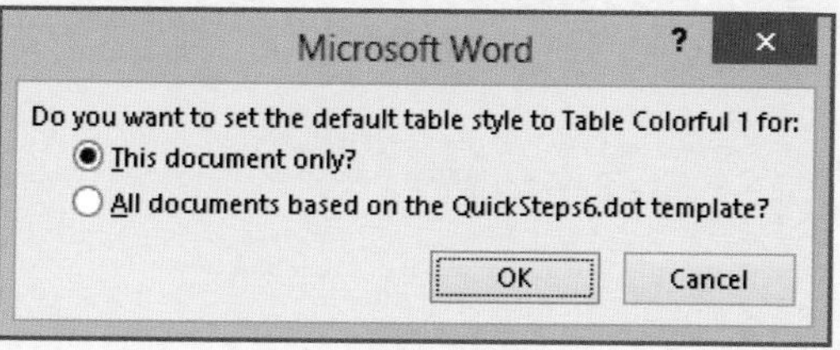

Delete a Style

1. In the Table Tools Design tab Table Styles group, scroll through the table styles gallery, and right-click the style you want to delete.
2. Click **Delete Table Style**, and click **Yes** to confirm the action. The style is removed from the gallery.

QuickSteps to...

- Add Pictures from a Computer
- Use the Picture Tools Format Tab
- Crop Unwanted Areas of a Photo
- Position "In-Line" Pictures
- Reduce a Picture's File Size
- Wrap Text Around a Picture
- Add Shapes
- Use Color Effects
- Work with Curves
- Add Special Effects to Text
- Create a Diagram
- Add Objects from Other Programs
- Take Screenshots
- Resize and Rotate Illustrations Precisely
- Position Illustrations
- Use Handles and Borders to Position Objects
- Position Illustrations Other Ways
- Combine Illustrations by Grouping

Chapter 7

Working with Illustrations

Illustration is a term used to describe several forms of visual enhancements that can be added to a document. Illustrations include pictures, clip art, drawings, shapes, SmartArt, charts, and screenshots. In this chapter you will learn how to insert, format, and manage illustration files, such as digital photos and clip art images. You will see how to create your own drawings directly on a document and how to combine them with built-in shapes. In addition, you will see how to embed charts and screenshots alongside your text and how to produce organizational charts and other business-oriented diagrams.

WORK WITH PICTURES

Pictures, which include both digital photos and *clip art* (small drawings or commercial photos), are separate files that can be manipulated in a number of ways once you have them within Word. You can organize your picture collections, resize images, and move them into the exact positions that you want.

Add Pictures from a Computer

You can browse for picture files, use the online libraries to assist you, drag them from other locations, or import them directly from a scanner or digital camera.

Browse for Pictures

1. Place your insertion point in the Word paragraph or table where you want to insert the picture.

2. Click **Insert | Pictures** in the Illustrations group. The Insert Picture dialog box appears, as shown in Figure 7-1.

3. Browse to the picture you want, and select it. (If you do not see your pictures, click the **Change Your View** down arrow on the dialog box toolbar, and click **Large Icons** or a larger size.)

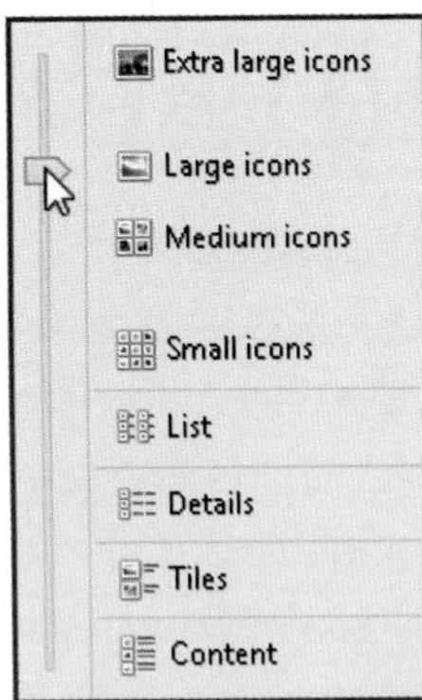

4. Click **Insert**. The picture is displayed in the document.

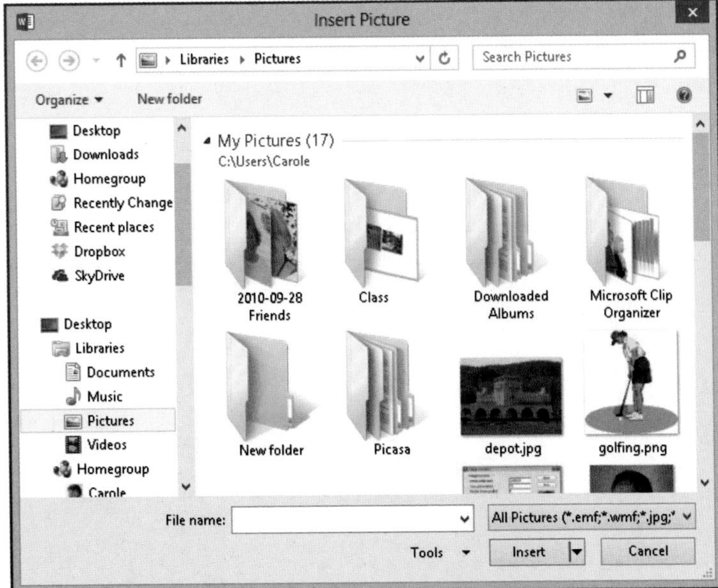

Figure 7-1: ***The Insert Picture dialog box displays thumbnails of picture files accepted by Word.***

NOTE Pictures are files that are produced by a device, such as a digital camera or scanner, or that are created in a painting or drawing program, such as Microsoft Paint or Adobe Illustrator. In either case, the files are saved in a graphic format, such as JPEG or GIF (popular formats used on the Internet) or TIF (used in higher-end printing applications). Table 7-1 lists the graphic file formats supported by Word.

Table 7-1: Picture File Formats Accepted by Word

File Type	Extension
Computer Graphics Metafile	CGM
Encapsulated PostScript	EPS
Graphics Interchange Format	GIF
Joint Photographic Expert Graphics	JPG, JPEG, JFIF, JPE
Macintosh PICT/Compressed	PCT, PICT/PCZ
Portable Network Graphics	PNG
Tagged Image File Format	TIF, TIFF
Windows Bitmap	BMP, RLE, DIB
Windows Enhanced Metafile/Compressed	EMF/EMZ
Windows Metafile/Compressed	WMF/WMZ
WordPerfect Graphics	WPG

NOTE Often, when you insert a picture or illustration, it is not the size that you want it to be. You can easily make a picture the size you want by first clicking it to select it (sizing handles are displayed when a photo is selected), and then dragging the sizing handles to resize or rotate the image.

1 2 3 4 5 6 7 8 9 10

TIP Besides using the Insert Pictures command in Word to add pictures, you can drag picture files from the desktop or Windows Explorer into an open document. To best do this, display a window showing where you want to insert the image in Word and another of Windows Explorer showing where your file is located. Drag the picture from Windows Explorer to the location in the Word document where you want it, as shown in Figure 7-2.

Add Clip Art

You can search for clip art and other images online or in your SkyDrive or computer. If one possibility doesn't provide the results you want, try another one.

1. Place your insertion point in the paragraph or table where you want to insert the picture.

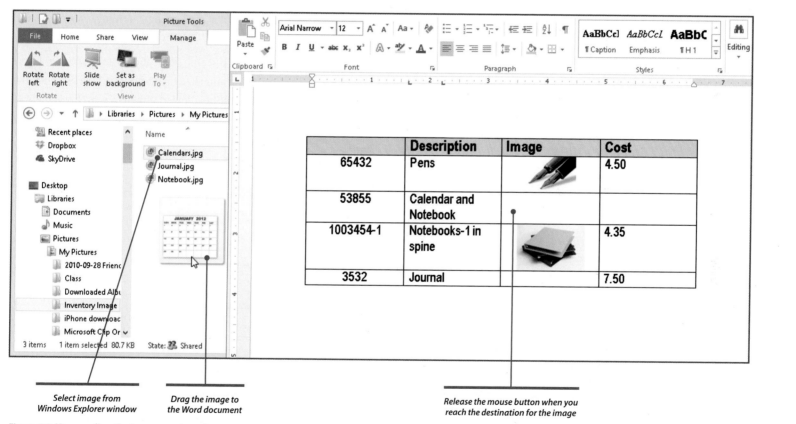

Select image from Windows Explorer window

Drag the image to the Word document

Release the mouse button when you reach the destination for the image

Figure 7-2: ***You can directly drag any art you have on your computer to an open Word document.***

2. Click **Insert | Online Pictures** in the Illustrations group. The Insert Pictures dialog box opens. You have these options:

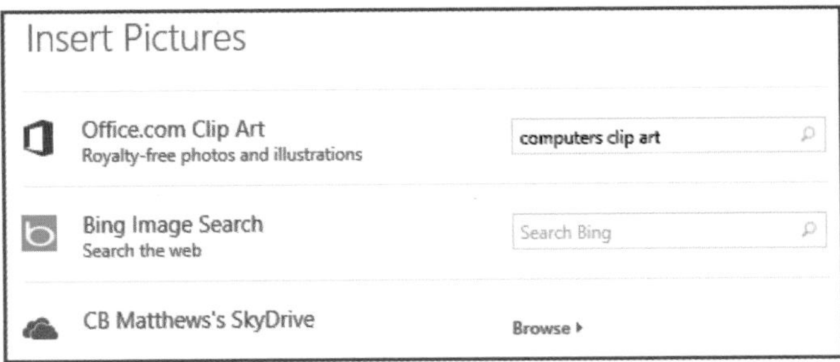

- **Office.com Clip Art** To search Office.com, type a category of clip art you want to find in the Search text box and click **Search** (the search icon) to find free clip art online. You'll see the results of the search, which contain both photos and drawings, as shown in the example in Figure 7-3. Select the image you want, and click **Insert**.

TIP Add something like the word "drawings" to your search category to find just graphic images rather than photos.

- **Bing Image Search** To search the Internet, type your search criteria in the Search text box and click the **Search** icon. You'll see the results of the search. Select your image, or type another criterion and try again. When you find the one you want, click it.
- ***Yourname* SkyDrive** To search your SkyDrive folders, click **Browse**. Find the folder containing the image you want and double-click it.
- **Also Insert From** To search your photos and videos in Flickr (a website for storing and sharing photos and videos), click the two-dot icon. You will be allowed either to search your Flickr account for an image or to sign up for an account if you don't have one.

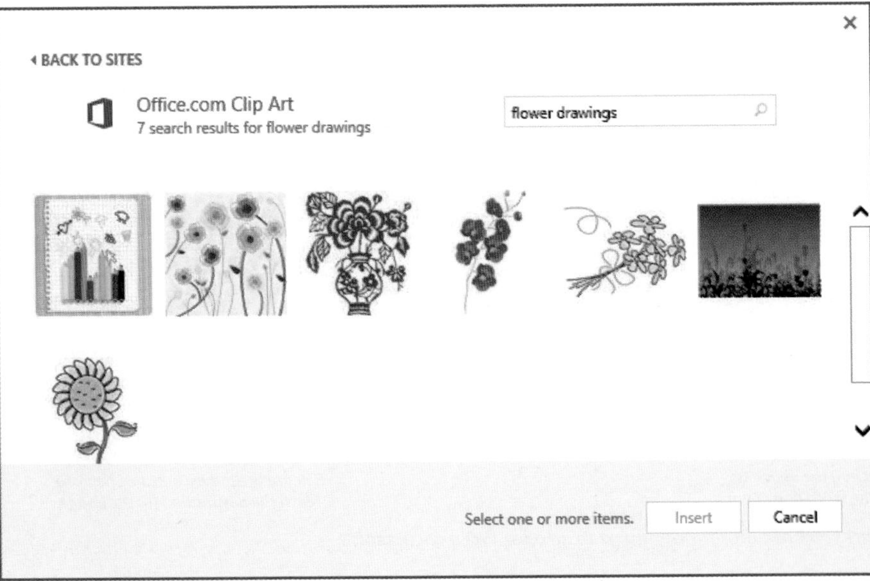

Figure 7-3: ***You can search the online library for clip art and photos.***

3. After inserting the image you want, you can resize or rotate it as needed. When you are ready, click **Back To Site** or **Close** to return to the dialog box in Figure 7-2.

Add Pictures Directly

In addition to adding pictures to Word from files on your computer or from clip art, you can bring pictures directly into Word from a camera plugged into your computer.

1. Place your insertion point in the paragraph or table where you want to insert the picture.
2. Make sure that the digital camera is connected to your computer and is turned on.
3. Click **Insert | Pictures** in the Illustrations group. The Insert Picture dialog box appears.
4. Drag the Folders pane to the top of its area, and select the device that represents your camera. This may be called a "removable storage," as shown in Figure 7-4.
5. Double-click the picture you want to use. The picture will appear in Word.
6. On the Picture tools Format tab, you can adjust custom settings, such as adjusting brightness and contrast or choosing to display the image with various borders and effects, as you can see in Figure 7-5. (If the Format tab is not visible, click the picture to select it.)

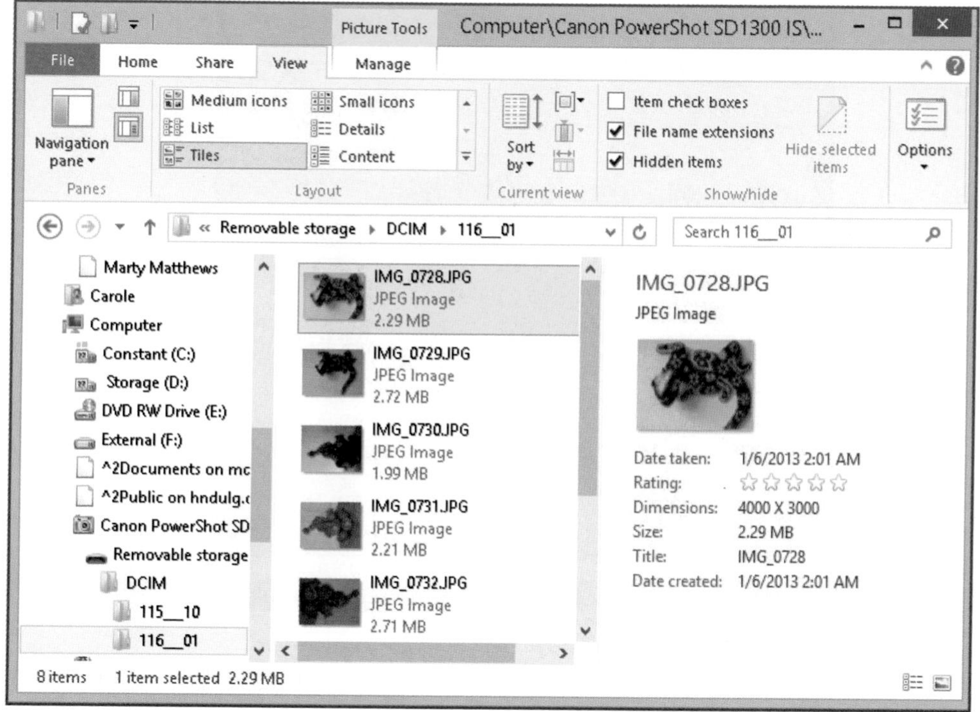

Figure 7-4: ***Plugging your camera into your computer makes it an extension of the computer and allows you to get pictures directly from it.***

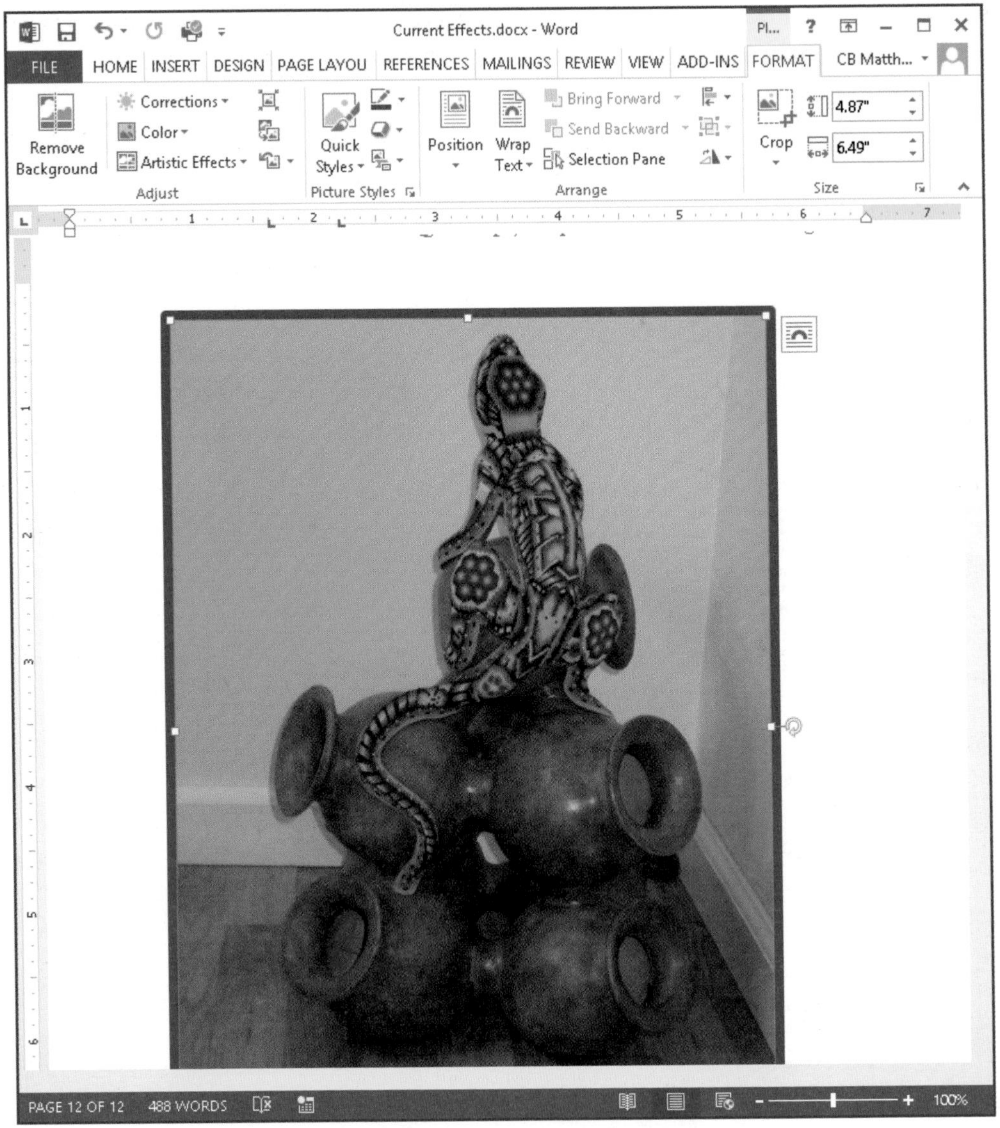

Figure 7-5: ***After bringing a picture into Word, you can set several image properties.***

TIP If you have plugged in and turned on your camera and everything looks like it should be working but you can't find it, in Windows 8 click the lower-right corner | **Settings** | **Control Panel**. (In Windows 7, click **Start** | **Control Panel**.) In Control Panel Category view, click **Hardware And Sound**, and click **Devices And Printers**. If your camera is not listed, click **Add A Device**. Select your camera, click **Next**, enter a name for the device, and click **Finish**.

CAUTION! Material you copy from the Internet, books, magazines, and other sources is normally protected by copyright; therefore, before you put it on your website or use it for any commercial purpose, be sure to check the licensing agreement or contact the copyright owner.

Use the Picture Tools Format Tab

Pictures are manipulated primarily by using the Picture Tools Format tab, shown in Figure 7-6. The Format tab automatically appears when an illustration is selected in a document. The tab has four groups that allow you to adjust the characteristics of an image, determine its style, remove its background, arrange an image on a page or in relation to other images or text, and size an image. In addition, the two Dialog Box Launchers in the Picture Styles and Size groups provide a number of other settings.

Crop Unwanted Areas of a Photo

You can remove areas from a picture that you do not want by using the Crop tool on the Picture toolbar.

1. Open and select the picture you want to crop. See "Add Pictures from a Computer" earlier in this chapter.
2. Click **Picture Tools Format** | **Crop** in the Size group, and click **Crop** from the menu. The picture redisplays with eight sizing handles on the corners and sides, and the mouse pointer becomes a four-headed arrow.
3. Place the cropping tool over one of the eight sizing handles (it will morph into an angle or T icon while you drag), and drag the tool so that the area of the picture is cut away or cropped by what you have dragged over, as shown in Figure 7-7.

Linking Picture Files

Pictures are *embedded* by default when inserted in a document. Embedding means that the picture files become part of the Word file and their file size is added to the size of the saved Word document. In a document with several high-resolution pictures, the document's size can quickly rise to several megabytes (the greater the number of pixels in a picture, the higher the resolution and the larger the file size). To dramatically reduce the size of a document that contains pictures, you can *link* to the picture files instead. In this case, the addresses of picture files are retained in the document file, not the pictures themselves. (Alternatively, you can reduce the resolution and compress embedded pictures, although the reduction in file size won't be as large as with linked files. See the section "Reduce a Picture's File Size," later in the chapter.) Another characteristic of linked picture files is that any changes made and saved in the source file will be updated in the Word document. Linking does have the downside of requiring the picture files to remain in the same folder location they were in when the link was created. In addition, documents with linked files are not suitable for sharing outside your local network.

1. To link a picture file when you are inserting a picture into a document, click **Insert** | **Picture** in the Illustrations group to open the Insert Picture dialog box.
2. Click the **Insert** down arrow in the lower-right corner, and click **Link To File**.

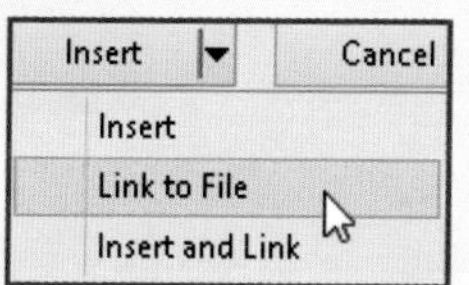

1 2 3 4 5 6 7 8 9 10

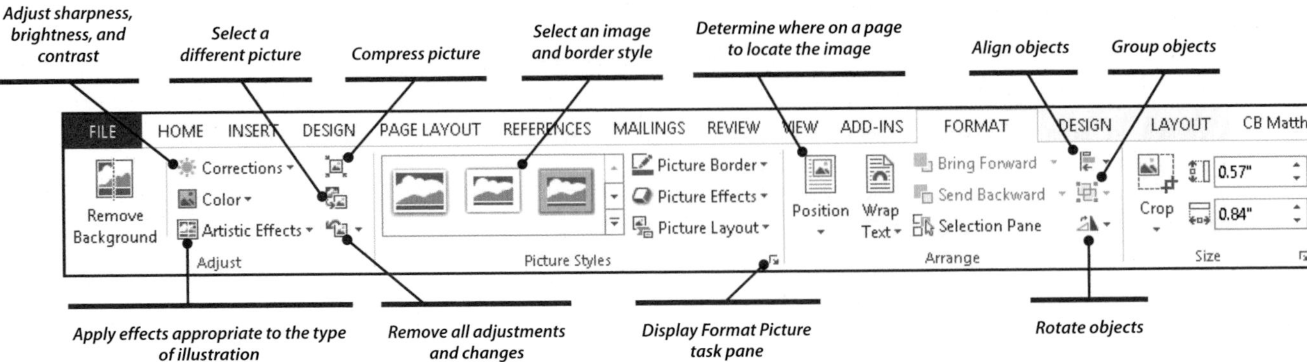

Figure 7-6: **The Picture Tools Format tab is your one-stop venue for accessing picture-related options.**

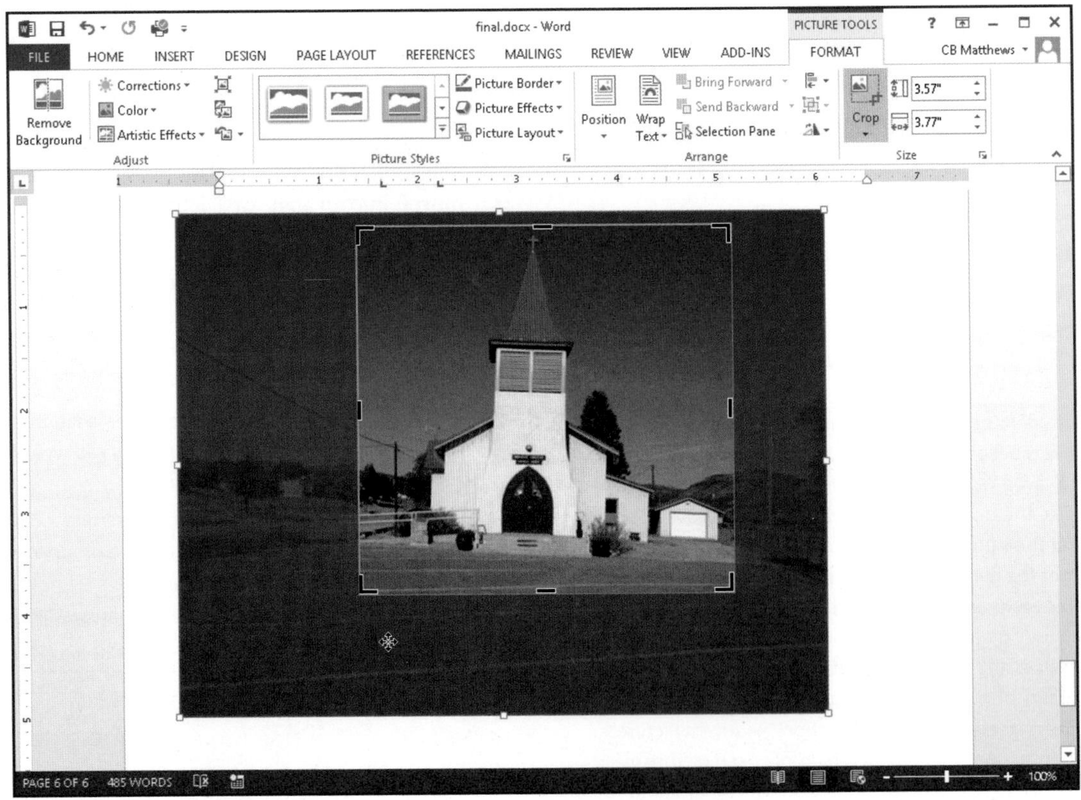

Figure 7-7: **Cropping removes the area of a picture outside where the cropping handle has been dragged.**

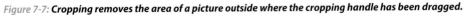

4. Release the mouse button. The area of the picture is shown as it will be cropped. While the cropping handles are still shown, you can drag them to a different location and consider that cropping.
5. To complete the cropping and turn off the Crop tool, press **ESC** or click outside of the image. If you change your mind after you complete the cropping, click **Undo** in the Quick Access toolbar or press **CTRL+Z** to reverse the cropping.

TIP You can crop to a shape to create some interesting effects. Click **Picture Tools Format | Crop To A Shape** in the Size group.

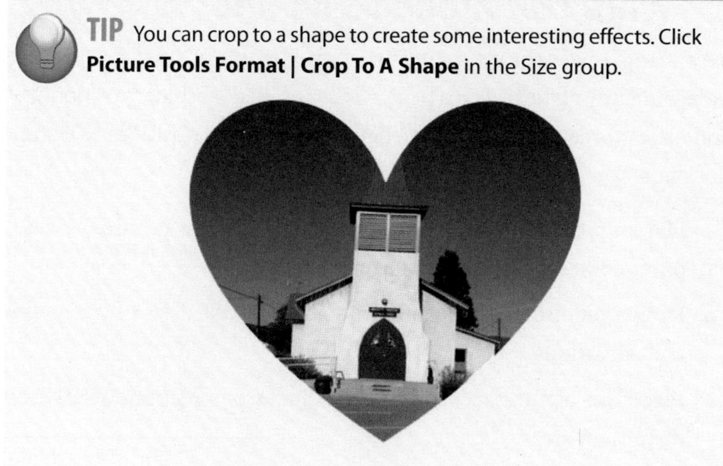

Position "In-Line" Pictures

When you insert a picture, by default, the image is positioned in a paragraph similar to a character you enter from the keyboard; that is, the bottom of the image is aligned with the bottom of the text line at the insertion point. The paragraph will expand vertically the height of the picture and "push" any other text or objects down the page. The picture is "in-line with text" and maintains its *relative* position to surrounding content as text and other objects are added to or removed from the page. (You can change this orientation, however. See "Wrap Text Around a Picture.")

Align Pictures

When a picture is in-line with text, it will respond to paragraph formatting. Use one of the following paragraph-formatting tools to align pictures with text (see Chapter 3 for details on how to format paragraphs):

- Click **Home** and then one of the paragraph alignment tools in the Paragraph group.
- Use the Paragraph dialog box, which is opened by either right-clicking the paragraph for its context menu or clicking **Home | Dialog Box Launcher** in the Paragraph group.
- Use tabs and indents, which are set in the horizontal ruler or the Tabs dialog box (opened from the Paragraph dialog box or by double-clicking a tab on the ruler).

Move Pictures

1. Click the picture you want to move to select it.
2. Drag the picture to a new paragraph or table cell.

TIP You can add a caption to inserted pictures to give a uniform appearance to your picture identifiers. Right-click a picture and click **Insert Caption**. In the Caption dialog box, choose a label (create your own labels by clicking **New Label**), where you want the caption, and a numbering format. You can also have Word use AutoCaption to automatically add a caption based on the type of picture or object inserted.

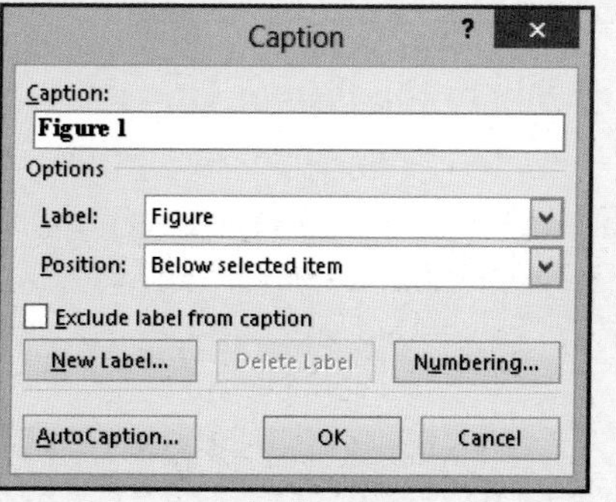

1 2 3 4 5 6 7 8 9 10

Reduce a Picture's File Size

Pictures embedded in a document add to the document's file size. Just a few high-resolution pictures or several lower-resolution pictures can quickly increase a document's file size beyond the threshold established by many email servers and network administrators. To mitigate file size "bloat," you have a few options available to you. (An alternative method of reducing the impact of inserted pictures is to link the pictures to the document. See the QuickFacts "Linking Picture Files" earlier in this chapter for more information.)

1. Open the document that contains the picture whose file size you want to reduce, and select the picture.
2. Click **Picture Tools Format | Compress Pictures** in the Adjust group.

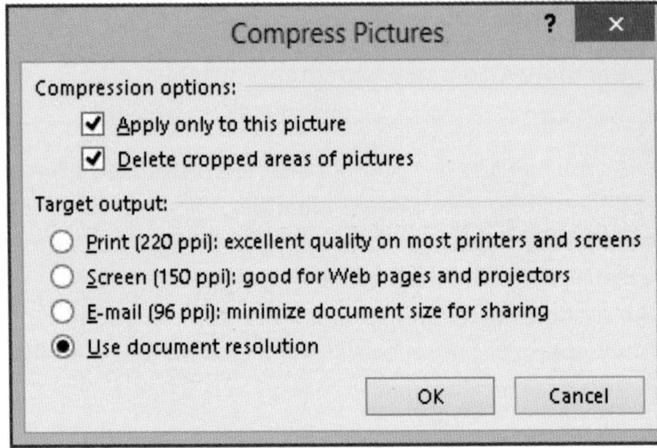

3. Click **Apply Only To This Picture** if that is what you want (versus applying it to all the pictures in the document).
4. Choose whether to delete cropped areas of pictures, which removes any cropped areas not only from view, but totally from the document.
5. Choose whether the target output should be:
   - Printing the document
   - Viewing it on the screen
   - Sending it via email
   - Current document resolution

   For each option but the last, the resolution of the resulting image is shown in pixels per inch (ppi). The greater the ppi, the higher the resolution.
6. Click **OK** to close the Compress Pictures dialog box.

Wrap Text Around a Picture

Wrapping text around a picture requires positioning a picture independently of the text on a page, which is called "absolute positioning," and offers three features that the default paragraph-positioning feature does not. You can:

- Place a picture in a document so that it keeps its position, even if other content shifts on the page
- Drag a picture to any location on a page, regardless of paragraph considerations
- Place the picture according to distances or positions relative to document areas

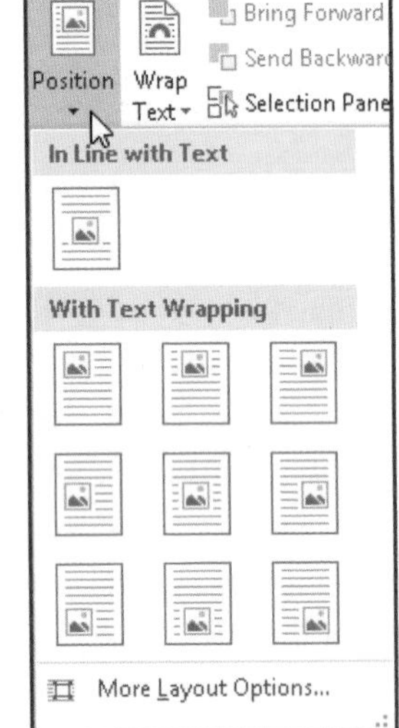

To position a picture absolutely:

1. Click the picture to select it. Click **Picture Tools Format | Position** in the Arrange group.
2. Click any wrapping style, except In Line With Text. You can now drag the picture to anywhere in the document.

TIP Pictures that are in-line with text are, in a sense, treated like a big character and have paragraph-formatting characteristics. Pictures can also be positioned independently of text and display either on top of the text or behind it. Click **Picture Tools Format | Position | More Layout Options**.

CREATE DRAWINGS

Drawings may be composed of prebuilt shapes, text you add effects to, and renderings you put together using one or more drawing tools. You can manipulate drawings by altering their position, size, color, shape, and other characteristics using the Drawing Tools Format tab, shown in Figure 7-8. You can choose premade illustrations or *shapes;* add styles, color, and effects; and position and size illustrations using the tools available in the Drawing Tools Format tab.

Drawings are created within a drawing canvas, which is a rectangular area where you can move and size multiple drawings as one object. To start a new drawing:

Open a new drawing canvas. Click **Insert | Shapes** in the Illustrations group, and then, at the bottom of the drop-down menu, click **New Drawing Canvas**.

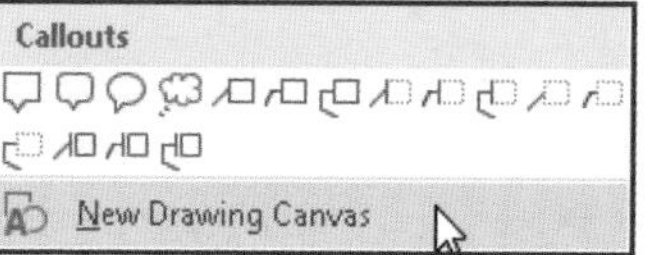

–Or–

Start with one of the many prebuilt shapes on the Shapes drop-down menu, and a drawing canvas will be created for you.

TIP Several other shapes are available from clip art collections. Click **Insert | Online Pictures** in the Illustrations group. In the Search text box, type autoshapes and click the **Search** icon. You'll see a list of resulting autoshapes.

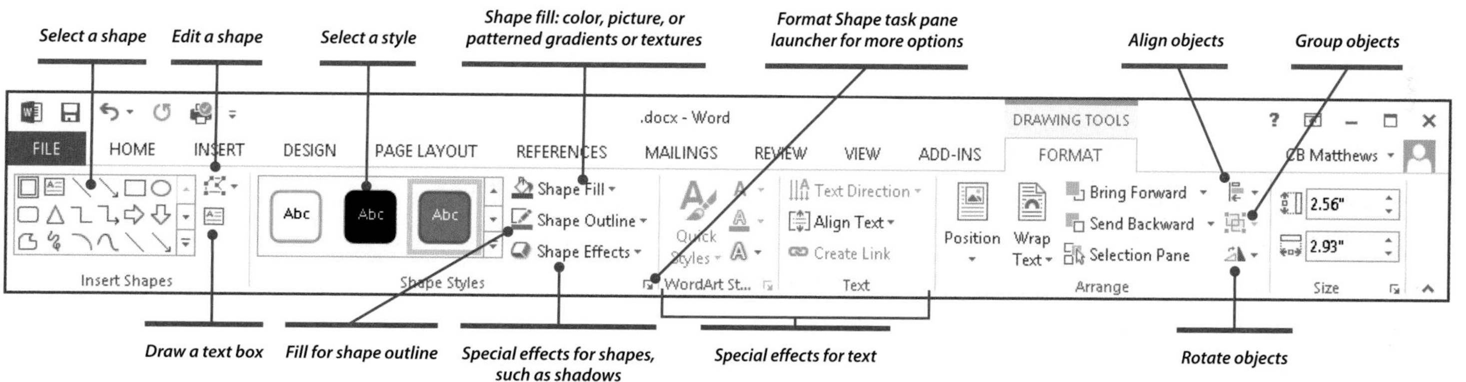

Figure 7-8: ***The Drawing Tools Format tab provides tools to create and insert drawings and to apply effects.***

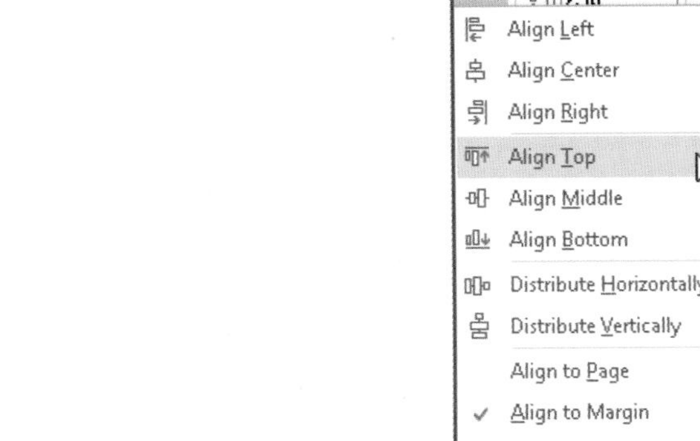

Figure 7-9: ***Aligning objects allows you to position your drawing object more precisely.***

> **TIP** Click **Drawing Tools Format | Align Objects** in the Arrange group to find a number of options that help with the relative placement of several objects. These allow you to align a common edge of several objects or to evenly distribute them, as seen in Figure 7-9.

Add Shapes

Shapes are prebuilt drawings that you can select, or you can create your own by modifying existing shapes or drawing your own freeform shapes. The prebuilt shapes and tools for creating your own are added either from the Insert tab Illustrations group or, with a drawing canvas open and selected, from the Drawing tools Format tab Insert Shapes group.

1. Click **Insert | Shapes** in the Illustrations group to open the Shapes drop-down menu.
2. Choose a shape by:

   Clicking a shape from one of the several categories

   –Or–

   Clicking one of the lines or basic shapes to begin your own shape
3. Drag the mouse crosshair pointer in the approximate location and size you want. In the case of freeform tools, see "Work with Curves."

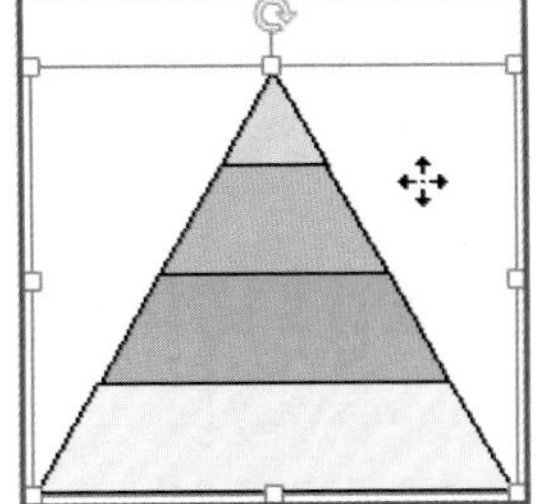

Use Color Effects

Color can be added to interior fills, borders, and text in various shades, gradients, textures, and patterns.

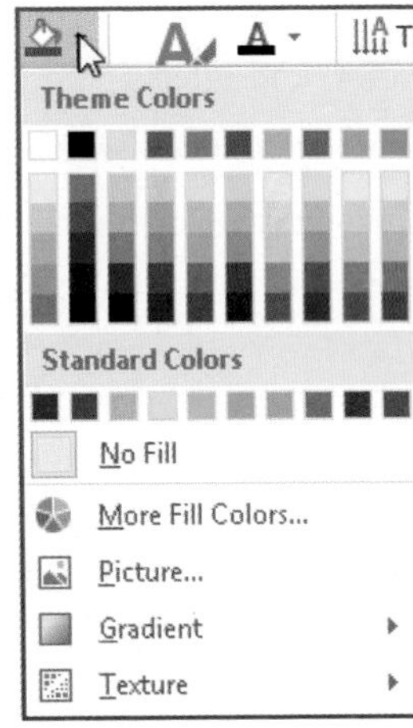

1. Click a drawing to select it.
2. Click **Drawing Tools Format | Shape Fill** or **Shape Outline** in the Shape Styles group. (The Drawing Tool Format toolbar is show earlier in Figure 7-8.)

A menu of coloring options opens. Depending on what attribute you want to format, you will see all or part of the following options.

Select a Color Quickly

Click one of 10 standard colors or one of the 60 theme colors in the color matrix on the drop-down menu.

–Or–

Click **More (*Fill* or *Outline*) Colors** to have access to more than 140 standard colors and many more custom colors.

Set Gradients

A gradient is the gradual blending of two colors, such as white and blue, where blues fades into white.

1. Click **Gradient** on the Shape Fill drop-down menu to open the submenu of basic gradient options.
2. Click **More Gradients** to open the Format Shape task pane.
3. Click **Shape Options** beneath the Format Shape title, if it is not already selected.
4. Select **Gradient Fill** under Fill, as shown in Figure 7-10.
5. Click **Preset Gradients** and select one of the gradient color schemes from the drop-down list box.

   –Or–

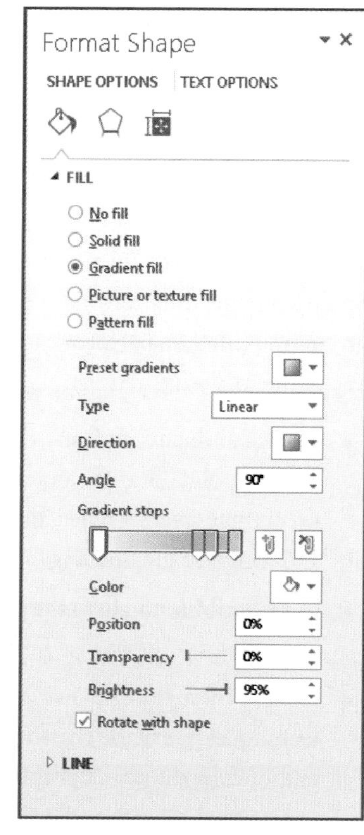

Figure 7-10: ***You can blend colors to create gradient fills.***

To manually create a gradient effect:

1. Click a gradient stop, and click **Color** to open the color palette, and then click a color. Repeat this for each of the gradient stops you want.
2. To add a stop, double-click the gradient bar or click the **Add Gradient Stop** button on the right. To delete a stop, drag it off the gradient bar or click the **Remove Gradient Stop** button.
3. Select a type of fill and its direction and angle, if applicable.
4. For each of the gradient stops, you can use the Position spinner to precisely set the location of the stop on the gradient bar.
5. Also, for each gradient stop, you can use the relevant slider or the spinner to set the degree of brightness and transparency.
6. When you are done, click **OK**.

Use a Picture to Fill Your Drawing

With a shape in Word that you want to fill with a picture:

1. Select the shape.
2. Click **Drawing Tools Format | Shape Fill | Picture** in the Shape Styles group. The Insert Pictures dialog box appears.

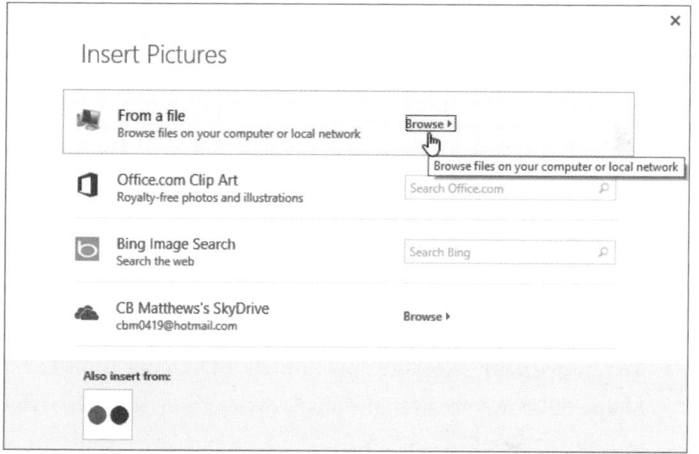

3. Click **Browse** on the From A File option to find the picture you want.
4. Then select it, and click **Insert**. The picture will be inserted into the background of the drawing shape.

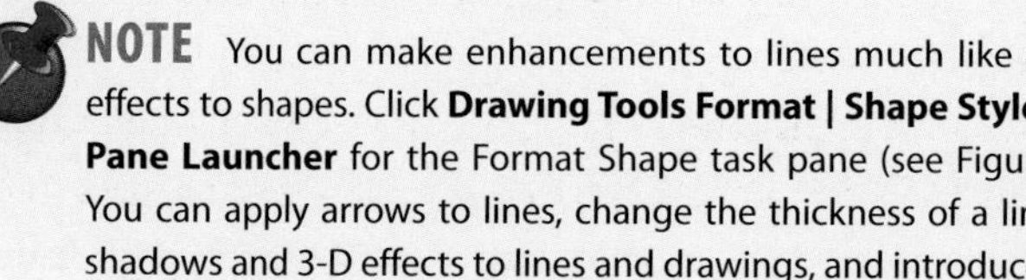

NOTE You can make enhancements to lines much like adding effects to shapes. Click **Drawing Tools Format | Shape Styles Task Pane Launcher** for the Format Shape task pane (see Figure 7-8). You can apply arrows to lines, change the thickness of a line, add shadows and 3-D effects to lines and drawings, and introduce other enhancements. The tools work similarly—select the line or drawing by clicking it, and then click the tool whose effect you want.

1 2 3 4 5 6 7 8 9 10

CAUTION! Do not remove the border or line around a drawing unless you have first added a fill. Without the line and a fill, the drawing is invisible, except for the handles that display when it's selected.

Color Text in a Text Box

1. Select the text to be colored by double-clicking or dragging. If you have trouble selecting the text you want, set your insertion point at the beginning or end of the selection, and press and hold CTRL+SHIFT while using the arrow keys to select the remaining characters.
2. On the mini toolbar (displayed when you select the text and place your pointer over the toolbar's vague outline), click the **Font Color** down arrow, and click the color you want from the color matrix. Your selected text is colored, and the Font Color button displays the selected color so that you can apply that same color to additional objects by just clicking the button.

Remove Effects

- **To remove a fill**, select the drawing. Click **Drawing Tools Format | Shape Fill** down arrow in the Shape Styles group, and click **No Fill**.
- **To remove the outline border** around a drawing, select the drawing. Click **Drawing Tools Format | Shape Outline** down arrow in the Shape Styles group, and click **No Outline**.
- **To remove text coloring**, select the text, in the mini toolbar click the **Font Color** down arrow, and click **Automatic**. The text will turn black.

Work with Curves

To find the freeform tools used to draw curved shapes, click **Insert | Shapes** in the Illustrations group. On the Shapes drop-down menu under Lines or Recently Used Shapes, you'll see the available freeform tools. (You will find that shapes are displayed in the Recently Used Shapes area after you have used them.)

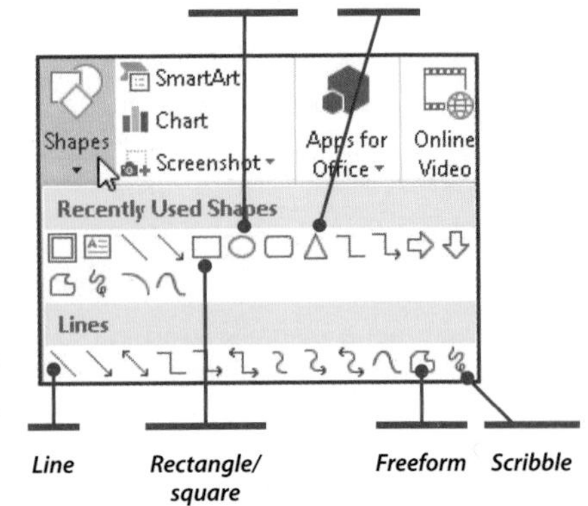

Create a Curve

To create a curve, click **Insert | Shapes** in the Illustrations group. You can then perform any of the following actions:

- Click **Curve** and click the crosshair pointer to establish the curve's starting point. Drag the pointer and click at each change in direction to continue creating other curvatures. Double-click to set the end point and complete the drawing.
- Click **Scribble** and drag the pencil icon to create the exact shape you want. Release the mouse button to complete the drawing.
- Click **Freeform** and use a combination of curve and scribble techniques. Click the crosshair pointer to establish curvature points, and/or drag the pencil pointer to create other designs. Double-click to set the end point and complete the drawing.

Adjust a Curve

1. Select the curve to be adjusted.
2. Click **Drawing Tools Format | Edit Shapes** in the Insert Shapes group, and click **Edit Points**. Black squares (*vertices*) appear at the curvature points. You have these options:
   - Drag a vertex to reconfigure its shape.
   - Pull out the two curve handles (the white squares) and rotate them to change the degree and angle of the curve.
3. Change any other vertex, and click outside the curve when finished.

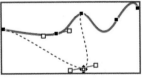

Close a Curve

Manually closing a curve is not always easy, so Word gives you an automated way to do it.

1. After completing a shape, right-click the curve and click **Edit Points**.
2. Right-click the curve again, and click **Close Path**.

Add Special Effects to Text

Special text effects, as shown in Figure 7-11, can be added easily to text using WordArt to simulate a graphic artist's professional touch.

NOTE Another "WordArt Effects" on the Home tab adds the ability to experiment with additional effects, such as outlines, shadows, reflections, glows, and more. You can get to these effects by clicking **Home | Text Effects** in the Font group. The effects can be seen on selected text as you mouse over them.

Apply a WordArt Effect

1. Click **Insert | Insert WordArt** in the Text group to display the WordArt gallery of text styles, shown in Figure 7-11.
2. Click a style that's close to what you want (you can "tweak" it later). The text "YOUR TEXT HERE" appears in a box with drawing handles.

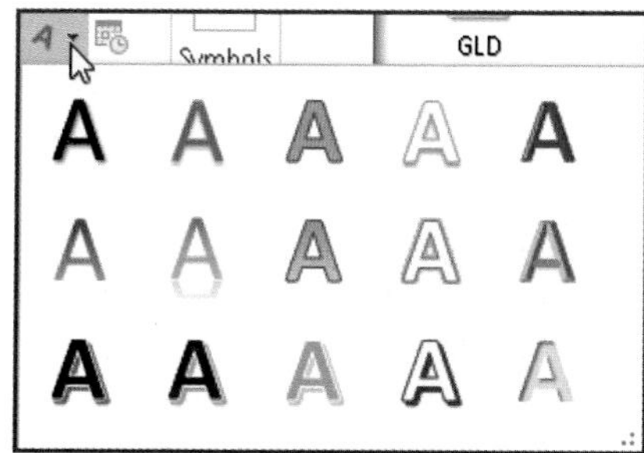

Figure 7-11: ***The WordArt gallery provides special effects that can be applied to text.***

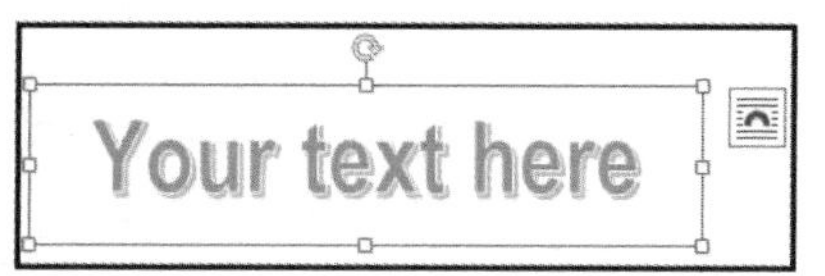

3. Select the text and overtype it with the text you want. Then select that text, and use the:
   - Home tab Font and Paragraph groups to format the text
   - Drawing Tools Format tab WordArt Styles and Text groups to adjust the text fill and outline colors and/or the text effects, as explained next
4. The text is displayed with the effect you have selected.

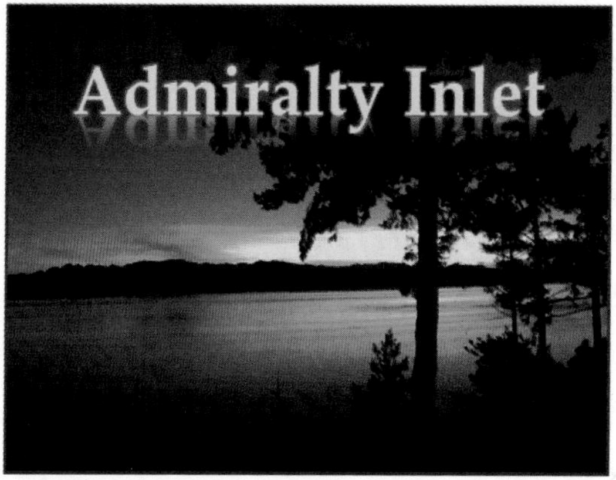

Use Drawing Tools with WordArt

The Drawing Tools Format tab, shown earlier in Figure 7-8, displays when you select text that has a WordArt effect applied to it. Use its options to apply different styles, effects, and alignment.

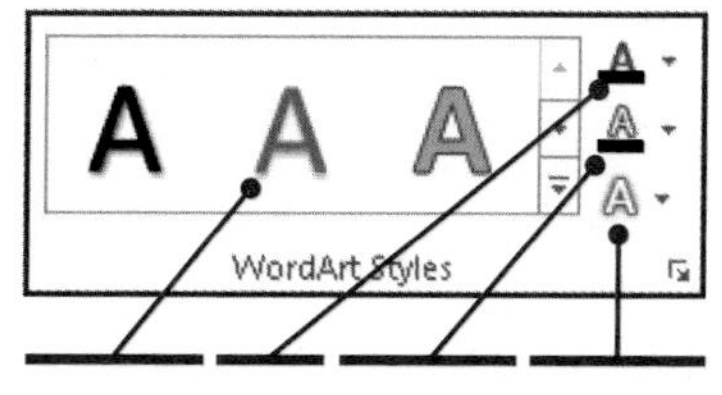

- In the WordArt Styles group, click a **Quick Styles** thumbnail (or if the window is maximized, click **More Styles**) to display the same WordArt gallery you originally saw from the Insert tab WordArt option. Point at a different WordArt style to preview the effects on your text. Click the style to apply it.

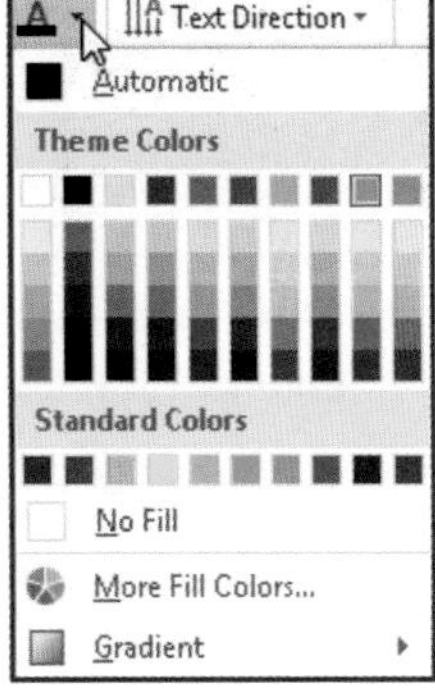

- Click **Text Fill** to open the standard color chart, and point at a color or a gradient to preview it on your text (see "Use Color Effects" earlier in this chapter). Click the selection to make it permanent.
- Click **Text Outline** to open the standard color chart, and point at a color, line weight, or line type to preview it on your text. Click a selection to make it permanent.
- Click **Text Effects** to open a drop-down menu of effects, each of which opens a submenu with a number of options for the particular effect, and at the bottom, an option to open the Format Text Effects dialog box. Click a selection to make it permanent.

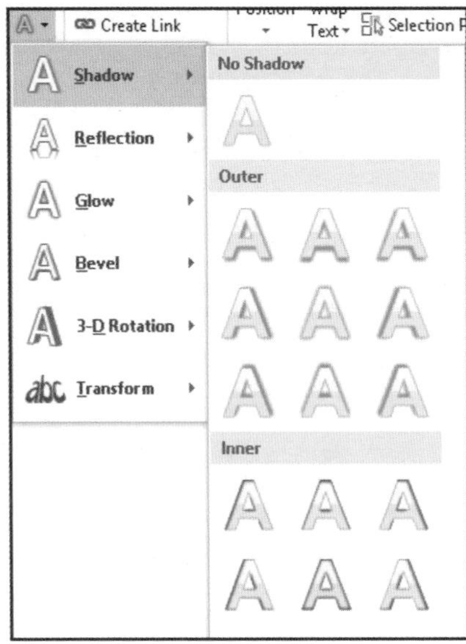

- Click **Text Effects** and then click **Transform** to open a drop-down menu of text transformations that wrap and curve text. Click the selection to make it permanent.

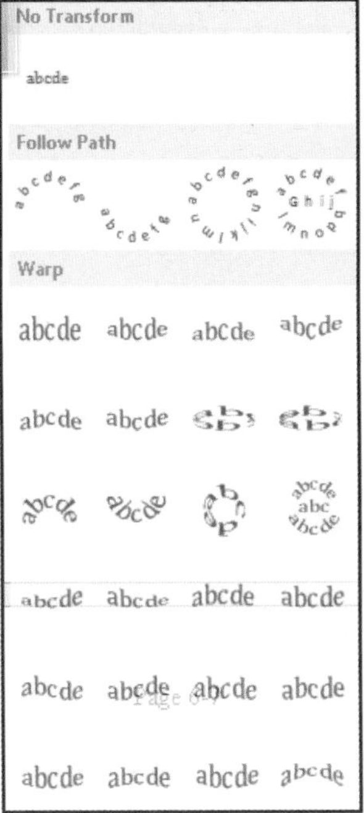

- Click the **WordArt Styles Task Pane Launcher** to open the Format Shape task pane. This provides a comprehensive set of controls to manually set WordArt shadow, reflections, glow, soft edges, and 2-D formats and rotation, as shown in Figure 7-12.
- In the Drawing Tools Format tab, click **Align Text** and click one of the several vertical alignment formats.

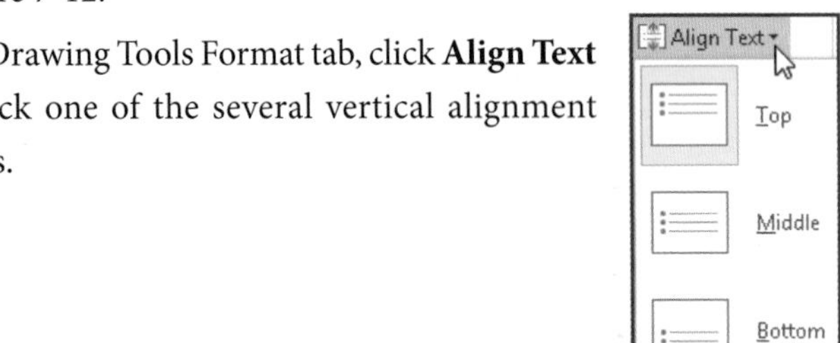

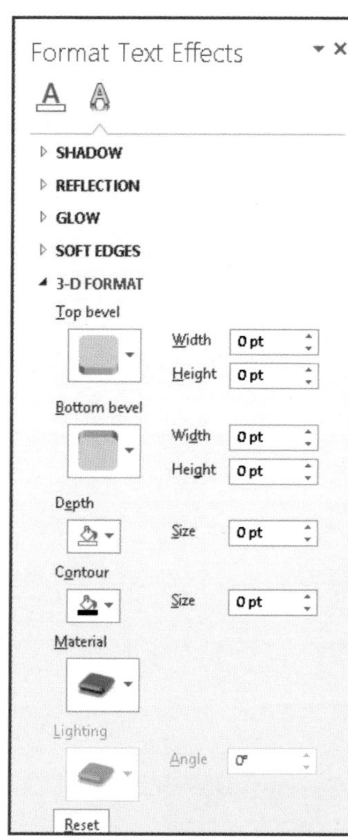

Figure 7-12: ***Word provides both quick and detailed ways to create amazing effects using shadows, reflections, and so forth.***

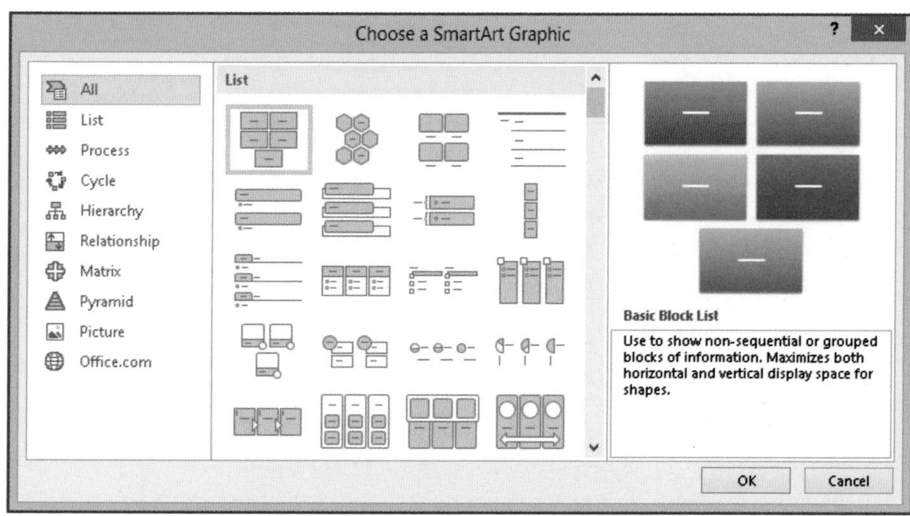

Figure 7-13: ***SmartArt allows you to easily create a number of diagram types, such as organizational charts.***

Create a Diagram

You can quickly create and modify several different types of diagrams, some of which are easily interchangeable. One type, an organization or hierarchy chart, provides special tools and features that streamline the structuring of this popular form of charting.

1. Click **Insert | SmartArt** in the Illustrations group. The Choose A SmartArt Graphic dialog box appears, as shown in Figure 7-13.

2. Click **Hierarchy** in the left column, and then double-click the organization chart, which is on the top left. The start of an organization chart and the SmartArt Tools Design tab will be displayed, as shown in the example chart in Figure 7-14. You can then personalize your chart by doing one or more of the following:
   - To restructure the organization chart, click the highest level, or *manager,* position in your chart, and in the SmartArt Tools Design tab, click **Layout** in the Create Graphic group to open a menu of hierarchical options. Click the structure that best matches your organization.

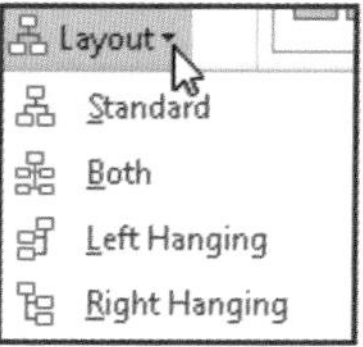

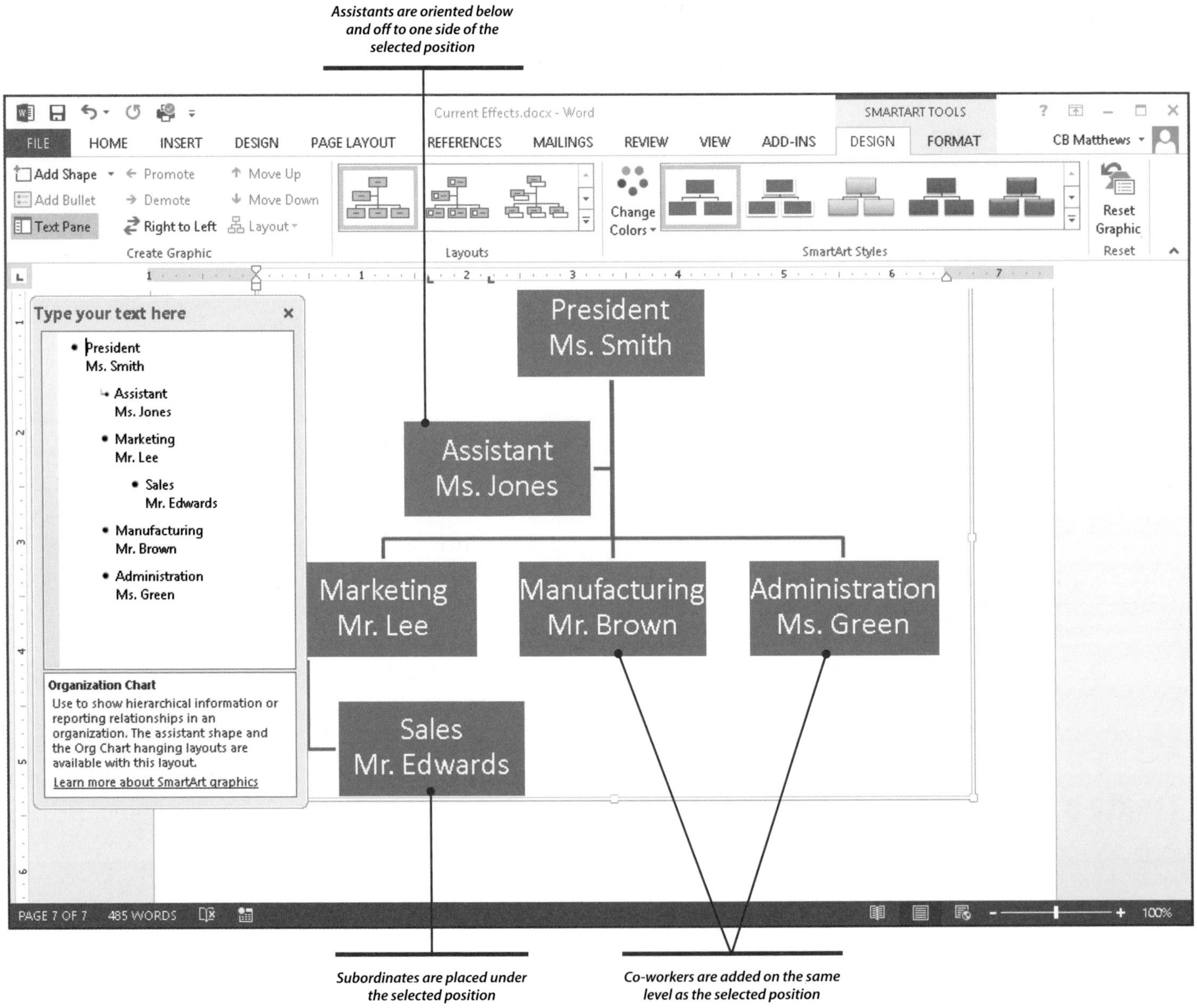

Assistants are oriented below and off to one side of the selected position

Subordinates are placed under the selected position

Co-workers are added on the same level as the selected position

Figure 7-14: **Organization charts are easily laid out and formatted using SmartArt in Word.**

- To add a new position to your chart, click a current box that the new one is related to on the chart. In the Create Graphic group, click **Add Shape** and select the type of new position you want to add to the current structure. For a higher level, click **Add Shape Above**; for a subordinate level, click **Add Shape Below**; for a co-worker level, click either **Add Shape Before** or **Add Shape After**; and for an assistant, click **Add Assistant**.
- To place text in a shape after adding a new shape or selecting one, simply start typing. You can also click **Text Pane** ("Type Your Text Here") in the Create Graphic group to open it, if it isn't already, and type text there. Type the name, title, and/or other identifiers for the position. The font size will change to fit the text box. Press **SHIFT+ENTER** after each line for a subordinate line (like a position after a name) that is spaced close to the previous line, or press **ENTER** for a second line equally spaced in the box. Format text in the shapes as you would standard text, using the Home tab and its associated options.
- Click **Right To Left** in the Create Graphic group to flip the entire chart so the names and shapes on the right are switched with the ones on the left. (You can switch it back since the button changes to "Left to Right.")
- Click **Promote** or **Demote** in the Create Graphic group to move a shape and its text up or down in the organization chart.
- Point at any of the alternative SmartArt styles to see how your chart would look with a color or effects change. Click the layout, color, or style to apply it.
- If you make a "permanent" change, as just described, you can return to the previous layout, color, or style by pressing **CTRL+Z** or by clicking **Reset Graphic** in the Reset group.
- To select a group of shapes and their text so that they can be acted upon all at once, hold down **CTRL** while clicking each shape (including the connecting lines).
- Click the **SmartArt Tools Format** tab to display several options for changing the shape and its text, as shown in Figure 7-15.

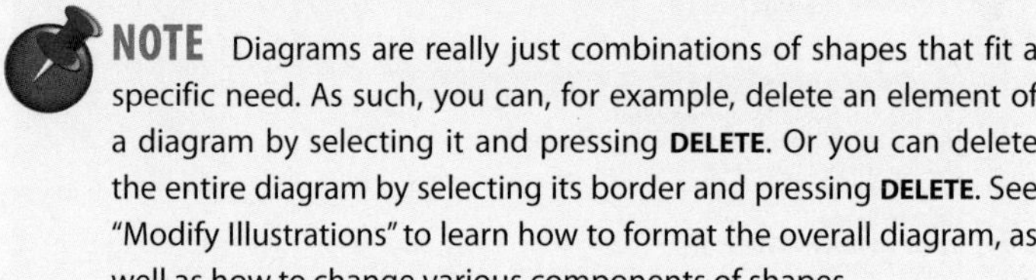

NOTE Diagrams are really just combinations of shapes that fit a specific need. As such, you can, for example, delete an element of a diagram by selecting it and pressing **DELETE**. Or you can delete the entire diagram by selecting its border and pressing **DELETE**. See "Modify Illustrations" to learn how to format the overall diagram, as well as how to change various components of shapes.

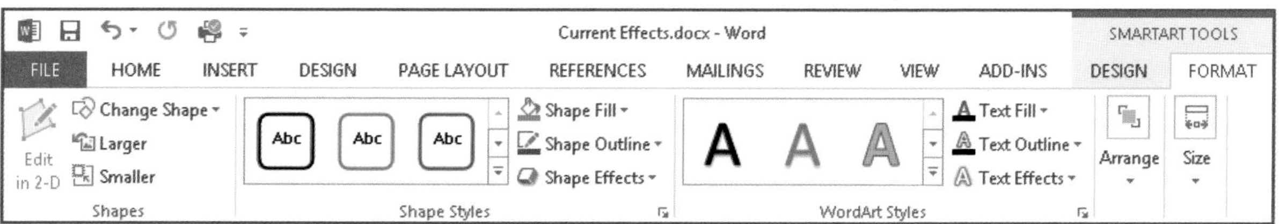

Figure 7-15: ***Quickly redesign the overall appearance of your organization chart.***

Add Objects from Other Programs

You might want to include the product of another program in a document as an illustration. The major difference between adding the illustration as an *object* (these are technically *OLE objects,* named for "object linking and embedding," which is the technology involved) and copying and pasting it is that an object maintains a link to the program that created it. This means that in addition to changing formatting and other illustration options, you can change the *content* using the menus, task panes, and other tools of the originating program while Word is still open.

1. Click **Insert | Object** in the Text group. If a context menu opens, click **Object** again. The Object dialog box appears.

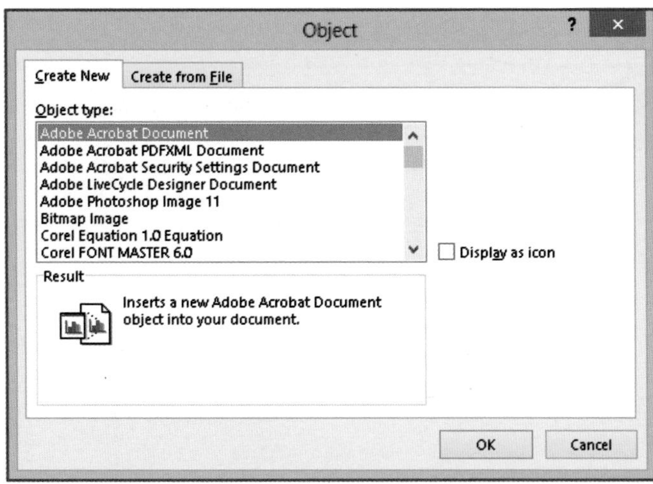

2. Choose whether to create a new object or use an existing one:
   - Click the **Create New** tab, select an object type, and click **OK**.
   - Click the **Create From File** tab, click **Browse**, locate an existing object, and click **OK**.

   Depending on the object, it opens in Word either in an image of what it is or in its original form, with the ribbon, toolbars, menus, and other tools taking on those of the object's originating program, as shown in Figure 7-16. If you see the image only, double-click the image to display it in its original form with its original tools.

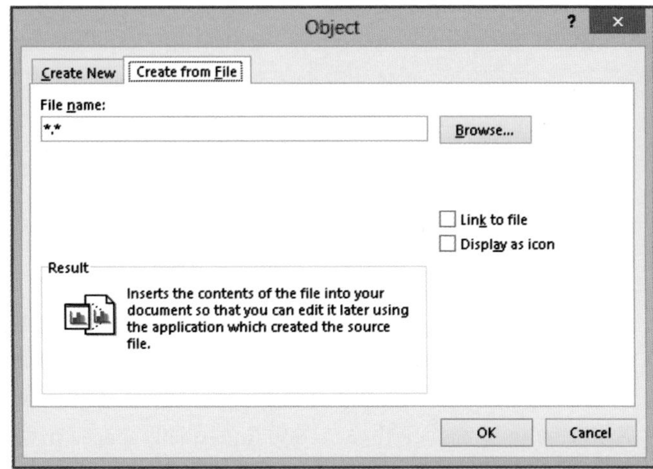

3. With the originating program open in Word, add content and apply design and formatting changes using the original tools.
4. When you are ready to return to Word, click the page outside the object. To reopen the object, double-click it.

TIP If you create an object from an existing file using the Create From File tab, you can create a *link* between the object in Word and the original file by clicking **Link To File** in the Object dialog box as you are bringing the object onto the document.

Take Screenshots

Screenshots (also called screen captures and screen grabs) allow you to copy a portion of what you see on your screen, be it an icon, window, or the entire screen. In Word, you can select any open windows to capture (except for Word itself, unless you have another Word window open), or you can drag a selection rectangle across whatever area of the screen

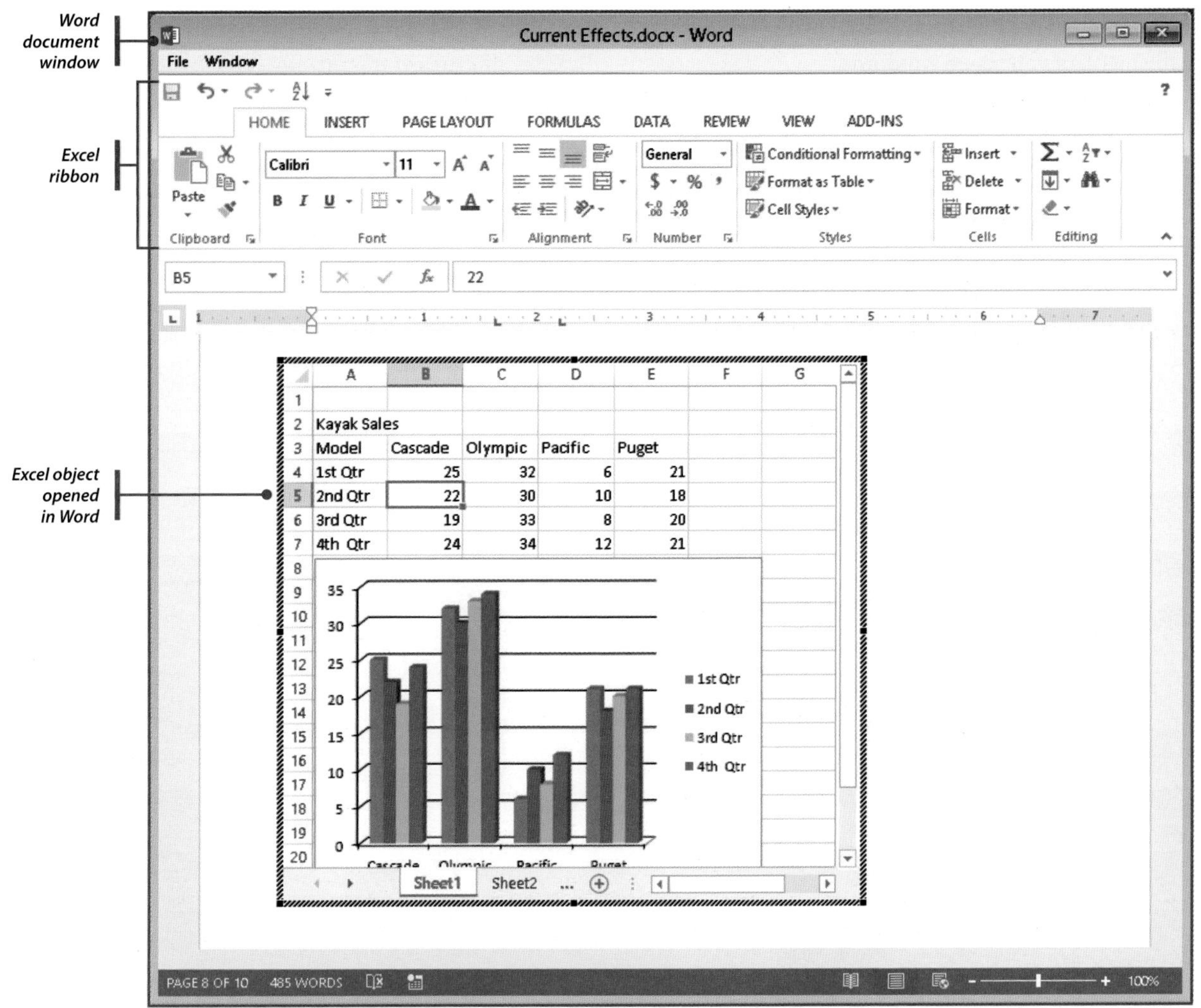

Figure 7-16: ***Many objects inserted in a document allow you to use their menus and toolbars within Word, such as this chart, which uses the tools from Excel.***

you want. The capture is placed in your document and can be modified using the Picture Tools formatting features.

1. Minimize the Word window and arrange your desktop with the program(s), window(s), and object(s) you want to capture.
2. Restore the Word window, place the insertion point where you want the screenshot, and click **Insert | Screenshot** in the Illustrations group. A menu of options is displayed, as described next.

- To capture a particular open window, select one of the windows shown in the menu of your open windows.

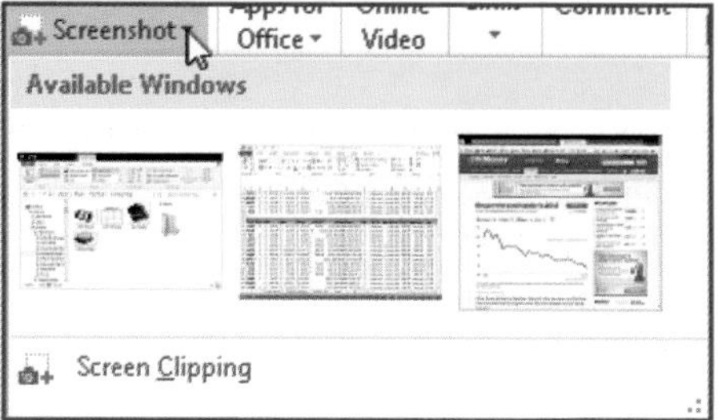

- Click **Screen Clipping**. Use the large black cross to drag across the area you want, and release the mouse button when finished. This way you can capture several windows or the whole screen, as shown in Figure 7-17.

3. In both cases, the image you selected is displayed on your worksheet surrounded by selection handles.

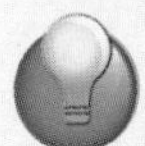

TIP When doing manual screenshots, drag over a slightly larger area than what you're looking to capture. You can more easily crop the picture to a smaller, precise size after it's in Word than you can add more image back in.

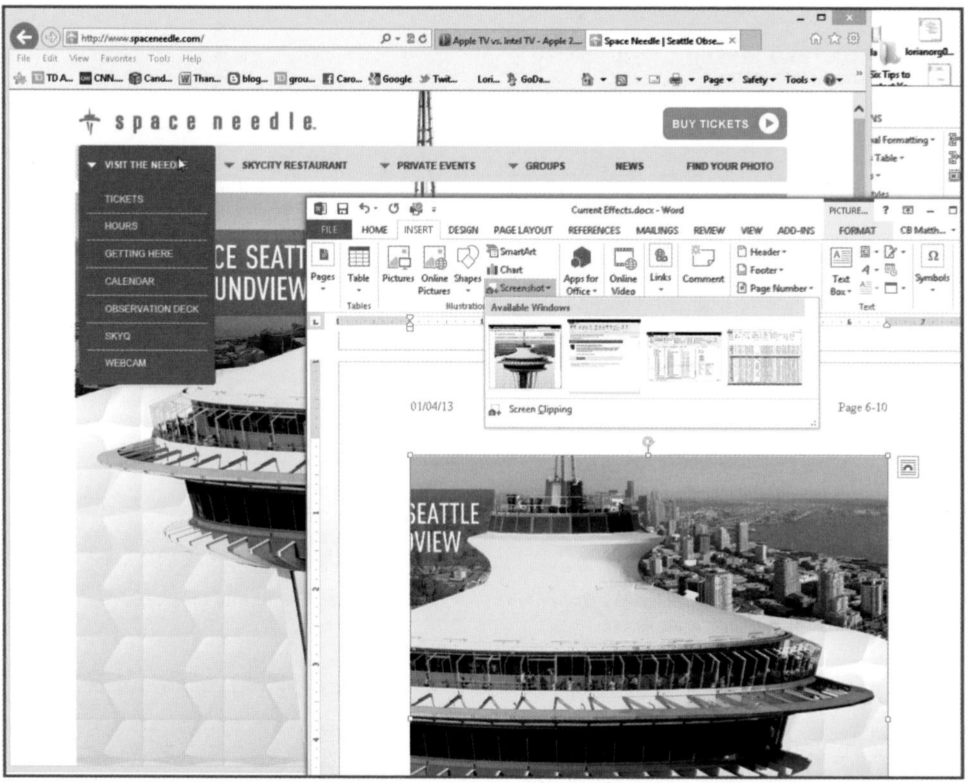

Figure 7-17: ***Screenshots are a powerful tool, allowing you to use your screen to provide visual additions to your document.***

CAUTION! Enlarging an image beyond the ability of the pixels to span it can distort the image.

TIP Display the Word rulers to help you draw, align, and arrange drawings more precisely. Click **View | Ruler** in the Show group.

MODIFY ILLUSTRATIONS

Pictures, drawings, and shapes share a common Format task pane, although not all of the features and options are available for every type of illustration you can add to a Word document. This section describes formatting and other modifications you can apply to illustrations.

Resize and Rotate Illustrations Precisely

You can change the size of illustrations by setting exact dimensions and rotating them. (You can also drag handles to change them interactively. See "Use Handles and Borders to Position Objects" later in this chapter for ways to resize and rotate illustrations with a mouse.)

1. Click the illustration you want to resize to select it.
2. Click **Picture** (or other type of illustration) **Tools Format | Size Dialog Box Launcher** in the Size group. (For some illustrations, such as an organization chart, the Size Dialog Box Launcher will not exist. Also, for some, a task pane is displayed rather than a dialog box.)

3. Click the **Size** tab, shown in Figure 7-18, and if it isn't already selected, click the **Lock Aspect Ratio** check box to size the illustration proportionally when entering either width or height values.
   - Under Rotate, enter a positive (rotate clockwise) or negative (rotate counterclockwise) number of degrees of rotation if you want to rotate the image.
   - Under either Height or Width, enter the height or the width dimension, or use the spinners to increase or decrease one of the dimensions from its original size.
   - Under Scale, enter a percentage for either the height or the width to increase or decrease it, or use the spinners to increase or decrease the percentage of the original picture size.
4. Click **OK**. The picture will resize and/or rotate according to your values.

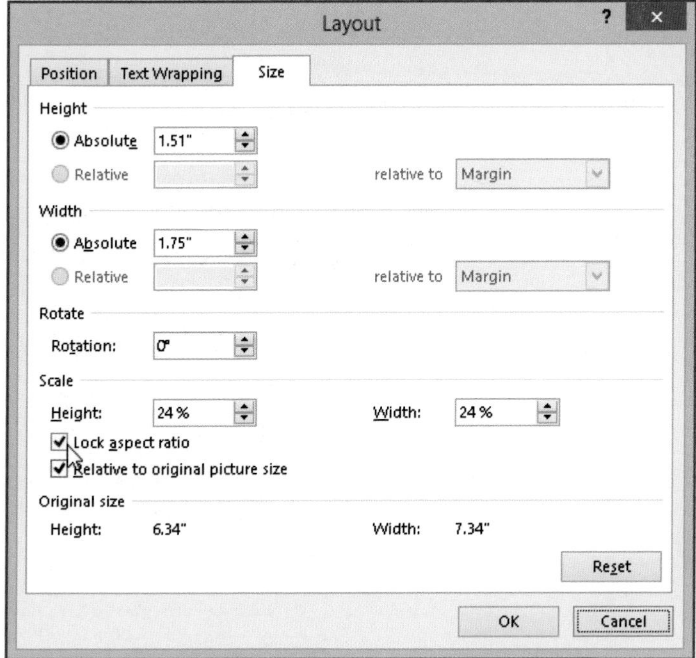

Figure 7-18: ***You can size an illustration to exact dimensions in its Layout dialog box.***

TIP After you change a picture from its default style of being in-line with the text to a style that supports absolute positioning, it is difficult to return to the default style. It's easiest to just delete the picture and reinsert it.

NOTE The default wrapping option (In Line With Text) is the only style that provides paragraph-like formatting to position pictures. If you change to any of the other wrapping styles, you can position the picture absolutely, that is, by dragging it into position or by selecting positions relative to document areas, such as margins or paragraphs.

Position Illustrations

Illustrations (including pictures that use absolute positioning) can be positioned anywhere in the document by dragging or setting values. In either case, the illustration retains its relative position within the document as text and other objects are added or removed. You can override this behavior by anchoring the illustration to a fixed location. You can also change how text and other objects "wrap" around the illustration. Figure 7-19 shows several of these features.

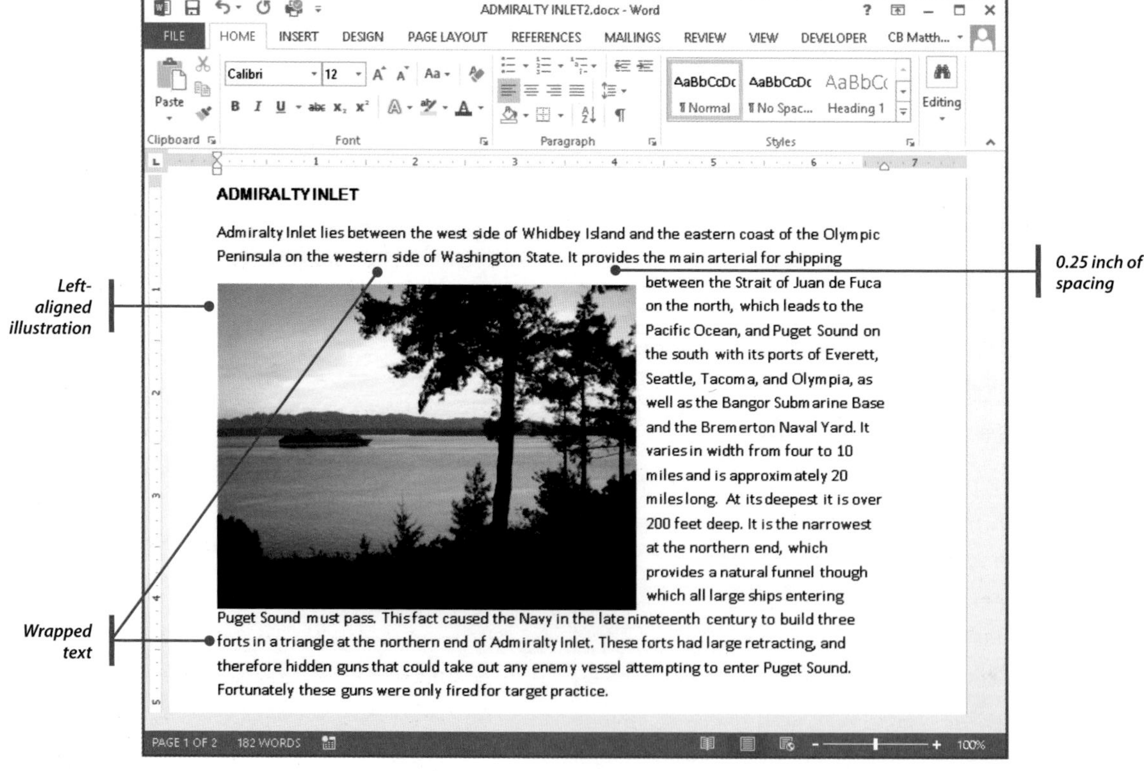

Figure 7-19: ***You can easily arrange text and illustrations in several configurations using dialog box options.***

QuickFacts

Understanding Illustration Positioning

When you position an illustration (picture, clip art, drawing, or shape) on the page, the position can be *inline,* or *relative,* to the text and other objects on the page, where the illustration moves as the text moves, like a character in a word. The alternative is *absolute* positioning, where the illustration stays anchored in one place, regardless of what the text does. If the illustration uses absolute positioning, you can then specify how text will wrap around the illustration, which can be on either or both sides or along the top and bottom of the illustration. Also, for special effects, the text can be all either on top of the illustration or underneath it.

If you find that the movement of the illustration is not as you intended, or if you want to change the way the illustration behaves as you add text, you can adjust the object easily by using the Layout dialog box. To display it, choose one of the following methods:

- Right-click the illustration and from the context menu, select **Wrap Text | More Layout Options**. The Layout dialog box is displayed, as seen in Figure 7-20. On the Position tab, you'll see horizontal and vertical absolute position options. On the right, you'll see what the illustration is positioned relative to: the margin, page, paragraph, or column. See "Position an Illustration Relative to Areas in a Document," later in this chapter. On the Text Wrapping tab, you'll find spacing controls.
- Click the **Layout Format** icon that appears when you select an object, and select **See More** at the bottom of the menu. The Layout dialog box is displayed.
- Click **Picture** (or object name) **Tools Format | Wrap Text** in the Arrange group, and click **More Layout Options**.

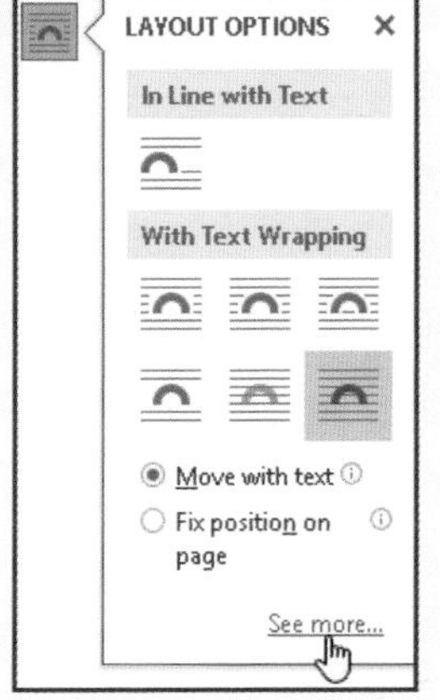

NOTE When you right-click an illustration, you may open a couple of context menus. If the one you're searching for does not open, right-click in a different place on the menu. It can be tricky, so persevere!

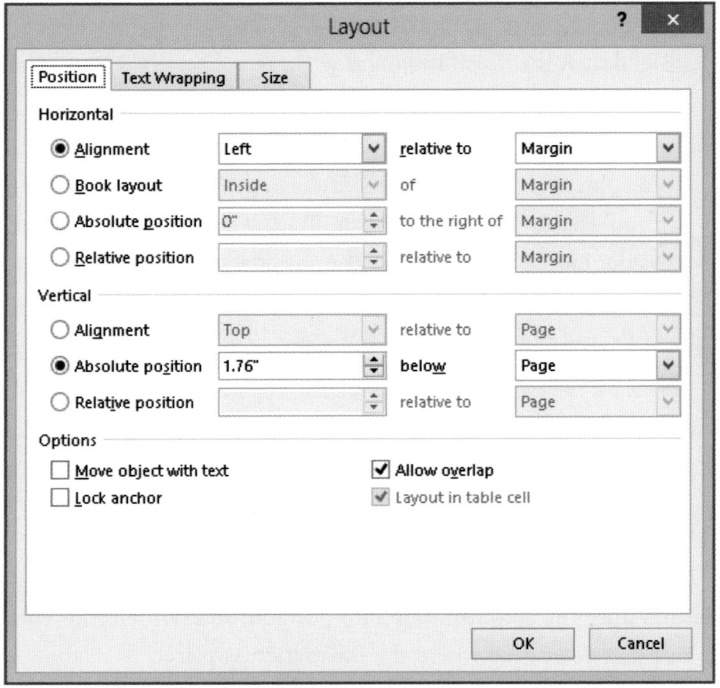

Figure 7-20: ***Using absolute positioning, you can choose where to place an illustration relative to other objects in the document.***

Change How Text Wraps Around an Illustration

By default, most illustrations come into a document in-line with the text, like just another character. In this mode, you can't control how the text flows, or *wraps,* around the illustration or where the illustration will be on the page if you change the text. You can change this behavior, however, to gain control of how the illustration and the text relate to each other.

1. Select the object, such as an illustration, that you want to wrap text around.
2. To quickly select an alternative text-wrap option, click the **Layout Options** icon that appears when you select the object. Select the option you want and click **Close** to remove the menu.

—Or—

Right-click the illustration and click **Wrap Text | More Layout Options**. The Layout dialog box is displayed.

3. Click the **Text Wrapping** tab, shown in Figure 7-21, and under Wrapping Style, click one of the styles to wrap as the icons indicate (if you select In Line With Text, the illustration will lose its absolute-positioning ability and can only be positioned using paragraph-like options, plus tabs, text, and spaces on the left).
4. Click where you want text to wrap, and under Distance From Text, click the relevant spinners to enter the distances you want between the text and the illustration.
5. Click **OK** to accept the wrapping style and other settings and to close the dialog box.

Position an Illustration Relative to Areas in a Document

Besides dragging an illustration into position, you can select or enter values that determine where the illustration is placed in relation to document areas.

1. Select the illustration that you want to position.
2. Click **Picture** (or other object name) **Tools Format | Wrap Text** in the Arrange group. Click **More Layout Options**, and click the **Position** tab. Select or enter the horizontal- and vertical-positioning entries by selecting them from the drop-down menus, entering the values, or using the spinners to increase or decrease distances, as shown earlier in Figure 7-20.
3. To anchor an illustration in place, regardless of whether other content is added or removed—for example, an illustration you want in the upper-left corner of a specific page—click the **Lock Anchor** check box, and clear all other options.
4. Click **OK** to close the Layout dialog box.

TIP When an illustration uses absolute positioning, an anchor icon may be displayed. If the anchor is locked, a padlock icon may also be displayed. If you don't see the anchor icon and the illustration is using absolute positioning, click **File | Options | Display** in the left column. Under Always Show These Formatting Marks, click the **Object Anchors** check box or click **Show All Formatting Marks**. Click **OK** to display anchor icons in the document.

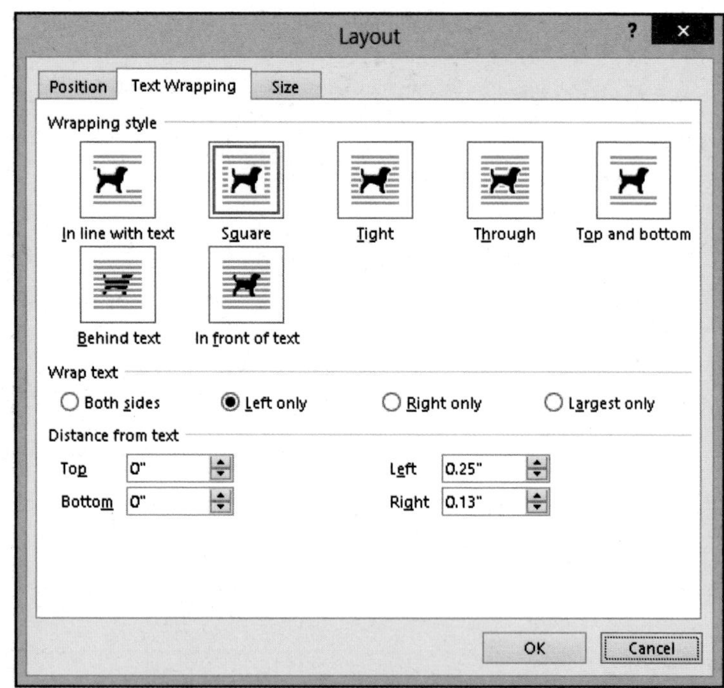

Figure 7-21: ***Word allows you to determine with some precision how text and illustrations interact.***

Use Handles and Borders to Position Objects

Objects, such as pictures, drawings, shapes, or text boxes, are easily manipulated using their sizing handles and borders.

Select and Rotate an Illustration

You select an illustration by clicking it. Handles appear around the illustration and allow you to perform interactive changes. The Layout Options icon also displays. Even text boxes and their text behave similarly (click **Insert | Text Box** in the Text group).

- Click in a text box. A dotted border with handles appears around the perimeter of the text box. Drag the rotation handle at the top, and the text box and its text will rotate. Hold SHIFT when dragging to rotate in 15-degree increments.

- Place the mouse pointer in the text in a text box; it will become an I-beam pointer. Click it to place an insertion point, or drag across the text to select it. The mini toolbar will appear, letting you make a selection to change the formatting.

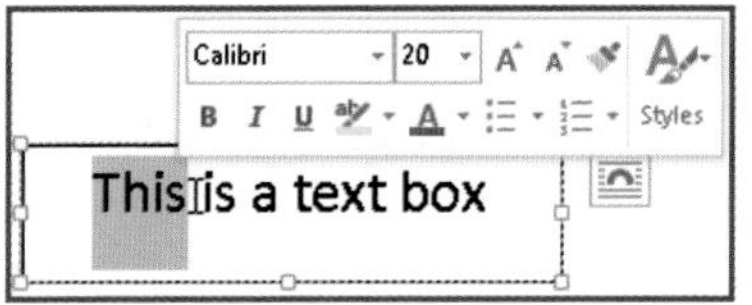

Resize an Illustration

Drag one of the square or round sizing handles surrounding the illustration—or at either end of it, in the case of a line—in the direction you want to enlarge or reduce the illustration. Your pointer will become a larger +. Hold SHIFT when dragging a corner sizing handle to change the height and length proportionately (if you have Lock Aspect Ratio selected in the Size tab of Format Pictures, the picture will remain proportionally sized without pressing SHIFT).

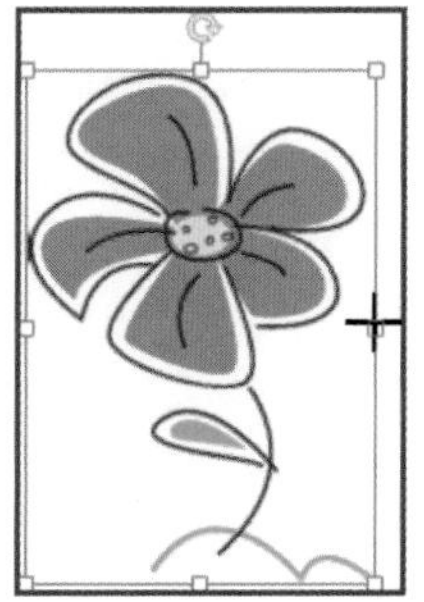

Position Illustrations Other Ways

While illustrations can be positioned absolutely by simply dragging them or choosing placement relative to other objects in a document, Word also provides a number of other techniques that help you adjust where an illustration is in relation to other illustrations.

Move Illustrations Incrementally

Select the illustration or group of illustrations (see "Combine Illustrations by Grouping"), hold CTRL, and press one of the arrow keys in the direction you want to move the illustration by very small increments (approximately .01 inch).

Reposition the Order of Stacked Illustrations

You can stack illustrations by simply dragging one on top of another. Figure 7-22 shows an example of a three-illustration stack. To reposition the order of the stack, right-click the illustration you want to change, click **Bring To Front** or **Send To Back** on the context menu, and then click one of the following:

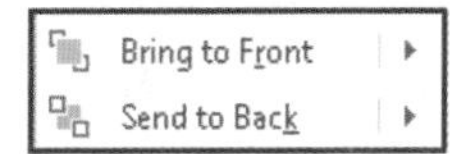

- **Bring To Front** moves the illustration to the top of the stack.
- **Send To Back** moves the illustration to the bottom of the stack.
- **Bring Forward** moves the illustration up one level (same as Bring To Front if there are only two illustrations in the stack).
- **Send Backward** moves the illustration down one level (same as Send To Back if there are only two illustrations in the stack).
- **Bring In Front Of Text** moves the illustration on top of overlapping text.
- **Send Behind Text** moves the illustration behind overlapping text.

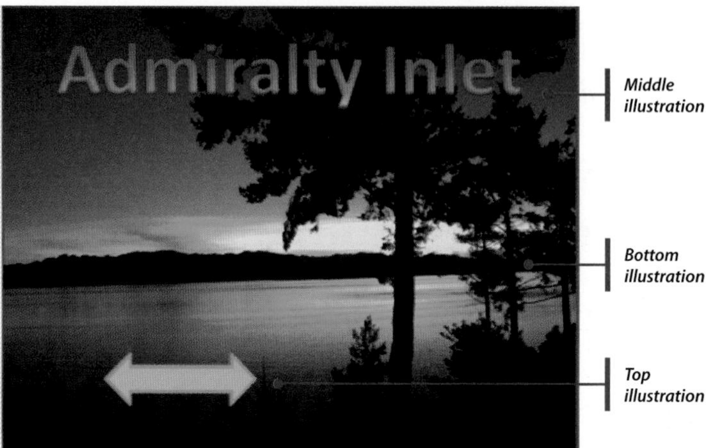

Figure 7-22: ***You can change the order of stacked illustrations to achieve the look you want.***

Align Illustrations

To align two or more illustrations relative to one another, select the illustrations by holding down SHIFT. Click **Picture** (or **Drawing**) **Tools Format | Align** in the Arrange group and click one of the alignment choices.

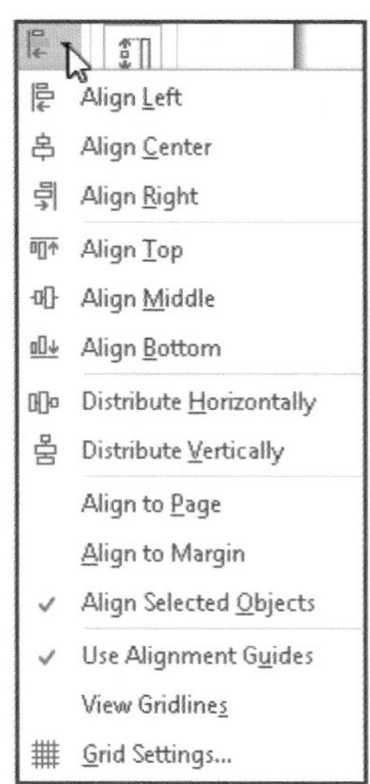

Evenly Space Illustrations

Select the illustrations by holding down SHIFT. Click **Picture** (or **Drawing**) **Tools Format | Align** in the Arrange group, and then click **Distribute Horizontally** or **Distribute Vertically**, depending on their orientation.

Combine Illustrations by Grouping

You can combine illustrations for any number of reasons, but you typically work with multiple illustrations to build a more complex rendering. To avoid losing the positioning, sizing, and other characteristics of the individual components just when you have them perfectly calibrated, you can group them so that they are treated as one object.

Group Illustrations

1. Select the illustrations to be grouped by clicking the first illustration and then holding down SHIFT while selecting other drawings and pictures.
2. Click **Picture** (or **Drawing**) **Tools Format | Group** in the Arrange group, and then click **Group** again.

—Or—

Right-click one of the selected illustrations, click **Group**, and click **Group** again.

A single set of selection handles surrounds the perimeter of the illustrations. Coloring, positioning, sizing, and other actions now affect the illustrations as a group instead of individually.

Ungroup Illustrations

To separate a group into individual illustrations, select the group. Click **Picture** (or **Drawing**) **Tools Format | Group** in the Arrange group and click **Ungroup**.

—Or—

Right-click the group, click **Group**, and click **Ungroup**.

QuickSteps to...

- Use Microsoft Form Templates
- Modify a Template
- Create a Form
- Use a Form
- Translate a Word or Phrase
- Translate Selected Text
- Translate an Entire Document
- Create a Chart
- Determine the Chart Type
- Select Chart Items
- Work with Chart Items
- Format Chart Items
- Format Text
- Work with the Data Table

Chapter 8

Using Special Features

Word comes with a number of special features that facilitate communications. Forms, which you can quickly generate in Word, provide the means to gather information. Language is no barrier, as Word can translate words and even entire documents. When working with data in Word, you can use Excel's charting capability to create a chart and embed it in Word to provide a more visual representation of data than that provided by a table.

WORK WITH FORMS

If you want to collect a consistent set of information from a number of people, an easy way is to use a form that asks for just the information you want. You can, of course, use Word's normal features, especially tables (see Chapter 6), to create a fairly good form. However, Word has some specialized tools that you can use to create professional-looking forms and allow someone using Word 2007 and later versions to interactively fill out the form. Using these same tools, Microsoft has both built in and included on Microsoft Office Online a number of form templates for various purposes. You can use these templates as is, you can modify them, and you can create your own forms from scratch.

Use Microsoft Form Templates

You can use the Microsoft Office Online form templates directly from Word, as explained in Chapter 2, or you can download and store them on your computer, where they are available from My Templates.

1 2 3 4 5 6 7 8 9 10

You can access Microsoft-provided templates directly from Word.

1. Click **File | New**, and type Forms in the Search For Online Templates (Office.com) Search text box. Microsoft Office Online is searched, and a list of forms is presented.
2. Under the list on the right, click the Category name of form that you want. For example, click **Business**.
3. Scroll down, reviewing the forms that are available to you, and click the form that you want to use. For example, click **Direct Deposit Authorization**, as shown in Figure 8-1.

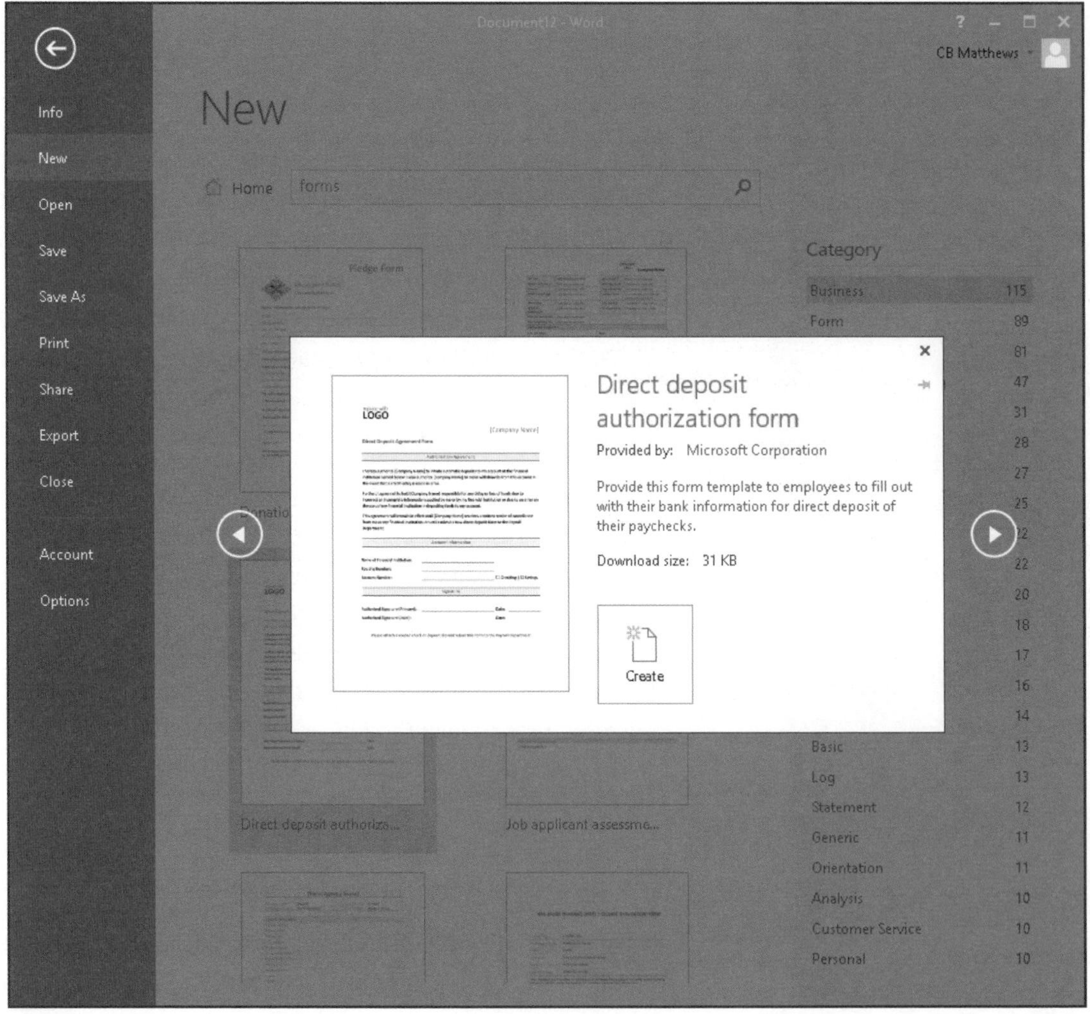

Figure 8-1: ***Microsoft Office Online provides a number of form templates for your use.***

4. Click **Create**. The form is downloaded and then opened in Word.
5. Click **File | Save As**. Click **Computer** (or other storage location) and then find the path to the folder under which you want the document saved.
6. If you want to use the form only once, leave the default type: Word Document.

   –Or–

   If you want to use the form a number of times or modify it, change the default type to Word Template.
7. In either case, after selecting a folder in which to store the form, enter a filename, and click **Save.** See "Use a Form" later in this chapter.

Modify a Template

The content controls that you can fill out or select on a Microsoft form template are created or modified using the content controls on the Developer tab in Word.

1. If you don't see the Developer tab, click **File | Options | Customize Ribbon** in the left pane. At the top of the right column, select **Main Tabs**, about halfway down the right column, click the **Developer** check box to select it, and click **OK**. The Developer tab will appear on your ribbon tabs.

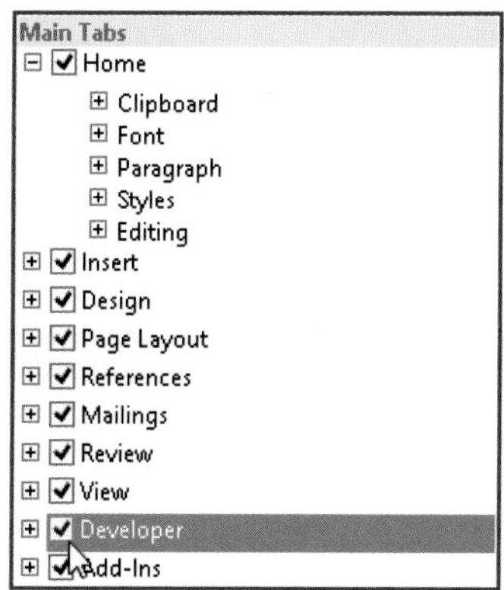

2. Open a Microsoft form template, and save it as a template, as explained in "Use Microsoft Form Templates" earlier in this chapter.
3. Click **Developer | Design Mode** in the Controls group, and take a minute to explore the form. Most forms are based on a table format. If the form is not already clear enough, you might be able to see it more easily if you right-click a section of the form, click **Table Properties | Borders And Shading | All**, and click **OK** twice. You can see an example of a form in in Figure 8-2. (If the border lines do not show up, make sure the color of the lines is black.)
4. You have these options when modifying a form:
   - Click in the content controls, and change the existing text or label simply by selecting it and typing new text.
   - Change the properties of the table, row, column, or cell, or introduce alternative text for people with disabilities. Right-click a table, row, column, or cell and click **Table Properties** from the context menu. You'll see the following dialog box.

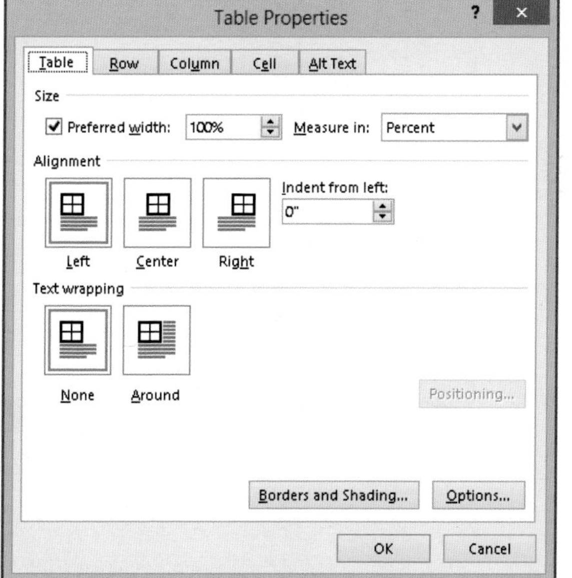

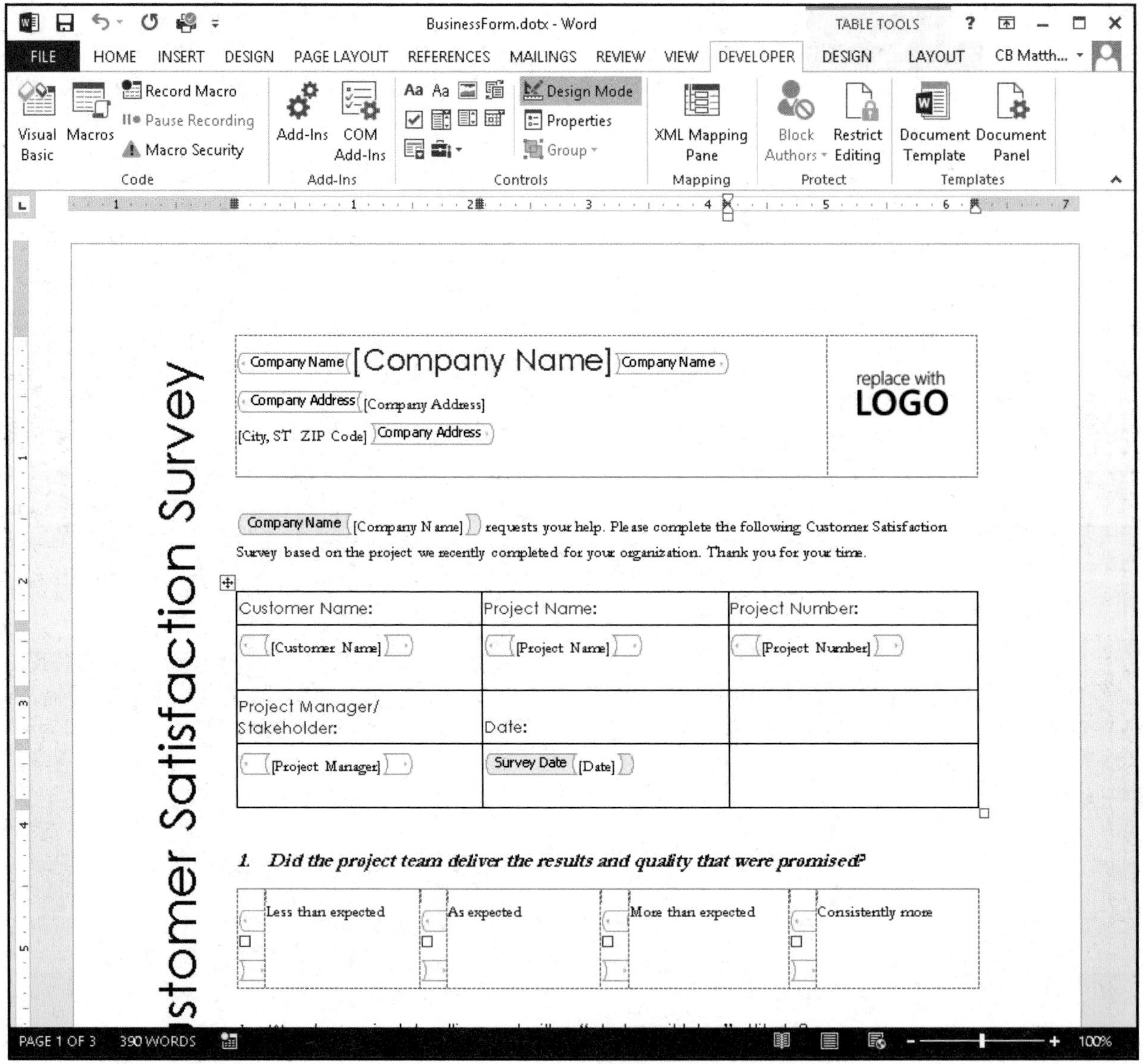

Figure 8-2: **_Many Microsoft Office Word form templates are built using tables and can be easily modified._**

- Delete a row or column by selecting and deleting it. You can also split and merge table cells to create fewer or more cells to hold content controls. (See Chapter 6 for information on how to work with tables.)
- You can add various kinds of content controls, as described in the next section "Create a Form."

5. When you have the form template the way you want it, click **File | Save As | Computer** or other storage area. Under Current Folder, click the **Custom Office Templates** folder or other storage folder. Click the **Save As Type** down arrow, click either **Word Template (*.dotx)** to create a template for use with Word 2007 through 2013 or **Word 97-2003 Template (*.dot)** to create a template that can be used with previous versions of Word.
6. Adjust the filename as desired, and click **Save**.

NOTE If you choose to save a document or form in .dot format, you will see a message showing you the features that will have to be removed or altered in order to be compatible with the older version of Word templates.

Create a Form

Your first step in creating a form is to decide how the form is to be used. Is it going to be printed and filled out by hand; is it going to be filled out using Word and, if so, what is the oldest version of Word that will be used; or will it be filled out in a browser over either an intranet or the Internet?

Second, are you going to use an existing layout in one of Microsoft's templates or design your own layout, perhaps using a table to provide the overall structure? You then need to add content controls (Microsoft calls them just "controls") to the form, but you determine which set of controls to use.

Lay Out a Form

Laying out a form is one way of visualizing how the information you want to collect will appear. That is why it is so helpful to at least look at, if not start with, a form that is already completed. If you don't use an existing form, start by listing all of the content controls you want on the screen. Then assign a type of control to each content item.

- **Labels** are typed like any other text.
- **Text content controls** allow the entry of text onto the form.
- **Check boxes** allow the selection of several options in a group.
- **Option buttons** allow the selection of one option in a group.
- **Spinners** allow the selection of a number in a series.
- **Combo boxes** (or drop-down lists) allow the selection of one item in a list, the first item of which is displayed, or they can type their own information.
- **List boxes** allow the selection of one item in a list where all items are displayed.
- **Command buttons** perform an action when clicked, such as saving or resetting the form.
- **Picture (or image)** allows the attachment of a picture or image when the form is filled out.

Next, sketch out the form so that you have a rough idea what will go where, and then create a table that has the general layout of the form (see Chapter 6 for information on creating tables). You can split and merge cells in the table to create the final form layout.

Select Content Controls

In the Developer tab Controls group, you have a choice of three different sets of form content controls: those that are fully operational in Word 2007 through 2013 forms, those that are designed to be used with

Word 2003 and later forms, and those that were designed to be used in forms created in Word 97 and later. These are grouped into the following:

- Controls that must be saved in a .dotx file and accessed and used in Word 2007, 2010, and 2013. These are available in the Developer tab Controls group itself.
- ActiveX controls that can be saved either in a .dot or .dotx file and accessed and used in Word 2003 to Word 2013. These are available in the lower part of the Legacy Tools flyout menu. (Legacy Tools is at the bottom-right corner in the Developer tab Controls group.)

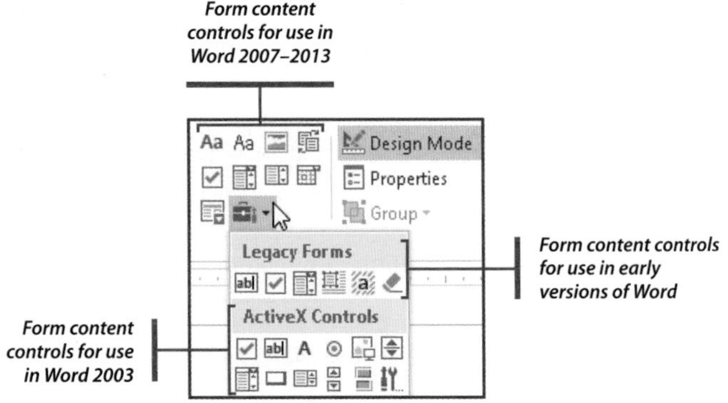

- Legacy form controls that can be saved either in a .dot or .dotx file and accessed and used in Word 97 through Word 2013. These are available in the upper part of the Legacy Tools flyout menu.

Choosing the type of controls to use depends a lot on how the form will be used. If you are going to print the form and have it manually filled out, then any of the controls will work. If the form will be filled out using Word, then you need to decide which versions of Word the form will support. Similarly, if the form will be filled out using a browser, you will need to decide which browsers you will support. The latest controls for use with Word 2007 to 2013 only work with the latest browsers. The ActiveX controls for use with Word 2003 work with more browsers, but far from all of them.

The simple answer, of course, is to use the oldest set of controls. The problem is that these controls are the most limited and, therefore, restrict what you can do on the form. The controls for Word 2007–2013 are the least problematical if the person filling out the form will be using those products. You need to determine which solution best meets your needs.

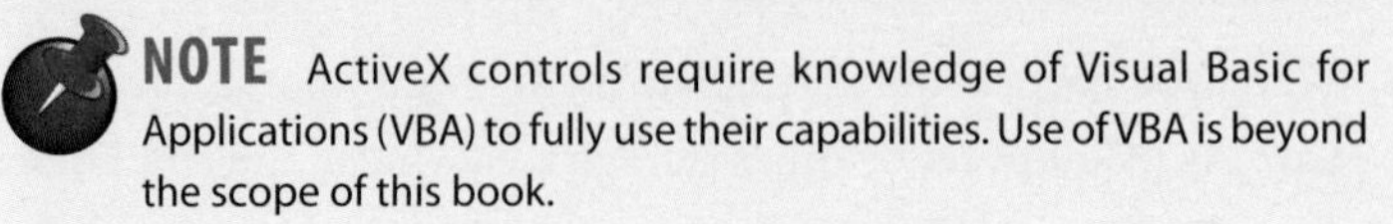

NOTE ActiveX controls require knowledge of Visual Basic for Applications (VBA) to fully use their capabilities. Use of VBA is beyond the scope of this book.

Insert Content Controls

The actual inserting of a content control is anticlimactic.

1. Click in the table cell where you want a label for a content control, and type the label.
2. Click in the table cell next to the label. In the Developer tab Controls group, click the control you want to use in that particular content control.
3. Repeat steps 1 and 2 for each content control in the form (see Figure 8-3).

Set Content Control Properties and Save a Template

Once you have added the controls that you want in each content control, you need to set the properties for those controls. The following steps are

Information Request						Date:	Click here to enter a date.
First Name:	Click here to enter text.			Last Name:	Click here to enter text.		
Address:	Click here to enter text.						
Phone:	Click here to enter text.			E-mail:	Click here to enter text.		
Model:	Choose an item.			Serial Number:	Click here to enter text.		
Type of Info Requested:	Click here to enter text.						
Requests:	Catalog: ☐	Spec Sheet: ☐		Phone Call: ☐		Web Site: ☐	

Figure 8-3: ***A simple form in design mode created using Word controls***

based on using the upper-left area of the Controls group. The Properties dialog boxes differ, depending on the controls used.

1. Click the control you want to work with, and click **Developer | Properties** in the Controls group. The properties dialog box for the control will appear.
2. Select or enter the information needed for that control. For example, the following illustration shows the properties dialog box for a check box that allows you to specify the reason for the request.

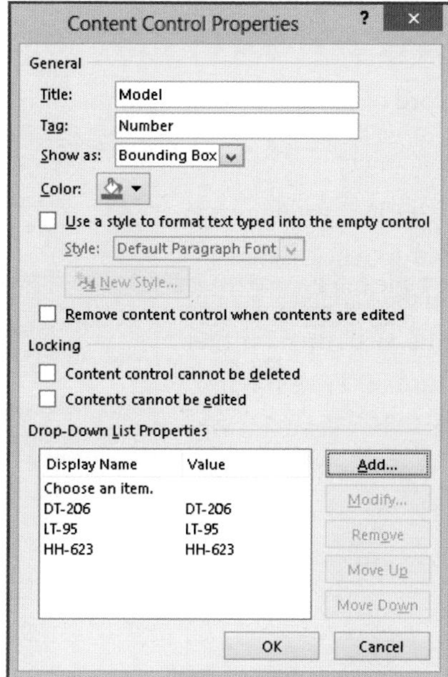

3. When the form is the way you want it, click **File | Save As | Computer** (or whatever your storage device is), and select **Custom Office Templates** under Current Folder to select the templates folder.

NOTE If your document is not a template, you'll not see the Current Folder. In that case find a folder and save the document as a template (see Chapter 2) It will be saved in the Custom Office Templates folder, not the one you initially choose.

- In the Save As dialog box, opposite Save As Type, select **Word Template (*.dotx)** if your template will be used with Word 2007 to 2013.
- Select **Word 97-2003 Template (*.dot)** for earlier versions of Word.
- Adjust the filename as desired.

4. Click **Save**.

Use a Form

Once you have created a form and saved it as a template, it can be used on any computer with a version of Word that is appropriate for the type of content controls used on the form.

1. In Word, click **File | New**. Click the **Personal** tab and double-click your template. The form will open as a document.

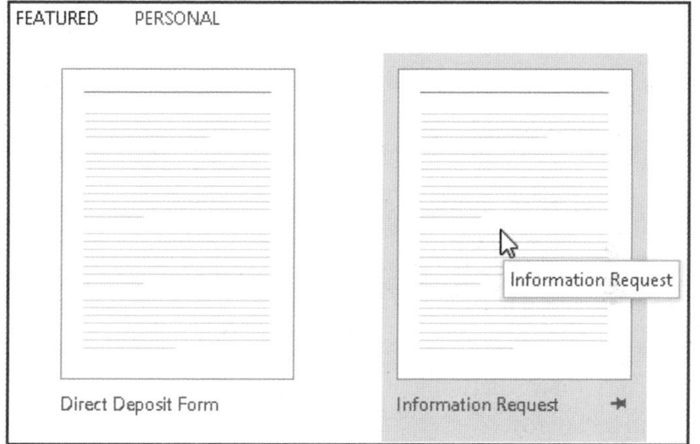

2. Click in the first content control, and enter the information requested. Press TAB to move to the next content control.
3. Repeat step 2 until all content controls are filled in. Figure 8-4 shows the form after it is filled out.

1 2 3 4 5 6 7 8 9 10

Information Request						Date:	2/14/2013
First Name:	Joseph			Last Name:	Martin		
Address:	1422 N.E. 24th Ave Denver, CO 80012						
Phone:	303-555-1234			E-mail:	joemartin@anisp.com		
Model:	DT-206			Serial Number:	123-4567-05		
Type of Info Requested:	Parts list						
Requests:	Catalog:	☒	Spec Sheet:	☐	Phone Call:	☒	Web Site: ☐

Figure 8-4: ***When you design a form, consider how easy it will be to gather information from it.***

4. When the form is filled out, click **File | Save As | Computer** (or whatever your storage device is, and select the folder where you want the filled-out form stored.
   - In the Save As dialog box, opposite Save As Type, select **Word Document (*.docx)** if your template will be used with Word 2007 to 2013.
   - Select **Word 97-2003 Document (*.doc)** for earlier versions of Word.
   - Adjust the filename as desired.
5. Click **Save**.

TRANSLATE TEXT

Word's Translate feature allows you to choose the original and translated languages and whether you want to translate the whole document, selected text, or a word or phrase. This process uses either a bilingual dictionary, for smaller amounts of text, or a computer translation service offered by Microsoft.

> **NOTE** If you choose a language that does not display its translated words correctly, you might have to install additional language-support software. Go to the Microsoft Office website (office.microsoft .com), and search for "proofing tools." You can download a number of different options.

Translate a Word or Phrase

To translate a word or phrase, the Mini Translator is your best option.

1. Open the document in Word with which you want translation help.
2. To establish the language to be translated to, click **Review | Translate** in the Language group and click the last entry on the menu: **Choose Translation Language**. The Translation Language Options dialog box opens. Click the **Translate To** down arrow and choose the language.

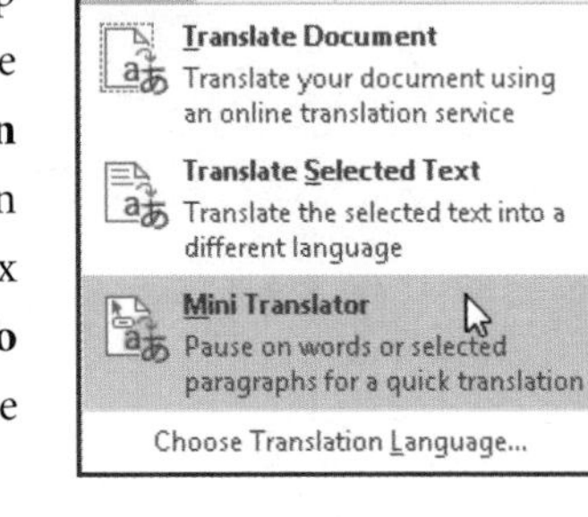

3. In the Language group, click **Translate | Mini Translator**.
4. Point at the word or select the phrase to be translated. The Mini Translator's bilingual dictionary will faintly appear. Move your mouse into it to see the translation.

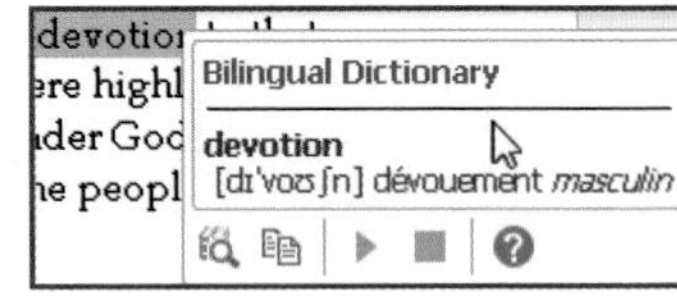

5. To translate another word or phrase, point at or select it, and the Mini Translator will display the translation.

NOTE The Mini Translator's bilingual dictionary translation is fine for words or short translations, but the literal translation may lose the "sense" of the words. For a more "true" translation, use the online machine translation services that are offered. See "Translate Selected Text" and "Translate an Entire Document" for more information.

Translate Selected Text

To translate larger sections of text:

1. Open the document in Word, and select the section(s) of text you want translated.
2. Click **Review | Translate | Translate Selected Text** in the Language group.

   –Or–

   Right-click your selected text, and click **Translate**.

   In either case, the Research task pane appears on the right side of the Word window with the Translation option selected.
3. Under Translation, click the **From** and **To** down arrows, and click the language the text is in (From) and the language you want it translated into (To). The results are displayed in the Microsoft Translator section of the Research task pane, as shown in Figure 8-5.

Translate an Entire Document

To translate a complete document, you can send the document unencrypted over the Internet to a Microsoft computer translator.

1. Open the document in Word to be translated and establish your language options as described in "Translate a Word or Phrase."
2. Click **Review | Translate | Translate Document** in the Language group. A Translate Whole Document message is displayed.

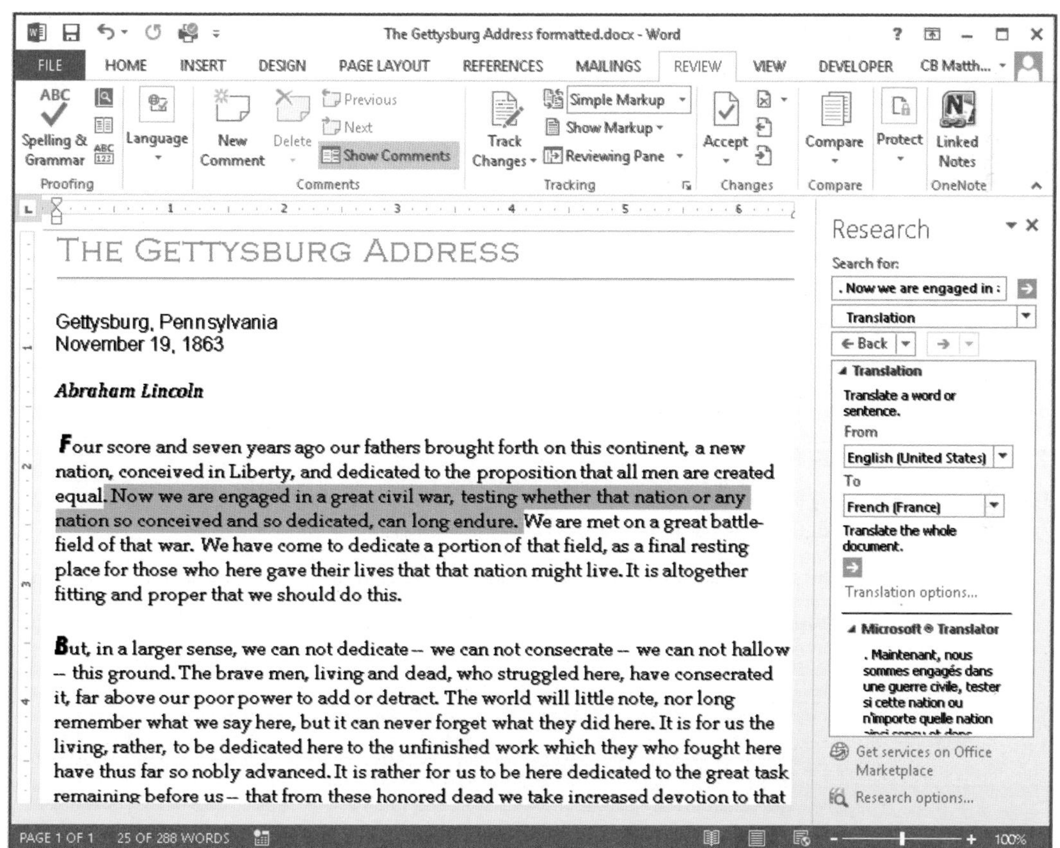

Figure 8-5: ***Word provides the ability to translate a number of languages using both bilingual dictionaries and machine translation.***

1 2 3 4 5 6 7 8 9 10

3. Click **Send** to send the document unencrypted over the Internet.
4. Your browser opens to the Windows Live Translator with the document translated using machine translation, similar to that shown in Figure 8-6.
5. To see how a particular section has been translated, click the Views **Side by Side** icon, as shown in Figure 8-6 (you can also see an error in the translation caused by the leading—enlarged letters on each paragraph that the translator guesses at). You may also choose other views: **Top/Bottom**, showing the original on top and the translation

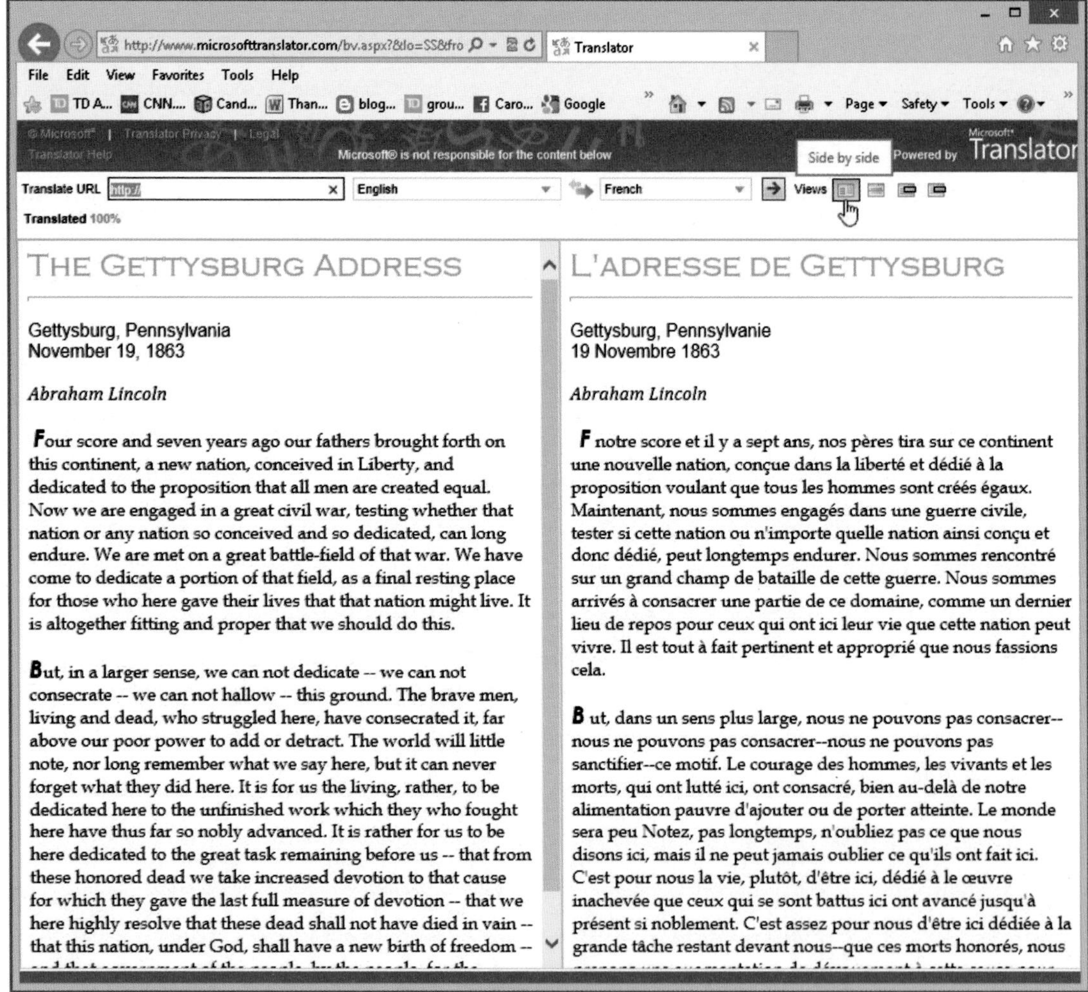

Figure 8-6: ***Your document is quickly translated by Microsoft's computer translation service. Notice the error caused by the leading enlarged letters.***

on the bottom; **Original With Hover Translation**, displays the translation as you hover your mouse over the original text; or **Translation With Original Hover**, displays the original when you hover the mouse over the translation.

Translation
notre score et il y a sept ans, nos pères tira sur ce continent une nouvelle nation,
Four score and seven years ago our fathers brought forth on t
proposition that all men are created equal. Now we are engag
conceived and so dedicated, can long endure. We are met on a

6. You can copy and paste the translation into your Word document.

NOTE Machine translation is free, but it is, of course, less than perfect due to the rigid rules a machine must follow.

WORK WITH CHARTS

Word 2013 uses Excel 2013's extensive chart-building capability to embed a chart in a Word document. You have the full functionality of the chart program available to you, as shown in Figure 8-7. After the chart is created, you can change how your data is displayed—for example, you can switch from column representation to a line chart. In addition, you can add or remove chart items, such as titles, axes, legends, and gridlines, as well as format text and several of the chart items with color and other attributes.

NOTE The terms *chart* and *graph* can be used interchangeably; they mean the same thing here; however, there are differences outside of charting.

Create a Chart

Charts are created from Word by initially opening the charting capability in Excel and using a sample table there to embed and display a chart of that data in Word. This chart can be easily formatted and reconfigured to meet your needs. You can then replace the sample data with the real data you want displayed, either by typing the data or by cutting and pasting it.

1. In Word, open the document and click the insertion point where you want the chart displayed.
2. Click **Insert | Chart** in the Illustrations group. Chart The Insert Chart dialog box appears.

QuickFacts

Understanding Data Series and Axes

There are a few guidelines for setting up data for charting, as well as some assumptions that are used:

- Text, which is used solely to create labels, should only be in the topmost row and/or the leftmost column. Text encountered in the table outside these two areas is charted as zero.
- Each cell must contain a *value* (or data point). Values in the same row or column are considered to be related and are called a *data series*. The first data series starts with the first cell in the upper-left corner of the selected data that is not text or formatted as a date. Subsequent data series are determined by continuing across the rows or down the columns.
- If it is determined that there is a greater number of rows or columns selected, the lesser number is assumed to be the data series, and the greater number is assumed to be categories that are plotted on the horizontal, or category, (X) axis. In Figure 8-7, there are three columns and four rows of data. As a result, the rows become categories and the columns become data series. When the number of rows and columns are equal, this same pattern is the default.
- The vertical, or value, (Y) axis displays a scale for the values in the data series.
- To swap the categories and data series, click **Chart Tools Design | Switch Row/Column** in the data group.

1 2 3 4 5 6 7 8 9 10

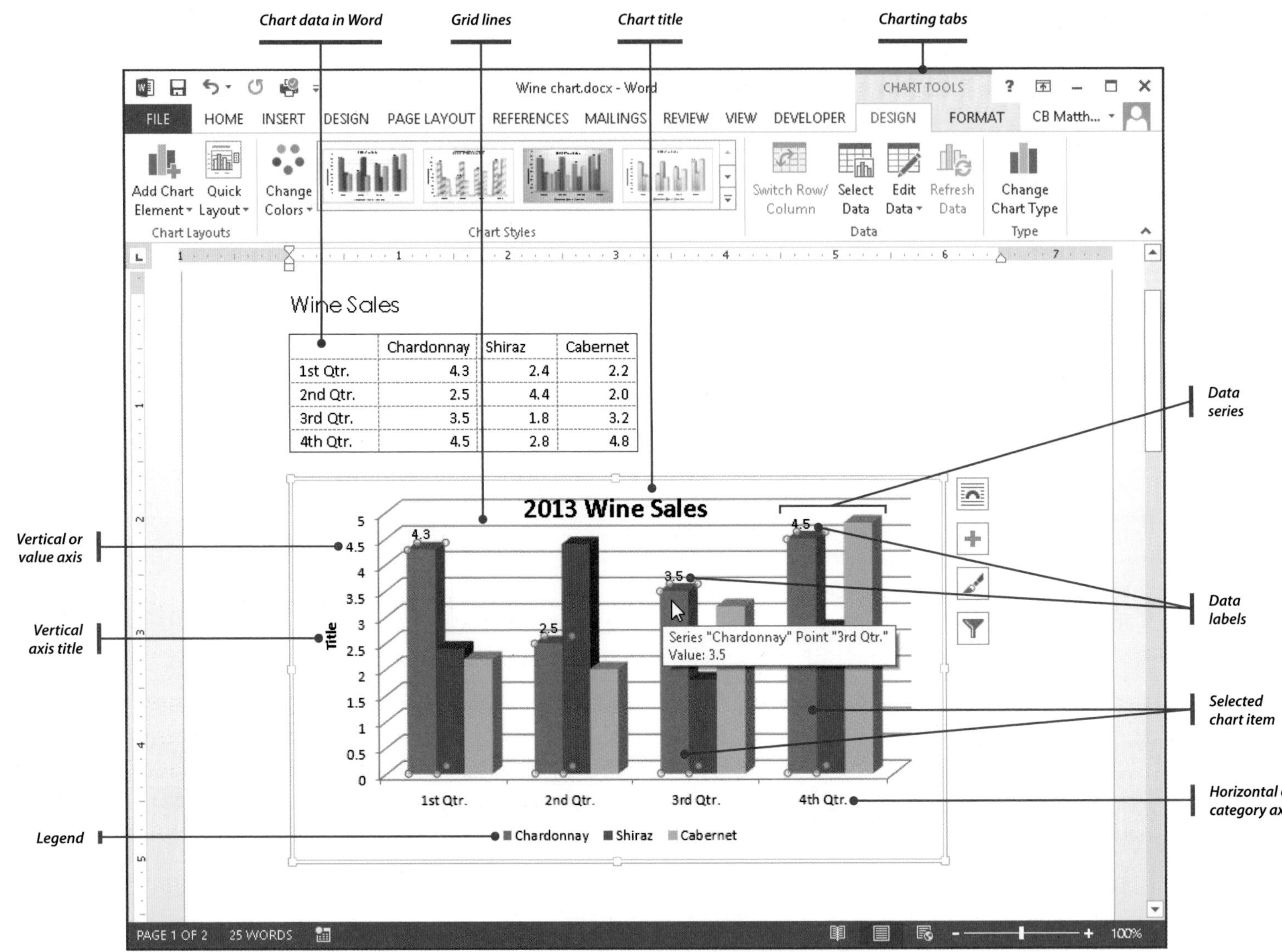

	Chardonnay	Shiraz	Cabernet
1st Qtr.	4.3	2.4	2.2
2nd Qtr.	2.5	4.4	2.0
3rd Qtr.	3.5	1.8	3.2
4th Qtr.	4.5	2.8	4.8

Figure 8-7: ***Word 2013 uses Excel 2013's chart tools to display your data in a Word document.***

3. In the Insert Chart dialog box, first click the type of chart you want in the left column, and then click the variations of that type above the preview of the chart in order to see how each will represent your data.

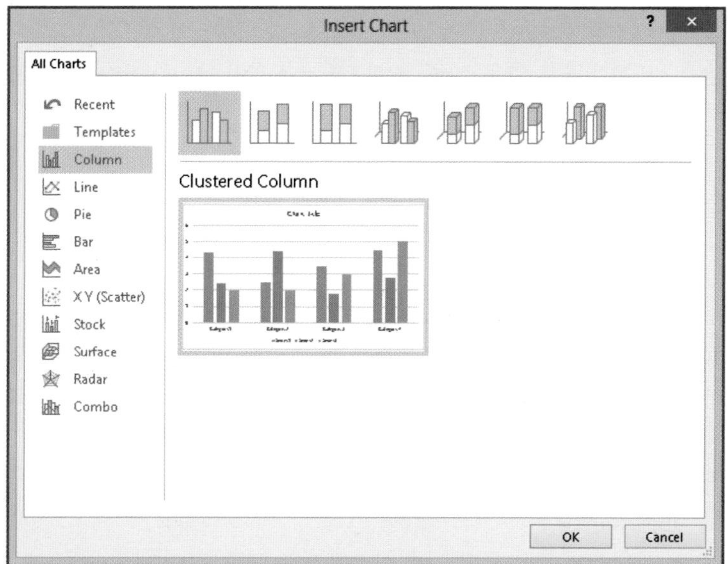

4. Double-click the variation you want.

   Excel opens and displays a table of sample data, while in Word, a chart of the type you specified displays the sample data graphically, with Excel tools in the ribbon. Figure 8-8 shows the two windows, the chart on top and the data beneath.

5. You can replace the data in the Excel window by typing over it or by copying data from another table, perhaps in Word, to the Excel table.

Chart Title

Chart in Microsoft Word

	A	B	C	D
1		Series 1	Series 2	Series 3
2	Category 1	4.3	2.4	2
3	Category 2	2.5	4.4	2
4	Category 3	3.5	1.8	3
5	Category 4	4.5	2.8	5

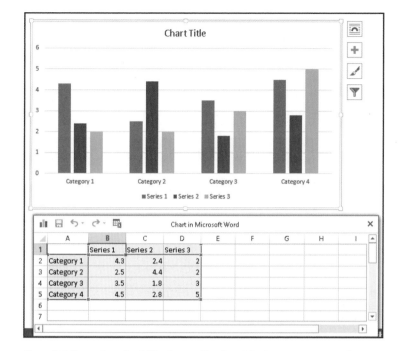

Figure 8-8: ***To create a chart, Word opens Excel, and the two programs can be displayed side by side.***

To directly replace the data in the Excel window, type your data over the sample data. To copy another table's data with one that exists in Word, select the Word table, copy it, click the upper-left cell in the Excel table, and paste the Word table there.

	Chardonnay	Shiraz	Cabernet
1st Qtr.	4.3	2.4	2.2
2nd Qtr.	2.5	4.4	2.0
3rd Qtr.	3.5	1.8	3.2
4th Qtr.	4.5	2.8	4.8

Chart in Microsoft Word

	A	B	C	D
1		Series 1	Series 2	Series 3
2	Category 1	4.3	2.4	2.2
3	Category 2	2.5	4.4	2
4	Category 3	3.5	1.8	3.2
5	Category 4	4.5	2.8	4.8

Word data transferred to Excel

Determine the Chart Type

In Excel, there are 10 standard chart types available to display your data. Each chart type has three or more variations you can choose. In addition, you can create a custom chart type based on changes you've made to a chart. Table 8-1 describes the different chart types.

Table 8-1: Chart Types

Chart Type	Function
Column	Compares trends in multiple vertical data series in columnar configurations, such as clustered columns, stacked columns, 3-D clustered columns, etc.
Line	Displays the chart's data in lines from left to right. The lines may contain markers of the data points or be in 3-D.
Pie and Doughnut	Displays one data series (pie) or compares multiple data series (doughnut), either as part of a whole or 100 percent.
Bar	Shows the data series in bars, similar to the Colum charts, only horizontal instead of vertical.
XY (Scatter), Bubble	Displays pairs of data to establish concentrations. The points may be joined by smooth or straight lines, or seen as bubbles—which may be in 3-D.
Area	Shows the magnitude of change over time; useful when summing multiple values to see the contribution of each. The areas can be stacked and in 3-D.
Radar	Connects changes in a data series from a starting or center point with lines, markers, or a colored fill.
Surface	Compares trends in multiple data series in a continuous curve; similar to a line chart with a 3-D visual effect.
Combo	Combines other chart types, such as column and line, or column and stacked area.
Stock	Displays three sets of values, such as open, high, low, and closing stock prices in a bar or candle style. Volume is added for two variations.

Change the Chart Type

1. Click in the chart to select it.
2. Click **Chart Tools Design | Change Chart Type** in the Type group.
3. In the Change Chart Type dialog box, double-click a different chart type to view it in the Word document.
4. Repeat steps 2 and 3 as many times as needed to find the correct chart type for your data.

Create a Chart Template

After you have applied formatting and added or removed chart items, your chart may not resemble any of the standard chart types provided by Excel. To save your work as a template so that you can build a similar chart at another time:

1. Create and customize the chart in Word, as described earlier in this chapter.
2. When the form is the way you want it, click the chart so that it is selected. Right-click a corner-sizing handle, and select **Save A Template** from the context menu.
3. In the Save Chart Template dialog box, replace the highlighted filename with your own, and verify that the Save As Type is **Chart Template Files (*crts)**.
4. Click **Save**.

Use a Chart Template

You can use a chart template, either when creating a new chart or by making an existing chart look like the template.

1. Create and save a chart as a template, as described in the previous section.

2. In a new document, either:

   Click in the document at the location where you want the chart. Click **Insert | Chart** in the Illustrations group.

   –Or–

   Select the chart in the document that you want to change, and click **Chart Tools Design | Change Chart Type** in the Type group.

   In either case, the chart type selection dialog box will appear (labeled either "Change Chart Type" or "Insert Chart").

3. Click **Templates** in the left column, and then double-click the template you want to use on the right.

Delete a Chart Template

You can delete a chart template from your folder of templates.

1. In any document open in Word, click **Insert | Chart** in the Illustrations group.
2. Click **Templates** in the left column.
3. Click **Manage Templates** at the bottom of the left column, find and right-click the template you want to remove, and click **Delete** on the context menu.

Select Chart Items

Before you can work on an item in a chart, you must select it. You can select items using the icons on the chart itself, the Chart Tools Layout or Format tabs, the keyboard, or by clicking the item with the mouse. When selected, items will display small, round handles (for some items, these are sizing handles; for others, they just show that they have been selected). When an item is selected, you can then access various menus and commands allowing you to change, add, or remove them. See "Work with Chart Items" for how to change specific items.

Select Chart Items Using the Mouse and Keyboard

The simplest way to select a chart element may be to simply click it. A set of selection handles will appear around the selected item.

- Click once to select all elements of a series.
- Click twice to select one single element in the series.
- Use the arrow keys on your keyboard to cycle through the chart items if you are having difficulty selecting the exact element.
- After an element is selected, right-click it to see a context menu with options for changing it (see "Work with Chart Items").

Select Chart Items Using Chart Icons

When you select a chart by clicking it, the handles appear, as do four icons to the right of the chart itself, as shown in Figure 8-9. These icons are one way to access the chart's elements, styles, colors, and values that you want to change or hide.

You have these options:

- Click **Layout Options** to position the chart within surrounding text. Click **See More** on the bottom of the context menu to open the Layout dialog box and change the layout position using horizontal and vertical positions relative to the page, column, or margin; text wrapping; and size (height and width).
- Click **Chart Elements** to display or hide an element by clearing the check box or leaving it filled in, respectively, and to display a menu for changing the element itself by clicking the arrow that displays when you mouse over an item. (See Figure 8-9.) Click **More Options** to open a task pane for changing the specific element.

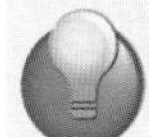

TIP You can get the same menus and submenu as the Chart Elements icon by clicking **Chart Tools Design | Add Chart Element** in the Chart Type group.

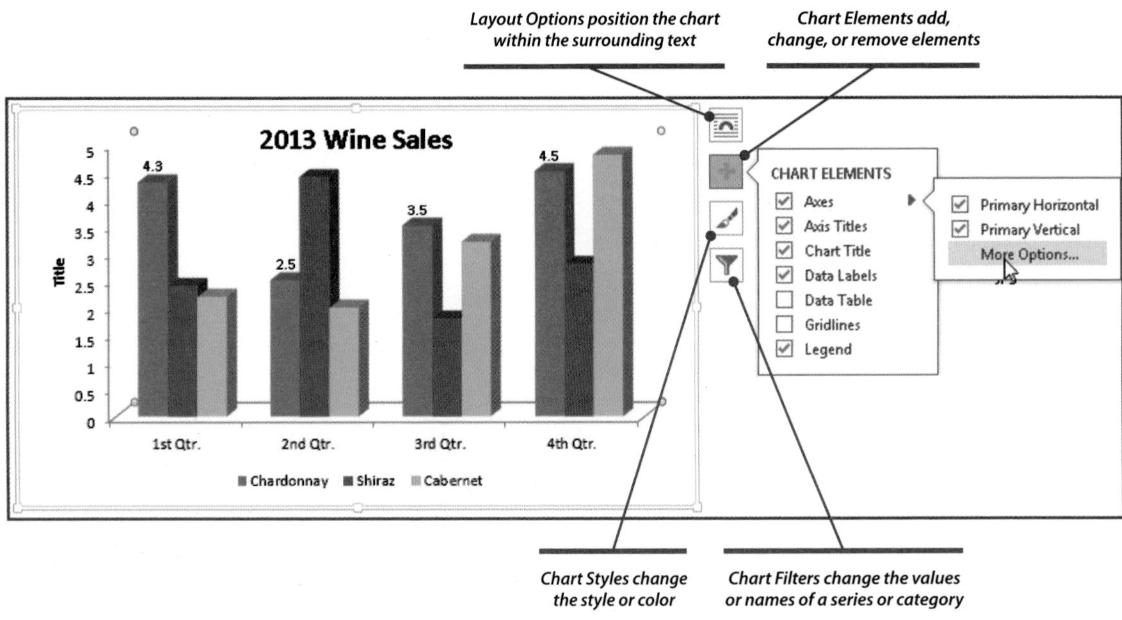

Figure 8-9: **The icons on the chart provide a quick way to access the element to add or change them.**

- Click **Chart Styles** to change the current style. Mouse over the options to see how they will look in your chart.

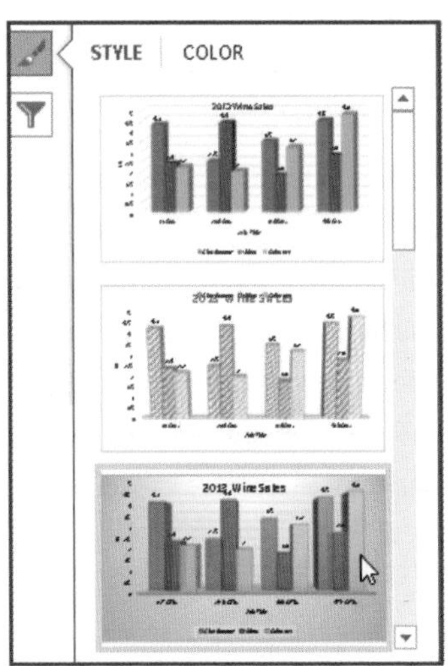

- Click **Chart Filters | Values** to see one series or category as you mouse over the options. You can click **Select Data** at the bottom to change it in the data source. Click **Chart Filters | Names | Select Data** to change names in the data source.

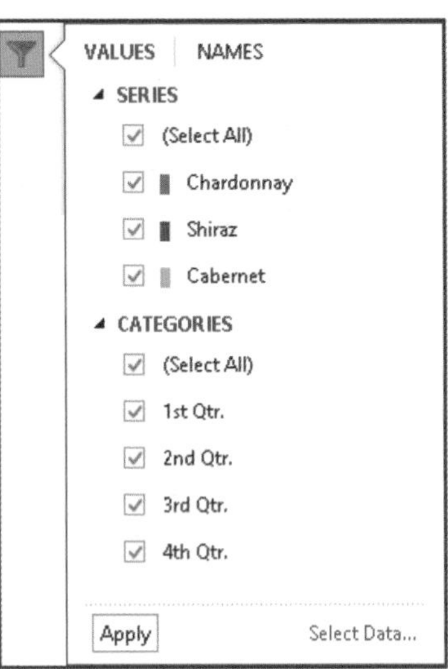

TIP If some or all of the icons should disappear while you are working with a chart, simply click in the chart again to redisplay them.

Select Chart Items from the Format Tab

1. Click the chart you are working on.
2. Click **Chart Tools Format | Chart Elements**, which is the top option in the Current Selection group (its name changes depending on what is currently selected in the chart). Click the item you want to select (such as Chart Title or Vertical (Value) Axis).
3. Click **Format Selection** in the Current Selection group. A task pane is displayed with options for changing the selected item.

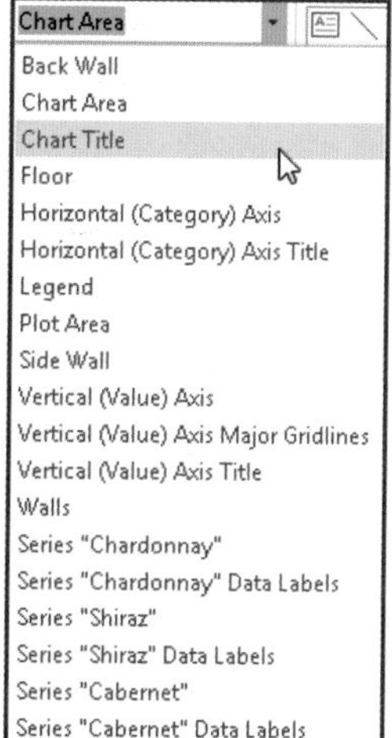

TIP The chart item displayed at the top of the Current Selection group in the Chart Tools Format tab changes as you select an element on the chart. For example, when you select a column in a column chart, the option will be "Series *name*"; when you select an axis, the option will be "*named* Axis"; when you select a legend, the option will be "Legend." You can also use this technique to select an element that you may not easily be able to click or select any other way. You click the element in this drop-down list, and then click **Format Selection** to display a task pane where it can be formatted.

Work with Chart Items

You can add or modify items on a chart to help clarify and emphasize the data it represents.

1. In an open Word document, click to select the chart you want to work on.
2. Using the chart icons, Chart Tools Format tab, or clicking directly on the chart, select the chart item you want to work on, as described in "Select Chart Items."

Add or Change a Chart Title

1. With the chart selected, click the **Chart Elements** icon to the right of the chart.
2. To add a chart title, click the option to place a check mark in the check box. If a check mark is already there, you have a chart title already. If you just want to change the text, click in it and type your new text.
3. To position the title, with your mouse on the option, click the **Chart Title** right arrow. A submenu will open.

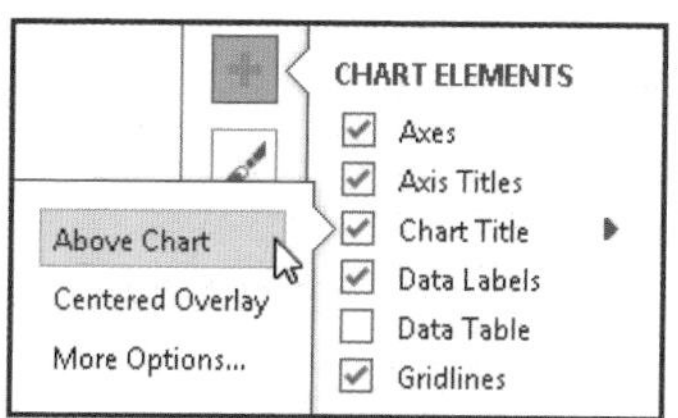

4. Click either **Centered Overlay** or **Above Chart** to position the title on the chart. If the title already exists, the text box will be selected and placed where you specified. If the title is new, the words "Chart Title" will appear in a selected text box placed on the chart where you specified.

1 2 3 4 5 6 7 8 9 10

5. Click in the title text box, select the existing text to be changed, and type your new title. Word's mini toolbar will appear to help with formatting the text.

6. To change all options for formatting the chart title, click the **Chart Elements icon | Chart Title | See More**. The Format Chart Title task pane is displayed, as seen in Figure 8-10. Using this you can change the text box or the text itself by varying the fill, color, borders, transparency, size, and more.

NOTE The Format Chart Title task pane can also be displayed by selecting the chart, clicking **Chart Tools Format | Chart Elements** in the Current Selection group, clicking **Chart Title** from the drop-down menu, and then clicking **Format Selection** in the Current Selection group.

Add or Change an Axis Title

You may have one or two axis titles for vertical or horizontal axes.

1. With the chart selected, click the **Chart Elements** icon to the right of the chart.
2. To add two new axis titles, click **Axis Title** to place a check mark in the check box. Two axis title text boxes will appear. At this point, if all you want is to insert two titles, you can simple click in each and type the names you want.
3. If you want to specify which axis you want, perhaps to work with one at a time, mouse over and click the **Axis Titles** right arrow. A submenu will open.

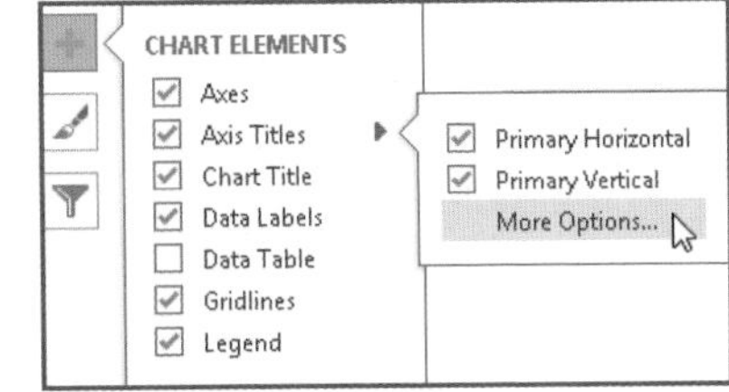

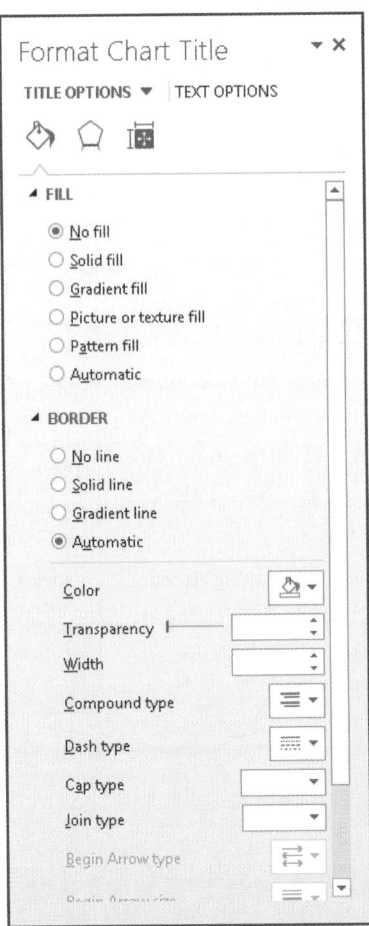

Figure 8-10: ***The Format Chart Title task pane allows you to change the text box and text with fill, borders, special effects, and alignment possibilities.***

4. To add axis titles, click either **Primary Horizontal** or **Primary Vertical** to specify which axis you want to add the title on the chart. If the title already exists, the text box will be selected. If the title is new, the words "Axis Title" appear in a selected text box placed on the chart where you specified.

Axis Title

5. Click in the title text box, select the existing text to be changed, and type your new title. Word's mini toolbar will appear to help with formatting the text.
6. To change all options for formatting the axis title, click the **Chart Elements icon | Axis Titles | the submenu arrow on the right | More Options**. The Format Axis Title task pane is displayed, similar to Figure 8-10. Using this you can change the text box or the text itself by varying the fill, color, borders, transparency, size, and more.

TIP You can also display the chart elements task panes with the Design tab. Click **Chart Tools Design | Add Chart Element** in the Chart Layouts group. Select the chart element from the menu, and a submenu is displayed. Click **More *element name* Options** to show the task pane.

Move the Legend

1. With the chart selected, click the **Chart Elements** icon to the right of the chart.
2. To simply add a legend, place a check mark next to the **Legend** option.
3. To position it, mouse over the **Legend** option and click the right arrow. A submenu will open.

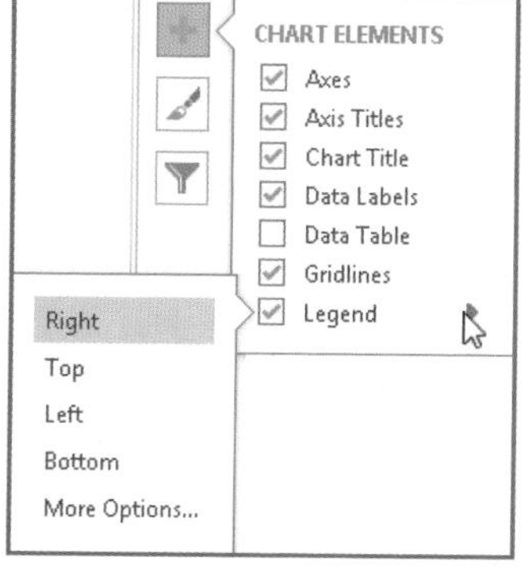

4. Click **Right**, **Top**, **Left**, or **Bottom** to position the legend on the chart. You can mouse over the options to see how each position will look before you click the one you want.
5. To change all options for formatting the axis title, click the **Chart Elements icon | Legend | More Options**. The Format Legend task pane is displayed, similar to Figure 8-10. Using this you can change the text box or the text itself by varying the fill, color, borders, transparency, size, and more.

Show Data Labels

Data labels are the actual numbers that generate the elements on a chart. For example, if you have a bar on a bar chart that represents 4.5 units sold, the data label, which you can optionally add to the chart, would be "4.5." You can choose to display them on the chart as simple values, or to place them in callouts. Figure 8-9, shown earlier, shows the data labels as simple numbers.

1. With the chart selected, click the **Chart Elements** icon to the right of the chart.
2. To simply add data labels to the chart, place a check mark next to the **Data Labels** option. You will see the values from your data source on the chart.
3. Mouse over the **Data Labels** option, and you'll see an arrow to the right. Click it for a submenu. To display the data labels as callouts, click **Data Callout**. You'll see the callouts on the chart.

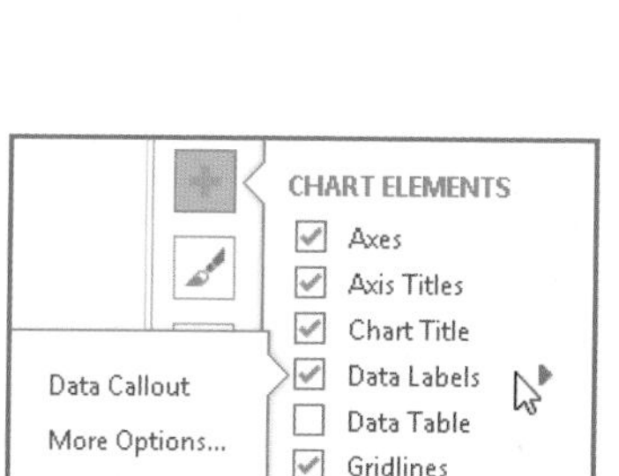

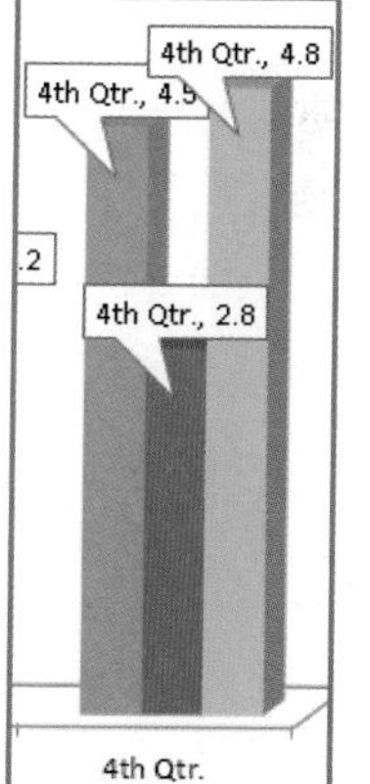

4. To change all options for formatting the data labels, click the **Chart Elements icon | Data Labels | More Options**. The Format Data Label task pane is displayed, similar to Figure 8-10. Using this you can change the text with fill, color, outlines, transparency, and more. You can also change what the label contains, such as a value or category name. You can specify the fill, color, special effects, and alignment of the data labels. And you can specify what kind of number the value will be (currency, general number, date, etc.).

Format Chart Items

Each chart item has a number of attributes that can be formatted, such as the color, the fill, the line style, and the alignment. These attributes are set in the Format task pane for that item, as shown in Figure 8-11. Table 8-2 shows the formatting options that are available in the Format task pane for each item.

To open the Format task pane for a chart item:

- Select the chart, and click the **Chart Elements** icon to the right of the chart . Select the element, mouse over the item, click the down arrow to the right, and select **More Options** on the submenu.

  –Or–

- Click a chart and then click **Chart Tools Format | Chart Element** top option in the Current Selection group (the name will depend on what is selected), and select an element. Then click **Format Selection** in the Current Selection group.

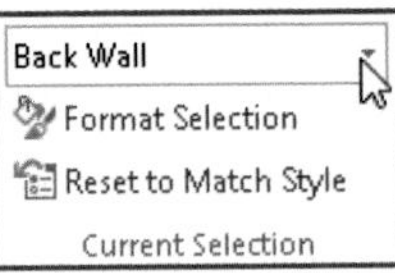

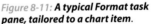

  –Or–

- Right-click the item on the chart, and click **Format *(element name)***.

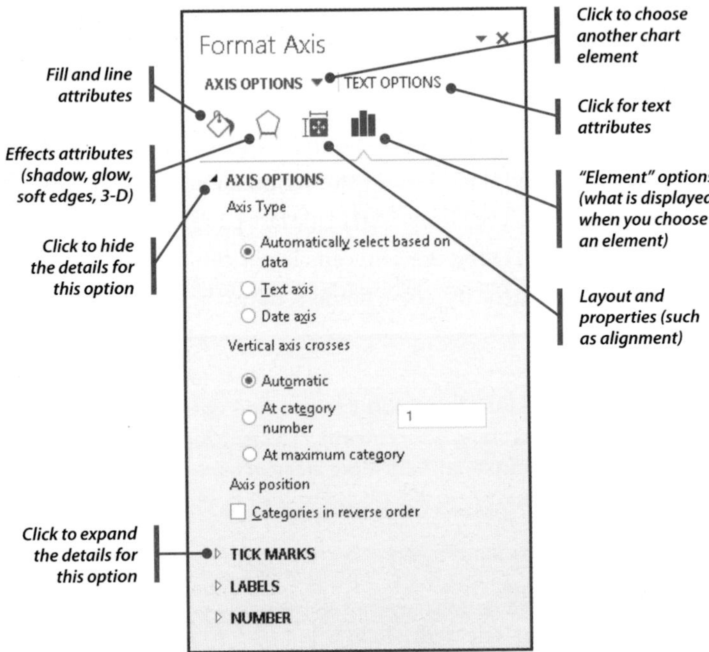

Figure 8-11: ***A typical Format task pane, tailored to a chart item.***

NOTE The options on the Format *elements* task pane will vary, depending on the type of chart. For instance, a pie chart will have different options than a bar chart. In addition, the attributes within an option will be different. For example, the fill attributes for a pie chart are different from those for a bar chart.

Format Text

You may have noticed that there is no capability to format text in the various chart item task panes. To format text:

- Select a chart item (see "Select Chart Items"), and in the Home tab Font group, use the formatting options or click the **Dialog Box Launcher** to open the Font dialog box.

Table 8-2: Formatting Options Available to Chart Items

Formatting Options	Description	Applies To
Number	Provides the same number formats as the Format Cells Number tab, such as currency, accounting, date, and time.	Axis, data labels
Fill	Provides options for solid-color fill, gradient colors and options, picture, or texture fill, as well as pattern fill and degrees of transparency.	Axis, chart area, data labels/series, data tables, legend, plot area, titles, walls/floors
Line or Border Color	Offers solid or gradient lines and options, as well as color choices and degrees of transparency.	Axis, chart area, data labels/series, data tables, error bars, grid lines, legend, plot area, titles, trend lines, walls/floors
Line or Border Style	Provides options for width, dashed, and compound (multiple) lines, as well as styles for line ends and line joins.	Axis, chart area, data labels/series, data tables, error bars, grid lines, legend, plot area, titles, trend lines, walls/floors
Shadow	Provides preset shadow styles and controls for color, transparency, size, blur, angle, and distance.	Axis, chart area, data labels/series, data tables, legend, plot area, titles, trend lines, walls/floors
Glow and Soft Edges	Provides presets for glow and soft edges and controls for color, transparency, and size.	Axis, chart area, data labels/series, data tables, legend, plot area, titles, trend lines, walls/floors
3-D Format	Adds a 3-D effect to shapes; provides top, bottom, material, and lighting presets and controls for depth and contour color and size or degree.	Axis, chart area, data labels/series, data tables, legend, plot area, titles, walls/floors
3-D Rotation	Provides angular rotation and perspective adjustments, as well as positioning and scaling controls.	Walls/floors
Alignment	Vertically aligns, rotates, and stacks text.	Axis, data labels, titles, legends
Alt Text	Provides a text title and description of the chart and the information it contains. This can be read to a person with a visual disability.	Chart area

–Or–

- Right-click a chart item, and either use the mini font toolbar that appears, or click **Font** to open the Font dialog box.

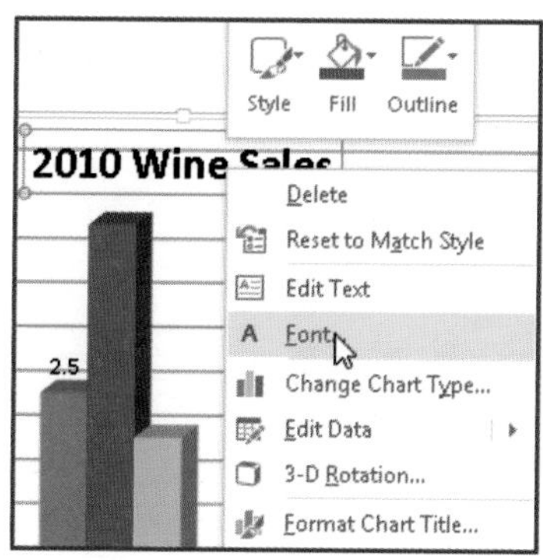

Work with the Data Table

In addition to the chart data in Excel, and possibly the original data in Word, you can display a *data table* as part of a chart with the same data. Data tables are for display only and simply reflect the data in Excel. The values in a data table cannot be changed on the chart without changing them in Excel. Figure 8-12 shows a chart with a data table that includes a legend.

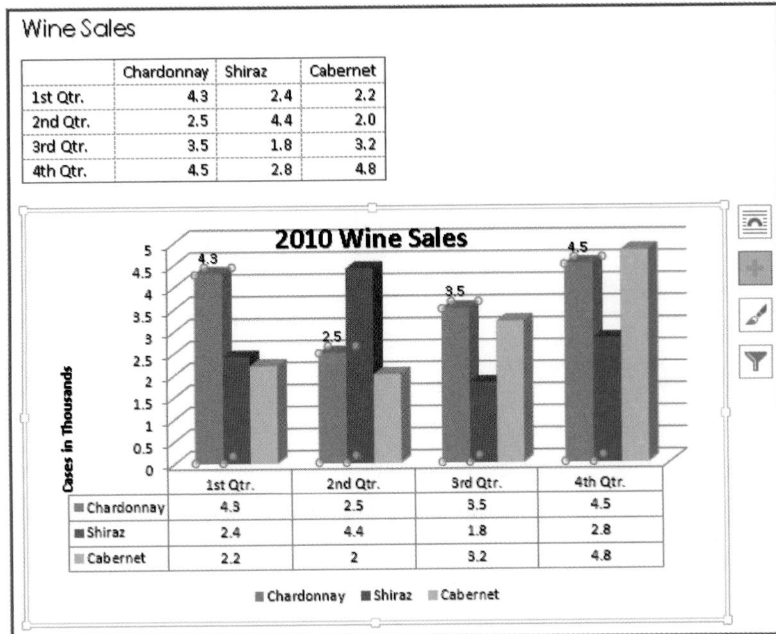

Wine Sales

	Chardonnay	Shiraz	Cabernet
1st Qtr.	4.3	2.4	2.2
2nd Qtr.	2.5	4.4	2.0
3rd Qtr.	3.5	1.8	3.2
4th Qtr.	4.5	2.8	4.8

	1st Qtr.	2nd Qtr.	3rd Qtr.	4th Qtr.
Chardonnay	4.3	2.5	3.5	4.5
Shiraz	2.4	4.4	1.8	2.8
Cabernet	2.2	2	3.2	4.8

Figure 8-12: ***Data tables add precision to the information presented in a chart.***

Display the Data Table

1. Click the chart in Word to select it.
2. Click the **Chart Elements** icon, second icon down on the right of the table.
3. Click **Data Table**, mouse over it for the arrow on the right, and then choose between **With Legend Keys** or **No Legend Keys**.

The chart and data are displayed in Word.

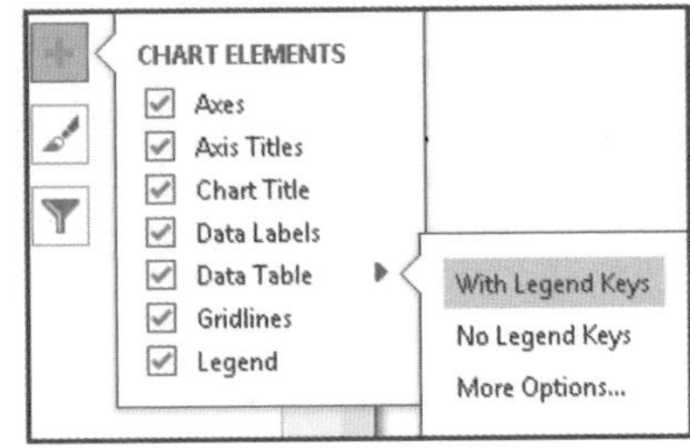

Format a Data Table

A data table can be formatted in the same way as any other chart element.

- Right-click the data table and click **Format Data Table**.

  –Or–

- With the data table selected (see "Select Chart Items"), click **Chart Tools Format | Format Selection** in the Current Selection group.

CAUTION! Be sure you select the correct element or you won't get the correct submenu.

QuickSteps to...

- Create a Webpage
- Save Word Documents as Webpages
- Use Word to Create HTML Elements
- Configure Web Options in Word
- Insert a Hyperlink
- Verify How a Page Will Look
- Remove Personal Information from the File Properties
- Remove Word-Specific Tags from a Document

Chapter 9

Creating Webpages

You can use Word 2013 to create and save documents as webpages. These features enable you to put Word documents on a website or an intranet site (a website that is internal to an organization) in a format in which they can be viewed using a web browser, such as Internet Explorer. Word also allows you to work with existing webpages and provides a number of settings to control them.

CREATE AND SAVE A WEBPAGE IN WORD

Word provides the means to produce a moderate quantity of webpages, including the ability to save documents as webpages, view a document as a webpage, and set a number of options unique to webpages.

TIP If you have a modest number of webpages to produce, Word offers a reasonable tool to do that. If you have a more extensive job, dedicated web tools, like Microsoft Expression Web, Adobe Dreamweaver, WordPress, and Aptana Studio, are more appropriate.

NOTE Instead of starting a new webpage from scratch in Word, you can create a webpage by opening an existing Word document and then saving it as a webpage. See "Save Word Documents as Webpages" for details.

1 2 3 4 5 6 7 8 9 10

Create a Webpage

Creating a webpage in Word consists of creating a document page as you would for any other document, viewing it as a webpage, and then saving it as a webpage. Such a page can then be viewed with a browser, such as Microsoft Internet Explorer. You can create a webpage from scratch—a blank page. Or you can start with an existing document or a template that you modify for your own purposes.

1. You may be starting from a variety of places:
   - If you are starting your webpage from scratch, open Word and click **Blank Document** or the template you'll be using.
   - If you are starting from an existing document, but not the one you want to use as the webpage, click **File | New**. Then click **Blank Document** or the template you want.
   - If you are starting with an existing document that you want to use, continue to step 2.
2. Click **View | Web Layout** in the Views group.
3. Create or modify the content on the page using standard Word techniques, as described in the earlier chapters of this book. For example:
   - To enter text, type it as usual.
   - To apply a style, select a style from the Quick Styles gallery in the Home tab Styles group.
   - To apply direct formatting (for example, bold or italic), select the text to which you want to apply it, and then click the appropriate button in the Home tab Font group.
   - To create tables and add pictures and other graphic elements, use Word's extensive table creation and graphics tools.
4. Save the document, as described in "Save Word Documents as Webpages."

TIP While you generally want to view a document intended to be a webpage as a webpage, there is no requirement to do so. You can look at it in any of the views in the View tab Document Views group.

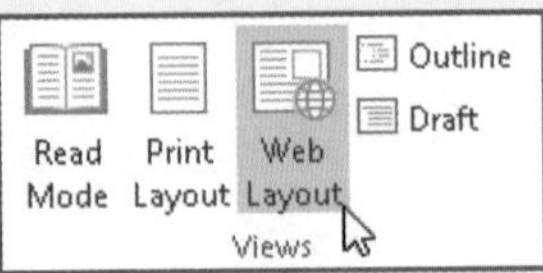

Understanding HTML and How Word Uses It

Many webpages, including those created with Word, use HTML to specify how the page will look and behave in a web browser. It is a standardized computer language used for displaying pages on websites.

Understand HTML

HTML (Hypertext Markup Language) is responsible for many of the wonders of the Web. It enables you to specify the contents of a webpage and control how it looks and behaves in a web browser. All modern computer operating systems have browsers, so pages created using HTML can be displayed on almost any computer. An HTML file consists of plain text and pictures with *tags*, or formatting codes, that specify how the text or pictures will look on the page.

For more information on HTML, see *HTML, XHTML, and CSS QuickSteps*, by Guy Hart-Davis (McGraw-Hill Professional, 2010).

Understand How Word Uses HTML

Word uses HTML to create web content, automatically applying all necessary tags when you save a file in one of the web formats. It uses standard HTML tags for creating standard HTML elements (such as headings, paragraphs, and tables) that will be displayed by a web browser. It uses custom, Word-specific tags for saving Word-specific data in a web-compatible format.

This combination of standard and custom tags enables Word to save an entire document as a webpage. Saving all the information like this allows what is called *round-tripping,* saving a file with all its contents and formatting so that the file can both be used as a webpage and be reopened by the application that created the file with exactly the same information and formatting as when it saved the file.

Round-tripping enables you to create HTML documents (.html files) instead of Word documents (.docx files). However, you should remember that the Word-specific data is saved along with the HTML data. Any visitor to your website can view the entire source code for a webpage, including any Word-specific data, by using a View Source command in a browser.

Word enables you to remove the Word-specific tags from a webpage you save (see "Remove Word-Specific Tags from a Document" later in this chapter). You may also choose to use Word to create specific HTML elements that you then paste into another HTML editor, such as Windows Notepad, where you can integrate them with the code you directly enter. (See "Use Word to Create HTML Elements" later in this chapter.)

Save Word Documents as Webpages

To save an existing Word document that is open in your Word window as a webpage:

1. Click **File | Save As**.
2. Click **Computer** or another storage area where you want to save the file. Under Recent Folders, click your folder or find the path to the folder you want.
3. In the Save As dialog box, click the **Save As Type** down arrow, and click the file format you want to use. (Your choices are Single File Webpage; Webpage; or Webpage, Filtered. See the "Choosing Suitable Web File Formats" QuickFacts for a discussion of the available formats.)
4. In the File Name text box, type the filename. If you want to use the .html extension instead of the .htm extension (for a file in either the Webpage format or the Webpage, Filtered format) or the .mhtml extension instead of the .mht extension (for a file in the Single File Webpage Format), type the extension as well.
5. To enter or change the page title, which is what appears in the title bar of the browser, click **Change Title**. In the Enter Text dialog box, click in the **Page Title** text box, and type the new title. Click **OK**. (Figure 9-1 shows the page title dialog box and button.)
6. Click **Save**. Word saves the document as a webpage.

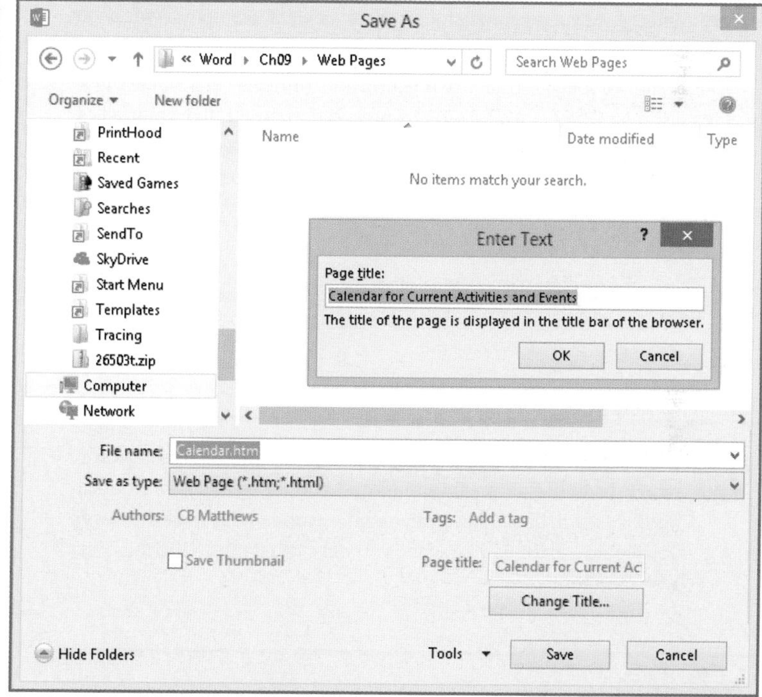

Figure 9-1: ***Word's Save As dialog box for saving webpages includes the Page Title area and the Change Title button.***

1 2 3 4 5 6 7 8 9 10

QuickFacts

Choosing Suitable Web File Formats

Word offers three HTML formats to choose from; before you save a file in HTML, you should understand how the formats differ from each other and which format is suitable for which purposes. Word offers the Single File Webpage format; the Webpage format; and the Webpage, Filtered format. (Also see the "Understanding HTML and How Word Uses It" QuickFacts.)

Webpage Format

The Webpage format creates an HTML file that contains the text contents of the document, together with a separate folder that contains the graphics for the document. This makes the webpage's HTML file itself smaller, but the page as a whole is a little clumsy to distribute because you need to distribute the graphics folder as well. The folder is created automatically and assigned the webpage's name followed by *files*. For example, a webpage named Products.htm has a folder named Products_files.

Files in the Webpage format use the .htm and .html file extensions. These files also use Office-specific tags to preserve in an HTML format all of the information the file contains. This is the classic way that webpages are prepared, and may be required in some hosting situations. You would use it when you have a hosting requirement to do so or you want a separate graphics file.

Single-File Webpage Format

The Single File Webpage format creates a web archive file that contains all the information required for the webpage: all the text contents and all the graphics. Use the Single File Webpage format to create files that you can easily distribute, for example, to be accessed for editing and comments by others.

Files in the Single File Webpage format use the .mht and .mhtml file extensions. These files use Office-specific tags that preserve in an HTML format all of the information the file contains.

Webpage, Filtered Format

The Webpage, Filtered format creates an HTML file that contains the text contents of the document, together with a separate, automatically named folder that contains the graphics for the document. However, this format removes Office-specific tags from the document. Removing these tags reduces the size of the file, but the file uses items such as document properties and Visual Basic for Applications (VBA) code, so this format is not useful for round-tripping complex documents (bringing them back into Word and editing them).

Use this format when you want the purest form of a webpage that cannot be reviewed in Word (it can still be viewed in a text editor).

Files in the Webpage, Filtered format use the .htm and .html file extensions.

NOTE Word also offers one other web-related file format, .xml, which uses the eXtensible Markup Language (XML) to organize and work with data. XML is beyond the scope of this book; however, you would use this format when you want to have access to the latest web features.

NOTE You must set the web options separately for each Office application. The settings you make in Word don't affect the settings in Excel, PowerPoint, or other applications.

Use Word to Create HTML Elements

If you choose not to use Word as your main HTML editor, you may still want to use it to create some HTML elements so that you can include them in your webpages.

1. Open an existing document, or create a new document, that contains the desired content.
2. Save the Word document in one of the HTML formats.
3. View the resulting page in your browser.

4. View the source code of the webpage. For example, in Internet Explorer, click **View | Source** (in Internet Explorer 7 or 8, you must first turn on the menus by pressing ALT).
5. Find and select the code for the element you want to copy, and then issue a copy command (for example, press CTRL+C).
6. Switch to your HTML editor, position the insertion point, and then issue a paste command (for example, press CTRL+V).
7. Close Word and your browser if you have finished working with them.

WORK WITH WEBPAGES IN WORD

Word provides a number of tools and settings that allow you to work with webpages and implement the features you want on a website.

Configure Web Options in Word

Before you start using Word to create webpages, you must configure the web options in Word. These options control how Word creates webpages. Once you've specified the options you want, you probably won't need to change them. If you do need to change them for a particular file, you can do so when you're saving the file as a webpage.

Display the Web Options Dialog Box

To configure web options, first display the Web Options dialog box.

1. Click **File | Options**. The Word Options dialog box appears.
2. Click **Advanced** in the left column, scroll down the right side to near the bottom of the page, and then click **Web Options**. The Web Options dialog box appears, as shown in Figure 9-2.
3. You'll have these areas where you can establish defaults for your webpages:
   - **Browsers** Set defaults for browsers you wish to support with your webpages.

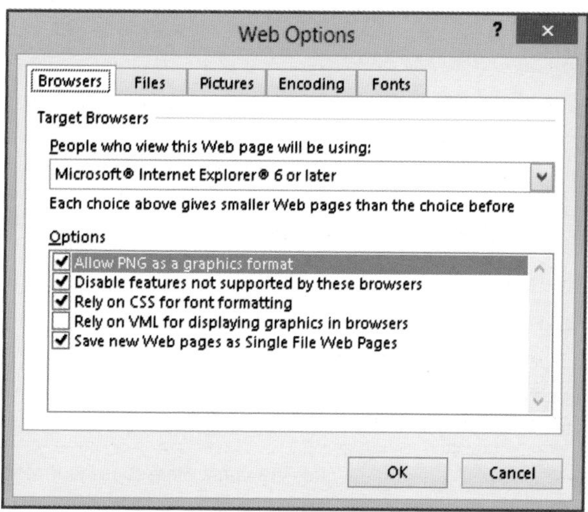

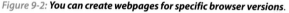

Figure 9-2: ***You can create webpages for specific browser versions.***

   - **Files** Set defaults relating to files and locations, and the default editor for webpages created in Word and using other tools.
   - **Pictures** Set screen size and pixels per inch for images used on the webpages.
   - **Encoding** Set the encoding standard used for the current document and identify the standard used for saving documents. Saves all webpages with the default encoding standard.
   - **Fonts** Identify the language character set to be used and the font name and size for webpages.
4. Choose options, as discussed in the following subsections, click **OK** to close the Web Options dialog box, and then click **OK** to close the Word Options dialog box.

Choose Options on the Browsers Tab

Figure 9-2 shows the Browsers tab of the Web Options dialog box for Word. Table 9-1 explains the options.

1 2 3 4 5 6 7 8 9 10

Table 9-1: Default Options Available on the Browsers Tab

Option	Explanation
Allow PNG As A Graphics Format	Enables webpages to contain graphics in the PNG format. All current browsers can display PNG graphics.
Disable Features Not Supported By These Browsers	Turns off HTML features the browsers don't support.
Rely On CSS For Font Formatting	Uses Cascading Style Sheets (CSS) for font formatting.
Rely On VML For Displaying Graphics In Browsers	Uses Vector Markup Language (VML) for displaying graphics.
Save New Webpages As Single File Webpages	Uses the Single File Webpage format for saving new files.

The best way to select the options is to click the **People Who View This Webpage Will Be Using** drop-down list and select the earliest browser version that you want to support. The choice you make in this list automatically selects the appropriate check boxes in the Options group box. You can then select or clear check boxes manually to fine-tune the choices you've made.

- Choosing **Microsoft Internet Explorer 6.0**, which came with Windows XP, provides a reasonable baseline for most websites and provides the largest feature set.
- If you want maximum browser compatibility, choose **Microsoft Internet Explorer 5.0**, which came with Windows 2000/ME; however, the percentage of users that will be picked up is less than 1 percent.
- To support Mozilla Firefox and Google Chrome, which you should, choose **Microsoft Internet Explorer 6.0 Or Later**.

TIP In October 2012, Internet Explorer had approximately 26 percent of the browser market. (In 2009, Internet Explorer had 41 percent, so you can see how the browser market is shifting.) Mozilla Firefox had approximately 23 percent; Google Chrome had 37 percent; and other browsers had 14 percent altogether. These figures show that choosing Microsoft Internet Explorer 6.0 Or Later on the Browsers tab of the Web Options dialog box and then checking to verify how your webpages look and work with Google Chrome and Mozilla Firefox will ensure that your pages are viewable by the vast majority of people online.

Choose Options on the Files Tab

On the Files tab of the Web Options dialog box, choose options for controlling how Word handles filenames and file locations for the webpages you create, and specify whether to use Office as the default editor for webpages created by Word. Figure 9-3 shows the Files tab of the Web Options dialog box.

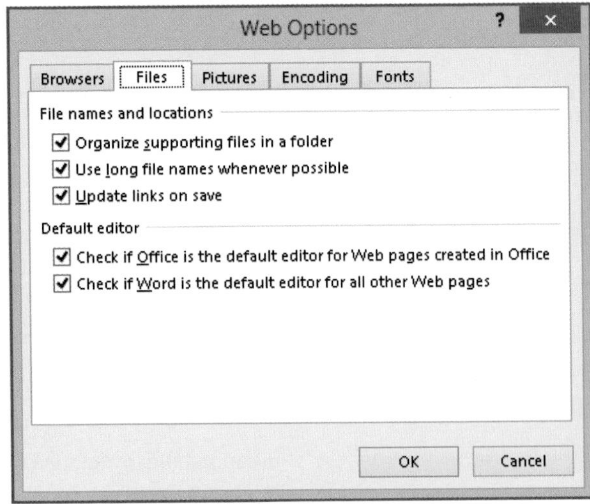

Figure 9-3: ***The Files tab of the Web Options dialog box determines where web files are stored and how the files are edited.***

The following options are included in the Files tab:

- Select **Organize Supporting Files In A Folder** if you want the application to save graphics and other separate elements in a folder that has the same name as the webpage plus "_files"—for example, the webpage named "products.html" receives a folder named "products_files." The application automatically creates a file named "filelist.xml" that contains a list of the files required for the webpage.
- Clear the **Use Long File Names Whenever Possible** check box to prevent the application from creating long filenames that include spaces, which may not be compatible with the web server you're using. It's best to keep filenames short and to use underscores instead of spaces when you need to separate parts of the filename.
- Click the **Update Links On Save** check box if you want the application to automatically check each link and update any information that has changed each time you save the file. In most cases, this automatic updating is helpful.
- Click the **Check If Office Is The Default Editor For Webpages Created In Office** check box if you want Internet Explorer to check if Word is your default HTML editor for webpages created by Word when you click the Edit button in Internet Explorer. Clear this check box if you want to use another application to edit the webpages you've created with Word.
- Click the **Check If Word Is The Default Editor For All Other Webpages** check box if you want Internet Explorer to open Word for the editing of all non-Office–created webpages. Clear this check box if you want to use another application for this function.

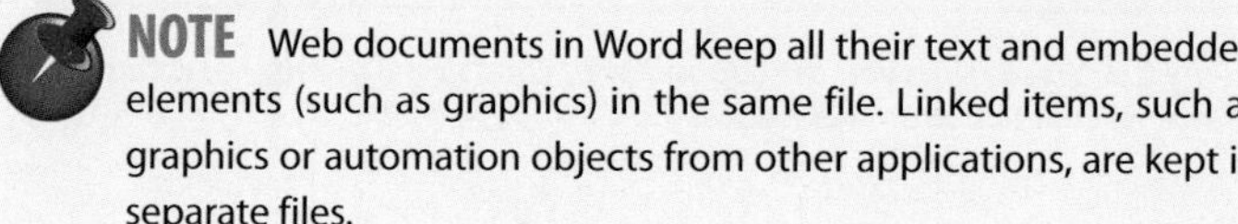

NOTE Web documents in Word keep all their text and embedded elements (such as graphics) in the same file. Linked items, such as graphics or automation objects from other applications, are kept in separate files.

NOTE Keeping the supporting files together in a folder is usually helpful, because you can move the webpage and its supporting files easily to another folder. If you clear the Organize Supporting Files In A Folder check box, Word saves the graphics and other separate elements in the same folder as the webpage. This behavior tends to make your folders harder to manage, as you cannot see at a glance which supporting files belong to which webpage. However, if you do not have permission to create new folders in the folder in which you are saving your webpages (for example on an intranet site), you may need to clear the Organize Supporting Files In A Folder check box so that Word does not attempt to create new folders for your webpages.

Choose Options on the Pictures Tab

On the Pictures tab of the Web Options dialog box (**File | Options | Advanced |Web Options**), choose options for the pictures you include in your webpages:

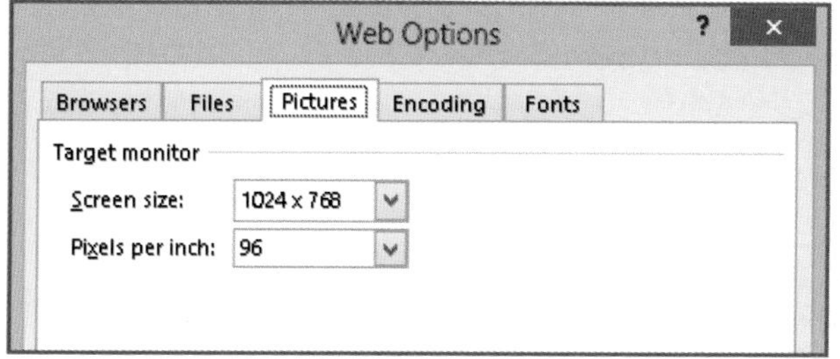

- In the Screen Size drop-down list, select the minimum resolution that you expect most visitors to your website to be using. For most websites, the best choice is 1024 × 768, a resolution that almost all monitors manufactured since 2004 support. If you're creating an intranet site whose visitors will all use monitors with a higher resolution than 1024 × 768, you can choose a higher resolution.
- In the Pixels Per Inch drop-down list, select the number of pixels per inch (ppi) to use for pictures in your webpages. The default setting is 96 ppi, which works well for most pages. You can also choose 72 ppi or 120 ppi.

Choose Options on the Encoding Tab

The Encoding tab of the Web Options dialog box lets you specify which character-encoding scheme to use for the characters in your webpages. Word in North America and Western Europe uses the Western European (Windows) encoding by default. This works well for most purposes, but you may prefer to choose Western European (ISO) for compliance with the ISO-8859-1 standard for a more European flavor or Unicode (UTF-8) for compliance with the Unicode standard and many languages outside North America and Western Europe. You must have saved your document before this option is available.

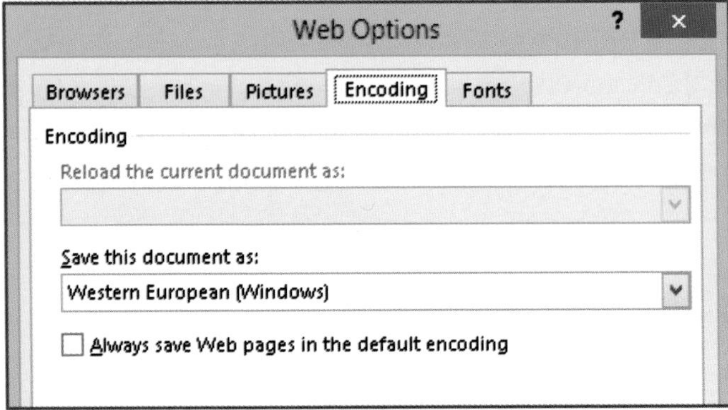

Select the encoding you want in the **Save This Document As** drop-down list. Then, if you always want to use this encoding, click the **Always Save Webpages In The Default Encoding** check box. Selecting this check box disables the Save This Document As drop-down list.

NOTE *Unicode* is a scheme for representing characters on computers. For example, a capital A is represented by 0041 in Unicode, and a capital B is represented by 0042. *UTF-8* is the abbreviation for Universal Character Set Transformation Format 8-Bit. *ISO* is the acronym for the International Organization for Standardization.

Choose Options on the Fonts Tab

The Fonts tab of the Web Options dialog box (**File | Options | Advanced | Web Options**), shown in Figure 9-4, offers the following options:

- **English/Western European/Other Latin Script** item, unless you need to create pages in another character set, such as Arabic.
- **Proportional Font** drop-down list and its **Size** drop-down list to specify the proportional font and font size for your pages.
- **Fixed-Width Font** drop-down list and its **Size** drop-down list to specify the monospaced font and font size.

After you finish choosing settings in the Web Options dialog box, click **OK** to close the dialog box, and then click **OK** to close the Options dialog box.

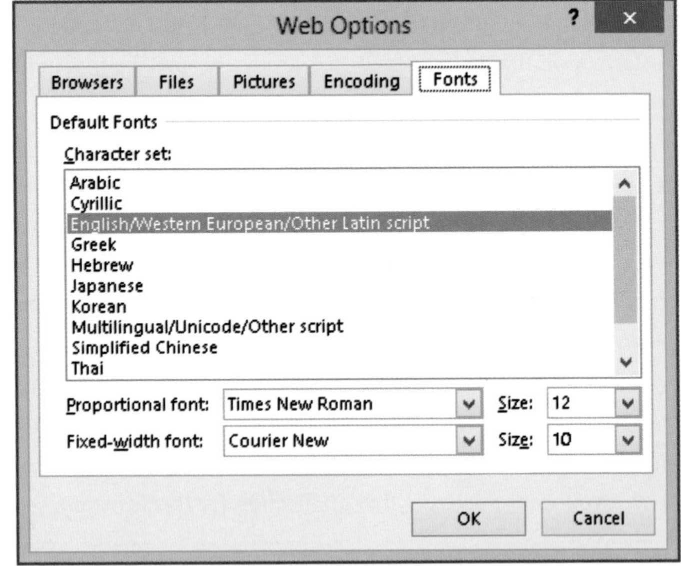

Figure 9-4: ***Word gives you the capability of choosing a number of different character sets to use on webpages.***

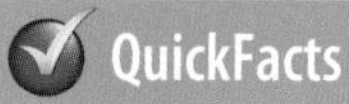

Understanding Hyperlinks

Hyperlinks provide the means to switch, or "jump," from one webpage to another or from one location on a webpage to another location on the same page. Hyperlinks can also be used to open files such as pictures and programs. The billions of hyperlinks on all the webpages on the Internet are what give the Web its name. On a webpage, a hyperlink can be a word or words, a graphic, or a picture that, when clicked, tells the browser to open a new page at another site whose address is stored in the hyperlink. A hyperlink's address is called a *URL*, or Uniform Resource Locator. A URL is used by a browser to locate and open a webpage or file. An example of a URL is http://en.wikipedia.org/wiki/Warren_Buffett#Acquisitions.

- The "http://" identifies the site as using Hypertext Transfer Protocol (HTTP), a set of standards for communication and identification.
- Next, there is often "www," which identifies the site as being on the Internet or World Wide Web; although, frequently, as in this case, the space used by "www" in a URL contains other information used to identify a major segment of the website. In this case, the "en" identifies the English language area.
- "wikipedia.org" is a *domain name* that is the principle identifier of a website.
- "/wiki/" is a folder name identifying a subarea within a site.
- "Warren_Buffett" is a webpage in the wiki folder in the website. (Warren Buffett is one of the most successful of American investors.)
- "#Acquisitions" is a particular location on the webpage, and is called a *bookmark*.

Insert a Hyperlink

There are several different types of hyperlinks. All of them are inserted on a page in Word by first displaying the Insert Hyperlink dialog box, as described here. You then need to follow the steps in the subsequent sections for the particular type of hyperlink you want to create.

1. In a Word web document, select the text or graphic where you want the hyperlink to appear.
2. Click **Insert | Hyperlink** in the Links group. The Insert Hyperlink dialog box appears (see Figure 9-5). (If your screen is full size, you'll see the Hyperlink command as listed. If your screen is smaller, you'll see the Hyperlink command included in a Link command, as follows: click **Insert | Link | Hyperlink**.)

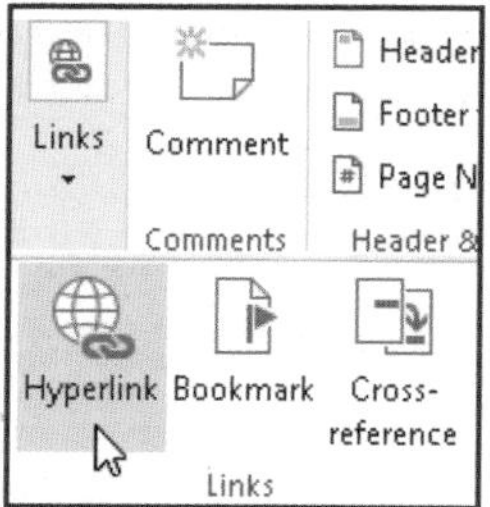

3. Complete the hyperlink by following the steps in one of the following sections, depending on whether you want to create a hyperlink to an existing file or webpage, to a place in the current document, to a new document, or to an email address.

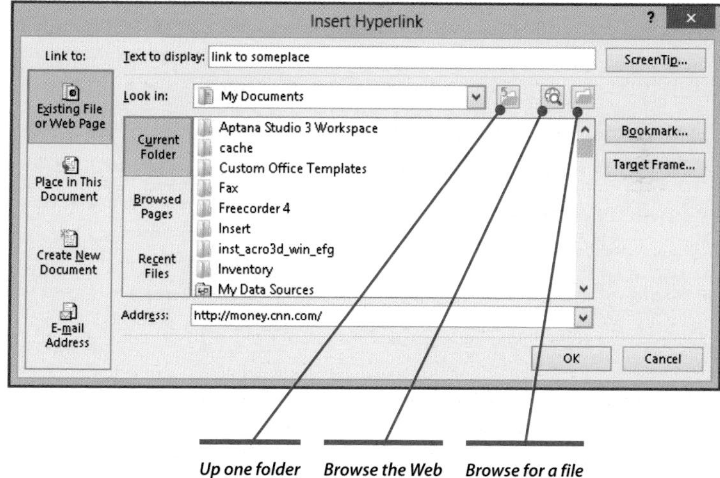

Figure 9-5: ***The Insert Hyperlink dialog box enables you to create hyperlinks to webpages, places within the same file, files, or email addresses.***

Create a Hyperlink to an Existing File or Webpage

To create a hyperlink to an existing file or webpage:

1. In the Link To column on the left, click the **Existing File Or Webpage** button, if it is not already selected.
2. Navigate to the file or webpage in one of these ways:
   - Use the **Look In** drop-down list (and, if necessary, the **Up One Folder** button) to browse to the folder.
   - Click the **Browse The Web** button to open a window in a web browser on your computer, browse to the page or pages to which you want to link, and then switch back to the Insert Hyperlink dialog box. Some browsers, such as Internet Explorer, will automatically enter the URL in the Address text box. If you use a different browser, you need to copy and paste the URL into the Address text box. If a browser is opened by selecting Insert Hyperlink and you want to use a different one, close the open browser and open the one you want to use.

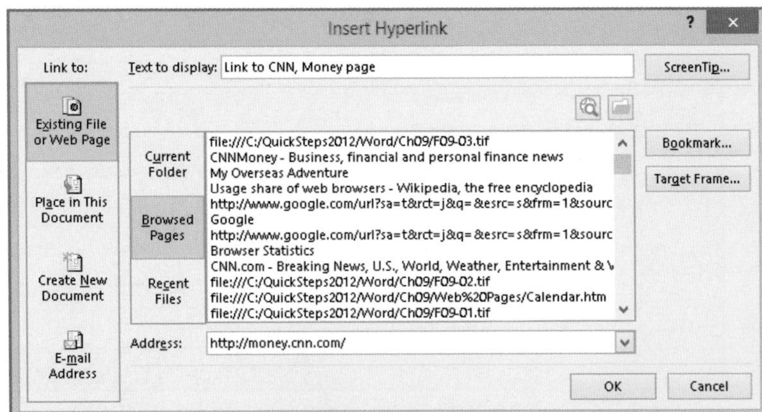

Figure 9-6: ***Clicking the Browsed Pages button will give you a list of the webpages and files that you have viewed with the browser so that you can select one of them for a hyperlink.***

   - Click the **Current Folder** button to display the current folder. Click the **Browsed Pages** button to display a list of webpages you've browsed recently. Click the **Recent Files** button to display a list of local files you've worked with recently.

   –Or–

   Select the address from the **Address** drop-down list.
3. If needed, change the default text in the **Text To Display** text box to the text you want displayed for the hyperlink. (This is the text that the user clicks to access the linked page.) If you have selected text instead of a graphic, for example, on your webpage, it will appear here and may not need to be changed.
4. To add a ScreenTip to the hyperlink, click **ScreenTip**, type the text in the Set Hyperlink ScreenTip dialog box, and then click **OK**.

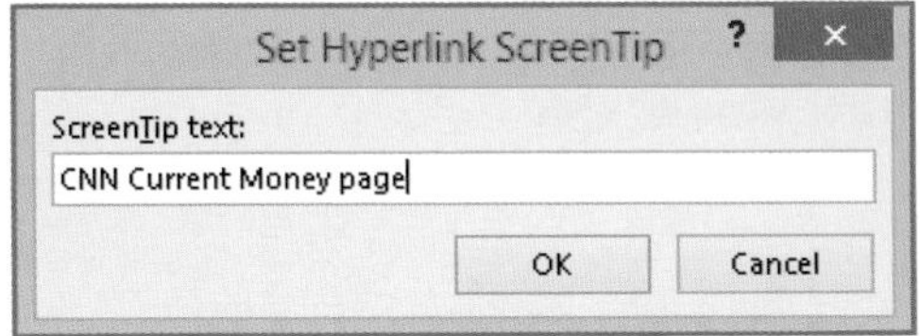

5. To make the hyperlink connect to a particular location in the page rather than simply to the beginning of the page, click **Bookmark** and choose the location in the Select Place In Document dialog box (see "Create a Hyperlink to a Place in the Current Document").
6. Click **OK**. Word inserts the hyperlink.

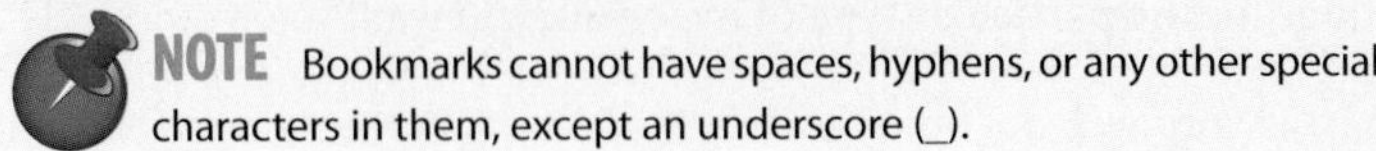

NOTE Bookmarks cannot have spaces, hyphens, or any other special characters in them, except an underscore (_).

Create a Hyperlink to a Place in the Current Document

To create a hyperlink to a place in the current document:

1. In the Link To column, click the **Place In This Document** button.
2. Under Select A Place In This Document, click a heading or a bookmark that is displayed (see Figure 9-7). If there are multiple items available, click the **plus sign** (+) to expand the list or **minus sign** (–) to collapse it.
3. If needed, click in the **Text To Display** text box and change the default text that you want displayed for the hyperlink. (This is the text that the user clicks to access the linked page.) If you have selected text instead of a graphic, that is what will be displayed. You may not want to change it in that case.
4. To add a ScreenTip to the hyperlink, click **ScreenTip**, type the text in the Set Hyperlink ScreenTip dialog box, and then click **OK**.
5. Click **OK**. Word inserts the hyperlink.

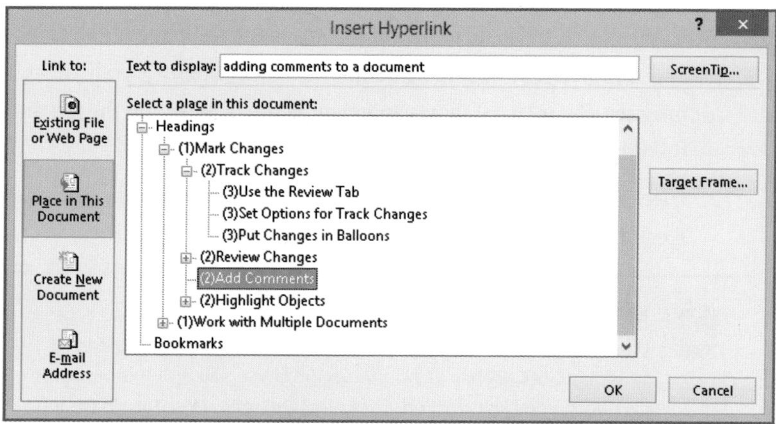

Figure 9-7: ***Word enables you to link to a particular place in either the current or a destination document—for example, to a heading or bookmark in a Word document.***

Create a Hyperlink to a New Document

To create a hyperlink to a new document:

1. In the Insert Hyperlink dialog box, in the Link To Column on the left, click the **Create New Document** button (see Figure 9-8).

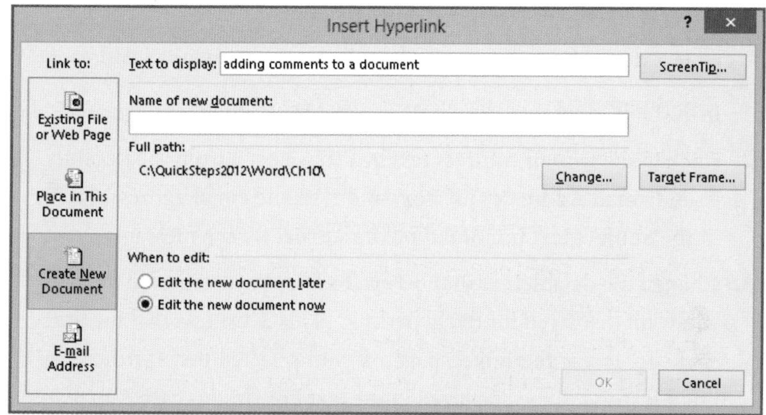

Figure 9-8: ***When you need to link to a new document, Word lets you create the new document immediately to ensure that it is saved with the correct name and location.***

2. Click in the **Name Of New Document** text box and type the filename and extension. Check the path in the Full Path area. If necessary, click **Change;** use the Create New Document dialog box to specify the folder, filename, and extension; and then click **OK**.
3. If needed, change the default text in the **Text To Display** text box to the text you want displayed for the hyperlink. (This is the text that the user clicks to access the linked page.) If you have selected text for the hyperlink instead of a graphic, it will be displayed in this field and you may not want it changed.
4. To add a ScreenTip to the hyperlink, click **ScreenTip**, type the text in the Set Hyperlink ScreenTip dialog box, and then click **OK**.

5. By default, Word selects the Edit The New Document Now option. If you prefer not to open the new document for editing immediately, click the **Edit The New Document Later** option to clear it.
6. Click **OK**. Word inserts the hyperlink.

Create a Hyperlink to an Email Address

To create a mailto hyperlink that starts a message to an email address:

1. In the Link To column, click the **E-mail Address** button (see Figure 9-9).
2. Click in the **E-mail Address** text box (or select it from the Recently Used E-mail Addresses list box) and type the email address. Click in the **Subject** text box and type the subject for the message.
3. Change the default text in the **Text To Display** text box to the text you want displayed for the hyperlink. (This is the text that the user clicks to access the linked page.) If you selected text instead of a graphic, this will be displayed in the text box. In this case, you may not want it changed.

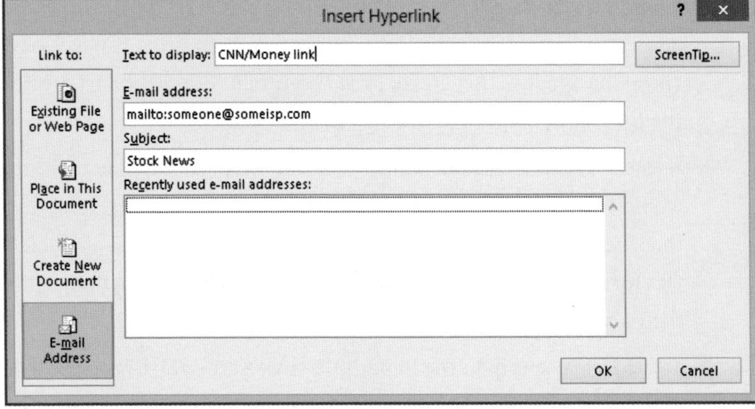

Figure 9-9: ***The Insert Hyperlink dialog box lets you quickly create a mailto hyperlink to an email address.***

4. To add a ScreenTip to the hyperlink, click **ScreenTip**, type the text in the Set Hyperlink ScreenTip dialog box, and then click **OK**.
5. Click **OK**. Word inserts the hyperlink.

TIP Email addresses you have recently used in other hyperlinks will be in the list of Recently Used E-mail Addresses at the bottom of the Edit Hyperlink dialog box. If you want to use one of them in another hyperlink, click it instead of typing it again in the E-mail Address text box.

NOTE The "mailto:" entry in front of the email address tells a browser to open the default email program, open a new message, and place the address in the "To" line.

Verify How a Page Will Look

After you have saved a Word document as a webpage, you'll probably want to check how it looks in your browser.

1. In Windows, navigate to the folder where the webpage file is stored, and double-click the web document. It will open in your default browser. Figure 9-10 shows an example file in Word on the left and then the file being previewed in Internet Explorer.
2. After viewing the webpage, click **Close** to remove the Internet Explorer window.

NOTE Word automatically creates a hyperlink when you type a URL, email address, or a network path in a document and then press **SPACEBAR, TAB, ENTER,** or a punctuation key. If you find this behavior awkward, you can turn it off: Click **File | Options | Proofing** in the left column, click **AutoCorrect Options**, click the **AutoFormat As You Type** tab, clear the **Internet And Network Paths With Hyperlinks** check box, and then click **OK** twice.

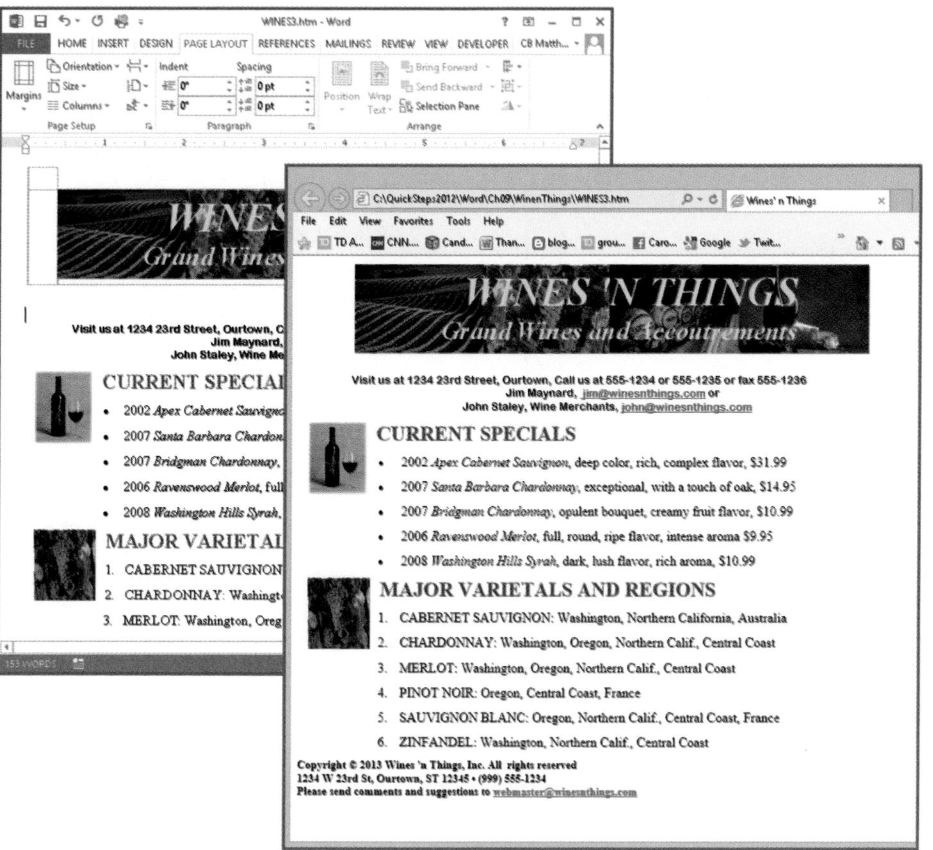

Figure 9-10: ***Previewing a webpage enables you to identify problems with your webpages while you are still working on them in Word. Here, the original document in Word is shown on the left.***

Remove Personal Information from the File Properties

When creating a webpage that you will place on a website (as opposed to a site on a local network), it's a good idea to remove the personal information that Word includes by default in documents, which might include your name, company name, date, and comments. To remove this information:

1. Click **File | Info | Check For Issues | Inspect Document**. The Document Inspector dialog box opens.
2. Select the type of data you want to check for (the default is to check all of the options), and click **Inspect**. The Document Inspector dialog box appears and may show information you want to remove, as shown in Figure 9-11.

1 2 3 4 5 6 7 8 9 10

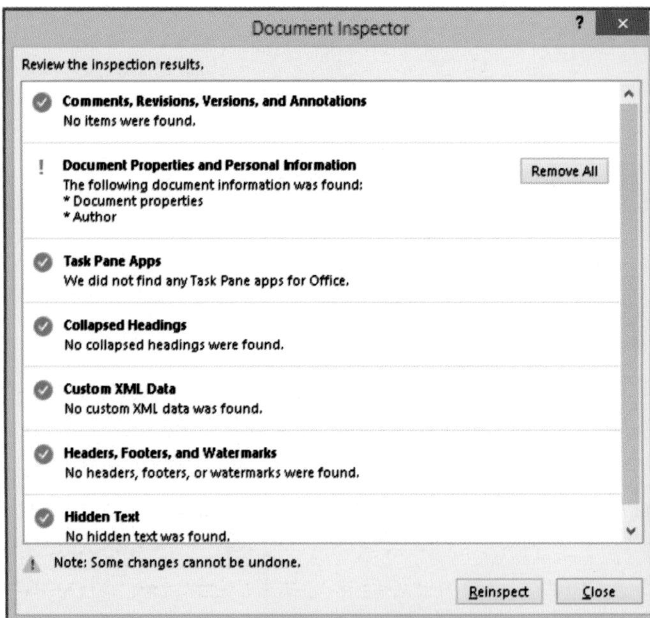

Figure 9-11: ***Inspect and remove any personal information in the webpages you save.***

3. Click **Remove All** for all the information you want removed. Click **Close.**
4. Save the document, as described in an earlier section of this chapter.

Remove Word-Specific Tags from a Document

As discussed earlier in this chapter, Word uses custom HTML tags to store the Word-specific data required to save the entire Word document in an HTML format. Saving this data is good if you want to be able to again edit the document in Word with all its features present, but you don't need this extra data when you're using Word on a one-time basis to create pages for your website.

To remove the Word-specific tags from a document:

1. When you are ready to save the document one final time after you are sure it is the way you want it, click **File | Save As | Computer**, or whatever storage place you want. Find the path to the folder within which you'll save the file.
2. Click the **Save As Type** down arrow, and click the **Webpage, Filtered** format.
3. Click **Save**. A Microsoft Office Word dialog box appears, telling you that Office-specific tags will be removed. Click **Yes**. (If you click No, the save will not occur. You will be able to change the Save As Type setting.)

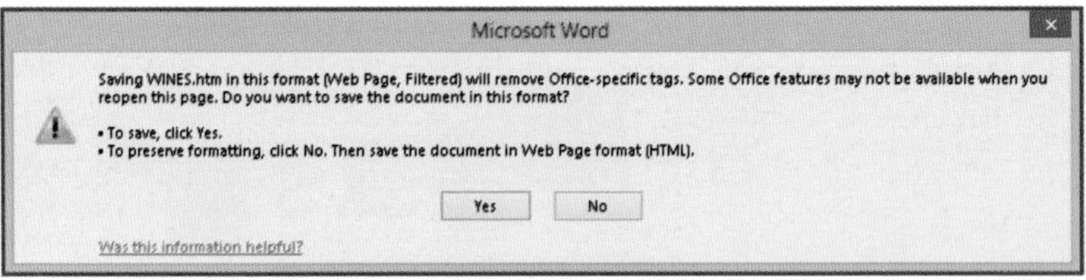

4. Depending on the browser settings you have chosen in the Web Options dialog box, you may also see warnings about features that will be removed from the Word document. Click **Continue** if you want to proceed anyway; click **Cancel** if you want to choose another format.

If you wish to go beyond the basic webpage building you can do in Word, two books can be of help. The first, mentioned earlier, is *HTML, XHTML, and CSS QuickSteps,* by Guy Hart-Davis, which provides a good foundation in website creation; the second, *Dynamic Web Programming: A Beginner's Guide,* by Marty Matthews, provides the tools to create an interactive website, including using an online database to provide information to the website and collect information from it. Both books are published by McGraw-Hill Professional. You can learn more on our website, http://matthewstechnology.com.

QuickSteps to...

- Track Changes
- Review Changes
- Add Comments
- Highlight Text
- Save Several Copies of a Document
- Compare Documents

Chapter 10

Using Word with Other People

In the first nine chapters of this book, we've talked about the many ways you can use Word on your own. In this chapter we'll talk about how you can use Word with other people. Word has a number of features that allow multiple people to work on the same document and see what each other has done. These include marking changes, both additions and deletions that multiple people make to a document; adding comments to a document; highlighting words, lines, and paragraphs of a document; having multiple versions of a document; and comparing documents.

MARK CHANGES

When two or more people work on a document, it is helpful to see what the other people have done without having to read every word and accurately remember what the document said before it was changed. You can do this in Word by using the Track Changes feature. *Track Changes* identifies the changes (additions, modifications, or deletions) made to a document by everyone who works on it. Each person is automatically assigned a color, and their changes are noted in that color. For example, Figure 10-1 shows a section of a document in the editing process. After all the changes are made, they can be accepted or rejected, either one at a time or all at once.

1 2 3 4 5 6 7 8 9 10

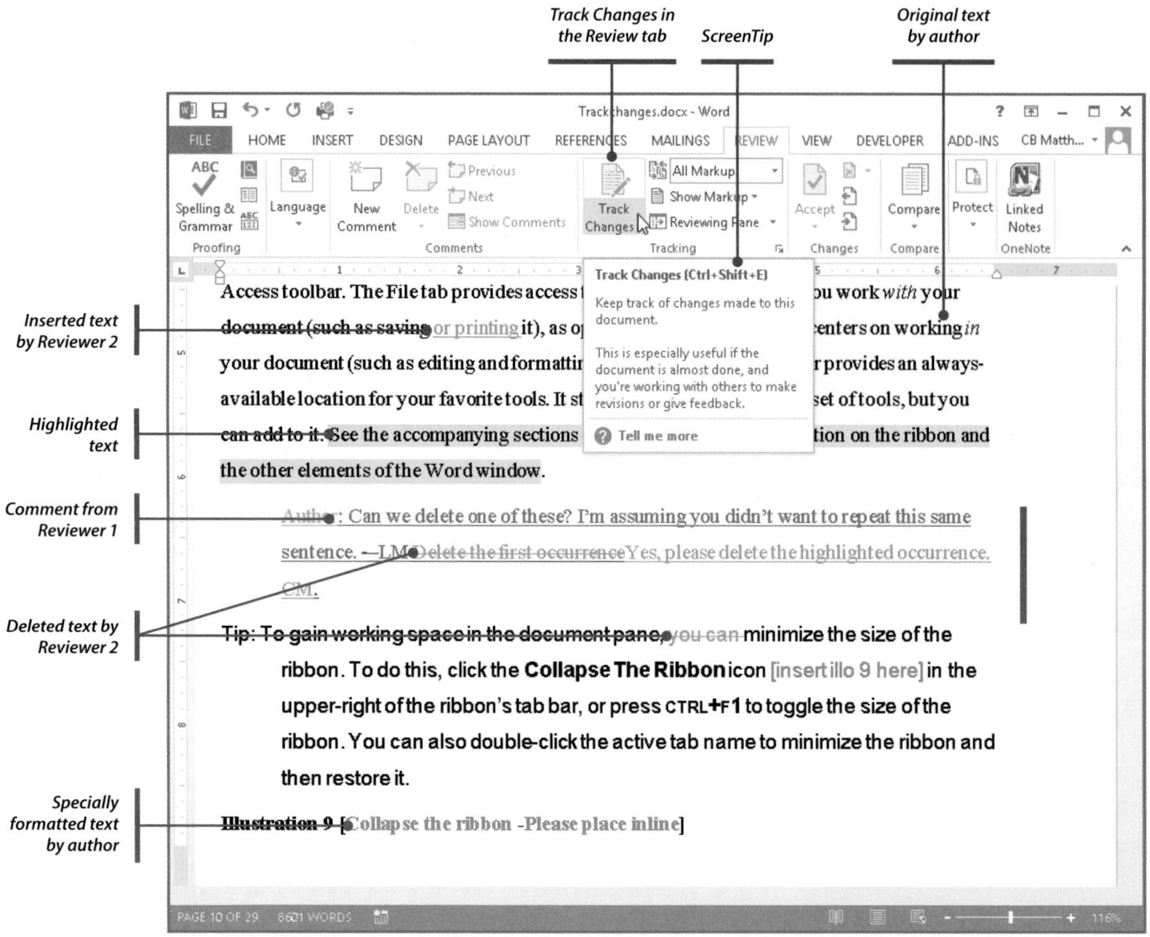

Figure 10-1: ***By using Track Changes, multiple people can make changes to a document, and you can see what each has done.***

TIP For major collaboration of multiple people and even teams, Microsoft has a product called SharePoint 2013 under which all the Office 2013 products run. See *SharePoint 2010 QuickSteps* (McGraw-Hill Professional, 2010) for more information.

TIP By pointing your mouse at a change, you can see who made the change and the date and time it was made.

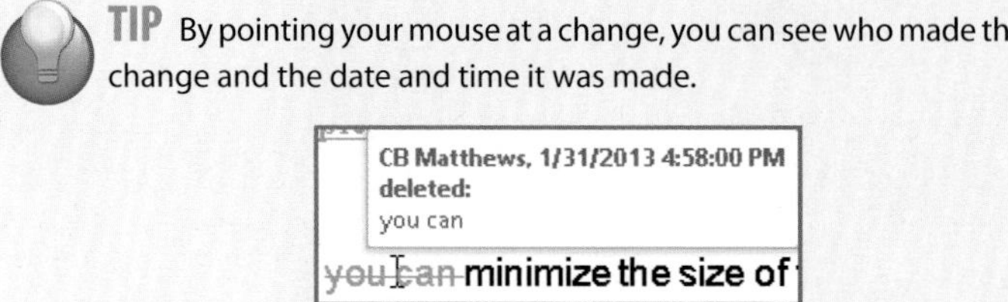

Track Changes

To use Track Changes, you must turn it on. Prior to this, anything anyone types looks like ordinary text, and there is no way of telling the difference between the new text and what was on the page before the change was made. Once Track Changes is turned on, however, you can choose how to display anything that anyone types or does to the document. You can choose for it to be shown in the color automatically assigned to that person; furthermore, the changes are fully reversible, if desired. To turn on Track Changes:

> In the document to be edited, click **Review | Track Changes** in the Tracking group.
>
> 
>
>
> –Or–
>
> Press **CTRL+SHIFT+E**.

The Review tab provides a number of features that you can use as you and others edit a document, as shown in Figure 10-2. You have these choices in the Tracking group:

- To choose what is to be included in the revision marks, click **Show Markup** and set your options.
- To set your display of revisions, click **Display For Review** and select your preference.
- To view revisions in a separate reviewing pane, click the **Reviewing Pane** down arrow and choose your preference.
- To set the Track Changes options, click the **Change Tracking Options** Dialog Box Launcher.

As you and others type, the changes will be recorded and displayed according to your preferences. See "Set Options for Track Changes" to set defaults and other settings.

Set Options for Track Changes

Word gives you a number of options for how changes are displayed with Track Changes. These are set in the Track Changes Options dialog box, shown in Figure 10-3. To open this dialog box and set the options:

1. Click **Review | Change Tracking Options** Dialog Box Launcher in the lower-right corner of the Tracking group. The Track Changes Options dialog box is displayed.

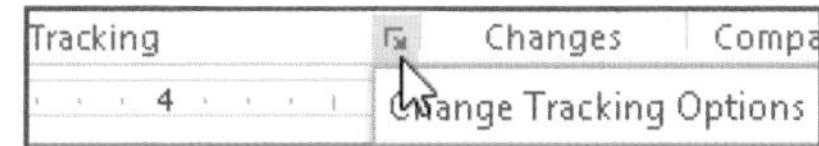

2. To show changes to an element, such as comments, a check mark must be in the check box, as it is by default. To suppress displaying changes for an element, clear the check box.

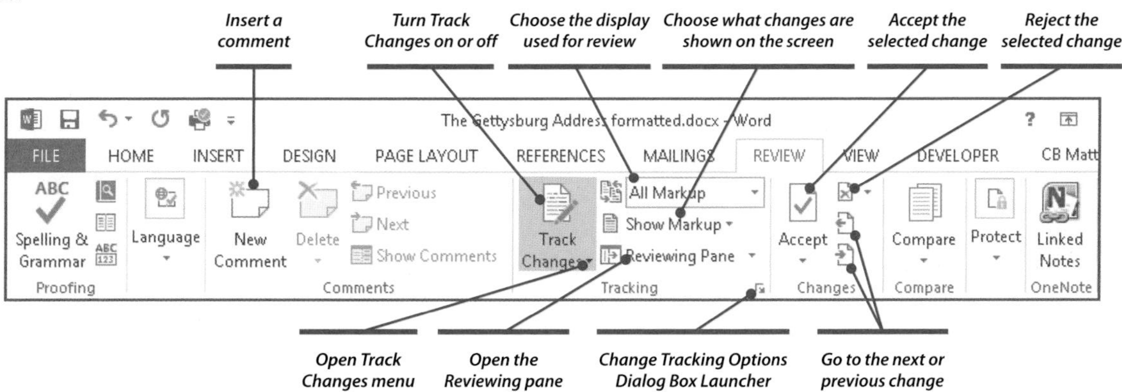

Figure 10-2: ***The Review tab can be used to go through an edited document and accept or reject changes.***

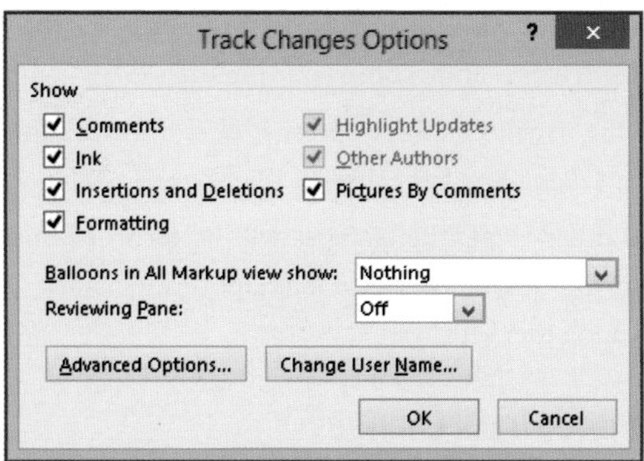

Figure 10-3: ***You can track changes by showing the revisions for selected changes in balloons, as well as in a reviewing pane or in the document. Clicking Advanced Options provides more choices.***

3. When you have selected **All Markup** in the Review tab Tracking group for your choice of what to show as tracked changes, you can further qualify this by selecting what is to be shown in balloons. Click the **Balloons In All Markup View Show** down arrow and select an option:
   - **Revisions** to show revisions in the balloons
   - **Nothing** to not use balloons to show changes
   - **Comments And Formatting** to show any comments and formatting in balloons
4. Click the **Reviewing Pane** down arrow and select **Vertical**, **Horizontal**, or **Off** to show revisions in a horizontal reviewing pane below the document, to show them in a vertical reviewing pane to the left of the document, or not to show revisions in a reviewing pane at all.
5. To change the name that is displayed when you make changes to the document, refer to "Set Your Tracking Changes Name."
6. To select additional changes affecting colors for each of the reviewers and other formatting specifics, refer to "Change Advanced Track Change Options."
7. Click **OK** to close the Track Changes Options dialog box.

Set Your Tracking Changes Name

To identify yourself to other people who are reviewing shared documents, you can set your name to be one that others in the editing group will recognize.

1. Click **Review | Change Tracking Options** Dialog Box Launcher in the lower-right corner of the Tracking group. The Track Changes Options is displayed, as shown in Figure 10-4.
2. Click **Change User Name**. The Word Options dialog box is displayed with the general pane selected.

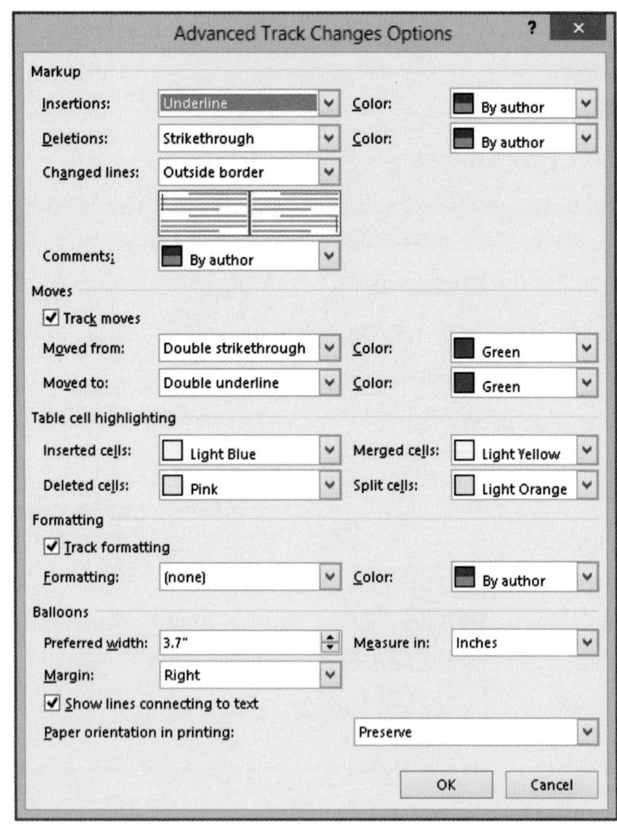

Figure 10-4: ***While you can select colors for each type of change, the best practice is to let Word automatically select the color for each reviewer***

3. Under Personalize Your Copy Of Microsoft Office, click in the **User Name** text box and type the name you want.
4. Click in the **Initials** text box and type your initials.
5. Click **OK** twice to close the two dialog boxes.

Change Advanced Track Change Options

1. Click **Review | Change Tracking Options** Dialog Box Launcher in the Tracking group.
2. Click **Advanced Options**. The Advanced Track Changes Options dialog box is displayed.
3. Open the **Insertions**, **Deletions**, **Changed Lines**, and **Comments** drop-down lists to review and change the options for displaying each of these items. Also, you can change the colors used for each of these.
4. Review and consider how moving text, changing tables, and revising formatting are handled, and make any changes you want. (Balloons are discussed in the following section.)
5. When you are done, click **OK**.

Put Changes in Balloons

Word gives you two ways of viewing changes, both on the screen and when you print out the document. One is an in-line method, where the changes are made within the original text, as shown earlier in Figure 10-1. The other is to put changes in balloons to the right of the text, as shown in Figure 10-5. You can see the balloonish shape when an item is selected. What is in the balloon and what is in the text depends on your choice in the Review tab's Display For Review drop-down list. The default option, shown in Figure 10-5, is All Markup, which shows the text with the final wording and the balloons with all revisions. The options available in the Display For Review drop-down list are described in Table 10-1.

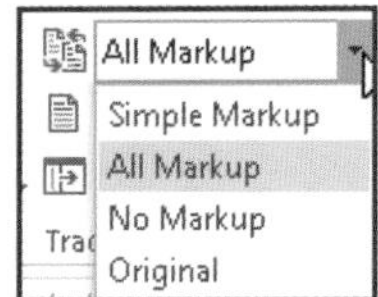

Table 10-1: Display For Review Options

Display Option	What Is in the Text	What Is in the Balloon
Simple Markup	Final text with insertions, with a line displayed on the modified line rather than the actual changes.	Nothing
All Markup	Final text with markups inline in the document, as shown in Figure 10-1.	Insertions, deletions, formatting
No Markup	Original text with modifications but nothing to indicate what they are.	Nothing
Original	Original text without markings.	Nothing

Turn Balloons On or Off

You can quickly turn the balloon changes on or off.

Click **Review | Show Markup** in the Tracking group, and then on the menu click **Balloons | Show Revisions In Balloons**.

NOTE You can also click **Review | Change Tracking Options** Dialog Box Launcher in the Tracking group. Then click the **Balloons In All Markup View Show** down arrow and select **Nothing** (the default) to turn off balloons, click **Revisions** to turn on balloons, or click **Comments And Formatting** to use balloons in that way. Click **OK** to close the dialog box.

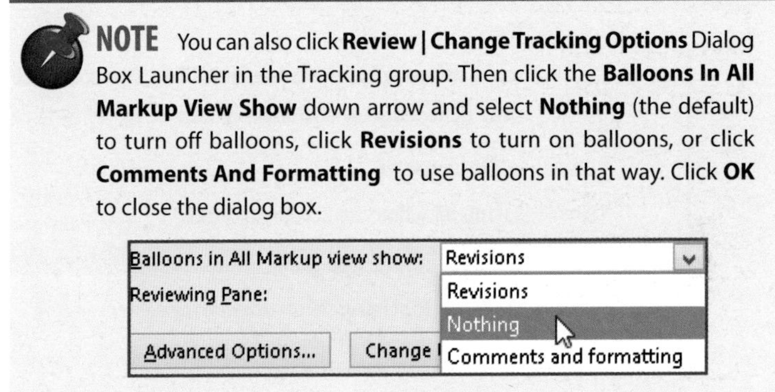

Control Balloon Size and Positioning

If you choose to turn balloons on, you can control their size and position them.

1. Click **Review | Change Tracking Options Dialog Box Launcher** in the Tracking group. Then click **Advanced Options.**

1 2 3 4 5 6 7 8 9 10

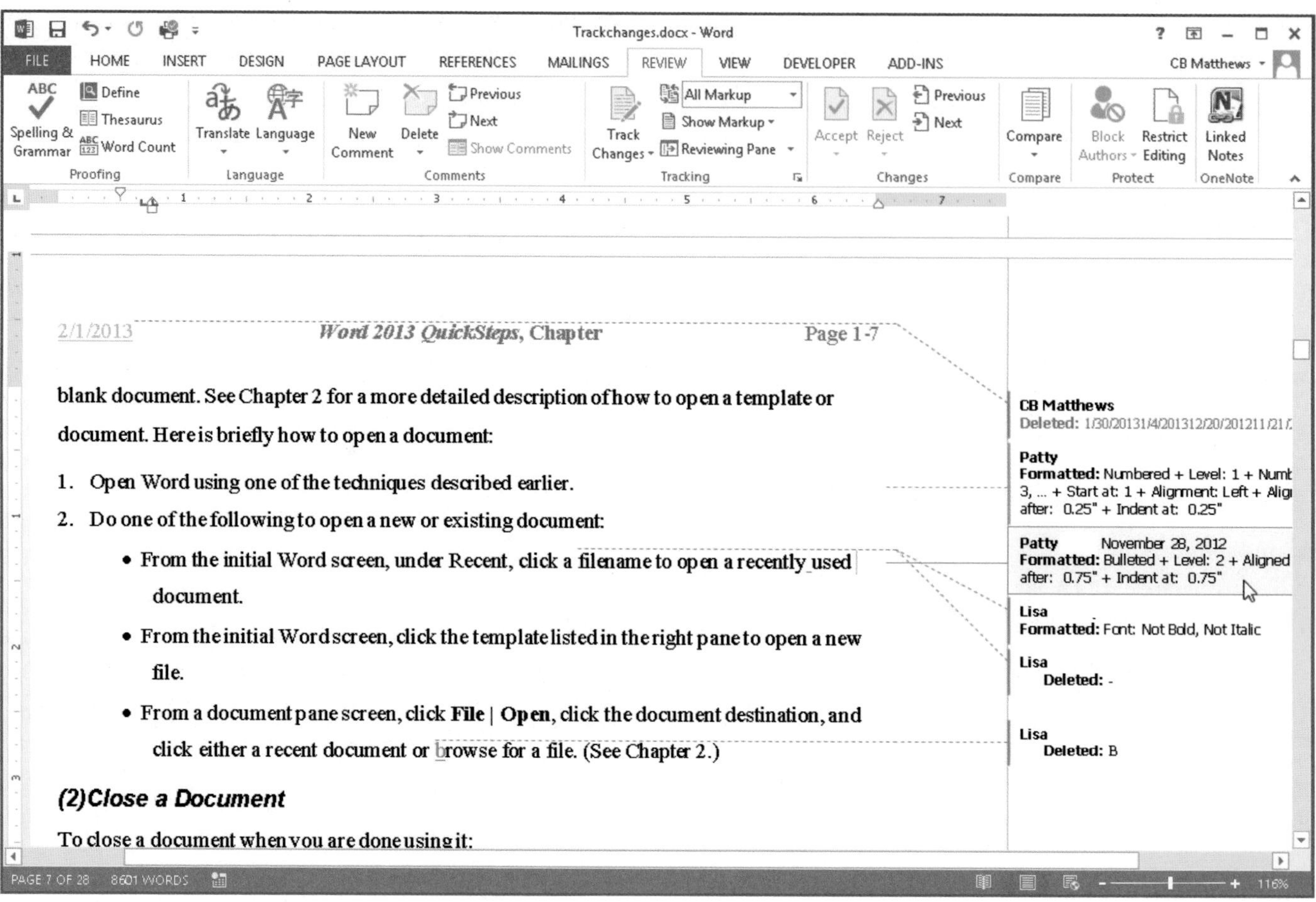

Figure 10-5: ***Using balloons for changes can provide for easier reading of the final text and can show changes in insertions, deletions, or formatting, but it can be harder to see what has been changed.***

2. Beneath Balloons, you have these options:
   - **Preferred Width** Set how wide the balloon task pane is to be. Click **Measure In** to choose between Percent and Inches.
   - **Margin** Determine in which margin (Right or Left) the balloons should be in.
   - **Show Lines Connecting To Text** Determine whether there are connecting lines between the balloons and the modified text.
   - **Paper Orientation In Printing** Determine whether to print a document with balloon changes in its normal portrait orientation, decide automatically when printing, or force it to be printed in landscape orientation to better keep the original text size.
3. When you are done with the balloon-related settings, click **OK** twice.

TIP If you want to quickly hide all the changes in a document, click **No Markup** in the Display For Review list found in the Tracking group. Click **All Markup** in the same list to reveal the changes again.

TIP If there are multiple reviewers on a single document, you can easily see who is represented by what color by clicking **Review | Show Markup | Specific People** in the Tracking group and clicking **All Reviewers**. You can use this to see only the changes made by specific people as well.

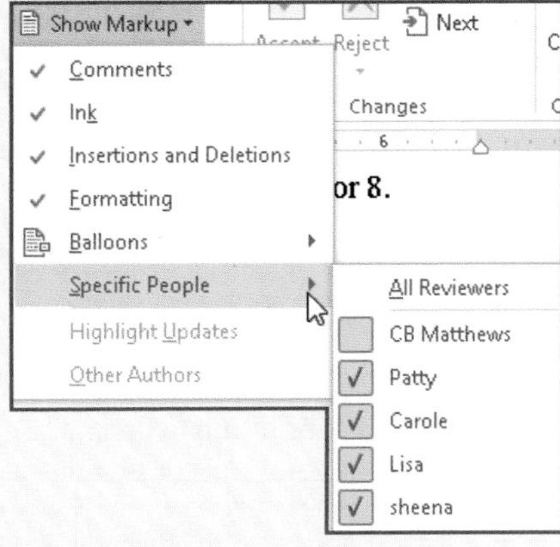

Review Changes

Once Track Changes has been turned on, any changes made to a document by adding, deleting, and reformatting the text are marked so that anyone can see them. The changes appear either in the text or in balloons in the margins. Once all changes have been made to a document, you will want to go through the document, look at the changes, and decide to accept or reject each one.

1. With the document you want to review, click **Review | Track Changes** in the Tracking group (see "Use the Track Changes" earlier in this chapter to turn the Track Changes feature on and off).
2. Press CTRL+HOME to position the insertion point at the beginning of the document. You have these choices available in the Changes group:
   - Click **Next** to find and select the first change.
   - Click **Previous** if you want to return to the previous change.
   - Click **Accept** if you want to make the change permanent.
   - Click **Reject** if you want to remove the change and leave the text as it was originally.
3. Repeat step 2 for each of the changes in the document. Each time you click Accept or Reject, you automatically move to the next change. (See "Create Reviewing Shortcuts" for creating keyboard shortcuts for these reviewing tasks.)
4. When you are finished, click **Save** on the Quick Access toolbar to save the reviewed document.

TIP If you want to accept all changes or reject all changes in a document, click the down arrow below or to the right of Accept or Reject in the Changes group, and click **Accept All Changes** or **Reject All Changes**.

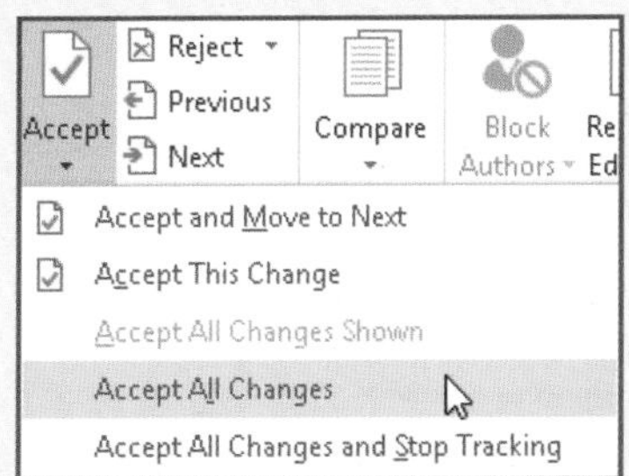

NOTE When you use Accept, Accept And Move To Next, Reject or Reject And Move To Next, you are automatically moved to the next change. You can use Next to move on without accepting or rejecting a change.

Create Reviewing Shortcuts

If you are going through a large document, looking at each change and accepting or rejecting it, clicking the mouse repeatedly on Accept or Reject can become tedious. A partial solution for this is to make keyboard shortcuts.

To assign shortcut keys to each of the three functions—Next, Accept, and Reject:

1. Click **File | Options | Customize Ribbon** in the left column, and opposite Keyboard Shortcuts at the bottom of the dialog box, click **Customize**. The Customize Keyboard dialog box appears.
2. Click **Review Tab** in the Categories list, click **AcceptChangesOrAdvance** in the Commands list, click in the **Press New Shortcut Key** text box, and press the key(s) you want to use. For example, press ALT+A for Accept (see Figure 10-6). Click **Assign**.

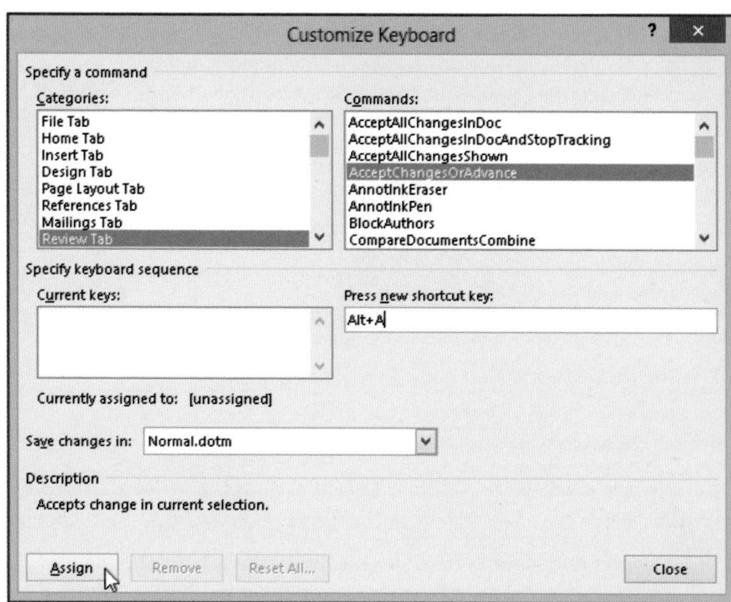

Figure 10-6: ***For some people, keyboard shortcuts are faster than clicking the mouse, especially if you use two hands.***

3. Repeat step 2, first for Next by clicking **NextChangeOrComment** in the Command list and assigning, for example, ALT+N; and then for Reject by clicking **RejectChangesOrAdvance** and assigning, for example, ALT+R, and clicking **Assign** for each.
4. When you are done, click **Close** and then click **OK**.
5. Open a document for which you want to review changes.
6. Press ALT+N to go to the first change. Then press either ALT+A to accept the change or ALT+R to reject the change and automatically move on to the next change. Repeat this for the remainder of the changes.

Use the Reviewing Pane

Word provides another way to look at changes using the Reviewing pane, shown in Figure 10-7. This pane opens at the left or at the bottom of the Word window and lists each individual change, with its type, the author, and the date and time the change was made (the latter is included only if the column is wide enough).

1. With the document you want to review open in Word, click **Review | Reviewing Pane** in the Tracking group to open it.

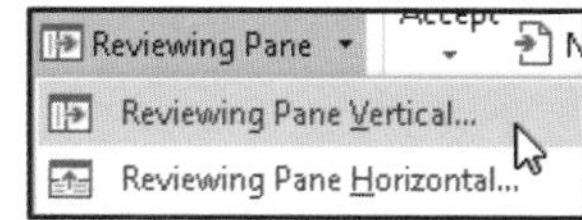

2. Scroll through and click the changes in the Reviewing pane to see them in the document, and/or use the **Next** and **Previous** buttons in the Changes group (or your shortcut keys) to display each change in the Reviewing pane, as well as to highlight them in the document pane.
3. When you are finished making changes, click **Save** on the toolbar.

Email a Document for Review

Often, when several people are working on a document, they exchange the document using email. Word makes using email with the reviewing process easy. You can both send out a document for review and return it with your changes.

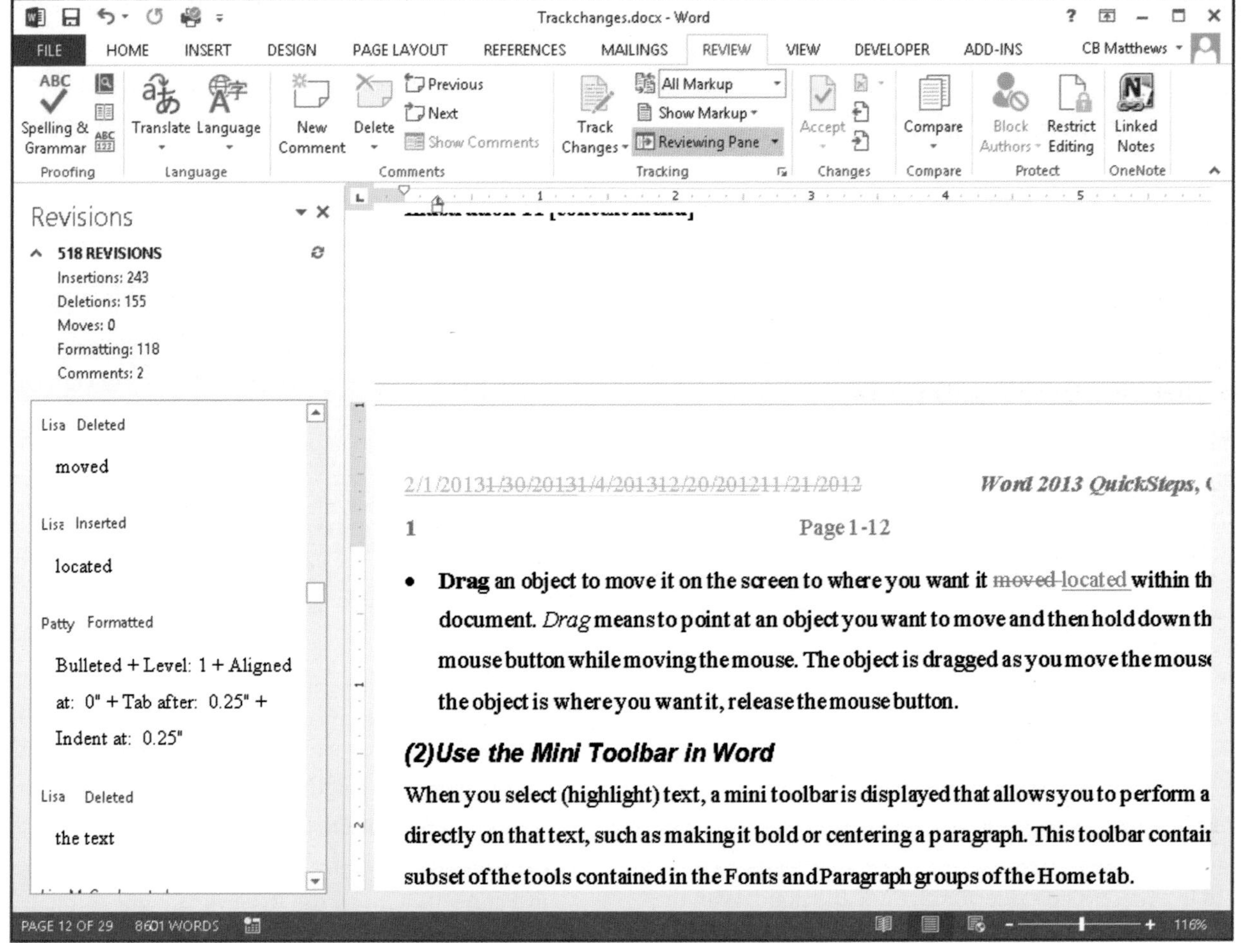

Figure 10-7: ***The Reviewing pane provides a detailed way of looking at each individual change.***

To send out the currently opened document for review:

1. Click **File | Share | Email**. Click **Send As Attachment**. The Email Message window opens with the Word document you want reviewed attached and shown as the subject (see Figure 10-8).
2. Fill in the name of the addressee, plus those who are to get copies, make any desired changes to the Subject line, and add a message. Then, when you are ready, click **Send**.

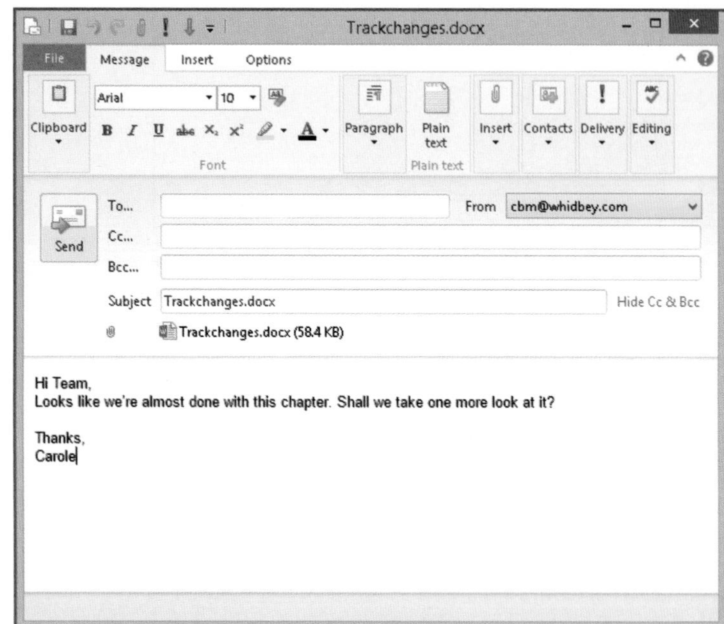

Figure 10-8: ***When you use the Send Using Email option in Word, an email message is opened and the Subject and Attachment lines are filled in for you.***

Save a Reviewed Document to the Cloud

When a document has been sent to you for review and you have finished making the changes you want, you can either email it back in the same way you received it, as described earlier, or save it to the cloud. With the document open in Word:

1. Click **File | Share | Invite People**, and click **Save To Cloud**.
2. Click your "cloud" destination, either on the SkyDrive or Other Web Location. You can browse to the folder you want, or it may be listed.
3. When you've found and clicked the folder to contain your document, click **Save**.

Add Comments

When you review or edit a document, you may want to make a comment instead of or in addition to making a change. If you have balloons turned on for any purpose, a new balloon will appear where you can type your comment. If you have balloons turned off (a setting of "Nothing" in the Track Changes Options dialog box), the Reviewing pane will open (if it isn't already) and a new comment area will appear.

To add a comment:

1. Open your document in Word, display the **Review** tab, and highlight the text to which the comment applies.
2. Click **New Comment** in the Comments group. A highlight will appear on the highlighted text along with your initials and sequential number at the end of the comments.

3. Depending on whether you are using a Reviewing pane or balloons, a place for you to type the comment will appear. You can type the comment of any length, and then click in the document pane to continue reviewing the document. Your comment will appear in the balloons on the right, as you can see in the top-right example in Figure 10-9, or in the Reviewing pane on the left, as shown in Figure 10-9.
4. If you wish, you can close the Reviewing pane by clicking **Review | Reviewing Pane** in the Tracking group, or clicking **Close** in the upper-right area of the Reviewing pane.

NOTE To find the comment that is associated with selected text in the document, click **Review | Next** or **Previous**, followed by **Previous** or **Next**. The comment in the Reviewing pane or balloon will be redisplayed next to the comment.

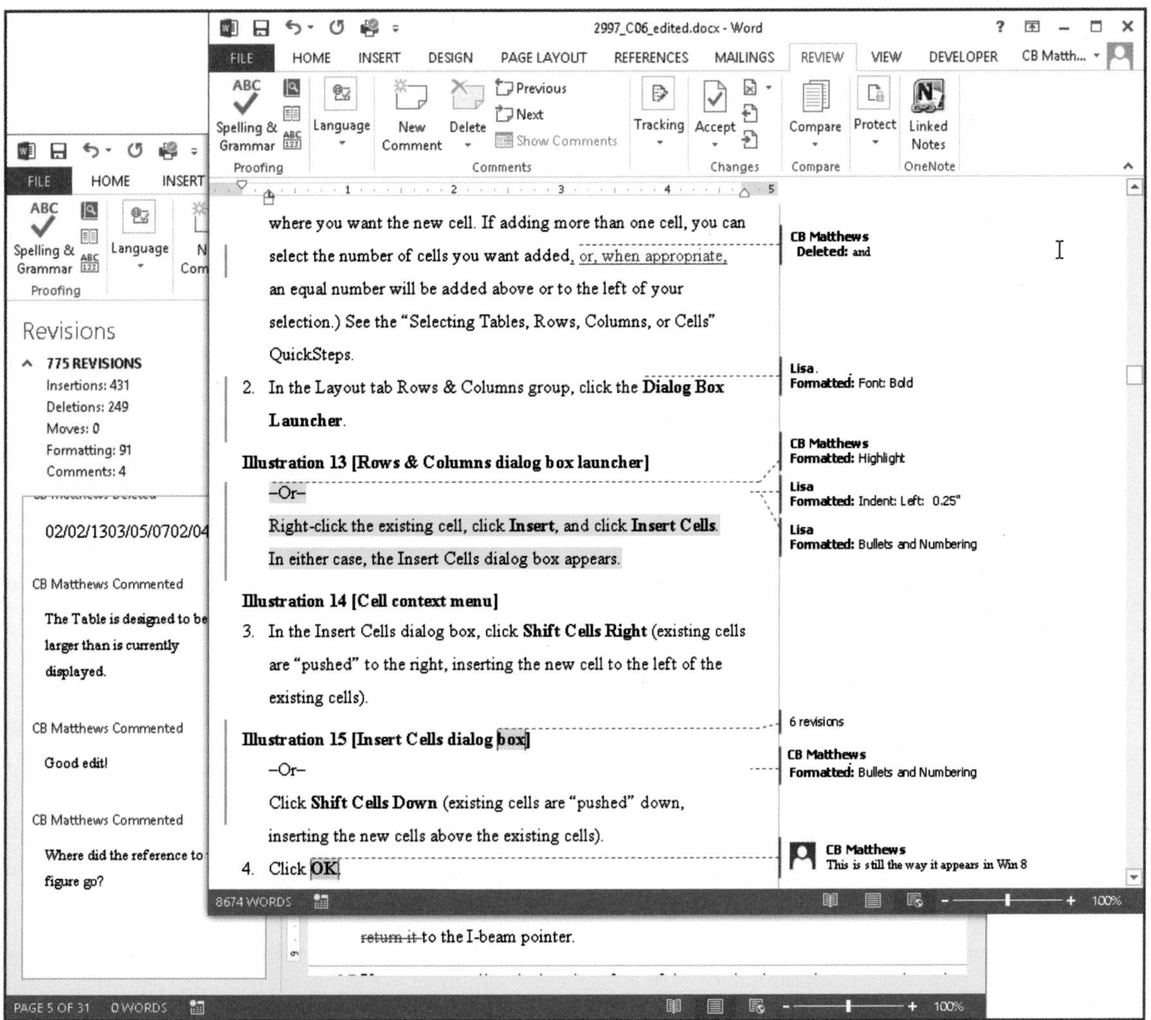
2997_C06_edited.docx - Word
FILE
HOME
INSERT
DESIGN
PAGE LAYOUT
REFERENCES
MAILINGS
REVIEW
VIEW
DEVELOPER
CB Matth...
Spelling & Grammar
Language
New Comment
Delete
Previous
Next
Show Comments
Tracking
Accept
Compare
Protect
Linked Notes
Proofing
Comments
Changes
Compare
OneNote
where you want the new cell. If adding more than one cell, you can select the number of cells you want added, or, when appropriate, an equal number will be added above or to the left of your selection.) See the "Selecting Tables, Rows, Columns, or Cells" QuickSteps.
2. In the Layout tab Rows & Columns group, click the Dialog Box Launcher.
Illustration 13 [Rows & Columns dialog box launcher]
–Or–
Right-click the existing cell, click Insert, and click Insert Cells. In either case, the Insert Cells dialog box appears.
Illustration 14 [Cell context menu]
3. In the Insert Cells dialog box, click Shift Cells Right (existing cells are "pushed" to the right, inserting the new cell to the left of the existing cells).
Illustration 15 [Insert Cells dialog box]
–Or–
Click Shift Cells Down (existing cells are "pushed" down, inserting the new cells above the existing cells).
4. Click OK.
CB Matthews
Deleted: and
Lisa
Formatted: Font: Bold
CB Matthews
Formatted: Highlight
Lisa
Formatted: Indent: Left: 0.25"
Lisa
Formatted: Bullets and Numbering
6 revisions
CB Matthews
Formatted: Bullets and Numbering
CB Matthews
This is still the way it appears in Win 8
8674 WORDS
100%
Revisions
775 REVISIONS
Insertions: 431
Deletions: 249
Moves: 0
Formatting: 91
Comments: 4
02/02/1303/05/0702/04
CB Matthews Commented
The Table is designed to be larger than is currently displayed.
CB Matthews Commented
Good edit!
CB Matthews Commented
Where did the reference to figure go?
return it to the I-beam pointer.
PAGE 5 OF 31
0 WORDS
100%

Figure 10-9: ***Comments allow you to explain why you made a change and appear in the balloons (top-right example) or the Reviewing pane (bottom-left example).***

TIP To quickly view a comment associated with your text if you have both your Reviewing pane and balloons disabled, simply select the highlighted comment (including the colored parentheses and your initials) and place your pointer over the selected text. The comment, along with the name of the person who made it and the date and time, will be displayed in a text box above or below the comment.

NOTE A comment can be deleted by locating it using **Review | Next** or **Previous** in the Changes group and then clicking **Reject**.

NOTE On a Tablet PC, you can use the tablet pen to handwrite comments (called "ink comments"). These are similar to the comments entered on a regular PC, except that they are handwritten instead of typed. In addition, you can use the tablet pen to directly mark in the document pane, not just in the comment areas (called "ink annotations"). For example, you might circle an incorrect phrase and write "Fixed?".

Highlight Text

As you review and change a document, you may want to highlight some text so you can discuss it in a comment or otherwise call attention to it (see Figure 10-1). You do this using the Highlight tool in the Home tab Font group. You can either select the Highlight tool first and then drag over the text to highlight it, or you can select the text to be highlighted first and then click the Highlight tool.

The highlighting that is placed on a page can be one of 15 different colors, so unless you want to use the default yellow, you need to select another color.

1. To select a color, click **Home | Text Highlight Color** down arrow in the Font group. The highlighting color palette will open.

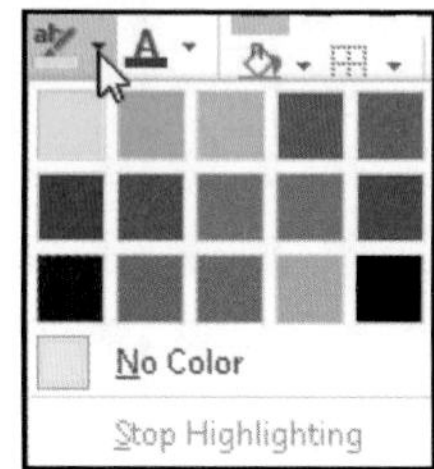

2. Click the color you want to use. The pointer will turn into a highlighter superimposed on the I-beam. Remember: You want whatever color text you are using to show up well on the color you choose (yellow is the most common).
3. Drag over the text you want to highlight if you have not already selected it.
4. Drag over as much and as many separate pieces of text as you want to highlight, also entering comments as needed (you will need to reselect the Highlight tool after you select another tool, such as New Comment). You will know you are still in highlight mode if your pointer is still the highlighted icon.
5. When you are done with the Highlight tool, you can press ESC, click **Highlight** again, or click **Home | Highlight** down arrow in the Font group and click **Stop Highlighting** to return to the normal I-beam insertion point.

NOTE You can remove highlighting by selecting the highlighted text, clicking the **Highlight** tool down arrow, and clicking **No Color**. Or, you can select the highlighted text again with the same selected color and it will remove the highlight from the text.

CAUTION Highlighting shows up when you print a document that contains it. This is fine with a color printer, but if you print on a black-and-white printer, the highlighting will be gray, which will make black text under the highlighting hard to read.

TIP To highlight several sections of text, it is easiest to first select the Highlight tool. To highlight a single piece of text, it is easiest to first select the text.

WORK WITH MULTIPLE DOCUMENTS

As you are going through the reviewing process with several people, it is likely that you will end up with multiple copies of a document. Word gives you a way of comparing these versions.

 Save Several Copies of a Document

First, you want to separately save each copy of the document with a unique name, giving you the ability to compare two copies of the document, as explained in the next section.

Save a Unique Copy

With the document for which you want to create different versions open in Word, click **File | Save As | Computer** (or other storage device), select the folder you want to use, or use **Browse** to find it. Then select the **Save As Type** format you want to use, enter a unique name, and click **Save**.

Open a Different Copy

With a document for which there are multiple copies open in Word, to open another copy, click **File | Open | Computer** (or select another device), select the folder in which the file is stored, select the file, and click **Open**.

 Compare Documents

If changes have been made to a copy of a document without using Track Changes, Word has the ability to compare the two and then merge them into a single document, with the differences shown as they would be with Track Changes.

1. In Word, open the first or original document.
2. Click **Review | Compare** in the Compare group, and then click **Compare** again. The Compare Documents dialog box will appear.

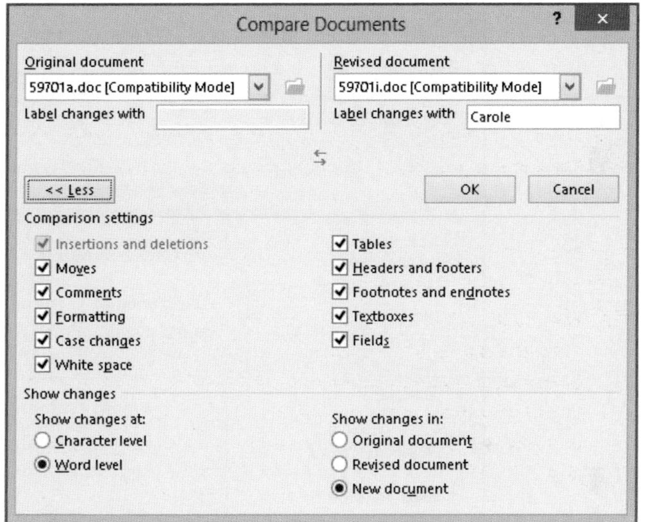

3. Click **More** to set several options:
   a. Select the types of differences you want to see and have reflected in the final document.
   b. Select whether you want to show changes at the character or word level.
   c. Select whether you want the combined changes in the original document, the revised document (the default), or a new document.

4. Select the original document and the revised document you want to compare and merge into the original, the revised, or a new document; make any changes to the settings that you want; and click **OK**.
5. With the default settings, a three-pane window will open and display the Reviewing pane with the revisions on the left, the compared document in the center, and the original document on the top right with the revised document below it, as you can see in Figure 10-10.
6. Scroll through the compared document pane, and click **Accept** or **Reject** in the Changes group, or use the keyboard shortcuts from the earlier section, to accept or reject the changes that have been made.
7. If you want to save the compared document under a new name, click **File | Save As | Computer** (or another storage device), select a folder, enter a name, and click **Save**.

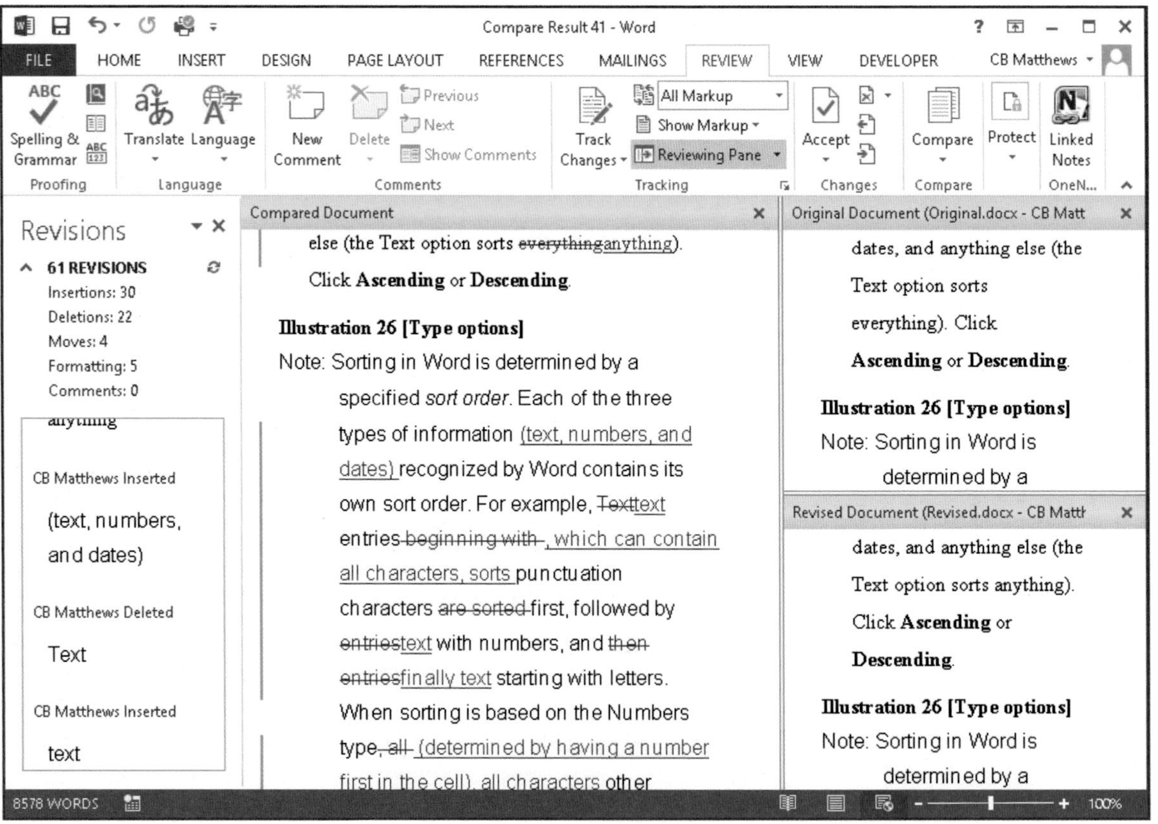

Figure 10-10: ***In a comparison window in Word, the three panes are synched so that scrolling one scrolls the other two.***

Index

Symbols

- < (beginning of word) wildcard, 51
- * (characters) wildcard, 51
- @ (copies of previous character) wildcard, 51
- > (end of word) wildcard, 51
- .* file extension, 37
- ? (single character) wildcard, 51
- \ (wildcard) wildcard, 51

A

- align left shortcut keys, 60
- align right shortcut keys, 60
- all caps shortcut keys, 60
- ALT key. *See* keyboard shortcuts
- %appdata%, relationship to templates, 102
- apps
  - starting in Start screen, 3
  - starting on desktop, 3
- AutoCorrect
  - adding entries, 119
  - configuring, 118–119
  - creating numbered lists with, 76–77
  - deleting entries, 119–120
  - Language dialog box, 119–120
  - Math, 127
- AutoFormat options
  - beginning of list, 121
  - bold style, 120
  - border lines, 120–121
  - bulleted lists, 120
  - fractions, 120
  - hyperlinks, 120
  - hyphens, 120
  - italic style, 120
  - numbered lists, 121
  - ordinals, 120
  - smart quotes, 120
  - straight quotes, 120
  - tables, 121
- AutoRecover feature, 56
- autoshapes, finding, 190
- axes, using with charts, 217
- axis titles, changing, 224

B

- background color, changing, 18
- blank documents, opening, 32–33. *See also* documents
- Blog Post template, 30
- BMP picture files, 180
- body fonts, 96
- Bold button, 9
- bold style
  - applying, 59, 61
  - autoformatting, 120
  - shortcut keys, 60
- border effects, applying to tables, 174–175
- border lines, autoformatting, 120–121
- borders
  - adding to text, 83–84
  - button, 59
- Browsers tab, Web options on, 234
- building blocks
  - creating, 121–122
  - deleting, 122
  - inserting, 122
- bullet shortcut key, 39
- bulleted lists
  - autoformatting, 120
  - changing to numbered lists, 81
  - creating before typing, 77
  - shortcut keys, 60
- bulleted steps, 9, 59
- bulleting, removing, 80
- bullets, customizing, 78–80

C

- camera, finding for pictures, 185
- capitalization
  - changing, 68
  - of each word, 68
  - lowercase, 68
  - sentence case, 68
  - toggle case, 68
  - uppercase, 68
- captions, adding to pictures, 187
- case, changing, 60
- [cc] (one in list) wildcard, 51
- [c-c] (one in range) wildcard, 51
- cell margins, changing in tables, 174
- cells
  - adding to tables, 160–161
  - changing text wrapping in, 171
  - creating spacing between, 174
  - merging in tables, 172
  - orienting text direction, 171
  - removing from tables, 161–162
  - splitting in tables, 172
- cent shortcut key, 39
- center alignment, 59–60, 69
- CGM picture files, 180

change case, 59–60
character formatting
  bold style, 61
  Font and Paragraph groups, 58–59
  font color, 62–63
  font sizes, 61–62
  italic style, 61
  mini toolbar, 60
  resetting text, 63
  selecting fonts, 60
  underlining text, 62
character spacing
  setting, 64–65
  text effects, 65–66
  using, 63–67
characters
  counting, 122–123
  moving to, 47
  selecting, 40
chart items
  3-D format, 227
  3-D rotation, 227
  alignment, 227
  alt text formatting, 227
  border color formatting, 227
  fill formatting, 227
  formatting options, 226–227
  glow formatting, 227
  line color formatting, 227
  number formatting, 227
  selecting, 221–223
  shadow formatting, 227
  soft edges formatting, 227
chart templates. *See also* templates
  creating, 220
  deleting, 221
  using, 220–221
chart titles
  adding, 223–224
  changing, 223–224
chart tools, 218
chart types
  area, 220
  bar, 220
  bubble, 220
  changing, 220
  column, 220
  combo, 220
  doughnut, 220
  line, 220
  pie, 220
  radar, 220
  stock, 220
  surface, 220
  XY (Scatter), 220
charts
  axes, 217
  changing axis titles, 224–225
  creating, 217–219
  data series, 217
  data tables, 227–228
  formatting text in, 226–227
  moving legends, 225
  showing data labels, 225–226
clearing formatting, 59
clip art
  adding, 181–183
  Bing Image Search, 182
  searching Office.com, 182
  searching SkyDrive folders, 182
Clipboard
  Office, 42–45
  Windows, 42, 45
close button, 6
closing documents, 4
cloud. *See* SkyDrive
color effects
  gradients, 191
  picture to fill drawings, 191
  removing, 192
color text, using with text box, 192
colors, selecting quickly, 190
Colors dialog box, displaying, 63
column width, changing in tables, 162–163
columns
  copying, 167
  creating in documents, 104–105
  inserting into tables, 161
  moving, 167
  removing from tables, 161–162
  selecting in tables, 160
  sorting, 165–166
  sorting by fields in, 166
commands
  adding, 13
  adding to Quick Access toolbar, 17
  changing keyboard shortcuts for, 18
  displaying, 13
  finding on ribbon, 13
  removing, 13
  repositioning, 16
comments
  adding to Track Changes, 252–254
  deleting from Track Changes, 254
comparing documents, 255–256
"Compatibility Mode," 11, 28
content controls, using with forms, 211–213
context menus
  identifying, 6
  opening for objects, 3

copies of documents, saving, 56
copy format shortcut keys, 60
copying
  columns, 167
  formatting, 85–86
  formulas, 168
  rows, 167
  tables, 166
  text, 42–43
  text formats, 9
copyright shortcut key, 39
counting
  characters, 122–123
  words, 122–123
CTRL key, using to select text, 40. *See also* keyboard shortcuts
curves
  adjusting, 192
  closing, 193
  creating, 192
customization files
  exporting, 13, 16
  importing, 13, 16
cutting text, 42

D

data series, using with charts, 217
data tables
  displaying, 228
  formatting, 228
decrease font size shortcut keys, 60
decrease indent, 59
deleted text, recovering, 45
deleting
  AutoCorrect entries, 119
  building blocks, 122
  chart templates, 221
  color effects, 192
  comments from Track Changes, 254
  endnotes, 112
  footers, 109–110
  footnotes, 112
  headers, 109–110
  highlighting, 123
  highlighting from Track Changes, 254
  section breaks, 103–104
  styles, 94
  table styles, 177
  tables, 170
  text, 41
desktop shortcut, creating, 3. *See also* shortcuts
diagrams, creating, 195–197
Dialog Box Launcher, 7, 59
dialog boxes, using to format pages, 86
DIB picture files, 180
dictionary, using, 23–24
display elements, selecting, 20–21
.doc file extension, 37
document pane
  gaining working space in, 8
  identifying, 6
document stats, 6
documents. *See also* blank documents; files
  adding identifying info to, 18–20
  closing, 4
  comparing, 255–256
  creating from "scratch," 5
  defined, 28
  entering text, 36–37
  faxing, 141–142
  importing, 36
  locating existing, 32
  moving around in, 45
  moving to beginning of, 47
  moving to end of, 47
  moving up and down in, 45
  opening, 4, 28–29
  opening existing, 32
  printing, 135–137
  saving, 56
  saving as templates, 56
  saving automatically, 56
  saving copies of, 255
  saving for first time, 53–55
  searching for in Word, 35
  selecting, 40
  translating, 24–26
  using mouse, 45
  using scroll bars, 45
  view buttons, 45
.docx file extension, 37
.dot file extension, 37, 211
.dotx file extension, 37
double-spacing, using, 74
Draft view, 10, 118
Drawing Tools, using with WordArt, 193–195
Drawing Tools Format tab, 189
drawings
  color effects, 190–192
  components, 189
  curves, 192–193
  diagrams, 195–197
  enhancing lines, 191
  finding autoshapes, 190
  objects from programs, 198
  screenshots, 198–200
  shape fill, 189
  shapes, 189–190
  styles, 189
  text boxes, 189

drawings (*cont.*)
text effects, 189, 193–195
using rulers with, 201
drop cap, create, 68–69

E

em dash shortcut key, 39
email, sending, 142–143
EMF picture files, 180
EMZ picture files, 180
en dash shortcut key, 39
endnotes
changing, 111
converting to footnotes, 112
deleting, 112
inserting, 110–111
envelopes
merging to, 151–152
printing, 137–140
EPS picture files, 180
equations
creating from scratch, 128
creating in text boxes, 127
formatting, 128
modifying, 125–126
Euro shortcut key, 39
exiting Word, 4

F

fax modem, using, 141–142
fax service, using, 141
file commands, locating on ribbon, 7
file extensions
.*, 37
.doc, 37
.docx, 37
.dot, 37
.dotx, 37
.htm, .html, .mht, mhtml, 37
.odt, 37
.pdf, 37
.rtf, 37
.txt, 37
.wpd, 37
.wps, 37
.xml, 37
File tab, 6–7
File view, displaying, 11–12
files. *See also* documents
browsing for, 5
defined, 28
opening from existing files, 28
opening from Word screen, 34
opening in Word window, 5
sorting, 36
Find and Replace, advanced, 49–50
Find command, using, 48
folders, finding quickly, 36
Font and Paragraph groups
bold, 59
borders, 59
bulleted steps, 59
center, 59
change case, 59
clearing formatting, 59
decrease indent, 59
Dialog Box Launcher, 59
font color, 59
font name, 59
font size, 59
grow font, 59
hiding formatting, 59
increase indent, 59
italics, 59
justify, 59
left align, 59
line spacing, 59
multilevel list, 59
numbered steps, 59
right align, 59
shading, 59
showing formatting, 59
shrink font, 59
strikethrough, 59
subscript, 59
superscript, 59
text effects, 59
text highlight color, 59
underline, 59
font color, 9, 59, 62–63
font defaults, resetting, 63
Font Dialog Box Launcher, accessing, 58–59
Font dialog box, opening, 60
font name, displaying, 9, 59
font size
changing, 61–62
decreasing, 9, 60
displaying, 9, 59
increasing, 9, 60
font theme set, customizing, 98
fonts
alphabetic, 61
sans-serif, 61
selecting, 60–61
serif, 61
symbols, 61
footers
creating from menus, 108–109
creating from scratch, 107–108

deleting, 109–110
editing, 109
going to, 108
footnotes
changing, 111
converting to endnotes, 112
deleting, 112
inserting, 110–111
form templates. *See also* templates
modifying, 209–211
using, 207–209
Format Painter, 9, 85
formatting, copying, 85–86
formatting marks, turning on, 84
forms
content controls, 211–213
laying out, 211
using, 213–214
formulas
assembling, 167–168
attributes, 167
cell references, 167
converting results, 168
copying, 168
displaying, 167
functions, 167
syntax, 167
fractions, autoformatting, 120

G

General options, setting, 21
GIF picture files, 180
Go To command, using, 47
Google Chrome, 234
gradients, setting, 191
grammar, checking, 52–53
graphic effects, themed, 99
graphs. *See* charts
groups
adding, 13–14
creating, 14
rearranging, 14
renaming, 13
repositioning tools in, 13
grow font, 59

H

hang paragraph shortcut keys, 60
hanging indent
creating, 71
making, 72
removing, 72
setting with rulers, 73
header rows, repeating, 169–170
headers
creating from menus, 108–109
creating from scratch, 107–108
deleting, 109–110
editing, 109
First Page option, 110
going to, 108
left and right, 110
Odd And Even Pages, 110
heading fonts, 96
heading levels shortcut keys, 60
Help feature, 6
Help system, online, 22
hiding formatting, 59
highlighting
applying, 123
changing colors, 123
finding in text, 123
removing, 123
removing from Track Changes, 254
horizontal lines, creating, 81, 83–84
horizontal scroll bar, 46
.htm, and .html file extension, 37
HTML (Hypertext Markup Language), 230–231
HTML elements, creating, 232–233
http://, explained, 237
hyperlinks
autoformatting, 120
to current documents, 239
described, 237
to email addresses, 240
to existing files, 238
inserting, 237
to new documents, 239–240
to webpages, 238
hyphenating text manually, 124
hyphenation rules, setting, 124
hyphens, autoformatting, 120

I

I-beam pointer, 6
identifying info, adding to documents, 18–20
IF/THEN/ELSE rule, using with merge, 150
illustrations. *See also* pictures
absolute positioning, 203–204
aligning, 206
grouping, 206
moving incrementally, 205
positioning, 202–204
reordering stacked, 205–206
resizing, 201, 205
rotating, 201, 205
selecting, 205
spacing evenly, 206

illustrations (*cont.*)
- ungrouping, 206
- wrapping text around, 203–204

images. *See* pictures
importing documents, 36
increase font size shortcut keys, 60
increase indent, 59
indent
- decreasing, 59
- increasing, 59

indenting
- bulleted lists, 71
- first line, 71–73
- hanging indents, 71
- numbered lists, 71
- paragraphs, 71

indents
- changing left, 71
- setting tabs with, 105–106
- setting using ruler, 105–106
- using ruler for, 73

index entries, tagging, 112–113
indexes
- defined, 112
- generating, 113

insert mode, using with text, 37
insertion point, 6, 37
Internet Explorer, 234
Italic button, 9
italic style
- applying, 59, 61
- autoformatting, 120

J

JFIF picture files, 180
JPE picture files, 180
JPEG picture files, 180
JPG picture files, 180
justified alignment, 59, 69

K

keyboard, using, 47
keyboard shortcuts. *See also* CTRL key
- align left, 60
- align right, 60
- all caps, 60
- bold, 60
- bullet character, 39
- bulleted list, 60
- cent symbol, 39
- centered alignment, 60, 69
- change case, 60
- changing for commands, 18
- for common characters, 39
- converting results of formulas, 168
- copy format, 60
- copying formatting, 86
- copying text, 42
- copyright symbol, 39
- cutting text, 42
- decrease font size, 60
- em dash, 39
- en dash, 39
- Euro symbol, 39
- Font dialog box, 60
- font name, 60
- formatting actions, 60
- Go To, 47
- hang paragraph, 60
- hanging indents, 72
- heading levels, 60
- hidden characters, 60
- increase font size, 60
- justified alignment, 69
- left alignment, 69
- left indent, 71
- Mark Index Entry, 112
- moving to beginning of documents, 47
- moving to bottom of windows, 47
- moving to browse objects, 47
- moving to characters, 47
- moving to end of documents, 47
- moving to top of windows, 47
- moving to words, 47
- moving up and down screens, 47
- paragraph formatting, 73
- pasting text, 42
- pound symbol, 39
- redoing actions, 44
- registered symbol, 39
- right alignment, 69
- saving files, 56
- table navigation, 164
- Thesaurus, 125
- toggling capitalization, 68
- toggling ribbon size, 8
- Track Changes, 245
- trademark symbol, 39
- undoing actions, 44–45

keywords, typing, 5

L

labels
- merging to, 152–154
- printing, 140–141

landscape orientation, 87
[lc-c] (not in range) wildcard, 51
left alignment, 59, 69

left indent
  changing, 71
  removing, 71
legends, moving in charts, 225–226
line breaks, inserting, 39–40, 75
line spacing
  double, 73–74
  in Font and Paragraph group, 59
  between paragraphs, 74–75
  setting, 73–76
  single, 73–74
  split pages, 76
lines
  lines, enhancing, 191
  moving to beginning of, 47
  moving to end of, 47
  selecting, 40
lowercase capitalization, 68

M

Mail Merge feature, explained, 143–144
Mail Merge Wizard. *See also* merging
  completing merge, 149–150
  fields, 145–146
  finalizing main document, 147–149
  identifying documents, 144–145
  name and address list, 146–147
  previewing merge, 149
  records, 145–146
  selecting recipients, 145
  selecting type, 144–145
  sorting recipients, 147
mail-merge letters, sending, 142
mail-merge process, 144
mailto: entry, explained, 240
margins
  changing for printing, 134–135
  changing in tables, 174
  setting, 85
Math AutoCorrect, using, 127
maximize screen button, 6
menus
  displaying submenus for, 9
  using, 9
merge document, inserting variable fields, 150
merging. *See also* Mail Merge Wizard
  to envelopes, 151–152
  to labels, 152–154
.mht and mhtml file extensions, 37
Microsoft Help, 6
mini toolbar
  components, 9
  displaying, 9, 60
  formatting commands, 60
  hiding, 9
  for text, 9
  text tools, 9
minimize screen button, 6
mirror margins, using, 87
mouse
  actions, 8
  click action, 8
  commands, 3
  double-click action, 8
  drag action, 8
  point action, 8
  right-click action, 8
  using, 8, 45
Mozilla Firefox, 234
multilevel lists
  creating before typing, 77
  defining, 81
  identifying, 59

N

{n,} (copies of previous character) wildcard, 51
{n,m} (copies of previous character) wildcard, 51
{n} (copies of previous character) wildcard, 51
navigation pane, finding text with, 48–49
Normal template
  explained, 28
  making changes to, 102
numbered lists
  autoformatting, 121
  changing to bulleted lists, 81
  creating before typing, 77
  creating with AutoCorrect, 76–77
numbered steps, 9, 59
numbering, removing, 80
numbers
  autoformatting, 120
  customizing, 78–80

O

objects
  adding from programs, 198
  aligning, 189
  grouping, 189
  moving on screen, 3
  opening, 3
  opening context menus for, 3
  positioning, 205
  rotating, 189
  selecting, 3
.odt file extension, 37
Office 365 versions, 21
Office 2013 versions
  Home & Business, 21
  Home & Student, 21
  Mobile, 22

Office 2013 versions (*cont.*)
- Professional, 21
- RT, 22
- Starter, 21
- Web Apps, 22

Office Clipboard
- adding items to, 43
- closing, 45
- deleting items on, 44
- displaying items in, 45
- opening, 43
- pasting items from, 43–44
- redoing actions, 44–45
- setting options, 44
- undoing actions, 44
- using, 42

Office.com, searching for clip art, 182
online Help system, accessing, 22
opening
- documents, 4
- files in Word window, 5
- Word from Start menu, 2

OpenType features. *See also* text
- contextual alternatives, 67
- number forms, 67
- setting, 66–68
- stylistic sets, 67

organization charts, creating, 195–197
Outline view, 10, 118
outlines
- creating, 117
- defined, 116

overtype mode, 38

P

page borders, adding, 84
page breaks, inserting, 39–40, 75
page formatting
- copying formatting, 85–86
- formatting marks, 84
- mirror margins, 87
- paper size, 87
- setting margins, 85
- setting vertical alignment, 88
- tracking inconsistency, 87–88

page orientation, determining, 87
Page Setup dialog box, 135
pages
- formatting from dialog boxes, 86–87
- navigating, 47

paper size, specifying, 87
paragraph alignment, setting, 69–72
Paragraph dialog box, displaying, 69, 74
paragraph formatting, resetting, 73
paragraph indents, setting with rulers, 73
paragraphs
- adding space between, 74–75
- indenting, 71

Paste Options smart tag, using, 42–43
pasting text, 42
.pdf file extension, 37
picture files, linking, 185
Picture Tools Format tab, 185–186
pictures. *See also* illustrations
- adding captions to, 187
- adding directly, 183–184
- aligning, 187
- browsing for, 179–180
- clip art, 181–183
- copyright concerns, 185
- cropping, 185–187
- default wrapping option, 202
- file formats, 180
- finding camera for, 185
- inserting, 181
- moving, 187
- positioning, 189
- positioning in line, 187
- reducing file sizes, 188
- resizing, 180
- selecting, 45
- setting image properties, 184
- using to fill drawings, 191
- wrapping text around, 188–189

pinning
- shortcuts to Start menu, 2
- shortcuts to taskbar, 2

PNG picture files, 180
portrait orientation, 87
pound shortcut key, 39
preferences
- display elements, 20–21
- General options, 21
- setting, 20–21

print jobs, customizing, 136–137
Print Layout view, 9, 118, 134
Print options, changing margins, 134–135
Print Preview
- exiting, 135
- moving from page to page, 135
- using, 132–133
- zooming in and out, 134

Print Settings area, 136
printers
- installing, 130
- Properties dialog box, 130–132
- setting default, 130
- verifying default, 130

printing
- documents, 135–137
- envelopes, 137–140

labels, 140–141
with Quick Print icon, 135

Q

Quick Access toolbar, 6
adding commands to, 17
adding to, 15
customization files, 16
customizing, 15–16
customizing for documents, 17
locating, 7
moving, 17
rearranging tools on, 17
removing tools, 16
repositioning, 16
repositioning commands, 16
repositioning tools, 16
Quick Print icon, adding, 135
quotes, autoformatting, 120

R

Read Mode view, 9, 118
registered shortcut key, 39
replacing text, 49
Reveal Formatting feature, 95
reviewing tracked changes, 249–251
ribbon, 6
adding commands, 15
adding groups, 14
adding tools, 15
collapsing, 6, 8
commands and tools, 13
commands and tools on, 7
contextual tab, 7
creating groups, 14
creating tabs, 14
customizing, 11, 13
Dialog Box Launcher, 7
display options, 6
exporting customization files, 13
features, 7
file commands, 7
File tab, 7
groups, 13
importing customization files, 13
main tabs, 11
minimizing, 8
Quick Access toolbar, 7
rearranging groups, 14
rearranging tabs, 14
repositioning tools in groups, 13
tabs, 6, 11, 13
tool tabs, 11
ribbon default, resetting, 14
ribbon groups, 6–7
right alignment, 59, 69, 72
RLE picture files, 180
rotating illustrations, 205
row height, changing in tables, 162–163
rows
adding to bottom of tables, 161
copying, 167
inserting into tables, 161
moving, 167
removing from tables, 161–162
selecting in tables, 160
.rtf file extension, 37
rulers
displaying, 73
setting hanging indents, 73
setting tabs with, 105–106
using for indents, 73
using with drawings, 201
rules
IF/THEN/ELSE, 150
using, 150
variable fields, 150

S

saving
copies of documents, 56, 255
documents, 56
documents for first time, 53–55
files on computers, 55
files to .dot format, 211
to new places, 55
to SkyDrive, 54
templates, 56
screens
moving down, 47
moving up, 47
screenshots, taking, 198–200
ScreenTips
hiding, 18
showing, 18
scroll arrows, 6, 46
scroll bars
identifying, 6
using, 45–46
scroll button, 6, 46
search features, using, 36
searching
advanced in Windows Explorer, 35
for documents in Word, 35
phrases, 47
words, 47
section breaks
changing types of, 104
deleting, 103–104

section breaks (*cont.*)
inserting, 40, 103
showing and hiding, 104
selected text, identifying, 40–41
selecting
objects, 3
text, 40–41
sentence case capitalization, 68
sentences, selecting, 40
shading
adding to text, 83–84
applying to tables, 174–175
button, 59
shape fill, using with drawings, 189
shapes
adding, 190
autoshapes, 190
SHIFT key. *See* keyboard shortcuts
shortcut keys. *See* keyboard shortcuts
shortcuts. *See also* desktop shortcut
pinning to Start menu, 2
pinning to taskbar, 2
using to start Word, 2–3
showing formatting, 59
shrink font, 59
SkyDrive
advantages, 34
getting for files, 53
saving to, 54
using, 34
SmartArt, creating diagrams with, 195–197
sort order, 165
sorting
data in tables, 164–165
by fields in columns, 166
files, 36
single columns, 165–166
spacing. *See* line spacing
special characters, inserting, 38–39
spelling and grammar checker, 52–54
split pages, handling, 76
Start menu
contents, 2
opening word from, 2
pinning shortcuts to, 2
sequences of items, 2
Start screen, starting apps in, 3
status bar, 6
strikethrough, 59
style sets, applying, 90–92
styles
applying, 90
applying to tables, 175–177
creating, 91, 93
defined, 90
inspecting, 95
modifying, 93–94
previewing, 95
restoring from gallery, 94
selecting, 9
submenus, displaying, 9
subscript, 59
superscript, 59
symbols, inserting, 38–39

T

table alignment, changing, 172–173
Table Eraser, 158, 162
table of contents
defined, 114
generating, 115–116
outlining tab, 114–115
placing text in, 114
tagging entries for, 114
table size, changing, 160–162
table styles
applying, 175–177
choosing default, 177
deleting, 177
table tools, contextual tabs, 158–159
tables
adding cells, 160–161
adding rows to bottom of, 161
aligning cell content, 170
applying border effects, 174–175
applying shading, 174–175
attributes, 158
autoformatting, 121
cells, 157
changing cell margins, 174
changing column width, 162–163
changing row height, 162–163
changing text wrapping, 171
column headings, 157
columns, 157
components, 157
contextual tabs, 157
converting text to, 168–169
converting to text, 169
copying, 166
creating, 152–154
drawing, 157
formatting, 170–171
hidden grid lines, 157
inserting columns, 161
inserting from dialog box, 157
inserting quickly, 157
inserting rows, 161
keyboard shortcuts, 164

merged cells, 157
merging cells, 172
move handle, 157
moving, 166
moving around in, 164
moving content around, 164
printing gridlines, 157
removing, 170
removing cells, 161–162
removing columns, 161–162
removing parts of, 162
removing rows, 161–162
repeating header rows, 169–170
resizing by dragging, 161
row headings, 157
rows, 157
selected cells, 157
selecting, 159–160
shading, 157
sizing handle, 157
sorting, 164–165
sorting cells, 164–165
splitting, 162
splitting cells, 172
typing text above, 164
uses for, 157
wrapping text around, 173–174
tabs
adding, 13
creating, 14
displaying text formatting, 107
rearranging, 14
renaming, 13–14
setting using measurements, 106
setting using ruler, 105–106
setting with leaders, 106–107
using, 9, 105–107
taskbar, pinning shortcuts to, 2
templates. *See also* chart templates; form templates
applying to new documents, 100
attachment of, 28
Blank Document, 30
Blog Post, 30
creating, 100, 102
default storage folder, 102
defined, 90
finding documents based on, 5
finding existing, 102
Ion Design, 30
listing, 100–101
Normal, 28, 102
saving documents as, 56
searching online, 31–32, 100
selecting, 30–32
Single Space, 30
text. *See also* OpenType features
converting tables to, 169
converting to tables, 168–169
copying, 42–43
cutting, 42
deleting, 41
entering, 36–37
finding with navigation pane, 48–49
formatting in charts, 226–227
inserting, 37–38
moving, 42–43
pasting, 42
replacing, 49
selecting, 9, 40–41
typing over, 37–38
underlining, 62
using insertion point with, 37
wrapping around illustrations, 203–204
wrapping around pictures, 188–189
wrapping around tables, 173–174
text boxes
drawing, 189
using color text with, 192
text effects, 59, 189
using, 65–66
WordArt, 193
text format,
copying, 9
displaying with tabs, 107
text highlight color, 9, 59
text tools, using, 9
theme colors, creating, 99
theme fonts, changing, 96, 98
themed graphic effects, changing, 99
themes
assigning to documents, 96
changing, 96–99
changing colors of, 96
customizing, 99–100
defined, 90
editing customizations, 100
Thesaurus feature, using, 22–23, 125
TIF picture files, 180
TIFF picture files, 180
title bar, 6
togglecase capitalization, 68
tools, adding to ribbon, 15
touch commands, 3
touch-sensitive screen, using, 3
Track Changes
Accept options, 249
adding comments, 252–254
Change User Name, 246–247
changing advanced options, 247
creating reviewing shortcuts, 250

Track Changes (*cont.*)
- emailing documents, 250–252
- highlighting text, 254–255
- identifying reviewers, 244
- interface, 244
- Reject option, 249
- removing highlighting, 254
- Review tab, 245
- reviewing changes, 249–252
- Reviewing pane, 250
- saving to cloud, 252
- setting options, 245–246
- using, 243–245
- using balloons, 247–249

trademark shortcut key, 39
translating
- documents, 25–26, 215–217
- phrases, 25, 214
- selected text, 215
- words, 25, 214

Translator, setting up, 24
.txt file extension, 37

U

underlining text, 9, 59, 62
Undo command, using, 45
Unicode, 236
uppercase capitalization, 68
URL (Uniform Resource Locator), 237
UTF-8, 236

V

vertical alignment, setting, 88
vertical scroll bar, 46
view buttons
- identifying, 6
- using, 118
- using with documents, 45

views
- displaying, 118
- Draft, 10, 118
- Outline, 10, 118
- Print Layout, 9, 118
- Read Mode, 9, 118
- Web Layout, 9, 118

W

web file formats, 231
Web Layout view, 9, 118
Web Options dialog box
- Browsers tab, 233–234
- displaying, 233
- Encoding tab, 236
- Files tab, 234–235
- Fonts tab, 236
- Pictures tab, 235

Webpage formats, 231
webpages
- creating, 230
- keeping files in folders, 235
- previewing, 240–241
- removing personal info from, 241–242
- removing Word-specific tags, 242
- saving Word documents as, 231

wildcard characters
- * (characters), 51
- ? (single character), 51
- @ (copies of previous character), 51
- \ (wildcard), 51
- < (beginning of word), 51
- > (end of word), 51
- [cc] (one in list), 51
- [c-c] (one in range), 51
- [lc-c] (not in range), 51
- {n,} (copies of previous character), 51
- {n,m} (copies of previous character), 51
- {n} (copies of previous character), 51

window background color, changing, 18
window design, changing, 18
windows
- moving to bottom of, 47
- moving to top of, 47

Windows 8, starting Word in, 4
Windows Clipboard
- reverting to, 45
- using, 42

WMF picture files, 180
WMZ picture files, 180
Word
- exiting, 4
- opening from Start menu, 2
- starting in Windows 8, 4
- starting using shortcut, 2–3

Word 2013, taking tour of, 5
word definitions, looking up, 23–24
Word Fields. *See* rules
Word window
- close button, 6
- collapsing ribbon, 6
- components, 5–6
- control menu, 6
- default, 6
- document pane, 6
- document stats, 6
- File tab, 6
- I-beam pointer, 6
- insertion point, 6
- maximize screen button, 6

Microsoft Help, 6
minimize screen button, 6
opening files in, 5
Quick Access toolbar, 6
ribbon, 6
ribbon display options, 6
ribbon groups, 6
scroll arrow, 6
scroll bar, 6
scroll button, 6
status bar, 6
tabs on ribbon, 6
title bar, 6
View buttons, 6
zoom slider, 6
WordArt, using Drawing Tools with, 193–195
words
counting, 122–123
moving to, 47
selecting, 40
.wpd file extension, 37
WPG picture files, 180
.wps file extension, 37
wrapping text, 203–204
writing aids
AutoCorrect, 118–119
AutoFormat, 120–121

X

.xml file extension, 37, 231

Z

zoom slider, 6
zooming in and out, 134